DIVINE ARABESQUE

DIVINE ARABESQUE

The Influence of Poe, Wagner, and Baudelaire on Debussy's Modernist Aesthetics

Matthew Brown

INDIANA UNIVERSITY PRESS

This book is a publication of

INDIANA UNIVERSITY PRESS
Herman B Wells Library
1320 East 10th Street
Bloomington, Indiana 47405 USA

iupress.org

For customers in the European Union with safety or GPSR concerns,
please contact Mare Nostrum Group B.V., Mauritskade 21D, 1091 GC
Amsterdam, The Netherlands. Email: gpsr@mare-nostrum.co.uk

First Printing 2026

Cataloging information is available from the Library of Congress.

ISBN 978-0-253-07455-3 (hdbk.)
ISBN 978-0-253-07456-0 (pbk.)
ISBN 978-0-253-07458-4 (ebook)

Contents

CONTENTS

Acknowledgments

This book has been in the works for some time. I came up with the idea of writing about Debussy and the arabesque several years ago and was lucky enough to receive a sabbatical from the Eastman School of Music in order to do so. Although I made considerable progress on the manuscript, I had put it on the back burner while I completed two coauthored volumes, one on Heinrich Schenker's conception of harmony and the other on Paul Dukas's opera *Ariane et Barbe-bleue*. With those volumes now in print, I have finally brought this project to completion. Seven of the chapters are entirely new: the introduction and chapters 1, 2, 5, 6, 9, and 10. Three more have been adapted from unpublished lectures and webinars: chapter 8 borrows from a very old paper, "*Pelléas, Nuages,* and *Le Rossignol*: Critical Concepts and Cognitive Consequences," that I codelivered with Linda Cummins at an AMS chapter meeting in the spring of 1995. Chapter 12 combines material from my paper "Pelléas, Mélisande, le grotesque et l'Arabesque," *Regards sur Debussy*, ed. Myriam Chimènes and Alexandra Laederich (Paris: Fayard, 2013), 137–50, and my talk "Debussy's Cinematic Obsessions," delivered at the joint meeting of AMS/SMT in San Antonio in 2018. Chapter 13 reworks a webinar, "Trauma and Grief in the Late Music of Claude Debussy," delivered online for City, University of London, in 2020. And the remaining four develop ideas that I touched on in earlier publications: chapter 3 expands on thoughts expressed in my books *Debussy's 'Ibéria': Studies in Genesis and Structure* (Oxford: Oxford University Press, 2003) and *Debussy Redux: The Impact of His Music on Popular Culture* (Bloomington: Indiana University Press, 2012) and my essay "*Japonism*, collecting, and the *Expositions Universelles*" for *Debussy in Context*, ed. Simon Trezise (Cambridge: Cambridge University Press, 2024). However, the latter includes new material and extensive musical analyses of several early songs by Debussy. Another essay from that collection, "Debussy Today," has ideas that I rework in the conclusion. Chapter 4 uses the voice-leading analyses of the *Prélude à L'Après-midi d'un faune* from my paper "Tonality and Form in Debussy's *Prélude à 'L'Après-midi d'un faune,'*" *Music Theory Spectrum* 15 (1993): 127–43 to shed new light on the arabesque qualities of Mallarmé's original poem, something I have never discussed in print before. Chapter 7 expands on material outlined in an essay, "Debussy's Violin Sonata and the Legacy of J. S. Bach," in *Debussy Studies 2*, ed. Barbara L. Kelly and David Code (Cambridge: Cambridge University Press, 2025), but does so in the context of the third rather than the first movement. And chapter 11 builds on analytical observations made in my earlier book, *Explaining Tonality: Schenkerian Theory and Beyond* (Rochester, NY: University of Rochester Press, 2005). As a side note, chapter 9 grew out of a joint project that I had started working on with David Code in 2018. Sadly, David passed away in the summer of 2022, before we were able to bring our thoughts to fruition.

I would also like to thank lots of people for their assistance. To begin with, I am extremely grateful to the two anonymous reviewers who read my original manuscript for Indiana University Press: their comments have been invaluable. I am likewise grateful to Jonathan Dunsby, Stephany Venturino, and François De Médicis for sharing their unpublished work with me and to François Delécluse for sending me a copy of his excellent dissertation. Thanks should also go to Shay Loya for arranging the webinar at City, University of London, Simon Trezise, Barbara Kelly, and Cambridge University Press for giving me permission to recycle material from several recent papers, Mark De Voto for permission to use his transcription of *Rondel chinois*, and Robert Orledge for permission to use his transcription of *La chute de la maison Usher*. Last, I would like to thank David Peter Coppen, Special Collections Librarian and Archivist at the Sibley Music Library, Eastman School of Music for providing me with scans of the draft for *La Mer*.

As regards the production of this book, I am extremely grateful to Jamal Rossi, former dean of the Eastman School of Music, and Peter Christensen, director of the Humanities Center at the University of Rochester; without their generous support, this project would not have come to fruition. I would also like to thank Allison Blair Chaplin and the team at Indiana University Press. It has been a great pleasure to work yet again with Sophia Hebert, Nancy Lila Lightfoot, and their colleagues. I would also like to thank two very dear friends—Mike Zachary and Christopher Winders—for engraving the musical examples. Their remarkable skills and dedication are much appreciated. And last, I would like to thank my wife, Elizabeth Steadman, who not only read through the entire book several times but also has been a constant source of strength and encouragement. I cannot imagine finishing this project without her support.

DIVINE ARABESQUE

I. Preliminaries

Introduction

Debussy's Concept of the Musical Arabesque

ARABESQUES CLEARLY PLAYED a pivotal role in the music of Claude Debussy (1862–1918) and did so because they were a crucial component of Symbolist aesthetics.[1] The term *arabesque* is usually associated with forms of ornamentation featuring regularly recurring geometric shapes or floral patterns which interlock to create a continuous design. Such ornaments, which were also known as moresques and grotesques, are typically found in artifacts from ancient Islamic culture, classical antiquity, and even Gothic and Renaissance Europe. Those artifacts take many forms: architectural designs, sculptures, furniture, textiles, manuscript illuminations, and book illustrations, to name but a few. For Symbolist artists and writers such as Edgar Allan Poe, Richard Wagner, Charles Baudelaire, Auguste Villiers de l'Isle-Adam, Gustave Moreau, Odilon Redon, Stéphane Mallarmé, Paul Verlaine, Joris-Karl Huysmans, Maurice Maeterlinck, Henri de Régnier, Gabriel Mourey, and Pierre Louÿs, arabesques provided a source of inspiration, a means for challenging common assumptions about the origins, categories, limits, structure, value, emotional impact, and expressive power of art, and even a point of departure for their distinctive brand of modernism.

Given Debussy's close ties to Symbolism, it is hardly surprising that the term *arabesque* regularly surfaces in discussions of him and his music. Among the most significant appears in Françoise Gervais's "La notion d'arabesque chez Debussy."[2] This paper, which was published in 1958, not only traces the term's history from the Renaissance to the twentieth century but also cites concrete examples from the music of Debussy and designs in Jules Bourgoin's *Les éléments de l'Art arab* (Paris: Librairie de Firmin-Didot, 1879). During the 1970s, Gervais's findings were amplified by other writers such as Claudia Maurer Zenck, Stefan Jarociński, Edward Lockspeiser, and Richard Langham Smith and more recently by the research of Jean-Jacques Eigeldinger, Jann Pasler, Linda

Cummins, Carolyn Potter, Elizabeth McCrombie, David J. Code, Gurminder Bhogal, François De Médicis, Jonathan Dunsby, and Stephanie Venturino, to name but a few.[3]

Despite differences in scope, current research usually connects the decorative aspects of Debussy's melodic writing with the interlocking geometric and floral patterns mentioned above. Bhogal's book *Details of Consequence: Ornament, Music, and Art in Paris* is a perfect case in point. As shown in figure 0.1, it presents a conceptual integration network for describing the conceptual metaphor LINE IS MELODY.[4] Having noted that not all highly decorated melodies are arabesques, Bhogal places musical arabesques in a generic space between visual design/visual perception and musical composition/aural perception. Like many before, she claims that the quintessential musical arabesque appears at the start of Debussy's *Prélude à L'Après-midi d'un faune*. The sinuous flute melody, which is given in example 0.1, begins by decorating the primary pitch, C# (mm. 1–3), before sliding down by step through B to A# across mm. 3–4. Remarkably, the stepwise descent C#–B–A# in mm. 3–4 is foreshadowed in the first three notes of mm. 1 and 2.

Debussy was not, of course, the first to compose ornate melodic arabesques: precedents can be found in works by other nineteenth- and early twentieth-century composers. Bhogal, for example, has found parallels between the decorative aspects of Debussy's "Reflets dans l'eau" (*Images*, Bk. 1, 1905) and those of piano pieces by Chopin, Liszt, and Fauré.[5] Meanwhile, Venturino and Dunsby have offered "a snapshot" of nineteenth-century arabesques for the keyboard: Schumann's *Arabeske*, Op. 18 (1839), Brisson's *L'Arabesque*, Op. 19 (1847), Liszt's *Schlummerlied mit Arabesken*, S 454 (1848), Gade's *Arabeske*, Op. 27 (1854), Bülow's *Arabesques en forme de variations sur un thème favori de l'opéra Rigoletto*, Op. 2 (ca. 1855), Vilbac's *Les Arabesques*, Op. 32 (1877), Jadassohn's *Four Arabesques*, Op. 53 (1877), and Heller's *Four Arabesques*, Op. 49 (1878).[6] And De Médicis has related the arabesque qualities of Debussy's melodic writing to that of Russian composers such as Balakirev, Rimsky-Korsakov, Borodin, Glazounov, and Tchaikovsky; he has compared the decorative flourishes in "Clair de lune" (*Suite Bergamasque*, 1890) and the *Prélude à L'Après-midi d'un faune* (1894) to those in Glazunov's *Oriental Rhapsody*, Op. 29 (1889), and Rimsky-Korsakov's Symphony No. 2, *Antar* (1868, rev. 1875 and 1891).[7]

At the same time, Eigeldinger has interrogated Debussy's own references to the term *arabesque*.[8] The earliest of these appear in letters to Eugène Vasnier (November 1885) and Prince André Poniatowski (February 1893) and associate arabesques with the vocal polyphony of Palestrina, Vittoria, and Lasso, which Debussy heard in Rome in the mid-1880s, while a recipient of the Prix de Rome.[9] Jumping ahead in time, Eigeldinger cites Debussy's review of a performance by Eugène Ysaÿe of Bach's Violin Concerto in G minor BWV 1056R. In his response, which was published in *La Revue blanche* in May 1901, Debussy contrasted the "divine arabesques" that Palestrina, Vittoria, and Lasso derived from Gregorian chant with the "more flexible, more fluid" arabesques imagined by Bach.[10] He expressed the same admiration for Bach's arabesques in other essays from 1902 and 1913.[11] Again, those opinions were not without precedent: as far back as 1805, Hans Georg Nageli described Bach's Keyboard Partita No. 6, BWV 830, as "a garland of Raphaelesque arabesques" depicting "organized chaos."[12]

Debussy did not, however, use arabesques exclusively for decorative purposes. Building on comments by Gervais and Eigeldinger, Jann Pasler has suggested that Debussy was less concerned with decorating individual lines and more with combining different lines contrapuntally and with allowing them to shape the harmonic, timbral, and formal structure of a work.[13] Others, however, have considered arabesques from a literary perspective. Gervais, for example, has described the influence of Jean Paul and E. T. A. Hoffmann on Schumann and Poe; like Cummins, she has

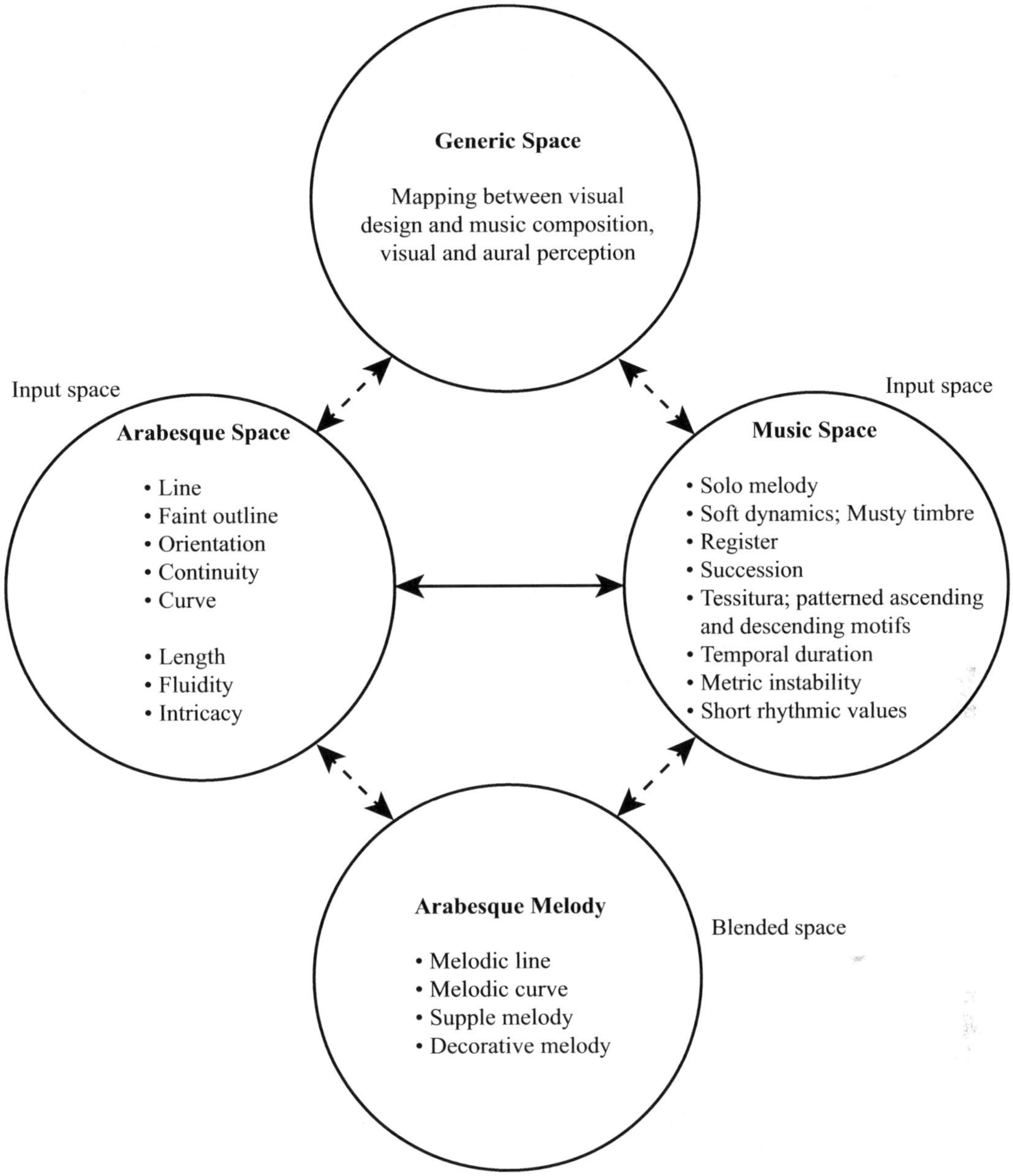
Generic Space
Mapping between visual design and music composition, visual and aural perception
Input space
Arabesque Space
• Line
• Faint outline
• Orientation
• Continuity
• Curve
• Length
• Fluidity
• Intricacy
Input space
Music Space
• Solo melody
• Soft dynamics; Musty timbre
• Register
• Succession
• Tessitura; patterned ascending and descending motifs
• Temporal duration
• Metric instability
• Short rhythmic values
Arabesque Melody
• Melodic line
• Melodic curve
• Supple melody
• Decorative melody
Blended space

Figure 0.1 Conceptual integration network for arabesque melodies

Très modéré
p doux et expressif

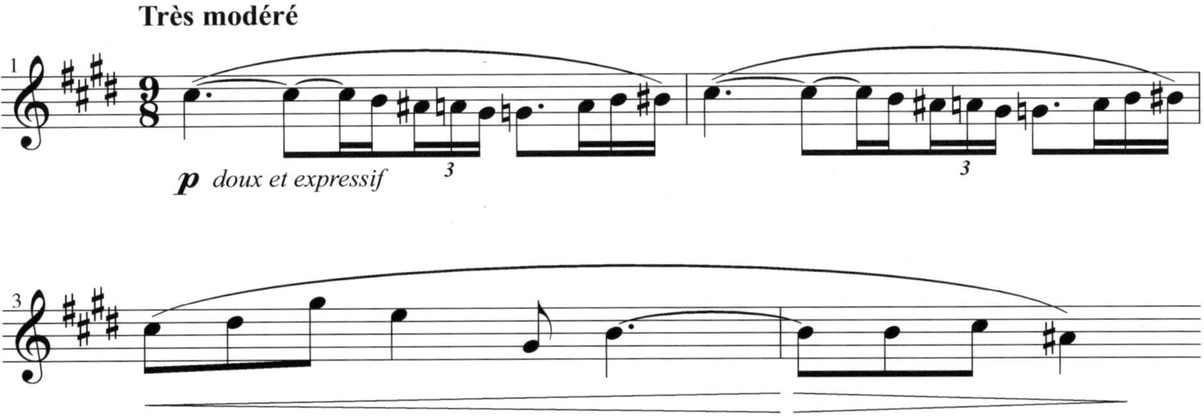

Example 0.1 Arabesque flute melody from Debussy, *Prélude à L'Après-midi d'un faune*, mm. 1–4

drawn attention to the influence of Poe's poems and stories on French Symbolism.[14] Cummins and Bhogal have likewise pointed to the impact of *Die Frühromantik* on French Symbolism, especially August Wilhelm Schlegel's influence on Baudelaire's concept of *correspondances* and Friedrich Schlegel's on the arabesque, particularly as regards Baudelaire's poem "Le Thyrse" (1862).[15] And Bhogal has rightly mentioned Wagner. It is well known, for example, that Wagner's concept of *Versmelodie* and the *Gesamtkunstwerk* shaped Symbolist views about the musicality of poetry and resonated with Baudelaire's concept of *correspondances*.[16] For his part, Baudelaire was instrumental in promoting Poe and Wagner in France by translating most of Poe's *Tales of the Grotesque and Arabesque* into French and by writing critical essays about both men.[17]

And yet Gervais, Cummins, and Bhogal do not consider the impact of Poe, Wagner, or Baudelaire in a systematic manner. Gervais says little about Poe and nothing about Schlegel, Wagner, or Baudelaire. Cummins discusses Friedrich Schlegel at length but says little about Poe or Baudelaire and nothing about Wagner. Bhogal invokes Wagner in general terms but largely ignores Poe, omitting his name and his work from her bibliography and index. This situation is regrettable because Wagner, Poe, Baudelaire, and indirectly Schlegel had a profound and lasting impact on Debussy.[18] For example, Debussy came under Wagner's spell as a student at the Paris Conservatoire (1872–84), thanks to the encouragement of his teachers Albert Lavignac and Ernest Guiraud and his benefactor Marguerite Wilson-Pelouze. He is known to have attended several prominent performances of act 1 of *Tristan et Isolde* and *Lohengrin* in Paris during 1887 and of *Parsifal, Die Meistersinger von Nürnberg*, and *Tristan und Isolde* in Bayreuth in the summers of 1888 and 1889. In February 1894, Debussy was even paid to participate in several "séances wagnériennes" at the home of Ernest Chausson's stepmother, Madame Philippe Escudier. These events centered on *Der Ring des Nibelungen, Tristan und Isolde, Die Meistersinger von Nürnberg*, and *Parsifal*.[19] Around the same time, Debussy singled out Poe as his favorite prose writer and Baudelaire as his favorite poet; he not only considered writing "a symphony on psychologically developed themes from various Poe tales" (1890) but even finished his *Cinq Poèmes de Baudelaire* (1887–89).[20] Fast-forward to 1917, and Poe, Wagner, and Baudelaire were still on his mind. Despite suffering from colon cancer, Debussy worked on his operatic version of Poe's "The Fall of the House of Usher" and complemented Wagner for being a great artist rather than a great composer.[21] And in the spring of 1917, he recycled a line from Baudelaire's poem "Harmonie du soir" as the title of his last piano piece: *Les soirs illuminés par l'ardeur du charbon*.[22]

More can also be said about Debussy's review of Bach's Violin Concerto in G minor BWV 1056R cited by Eigeldinger. Having praised Ysaÿe for his freedom of expression and gorgeous tone, Debussy shifted his attention to the piece itself.

[This] is a marvelous concerto—like so many others inscribed in the notebooks of the grand old Bach. Once again, one finds that almost the entire piece is pure 'musical arabesque,' or rather it is based on the principle of the "ornament," which is at the root of all kinds of art. (And the word "ornament" here has nothing to do with the ornaments one finds in musical dictionaries.) The primitives—Palestrina, Vittoria, Orlando di Lasso, etc.—had a sense of this divine "arabesque." They found the basis of it in Gregorian chant, whose delicate tracery they supported with twining counterpoints. In reworking the arabesque, Bach made it more flexible, more fluid, and despite the fact that the Great Master always imposed a rigorous discipline on beauty, he imbued it with a wealth of free fantasy so limitless that it still astonishes us today. In Bach's music it is not the character of the melody that affects us but rather the curve. More often still it is the parallel movement of several lines whose fusion stirs our emotions—whether fortuitous or contrived. Based on this conception of the ornamental, the music will impress the public as regularly as clockwork, and it will fill their imaginations with images.[23]

He added, "Perhaps we find it difficult to believe in anything so unnatural and artificial. Well, it is a good deal more 'natural' than all that silly wailing you find in opera."

This statement in fact makes five important claims about arabesques. First, having acknowledged that they are a form of ornamentation and that ornaments are essential features of all art, Debussy insisted that the ornaments are not bound to conventional norms. While musicians usually associate the principles of ornamentation with the addition of optional surface decorations (e.g., trills, turns, mordents, and other *Manieren*), he had something more abstract in mind, something that bites deeper into the fabric of the composition. To quote Gabriel Mourey, "In his words, as in life, and as also in his music, Debussy never abandoned his love of conciseness. He had in all things, a hatred of superfluous development, or useless ornament; none practiced better the art of finding just the correct phrase, the rightly placed word, or the expressive gesture. Debussy was a concentrated being who lived an intense inner life. He was not of those who talk a lot but say nothing."[24] For Debussy, such ideas are epitomized by the music of Bach, "where everything conspires wonderfully to highlight the central idea and where the delicacy of the inner parts never absorbs the principal line."[25]

Second, Debussy specifically linked arabesques to the principles of counterpoint and harmony. He put this idea into sharp relief in his letter to Eugène Vasnier (November 24, 1885): "I'm truly amazed at the effects [Palestrina and Lasso] can get simply from a vast knowledge of counterpoint. I expect you think of counterpoint as the most forbidding article in the whole of music. But in their hands it becomes something wonderful, adding an extraordinary depth to the meaning of words. And every now and then the melodic lines unroll and expand, reminding you of the illuminations in ancient missals."[26] Nearly two decades later, he echoed this point when discussing Bach's music: "He preferred the free play of sonorities whose curves, whether flowing in parallel; or contrary motion, would result in an undreamed-of flowering, so that even the least of his countless manuscripts bears an indelible stamp of beauty. That was the age of the 'wonderful arabesque' [*l'adorable arabesque*], when music was subject to the laws of beauty inscribed in the movements of Nature herself. Rather our time will be remembered as the era of the 'age of veneer' [*style plaqué*]."[27] And when writing to André Poniatowski in February 1893, Debussy proposed that harmony actually derived from counterpoint: "They sang a Palestrina mass for unaccompanied voices. It was extremely beautiful. . . . The shaping of the music is what strikes you, and the arabesques crossing each other to produce something which has never been repeated: harmony formed out of melodies!"[28] It is a claim that he foreshadowed in his well-known conversations with Guiraud (1889–90): "Counterpoint is not given to us for nothing. As the parts go forward we come across some splendid chords."[29]

Third, Debussy challenged traditional views of ornamentation by denying that it is possible to distinguish "main ideas" from "subordinate gestures" and by demanding that the former should always be understood contextually. He underscored the first point in a letter to his stepson Raoul Bardac dated February 24, 1906: "You know how little love I have for developmental padding. It's seen long service at the hands of the masters and it's time we started to replace it by a more rigorous selection of idea; the line needs to take more account of the value of those ideas on the orchestral and ornamental front and, above all, the ideas must breathe. So often they're overwhelmed by the richness or the banality of the frame."[30] On the matter of context, he noted in his essay "Du Précurseur" (*SIM*, March 15, 1913), "One chord, even if it's from a monumental piece of music, has no more significance in itself than one stone in a fine building. It's where it is placed that counts, and the way it throws into relief the flowing curves of the melodic line."[31]

Fourth, by suggesting that Bach imbued the arabesque "with a wealth of free fantasy," Debussy suggested that music should avoid preconceived formal schemes and unfold in a natural manner. It is an idea that he echoed in his famous "L'Entretien avec M. Croche" (*La Revue blanche*, July 1, 1901): "Search for discipline within freedom! Don't let yourself be governed by formulae drawn from decadent philosophies: they are for the feeble-minded."[32] Above all, he rejected the principles of *Formenlehre*, criticizing its advocates for their "silly obsession with over precise 'forms' and 'tonality.'"[33] Once again, Debussy followed Bach's lead: "Those severe old critics passed judgment and threatened terrible punishments for breath of the classical rules whose construction—they should have realized—was nothing less than mechanical. Did they not realize that no one could even go further than Bach, one of their judges, toward freedom and fantasy in both composition and form?"[34] On September 3, 1907, he even reminded Jacques Durand of Bach's genius: "Music is not, in its essence, something that can flow within a rigorous and traditional form. It is colours and rhythmicized time. . . . The rest is a joke invented by cold-blooded imbeciles on the backs of the Masters, who have almost always written only music for their own day! Only Bach approached the truth."[35] Like his illustrious predecessor, Debussy favored self-generating, quasi-improvised forms, labeling *La Mer* "Trois esquisses symphonique" and the opening of *L'Isle joyeuse* "quasi una cadenza."

And fifth, Debussy drew attention to the expressive and visual power of arabesques. As regards the music of Palestrina, Vittoria, and Lassus, he mentioned to André Poniatowski that, despite their strictness, "the effect is of utter whiteness, and emotions not represented (as has come to be the norm since) by dramatic cries but by melodic arabesques."[36] He expressed similar ideas in a letter to Pierre Louÿs (April 10, 1896): "Speaking personally, I find the book extraordinarily supple. The way you describe actions, too, is unique: you manage to make it all seem utterly human and perfectly harmonized at the same time (you know what I mean). And as for the beginnings and endings of the chapters, where you describe or arrest the arabesques of feeling and colour, they're magical."[37] At the same time, Debussy explained the parallels between images and sounds in his aforementioned letter to Raoul Bardac: "Collect impressions. Don't be in a hurry to write them down. Because that's something music can do better than painting: it can centralize variations of color and light within a single picture."[38] He had anticipated this view a few years earlier in *Gils Blas* (January 26, 1903): "For it is music alone that has the power to evoke imaginary scenes at will, to conjure up the intangible world of fantasies secretly shrouded within the mysterious poetry of the night, the thousand indistinguishable noises made by moonbeams caressing the leaves."[39] And in an interview with Emily Frances Bauer for *Harper's Magazine* (August 29, 1908), Debussy confessed to living "in a world of [the] imagination" and finding "an exquisite joy" when he searched through the recesses of his mind: "if anything original is to come from me, it can only come in that way."[40]

With Debussy's five claims in mind, this book shows that, through the influence of Schlegel, Poe, Wagner, and Baudelaire, the arabesque had an even greater impact on the composer's thinking than has previously been supposed. The book also departs from earlier accounts by suggesting that they rely on an overly narrow view of ornamentation, one that underestimates its contrapuntal, harmonic, and formal implications. To show how lines, chords, and motives interact with one another at the local and global levels, this book relies heavily, though not exclusively, on Schenkerian theory. Last, the book proposes that existing studies underestimate the extent to which arabesques provided Symbolist artists with a means for explaining the origins, nature, purpose, and meaning of art. Above all, it gave them a framework within which to challenge the traditional ways of distinguishing fine art from decorative art, Western art from non-Western art, and even so-called high art from low art and entertainment.

Expanding on Gervais's paper, chapter 1 offers a general overview of the arabesque. It describes how the term entered popular parlance in the sixteenth and seventeenth centuries when the fine arts were institutionalized in France. Having demonstrated how the term was originally used to describe visual designs, chapter 1 describes how Friedrich Schlegel and others reinterpreted it in literary terms. Schlegel's views were then transmitted to Debussy primarily through the writings of Poe, Wagner, and Baudelaire. Next, chapters 2–4 turn the spotlight on Debussy and the ways in which he embraced the arabesque. Since Debussy associated arabesques with the music of Bach, chapter 2 compares the decorative features of Bach's Violin Concerto in G minor BWV 1056R with those of Debussy's *Première Arabesque* for piano. Chapters 3 and 4 continue this line of inquiry by considering the polyphonic foundations of Debussy's early song *Rondel chinois* and his orchestral masterpiece the *Prélude à L'Après-midi d'un faune*. Once again, these chapters show how Debussy's conception of ornamentation extended well beyond that of surface melodic decoration to encompass matters of counterpoint, harmony, and form. Chapters 5–7 then address the issue of form by showing how successful arabesques use local details to determine a work's global form. They consider movements from three cyclic compositions: Debussy's *Quatuor à cordes, La Mer*, and the *Sonate pour violon et piano*.

Whereas chapters 2–7 deal with the compositional aspects of the arabesque as outlined in claims 1–3 from Debussy's review, chapters 8–13 explore its extramusical implications as delineated in claims 4–5. Chapters 8–10 consider Debussy's observation that arabesques can create a sense of fantasy. Since Symbolist writers often associated the fantastic with the fusion of literary genres and with the interpolation of texts within texts, these chapters show how Debussy followed suit by discussing his penchant for intertextuality and for enchaining these references for narrative purposes. Chapter 8, for example, demonstrates how he imbued the score of *Pelléas et Mélisande* with elements of the fantastic by including passages from other sources, such as songs and orchestral compositions. Similarly, chapter 9 describes how Debussy created the make-believe world of a children's toybox by casting *La Boîte à joujoux* as an elaborate potpourri of preexistent and newly created tunes. And chapter 10 demonstrates how Debussy used a chain of waltz sections, some alluding to preexistent works, to re-create the fantastic nocturnal setting of his ballet *Jeux*. Next, chapter 11 shows how Debussy distorted his arabesque to express the sense of melancholy pervading Baudelaire's poem "La Morte des amants," Verlaine's "L'Ombre des arbres," and Mallarmé's "Soupir." Chapter 12 addresses Debussy's claim that arabesques have the capacity to fill the mind with images in a quasi-cinematic manner by comparing the climaxes of *Pelléas et Mélisande* and Poe's "The Fall of the House of Usher" with the first kidnapping scene from Brian DePalma's Hitchcockian thriller *Obsession* (Columbia Pictures, 1976). Finally, chapter 13 riffs on Schlegel's comments about arabesques and confessions; it describes the traumatic experiences that Debussy faced during WWI and their impact on his unfinished opera *La chute de la maison Usher*. The conclusion reinforces the central thesis of this book: the arabesque provided Symbolist artists not only with a technical blueprint for how to create art but also with a means for challenging traditional divisions between fine art and decorative art, Western and non-Western art, and even art and entertainment. The concept of the arabesque, therefore, helps us understand how Debussy and other Symbolists opened the door to modernism.

Notes

1. François de Médicis, "Symbolism," in *Debussy in Context*, ed. Simon Trezise (Cambridge: Cambridge University Press, 2024), 69–78.

2. Françoise Gervais, "La notion d'arabesque chez Debussy," *La Revue musicale* 241 (1958): 3–22.

3. See Claudia Maurer Zenck, *Versuch über die wahre Art, Debussy zu analysieren*, Berliner musikwissenschaftliche Arbeiten (München: E. Katzbichler, 1974); Stefan Jarociński, *Debussy: Impressionism and Symbolism* (London: Eulenburg, 1976), 146; Edward Lockspeiser, *Debussy: His Life and Mind*, vol. 1, *1862–1902*, 2nd ed. (Cambridge: Cambridge University Press, 1978), 113–21; Claude Debussy, *Debussy on Music*, ed. François Lesure and trans. Richard Langham Smith (New York: Knopf, 1977), 31–32; Jean-Jacques Eigeldinger, "Debussy et l'idée d'arabesque musicale," *Cahiers Debussy* 12/13 (1988–89): 5–14; Jann Pasler, "Timbre, Voice Leading, Arabesque," in *Debussy in Performance*, ed. James R. Briscoe (New Haven, CT: Yale University Press, 2000), 225–55; Linda Cummins, *Debussy and the Fragment* (Amsterdam: Rodopi, 2006); Caroline Potter, "Debussy and Nature," in *The Cambridge Companion to Debussy*, ed. Simon Trezise (Cambridge: Cambridge University Press, 2003); Elizabeth McCombie, *Mallarmé and Debussy: Unheard Music, Unseen Text* (Oxford: Oxford University Press, 2003), esp. 99–102; David J. Code, "Debussy's Quartet in the Brussels Salon of 'La Libre Esthétique,'" *19th-Century Music* 30, no. 3 (2007): 257–87; David J. Code, "The 'Song Triptych': Reflections on a Debussyan Genre," in *Debussy's Resonance*, ed. François de Médicis and Steven Huebner (Rochester, NY: University of Rochester Press, 2018), 127–74; David J. Code, "Debussy, Discourse, Time," *Musical Quarterly* 100, no. 3–4 (Fall–Winter 2017): 340–98; Gurminder Kaur Bhogal, *Details of Consequence: Ornament, Music, and Art in Paris*, AMS Studies in Music (New York: Oxford University Press, 2013); Gurminder Kaur Bhogal, "Ephemeral Arabesque Timbres and the Exotic Feminine," in *Arabesque without End: Across Music and the Arts, from Faust to Shahrazad*, ed. Anne Leonard (New York: Routledge, 2022), 129–48; Eric Frederick Jensen, *Debussy* (Oxford: Oxford University Press, 2014); François De Médicis, "Debussy's *Faun* and the Russian Arabesque," paper delivered at Claude Debussy in 2018: A Centenary Celebration, Royal Northern College of Music, March 19, 2018; Stephanie Venturino, "Arabesque in French Music after Debussy," in *Arabesque without End: Across Music and the Arts, from Faust to Shahrazad*, ed. Anne Leonard (New York: Routledge, 2022), 149–72; Stephanie Venturino and Jonathan Dunsby, "The Evolution of Claude Debussy's Arabesque," in *Debussy Studies 2*, ed. Barbara Kelly and David J. Code (Cambridge: Cambridge University Press, 2025), 58–86.

4. Bhogal adapts the idea of a conceptual integration network (CIN) from Lawrence Zbikowski's *Conceptualizing Music: Cognitive Structure, Theory, and Analysis* (New York: Oxford University Press, 2002).

5. Bhogal, *Details of Consequence*, 118–37.

6. Venturino and Dunsby, "Evolution," figure 7.

7. De Médicis, "Debussy's *Faun*."

8. Eigeldinger, "Debussy et l'idée d'arabesque musicale," 5–14.

9. Claude Debussy, *Correspondance (1872–1918)*, ed. François Lesure and Denis Herlin, annotated by François Lesure, Denis Herlin, and Georges Liébert (Paris: Gallimard, 2005), 44–45 and 116; and trans. Roger Nichols in [Claude Debussy], *Debussy Letters*, ed. François Lesure and Roger Nichols, trans. Roger Nichols (Cambridge, MA: Harvard University Press, 1987), 14 and 42. See also Richard Langham Smith, "Notes," in [Claude Debussy], *Debussy on Music*, ed. François Lesure and trans. Richard Langham Smith (New York: Knopf, 1977), 31. For Debussy's interest in early music, see Catrina Flint de Médicis, "Early Music," in *Debussy in Context*, ed. Simon Trezise (Cambridge: Cambridge University Press, 2024), 281–90.

10. Claude Debussy, "Vendredi Saint—Le neuvième Symphonie," *La Revue blanche* (May 1, 1901), in *Monsieur Croche et autres écrits*, ed. François Lesure (Paris: Gallimard, 1987), 34; and Claude Debussy, "Good Friday—The Ninth Symphony," in *Debussy on Music*, ed. François Lesure and trans. Richard Langham Smith (New York: Knopf, 1977), 27.

11. Claude Debussy, "L'Orientation Musicale," *Musica* (October 1902), in Debussy, *Monsieur Croche*, 65; Debussy, "The Orientation of Music," in *Debussy on Music*, 84; Debussy, "De Goût," *SIM* (February 15, 1913), in *Monsieur Croche*, 228–29; Debussy, "Taste," in *Debussy on Music*, 277.

12. See Venturino and Dunsby, "The Evolution of Claude Debussy's Arabesque Idea," Table 3.7, 68–69.

13. Pasler, "Timbre, Voice Leading, Arabesque," 225–28.

14. Gervais, "La notion d'arabesque chez Debussy," 6; and Cummins, *Debussy and the Fragment*, 96, 130–32. See also Célestin Pierre Cambiaire, *The Influence of Edgar Allan Poe in France* (New York: Haskell House, 1970); Patrick F. Quinn, *Poe and France: The Last Twenty Years* (Baltimore: Edgar Allan Poe Society and Enoch Pratt Free Library, 1970), https://www.eapoe.org/papers/psblctrs/pl19691.htm; Patrick F. Quinn, *The French Face of Edgar Poe* (Carbondale: Southern Illinois University Press, 1971); and Harold Bloom, "Edgar Allan Poe (1809–1849)," in *The American Canon*, ed. David Mikics (New York: Library of America, 2019), 45–60.

15. Cummins, *Debussy and the Fragment*, 15–18, 47–54, 97–98; and Bhogal, "Precursors," in *Details of Consequence*, 69–71 and 65–66.

16. For Wagner's influence in France and on French opera, see Georges Servières, *Richard Wagner jugé en France* (Paris: La Librairie illustrée, 1898); Martine Kahane and Nicole Wild, *Wagner et La France: Exposition 26 octobre–26 janvier 1984* (Paris: Bibliothèque nationale, Théâtre National de L'Opéra de Paris, Herscher, 1983); Steven Huebner, *French Opera at the Fin De Siècle: Wagnerism, Nationalism, and Style* (Oxford: Oxford University Press, 1999) and Steven Huebner, "Wagnérisme," in *Debussy in Context*, ed. Simon Trezise, 88–97; and Jeremy Coleman, *Richard Wagner in Paris: Translation, Identity, Modernity* (Woodbridge: The Boydell Press, 2019).

17. For Baudelaire's relationship with Wagner, see Margaret Miner, *Resonant Gaps: Between Baudelaire and Wagner* (Athens; University of Georgia Press, 1995); and Joseph Acquisito, "Uprooting the Lyric: Baudelaire in Wagner's Forests," *Nineteenth-Century French Studies* 32, no. 3–4 (2004): 223–37.

18. For the influence of Poe and Baudelaire on Debussy, see Caroline Potter, "Relationships with Poets and Other Literary Figures," in *Debussy in Context*, ed. Trezise, 138–39.

19. See Debussy's letter to Henri Lerolle (January 31, 1894), *Correspondance*, 190.

20. Debussy, *Correspondance*, 154; Debussy, *Letters*, 51. See Lockspeiser, *Life and Mind*, 230; and Edward Lockspeiser, *Debussy et Edgar Allan Poe. Documents inédits* (Monaco: Éditions du Rocher, 1962).

21. See Debussy, "Lettre-Préface à *Pour la musique Français. Douze causeries*," in *Monsieur Croche*, 267 [267–68]; and Debussy, "Preface in the Form of a Letter to *Pour la musique Français. Douze causeries*," in *Debussy on Music*, 324 [324–25].

22. Denis Herlin, "*Les soirs illuminés par l'ardeur du charbon*: de Baudelaire à Debussy," in *Claude Debussy—Portraits et Études* (Hildesheim: Georg Olms, 2023), 497–504.

23. Debussy, "Vendredi Saint—Le neuvième Symphonie," in *Monsieur Croche*, 33–34; and Debussy, "Good Friday—The Ninth Symphony," in *Debussy on Music*, 26–27.

24. Gabriel Mourey, "Memories of Claude Debussy," *Musical News and Herald*, June 11, 1921, 747–48, in Roger Nichols, *Debussy Remembered* (London: Faber, 1992), 31; Debussy's letter to Ernest Chausson (October 23, 1893), in Debussy, *Correspondance*, 167–68; and Debussy, *Letters*, 58.

25. Debussy, *Correspondance*, 941; and Debussy, *Letters*, 166.

26. Debussy, *Correspondance*, 44–45; and Debussy, *Letters*, 14.

27. Debussy, "L'Orientation Musicale," *Musica* (October 1902), in *Monsieur Croche*, 65; and Debussy, *Debussy on Music*, 84. Debussy made a similar claim a decade later about the music of Bach: "on each new page of his innumerable works we discover new things we thought were born only yesterday—from delightful arabesques [*capricieuse arabesques*] to an overflowing religious feeling greater than anything we have since discovered." Debussy, "De Goût," *SIM* (February 15, 1913), in *Monsieur Croche*, 228–29; and Debussy, "Taste," in *Debussy on Music*, 277.

28. Debussy, *Correspondance*, 116; and Debussy, *Letters*, 42.

29. See Sylvie Douche, Appendix I, "Transcription littérale du carnet de notes de Maurice Emmanuel au suject des échanges Debussy-Guiraud (1889–1890)," in *Pelléas et Mélisande cent and après: études et documents*, ed. Christophe Branger, Sylvie Douche, and Denis Herlin (Lyon: Symétrie, 2012), 285 [279–87]; and Lockspeiser, *Debussy: His Life and Mind*, vol. 1, Appendix B, 208 [204–08].

30. Debussy, *Correspondance*, 941; and Debusssy, *Letters*, 166.

31. Debussy, "Du Précurseur," *SIM* (March 15, 1913), in *Monsieur Croche*, 232–35; and Debussy, "Precursors," in *Debussy on Music*, 283–84. Debussy echoed this view in a letter to René Lenormand concerning the latter's book *Étude sur harmonie modern* (July 25, 1912); see Debussy, *Correspondance*, 1532–33; and Debussy, *Letters*, 260.

32. Debussy, "L'Entretien avec M. Croche," *La Revue blanche* (July 1, 1901), in *Monsieur Croche*, 52–53; Debussy, "Conversation with M. Croche," in *Debussy on Music*, 48.

33. Debussy, "La musique en plein air," *La Revue blanche* (June 1, 1901), in *Monsieur Croche*, 46; Debussy, "Music in the Open Air," in *Debussy on Music*, 41.

34. Debussy, "Concerts Colonne—Societé des nouveaux concerts," *SIM* (November 1, 1913), in *Monsieur Croche*, 247; *Debussy on Music*, 296–97.

35. Debussy, *Correspondance*, 1030.

36. Debussy, *Correspondance*, 116; and Debussy, *Letters*, 42.

37. Debussy, *Correspondance*, 310; and Debussy, *Letters*, 84.

38. Debussy, *Correspondance*, 942; and Debussy, *Letters*, 166.

39. Debussy, "Titania," in *Monsieur Croche*, 84; and Debussy, "Titania," in *Debussy on Music*, 101.

40. Debussy, "Debussy parle de sa musique," in *Monsieur Croche*, 282–83; and Debussy, "Debussy Talks of His Music," in *Debussy on Music*, 233.

1

Arabesques, Moresques, and Grotesques

In her paper "La notion d'arabesque chez Debussy," Françoise Gervais posed an intriguing question: why did Debussy regard arabesques as "divine," "adorable," and "capricieuse"?[1] The answer for Gervais lies in understanding the arabesque's changing role in aesthetic theory. Building on this insight, this chapter starts by rewinding the clock to the sixteenth and seventeenth centuries when the terms *arabesque, moresque,* and *grotesque* were first used. Next, it describes how these concepts evolved in the visual arts in the first half of the eighteenth century through the works of William Hogarth, Karl Philipp Moritz, and Jean-Antoine Watteau and in the literary arts in the second half of the eighteenth century through the writings of Johann Wolfgang von Goethe, Immanuel Kant, and Friedrich Schlegel. Among other things, this section shows how Schlegel's conception of the arabesque, which anticipated the five claims outlined in the introduction, had a direct impact on the writings of Poe, Wagner, and Baudelaire. Having lingered on three specific works, Poe's "The Fall of the House of Usher" (1839), Wagner's essay "Music of the Future" (1860/1861), and Baudelaire's prose poem "Le Thyrse" (1863), the discussion ends by describing how Schlegel's image of the arabesque, as transmitted through Poe, Wagner, and Baudelaire, influenced Symbolist writers in the 1870s and 1880s, especially those linked to *La Revue Wagnerienne.* It was against this backdrop that Debussy cultivated the vision of arabesques described in the introduction.

According to most authorities, the term *arabesque* entered the vocabulary in the late sixteenth century.[2] Writing in 1611, Randle Cotgrave defined "rebeskes" as "small, and curious flourishing, . . . Arabian-like" and the related term *moresque* as "a rude or anticke painting, or carving, wherin the feet and tayles of beasts, &c, are intermingled with, or made to resemble, a kind of wild leaves, &c."[3] Figures 1.1a–1.1c illustrate what he had in mind: figure 1.1a shows a pair of rectilinear Islamic arabesques; figure 1.1b shows a floral arabesque like those used in ancient

Greece and Rome or Gothic Europe; and figure 1.1c gives two seventeenth-century designs, one including images of a vulture and a lion surrounded by intricate floral garlands and the other featuring three monstrous faces. As Antoine Furetière noted in his *Dictionnaire universel des arts et des sciences* (1702), the terms *arabesque, moresque,* and *grotesque* were often used interchangeably: "ARABESQUE. adj. Which is made in the manner of the Arabs. The curious go to see the Palace of Granada, because of the *Arabesque* ornaments, which are marvelous. Paintings and ornaments where there are no human figures are called *Grotesque, Moresque,* and *Arabesque.*"[4] But some used the term *grotesque* or *grotesco* for designs with images of animals and people. This usage is thought to have stemmed from Michel de Montaigne, who described his own *Essais* as "antike works and monstrous bodies, patched and hudled up together of divers members without any certaine or well-ordered figure, having neither order, dependencie, or proportion, but casual and framed by chance."[5]

When the word *arabesque* was originally coined, aestheticians largely endorsed a view of art set forth in classical antiquity and reimagined in the Renaissance. That view presupposed that art should imitate nature, though it might "correct" certain defects or anomalies.[6] Special attention was paid to art forms prized by the ancient Greeks and Romans: painting, music, sculpture, architecture, and poetry.[7] These forms came to be known as the fine or beaux arts and were institutionalized in 1648 when Cardinal Mazarin founded the Académie Royale de Peinture et de Sculpture. Established a decade or so later, the Prix de Rome gave students the opportunity to experience classical art firsthand and receive on-site training in anatomy, geometry, and perspective in the Eternal City.[8] The Académie de musique and the Académie d'architecture were founded in 1669 and 1671, respectively. The scope of these institutions was conveyed in a remarkable volume prepared by Charles Perrault entitled *Le cabinet des Beaux Arts* (1690).[9] This book identifies eight fine arts: eloquence, poetry, music, architecture, painting, sculpture, optics, and mechanics. The Académie Royale de Peinture et de Sculpture, Académie de musique, and Académie d'architecture eventually merged in 1816 to create the Académie des Beaux-Arts.

Founded in 1635 to promote the French language, the Académie Française likewise promoted classical ideals. In his *Trois Discours sur le poème dramatique* (1660), for example, Pierre Corneille (1606–84) famously extended the principles of dramatic unity advocated by Aristotle and Horace, demanding not only that dramas should have a distinct beginning, middle, and end and should ensure that the action resembles reality but also that the action should occur within a unified space. Despite these innovations, however, Corneille's writing was firmly inspired by classical models: "The weightiest theoretical legacy which antiquity and the Renaissance passed on to [the seventeenth and eighteenth centuries] was the ornamental conception of poetic style. Till the dawn of Romanticism, writers continued to regard the characteristics of verse as raiment

Figure 1.1 Arabesque, grotesque, moresque

Facing top, **Figure 1.1a** Claude-Aimé Chenavard, *Motifs Persans, Album de L'Ornemaniste* (Paris: Lenoir, 1832), plate 44

Facing middle, **Figure 1.1b** Claude-Aimé Chenavard, "Devant d'Autel," *Album de L'Ornemaniste* (Paris: Lenoir, 1832), plate 3

Facing bottom, **Figure 1.1c** Anonymous, grotesque, ca. seventeenth century

adorning the 'body' of a poet's thought. These include meter (usually), syntactical deviations from the prose norm, the sensuous effect of imagery on fancied sight, and of rhyme, onomatopoeia, and alliteration on the ear."[10]

The idea that art should imitate nature and emulate classical Greco-Roman models continued to hold sway in the eighteenth century through works such as Ephraim Chambers's *Cyclopaedie* (1728).[11] Indeed, as shown in figure 1.2a, the fine arts appear under the heading of "Artificial and Technical" knowledge: painting is on the far right under the rubric of "optics"; music is under the rubric of "phonics"; sculpture and architecture are under the rubric of "mechanics"; and poetry is on the bottom line under the rubric of "symbolical," along with grammar and rhetoric. Figure 1.2b offers a similar scheme from the celebrated *Encyclopédie* (1751–66) by Denis Diderot and Jean le Rond d'Alembert.[12] Inspired by Chambers, Diderot and d'Alembert located the fine arts within the sphere of the imagination and added engraving to the list of possible contenders. And, in his highly influential *Les Beaux Arts réduits à un même principe* (1746), Charles Batteux offered yet another plan, in which dance or "the art of gesture" replaced engraving in the category of fine art.[13]

One outcome of classifying art along these lines advocated by Chambers and his successors is that it posited an underlying continuity to Western culture, one that extended from the present all the way back to ancient Rome and Greece. A major disadvantage, however, is that it insulated the fine arts aesthetically and institutionally from artworks created by non-Western cultures as well as from decorative arts such as tapestry making, couture, mosaics, ceramics, metalwork, jewelry, furniture, bookbinding, and landscape architecture. Indeed, whereas the fine arts were lauded for both their formal properties (e.g., their sense of proportion, balance, and symmetry) and their capacity to stimulate the intellect, the decorative arts were primarily appreciated for their usefulness and for their ability to serve a specific function. Furthermore, many vernacular forms, such as posters, comic books, toys, flower arranging, puppetry, acrobatics, pantomime, magic

Figure 1.2 Classification of knowledge

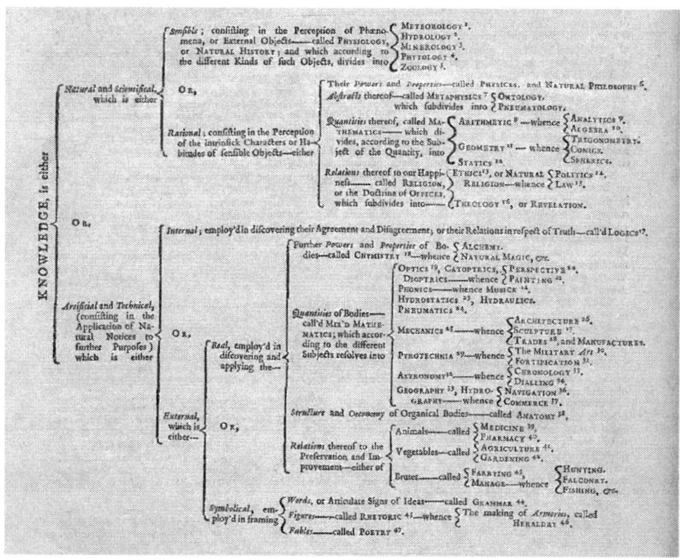

Figure 1.2a Ephraim Chambers, *Cyclopaedia* (London: J. Knapton et al., 1728)

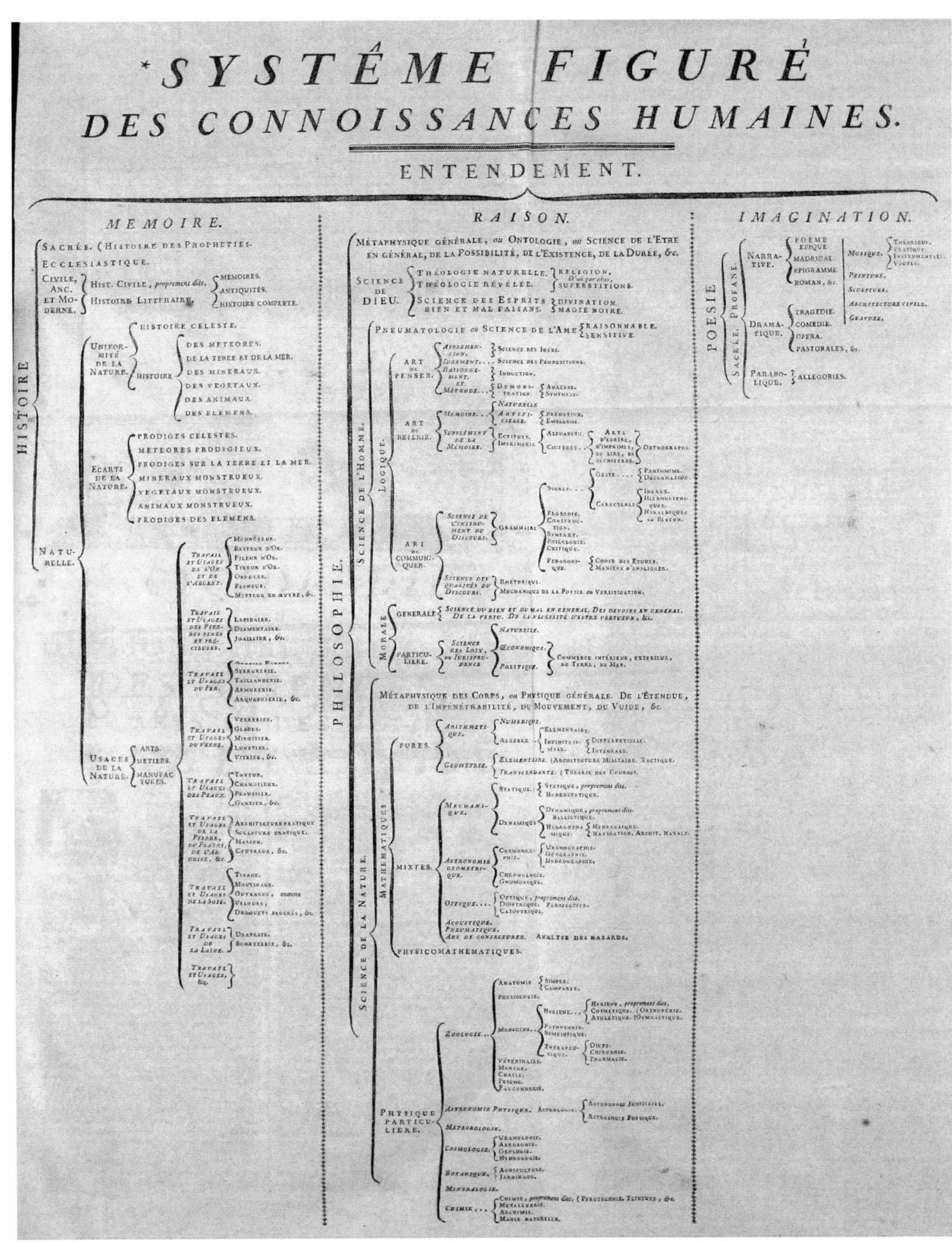

Figure 1.2b Denis Diderot and Jean le Rond d'Alembert, *Encyclopédie* (Paris: Chez Briasson, 1751–65)

Figure 1.3 Arabesques and eighteenth-century landscape architecture

Figure 1.3a *Turkish Mosque*, William Wrighte, *Grotesque Architecture or Rural Amusement* (London: Webley, 1767)

lantern shows, vaudeville, and cabaret, were dismissed as mere entertainment. With the advent of the Industrial Revolution, not only did these distinctions multiply—artists versus craftsmen, handmade versus machine-made products, and custom-made versus mass-produced objects—but decorative artists often relied on ornamentation as a means of adding value to their work, thereby prompting renewed interest in the arabesque, moresque, and grotesque, especially as borrowed from vernacular and non-Western sources.[14]

Such trends were especially striking in the field of landscape architecture, as demonstrated by William Wrighte's book *Grotesque Architecture or Rural Amusement* (1767).[15] This short treatise included plans, elevations, and sections for grottos, follies, and pavilions in a variety of styles, some vernacular (e.g., a hermit's cell), some ancient (e.g., an Augustine hermitage), and some exotic (e.g., a Chinese grotto). Figure 1.3a gives a good example of the latter: Wrighte's plan for a Turkish mosque. Figure 1.3b shows examples of buildings erected along the lines suggested by Wrighte at Kew Palace in southwest London: adorned with elaborately painted dragons, the Great Pagoda (completed in 1762) originally stood alongside a mosque (erected in 1760 but demolished in 1779), a re-creation of the Alhambra palace in Grenada (erected in 1760 but demolished in the 1820s), and the Temple of Victory (erected in 1759 but demolished in 1861). Designed by Sir William Chambers, the Great Pagoda was inspired by buildings and gardens he had encountered in 1748 on a trip to Canton (modern-day Guangzhou).[16]

Although the distinctions between fine art, decorative art, and entertainment persisted during the seventeenth and eighteenth centuries through the development of national academies, civic

Figure 1.3b *La Pagode, la Mosquée, l'Alhambra ou Temple Moresque dans les desert de Kew*, Georges Louis le Rouge, *Jardins Anglo-Chinois à la Mode* (Paris: 1788)

libraries, public concert halls and opera houses, museums and archives, conservatories, and so on, they were by no means accepted universally. On the contrary, European colonization of Africa, Asia, Central America, and the Caribbean, the migration of people to urban centers, the growth of the middle class, and the secularization of societies prompted some to question the legitimacy of those traditional distinctions. Charles Perrault was one of them. Born in 1628 and trained as a lawyer, Perrault worked as a supervisor of royal buildings for Louis XIV.[17] However, his reputation as a writer was such that he was elected to the Académie Française in 1671, where he soon became embroiled in the so-called Querelle des Anciens et des Modernes, which pitted supporters of classical literature against proponents of contemporary writing. Perrault clearly sided with the latter, as he made clear in philosophical tracts such as *Le Siècle de Louis le Grand* (1687) and *Parallèle des Anciens et des Modernes* (1688–92) and volumes of fairy tales such as *Contes en Vers* (1695) and *Histoires ou contes du temps passé* (1697). According to Jeanne Morgan Zarucchi, "[Perrault offered] his tales as modern rivals to the classical fables, superior in their moral character and pertinent to the interests of an adult, sophisticated audience. The delicate conceit of deprecating the tales as amusements for children, and signing the dedication of the prose tales with the initials of his son, was a common practice for authors of works in a lighter vein and was disregarded by his contemporaries."[18]

Another skeptic of the status quo was William Hogarth: he famously took issue with any suggestion that art could improve nature or that fine art might be distinguished from decorative art on purely formal grounds.[19] In his opinion, shapes created by nature were always superior to those created by artists: this prompted him to privilege serpentine lines over straight lines and champion the arabesque as an essential element of design. In his *Analysis of Beauty* (1753), for example, Hogarth urged readers to treat the surface of an object as if it were constructed from "so many shells of lines, closely connected together."[20] These lines can be configured in different ways. Some objects, such as cubes and pyramids, are comprised entirely of straight lines, while others, such as cylinders and cones, also require circular lines (fig. 1.4 [23]). Since straight lines

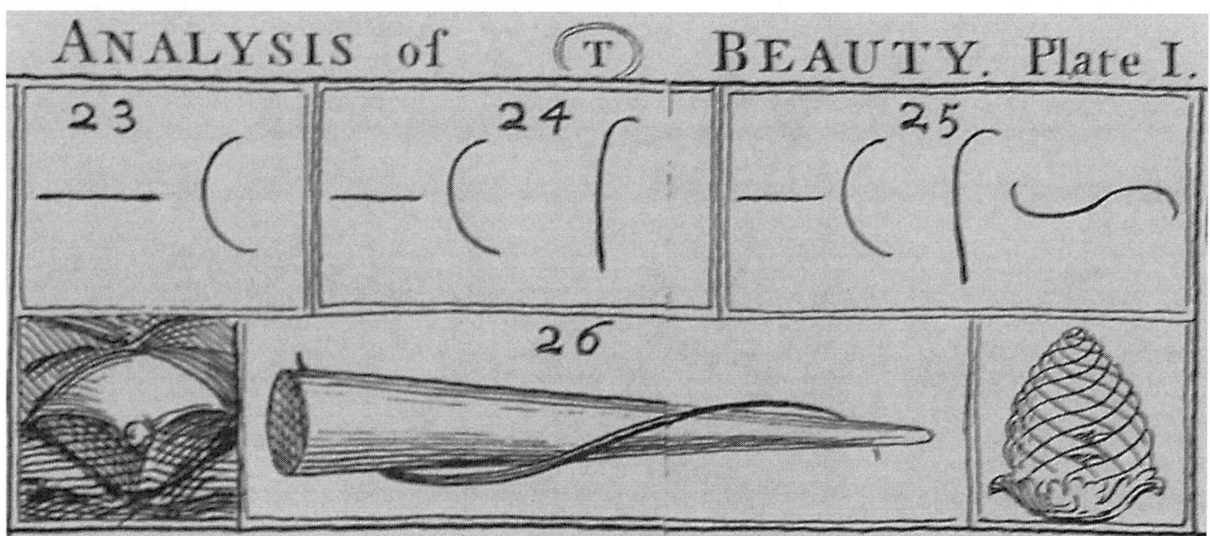

Figure 1.4 William Hogarth, *Analysis of Beauty*, Chapter 7. Combinations of straight, circular, waving, and serpentine lines

can vary only in length, Hogarth regarded them as less ornamental than circular lines, which can vary in length and degree of curvature. Next, he noted that vases and the capitals of columns and similar objects are composed of straight and circular lines as well as partly straight and circular lines (see fig. 1.4 [24]). Since these objects mix straight and circular lines, Hogarth regarded them as more ornamental than purely circular lines. He claimed that "ornamental" objects, such as flowers, also include waving lines (see fig. 1.4 [25]). These "lines of beauty" are more ornate than "compound lines" because they combine at least two contrasting curves. Finally, Hogarth suggested the most complex shapes, such as that of the human body, *combine* straight, circular, partly straight, partly circular, and waving lines to create so-called serpentine lines (see fig. 1.4 [26]). According to him, the serpentine lines add grace to beauty; their twists and turns enclose a variety of gestures, thereby giving them a unique capacity to inspire the imagination.

Hogarth's observation about the expressive power of serpentine lines was echoed by other eighteenth-century authors. In his *Vorbegriffe zu einer Theorie der Ornamente* (Berlin: Karl Matzdorff, 1793), for example, Karl Philipp Moritz noted, "Nothing is more tedious and tiresome than a military road going straight, where we see before us the objective to be reached in a direction that is always unique. A winding country path is more pleasant than a straight path."[21] Around the same time, Claude-Henri Watelet and Pierre-Charles Lévesque echoed this point of view:

Figure 1.5 Seventeenth- and eighteenth-century arabesques

Figures 1.5aa and 1.5ab Two designs from the eighteenth-century *Cahiers d'Arabesques*

Left, **Figure 1.5b** Anonymous, design for a panel, ca. 1775

Above, **Figure 1.5c** Leonardo Agostini, *Le Gemme Antiche figurate* (Rome: 1657–69)

"the beauty of contours consists in a continuous line, undulating, serpentine, always tending to roundness, and always prevented from achieving it by flat spots. The beauty of this line would be lost if it were constantly interrupted by the little shapes, the little folds, finally the little details that artists so energetically call the poverty, the miseries of nature."[22] And, according to Diderot, "The undulating line is the symbol of movement and life; the straight line is the symbol of inertia or immobility. It is the serpent that lives, or the icy serpent."[23]

The preference for complex serpentine lines expressed by Hogarth, Moritz, and Watelet and Lévesque fueled an explosion in arabesque designs in the fine arts. Figure 1.5a gives two examples from eighteenth-century *Cahiers d'Arabesques.* Dating from circa 1775, the arabesque panel in figure 1.5b is particularly ornate: it includes not only an array of floral, animal, and human motifs but also a thyrsus, an object that came to epitomize the concept of the arabesque.[24] Used in ancient Greek and Roman festivals and religious ceremonies, the thyrsus consists of a pole adorned with vines, ribbons, and tresses of flowers and topped with a pine cone and leaves. The face on the column at the center of figure 1.5b is most likely that of Dionysus/Bacchus, with whom the thyrsus is often associated. Such associations are brought to the fore in figure 1.5c; dating from the 1670s, this illustration shows a priest from the Temple of Bacchus carrying a thyrsus in one hand and a wine jug in the other.

Figure 1.6a shows an analogous image entitled *Feste Bacchique* by the French artist Jean-Antoine Watteau (1684–1721). Dating from the early eighteenth century, this design includes many of the same components as figure 1.5b: the head of Bacchus atop a column in the middle of the picture, flanked by two poles entwined with vines. The same passion for decoration can be seen

Figure 1.6 Arabesque designs by Antoine Watteau
and Jean-Baptiste Pillement

Figure 1.6a Antoine Watteau, *Feste Bacchique*

Figure 1.6b Jean-Baptiste Pillement, *Chinese Boats*, in Robert Sayer, *The Ladies Amusement: Or, The Whole Art of Japanning Made Easy* (London: Golden Buck, 1762), plate 107

in Watteau's *L'Embarquement pour Cythère* (1717) and his *Fêtes galantes*: these *highly* ornate arabesques present "poignant, arcadian visions of love in settings halfway between the real and the theatrical" and mark the change from baroque to rococo styles.[25] François Boucher (1703–70) and Jean-Baptiste Pillement (1728–1808) went on to incorporate Chinese, Indian, and other non-Western styles in their arabesques. Figure 1.6b gives Pillement's designs featuring Chinese boats as reproduced by Robert Sayer in his book *The Ladies Amusement: Or, The Whole Art of Japanning Made Easy* (1762).[26]

Although the terms *arabesque*, *moresque*, and *grotesque* were originally associated with the visual arts, they also appear in eighteenth-century literary sources, especially those by Johanne Wolfgang von Goethe, Immanuel Kant, and, above all, Friedrich Schlegel. The concept of the arabesque, as outlined in his *Dialogue on Poetry* (1799–1800) and *Literary Aphorisms* (1797–1800), became central in fact to Schlegel's theory of literary form; that theory not only provided him with a platform from which to criticize traditional explanations and classifications of art but anticipated each of Debussy's five claims.[27] First, Schlegel regarded arabesques not as "subordinate" forms of ornamentation but as "the oldest and most original form of human imagination."[28] Second, he believed that by weaving together several disparate lines of thought, arabesques are inherently contrapuntal in nature. In his novel *Lucinde* (1799), for example, such counterpoints are created by combining elements of different genres—"letters, confessions, dithyrambic fantasies, characteristics, allegory, idyll, and reflections."[29] Third, instead of differentiating between the ornamental and the structural, Schlegel insisted that arabesques create self-generating forms in which small details often determine larger structures: "transitions [are] unrecognizable, or at least not as stressed as breaks, for every position in the ornament is simultaneously that of another."[30] Fourth, Schlegel claimed that arabesques induce a sense of fantasy and release the mind from preconceived ideas and forms: "For this is the beginning of all poetry. To unravel the progression and laws of rationally thinking reason, and to transplant us once again in the beautiful confusion of the imagination, into the original chaos of human nature."[31] It was for this reason that Schlegel promoted two decidedly unconventional literary forms: the fragment and the prose poem.[32] And fifth, Schlegel proposed that arabesques can even conjure up colors, images, and sounds. When discussing Diderot's *The Fatalist*, for example, he declared, "No, it is the sacred breath which, in the tones of music, moves us. It cannot be grasped forcibly and comprehended mechanically, but it can be amiably lured by mortal beauty and veiled in it. The magic words of poetry can be infused with and inspired by its power."[33] Schlegel even saw arabesques as akin to confessions: "There would be true arabesques, which together with confessions . . . are the only romantic products of nature in our age."[34] This suggestion would soon be manifest in Thomas De Quincey's arabesque novel *Confessions of an English Opium Eater* (1822).[35]

Filtered through the writings of Jean Paul, E. T. A. Hoffmann, and other early German Romantics, Schlegel's conception of the literary arabesque had a direct impact on Edgar Allan Poe and his celebrated *Tales of the Grotesque and Arabesque* (1839).[36] Take, for instance, "The Fall of the House of Usher."[37] Following Aristotle, the story has a clear beginning, middle, and end. It begins when Roderick Usher is visited by a school friend; his remote and decaying mansion is flanked by dead trees, a stagnant tarn, and a rocky causeway. Roderick and his twin sister, Lady Madeline, are scarred physiologically and psychologically from the family's isolation and generations of inbreeding: he is hypersensitive to light, sound, smell, and taste; she is prone to deathlike cataleptic trances and appears only briefly after a visit from the family physician. Roderick and the friend become reacquainted in the middle of the story. Roderick performs some of his own musical compositions and explains his controversial belief that plants and stones are sentient. The scene closes when, late one evening, Roderick announces that Lady Madeline is dead. The two men take her body to the vault, which is located deep beneath the house at the end of a copper-lined corridor and behind a heavy iron door. After securing her body in a coffin, they come back upstairs. The story ends one dark and stormy night. Roderick's mental state has deteriorated rapidly since his sister's death. His friend tries to console him by reading "Mad Trist," a story by Sir Launcelot Canning. But after some terrifying sounds, the two men turn around to see Lady Madeline drenched in blood. They realize that they had accidentally buried her alive and that she has clawed her way to freedom. Roderick reaches out to her, but she collapses on him, killing him instantly. The friend rushes out of the house. While he is crossing the causeway, there is a violent flash of light and a terrible noise; Usher's ancestral home disappears under the swirling waters of the tarn.

Though organized along Aristotelian lines, "The Fall of the House of Usher" illustrates the idea of a literary arabesque in several ways. August Nigro points to Poe's intricate account of the house's exterior: "What Poe dramatizes in the Gothic action, he also effectively evokes in the arabesque imagery. The genealogical and psychological House of Usher is the architectural house of Usher: the cadaverous structure, with a 'barely perceptible fissure' running down its facade into the tarn that mirrors forth in even more foreboding and 'inverted images' the decadence of the House." Nigro adds, "It is an effective symbol: a fourfold pattern, halved by the fissure and quartered by the tarn's reflection. It is the Usher coat of arms, made more arabesque and grotesque by the order and arrangement of the stones that are overspread with fungi and surrounded by decaying trees."[38] Poe's portrait of Roderick is equally ornate.

> A cadaverousness of complexion; an eye large, liquid, and luminous beyond comparison; lips somewhat thin and very pallid, but of a surpassingly beautiful curve; a nose of a delicate Hebrew model, but with a breadth of nostril unusual in similar formations; a finely moulded chin, speaking, in its want of promi-nence, of a want of moral energy; hair of a more than web-like softness and tenuity; these features, with an inordinate expansion above the regions of the temple, made up altogether a countenance not easily to be forgotten. The now ghastly pallor of the skin, and the now miraculous lustre of the eye, above all things startled and even awed me.[39]

Poe continued, "The silken hair, too, had been suffered to grow all unheeded, and as, in its wild gossamer texture, it floated rather than fell about the face, I could not, even with effort, connect its Arabesque expression with any idea of simple humanity."[40]

At the same time, "The Fall of the House of Usher" illustrates Schlegel's insight about the contrapuntal nature of arabesques. A particularly beautiful example occurs near the end of the story when Poe interweaves the friend's recitation of Ethelred's encounter with the dragon with Lady Madeline's struggle for freedom. Each event in the former is correlated with one in the latter: the sound of Ethelred smashing the hermit's door lines up with that of Lady Madeline splitting open the coffin; the sound of him engaging the dragon with that of her opening the iron door; the sound of him dropping his shield with that of her crawling along the copper-lined corridor. The two threads then combine at the end of the story: "In an effective contrapuntal movement to the death embrace and collapse of Roderick and Lady Madeline, the house of Usher is rent asunder and, together with its morbid image in the tarn, collapses in a kaleidoscopic implosion into the dark waters, leaving behind the circular, but red-blood moon."[41] According to Freud's student Marie Bonaparte, "The legendary theme of the dragon, which must be killed to win some woman—with or without the aid of treasure—is as old as the world. It is the perfect expression of the Œdipus wish: the dragon, symbol of the father, is killed and the mother set free to belong to the victorious son. It is the theme of the legend of Perseus and Andromeda, of Siegfried and Brunhild."[42] The mother, symbolized by Madeline, punishes Roderick for his "infantile inces-tuous wishes towards his Mother."[43] Bonaparte also suggests that the black tarn represents "a transference from one who once existed: the dead mother who still survived in the unconscious memory of her son."[44] The dark waters allow the House of Usher to sleep forever, "brother with sister, mother with son."[45]

Poe likewise followed Schlegel in using local details to generate global structures. To quote H. P. Lovecraft, "Simple and straight-forward in plot, ['Ligeia' and 'The Fall of the House of Usher'] owe their supreme magic to the cunning development which appears in the selection and colloca-tion of every least incident."[46] Lovecraft specifically cites Roderick's excursus about the sentience of plants and stones. Although it initially seems like a non sequitur, Roderick's comment about "obscure life in inorganic things" captures the essence of the entire drama: "an abnormally linked trinity of entities at the end of a long and isolated family history—a brother, his twin sister, and their incredibly ancient house all sharing a single soul and meeting one common dissolution and the same moment."[47] And, predictable as the plots of gothic horror stories may be, Lovecraft insists that Poe essentially "[re]invented the short story in its present form," thereby elevating "disease, perversity, and decay to a level of artistically expressible themes."[48]

Following Schlegel's lead, Poe associated the arabesque with the fantastic. Above all, Poe was fascinated with the uncanny (*Das Unheimliche*), a concept cultivated by E. T. A. Hoffmann, discussed by Friedrich Wilhelm Joseph von Schelling (1842), and developed by Ernst Jentsch (1906) and Sigmund Freud (1919).[49] As Tzvetan Todorov notes, "'The Fall of the House of Usher' is an instance of the uncanny bordering on the fantastic."[50] He suggests that the uncanny surfaces in two ways. First, the story relies on two coincidences: "the resurrection of Usher's sister and the fall of the house after the death of its inhabitants."[51] Second, it relies on "an experience of limits" and deviations from the norm: "it is the extremely morbid condition of the brother and sister which disturbs the reader."[52] From a literary perspective, the fantastic also manifests itself in what John Barth refers to as "the contamination of reality by irreality" and "the text within the text."[53] One way in which Poe contaminates reality with irreality is by his references to external sources. Some, such as the epigram by Pierre-Jean de Béranger; the books by Jean-Baptiste Gresset, Niccolo Machiavelli, Emanuel Swedenborg, et al.; the nightmare paintings of Henry Fuseli; and the waltz by Carl Maria von Weber are real. But Canning's story "Mad Trist" is fictitious.[54] The most obvious example of a "text within the text" is, of course, Roderick's ballad "The Haunted Palace." This poem, which Roderick performs midway through "The Fall of the House of Usher," is a perfect example of what André Gide referred to as a *mise en abyme*: in this case it provides a smaller mirror image of what will happen in the story as a whole.[55] "The Haunted Palace" also stands out because it was first published as an independent poem in the *Baltimore Museum Magazine* in April 1839 and is widely believed to be based on a pseudo-Elizabethan verse by John Wolcot (1738–1819), a.k.a. "Peter Pindar."[56]

Finally, like Schlegel before him, Poe recognized that arabesques have the capacity to stir the emotions and function autobiographically. As Lovecraft rightly points out, many of Poe's most evocative ideas ultimately derive from his own psychology, notably his "depression, sensitiveness, mad aspiration, loneliness, and extravagant freakishness."[57] These are precisely the emotions Roderick felt in his bleak ancestral home and that Poe re-created with extraordinary precision in "The Fall of the House of Usher." Some have even claimed that Poe suffered from taphophobia, an extreme condition of claustrophobia due to the fear of being buried alive. Although this was probably not the case, it resonates perfectly with Schlegel's claims about the interconnections between arabesques and confessions and the fact that Poe finished "The Fall of the House of User" a couple years after he married his thirteen-year-old first cousin Virginia Clemm, his so-called "sister-wife," in 1836.[58]

Another author inspired by Schlegel's concept of the arabesque was the French poet and critic Charles Baudelaire. Like Poe before him, Baudelaire acquired a taste for the arabesque from reading German Romantic authors: he was especially fond of Hoffmann's *Der Sandmann* (1816) and *Das Fräulein von Scuderi* (1819).[59] Baudelaire even traced the concept of *correspondances*—the idea that sensory perceptions of one type (e.g., a sound, a smell, a color, or a movement) can trigger those of another—to a passage from Hoffmann's *Kreisleriana* (1814–15): "It is not only in dreams, or in the mild delirium which precedes sleep, but it is even awakened when I hear music—that the perception of an analogy and an intimate connexion between colours, sounds and perfumes. It seems to me that all these things were created by one and the same ray of light, and that their combination must result in a wonderful concert of harmony."[60] This concept would, of course, become the subject of his poem "Correspondances" from *Les Fleurs du mal* (1857) and raised the possibility of unifying artistic experiences in different domains—written, visual, aural, and so on—through the process of synesthesia.[61]

Sometime in the 1840s, Baudelaire's fascination with the arabesque intensified after he encountered the writings of Poe.[62] Clearly identifying with Poe's reputation as a *"poète maudit,"* Baudelaire especially enjoyed the American author's technical skills and masterful use of the arabesque.[63] Like Lovecraft, he drew attention to the tightly woven structure of Poe's stories: "throughout the whole composition not a single word must be allowed to intrude which is not also an intention and which does not aim, directly or indirectly, at completing a premeditated design."[64] These factors contributed to their strong sense of overall unity: "Everything in a poem as in a novel, everything in a sonnet as in a novelette, ought to contribute to the dénouement. A good writer has the last line already in his mind when he writes the first."[65] And Baudelaire delighted in Poe's use of details: "he analyses whatever is most transitory, weighs the imponderable and describes, in that detailed, scientific manner whose effects are so terrible, the whole imaginary atmosphere which floats around the man of nerves and leads him on to his downfall."[66] Baudelaire's admiration was so great that he set about translating Poe's short stories from English into French, starting with "Mesmeric Revelation" in 1848. Over the next seven years, he published further translations with "La chute de la Maison Usher" appearing serially in *Le Pays* on February 7, 9, and 13, 1855. Baudelaire subsequently gathered them up into sets: *Histoires extraordinaires* (1856), *Nouvelles histoires extraordinaires* (1857), *Aventures d'Arthur Gordon Pym* (1858), *Eureka* (1863), and *Histoires grotesques et sérieuses* (1865).[67] According to Gautier, Baudelaire's translations are perfect in almost every respect: "they possess a correspondence in style and thought so exact, a freedom so faithful yet so supple, that they produce the same effect as the original."[68]

Baudelaire's interest in the arabesque also affected his poetry, especially "Le Thyrse" (1863).[69] Published posthumously in *Le Spleen de Paris* and dedicated to Franz Liszt, this prose poem is the perfect manifestation of Schlegel's arabesque. The text, reproduced below, divides into three paragraphs that articulate a clear beginning, middle, and end. Paragraph 1 poses a simple question—"what is a thyrsus?"—and offers an obvious reply: according to myth, the thyrsus was a simple staff used by priests in religious rituals. Since the staff features entwined vines and flowers it encapsulates the concept of the arabesque. Next, paragraph 2 qualifies this answer by suggesting that the thyrsus symbolizes two universal aspects of artistic genius, with the staff representing the artist's sense of purpose and the vines and flowers representing their creativity. Finally, paragraph 3 pays homage to Liszt. Presented as a single sentence, it begins by addressing "Dear Liszt" directly and then spirals round in a serpentine fashion toward its final celebration of Liszt's immortality as a "philosopher, poet, and artist." By casting this final arabesque as a single sentence, Baudelaire illustrated Schlegel's claim that "a theory of the novel would have to be itself a novel."[70]

À Franz Liszt

    Qu'est-ce qu'un thyrse? Selon le sens moral et poétique, c'est un emblème sacerdotal dans la main des prêtres ou des prêtresses célébrant la divinité dont ils sont les interprètes et les serviteurs. Mais physiquement ce n'est qu'un bâton, un pur bâton, perche à houblon, tuteur de vigne, sec, dur et droit. Autour de ce bâton, dans des méandres capricieux, se jouent et folâtrent des tiges et des fleurs, celles-ci sinueuses et fuyardes, celles-là penchées comme des cloches ou des coupes renversées. Et une gloire étonnante jaillit de cette complexité de lignes et de couleurs, tendres ou éclatantes. Ne dirait-on pas que la ligne courbe et la spirale font leur cour à la ligne droite et dansent autour dans une muette adoration? Ne dirait-on pas que toutes ces corolles délicates, tous ces calices, explosions de senteurs et de couleurs, exécutent un mystique fandango autour du bâton hiératique? Et quel est, cependant, le mortel imprudent qui osera décider si les fleurs et les pampres ont été faits pour le bâton, ou si le bâton n'est que le prétexte pour montrer la beauté des pampres et des fleurs?

Le thyrse est la représentation de votre étonnante dualité, maître puissant et vénéré, cher Bacchant de la Beauté mystérieuse et passionnée. Jamais nymphe exaspérée par l'invincible Bacchus ne secoua son thyrse sur les têtes de ses compagnes affolées avec autant d'énergie et de caprice que vous agitez votre génie sur les cœurs de vos frères.—Le bâton, c'est votre volonté, droite, ferme et inébranlable; les fleurs, c'est la promenade de votre fantaisie autour de votre volonté; c'est l'élément féminin exécutant autour du mâle ses prestigieuses pirouettes. Ligne droite et ligne arabesque, intention et expression, roideur de la volonté, sinuosité du verbe, unité du but, variété des moyens, amalgame tout-puissant et indivisible du génie, quel analyste aura le détestable courage de vous diviser et de vous séparer?

Cher Liszt, à travers les brumes, par delà les fleuves, par-dessus les villes où les pianos chantent votre gloire, où l'imprimerie traduit votre sagesse, en quelque lieu que vous soyez, dans les splendeurs de la ville éternelle ou dans les brumes des pays rêveurs que console Cambrinus, improvisant des chants de délection ou d'ineffable douleur, ou confiant au papier vos méditations abstruses, chantre de la Volupté et de l'Angoisse éternelles, philosophe, poëte et artiste, je vous salue en l'immortalité![71]

Close reading of "Le Thyrse" reveals that Baudelaire addressed each aspect of the arabesque proposed by Schlegel, amplified by Poe, and reiterated by Debussy. For starters, he invoked the thyrsus to highlight the significance of ornamentation in art. In particular, he noted that the thyrsus is first and foremost a sacred artifact: "a sacerdotal emblem in the hands of the priests and priestesses when celebrating the godhead whose intermediaries and servants they are." Echoing Schlegel's claim that arabesques are "the oldest and most original form of human imagination," Baudelaire drew special attention to the spiritual dimension of the arabesque: "The arabesque design is the most spiritualistic of designs. . . . The arabesque design is the most ideal of all."[72] This observation resonates perfectly with Debussy's reference to the divine arabesque in his Good Friday review.

"Le Thyrse" likewise underscores Baudelaire's desire to challenge literary convention. One way it does so is by being cast as a prose poem, a form championed by Schlegel, rather than as alexandrines, the traditional scheme used throughout *Les Fleurs du mal*. Baudelaire celebrated the radical nature of the prose poem in "À Arsenne Houssaye," the opening poem of *Le Spleen de Paris*: "Which of us has never imagined, in his more ambitious moments, the miracle of a poetic prose, musical though rhythmless and rhymeless, flexible yet strong enough to identify with the lyrical impulses of the soul, the ebbs and flows of revery, the pangs of conscience?[73] It goes without saying, of course, that the staff of a thyrsus is disguised by vines and flowers—"sinuous and fugitive . . . hanging their heads like little bells or overturned goblets." But Baudelaire rejected any attempt to distinguish the ornamental from the structural: "And what imprudent mortal will ever dare to decide whether the flowers and the vine branches were created for the staff, or whether the staff is a pretext for displaying the beauty of the vine branches and the flowers?"[74]

Baudelaire was equally adamant that poets can create harmony by interweaving different lines of thought: "The poetic phrase can mimic (and thereby it touches upon the art of music and the science of mathematics) the horizontal line, the straight line up, the straight line down, it can climb steeply to the sky without breathlessness or perpendicularly down to hell with all the velocity of gravity, it can follow the spiral, decry the parable, or zigzag contained in a series of superimposed angles."[75] In the case of the thyrsus, this interplay is achieved by surrounding the straight line of the pole with the serpentine lines of the vines: "An amazing effect is created by this complex pattern of lines and colors, tender or brilliant. It is as if the curve and the spiral are wooing the straight line, around which they dance in silent admiration. It is as if all those delicate corollæ, all these chalices, in explosions of scent and colors, dance a mystical fandango around the hieratic wand." Or, in the words of Georges Poulet, "The poetic act is . . . a spiral that winds and unwinds around a directed thought."[76]

Also in keeping with Schlegel's views about the arabesque, Baudelaire implied that the thyrsus cultivates an aura of mystery and fantasy, with the pole symbolizing the artist's will (*volonté*) and the twisting vine representing their imaginations (*fantaisie*): "No nymph exasperated by the invincible Bacchus ever waved her thyrsus over the heads of her stampeded companions with as much energy as you wave the baton of genius over the hearts of your brother artists."[77] Once again, he expressed similar views elsewhere. In his essay "L'Œuvres et la vie de Delacroix," for example, he described the ineffable genius of Eugène Delacroix.

> You will be asking what is this strange, mysterious quality which Delacroix, to the glory of our age, has interpreted better than anyone else. It is the invisible, the impalpable, the dream, the nerves, the *soul*; and this he has done—allow me, please, to emphasize this point—with no other means but colour and contour; he has done it better than anyone else—he has done it with the perfection of a consummate painter, with the exactitude of a subtle writer, with the eloquence of an impassioned musician. It is, moreover, one of the characteristic symptoms of the spiritual condition of our age that the arts aspire if not to take one another's place, at least reciprocally to lend one another new powers.[78]

In the same vein, he suggested that Delacroix's paintings create a sense of aesthetic pleasure not just from their subject but also from their very design: "A well-drawn figure fills you with a pleasure divorced from its subject. Whether voluptuous or awe-inspiring, this figure will owe its entire charm to the arabesque which it cuts in space."[79]

Finally, Baudelaire treated the thyrsus as a symbol of the ways in which poets express their most profound thoughts and emotions: "Straight line and arabesque—intention and expression—unyielding will-power and the suppleness of the word—united in purpose, varied in means—the all-powerful and indivisible amalgam of genius—what analyst would be so bold as to divide or separate you?" For him, there is a causal connection between line and emotion: "The harmony, [balance of the lines], eurythmy of movements appear to the dreamer as necessities, as duties not only in relation to all beings in creation but also to himself . . . and the dreamer finds that he is endowed with a marvelous aptitude for understanding the immortal, universal rhythm."[80] Given the poem's dedication, it is tempting to assume that these lines celebrate the achievements of Franz Liszt. However, as David Ellison points out, by recalling a paragraph from Liszt's book on Wagner and quoted by Baudelaire in his essay "Richard Wagner et *Tannhäuser* à Paris," it is more likely that Wagner is "the protagonist behind the meandering, serpentine figuration of 'Le Thyrse.'"[81] When he positioned "the god behind his priest," Baudelaire recalled Wagner's allusions to the thyrsus in act 3 of *Tannhäuser* when "Tannhäuser relates his travails as pilgrim to Wolfram."[82] This connection is perfectly understandable given Baudelaire's personal friendship with Wagner and the fact that his essay was first published in *La Revue européenne* in the spring of 1861, just after the Paris production of *Tannhäuser* had been canceled.

Baudelaire's decision to connect the thyrsus with Richard Wagner is significant because it helps explain why the arabesque pervades so much discourse about music in the latter half of the nineteenth century. Baudelaire had, of course, read Richard Wagner's "Music of the Future" (1860/1861) before writing "Le Thyrse."[83] But given his lack of training in music, he decided to let Liszt speak on his behalf: "The spectator . . . will be in a position to find an uncommon interest in the following through the space of three acts the deeply-pondered, astonishingly skillful and poetically intelligent combinations, with which Wagner, *by means of several leitmotivs*, has tied *a melodic knot* which constitutes his whole drama. The twists and turns made by these phrases as they wind and interlace around the words of the poem, have an effect which is to the utmost degree moving."[84] Or, to borrow the image of the serpentine line, "There are phrases . . . which run through the opera like a poisonous snake, winding around its victims and fleeing before their holy champions."[85] Baudelaire went so far as to declare that "Wagner's music would still be a poetic work" because, like a well-constructed poem, "all its elements harmoniously wedded, mutually adapted, and . . . skillfully *concatenated*."[86] This declaration is, of course, a consequence of his belief in correspondances: "it would be by no means absurd at this point to argue *a priori*; for what *would be* truly surprising would be to find that sound *could not* suggest colour, that colours *could not* evoke the idea of a melody, and that sound and colour were *unsuitable* for the translation of ideas, seeing that things have always found their expression through a system of reciprocal analogy ever since the day when God uttered the world like a complex and indivisible statement."[87] Associating the thyrsus, the arabesque, and correspondances to Wagner's music also allowed Baudelaire to treat them as symbols of *modernity* in art: just as he used the thyrsus to convey the idea that artistic creativity requires both fantasy as symbolized by the twisting vines and purpose as symbolized by the staff, so he insisted that artworks rely on both innovation and tradition. He explained this duality as follows: "By modernity, I mean the ephemeral, the fugitive, the contingent, the half of art whose other half is eternal and the immutable."[88] For Baudelaire, Wagner epitomized modernity in art.[89]

Given that Symbolist writers and artists were ardent Wagnerians, it is hardly surprising that they frequently contributed to Édouard Dujardin's *Revue Wagnerienne*.[90] This remarkable periodical, which ran from February 1885 to July 1888, combined previously published items by Baudelaire and others with newly commissioned essays, poems, and illustrations by Villiers de l'Isle-Adam, Verlaine, Mallarmé, Huysmans, Swinburne, Redon, Mendès, and their less familiar acolytes. Wagner inspired them in various ways. His obsession with myths, legends, and fairy tales clearly fueled their interest in the universal aspects of human nature.[91] As he explained, myths provide "the greatest possible scope for revealing those inner psychic motives which alone can bring home the inevitability of the action since we ourselves feel them in our own hearts," and hence left him free "to deal with them in such a way that that very atmosphere would itself become the action."[92] By formulating the concept of *Versmelodie*, a synthesis between words and music that expresses both thought and feeling, Wagner foreshadowed the Symbolists' interest in the links between poetry and music: "The poet's handling of words subordinates their abstract conventional meaning to their elemental sensuous quality: through the organization of metre and quasi musical embellishment of rhyme his phraseology acquires a magical power of evoking and determining feeling."[93] Such interconnections also gave rise to the concept of the *Gesamtkunstwerk* by fusing elements of different media—poetry, music, dance, and the visual arts—into a single unified experience, and to Wagner's notion that "every genre (itself a multiple of one great art . . .) is defined by its own arabesque."[94] And Wagner fueled the Symbolists' dislike of standard forms by rejecting the traditional concept of a number opera, with its alternation between arias and recitatives, on the grounds that it forced the poet to "degrade both his subject and his poetry to the level of triviality castigated in that pronouncement of Voltaire: ['What is too stupid to be said, we sing.']"[95]

At the same time, Wagner insisted that music's expressive power ultimately stems from its melodic content: "*melody is the only form of music.* . . . To say that a piece of music has no melody is in a higher sense tantamount to saying that a composer has failed to create a form that grips and stirs our emotions."[96] Above all, he used particular melodic patterns or leitmotivs that denote the specific characters, locations, objects, and emotional states.[97] These patterns can be intensified in two ways. First, they can be superimposed contrapuntally: "through the so-called art of counterpoint each voice could be employed independently and expressively beneath the melody proper (the so-called *cantus firmus*)."[98] Second, they can be developed symphonically: "The modern symphony orchestra . . . will be intimately involved: it will embody the harmony which alone makes possible the melody's specific expression; it will maintain the melody in a state of uninterrupted flow so that the motives will be able to work with maximum effect upon the audience's feelings . . . through the richly varied development of all the motives it contained, into a continuous large-scale piece, which in itself constituted a single, perfectly coherent melody."[99] According to Wagner, "It is the musician who can bring this great Unsaid to sounding life, and the unmistakable form of his resounding silence is *endless melody* (*Die unendliche Melodie*)."[100]

It was during the heyday of the *Revue Wagnerienne* that Jean Moréas codified the tenets of Symbolism in a manifesto published in *Le Figaro* (September 18, 1886).[101] Having pointed to the pioneering efforts of Shakespeare, Stendahl, Balzac, Hugo, Flaubert, the Goncourts, and Zola, the document praised Baudelaire for being the "true forerunner" of Symbolism and the main source of inspiration for Mallarmé and Verlaine. Moréas celebrated their complex written styles, which embodied the arabesque through its synthesis "of unpolluted terms, periods which brace themselves alternating with periods of undulating lapses, significant pleonasms, mysterious ellipses, outstanding anacoluthia, any audacious and multiform surplus."[102] They also enlivened traditional poetic forms: "the ancient metric enlivened; a chaos learnedly ordered; the rhyme illucescente and beaten as a buckler of gold and bronze, to rhymes of unintelligible fluidity; the alexandrine with numerous and mobile stopping; the job of first certain numbers—seven, nine, eleven, thirteen—bold in the various rhythmic combinations of which they are the price."[103]

By the late 1880s, arabesques featured prominently in other artistic styles, including art nouveau. Indeed, Jean Pierrot notes, "The widespread use of the arabesque corresponds to a desire to saturate perception by drawing it into a maze of curves that submerges and obscures all solid forms. Like baroque art, with which it shares a similar dynamism, as well as a taste for ostentation and superabundance, Art Nouveau aims to provoke an impression of profusion in which the spectator's gaze becomes lost."[104] Although such trends can be found in the work of artists throughout Europe and America, the names that immediately spring to mind are Antoni Gaudi in Catalonia, Alphonse Mucha and Hector Guimard in France, William Morris and Aubrey Beardsley in England, Victor Horta and Paul Hankar in Belgium, and Louis Comfort Tiffany and Louis Sullivan in the US. Pierrot draws special attention to the theories of Eugène Grasset, a Swiss decorative artist who worked in Paris. Recalling Hogarth's *Analysis of Beauty*, Grasset's monumental treatise *Méthode de Composition Ornemental* (ca. 1900) not only distinguished designs based on straight lines (Vol. 1, Éléments rectilignes) and those based on curves (Vol. 2, Éléments courbes) but also emphasized the expressive power of curves and spirals: "It is not gold, any more than rarity or intrinsic value, that creates richness; it is the method of working even the most poverty-stricken material, and at very little cost, in order, once again, to avoid the visual flatness, coldness, and poverty that even the most costly material can present. . . . That once grasped, the way is open for the creation of true works of art, works upon which the hand can rest with refined and subtle pleasure, and which will not repel us like the eternally plain and polished glass of mirrors."[105] According to Pierrot, the profusion of curves and spirals "should express the anarchic upsurge of concealed layers of sensibility, so that there can be no doubt that such art contains a predominantly irrational element."[106] That irrational element might be entirely benign, as in the arabesque styles of the Pre-Raphaelites, the arts and crafts movement, and other genres of decorative art. But for those with more decadent tastes, they might unleash more troubling emotions: "Anxiety and dread, even perversity and morbidity, the eruption of the unconscious, baroque superabundance of forms expressed by means of an ever more complex network of arabesques, anti-naturalism, violent movement and deliberate visual excess, these are indeed the essential features to be found in the specifically decadent strain of fin-de-siècle art."[107] As this book makes clear, the same themes shaped Debussy's handling of the arabesque.

Notes

1. Françoise Gervais, "La notion d'arabesque chez Debussy," *La Revue musicale* 241 (1958): 4.

2. Ina Baghdiantz McCabe, *Orientalism in Early Modern France* (Oxford: Berg, 2008).

3. Randle Cotgrave, *A Dictionarie of the French and English Tongues* [1611] (Columbia: University of South Carolina Press, 1968).

4. Antoine Furetière, *Dictionnaire universel des arts et des sciences* (The Hague: Leers, 1702), https://books.google.com/books?id=nrdKAAAAcAAJ&printsec=frontcover#v=onepage&q&f=false.

5. The Art and Popular Culture Encyclopedia: Jan-Willem Geerinck's mind upload, "Montaigne was the first to apply the word 'grotesque' with reference to literature," http://www.artandpopularculture.com/Montaigne_was_the_first_to_apply_the_word_%22grotesque%22_with_reference_to_literature, accessed October 16, 2022.

6. A. J. Close, "Commonplace Theories of Art and Nature in Classical Antiquity and the Renaissance," *Journal of the History of Ideas* 30, no. 4 (1969): 467–86, esp. 469 and 472.

7. Larry Shiner, *The Invention of Art* (Chicago: University of Chicago Press, 2001), 79–88.

8. See Albert Boime, "The Prix de Rome: Images of Authority and Threshold of Official Success," *Art Journal* 44, no. 3 (1984): 281–89.

9. Charles Perrault, *Le cabinet des Beaux Arts* (Paris: G. Edelinck, 1690).

10. Emerson Marks, *Taming the Chaos: English Poetic Diction Theory Since the Renaissance* (Detroit, MI: Wayne State University, 1998), 55.

11. Ephraim Chambers, *Cyclopaedie*, 2 vols. (London: J. Knapton et al., 1728) with two supplement vols. in 1753. https://onlinebooks.library.upenn.edu/webbin/book/lookupname?key=Chambers%2C%20Ephraim%2C%20approximately%201680%2D1740.

12. Denis Diderot and Jean Le Rond d'Alembert, *Encyclopédie, ou Dictionnaire Raisonné des Sciences, des Arts, et des Métiers* (Paris: Chez Briasson, 1751–65).

13. Charles Batteux, *Les Beaux Arts réduits à un même principe* (Paris: Durand, 1746), https://gallica.bnf.fr/ark:/12148/bpt6k50428g.image.

14. Shiner, *Invention of Art*, 206–12.

15. William Wrighte, *Grotesque Architecture or Rural Amusement* (London: Henry Webley, 1767), https://openlibrary.org/works/OL16751738W/Grotesque_architecture_or_Rural_amusement.

16. Sir William Chambers, *Plans, Elevations, Sections, and Perspective Views of the Gardens and Buildings at Kew in Surry (1763)*, facsimile ed. (London: Gregg International, 1966).

17. Charles Perrault, *Memoirs of My Life*, ed. and trans. Jeanne Morgan (Columbia: University of Missouri Press, 1989).

18. Jeanne Morgan Zarucchi, "Note" to Appendix C, in Perrault, *Memoirs of My Life*, 120.

19. Richard Woodfield, "Introductory Note," in William Hogarth, *The Analysis of Beauty* (London: J. Reeves, 1753). A Scolar Press Facsimile (Ilkley: Scolar Press, 1969). See also Danièle Cohn, "Préface," in Karl Philipp Moritz, *Sur l'ornement*, ed. and trans. Clara Paquet (Paris: Éditions Rue d'Ulm, 2008), 15.

20. William Hogarth, *Analysis of Beauty*, 37.

21. Karl Philipp Moritz, *Sur l'ornement*, ed. and trans. Clara Paquet (Paris, Éditions Rue d'Ulm, 2008), 30.

22. Claude-Henri Watelet and Pierre-Charles Lévesque, "Détails," in *Dictionnaire des arts de peinture, sculpture et gravure*, vol. 1 (Paris: L. F. Prault, 1792; Geneva: Minkoff Reprints, 1972), 618–19.

23. Denis Diderot, "Pensées détachées sur la peinture, la sculpture, l'architecture et la poésie pour servir de suite aux Salons," in *Œuvres de Denis Diderot*, vol. 10, ed. Hippolyte Walferdin (Paris: J. L. J. Brière, 1821), 199, https://gallica.bnf.fr/ark:/12148/bpt6k9788771p/f181.ite. See also Nathalie Kremer, "The Broken Lines of Art. Diderot and Baudelaire on Painting," *Nouvelle revue d'esthétique* 25, no. 1 (2020): 147 [145–53].

24. This illustration is available from: https://commons.wikimedia.org/wiki/File:Drawing,_Arabesque_Design _for_a_Panel,_ca._1775_(CH_18159425).jpg.

25. Jeffrey Collins, "Watteau and the *Fête galante* by Martin Eidelberg, Barbara Anderman, Guillaume Glorieux, Michael Hochmann and François Moureau," *Eighteenth-Century Studies* 38, no. 4 (2005), 691 [691–96]. *Watteau et la Fête galante* Réunion des Musées Nationaux; Hors Collection edition (April 1, 2004); and Mary L. Meyers, *French Architectural and Ornament Drawings of the Eighteenth Century* (New York: Metropolitan Museum of Art, 1991).

26. Robert Sayer, *The Ladies Amusement: Or, The Whole Art of Japanning Made Easy* (London: Golden Buck, 1762), facsimile ed. (Newport: Ceramic Book, 1966).

27. Friedrich Schlegel, *Dialogue on Poetry and Literary Aphorisms*, trans., introduced, and annotated by Ernest Behler and Roman Struc (University Park: Pennsylvania State University Press, 1968). See also Patricia Stanley, "Hoffmann's 'Phantasiestücke in Callots Manier' in Light of Friedrich Schlegel's Theory of the Arabesque," *German Studies Review* 8, no. 3 (October 1985): 399–419; Alain Muzelle, "Arabesque et Roman dans l'oeuvre de Friedrich Schlegel," *Societes & Representations* Éditions de la Sorbonne 3, no. 10 (2000): 23–54; Bianca Theisen, "Early Romantic Poetics of Complex Form," *Studies in Romanticism* 42, no. 3 (Fall 2003): 305; Gurminder Kaur Bhogal, *Details of Consequence: Ornament, Music, and Art in Paris*, AMS Studies in Music (New York: Oxford University Press, 2013), 69–70; and Cordula Grewe, *The Arabesque from Kant to Comics*, Routledge Advances in Art and Visual Studies (New York: Routledge, 2021). Venturino and Dunsby discuss the significance of the arabesque in the writings of Goethe, Kant, and even Hanslick in "The Evolution of Claude Debussy's Arabesque."

28. Theisen, "Early Romantic Poetics," 305; and Schlegel, *Dialogue on Poetry*, 86.

29. Theisen, "Early Romantic Poetics," 311.

30. Niklas Lubmann, *Die Kunst der Gesellschaft* (Frankfurt a.m.: Suhrkamp, 1995), 195; and Niklas Lubmann, *Art as a Social System*, trans. Eva M. Knodt (Stanford, CA: Stanford University Press, 2000), 120, cited by Theisen, "Early Romantic Poetics," 311.

31. Schlegel, *Dialogue on Poetry*, 86.

32. See Jonathan Monroe, *A Poverty of Objects: The Prose Poem and the Politics of Genre* (Ithaca, NY: Cornell University Press, 1987), 45–71; Linda Cummins, *Debussy and the Fragment* (Amsterdam: Rodopi, 2006), 47–54.

33. Schlegel, *Dialogue on Poetry*, 99.

34. Schlegel, *Dialogue on Poetry*, 103.

35. Thomas De Quincey, *Confessions of an English Opium Eater* (London: Taylor and Hessey, 1822).

36. Edgar Allan Poe, *Tales of the Grotesque and Arabesque*, 2 vols. (Philadelphia: Lea and Blanchard, 1839). Many of these essays were later reprinted in *Tales of Mystery and Imagination & Humour; and Poems* (London: Henry Vizetelly, 1852). See also Gustav Gruener, "Notes on the Influence of E. T. A. Hoffmann upon Edgar Allan Poe," *Proceedings of the Modern Language Association* 19 (1904): 16–17; and Palmer Cobb, "The Influence of E. T. A. Hoffmann on the Tales of Edgar Allan Poe," *Studies in Philology* 3 (1908): 1–105. Jeffrey Meyers discusses Poe's tendency to borrow from earlier writers in *Edgar Allan Poe: His Life and Legacy* (New York: Cooper Square, 1992).

37. "The Fall of the House of Usher" seems to have been inspired by Hoffmann's *Das Majorat*; see Gruener, "Notes on the Influence," 16–17.

38. August J. Nigro, *The Diagonal Line: Separation and Reparation in American Literature* (Cranbury, NJ: Associated University Presses, 1984), 63.

39. Edgar Allan Poe, ed., "The Fall of the House of Usher," in *The Complete Tales and Poems of Adgar Allan Poe* (New York: Vintage, 1975), 234.

40. Poe, "The Fall of the House of Usher," 234.

41. Nigro, *Diagonal Line*, 63.

42. Marie Bonaparte, *The Life and Works of Edgar Allan Poe: A Psycho-Analytic Interpretation* (London: Imago, 1949), 249.

43. Bonaparte, *Life and Works*, 249.

44. Bonaparte, *Life and Works*, 243.

45. Bonaparte, *Life and Works*, 250.

46. H. P. Lovecraft, *The Annotated Supernatural Horror in Literature*, ed. S. T. Joshi (New York: Hippocampus, 2000), 45.

47. Lovecraft, *Annotated Supernatural Horror*, 45.

48. Lovecraft, *Annotated Supernatural Horror*, 43. According to Eve Kosofsky, "Once you know a novel is of the Gothic kind (and you can tell that from the title), you can predict its contents with an unnerving certainty." Eve Kosofsky Sedgwick, *The Coherence of Gothic Conventions* (London: Methuen, 1986), 9.

49. F. W. J. Schelling, *Historical-Critical Introduction to the Philosophy of Mythology*, trans. Mason Richey and Markus Zisselsberger with a foreword by Jason M. Wirth (Albany: State University of New York Press, 2007); Ernst Jentsch, "Zur Psychologie des Unheimlichen," *Psychiatrisch-Neurologische Wochenschrift* 8, no. 22 (August 25, 1906), 195–98 and 8, no. 23 (September 1, 1906): 203–5; Ernst Jentsch, "On the Psychology of the Uncanny," in *Uncanny Modernity. Cultural Theories, Modern Anxieties*, ed. Jo Collins and John Jervis, trans. Roy Sellars (Basingstoke: Palgrave Macmillan, 2008), 216–28; Sigmund Freud, *Das Unheimliche* (1919), ed. Oliver Jahraus (Ditzingen: Reclam, 2020); Sigmund Freud, *The Uncanny*, trans. David McLintock, with an introduction by Hugh Haughton (London: Penguin, 2003). For Freud's interpretation of Jentsch, see Nicholas Royle, *The Uncanny* (Manchester: Manchester University Press, 2003), 39–42 and 52.

50. Tzvetan Todorov, *Introduction à la littérature fantastique* (Paris: Seuil, 1970), 52–54; Tzvetan Todorov, *The Fantastic: A Structural Approach to a Literary Genre*, trans. Richard Howard with a new foreword by Robert Scholes (Ithaca, NY: Cornell University Press, 1975), 47–48. Interestingly, Joris-Karl Huysmans found in Poe's writings a "quality of strangeness" and "Byzantine flowers of thought." Joris-Karl Huysmans, *À Rebours* (Paris: Garnier-Flammarion, 1978), 206; Joris-Karl Huysmans, *Against Nature*, trans. Robert Baldick (Harmondsworth: Penguin, 1959), 180.

51. Todorov, *Introduction à la littérature fantastique*, 53; Todorov, *Fantastic*, 47–48.

52. Todorov, *Introduction à la littérature fantastique*, 53; Todorov, *Fantastic*, 48.

53. John Barth, "Tales within Tales within Tales," in *The Friday Book: Essays and Other Nonfiction* (Baltimore: Johns Hopkins University Press, 1984), 223. Barth also mentions two other devices: "the double" and "the voyage back in time."

54. For the record, Poe modified de Béranger's text by replacing the words "Mon cœur" with "Son cœur." It is now thought that Weber's waltz was composed by Karl Gottlieb Reissiger.

55. Lucian Dällenbach, *Le récit spéculaire. Essai sur la mise en abyme* (Paris: Éditions du Seuil, 1977), 24–25, 30–31, 63, 84.

56. https://www.eapoe.org/works/mabbott/tom1p071.htm.

57. Lovecraft, *Annotated Supernatural Horror*, 46.

58. Gerald J. Kennedy, *Poe, Death, and the Life of Writing* (New Haven, CT: Yale University Press, 1987), 58–59. See also Jan Bondeson, *Buried Alive: The Terrifying History of Our Most Primal Fear* (New York: Norton, 2002), esp. 118–36 and 208–14; Bonaparte, *Life and Works*, 237 and 243.

59. Rae Beth Gordon, *Ornament, Fantasy, and Desire in Nineteenth-Century French Literature* (Princeton, NJ: Princeton University Press, 1992), 5. See also Rosemary Lloyd, *Baudelaire et Hoffmann. Affinités et Influences* (Cambridge: Cambridge University Press, 1979); and Val Scullion, "Kinaesthetic, Spastic and Spatial Motifs as Expressions of Romantic Irony in E. T. A. Hoffmann's *The Sandman* and Other Writings," *Journal of Literature and Science* 2, no. 1 (2009): 1–22.

60. Charles Baudelaire, "Salon de 1846," in *Charles Baudelaire: Œuvres Complètes*, vol. II, ed. Claude Pichois, Bibliothèque de la Pléiade (Paris: Gallimard, 1976), 425; Baudelaire, "The Salon of 1846," in *Art in Paris 1845–1862: Salons and Other Exhibitions Reviewed by Charles Baudelaire*, ed. and trans. Jonathan Mayne, 2nd ed. (London: Phaidon, 1995), 51.

61. Kevin T. Dann, *Bright Colors Falsely Seen: Synaesthesia and the Search for Transcendental Knowledge* (New Haven, CT: Yale University Press, 1998).

62. See Célestin Pierre Cambiaire, *The Influence of Edgar Allan Poe in France* (New York: Haskell House, 1970); and Jonathan Culler, "Baudelaire and Poe," in *Critical Insights: The Poetry of Edgar Allan Poe*, ed. Steven Frye (Pasadena, CA: Salem, 2011), 188–209.

63. Baudelaire, "Edgar Allan Poe: Sa Vie et Ses Ouvrages" in *Œuvres Complètes*, II:249–318; Baudelaire, "Edgar Allan Poe: His Life and Works," in *The Painter in Modern Life and Other Essays*, ed. and trans. by Jonathan

Mayne (London: Phaidon, 2001), 70–92; and Baudelaire, "Notes Nouvelles sur Edgar Poe," in *Œuvres Complètes*, II:319–37; Baudelaire, "Further Notes on Edgar Poe" in *The Painter in Modern Life and Other Essays*, 93–110. For translations of Poe's other essays and poetry, see Edgar Poe, *Derniers Contes*, trans. F. Rabbe (Paris: Savine, 1887); and Edgar Poe, *Poésies complètes de Edgar Allan Poe*, trans. Gabriel Mourey (Paris: Dalou, 1889).

64. Baudelaire, "Notes Nouvelles," in *Œuvres Complètes*, II:329; Baudelaire, "Further Notes," 103.

65. Théophile Gautier, *Charles Baudelaire: His Life*, trans. Guy Thorne (London: Greening, 1915), 30.

66. Baudelaire, "Sa Vie et Ses Ouvrages," in *Œuvres Complètes*, II:317; Baudelaire, "His Life and Works," 90.

67. Baudelaire's translations are reprinted in Edgar Allan Poe, *Edgar Allan Poe, Œuvres en prose*, Bibliothèque de la Pléiade, ed. Y.-G. Le Dantec (Paris: Gallimard, 1951). For Baudelaire's translation of "Mesmeric Revelation" and "The Fall of the House of Usher," see Poe, *Œuvres en prose*, 211–22 and 337–57. Baudelaire also translated Poe's critical essays "Philosophie de l'ambeulement" and "La Genèse d'un poëme"; see Poe, *Œuvres en prose*, 970–78 and 979–97.

68. Gautier, *His Life*, 59–60.

69. According to Juliet Simpson, "[The arabesque] figures prominently in Baudelaire's aesthetic writings, notably in 'Le Peintre de la vie moderne' (1863), 'L'Essence du rire' (1855), 'Le Thyrse' (18[63]), and the *Fusées*." See Juliet Simpson, "Symbolist Aesthetics and the Decorative Image/Text," *French Forum* 25, no. 2 (May 2000): 194fn3.

70. Schlegel, *Dialogue on Poetry*, 102.

71. Baudelaire, "Le Thyrse," *Le Spleen de Paris*, XXXII, in *Œuvres Complètes*, vol. I, ed. Claude Pichois, Bibliothèque de la Pléiade (Paris: Gallimard, 1975), 335–36; Baudelaire, "The Wand," in Baudelaire, *Vol. II. The Poems in Prose and La Fanfarol*, trans. Francis Scarfe (London: Anvil Press Poetry, 1989), 144–47.

72. Baudelaire, "Fusées: IV, V," in *Œuvres Complètes*, I:652; "Flares: 5 and 6," in *Late Fragments: Flares, My Heart Laid Bare, Prose Poems, Belgium Disrobed*, ed. and trans. Richard Sieburth (New Haven, CT: Yale University Press, 2022), 85.

73. Baudelaire, "À Arsènne Houssaye," in *Œuvres Complètes*, I:275–276; "To Arsènne Houssaye," in *Baudelaire: The Poems in Prose and La Fanfarlo*, trans. Francis Scarfe (London: Anvil Press Poetry, Inc., 1989), 25.

74. Baudelaire, "Le Thyrse," in *Œuvres Complètes*, I:336; Baudelaire, "The Wand," in Baudelaire, *The Poems in Prose and La Fanfarol*, 145.

75. Baudelaire, "Préface III," *Reliquat et dossier de* Fleurs du mal, in *Œuvres Complètes*, I:183.

76. Georges Poulet, *Les Métamorphoses du cercle* (Paris: Plon, 1961), 426.

77. John E. Gale, "De Quincey, Baudelaire, and 'Le Cygne,'" *Nineteenth-Century French Studies* 5, nos. 3–4 (1977): 305 [296–307].

78. Baudelaire, "L'Œuvres et la vie de Delacroix," in *Œuvres Complètes*, II:744; "The Life and Works of Eugène Delacroix," 43.

79. Baudelaire, "L'Œuvres et la vie de Delacroix," in *Œuvres Complètes*, II:753; Baudelaire, "The Life and Works of Eugène Delacroix," in *The Painter in Modern Life*, ed. and trans. Jonathan Mayne (London: Phaidon, 2001), 52.

80. Baudelaire, "Le Poème du hachisch," *Les Paradis artificiels*, in *Œuvres Complètes*, I:432; "The Poem of Hashish," in Baudelaire, *Artificial Paradises*, trans. Stacy Diamond (New York: Carol, 1996), 65.

81. David Ellison, "Aesthetic Redemption: The Thyrsus in Nietzsche, Baudelaire, and Wagner," in *Ethics and Aesthetic in European Modernist Literature: From the Sublime to the Uncanny* (Cambridge: Cambridge University Press, 2001), 108, 110. Baudelaire, "Richard Wagner et *Tannhäuser* à Paris," in *Œuvres Complètes*, II:779–815; Baudelaire, "Richard Wagner and *Tannhäuser* in Paris," in *Painter in Modern Life*, 111–46, esp. 121 and 122. Enid Starkie, *Baudelaire* (New York: New Directions, 1958), 405. Mary Breatnach, "Baudelaire, Wagner, Mallarmé: Romantic Aesthetics and the Word-Tone Dichotomy," Word and Music Studies, vol. 4 (Amsterdam: Rodopi, 2003), 69–83. According to Miner, Baudelaire resorted to reading an English translation of *Oper und Drama* when writing his 1861 essay "Richard Wagner et Tannhäuser à Paris." See Margaret Miner, *Resonant Gaps: Between Baudelaire & Wagner* (Athens; University of Georgia Press, 1995), 65fn7.

82. Ellison, "Aesthetic Redemption: The Thyrsus in Nietzsche, Baudelaire, and Wagner," in *Ethics and Aesthetic in European Modernist Literature: From the Sublime to the Uncanny* (Cambridge: Cambridge University Press, 2001), 110.

83. Wagner's essay "Music of the Future" was originally published in French under the title "Lettre sur la musique." Richard Wagner, *Quatre poèmes d'opéras traduits en prose française, précédés d'une Lettre sur la musique [à Frédéric Villot, Paris, 15 septembre 1860] par Richard Wagner. Le Vaisseau fantôme, Tannhäuser, Lohengrin, Tristan et*

Iseult (Paris: A. Bourdillat, 1861; repr., Paris: Durand, 1893), LIX, XXXII; Robert L. Jacobs, trans., "Music of the Future," in *Three Wagner Essays* (London: Eulenburg, 1979), 24. For Wagner's use of the arabesque, see Michael Spitzer, *Metaphor and Musical Thought* (Chicago: University of Chicago Press, 2004), 299; and Hilda Meldrum Brown, *The Quest for the Gesamtkunstwerk and Richard Wagner* (Oxford: Oxford University Press, 2016), 56.

84. Baudelaire, "Richard Wagner et *Tannhäuser* à Paris," in *Œuvres Complètes*, II:801; Baudelaire, "Richard Wagner and *Tannhäuser* in Paris," in *Painter in Modern Life*, 132.

85. Baudelaire, "Richard Wagner et *Tannhäuser* à Paris," in *Œuvres Complètes*, II:802; Baudelaire, "Richard Wagner and *Tannhäuser* in Paris," in *Painter in Modern Life*, 133.

86. Baudelaire, "Richard Wagner et *Tannhäuser* à Paris," in *Œuvres Complètes*, II:803; Baudelaire, "Richard Wagner and *Tannhäuser* in Paris," in *Painter in Modern Life*, 133.

87. Baudelaire, "Richard Wagner et *Tannhäuser* à Paris," in *Œuvres Complètes*, II:784; Baudelaire, "Richard Wagner and *Tannhäuser* in Paris," in *Painter in Modern Life*, 116.

88. Baudelaire, "Le Peintre de la vie moderne: La Modernité," in *Œuvres Complètes*, II:695; Baudelaire, "The Painter in Modern Life: IV. Modernity," in *Painter in Modern Life*, 13.

89. See Andrea Gogröf-Voorhees, *Defining Modernism: Baudelaire and Nietzsche on Romanticism, Modernity, Decadence, and Wagner*, 2nd ed. (Frankfurt am Main: Peter Lang, 2004).

90. Édouard Dujardin, ed., *La Revue Wagnerienne*, 1885–88 (Genève: Slatkine, 1993). See also D. Hampton Morris, *A Descriptive Study of the* La Revue Wagnérienne *Concerning Richard Wagner* (Lewiston, NY: Edwin Mellen, 2002); Steven Huebner, Brendan King, and Charlotte Mandell, "The *Revue Wagnerienne*: Symbolism, Aetheteticism, and Germanophilia," in *Wagner and His World*, ed. Thomas S. Grey (Princeton, NJ: Princeton University Press, 2009), 372–90; Kelly J. Maynard, "Strange Bedfellows at the *Revue Wagnérienne*: Wagnerism at the Fin de Siècle," *French Historical Studies* 38, no. 4 (2015): 633–59; and Adeline Anastasia Heck, "Under the Spell of Wagner: *The Revue Wagnérienne* and Literary Experimentation in the Belle Epoque (1878–1893)," PhD diss., Princeton University, 2020.

91. See Bettina L. Knapp, "Baudelaire and Wagner's Archetypal Operas," *Nineteenth-Century French Studies* 17, nos. 1–2 (1988–89): 58–69.

92. Wagner, "Lettre sur la musique," in *Quatre poèmes d'opéras*, LIX, XXXII; Richard Wagner, "Music of the Future," in *Three Wagner Essays*, trans. Robert L. Jacobs (London: Eulenberg, 1979), 34.

93. Wagner, "Lettre sur la musique," in *Quatre poèmes d'opéras*, XXV; Wagner, "Music of the Future," in *Three Wagner Essays*, 23–24. See also Mary Breatnach, "Baudelaire, Wagner, Mallarmé: Romantic Aesthetics and the Word-Tone Dichotomy," in *Word and Music Studies* (Amsterdam: Rodopi, 2003), 4:69–83.

94. Bradford Cook, "Introduction," in *Mallarmé: Selected Prose Poems, Essays, & Letters*, trans. Bradford Cook (Baltimore: Johns Hopkins Press, 1956), xvi.

95. Wagner, "Lettre sur la musique," in *Quatre poèmes d'opéras*, LXIX; Wagner, "Music of the Future," in *Three Wagner Essays*, 23.

96. Wagner, "Lettre sur la musique," in *Quatre poèmes d'opéras*, LXV; Wagner, "Music of the Future," in *Three Wagner Essays*, 37.

97. Matthew Bribitzer-Stull, *Understanding the Leimotif: From Wagner to Hollywood Film* (Cambridge: Cambridge University Press, 2015).

98. Wagner, "Lettre sur la musique," in *Quatre poèmes d'opéras*, XXXVII; Wagner, "Music of the Future," in *Three Wagner Essays*, 25.

99. Wagner, "Lettre sur la musique," in *Quatre poèmes d'opéras*, LXXIII, LXVIII; Wagner, "Music of the Future," in *Three Wagner Essays*, 40, 38.

100. Wagner, "Lettre sur la musique," in *Quatre poèmes d'opéras*, LXXII–LXXIII; Wagner, "Music of the Future," in *Three Wagner Essays*, 40. See also Jed Rasula, "Endless Melody," *Texas Studies in Literature and Language* 55, no. 1 (2013): 36–52.

101. Jean Moréas, "The Manifesto of Symbolism (1886)." https://www.poetryintranslation.com/PITBR/French/MoreasManifesto.php (accessed July 11, 2025).

102. Moréas, "The Manifesto of Symbolism (1886)."

103. Moréas, "The Manifesto of Symbolism (1886)."

104. Jean Pierrot, *The Decadent Imagination 1880–1900*, trans. Derek Coltman (Chicago: University of Chicago Press, 1981), 230.

105. Eugène Grasset, Méthode de Composition Ornemental (Paris: Librairie Centrale des Beaux-Arts, ca. 1900), 2:160–61; Pierrot, *Decadent Imagination*, 231.
106. Pierrot, *Decadent Imagination*, 231.
107. Pierrot, *Decadent Imagination*, 231–32.

II. Decoration and Counterpoint

2

Debussy's *Première Arabesque* and the Legacy of J. S. Bach

SOONER OR LATER, any discussion of Debussy and the arabesque will want to consider his *Première Arabesque.* This perennial favorite of young pianists belongs to a group of short keyboard works that Debussy completed after returning home from his Prix de Rome in March 1887: those works include *Petite Suite* (1888–89), *Deux Arabesques* (1888–89), *Rêverie* (1890), *Tarentelle styrienne* (1890), *Ballade (Ballade slave)* (1890), *Valse Romantique* (1890), *Suite bergamasque* (1890), *Mazurka* (1890), and *Nocturne* (1892).[1] Like these other pieces, the *Première Arabesque* stands out for its lyricism and simple harmonic idiom; these qualities have allowed the piece and its cousin "Clair de lune" (*Suite bergamasque*) to become one of Debussy's most popular and recognizable compositions. For many listeners, these works epitomize classical music as a genre and provide a benchmark against which to measure the aesthetic success of other classical compositions. They also provide them with their first concrete examples of a musical arabesque.

What is not so clear, however, is why the piece was entitled arabesque or why it conforms with Debussy's own understanding of the term as described in the introduction. That explanation, which appeared in his review of Bach's Violin Concerto in G minor BWV 1056R, hinged on five specific claims about the nature of arabesques.

1. Arabesques are forms of ornamentation but are not bound to conventional norms.
2. Arabesques are inherently contrapuntal and create harmony when one contrapuntal thread interacts with another.
3. Arabesques blur the distinction between the ornamental and the structural because they require that local details have global implications.
4. Arabesques introduce an element of fantasy into art, thereby allowing artists to disguise and even replace traditional formal schemes.
5. Arabesques allow artworks to stir emotions and induce images in the mind of the listener.

But how exactly does one demonstrate theoretically and analytically the contrapuntal nature of the arabesque? How does one create harmony out of interacting melodic lines? How does one reveal the relationship between a work's local details and its global form? How does one show analytically that a complex surface structure is a disguised version of some familiar formal scheme? And how do composers use ornamentation to express emotions and induce images in the minds of the listener?

Not only are these questions intrinsically hard to answer, but, to complicate matters further, Debussy's letters and published essays are littered with diatribes against traditional music theory and analysis. Debussy denied, for example, that there was any need to resolve French sixth chords or to prohibit parallel octaves and fifths.[2] He also scoffed at the notion that music can be classified as either major or minor and that chords should be classified as perfect or imperfect: "Nothing is more mysterious than a perfect chord! Despite all theories, both old and new, we are still not sure, first why it is perfect, and second, why the other chords have to bear the stigma of being imperfect. Music ought therefore to free itself as quickly as possible from these little rituals with which the conservatories insist on encumbering it."[3] And the very idea of music analysis was anathema to him: "Grownups tend to forget that as children they were forbidden to open the insides of their dolls—a crime of high treason against the cause of mystery. . . . And yet they still insist on poking their aesthetic noses into things that don't concern them! Without their dolls to break open, they still try to explain things, dismantle them and quite heartlessly kill all their mystery."[4]

Despite these complaints, there is one approach that seems well equipped to explain the arabesque structure of Debussy's music: Heinrich Schenker's system of graphic analysis. The idea of using Schenkerian theory to analyze Debussy's music is not, of course, new: Adele Katz and Felix Salzer undertook this task as far back as the 1940s and early 1950s.[5] And yet, their work is still regarded by many as controversial. It is well known, for example, that Schenker had a deep personal antipathy toward Debussy and blamed him in part for what he regarded as the demise of classical music in the first decades of the twentieth century.[6] In a diary entry dated January 15, 1908, he singled out Debussy's cantata *La Damoiselle élue* (1887–88) as "a nothingness flowing far-and-wide; never once even the smallest semblance of form; sonorities suspended in the air; accordingly not impressing itself on the heart."[7] Three years later, he agreed to deliver a series of lectures demonstrating "the unhealthy state of form and counterpoint, cacophony, and the like, in the works of several composers (Strauss, Reger, and Debussy, etc.)."[8] Doubtless fueled by his shameful racism, Schenker intensified his criticisms after Austria and Germany signed an armistice in November 1918. In the preface to his edition of Beethoven's Piano Sonata Op. 101 (1923), he denounced Impressionist compositions, like those by Debussy, as "nothing but tonal noise (which, like any noise, represents an acoustic event, but not yet art."[9] And in the second volume of *Das Meisterwerk in der Musik* (1926), he declared that Debussy's finest scores paled beside the simplest minuet by Haydn.[10]

And yet, Schenker's concerns as a music theorist often resonate with Debussy's five claims about the arabesque, thereby indicating their potential value for analyzing Debussy's music. To begin with, Schenker clearly recognized the significance of ornamentation to musical composition and even made it a central feature of his theoretical writings. Schenker's first major treatise—*Ein Beitrag zur Ornamentik* (1904)—primarily deals with eighteenth-century music and the problems of realizing trills, mordants, turns, and other standardized ornaments or *Manieren*.[11] Schenker's next two treatises—*Harmonielehre* (1906) and *Kontrapunkt I* (1910)—address more abstract notions of ornamentation: the former ends with a chapter on improvising preludes and fantasies whereas the latter describes how Fuxian species counterpoint elaborates prototypical melodies or cantus firmi.[12] And in his essay "Der Kunst der Improvisation," *Das Meisterwerk in der Musik I* (1925), Schenker returned to the problems of improvising preludes and fantasies, paying special attention to the advice of C. P. E. Bach.[13] In the meantime, Schenker offered important insights about the principles of melodic diminution in *Kontrapunkt II* (1922), *Der freie Satz* (1935), and the posthumous essay "Von der Diminution" (1937).[14] Remarkably, the principles of elaboration and enlargement inspired him to develop his concepts of voice-leading transformations (*Stimmführungsverwandlungen*) and voice-leading levels (*Stimmführungsschichte*). By the end of his career, Schenker used these concepts to show how complex tonal surfaces might be derived by ornamenting simple tonal prototypes at the middle ground and background. He referred to these prototypes as Ursätze and their upper-voice melodies as Urlinien.

At the same time, Schenker also echoed Debussy by paying special attention to the contrapuntal foundations of music and to the idea that tonal harmonies are byproducts of voice leading. His thinking in this regard stemmed from his belief that melodies are "the primary element in music" and that in tonal contexts they are triadic in nature.[15] Schenker's interest in melody dated back at least to the 1890s, when he discussed the possibility of writing a history of melody with Eduard Hanslick, who discussed arabesques at several points in his *Vom Musikalisch-Schönen* (1854).[16] Schenker even began his paper "Der Geist der musikalischen Technik" (1895) with a section on melody.[17] Locally, Schenker claimed that melodic lines are fluent if they balance their use of repeated/pedal tones, stepwise successions, and leaps: according to him, stepwise successions derive from passing and neighbor tones and leaps from skipping between chord tones, shifting between registers, or switching from one "latent voice" to another.[18] Melodies that project more than one "latent voice" are known as polyphonic or compound melodies. Schenker also insisted that bass lines are melodic in conception and that they, too, are triadic in nature, just like the other voices.[19] By the time he completed *Der freie Satz*, Schenker had come to the conclusion that harmonic progressions are inextricably bound up with counterpoint: "All the transient harmonies which appear in the course of a work have their source in the necessities of voice leading."[20]

Again like Debussy, Schenker was adamant that a work's local details should guide its global form. Such relationships stemmed from the fact that, in his opinion, successful melodies balance the "pleasure the ear derived from repetition—a joy in recognition itself" with "the ever stronger desire of music to follow its own course, to strive towards expansion of content."[21] One way to create such relationships is through the use of what Schenker referred to as concealed repetitions (or *Der verborgene Wiederholungen*): instead of treating motives as purely surface phenomena, he claimed that they can also be projected, albeit in disguised forms, across large swathes of music.[22] As these enlargements become more extensive and more heavily disguised, so the original patterns may become increasingly difficult to discern. And yet, Schenker insisted that concealed repetitions are "fully as effective as the simpler repetitions; they, too, sprang only from the blood relationship of statement and variant, almost beyond the composer's volition—but they remained concealed."[23] Given his abstract view of motivic relationships, it is not perhaps surprising that Schenker rejected traditional distinctions between main ideas and developmental padding: "One cannot speak of 'melody' and 'idea' in the work of the masters; it makes even less sense to speak of 'passage,' 'sequence,' 'padding,' or 'cement' as if they were terms that one could possibly apply to art. Drawing a comparison to language, what is there in a logically constructed sentence that one could call 'cement'? How does one distinguish an 'idea' from 'cement'?"[24]

Schenker likewise shared Debussy's skepticism about traditional accounts of musical form or *Formenlehre*.

> Coherence in language does not arise from a single syllable, a single sword, or even from a single sentence; despite the correspondence of words and things, every coherent relationship in language depends upon a meaning hidden in a background. Such meaning achieves no fulfillment with mere beginnings. Similarly, music finds no coherence in a "motive" in the usual sense [*Der freie Satz*, §50, 51–53; *Free Composition*, 26–27] Thus, I reject definitions which take the motive as their starting point and emphasize the manipulation of the motive by means of repetition, variation, extension, fragmentation and dissolution. I also reject those explanations which are based upon phrases, phrase-groups, periods, double-periods, themes, antecedents, and consequents.[25]

Instead, he maintained that the form of a piece depended on the relationships between the whole and the individual parts: "differences in prolongations lead to differences in form."[26] Such prolongations are fulfilled by diminution: "Obviously, we do meet repetitions, but in contrast to the motivic repetitions in the conventional theory of form, those which I describe are usually concealed. Such repetitions make possible far-reaching extensions and the organic connections of distant points."[27]

Last, Debussy and Schenker both agreed about the imagination's vital role in music making and about music's great capacity to express emotions and induce images. In the first case, Schenker noted at the start of *Der freie Satz*: "The power of [the] will and imagination which lives through the transformation of a masterwork reaches us in our spirit as a power of imagination—whether we have specific knowledge of the fundamental structure and the transformation or not. The life of the transformation conveys its own nature to use."[28] A few lines later, he commented on music's expressive power: "In the art of music, as in life, motion toward the goal encounters obstacles, reverses, disappointments, and involves great distances, detours, expansions, interpolations, and, in short, retardations of all kinds."[29] He continued: "As the image of our life motion, music can approach a state of objectivity, never, of course, to the extent that it need abandon its own specific nature as an art. Thus it may almost evoke pictures or seem to be endowed with speech: it may pursue its course by means of associations, references, and connectives: it may use repetitions of the same tonal succession to express different meanings: it may simulate expectation, preparation, surprise, disappointment, patience, impatience, and humor."[30]

Since Bach's Violin Concerto in G minor BWV 1056R epitomized Debussy's conception of "pure 'musical arabesque,'" and since it confirms Jean Pierrot's claim about the similarities between Symbolist arabesques and the superabundance of baroque art, it seems appropriate to begin by seeing how the music satisfies each of the five points mentioned above, starting with its use of ornaments.[31] For convenience, example 2.1 presents the opening phrase of the "Largo" (mvt. 2). Even from a brief glance at the score, one is struck by the decorative quasi-improvised character of the solo violin part in mm. 1–3. Some of the violin's decorations are traditional *Manieren*: a lower mordent on the down beat of m. 1, a grace note on the third beat on m. 1, a trill on the fourth beat of m. 2, and another grace note on the downbeat of m. 3. But some are woven more deeply into the fabric of the composition. As regards its overall trajectory, the violin melody descends by step from D (m. 1) through C (m. 1) to B♭ (m. 2). Each note is elaborated by sixteenth-note flourishes: D with the rising pattern D–E♭–F–G; C with a similar pattern, C–D–E♭–F; and B♭ with the sixteenth notes B♭ and G an octave higher. And in mm. 2–3 the violin elaborates the note E♭ with the turn figure E♭–F–E♭–D–E♭ on beats 2–3, decorates it with the arpeggiated pattern

E♭–C–A–F–E♭ on beats 3–4, and reinforces it with a lower neighbor E♭–D–E♭ on beat 4. The melody eventually lands on D, which it extends by means of a *tierce coulée* D–C–B♭. When the opening theme from mm. 1–3 returns halfway through m. 15, it is even more highly decorated. As shown in example 2.2, the violin part ornaments the ascending stepwise strings D–E♭–F–G and C–D–E♭–F in mm. 15–16 with incomplete lower neighbor tones and the tierce coulée with an undulating thirty-second note pattern. The result is a serpentine line that slithers effortlessly from beginning to end. It is a perfect example of a musical arabesque.

Whereas examples 2.1 and 2.2 demonstrate the ornamental character of the violin solo, the voice-leading reduction in example 2.3 suggests that it is a polyphonic or compound melody. As mentioned earlier, polyphonic melodies are linear patterns that appear on the surface of the music as a single continuous thread but are actually created by shifting from one implied or latent contrapuntal voice to another. In the case of the main theme of the "Largo," the solo violin articulates two distinct contrapuntal threads: a latent soprano voice F–G–F–E♭–D and a latent

Example 2.1 Bach, "Largo," Violin Concerto in G minor, BWV 1056R, mvt. 2, mm. 1–3

Example 2.2 Bach, "Largo," Violin Concerto in G minor, BWV 1056R, mm. 15–19

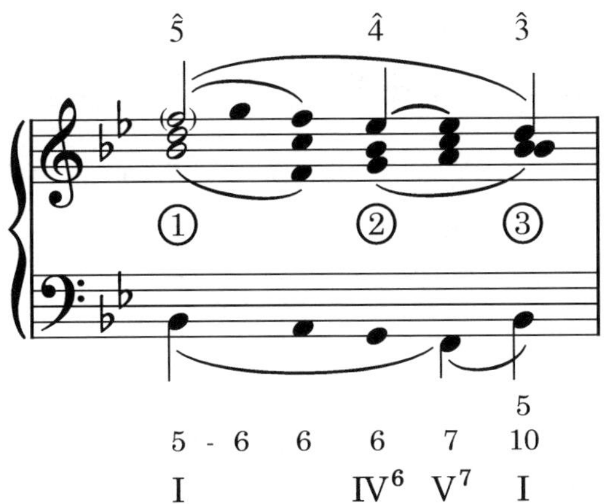

Example 2.3 Essential voice leading, Bach, "Largo," Violin Concerto in G minor, BWV 1056R, mm. 1–3

alto voice D–C–B♭–C–B♭. According to this reading, the sixteenth-note diminutions D–E♭–F–G and C–D–E♭–F in m. 1 connect the latter with the former and, in so doing, illustrate a technique that Schenker referred to as motion from an inner voice (or *Untergreifen*). Example 2.3 also shows how these latent voices, which both proceed by step, are supported by a stepwise descent B♭–A–G–F–B♭ in the bass. Together with the tenor voice B♭–F–G–A–B♭, these four contrapuntal lines create the functional progression I–IV⁶–V⁷–I and demonstrate Debussy's notion that harmony is formed out of melodies.

The voice-leading sketch in example 2.4 captures another idea promoted by Schlegel, Poe, and Baudelaire: local details should determine global forms. This is precisely what happens when the main theme of the "Largo" returns near the end of the movement: not only do mm. 15–17 present a varied repetition of mm. 1–3, but they are also extended by two measures leading to a weak authentic cadence in mm. 18–19. The extension is achieved quite simply; by adding a flattened seventh A♭ to the violin part at the end of m. 17, the supporting B♭ triad tonicizes an E♭ sonority

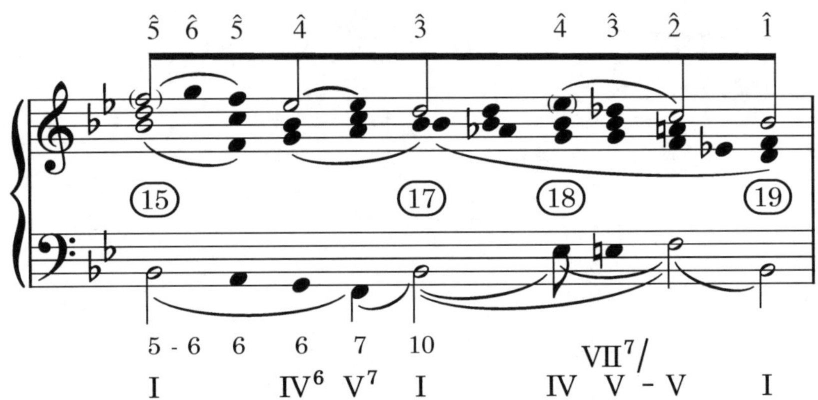

Example 2.4 Essential voice leading, Bach, "Largo," Violin Concerto in G minor, BWV 1056R, mm. 15–19

Example 2.5a Bach, "Largo," Violin Concerto in G minor, BWV 1056R, mm. 3–7

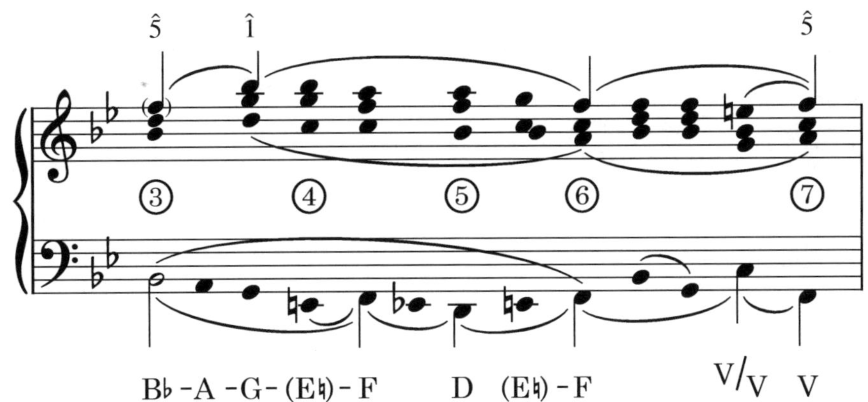

Example 2.5b Essential voice leading, Bach, "Largo," Violin Concerto in G minor, BWV 1056R, mm. 3–7

on the downbeat of m. 18. But the effects of this chord are immediately thwarted when the bass line ascends from E♭ through E♮ to F to create the progression I–IV–VII⁷/V–V–I. Remarkably the bass line B♭–A–G–F from mm. 15–17 recurs in the alto as B♭–A♭–G–F–(E♭–D) in mm. 17–19. A similar strategy can be seen earlier when the movement modulates locally from B♭ major to F major in mm. 3–7. As shown in examples 2.5a–2.5b, the bass descends from B♭ through A, G, and E♮ to F in mm. 3–4. It then continues down through E♭ to D in m. 5 before returning to F in m. 6 to set up an emphatic authentic cadence in the dominant key in mm. 6–7. Just as the bass line B♭–A–G–E♮–F appears in mm. 3–4, so it appears in augmentation in the soprano as B♭ (m. 3)–A♭ (m. 4)–G (m. 5)–F (m. 6)–E♮ (m. 6)–F (m. 7).

As regards the element of fantasy and the notion of a "text within the text," perhaps the most striking example occurs in the last three bars of the movement; mm. 19–21 not only provide a link with the final movement but also offer a fleeting allusion to the opening movement. The first point is illustrated in example 2.6. The score (ex. 2.6a) and voice-leading sketch (ex. 2.6b) show how mm. 19–21 modulate from B♭ major, the tonic of the "Largo," to G minor, the home key of the third and final movement. This modulation is achieved by taking the familiar bass pattern B♭–A–G–F and extending through E♭ to D for a Phrygian half cadence in G minor (mm. 20–21). The soprano likewise expands the pattern (F)–G–F–E♭–D by adding the cadential tones C–D on the end. Meanwhile, the second point is illustrated in example 2.7: it shows how the voice leading of this passage recalls a similar cadence in G minor in mm. 79–82 of the first movement. Notice how the bass line from the preceding movement begins on G and then descends from A♭ through G and F to E♭ and D before leaping back up to G. By recycling elements of the first movement and providing a transition to the third movement, the final measures of the "Largo" remind the listener that Bach conceived of his concerto in some sense as a unified whole and that further interconnections might be found between the individual movements.

Finally, the "Largo" from Bach's Violin Concerto in G minor BWV 1056R illustrates Debussy's claims about the expressive power of tonal counterpoint, something that several filmmakers have exploited to great effect.[32] In this regard, it is helpful to recall a statement from *Der freie Satz,* in which Schenker evoked ideas expressed by the likes of Hogarth, Moritz, Watelet, Lévesque, and Diderot: "In the art of music, as in life, motion toward the goal encounters obstacles, reverses,

Example 2.6a Bach, "Largo," Violin Concerto in G minor, BWV 1056R, mm. 19–21

disappointments, and involves great distances, detours, expansions, interpolations, and, in short, retardations of all kinds."[33] Such delays are readily apparent in the middle portion of the "Largo," notably in mm. 7–15. As shown in Example 2.8, the passage begins in the dominant key of F major and ends with a half cadence on F in B♭ major. Instead of being connected directly, these sonorities are linked circuitously by a local modulation from F major to C minor in mm. 8–11. Having cadenced in C in mm. 10–11, the bass descends by step through B♭, A♭, G, and an implied F to E♭ in m. 13, and from E♭ to C and then from C through B♭, A♮, and G, to a half cadence on F in mm. 14–15. This digression not only delays the start of the reprise but also allows the solo violin to present some of its most elaborate and expressive diminutions.

Given Debussy's hostility toward the hegemony of German music, it may seem strange that he specifically associated the concept of the arabesque with Bach's compositions. And yet, the

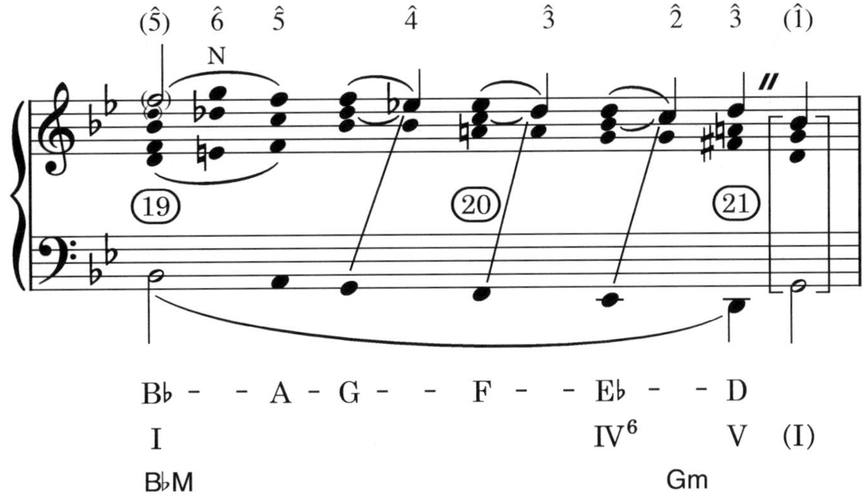

Example 2.6b Essential voice leading, Bach, "Largo," Violin Concerto in G minor, BWV 1056R, mm. 19–21

Example 2.7 Bach, "Largo," Violin Concerto in G minor, BWV 1056R, mm. 79–82/83

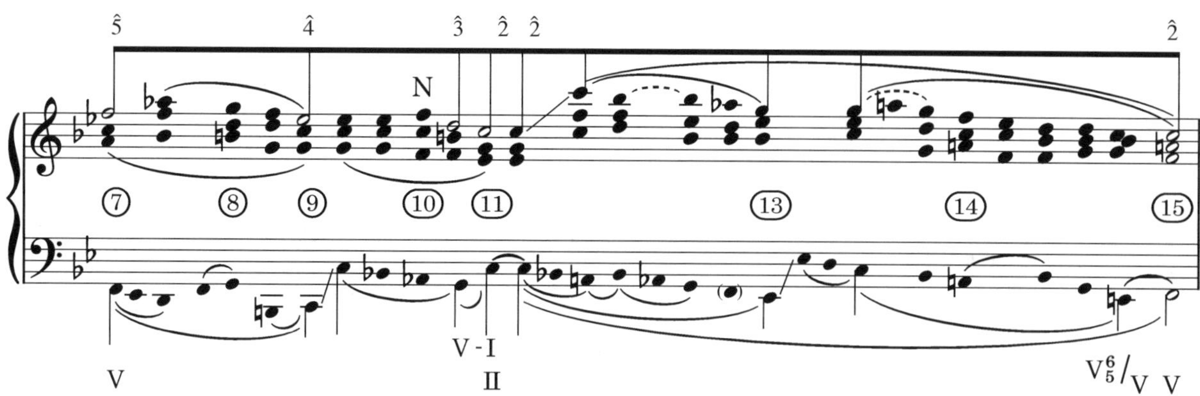

Example 2.8 Essential voice leading, Bach, "Largo," Violin Concerto in G minor, BWV 1056R, mm. 7–15

decision is perfectly understandable within the context of his own musical background. Many of Debussy's early musical experiences involved the works of Bach. Antoinette Mauté, his piano teacher from 1871 to 1872, encouraged him to perform Bach's keyboard music and apparently played this repertory "as it is never played today, with vitality."[34] Later, as a student at the Paris Conservatoire, not only did he learn an array of Bach's compositions, including the *Toccata and Fugue* in G minor (BWV 915), the *Chromatic Fantasy and Fugue* in D minor (BWV 903), and Liszt's transcription of the organ prelude in A minor (BWV 543), but he also received extensive training in figured bass and fugue.[35] When playing piano duet arrangements of Bach's organ works with him, fellow student Paul Vidal recalled how Debussy avoided conventional realizations, "inventing solutions that were ingenious, elegant and delightful but totally unacademic."[36] Later in life, Debussy continued to praise Bach not only in concert reviews and essays, such as the one from *La Revue blanche* (May 1, 1901) mentioned earlier, but also in his personal letters, such as the one to Durand cited above (September 3, 1907).

Although Debussy's *Première Arabesque* initially seems worlds apart from the "Largo" of Bach's Violin Concerto in G minor, close inspection soon reveals that it embodies the concept of the arabesque in many of the same ways.[37] Consider, for a moment, the matter of *Manieren* and written-out decorations. Whereas the *Première Arabesque* tends to avoid the former, it does include numerous instances of the latter. Example 2.9a, for instance, shows that the theme from mm. 6–9 is decorated with escape tones (e.g., F# and C# in mm. 6 and 8) and lower neighbor tones (e.g., the pattern E–D#–E in m. 10). Example 2.9b shows that similar lower neighbor pattern appears in the secondary theme in mm. 39–42. Another common ornament is the turn: example 2.9a gives some obvious instances from m. 10 (B–A–B–C#) and m. 12 (D#–C#–D#–E).

Just like the "Largo" from Bach's Violin Concerto, the reprise features an ornamented version of the main theme. Example 2.10a shows the original theme as it appears at the start of the movement in mm. 1–6. As with Bach's theme, this one is supported by a long stepwise descent in the bass from C# in m. 1 through B, A, G#, F#, E, D, and C#, to B in m. 5. When this material returns in m. 87, however, it is recomposed and elaborated in the manner shown in example 2.10b. Among other things, mm. 1–2 reappear twice in mm. 87–88 and 89–90, the second version being highly decorated mostly with (e.g., A–B–C# in m. 89) or suspensions (e.g., A–G# in m. 89 on beats 3–4, G#–F# and F#–E in m. 90).

Example 2.9a Debussy, *Première Arabesque*, mm. 6–13

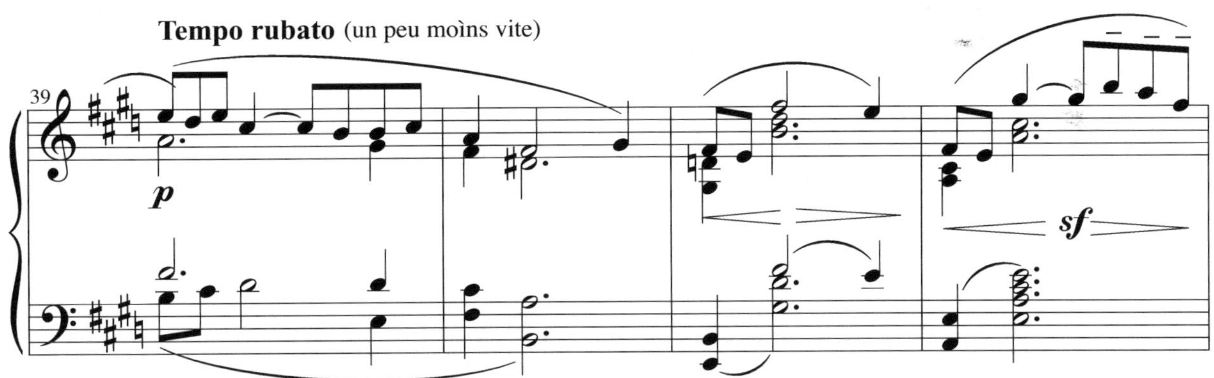

Example 2.9b Debussy, *Première Arabesque*, mm. 39–42

Debussy's *Première Arabesque* also relies heavily on polyphonic melodies. The opening gesture is a good case in point. As shown in example 2.11, it first appears in mm. 1–3 as a single string of triplet eighth notes (ex. 2.11a) but returns in mm. 17–19 as a polyphonic texture comprised of an essential soprano, which descends from A through G# and F# to E; an essential alto, which descends from E through D and C# to B; and an essential bass, which descends from C# through B and A to G# (see ex. 2.11b). Although the resulting chords can be assigned harmonic functions using roman numerals, example 2.11c suggests that they can also be explained contrapuntally as passing chords between IV^6 at the start of m. 1 and a perfect authentic cadence V^{9}7–I in E

Example 2.10a Debussy, *Première Arabesque*, mm. 1–6

major in mm. 6–8. Examples 2.11d–2.11e show how later statements of the main theme in mm. 17–26 and 87–99 can be explained in similar terms: the former culminates in a perfect authentic cadence in A major in mm. 25–26 and the latter in an emphatic perfect authentic cadence in E major in mm. 95–99. Such parallel voice-leading patterns clearly resemble those found in the "Largo" from Bach's Violin Concerto in G minor.

Besides showing how functional progressions derive from stepwise voice leading, examples 2.11c–2.11e also reinforce the idea endorsed by Schlegel, Poe, and Baudelaire that arabesques use surface details to illuminate global structures. Consider, for instance, the case of the descending fourth-span A–G#–F#–E in example 2.11c. Although this gesture appears in eighth notes in mm. 5–6, it is enlarged and concealed as a string of half notes in mm. 1–2. Example 2.11c also shows how the same pattern returns in mm. 4–6 and how it is transposed as E–D#–C#–B over the tonic

Example 2.10b Debussy, *Première Arabesque*, mm. 87–95

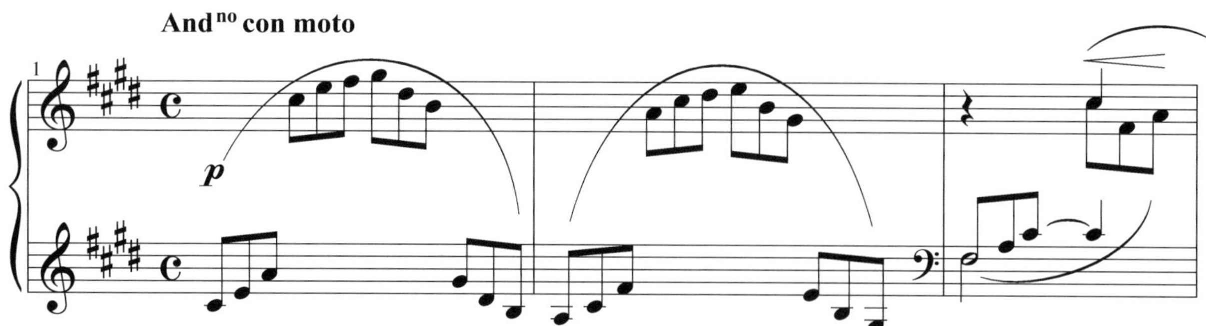

Example 2.11a Debussy, *Première Arabesque*, mm. 1–3

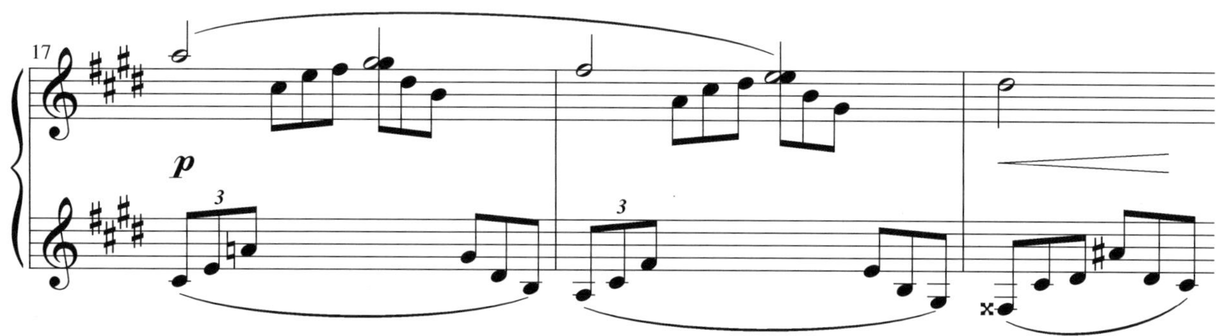

Example 2.11b Debussy, *Première Arabesque*, mm. 17–19

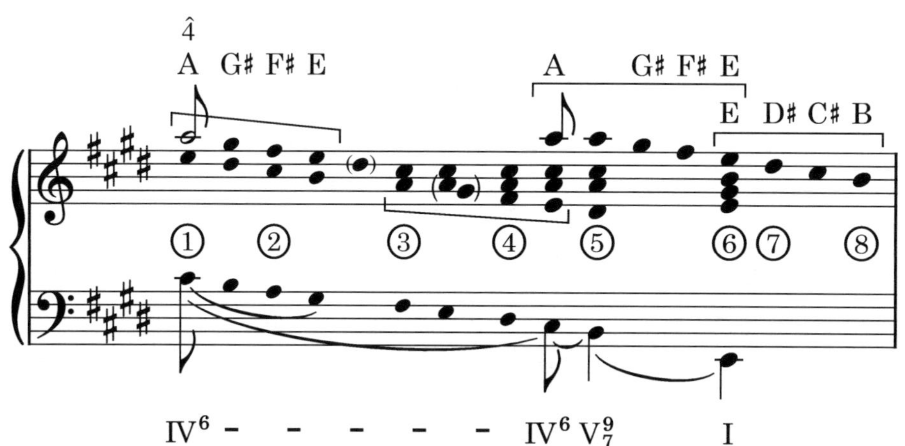

Example 2.11c Essential voice leading, Debussy, *Première Arabesque*, mm. 1–8

chord in mm. 6–8. Remarkably, these descending fourth spans are treated in slightly different ways later in the movement. When the main theme returns in m. 17, example 2.11d shows how it articulates two versions of the fourth-span A–G#–F#–E in mm. 17–18 and 21–24 followed by a new extended version A–G#–F#–E–D♮–C# for the cadence in A major in mm. 24–26. And

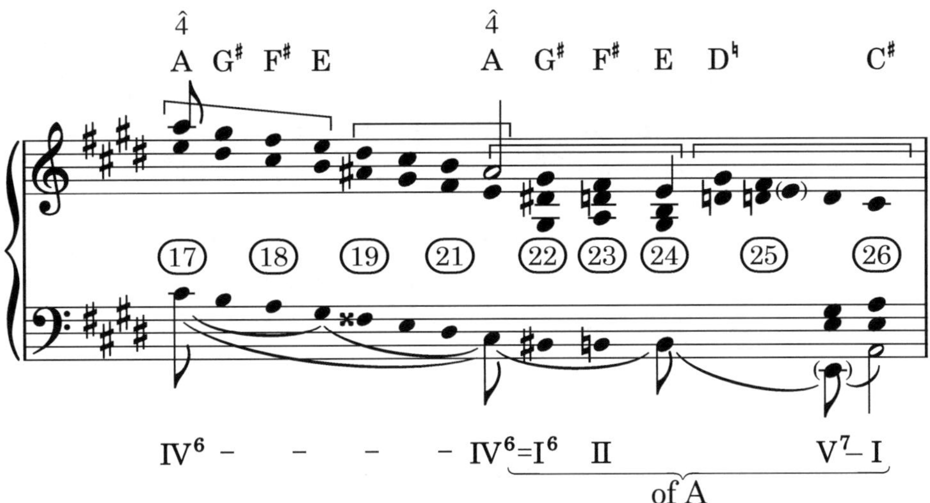

Example 2.11d Essential voice leading, Debussy, *Première Arabesque*, mm. 17–26

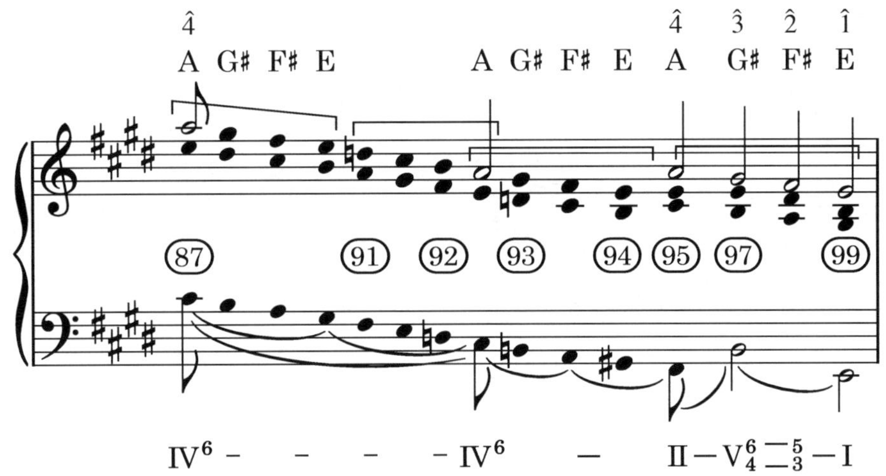

Example 2.11e Essential voice leading, Debussy, *Première Arabesque*, mm. 87–99

when the theme reappears for the last time in mm. 87–99, example 2.11e shows how it includes three distinct versions of the original fourth-span A–G#–F#–E: unadorned and decorated versions in mm. 87–90, another version in mm. 92–94, and an augmented version A (mm. 95–96)–G# (m. 97)–F# (m. 98)–E (m. 99). Finally, example 2.12 suggests another parallel between the three principal statements of the main theme: just as mm. 6–16 prolong the tonic by a chain of ascending parallel tenths in the tenor and bass G#/E–A/F#–B/G#–C#/A♮–C#/A#–(D/B)–E/C# (see ex. 2.12a), so mm. 31–37 consolidate the tonic E major by an analogous chain of ascending parallel thirds in the soprano and alto A/F#–B/G#–C#/A–D#/B–E/C#–F#/D#–G#/E–A/F#–B/G#–C#/A–D#/G–G#/E over predominant and dominant harmonies (see ex. 2.12b).

Also echoing Schlegel's five precepts and Debussy's statement about the nature of arabesques, the *Première Arabesque* conjures up elements of the fantastic. One way in which it does so is

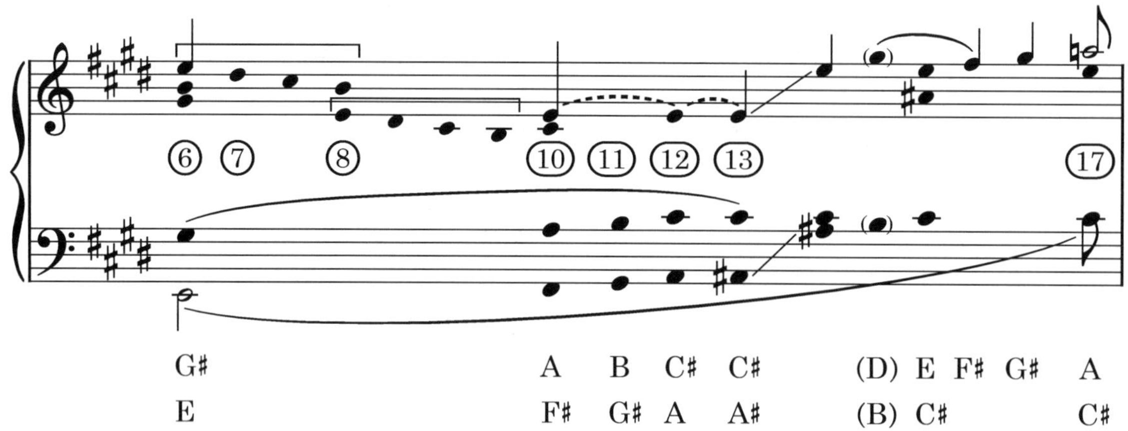

Example 2.12a Essential voice leading, Debussy, *Première Arabesque*, mm. 6–17

Example 2.12b Debussy, *Première Arabesque*, mm. 34–37

by alluding to other related pieces, such as its companion movement, the *Deuxième Arabesque*. Compare, for instance, the stepwise descent of the bass C#–B–A–G# at the start of the *Première Arabesque* as given in example 2.13a with the stepwise descent C–B–A–(D)–G at the start of the *Deuxième Arabesque* as given in example 2.13b. Interestingly, both passages do not start on the tonic, thereby leaving the listener momentarily in doubt about what the tonic chord might be and when it might enter. Similarly, the string of parallel ascending spans from mm. 34–37 of the *Première Arabesque* as given in example 2.13c resembles those from mm. 91–94 of the *Deuxième Arabesque* as given in example 2.13d. And examples 2.13e–2.13g show how mm. 63–70 from the *Première Arabesque* resemble not only mm. 38–41 from the *Deuxième Arabesque* but also, albeit obliquely, the opening measures of Schumann's *Arabeske*, Op. 18. The latter connection is

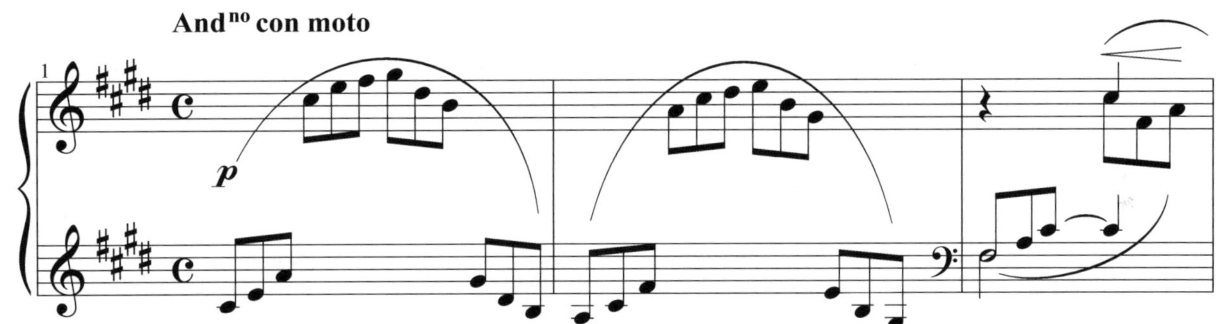

Example 2.13a Debussy, *Première Arabesque*, mm. 1–3

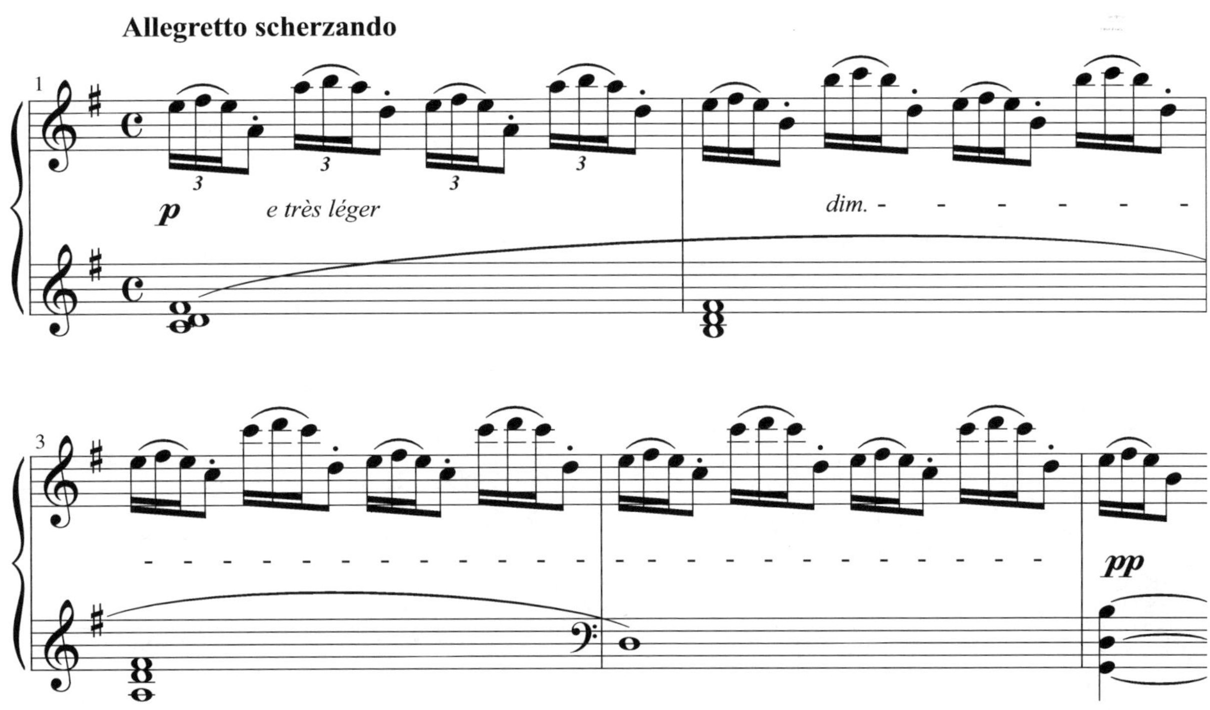

Example 2.13b Debussy, *Deuxième Arabesque*, mm. 1–5

Example 2.13c Debussy, *Première Arabesque*, mm. 34–37

Example 2.13d Debussy, *Deuxième Arabesque*, mm. 91–94

Example 2.13e Debussy, *Première Arabesque*, mm. 63–70

especially interesting because, as Roy Howat has noted, Debussy's *Arabesques* mimicked the ways in which Schumann overlaid slower-moving inner melodies "with surface tracery and melodic ornamentation."[38] According to Howat, Debussy never lost his love of such textures, which he also associated with music "ranging from J. S. Bach to Javanese gamelan." The choice of Schumann's *Arabeske* as a model is, of course, all the more telling given Schumann's own connections to Schlegel, Jean Paul, E. T. A. Hoffmann, and other early nineteenth-century German Romantics. It may well have influenced Debussy's decision to transcribe Schumann's *Six etudes en forme de canon pour piano ou orgue à pédales* (Op. 56) for two pianos in 1891, a work that is clearly arabesque in nature and surely influenced by Bach.

Example 2.13f Debussy, *Deuxième Arabesque*, mm. 38–41

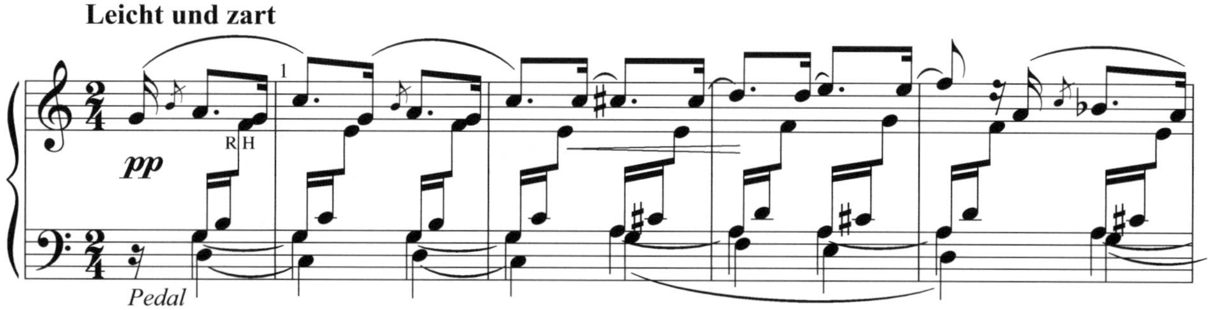

Example 2.13g Schumann, *Arabesk*, mm. 1–4

Finally, the *Première Arabesque* captures Debussy's point about the expressive power of tonal counterpoint and Schenker's claims about the ways in which detours, expansions, and other retardations create a sense of musical tension. To begin with, the piece does not start unambiguously on the tonic E major; as shown in example 2.11c, it actually starts on IV^6 and arrives on a root position tonic triad only at the perfect authentic cadence in m. 6. By delaying the definitive arrival of the tonic chord until m. 6, the passage fills the listener with a sense of expectation typical of an arabesque. The fact that the underlying progression is created by strings of parallel voices only increases this sense of uncertainty. Debussy's decision to begin the opening gesture on an inverted

Example 2.14 Essential voice leading, Debussy, *Première Arabesque*, mm. 39–46

subdominant sonority is even more remarkable because it anticipates the strong moves to A major in the middle section of the *Première Arabesque*, especially in mm. 39–70. In the case of mm. 39–42, example 2.14 shows how it is generated from the same stepwise patterns as those found in the work's outer sections: the soprano voice descends an octave from E to E and ends with the fourth-span A–G#–F#–E. As before this fourth it is supported by an alto voice set in parallel thirds. Having cadenced in A, the soprano again descends an octave from E to E though it ends with a perfect authentic cadence in E major, with the fourth-span A–G#–F#–E appearing in the bass in mm. 44–46. Significantly, Debussy repeated mm. 39–46 nearly verbatim in mm. 55–62.

The preceding discussion has described some of the many ways in which the "Largo" from Bach's Violin Concerto in G minor BWV 1056R and Debussy's *Première Arabesque* both allude to the concept of the arabesque as it was understood by Schlegel, Poe, Baudelaire, and even Debussy himself. Those allusions stem from the works' highly decorated melodic lines, their complex contrapuntal structures, their tendency to generate global forms from surface details, their infusions of the fantastic, and their expressive power. But given that Symbolist writers and artists invoked the concept of the arabesque to subvert the ways in which art was traditionally classified and institutionalized, we are left to answer a couple of obvious questions: how do the *Deux Arabesques* challenge the musical status quo? How do they fulfill the modernist agenda set forth by Schlegel, Poe, Baudelaire, and Debussy?

Taken at first sight, these questions are not easy to answer. When compared to other works written in the 1880s and 1890s, such as the *Ariettes oubliées* (1885–87) and *Cinq poèmes de Charles Baudelaire* (1887–89), the *Première Arabesque* doesn't seem particularly revolutionary and seems hardly capable of undermining the ways in which art was typically classified and institutionalized. On the contrary, Roger Nichols has even dismissed Debussy's early keyboard works like this one as "jejune in both content and technical expression."[39] And yet, the issue is a good deal more complex than it might initially seem. While the *Première Arabesque* may not achieve the levels of complexity displayed by the *Ariettes oubliées* and *Cinq poèmes de Charles Baudelaire*, it is certainly not without merit and cannot be dismissed simply as vernacular music. Rather, the piece seems to fall under the rubric of decorative art; it is the sort of music that bourgeois audiences might play in the comfort of their own home. This was the same social group that would soon shop for fine china and glassware, oriental rugs, Art Nouveau furniture, upscale fashions, gourmet food, and so on at fashionable stores such as the celebrated Galeries Lafayette. And it was in the hope of attracting such audiences and finding a publisher for his works that Debussy sometimes performed his early piano works in bourgeois salons.[40] Jacques Durand was sufficiently confident about the work's marketability that he purchased the rights to the *Deux Arabesques* for two hundred francs in October 1891, a sum that rivaled the one he paid for the rights of the *Quatuor* in 1894.[41] As Howat notes, the *Deux Arabesques* were not initially bestsellers: in between 1891 and 1902 Durand sold only twelve hundred copies.[42] The situation changed dramatically, however, after the successful premiere of *Pelléas et Mélisande* in 1902: over the next seven years, sales exploded to around fifty thousand copies.

Treating the *Deux Arabesques* and Debussy's other salon works as decorative art calls to mind Baudelaire's decision to focus his essay "Le Peintre de la vie moderne" on the commercial art of Constantin Guys, or Monsieur G., rather than the celebrated canvases of an Establishment painter such as Eugène Delacroix.[43] Working for many years in England, Guys made drawings and watercolors that were subsequently engraved and reproduced in magazines such as *The Illustrated London News* and others. Not only did Guys travel widely, producing images of exotic countries and foreign wars, but he also cruised the streets of Paris, sketching images of everyday life in the French capital. According to Baudelaire, "Monsieur G. has deliberately filled a function which other artists disdain, and which a man of the world above all others could carry out. He has gone everywhere in quest of the ephemeral, the fleeting forms of beauty in the life of our day, the characteristic traits of which, with the reader's permission, we have called 'modernity.'"[44] To achieve this goal, Guys adopted working methods ideally suited to that mission, methods that forced him to "see things broadly" and consider "their total effect": "Monsieur G brings an instinctive emphasis to his making of the salient or luminous points of an object (which may be salient or luminous from the dramatic point of view) or of its principal characteristics, sometimes with a degree of exaggeration which aids the human memory; and thus, under the spur of so forceful a prompting, the spectator's imagination receives a clear-cut image of the impression produced by the external world upon the mind of Monsieur G."[45] According to Baudelaire, Guys was able to capture the transient, fleeting, contingent aspects of modern life because he had a vision that is both "synthesizing and abbreviative" and that was firmly imprinted on his memory. Guys had to mediate between "the will to see all and forget nothing" and the faculty of memory "which has formed the habit of a lively absorption of general color and of silhouette, the arabesque of contour."[46] Baudelaire found a "fire" in Guys's manner of execution, "an intoxication of the pencil or the brush, amounting almost to a frenzy." As he explained, "It is a fear of not going fast enough, of letting the phantom escape before the synthesis has been extracted and pinned down; it is a terrible fear which takes possession of all great artists and gives them such a passionate desire to become masters of every means of expression so that the orders of the brain may never be perverted by the hesitations of the hand and that finally execution, ideal execution, may become as unconscious and spontaneous as is digestion for a healthy man after dinner."[47]

Such methods clearly differed from those used by painters in the fine arts who traditionally worked with models posing for them in studios and instead resembled those used by Baudelaire's close friend Édouard Manet, as well as generations of Impressionist, Post-Impressionist, and Symbolist painters. By lauding the aesthetic value of Guys's work, Baudelaire shifted attention away from what he saw as the artificiality and contrived nature of much so-called fine art and onto the authenticity and abbreviated quality of much commercial art. Debussy's forays into salon music do much the same; they remind us that he rejected the concept of high art as defined institutionally by the Académie des Beaux-Arts or the Paris Conservatoire. This much is clear from Debussy's review of Eugène Ysaÿe's performance of Bach's Violin Concerto in G minor BWV 1056R at the *Concerts spirituels* on Good Friday (April 5) 1901, which was described at length in the introduction. Before commenting on the significance of the arabesque, Debussy deliberately mocked the rationale behind the concert: "One never quite knows how the same old things could suddenly be played 'spiritually.'"[48] He then poked fun at the cult of the virtuoso: "The attraction that binds the virtuoso to his public seems much the same as that which draws the crowds to the circus: we always hope that something dangerous is going to happen. M. Ysaÿe is going to play the violin with M. [Édouard] Colonne on his shoulders. Or M. [Raoul] Pugno will finish by seizing the piano between his teeth. . . . None of these acrobatics materialized." Simply put, traditional concerts are not the best environments in which to appreciate art: "devoted music lovers still [have] to put up with neighbors more interested in orchestral pantomime than in anything really artistic."

Notes

1. See Roy Howat, "Foreword," in *Danses bohémienne, Dances (Tarentelle styrienne), Ballade (Ballade slave), Valse Romantique, Suite bergamasque, Rêverie, Mazurka, Deux Arabesques, Nocturne*, Oeuvres complètes de Claude Debussy, sér. I, vol. 1 (Paris: Durand, 2000), xx.

2. See Douche, "Transcription littérale du carnet de notes de Maurice Emmanuel au sujet de échanges Debussy-Guiraud (1889–1890)," in *Pelléas et Mélisande cent and après: études et documents*, Palazzetto Bru Zane, Centre de musique contemporaine Française, ed. Jean-Christophe Branger, Sylvie Douche, and Denis Herlin (Lyon: Symétrie, 2013), 279–87; Edward Lockspeiser, *Debussy: His Life and Mind*, vol. 1, *1862–1902*, 2nd ed. (Cambridge: Cambridge University Press, 1978), Appendix B, 204–8.

3. Claude Debussy, "A propos de 'Muguette.'—Au Concert Lamoureux," *Gil blas* (March 23, 1903), in *Monsieur Croche et autres écrits*, ed. François Lesure (Paris: Gallimard, 1987), 133–34; Claude Debussy, "Apropos de 'Muguette.'—At the Concert Lamoureux," in *Debussy on Music*, ed. François Lesure and trans. Richard Langham Smith (New York: Knopf, 1977), 155. See also Claude Debussy, "La musique en plein air," in *Monsieur Croche*, 46; Claude Debussy, "Music in the Open Air," in *Debussy on Music*, 41.

4. Claude Debussy, "Le 'Faust' de Schumann," in *Monsieur Croche*, 23; Claude Debussy, "At the Concerts Colonne: Schumann's *Faust*," in *Debussy on Music*, 13.

5. Adele Katz, *Challenge to Musical Tradition* (New York: Knopf, 1945); Felix Salzer, *Structural Hearing* (New York: Charles Boni, 1952), 222ff; David Carson Berry, "The Role of Adele T. Katz in the Early Expansion of the New York 'Schenker School,'" *Current Musicology* 74 (2002): 103–51. See also Boyd Pomeroy, "Debussy's Tonality: A Formal Perspective," in *The Cambridge Companion to Debussy*, ed. Simon Trezise (Cambridge: Cambridge University Press, 2003), 155–78; Matthew Brown, *Explaining Tonality: Schenkerian Theory and Beyond* (Rochester, NY: University of Rochester Press, 2005), 171–208; and John Koslovsky and Matthew Brown, "History and Tonal Coherence in Debussy's 'La Fille aux Cheveux de lin' and 'Bruyères,'" *Rivista di Analisi e Teoria Musicale* 18, no. 2 (2012): 35–54.

6. See https://schenkerdocumentsonline.org/search/?fq=all&kw=debussy.

7. See https://schenkerdocumentsonline.org/documents/diaries/OJ-01-07_1908-01/r0009.html.

8. See https://schenkerdocumentsonline.org/documents/diaries/OJ-01-10_1911-06/r0001.html.

9. Heinrich Schenker, *Erläuterungsausgabe der Sonate Op. 101, Ludwig van Beethoven* (Vienna: Universal, 1921), 23; Schenker, *Piano Sonata in A Major, Op. 101. Beethoven's Last Piano Sonatas. An edition with elucidations*, vol. 4, trans., ed., and annotated by John Rothgeb (New York: Oxford University Press, 2015), 10fn7.

10. Schenker, "Vermischtes," *Das Meisterwerk in der Musik II* (Munich: Drei Masken, 1926); "Miscellanea," trans. Ian Bent, in *The Masterwork in Music*, ed. William Drabkin (Cambridge: Cambridge University Press, 1996), 2:130.

11. Schenker, *Ein Beitrag zur Ornamentik* (Vienna: UE, 1904/1908); Schenker, "A Contribution to the Study of Ornamentation," ed. and trans. Hedi Siegel, *Music Forum* 4 (1976): 1–139.

12. Schenker, *Harmonielehre*, Neue musikalische Theorien und Phantasien, vol. 1 (Stuttgart and Berlin: Cotta, 1906), §§181–82, 445–52; Schenker, *Harmony*, ed. Oswald Jonas and trans. Elisabeth Mann Borgese (Chicago: University of Chicago Press, 1954), 336–42; and Schenker, *Kontrapunkt I*, Neue musikalische Theorien und Phantasien (Stuttgart and Berlin: Cotta, 1910), 2:384; *Counterpoint I*, ed. John Rothgeb and trans. John Rothgeb and Jürgen Thym, rev. ed. (Ann Arbor, MI: Musicalia, 2001), 296.

13. Schenker, "Der Kunst der Improvisation," in *Das Meisterwerk in der Musik I* (Munich: Drei Masken, 1925), 11–40; Schenker, "The Art of Improvisation," in *The Masterwork in Music I*, ed. William Drabkin and trans. Richard Kramer (Cambridge: Cambridge University Press, 1994), 2–19.

14. Schenker, *Kontrapunkt II*, Neue musikalische Theorien und Phantasien 2 (Vienna: Universal, 1922); and Schenker, *Der freie Satz*, Neue musikalische Theorien und Phantasien 3 (Vienna: Universal, 1935), §§251–66, 150–74; Schenker, *Free Composition*, ed. and trans. Ernst Oster (New York: Longman, 1979; Hillsdale, NY: Pendragon, 2001), 93–107; and Schenker, "Von der Diminution," *Der Dreiklang 4/5* (1937): 93–98.

15. Schenker, *Harmonielehre*, §88, 214; Schenker, *Harmony*, 168.

16 Venturino and Dunsby suggest that Debussy may have known Charles Bannelier's French translation, *Du beau dans la musique: essai et réforme de l'esthétique musicale par Edouard Hanslick* (Paris: Brandus, 1877); "The Evolution of Claude Debussy's Arabesque Idea," in *Debussy Studies 2*, ed. Barbara Kelly and David J. Code (Cambridge: Cambridge University Press, 2025), 68, fn28.

17. Schenker, "Der Geist der musikalischen Technik," in Hellmut Federhofer, *Heinrich Schenker als Essayist und Kritiker: Gesammelte Aufsätze, Rescensionen und kleinere Berichte aus den Jahren 1891–1901* (Hildesheim: Olms, 1990), 135–54; William Pastille, trans., "The Spirit of Musical Technique," in Nicholas Cook, *The Schenker Project* (Oxford: Oxford University Press, 2007), 319–32.

18. Schenker, *Kontrapunkt I*, Part 1, Chapter 2, §20, 133–35; Schenker, *Counterpoint I*, 94–95.

19. Schenker, *Harmonielehre*, §88, 214, 218; Schenker, *Harmony*, 168, 172–73.

20. Schenker, *Der freie Satz*, §79 and §84, 63 and 64; Schenker, *Free Composition*, 35.

21. Schenker, *Der freie Satz*, §254, 161; Schenker, *Free Composition*, 99.

22. For Debussy's use of concealed repetitions in the *Prélude à L'Après-midi d'un faune*, see Charles Burkhart, "Schenker's 'Motivic Parallelisms,'" *Journal of Music Theory* 22, no. 2 (1978): 145–75.

23. Schenker, *Der freie Satz*, §254, 161; Schenker, *Free Composition*, 99.

24. Schenker, *Der freie Satz*, §50, 51; Schenker, *Free Composition*, 27.

25. Schenker, *Der freie Satz*, §308, 212–13; Schenker, *Free Composition*, 131.

26. Schenker, *Der freie Satz*, §308, 213; Schenker, *Free Composition*, 131.

27. Schenker, *Der freie Satz*, §308, 213; Schenker, *Free Composition*, 131–32.

28. Schenker, *Der freie Satz*, Chapter 1.3, 19; Schenker, *Free Composition*, 6.

29. Schenker, *Der freie Satz*, Chapter 1.3, 18; Schenker, *Free Composition*, 5.

30. Schenker, *Der freie Satz*, 19; Schenker, *Free Composition*, 5.

31. Pierrot, *The Decadent Imagination 1880–1900*, trans. Derek Coltman (Chicago: University of Chicago Press, 1981), 230. For the impact of arabesques on eighteenth-century music, see Xavier Bisaro, "L'arabesque musicale: un non-sens? Étude de l'applicabilité d'un concept debussyste à la musique du XVIII e siècle," *Musurgia* 17, no. 2 (2010): 21–39.

32. See *Slaughterhouse Five* (1972), *Hannah and Her Sisters* (1986), *Primal Fear* (1996), and *Lara Croft: Tomb Raider* (2001).

33. Schenker, *Der freie Satz*, 18; Schenker, *Free Composition*, 5.

34. François Lesure, *Claude Debussy* (Paris: Klincksieck, 1994), 20; François Lesure, *Claude Debussy: A Critical Biography*, Eastman Studies in Music 159, ed. and trans. Marie Rolf (Rochester, NY: University of Rochester Press, 2019), 10. Debussy also enjoyed the way in which Pierre Louÿs played Bach: "nobody else plays me Bach with those delightfully imaginative touches with which you alone know how to adorn such antiquities." Letter to Pierre Louÿs of July 20, 1894, in Debussy, *Correspondance*, 215.

35. John R. Clevenger, "Debussy's Paris Conservatoire Training," in *Debussy and His World*, ed. J. F. Fulcher (Princeton, NJ: Princeton University Press, 2001), 299–361, esp. 314ff; Roy Howat, "Foreword," in *Debussy: Images (1894—dédiées à Y. Lerolle), Pour le piano, Children's Corner*, Œuvres Complètes de Claude Debussy, sér. 1, vol. 2

(Paris: Durand, 1998), XX; Julia Liu and Kenji Fujimura, "Music Education and the Prix de Rome," in *Debussy in Context*, ed. Simon Trezise (Cambridge: Cambridge University Press, 2024), 159–66. See also Matthew Brown, "Follow the Leader: Debussy's Contrapuntal Games," in *Debussy's Resonance*, ed. François de Médicis and Steven Huebner (Rochester, NY: University of Rochester Press, 2018), 383–406; and "Debussy's Violin Sonata and the Legacy of J. S. Bach," in *Debussy Studies 2*, ed. Barbara L. Kelly and David Code (Cambridge: Cambridge University Press, 2025).

36. Paul Vidal, "Souvenirs d'Achille Debussy," *Revue Musicale* 7 (1926): 10–16; Roger Nichols, *Debussy Remembered* (London: Faber, 1992), 6, 8.

37. For an alternative Schenkerian analysis of the *Première Arabesque*, see Richard S. Parks, *The Music of Claude Debussy* (New Haven, CT: Yale University Press, 1989), 5–10.

38. Roy Howat, "Foreword," in *Deux Arabesques, Œuvres Complètes*, sér. 1, vol. 1, ed. Roy Howat (Paris: Durand, 2008).

39. Roger Nichols, *Debussy*, Oxford Studies of Composers 10 (Oxford: Oxford University Press, 1973), 15–16.

40. For a general survey of Parisian salons at the end of the nineteenth century, see Cécile Tardif, "Fauré and the Salons," in *Regarding Fauré*, ed. Tom Gordon (Amsterdam: Gordon and Breach, 1999), 1–14. Although Debussy was no fan of bourgeois salons, he apparently performed his *Petite Suite* at one with his future publisher, Jacques Durand, in March 1889. This might have been at the home of Count and Countess Henri de Saussine; see Philippe Jullian, *Prince of Aesthetes: Count Robert de Montesquiou 1855–1921*, trans. John Haylock and Francis King (New York: Viking, 1968), 163.

41. See Denis Herlin, "An Artist High and Low, Or Debussy and Money," trans. Vincent Giroud, in *Rethinking Debussy*, ed. Elliot Antokoletz and Marianne Wheeldon (New York: Oxford University Press, 2011), 153; and Denis Herlin, "Publishers," in *Debussy in Context*, ed. Simon Trezise (Cambridge: Cambridge University Press, 2024), 143–49. Debussy, *Correspondance*, 192.

42. Howat, "Foreword," in *Deux Arabesqes*.

43. "How Delacroix Went from Lycée Dropout to Establishment Favourite," *The Art Newspaper*, April 12, 2018, https://www.theartnewspaper.com/2018/04/12/how-delacroix-went-from-lycee-dropout-to-establishment-favourite.

44. Baudelaire, "Le Peintre de la vie moderne: XIII Les Voitures," in *Charles Baudelaire: Œuvres Complètes*, Vol. II, ed. Claude Pichois, Bibliothèque de la Pléiade (Paris: Gallimard, 1976), 683–724; Baudelaire, "The Painter of Modern Life: XIII Carriages," in *The Painter of Modern Life*, ed. and trans. Jonathan Mayne (London: Phaidon, 2001), 40.

45. Baudelaire, "Le Peintre de la vie moderne: V L'Art mnémonique," in *Œuvres Complètes*, II:698; Baudelaire, "The Painter of Modern Life: V Mnemonic Art," 15–16. Baudelaire did, however, admit one exception—namely, situations, such as the Crimean War, when it was necessary for Guys to "take immediate, hasty notes, and to fix the principal lines of a subject." Baudelaire, "Le Peintre de la vie moderne: V L'Art mnémonique," in *Œuvres Complètes*, II:698; Baudelaire, "The Painter of Modern Life: V Mnemonic Art," 16.

46. Baudelaire, "Le Peintre de la vie moderne: V L'Art mnémonique," 698; Baudelaire, "The Painter of Modern Life: V Mnemonic Art," 16.

47. Baudelaire, "Le Peintre de la vie moderne: V L'Art mnémonique," 699; Baudelaire, "The Painter of Modern Life: V Mnemonic Art," 17.

48. Debussy, "Vendredi Saint," in *Monsieur Croche*, 33; "Good Friday," in *Debussy on Music*, 26.

3

Exoticism, Escapism, and Ennui

ONE REASON WHY the concept of the arabesque is helpful for understanding Debussy's music is that it offers a way to explain his love of the exotic. And rightly so: when coined in the sixteenth century, the terms *arabesque* and *moresque* were specifically introduced to describe decorative patterns borrowed from non-Western cultures, especially those from the Middle East. Arabesque designs became increasingly common during the seventeenth and eighteenth centuries because France and its European neighbors actively pursued expansionist policies.[1] Starting under the rule of Louis XIV (1643–1715), France extended its borders by colonizing territories in India, the Caribbean, and Central America. This process only accelerated in the nineteenth century: after occupying Egypt and the Iberian Peninsula during the Napoleonic Wars, France went on to control large swathes of North and West Africa, Madagascar, Indochina, and the South Pacific.[2] Meanwhile, French companies expanded their global interests. For example, the founding of the French East India Company in September 1660 encouraged the importation of exotic spices, silks, porcelain, and tea from China, India, and Japan.[3] The French government stimulated international trade even further by hosting a series of Expositions Universelles starting in 1855 and continuing in 1867, 1878, 1889, and 1900.

The goal of this chapter is to show how objets d'art imported from one particular non-Western nation had a direct impact on Symbolist conceptions of the arabesque and the "Other." That nation is Japan. It begins by showing how Japanese objets d'art flooded Paris in the decades following Baudelaire's death in 1867, thereby giving rise to a movement known as Japonisme. Next, the discussion shows how Japonisme resonated with the ways in which Schlegel, Poe, and Baudelaire invoked the arabesque and the Other to challenge current Western distinctions between fine and decorative art and between artist and artisan. The final parts then look at Debussy's long-standing interest in non-Western cultures. They not only offer a detailed analysis of a song from the Vasnier

Songbook but also highlight the ways in which Debussy, like Schlegel, Poe, and Baudelaire, used non-Western elements to challenge traditional Western aesthetic values.

When assessing the impact of Japonisme on Symbolist aesthetics, it is important to remember that French audiences had been interested in Japanese art since at least the seventeenth century when they first tried to establish diplomatic and trade agreements with Japan (see figs. 3.1a–3.1ca–cb). But those efforts were thwarted when Japan embarked on a policy of Sakoku: starting in the mid-seventeenth century the country closed its borders to other nations. The situation suddenly changed in the mid-1850s when Commodore Matthew Perry entered Edo Bay in 1854 and when the Crimean War (1854–56) pitted France and Great Britain against Russia.[4] On behalf of France, Baron Jean-Baptiste-Louis Gros went to Japan to sign a Treaty of Amity and Commerce between the two countries in 1858. Over the next few decades, especially during the Meiji Restoration (1868–1889), Japan rapidly transformed from an agrarian economy into a major industrial power that exported and imported goods to and from the entire globe. It formed political and financial alliances with France following the latter's defeat in the Franco-Prussian War (1870–71) as well as with Britain and the US.[5] Japan also had colonial ambitions that created tensions with Russia; victory in the Russo-Japanese War of 1904–5 gave them control of Korea and forced Russia to evacuate southern Manchuria.

Having flirted with chinoiserie and japanning in the 1740s and 1750s, French consumers succumbed to Japonisme in the 1850s when Félix Bracquemond and Claude Monet first discovered Japanese prints (*estampes*). The craze exploded a decade later with the opening of La Porte Chinoise in Paris by Louise DeSoye in 1862.[6] DeSoye's boutique and *salon de thé* became a magnet for the likes of Bracquemond, Gautier, Baudelaire, the Goncourts, Manet, Fantin-Latour, Degas, Whistler, Tissot, and Zola.[7] Philippe Burty, another regular at La Porte Chinoise, is widely credited with both popularizing the term *Japonisme* and founding the Société japonaise du Jinglar de Sèvres in 1867. Dealers and collectors such as Enrico Cernuschi, Théodore Duret, Emile Guimet, Philippe Sichel, and Siegfried Bing toured China and Japan to acquire materials of their own. Bing opened his first shop in 1885 and his famous Maison de l'Art Nouveau in December 1895. The influence of Japonisme can be felt on most major artists of the period: first-generation Impressionists (e.g., Manet, Degas, Whistler, and Fantin-Latour); plein air Impressionists (e.g., Monet and Pissarro; Symbolists such as Redon and Moreau); Post-Impressionists (e.g., Gauguin, Van Gogh, and Toulouse-Lautrec); Les Nabis (e.g., Bonnard, Vuillard, and Denis); and even pointillists (e.g., Seurat and Signac).[8] Also smitten were prominent writers such as Verlaine, Mallarmé, Huysmans, Loti, and Proust.[9] And, long before *Madame Butterfly* was performed in French at the Opéra-Comique in 1906, Parisians were treated to "Japanese" operas such as Saint-Saëns's *La princesse jaune* (1872), Lecocq's *Kosiki* (1876), and Messager's *Madame Chrysanthème* (1893).

Just as Japonisme followed chinoiserie and japanning, Symbolist views of the Other have their origins many decades earlier. Indeed, it was during his time in Paris (1802–4) that Friedrich Schlegel first studied Sanskrit and connected the fantastic elements of the arabesque with orientalism and Romanticism. According to him, arabesques allow readers "to cancel the progression and laws of rationally thinking reason," and transplant themselves "into the beautiful confusion of imagination, into the original chaos of human nature, for which I know as yet no more beautiful symbol than the motley throng of Ancient Gods."[10] To fuel this new mythology, "the other mythologies must also be reawakened according to the measure of their profundity, their beauty, and their form. If only the treasures of the Orient were as accessible to us as those of Antiquity. What new source of poetry could then flow from India if a few German artists with

Figure 3.1 Images of Japanese culture in eighteenth-century France

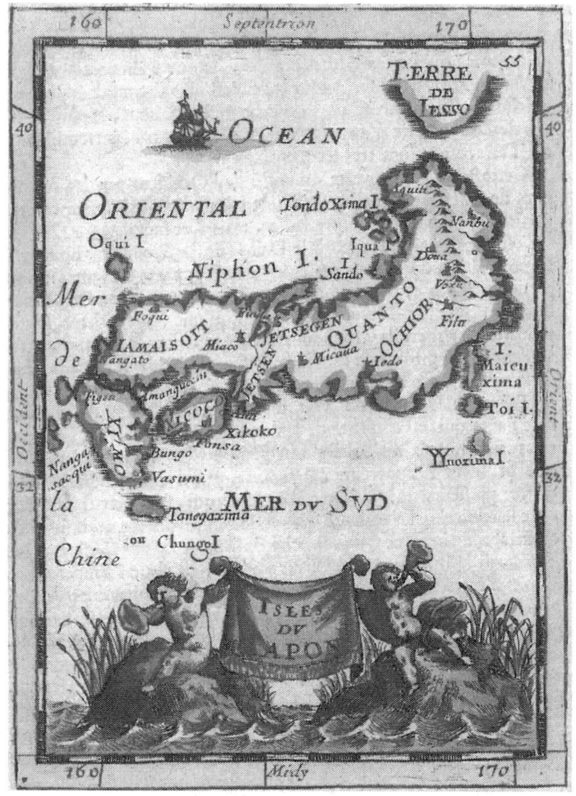

Top left, **Figure 3.1a** Allain Manesson Mallet, "Map of Japan," *Description de l'Univers* (Paris: Denys Thierry, 1683)

Top right, **Figure 3.1b** Allain Manesson Mallet, "Emperor of Japan," *Description de l'Univers* (Paris: Denys Thierry, 1683)

Bottom left, **Figure 3.1cb** "La Pagode des Singes," Cérémonies et coutumes religieuses de tous les peuples du monde (Amsterdam: J. F. Bernard, 1723–28)

Bottom right, **Figure 3.1ca** Bernard Picart, "La Divinité Supreme," "Xaca autre Divinité du Japon"

their catholicity and profundity of mind, with the genius of translation which is their own, had the opportunity which a nation growing ever more dull and brutal barely knows how to use. In the Orient we must look for the most sublime form of the Romantic, and only when we can draw from the source, perhaps will the semblance of southern passion which we find so charming in Spanish poetry appear to us occidental and sparse."[11]

But what did Schlegel really know about the orient? Not, it seems, very much. A specialist in philology, Schlegel had no firsthand experience of India; on the contrary, Edward Said has noted that Schlegel's *Über die Sprache und Weisheit der Indier* was actually the product of "hours spent in Paris libraries."[12] Since Germany had no significant presence in India, the Levant, or North Africa, there could be no "close partnership . . . between Orientalists and a protracted, *national* interest in the orient."[13] To a large extent, German accounts of the Orient were based on scholarly studies of classical antiquity: "it was made the subject of lyrics, fantasies, and even novels, but it was never the actual."[14] Some have even accused Schlegel of racism because of his allusions to the concept of an Aryan race.[15] Certainly, the message of tolerance found in texts like Chamber's *Cyclopaedie* presumed that, due to its scientific and artistic achievements, "Europe is the most 'civilized' part of the world, thereby giving rise to the notorious concept of the 'Noble savage.'"[16] And yet, Dorothy M. Figueira has offered a more nuanced response: "[Schlegel's] search for inspiration in Indian models implied the questioning of the dominant Western cultural values, as well as a dependence on what cultural ostensibly values assure in terms of self-realization. Although his quest manifested an arrogance which was endemic to his Europeanism, it would be wrong to view Schlegel's India reception solely in light of his political entitlement. It should be recognized that he also exhibited a will to be spiritually converted and empowered by India."[17] According to her, Schlegel's shortcomings ultimately stem from "an incomplete understanding" of Sanskrit: "Schlegel went to India not as a fanatic, but under the banner of an ultimately faulty science."[18]

Whatever Schlegel's motivations may have been for studying Sanskrit, Said is surely right to claim that in treating the Orient as the "Other," Schlegel sparked a sense of fantasy in the European mind, and Figueira is correct to suggest that by embracing the Other, Schlegel implicitly questioned the universality of Western cultural values. And it was these particular ideas—engaging the Other and criticizing Western values—that had such a profound influence on Edgar Allan Poe. Indeed, although Poe spent most of his adult life on the East Coast of the US between Boston and South Carolina, he embraced the exotic in several ways. One was by writing reviews of travelogues, such as John Lloyd Stephens's *Incidents of Travel in Egypt, Arabia Petraea, and the Holy Land* (1837) and Washington Irving's *The Crayon Miscellany* (1835). Another was by setting stories in distant lands.[19] Poe's novel *The Narrative of Arthur Gordon Pym* (1838) describes how Pym sails toward Antarctica and lands on the remote island of Tsalal. Pym is struck not only by the island's mysterious flora and fauna but also by its complete lack of the color white.[20] The indigenous population are, in fact, completely black, even their teeth! Equally fascinating is the short story "Silence—A Fable" (1837).[21] Set in another exotic land, it describes a cacophonous landscape in which nothing is quiet. A man sits desolately on a rock where, after being tormented by one tumultuous experience after another, he is finally cursed with complete silence. And a third way in which Poe embraced the Other was by placing characters in disturbing situations within an otherwise familiar environment. In the case of "The Man of the Crowd" (1840), for example, that environment is Victorian London. Poe's point is simple: it is possible to identify with the Other simply by living outside the mainstream of modern society. The resulting anxiety and sense of alienation may well have been prompted by Poe's own experiences as a schoolboy in Scotland and England.

Given Baudelaire's ambivalence toward the modern world, it not surprising that Poe became his main role model: "in Poe . . . Baudelaire found the prototype of le poète maudit, the poet as the outcast of society—the type which was to realize itself, in different ways, in Verlaine and Rimbaud, the type of which Baudelaire saw himself as a distinguished example."[22] Like Poe, Baudelaire was fascinated by the possibility of losing oneself in the midst of the crowd as he indicated in his short prose poem "Les Foules" (1861/1862).[23] He also shared Poe's love of the unexpected: "the elements of surprise and astonishment are an essential portion and characteristic of beauty."[24] And Baudelaire specifically associated the Other with the exotic: after encountering Chinese objets d'art at the Exposition Universelle of 1855, he famously declared "*The beautiful is always strange.*"[25] Such ideas clearly resonate with Baudelaire's concept of the flâneur. To deal with the instability of modern urban environments, flâneurs seek distractions (or "divertissements"). They crave fleeting moments of liberation in the eternal continuum, brief releases from their dull and tedious lives.[26] Such distractions might be inspired by physical interactions, imported objets d'art from foreign climes, or fantastic leaps of the imagination, perhaps involving the supernatural as in seances or induced by drugs as in Baudelaire's *Les Paradis artificiels*, a text inspired by Thomas De Quincey's *Confessions of an English Opium Eater* (London: Taylor and Hessey, 1821/1822).[27] The latter were clearly at odds with prevailing codes of conduct, especially those promulgated by the Catholic Church, which still held sway throughout France.

Baudelaire showed how the exotic can provide the flâneur with an appropriate diversion in his essay "Le Peintre de la vie moderne." When describing the ways in which commercial artist Constantin Guys reports from foreign countries, Baudelaire offered a particularly vivid response to Guys's depiction of a royal procession in Constantinople (see fig. 3.2).

> Turkey too has provided our beloved Monsieur G. with some admirable working-material: the festivals of the Bairam, those gloomy, rain-soaked splendours, in the midst of which, like a pale sun, can be discerned the endless *ennui* of the late sultan; drawn up on the sovereign's left, the officers of the civil order; on his right, those of the army, of whom the leader is Said Pasha, sultan of Egypt, at that time present in Constantinople; solemn processions and cavalcades moving in order towards the little mosque near the palace, and in the crowd Turkish functionaries, real caricatures of decadence, quite overwhelming their magnificent steeds with the weight of their fantastic bulk; massive great carriages, rather like coaches of the time of Louis XIV, but gilded and decked out in a bizarre Oriental manner, from which every now and then there dart curiously feminine glances, peeping out from between the strict interval left by bands of muslin stuck over the face; the frenzied dances of the tumblers of the 'third sex' (never has Balzac's comical expression been more applicable than in the present instance, for beneath this throbbing, trembling light, beneath the agitation of these ample garments, beneath the blazing rouge on these cheeks, in these hysterical, convulsive gesture, in these floating, waist-long tresses, it would be difficult, not to say impossible, to guess that virility lay hid); finally the *femmes galants* (if at least it is possible to speak of 'gallantry' in connection with the East), who generally consist of Hungarians, Wallachians, Jewesses, Poles, Greeks and Armenians—for under a despotic government it is the subject races, and amongst them, those in particular that have the most to endure, that provide most candidates for prostitution.[28]

Instead of explaining the picture's formal properties, Baudelaire recalls the fantasies that the image of the procession stirred in his mind. Notice, too, the arabesque quality of Baudelaire's account; cast as a single sentence containing nearly three hundred words, it recalls the final sentence of "Le Thyrse," which was written that same year.[29]

Figure 3.2 Constantin Guys, *Procession of the Sultan at the Festival of the Bairam, Constantinople*

Freeman G. Henry has suggested Baudelaire's escapist tendencies were already apparent in *Les Fleurs du Mal* and stemmed in part from events in the poet's life, such as his love of eighteenth-century literature, his longtime relationship with the Haitian-born actress and dancer Jeanne Duval, and his aborted trip to Calcutta as a youth.[30] According to Henry, *Les Fleurs du Mal* reveals "an interrelated evolution of exotic fantasies, escapism, and poetic visions."[31] That evolution corresponds to "an autobiographical account of real and illusory experiences" in which "the poet's escapism passes through several hierarchical stages, each one characterized by the same cyclical process—illusion, realization, rejection, ennui, and the search for illusion on a higher, more sophisticated plane."[32] This point resonates perfectly with Schlegel's claim that arabesques are akin to confessions. Henry also noted that the poems in *Les Fleurs du Mal* frequently refer to voyages, deserts, and the sea: by connecting such images with the lure of the unknowable and the impossible, the texts specifically link escapism with the exotic and the visionary.[33] Henry even claimed Baudelaire became a poet in large part because he was dissatisfied with life itself: "poetry would soon become for him a means of escape from the terrible ennui of his . . . 'nervous idleness.'"[34] When that wasn't enough, there was always "the exotic attraction of death."[35]

Schlegel, Poe, and Baudelaire were not, of course, alone in treating exoticism and arabesques as a means for escaping the hegemony of Western aesthetic values; their decision to treat the bizarre and the Other as beautiful was echoed by other artists working in numerous other domains. Many visual artists were inspired by the countless Japanese woodblock prints (estampes) and objets d'art that flooded Parisian boutiques starting in the 1860s. In response, they started to replace Western techniques, modes of composition, and motifs with those derived from Japanese art. Théodore Duret described this trend in his essay "The Impressionist Painters" (1878): "As soon as people looked at Japanese pictures, where the most glaring, piercing colors were placed side by side, they finally understood that there were new methods for reproducing certain effects of nature which had been neglected or considered impossible to render until then, and which might be good to try."[36] A few years later, Jules Laforgue explained how these new methods rejected traditional concepts of line, light, relief, perspective, and chiaroscuro as childish classifications.[37] Instead, they flatten out their images, emphasize bright colors and empty spaces, replace horizontal forms with vertical images (e.g., scrolls) and polytychs (e.g., screens and fans), blur the boundaries between image, border, and frame, and focus on commonplace subjects, the ephemeral, and the transcendental.[38] They also promoted the Sino-Japanese concept of "Ma," or negative space, in which specific areas of a design are left blank. Such trends are on perfect display in the images given in figure 3.3. Figures 3.3a–3.3b show two etchings from Félix Buhot's collection "Japonism: Dix Eaux-Fortes," the second of which was owned by Philippe Burty. For comparison, figure 3.3c shows Kono Bairei's woodblock print "The Night Heron" from the early 1880s and figure 3.3d shows Katsushika Hokusai's woodblock print "Frog and Bird," from the first half of the nineteenth century. Figure 3.3e shows a porcelain toad owned by Debussy that he affectionately named Arkel. Since Japan was isolated geographically and linguistically from France and the French language, the influence of Japonisme on French literature was inconsistent and often mimicked features taken from the visual arts. Indeed, as Elwood Hartman points out, they shaped not only the choice of "vocabulary, similes, syntactical constructions, [and] themes" but also the use of "short sentences, broken structure, verbless phrases, and colorful nouns."[39] Some have even linked the development of the short story to the concision of estampes and the principles of variation in Maeterlinck's verse to Hokusai's "Thirty-Six Views of Mount Fuji" and Monet's series paintings of Rouen Cathedral.[40]

Ultimately, however, Western artists appropriated Japanese elements for narcissistic and opportunistic reasons to escape from traditional conceptions of art. Few, if any, had direct knowledge of Japan, and few understood the Japanese language.[41] Gerald Needham has even suggested that French artists exploited Japonisme not because Japanese elements were especially novel but rather because they "corresponded with the effects they had [already] noticed and admired in their own environment."[42] According to him, "cut-off compositions and silhouetting occurred in photography; the black outlines adopted by the Pont-Aven artists appeared in the Medieval

Figure 3.3 Japanese designs and their influence in the late nineteenth century

Facing top left, **Figure 3.3a** Félix Buhot, "Japonism: Dix Eaux-Fortes," etching, 1883

Facing top right, **Figure 3.3b** Félix Buhot, "Japonism: Dix Eaux-Fortes," etching, 1883

Facing bottom left, **Figure 3.3c** Kono Bairei (1844–95), "The Night Heron," early 1880s

Facing bottom right, **Figure 3.3d** Katsushika Hokusai (1760–1849), "Frog and Bird," woodblock print

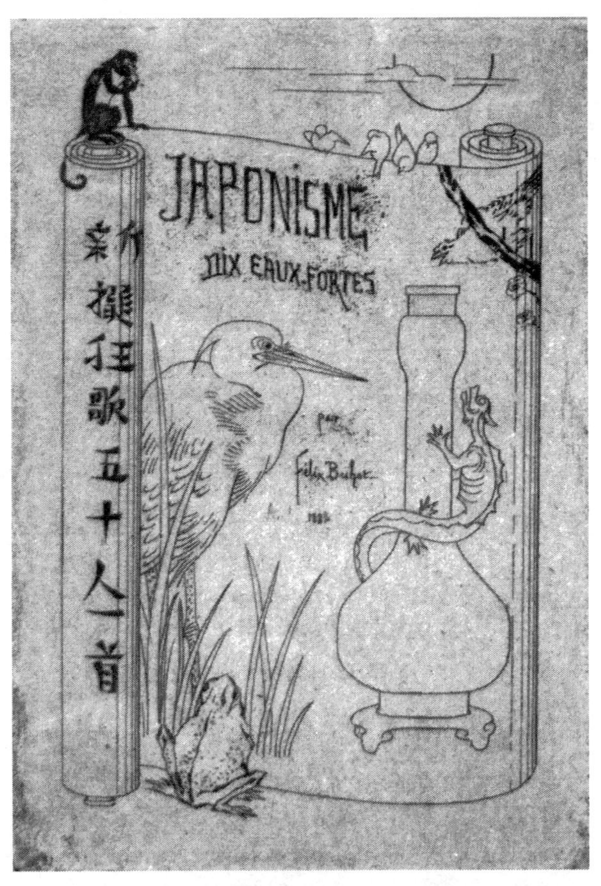

Figure 3.3e Debussy's toad "Arkel"

art they admired in the churches in Brittany; and certain daring composition had been created by French caricaturists of the mid-century." And, like similar forms of exoticism, Japonisme allowed Western artists to explore topics often regarded as taboo: it was more acceptable to paint a Japanese geisha than a Parisian prostitute.[43] Guys and others even produced erotic drawings in the manner of Japanese pillow-books, or *shunga*.[44] Carl Dahlhaus has echoed Needham's points in his discussion of exoticism in the nineteenth century. According to Dahlhaus, composers were entirely self-serving in their interest in exotic music and were motivated by a desire to avoid the traditional techniques and forms of Common-Practice tonality: "pentatonicism, the Dorian sixth and Mixolydian seventh, the raised second and augmented fourth, non-functional chromatic coloration, and finally bass drones, ostinatos, and pedal points [serve] as central axes."[45] To add an air of verisimilitude, they might also incorporate distinctive rhythmic clichés, melodic decorations, and scale types from the specific milieu in question, information about which was widely available through a variety of secondary sources. Even Schenker recognized the significance of exoticism in fin de siècle composition: not only did he discuss the status of so-called exotic scales, such as the "Japanese" scale (D E F G A B C D), the "Chinese" scale (F G A B C D E F), and the "Chinese whole-tone scale" (F G A B C♯ D♯ F) near the beginning of *Kontrapunkt 1* (1910), but he even owned a copy of Y. Nagai and K. Kobataki's *Japanese Popular Music* (see fig. 3.4).[46]

Taken together, the interrelations between exoticism, escapism, and ennui described by Schlegel, Poe, and Baudelaire, along with the musical devices enumerated by Dahlhaus, provide an appropriate backdrop against which to consider Debussy's interest in non-Western art and the ornamental character of one specific composition: *Rondel chinois*. Written in 1881, the song was inspired by and dedicated to Madame Marie-Blanche Vasnier, whom he met around 1880.[47] An aspiring singer, she was married to Eugène Vasnier, a noted Parisian architect, building contractor, and connoisseur of art. The song itself, whose text follows, is based on a short poem by Marius Dillard that was originally published in *Union Littéraire des poètes et des prosateurs* on May 5, 1875.[48] It describes a lake somewhere in China. A lady sleeps on a gilded boat, perhaps like the one shown in figure 1.6b, veiled in crepe and surrounded by azaleas, water lilies, and bamboo. From a veranda on the shore, a mandarin spies her through his owl-like eyes. Dillard cast this simple narrative in the form of a rondel: the first and second stanzas have four lines, with the opening couplet of the former recurring as the final couplet of the latter, whereas the third stanza has five lines, with the extra line recalling the opening line of the first stanza and the third line of the second.[49]

Rondel chinois
Sur le lac bordé d'azalée
De nénuphar et de bambou
Passe une jonque d'acajou
À la pointe d'or effilée.
    Une Chinoise dort voilée
D'un flot de crêpe jusqu'au cou.
Sur le lac bordé d'azalée,
De nénuphar et de bambou.
    Sous la véranda dentelée
Un mandarin se tient debout
Fixant de ses yeux de hibou
La dame qui passe isolée
Sur le lac bordé d'azalée.

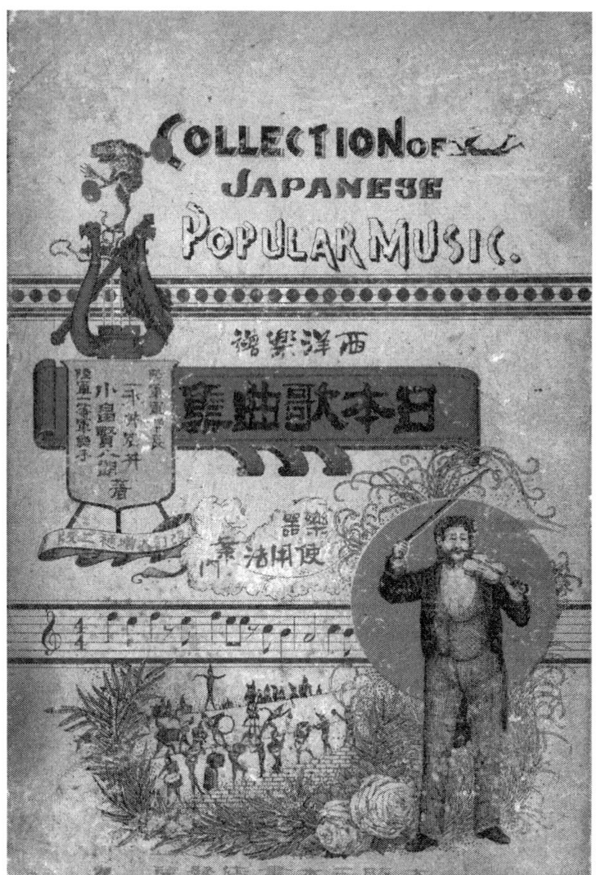

Left, **Figure 3.4aa** Y. Nagai and K. Kobataki's *Japanese Popular Music* (Osaka: Miki, 1893)

Right, **Figure 3.4ab** Cover

Besides demonstrating a love of the exotic, Debussy's setting of *Rondel chinois* is significant here because it illustrates the strong associations described by Schlegel between arabesques and the exotic, between arabesques and self-generating forms, and between arabesques and counterpoint. As regards the former, example 3.1a shows that the song is highly decorated: it starts with an elaborate vocalization in mm. 1–3 that is echoed by the piano in mm. 4–6. This pattern, which spans an octave A–A, highlights F♯ and E, the latter being emphasized by a trill on the downbeat of m. 2. This decoration provides a delightful foretaste of two prominent trills that appear later in the song: one on a high G♯ in mm. 32–33 (see ex. 3.1b) and another on a high A at the end of the song in m. 44 (see ex. 3.1c). These elaborations were surely designed to show off Vasnier's agile coloratura voice. Example 3.1c also includes several written-out ornaments, such as the turn figures in A–B–A–G and E–D–E–G in m. 45 and A–B–A–G–A in m. 46. Examples 3.1a–3.1c also indicate that these melodic arabesques are polyphonic in nature. In the case of example 3.1a, the vocalization seems to imply three latent voices: a latent soprano descending from A through F♯ to E, a latent alto voice beginning on C, and a latent tenor voice starting on A. The identity of these voices is even confirmed in the right hand of the piano in mm. 1–3, which suggests that the soprano voice may ultimately descend by step (A)–G♮–F♯–E, the alto C♯–A–G♯, and the tenor

Left, **Figure 3.4ba** Two songs in Western notation, page 2

Right, **Figure 3.4bb** Two songs in traditional notation, page 3

A–F♯–E over a stepwise descent in the bass E–D–C–B. Next, mm. 4–6 invert the contrapuntal framework of mm. 1–3 at the octave: the vocalization now appears in the bottom of the left hand. Example 3.1d shows a similar process in mm. 7–10: the vocal arabesque in m. 9 is echoed an octave lower in the piano in m. 10.

Also in line with Schlegel's testimony, Debussy's music seems to grow out of melodic arabesques in a self-generating manner so that local details determine a song's global form. Debussy's music for *Rondel chinois* can in fact be subdivided into two types: sections that set Dillard's original text and those that include textless vocalizations. The former are listed in example 3.2: Verse 1 (mm. 11–18), Verse 2 (mm. 19–26), and Verse 3 (mm. 32/33–42). These sections have several important things in common. First, they are all tonally closed. Verses 1 and 3 both are in A minor and end on a Picardy third (see ex. 3.2a–3.2b). In each case, the tonic is projected by means of a local progression I–♭II–V^{4}3–I♯ in A minor; the Phrygian ♭II sonority is not only decorated by an added sixth G, which reinforces the melody's pentatonic character, but also tonicized by an applied dominant in which the seventh E♭ is enharmonically respelled as D♯. The main difference between Verses 1 and 3 is that the latter repeats mm. 39–40 in mm. 41–42 in order to accommodate the extra line of text in Dillard's poem. Verse 2, meanwhile, is in C major (see ex. 3.2c): this local tonic is

Example **3.1a** *Rondel chinois*, mm. 1–6

Example **3.1b** *Rondel chinois*, mm. 30–32

Example 3.1c *Rondel chinois*, mm. 44–46

Example 3.1d *Rondel chinois*, mm. 7–10

clearly articulated both by a pedal tone C^5 buried in the right hand of the piano and by a perfect authentic cadence in the piano at the end of the verse in mm. 25–26. The passage also includes a couple of chromatic alterations: the A♭ in m. 20 is a simple coloration, whereas the B♭ in mm. 23 and 25 helps to tonicize F. Second, the verses all use the same motive: A–E–C–B–A for Verses 1 and 3 (see the voice parts in mm. 11 and 33); and C–G–E–D–E–C for Verse 2 (see the middle register of the piano in mm. 19, 21, and 22). To smooth over the transition between Verse 2 and Verse 3, variant of the motive A–E–D–C–D–E–F–A appear in the right hand of the piano in mm. 23–25 (see ex. 3.2c).

While example 3.2 shows how Debussy's setting of *Rondel chinois* articulates the strophic structure of Dillard's text, it nonetheless frames each strophe with passages of wordless vocalizations: Verse 1 is preceded by an introduction (mm. 1–10); Verse 2 is followed by a transition section (mm. 27–32); and Verse 3 is succeeded by a brief coda (mm. 42–46).

Whereas example 3.1b confirms that the coda basically spins out the final tonic chord, the introduction and transition stand out because they elaborate similar progressions from III to V♯

Example 3.2 Harmonic structure of Debussy, *Rondel chinois* (1)

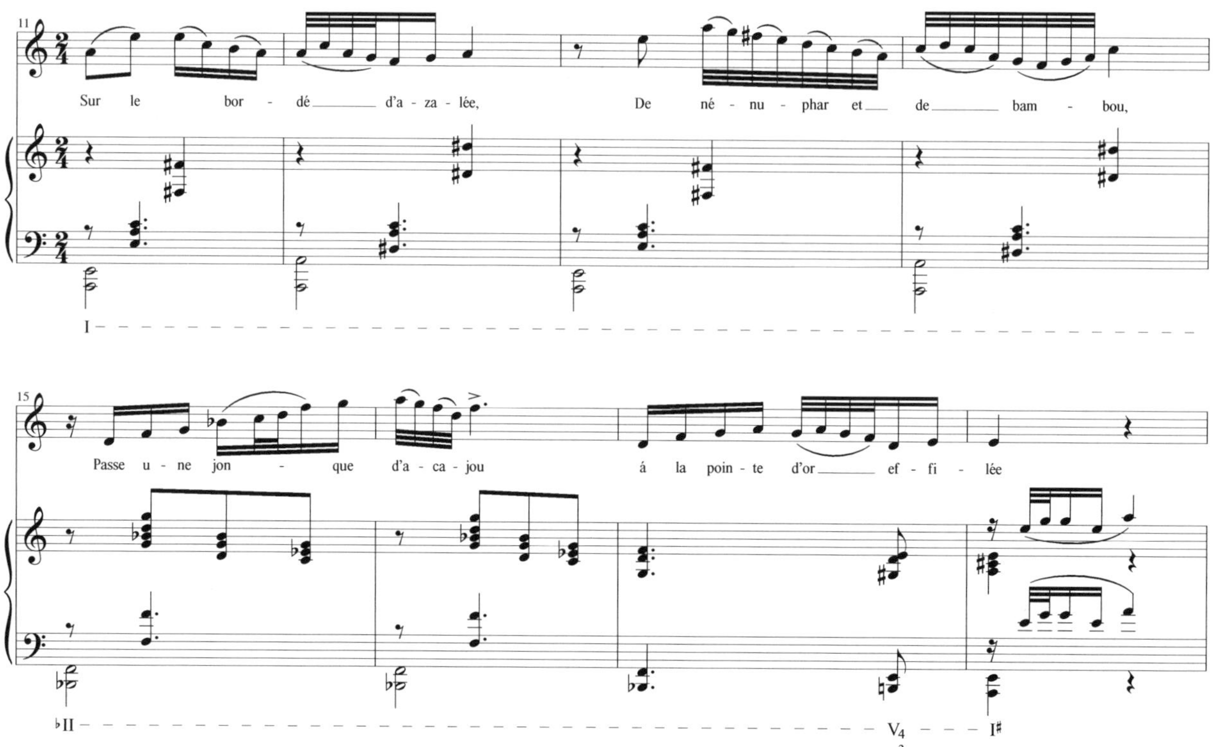

Example 3.2a Verse 1, mm. 11–18

in A minor (see ex. 3.3a). In the case of the introduction, this progression appears in mm. 7–10. In the transition, the situation is more complex: unlike mm. 7–10 where the two sonorities appear in immediate succession, the C major sonority in m. 26 connects to the E major chord in m. 32 by a string of chromatic parallel first inversion triads in the upper voices. These triads, which are supported by a string of descending thirds G♭/E♭–D/B–B♭/G–G♭/E♭–(G♯)/E in the middle register, imply a cycle of descending thirds C (III)–A♭ (♭VII)–E♮ (V♯)–C (III)–A♭ (♭VII)–E♮ (V♯) in the bass (see ex. 3.3b).[50] Besides foreshadowing the underlying large-scale motion III to V♯ in the transition, the introduction also presents certain motivic patterns that recur later in the song. A good case in point is the descending spans A–G–F♯–E (mm. 1–6) and its chromatic variant A–G–F–E (mm. 7–11). The voice-leading analysis given in example 3.4 shows how these patterns recur throughout the rest of the song, often appearing nested inside one another at different levels of musical organization.[51]

What, then, does *Rondel chinois* reveal about Debussy and exoticism? How does it shed light on his understanding of the arabesque? Though the *Rondel chinois* does indeed include pedal tones, pentatonic collections, and other melodic decorations that might have reminded Parisian audiences of Chinese music, those patterns can be found in other early songs by Debussy, such as *Séguidille* (1882) and *Les Elfes* (1881), that evoke other locales and even other worlds. Some of these interconnections are shown in example 3.5. Examples 3.5a–3.5b show that the Phrygian

Example 3.2b Verse 3, mm. 33–46 [mm. 33–36 = 1–4])

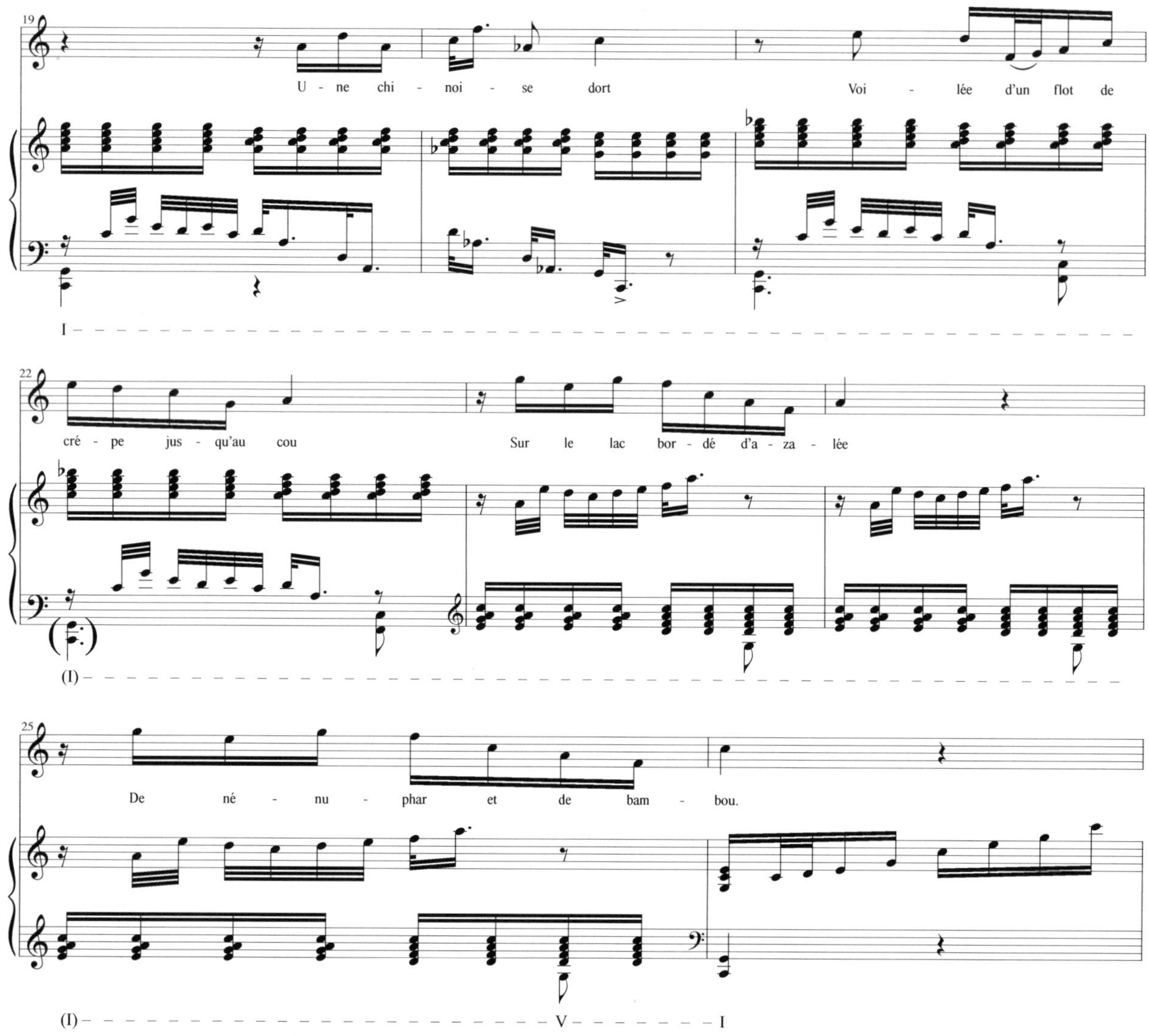

Example 3.2c Verse 2, mm. 19–26

collection E–F–G–A–B–C–D appears in mm. 7–8 of *Rondel chinois* and mm. 17–24 of *Ségui-dille* and examples 3.5c–3.5e that the melodic lines in *Rondel chinois*, *Séguidille*, and *Les elfes* are decorated with the same turn figures.[52] Not only are these patterns extremely generic in nature, but they adorn melodies that are not necessarily exotic in nature. Similarly, Examples 3.5f–3.5h show selected passages from *Rondel chinois*, *Séguidille*, and *Les elfes* in which the upper voices proceed chromatically in chains of parallel thirds and sixths. And examples 3.5i–3.5j indicate that the high trills in *Rondel chinois* also appear in *Séguidille*. Since these technical devices are often the same "regardless of the milieu being depicted," it seems that Debussy's first experiments in exotica were not based on any intimate knowledge of music from other cultures; instead, they were motivated by a desire to compose decorative music based on the principle of the arabesque. Marie Rolf confirms this suspicion by observing that the main motive used in Verses 1 and 3 of

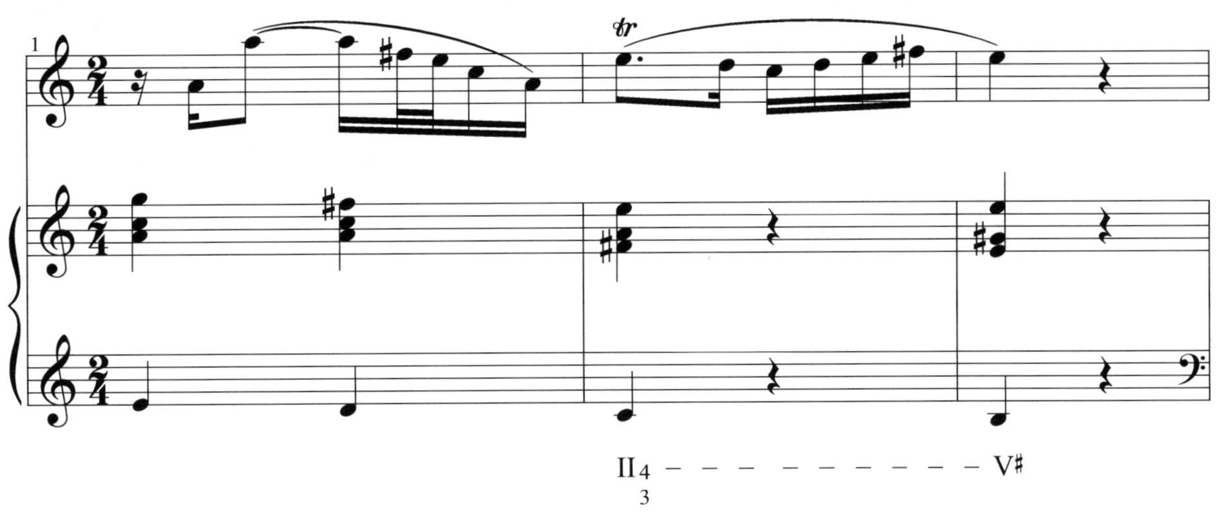

Example 3.3a Introduction, mm. 1–10

Example 3.3b Transition, mm. 27–32

Rondel chinois is almost a carbon copy of that of another song from 1882, *Fête galante* (see ex. 3.6). This song, which is based on a poem by Théodore de Banville, doesn't have any obvious allusions to other cultures; on the contrary, it conjures up images of amorous arabesques in Watteau's *L'Embarquement pour Cythère* and underscores, yet again, the extent of Debussy's infatuation with Mme Vasnier.[53]

Debussy continued to cultivate his interests in non-Western music throughout the remainder of his career.[54] In 1884, for example, he read Huysman's recently published novel *À Rebours* (1884), a work that lauded the writings of Poe and Baudelaire for their "strangeness" and "strange magic."[55] Soon after, he would even meet Huysmans and other leading Symbolists at Edmond Bailly's Librarie de l'Art Indépendent and at Mallarmé's famous *mardis*, where he is known to have discussed Japanese prints with the sculptor Camille Claudel around 1890. Many of these writers were also interested in the occult and metaphysical views other than those associated with

Example 3.4 Essential voice leading, Debussy, *Rondel chinois*, mm. 1–46

Catholicism.[56] Debussy also encountered a Javanese gamelan and the Théâtre Annamite from Vietnam and may well have attended performances of Japanese dance music and the Kabuki play *The Geisha and the Samurai* at the Exposition Universelle of 1900.[57] According to Jean-Michel Nectoux, Debussy also visited several exhibitions in the 1880s and 1890s and a showing of the Bing collection at the Galerie Durand-Ruel in May 1906.[58] After viewing a new exhibition in the summer of 1910, he noted, "Another very personal thing is the Chinese exhibition at the Pavillon Marsan that I just saw. . . . It cannot be described nor expressed, but I have never, or rarely, seen one attain such refined beauty."[59] Debussy's interest in the music of China and Japan was surely fueled by his friendship with Louis Laloy, whom he befriended in 1902 and who was an expert in Chinese music.[60] A regular at Debussy's house after marrying the Armenian pianist Susanik Babaïan in 1906, Laloy completed a short monograph on Chinese music in 1910 that includes several observations about music from Japan.[61]

All the while, Debussy assembled his own personal collection of exotic objets d'arts from various Parisian boutiques, such as La Porte Chinoise and L'Empire Chinois, often spending housekeeping money, much to the chagrin of his partners.[62] Jacques Durand, for example, remembered visiting Debussy's house in 1904 or early 1905: "His study was on the ground floor, with spacious bay windows which flooded it with light, and it opened out on to the garden which surrounded the house. The wide table on which he used to work was cluttered with high-class Japanese objects. His favorite was a porcelain toad which he called his fetish and which he took

Example 3.5 Recurring patterns in Debussy's *Rondel chinois*, *Séguidille*, and *Les elfes*

Example 3.5a Phrygian collection in *Rondel chinois*, mm. 7–10

Example 3.5b Phrygian collection in *Séguidille*, mm. 17–25

Example 3.5c Turn figure in *Rondel chinois*, mm. 41–42 and 46

88

Example 3.5d Turn figure in *Séguidille*, mm. 21–23 and 57–58

Example 3.5e Turn figure in *Les elfes*, mm. 1–3

Example 3.5f Parallel 3rds/6ths in *Rondel chinois*, mm. 27–32

Example 3.5g Parallel 3rds/6ths in *Séguidille*, mm. 87–91

Example 3.5h Parallel 3rds/6ths in *Les elfes*, mm. 63–65

Example 3.5i Trill in *Rondel chinois*, mm. 44–46

Example 3.5j Trill in *Séguidille*, mm. 13–25

Example 3.6 Motivic connections between Debussy's *Rondel chinois* and *Fête galante*

with him when he moved, claiming he could not work unless it was in sight. Many was the time he lamented to the difficulty of taking his worktable with him on holiday."[63] Durand added, "I also remember, in his study, a certain coloured engraving by Hokusai, representing the curl of a giant wave. Debussy was particularly enamored of this wave. It inspired him while he was composing *La Mer*, and he asked us to reproduce it on the cover of the printed score." Debussy's personal collection of Japanese artifacts also included a koto and a lacquer panel featuring two "poissons d'or."[64] Most experts acknowledge that this collection had an impact on the decorative aspects of Debussy's music. David Code has suggested that Debussy's penchant for presenting his songs in triptychs may have been inspired by three-part Japanese prints, of which thousands were

Example 3.7 Similarities between Debussy's *Le Matelot qui tombe à l'eau* and "Poissons d'or," *Images*, sér. 2

Example 3.7a Debussy, *Le Matelot qui tombe à l'eau*, mm. 1–2

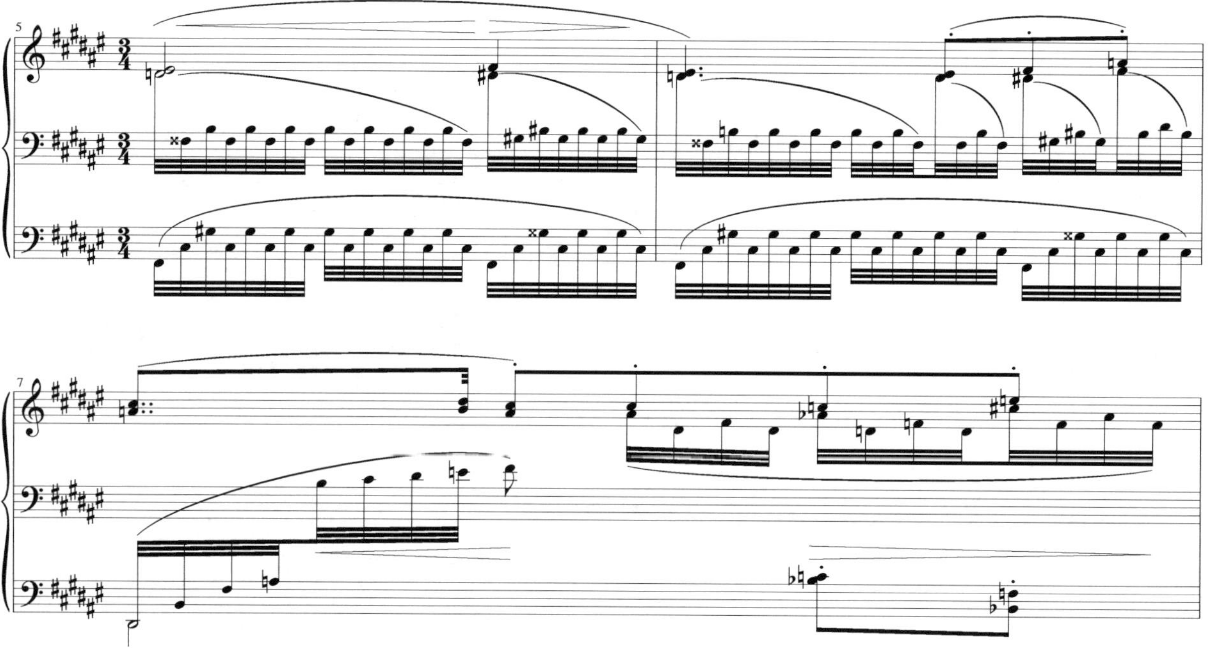

Example 3.7b Debussy, "Poissons d'or," mm. 5–7

produced in the eighteenth and nineteenth centuries.[65] In the case of *La Mer*, the first edition included a doctored version of Hokusai's "Under the Wave off Kanagawa" (Thirty-Six Views of Mount Fuji) on the cover, and the first movement begins with a string of exotic sounds that recall the opening of "Pagodes" (*Estampes*, 1903) and the tuning system of the Paris Conservatoire's Javanese gamelan.[66] Similarly, Robert Waters has suggested that the opening chords of "Et la lune descend sur le temple qui fut" (*Images*, sér. 2, 1907) resemble those produced on the shō, a mouth organ often used in Japanese *gagaku*.[67] It is also possible that Debussy had the sounds of a koto in mind when composing mm. 441–450 of *Jeux* (1912–13): not only does the harp part re-create the koto's distinctive twang, but it was written about the same time as Stravinsky's *Three Japanese Lyrics*.[68] And it is widely believed that Debussy's piano piece "Poissons d'or" (*Images*, sér. 2) was inspired by the lacquer panel in his personal collection. As shown in example 3.7, the opening arpeggios resemble the piano part of his early song *Le Matelot qui tombe à l'eau*, which he completed in 1882.

In short, Debussy's interest in the exotic was motivated by the same escapist tendencies and feelings of ennui as other Symbolist writers. Debussy was the quintessential flâneur with no authentic understanding of Japan or of any other culture. He was an armchair observer who projected himself onto such repertories as much as he borrowed from them. Composing exotic music gave him justification for employing many of the musical techniques that he had already found in the music of Bach and many of the aesthetic principles outlined by Schlegel, Poe, and Baudelaire. These included emphasizing the ornamental character of music, focusing on the contrapuntal aspects of music, finding new ways for local details to generate global forms, and creating a fantasy by alluding to diverse styles and idioms. That these principles are all embodied in the concept of the arabesque underscores that Debussy was less interested in providing an authentic image of other cultures and more in challenging the status quo. That dissatisfaction with the French musical establishment, which became increasingly apparent after Debussy was awarded a Prix de Rome by the Académie des Beaux-Arts, remained with him for the rest of his life.[69] It often bubbled up when he wrote about the value of non-Western music. Six years after attending the Exposition Universelle of 1889, for example, he recalled those visits in a letter to Pierre Louÿs dated January 22, 1895: "Remember the music of Java which contained every nuance, even the ones we no longer have names for. There tonic and dominant had become empty shadows of use only to stupid children."[70] And in an essay for *SIM* (February 15, 1913): "Javanese music obeys laws of counterpoint that make Palestrina seem like child's play. And if one listens to it without being prejudiced by one's European ears, one will find a percussive charm that forces one to admit that our own music is not much more than a barbarous kind of noise more fit for a travelling circus."[71] Exoticism and the arabesque thus provided Debussy with a means for challenging the ways in which classical music was institutionalized in French society. They were part and parcel of his modernist agenda.

Notes

1. See Ina Baghdiantz McCabe, *Orientalism in Early Modern France* (Oxford: Berg, 2008).
2. See Lola San Martín Arbide, "Beyond Paris," in *Debussy in Context*, ed. Simon Trezise (Cambridge: Cambridge University Press, 2024), 25–33.
3. See E. H. Pritchard, "The Struggle for Control of the China Trade during the Eighteenth Century," *Pacific Historical Review* 3, no. 3 (1934): 280–95.
4. Meron Medzini, *French Policy in Japan during the Closing Years of the Tokugawa Regime* (Cambridge, MA: Harvard University Press, 1971), 9.

5. See John Albert White, *Transition to Global Rivalry: Alliance Diplomacy and the Quadruple Entente, 1895–1907* (Cambridge: Cambridge University Press, 1995).

6. For a general overview, see Michael Sullivan, *The Meeting of Eastern and Western Art* (Berkeley: University of California, 1989); Elwood Hartman, "Japonisme and Nineteenth-Century French Literature," in "East-West Issue," special issue, *Comparative Literature Studies* 18, no. 2 (1981): 141–66; and Nicola Saravese, *Eurasian Theatre: Drama and Performance between East and West from Classical Antiquity to the Present*, trans. Richard Fowler, rev. and ed. Vicki Ann Cremona (Holstebro: ICARUS, 2010).

7. Elizabeth Emery, "Madame Desoye, 'First Woman Importer' of Japanese Art in Nineteenth-Century Paris," *Journal of Japonisme* 5, no. 1 (2019): 1–46; and Elizabeth Emery, *Reframing Japonisme: Women and the Asian Art Market in Nineteenth-Century France, 1853–1914* (London: Bloomsbury, 2022).

8. See Gerald Needham, "Japanese Influence on French Painting 1854–1910," in *Japonisme. Japanese Influence on French Art 1854–1910*, ed. Gabriel P. Weisberg (Kent, OH: Kent State University Press, 1975), 115–39; and Frank Whitford, *Japanese Prints and Western Painters* (New York: Macmillan, 1977), 96–233.

9. Hartman, "Japonisme," 146.

10. Friedrich Schlegel, *Dialogue on Poetry and Literary Aphorisms*, trans., introduced, and annotated Ernest Behler and Roman Struc (University Park: Pennsylvania State University Press, 1968), 86.

11. Schlegel, *Dialogue on Poetry*, 86–87.

12. Edward Said, "Introduction," in *Orientalism* (New York: Random House, 1978), 19.

13. Said, "Introduction," 19.

14. Said, "Introduction," 19.

15. See Martin Bernal, *Black Athena: The Afroasiatic Roots of Classical Civilization* (New Brunswick, NJ: Rutgers University Press, 1987), 230.

16. Devin J. Vartija, *The Color of Equality: Race and Common Humanity in Enlightenment* (Philadelphia: University of Pennsylvania Press, 2021), 83.

17. Dorothy M. Figueira, "The Politics of Exoticism and Friedrich Schlegel's 'Metaphorical Pilgrimage to India,'" *Monatshefte* 81, no. 4 (Winter 1989): 431. For Schlegel's alleged racism, see Bernal, *Black Athena*, 230.

18. Figueira, "Politics of Exoticism," 431.

19. Brian Yothers points to Poe's short stories, such as "MS. Found in a Bottle" (1833), "The Journal of Julius Rodman" (1840), and "The Unparalleled Adventure of One Hans Pfaall" (1835). See Brian D. Yothers, "Poe's Poetry of the Exotic," *Critical Insights: The Poetry of Edgar Allan Poe*, ed. Steven Frye (Pasadena, CA: Salem, 2010), 19.

20. For an extended critique of this work, especially its racist overtones, see Toni Morrison, *Playing in the Dark: Whiteness and the Literary Imagination* (New York: Vintage, 1993), 31–59. For Baudelaire's translation of Poe's novel, see Edgar Allan Poe, *Edgar Allan Poe, Œuvres en prose*, trans. Charles Baudelaire, Bibliothèque de la Pléiade, ed. Y.-G. Le Dantec (Paris: Gallimard, 1951), 495–691.

21. For Baudelaire's translation of this story, see Poe, *Edgar Allan Poe, Œuvres en prose*, 480–83.

22. T. S. Eliot, "From Poe to Valéry," *Hudson Review* 2, no. 3 (1949): 337.

23. Baudelaire, "'Les Foules', *Le Spleen de Paris*, XII," in *Charles Baudelaire: Œuvres Complètes*, vol. I, ed. Claude Pichois, Bibliothèque de la Pléiade (Paris: Gallimard, 1975), 291–92; Baudelaire, "Crowds," in *Vol. II. The Poems in Prose and La Fanfarol*, ed. and trans. Francis Scarfe (London: Anvil Press Poetry, 1989), 58–59. See Marit Grøtta, *Baudelaire's Media Aesthetics: The Gaze of the Flâneur and Nineteenth-Century Media* (London: Bloomsbury, 2015), 5.

24. Baudelaire, "Fusées: VIII," in *Œuvres Complètes*, I:656; Baudelaire, "Flares: 12," in *Late Fragments: Flares, My Heart Laid Bare, Prose Poems, Belgium Disrobed*, ed. and trans. Richard Sieburth (New Haven, CT: Yale University Press, 2022), 89.

25. Baudelaire, "L'Exposition universelle de 1855 vue par Baudelaire," in *Charles Baudelaire: Œuvres Complètes*, vol. II, ed. Claude Pichois, Bibliothèque de la Pléiade (Paris: Gallimard, 1976), 578; Baudelaire, "The Exposition Universelle," in *Art in Paris 1845–1862: Salons and Other Exhibitions Reviewed by Charles Baudelaire*, ed. and trans. Jonathan Mayne, 2nd ed. (London: Phaidon, 1995), 124. See also Jennifer Yee, "Baudelaire and the Chinese Object," *L'Esprit Créateur* 58, no. 1 (2018): 101–13.

26. See Hartman, "Japonisme," 153.

27. See Mohammed Hamdan, "The Gift of Drugs: Oriental Geographies and Decolonizing Space in Thomas De Quincey's Confessions of an English Opium-Eater," *Janus Unbound: Journal of Critical Studies* II, no. 1 (Winter 2022): 63–68.

28. Baudelaire, "Le Peintre de la Vie Moderne: VII Pompes et Solennites," in *Œuvres Complètes*, II:704; Baudelaire, "The Painter of Modern Life: VII Pomps and Circumstances," in *The Painter in Modern Life*, ed. and trans. Jonathan Mayne (London: Phaidon, 2001), 21–22.

29. Baudelaire, "Richard Wagner et *Tannhäuser* à Paris," in *Œuvres Complètes*, II:784–86; Baudelaire, "Richard Wagner and *Tannhäuser* in Paris," in *The Painter in Modern Life*, 116–18. Enid Starkie, *Baudelaire* (New York: New Directions, 1958), 405; Margaret Miner, *Resonant Gaps between Baudelaire and Wagner* (Athens: University of Georgia Press, 1995).

30. Freeman G. Henry, "Les Fleurs du Mal and the Exotic: The Escapist Psychology of a Visionary Poet," *Nineteenth-Century French Studies* 8, nos. 1/2 (1979–80): 62–63. See also Robert Vivier, *L'Originalité de Baudelaire*, 3rd ed. rev. (Brussels: Palais des Académies, 1965), 194–95; and see Yvan Landis, *Baudelaire at 20 Years Old: The Journey to India* (Nogent-sur-Marne: Storia Editions, 2019).

31. Henry, "Les Fleurs du Mal and the Exotic," 63.

32. Henry, "Les Fleurs du Mal and the Exotic," 63.

33. Henry, "Les Fleurs du Mal and the Exotic," 66.

34. Henry, "Les Fleurs du Mal and the Exotic," 67.

35. Henry, "Les Fleurs du Mal and the Exotic," 63.

36. Théodore Duret, "The Impressionist Painters" (1878), in Linda Nochlin, *Impressionism and Post-Impressionism 1874–1904*, Sources & Documents in the History of Art Series (Englewood Cliffs, NJ: Prentice-Hall, 1966), 9 [7–10].

37. Jules Laforgue, "Impressionism" (1883), in Nochlin, *Impressionism*, 14–20. Laforgue was apparently inspired by the research of Charles Henry; see Roy Howat, *Debussy in Proportion: A Musical Analysis* (Cambridge: Cambridge University Press, 1983), 164–65.

38. See Needham, "Japanese Influence," 116ff; and Hartman, "Japonisme," 147.

39. Hartman, "Japonisme," 150.

40. Sadakichi Hartmann, *Japanese Art* (Boston, MA: L. C. Page, 1904), 160–63.

41. See Earl Miner, *The Japanese Tradition in British and American Literature* (Princeton, NJ: Princeton University Press, 1958), 45; and Hartman, "Japonisme," 149.

42. Needham, "Japanese Influence," 116.

43. See Hollis Clayson, *Painted Love. Prostitution in French Art of the Impressionist Era* (New Haven, CT: Yale University Press, 1991).

44. Baudelaire, "Le Peintre de la Vie Moderne: XII Les Femmes et les Filles," in *Œuvres Complètes*, II:718–22; Baudelaire, "The Painter of Modern Life: XII, Women and Prostitutes," in *The Painter in Modern Life*, 34–38. See also Clayson, *Painted Love*, 2.

45. Carl Dahlhaus, *Nineteenth-Century Music*, trans. J. Bradford Robinson (Berkeley: University of California Press, 1989), 306. See also Ralph P. Locke, "A Broader View of Musical Exoticism," *Journal of Musicology* 24, no. 4 (2007): 477–521; and Richard E. Mueller, *Beauty and Innovation in La Machine Chinoise: Falla, Debussy, Ravel, Roussel* (Hillsdale, NY: Pendragon, 2018).

46. Heinrich Schenker, *Kontrapunkt I*, Neue musikalische Theorien und Phantasien 2 (Stuttgart: Cotta, 1910), part 1, chap. 1, §5, 30–37; Heinrich Schenker, *Counterpoint I*, ed. John Rothgeb and trans. John Rothgeb and Jürgen Thym, rev. ed. (Ann Arbor, MI: Musicalia, 2001), 20–24. See Heinrich Hinterberger, *Enthaltend die Bibliothek des Herrn Dr. Heinrich Schenker*, Wien Katalog XII (Vienna: Antiquariat Hinterberger, ca. 1935), 14; and Brown, "Schenker and the 'Myth of Scales,'" in *Explaining Tonality: Schenkerian Theory and Beyond* (Rochester, NY: University of Rochester Press, 2005), 140–70.

47. James R. Briscoe, "Debussy's Earliest Songs," *College Music Symposium* 24, no. 2 (Fall 1984): 81–95. Jann Pasler, "Revisiting Debussy's Relationships with Otherness: Difference, Vibrations, and the Occult," *Music & Letters* 101, no. 2 (2020): 321–42; Marie Rolf, "Oriental and Iberian Resonances in Early Debussy Songs," in *Debussy's Resonance*, ed. François de Médicis and Steven Huebner (Rochester, NY: University of Rochester Press, 2018), 278–81.

48. Rolf, "Oriental and Iberian Resonances," 275.

49. Rolf, "Oriental and Iberian Resonances," 278.

50. See Heinrich Schenker, *Der freie Satz*, Neue musikalische Theorien und Phantasien, vol. 3 (Vienna: Universal, 1935), §§230 and 246, 133–34 (fig. 100.6) and 144 (fig. 110); Heinrich Schenker, *Free Composition*, ed. and trans. Ernst Oster (New York: Longman, 1979), 82 and 89–90.

51. Charles Burkhart, "Schenker's 'Motivic Parallelisms,'" *Journal of Music Theory* 22, no. 2 (1978): 151–55.

52. Dahlhaus, *Nineteenth-Century Music*, 306.

53. Rolf, "Oriental and Iberian Resonances," 279–80; James R. Briscoe, "Debussy 'd'après' Debussy: The Further Resonance of Two Early 'Mélodies,'" *19th-Century Music* 5, no. 2 (1981): 110–16. See also Emma Adlard, "Debussy, 'Fêtes galantes,' and the Salon of Marguerite de Saint-Marceaux," *Musical Quarterly* 96, no. 2 (2013): 178–218. It is worth noting that Baudelaire praised the arabesque qualities of Watteau's paintings in several essays and conveyed the mood of Watteau's *Fêtes galantes* in his poem "Un voyage à Cythère," *Les Fleurs du Mal*, CXIV, in *Œuvres Complètes*, I:117–19.

54. For Debussy's interest in Spanish music, see Matthew Brown, *Debussy's 'Ibéria': Studies in Genesis and Structure* (Oxford: Oxford University Press, 2003), 36–64.

55. Joris-Karl Huysmans, *À Rebours* (Paris: Garnier-Flammarion, 1978), 206, 110; Joris-Karl Huysmans, *Against Nature*, trans. Robert Baldick (Harmondsworth: Penguin, 1959), 180, 69.

56. Jann Pasler, "Revisiting Debussy's Relationships," 321–42.

57. See Anik Devriè, "Les musiques d'extrême orient à l'exposition universelle de 1889," *Cahiers Debussy* 1 (1977): 24–37; Annegret Fauser, *Musical Encounters at the 1889 Paris World's Fair* (Rochester, NY: University of Rochester Press, 2005), 165; and François Lesure, *Claude Debussy* (Paris: Klincksieck, 1994), 103–6; François Lesure, *Claude Debussy: A Critical Biography*, ed. and trans. Marie Rolf, Eastman Studies in Music 159 (Rochester, NY: University of Rochester Press, 2019), 82–83. Edmond Bailly, *Le pittoresque musical* à *l'exposition* (Paris: Editions de l'Humanité Nouvelle, 1900), 30; and Julien Tiersot, *Notes D'Ethnographie Musicale*, Série 1 (Paris: Fischbacher, 1905), 7–38. This material appeared earlier in *Ménestel* 1900–2.

58. Jean-Michel Nectoux, *Harmonie en bleu et or: Debussy, la musique et les arts* (Paris: Fayard, 2005), 190.

59. See Debussy's letter to Durand (July 8, 1910). Claude Debussy, *Correspondance (1872–1918)*, ed. François Lesure and Denis Herlin, annotated by François Lesure, Denis Herlin, and Georges Liébert (Paris: Gallimard, 2005), 1300; Michel Duchesneau, "Debussy and Japanese Prints," in *Debussy's Resonance*, ed. François de Médicis and Steven Huebner (Rochester, NY: University of Rochester Press, 2018), 304.

60. Deborah Priest, *Louis Laloy (1874–1944) on Debussy, Ravel, and Stravinsky* (Aldershot: Ashgate, 1999), 6–24.

61. Louis Laloy, *La musique chinoise*, Collection "Les musiciens célèbres" (Paris: Henri Laurens, 1910), esp. 119.

62. Duchesneau, "Debussy and Japanese Prints," 304. See also H. Hazel Hahn, "Consumption and Leisure," in *Debussy in Context*, 45–55.

63. Jacques Durand, *Quelques souvenirs d'un éditeur*, vol. 2 (Paris: Durand, 1924–25), 90–93; Roger Nichols, trans., *Debussy Remembered* (London: Faber, 1992), 194–95.

64. See Roy Howat, "Debussy and the Orient," in *Recovering the Orient. Artists, Scholars, Appropriations*, ed. Andrew Gerstle and Anthony Milner (Reading: Harwood, 1994), 70.

65. David Code, "The 'Song Triptych': Reflections on a Debussyan genre," in *Debussy's Resonance*, ed. François de Médicis and Steven Huebner (Rochester, NY: University of Rochester Press, 2018), 127–74.

66. See Matthew Brown, *Debussy Redux: The Impact of His Music on Popular Culture* (Bloomington: Indiana University Press, 2012), 140–47. For details about the Paris Conservatoire's gamelan, see Julien Tiersot, *Musiques pittoresques: Promenades musicales à l'Exposition de 1889* (Paris: Fischbacher, 1889), 31–47; Léon Pillaut, "Le Gamelan javanais," *Le Ménestrel*, July 3, 1887, 244–45; and Richard Mueller, "Javanese Influence on Debussy's *Fantaisie* and Beyond," *19th-Century Music* 10, no. 2 (1986): 157–86.

67. Robert F. Waters, "Emulation and Influence: Japonisme and Western Music in fin de siècle Paris," *Music Review* 55, no. 3 (1994): 224.

68. See Brown, *Debussy Redux*, 140–43.

69. See, for example, Debussy's interview with Guiraud and his conversations with *Monsieur Croche*: Claude Debussy, "L'Entretien avec M. Croche," *La Revue blanche* (July 1, 1901), in *Monsieur Croche et autres écrits*, ed. François Lesure (Paris: Gallimard, 1987), 49, and Debussy, "De quelques superstitions et d'un opera," *La Revue blanche* (November 15, 1901), in *Monsieur Croche*, 54, 55; Claude Debussy, "Conversation with M. Croche," in *Debussy on Music*, ed. François Lesure and trans. Richard Langham Smith (New York: Knopf, 1977), 45, and Debussy, "About a Few Superstitions of Ours and an Opera," in *Debussy on Music*, 51, 52.

70. Debussy, *Correspondance*, 237; and Claude Debussy, *Debussy Letters*, ed. François Lesure and Roger Nichols, trans. Roger Nichols (Cambridge, MA: Harvard University Press, 1987), 76.

71. Debussy, "Du Goût," *SIM* (February 15, 1913), in *Monsieur Croche*, 229; "Taste," in *Debussy on Music*, 278.

4

Prélude à L'Après-midi d'un faune

ON DECEMBER 20, 1894, Debussy invited Stéphane Mallarmé to attend the premiere of the *Prélude à L'Après-midi d'un faune*: "[Dear master], I need not tell you how happy I should be if you were kind enough to honour with your presence the arabesque which, by an excess of pride perhaps, I believe to have been dictated by the flute of your faun."[1] This request, though brief, is telling on several counts. For one thing, it proved successful: Mallarmé did indeed attend the performance, which took place two days later on December 22 at la salle d' Harcourt in Paris. That event was presented by the Societé nationale de la musique and conducted by Gustave Doret.[2] For another, the request reveals that Debussy consulted Mallarmé about the score and sought the poet's approval. The two men had known each other since 1889 or 1890; Debussy soon became a regular at Mallarmé's *mardis*, attending them up until the poet's death in 1898.[3] It was soon after the two men met that they began to collaborate on a dramatic presentation of "L'Après-midi d'un faune." The idea of staging the work was not, in fact, new: when Mallarmé finished the first version of his poem entitled "Monologue d'un faune" or "Le Faune, intermède héroïque" in 1865, he mentioned to his friend Henri Cazalis that it was "pure theatre; it will not be *playable on the stage*, but it *needs the stage*."[4] He even hoped to see it performed at the Comédie Française.[5] But it was not until 1890–91, long after the poem's publication in 1876, that this desire came to fruition: on February 27, 1891, Mallarmé scheduled a performance at Paul Fort's Théâtre d'Art partly as a joint fundraiser for Paul Verlaine and for Paul Gauguin, who was about to set sail for Tahiti.[6] Debussy was slated to contribute "a new kind of incidental music, which he called *Prélude, Interludes et Paraphrase finale pour L'Après-midi d'un faune*."[7] Unfortunately, that project never materialized.

While his invitation to Mallarmé demonstrates that Debussy had the concept of the arabesque in mind when he composed the *Prélude à L'Après-midi d'un faune*, it remains to be seen whether the same can be said of Mallarmé's original poem. There are, of course, good reasons for suspecting that this is indeed the case. As one of the leading proponents of Symbolism, Mallarmé was a devotee of Poe, Baudelaire, and Wagner. He evidently encountered the works of Poe and Baudelaire for the first time in 1860 when he was just eighteen years old and began translating Poe's verse into French soon afterward.[8] Fifteen years later, in 1875, Mallarmé published his French version of "The Raven," adorned with illustrations by his friend Édouard Manet. In the following years, Mallarmé not only translated other poems by Poe but also wrote an homage entitled "Le Tombeau d'Edgar Poe" (1877).[9] Poe's influence can also be felt in Mallarmé's own verse. In "Le Phénomène future," for instance, he re-created the desolate landscape of "The Fall of the House of Usher," and when writing his *Hérodiade* he set out to make it "worthy of Poe" and something "his admirers will not surpass."[10] When Mallarmé famously proclaimed that "to *name* an object is to remove three-quarters of a poem's joy that it develops bit by bit: to *suggest* it, that is ideal," he echoed a view that Poe hinted at near the end of his essay *Philosophy of Composition*.

> Two things are invariably required—first, some amount of complexity, or more properly, adaptation; and, secondly, some amount of suggestiveness—some undercurrent, however indefinite, of meaning. It is this latter, in especial, which imparts to a work of art so much of that *richness* (to borrow from colloquy a forcible term), which we are too fond of confounding with *the ideal*. It is the excess of the suggested meaning—it is the rendering this the upper instead of the undercurrent of the theme—which turns into prose (and that of the very flattest kind), the so-called poetry of the so-called transcendentalists.[11]

Baudelaire's impact on Mallarmé was no less profound and is readily apparent in his experiments with the prose poem, such as "Plainte d'automne" (1864), which he dedicated to Baudelaire, as well as in his frequent allusions to the arabesque and the thyrsus in "La Musiques et les Lettres" (1895), "Crise en verse" (1895?), "La Musiques et les Lettres" (1895), and other critical essays.[12] Mallarmé even wrote "Le Tombeau de Charles Baudelaire" (1877).[13]

After reading Baudelaire's essay "Richard Wagner et *Tannhäuser* à Paris" (1861), Mallarmé also came under Wagner's spell, so much so that he contributed several responses to *La Revue Wagnérienne*. He, too, was fascinated by the ways in which Wagner used music not only to describe a particular scene but also to explain why the scene induces a particular emotional response in the listener.[14] According to Théodore de Wyzéwa, Wagner achieved this goal through his use of line and color, two elements that Baudelaire specifically associated with the arabesque: "Today these colors and lines, which belong to the technique of painting, can be applied to two very different modes, one sensory and descriptive that re-creates the exact appearance of objects, the other emotional and musical, which neglects the object these colors and these lines represent, utilizing them only as emotional signs, marrying them to one another with the sole purpose of producing within us, through their free play, an impression that like of a symphony."[15] Mallarmé largely agreed. In an essay entitled "Richard Wagner, rêverie d'un poète français," he complimented Wagner for creating a form of music "that possesses of that art only the observance of some very complex laws. At first only the variable and the innate, mixes the colors and lines of character with timbres and themes into a richer ambience for Dreams than any song here below, a god dressed in the invisible folds of a fabric of chords."[16] And yet, though sympathetic to the concept of the *Gesamtkunstwerk*,

> **Colorées ainsi se prouvent à mon regard exempt d'antérieur aveuglement les Cinq :**
>
> **A, noir ; E, blanc ; I, bleu ; O, rouge ; U, jaune ;**
>
> dans la très calme royauté de Cinq durables lieux s'épanouissant monde aux soleils : mais l'A étrange en qui s'étouffe des Quatre autres la propre gloire, pour ce qu'étant le désert il implique toutes les présences.
>
> D'où, à l'esprit qui me suivit (introublé désormais si des Instruments pères lui sont présentes les Couleurs, plus haut régnantes) selon la logique apparaît la conclusion voulue, disant :
>
> **A, les orgues ; E, les harpes ; I, les violons ; O, les cuivres ; U, les flûtes ;**
>
> et : c'est en allant quérir selon l'ordre de ma vision chantante les mots où le plus souvent se nombre la Voyelle maîtresse demandée, que l'immatérielle obéissance vibrera de l'Instrument au timbre qui sied.

Figure 4.1 René Ghil, *Traité du verbe* (Paris: Giraud, 1886), 28

Mallarmé rejected Wagner's claim that music is superior to the other arts.[17] Through its use of rhythm, color, and line and its association with specific ideas, he regarded poetry as the apotheosis of music: "Through the act of reading, a solitary tacit concert is performed for the spirit, which regains, with a lesser sonority, signification: none of the mental ways to exalt a symphony will be left out—just rarified from the act of thought, that's all. Poetry, close to the idea, is music par excellence—[and] doesn't admit inferiority."[18] Mallarmé underscored the latter point in a letter to René Ghil (March 7, 1885), in which he responded to the latter's claim that vowels can convey colors and even orchestral sounds (see fig. 4.1): "in this act of restitution which we [poets] must perform, in which everything is [traced] back from music, its rhythms which are merely those of reason, its very colorings which is that of our passions evoked by revery, you let the old dogma of poetry disappear somewhat. . . . Your phrases are those of a composer rather than a writer."[19]

Just as Wagner drew extensively on myths and legends for his inspiration, so, too, did Mallarmé. "L'Après-midi d'un faune" is a good case in point, being inspired by Pan's famous encounter with the nymph Syrinx. Mallarmé's retelling of the story is set in Sicily near Mount Etna and is transcribed here in full.[20] A young faun has spent the morning gathering reeds at the edge of a marsh in order to make a syrinx, or reed flute. Peering through a bank of rushes, he sees some white forms resting beside a lake. The white forms turn out to be a group of nymphs; when the faun starts to tune his flute, most of them run away or dive into the water. Two remain, however, clasping each other by the arms. The faun runs over and carries them off into a nearby thicket, dropping his flute along the way. The image of the nymphs then fades from the faun's mind as he wakes up from a wine-induced slumber in the hazy afternoon sun. The faun can't remember when he fell asleep and isn't sure whether he really saw the nymphs or whether he simply imagined them in a dream.

Stéphane Mallarmé, *Le Faun*

1 Ces nymphes, je les veux perpétuer.
   Si clair,
2 Leur incarnat léger, qu'il voltige dans l'air
3 Assoupi de sommeils touffus.
   Aimai-je un rêve?
4 Mon doute, amas de nuit ancienne, s'achève
5 En maint rameau subtil, qui, demeuré les vrais
6 Bois même, prouve, hélas! que bien seul je m'offrais
7 Pour triomphe la faute idéale de roses—
8 Réflchissons . . .
   ou si les femmes dont tu gloses
9 Figurent un souhait de tes sens fabuleux!
10 Faune, l'illusion s'échappe des yeux bleus
11 Et froids, comme une source en pleurs, de la plus chaste:
12 Mais, l'autre tout soupirs, dis-tu qu'elle contraste
13 Comme brise du jour chaude dans ta toison?
14 Que non! par l'immobile et lasse pâmoison
15 Suffoquant de chaleurs le matin frais s'il lutte,
16 Ne murmure point d'eau que ne verse ma flûte
17 Au bosquet arrosé d'accords; et le seul vent
18 Hors des deux tuyaux prompt à s'exhaler avant
19 Qu'il disperse le son dans une pluie aride,
20 C'est, à l'horizon pas remué d'une ride,
21 Le visible et serein souffle artificiel
22 De l'inspiration, qui regagne le ciel.

23 Ô bords siciliens d'un calme marécage
24 Qu'à l'envi de soleils ma vanité saccage,
25 Tacite sous les fleurs d'étincelles, CONTEZ
26 *« Que je coupais ici les creux roseaux domptés*
27 *Par le talent; quand, sur l'or glauque de lointaines*
28 *Verdures dédiant leur vigne à des fontaines,*
29 *Ondoie une blancheur animale au repos:*
30 *Et qu'au prélude lent où naissent les pipeaux,*
31 *Ce vol de cygnes, non! de naïades se sauve*
32 *Ou plonge . . . »*
   Inerte, tout brûle dans l'heure fauve
33 Sans marquer par quel art ensemble détala
34 Trop d'hymen souhaité de qui cherche le *la*:
35 Alors m'éveillerai-je à la ferveur première,
36 Droit et seul, sous un flot antique de lumière,

37   Lys! et l'un de vous tous pour l'ingénuité.
38   Autre que ce doux rien par leur lèvre ébruité,
39   Le baiser, qui tout bas des perfides assure,
40   Mon sein, vierge de preuve, atteste une morsure
41   Mystérieuse, due à quelque auguste dent;
42   Mais, bast! arcane tel élut pour confident
43   Le jonc vaste et jumeau dont sous l'azur on joue:
44   Qui, détournant à soi le trouble de la joue,
45   Rêve, dans un solo long, que nous amusions
46   La beauté d'alentour par des confusions
47   Fausses entre elle-même et notre chant crédule;
48   Et de faire aussi haut que l'amour se module
49   Évanouir du songe ordinaire de dos
50   Ou de flanc pur suivis avec mes regards clos,
51   Une sonore, vaine et monotone ligne.

52   Tâche donc, instrument des fuites, ô maligne
53   Syrinx, de refleurir aux lacs où tu m'attends!
54   Moi, de ma rumeur fier, je vais parler longtemps
55   Des déesses; et par d'idolâtres peintures,
56   À leur ombre enlever encore des ceintures:
57   Ainsi, quand des raisins j'ai sucé la clarté,
58   Pour bannir un regret par ma feinte écarté,
59   Rieur, j'élève au ciel d'été la grappe vide
60   Et, soufflant dans ses peaux lumineuses, avide
61   D'ivresse, jusqu'au soir je regarde au travers.

62   O nymphes, regonflons des SOUVENIRS divers.
63   *« Mon œil, trouant le joncs, dardait chaque encolure*
64   *Immortelle, qui noie en l'onde sa brûlure*
65   *Avec un cri de rage au ciel de la forêt;*
66   *Et le splendide bain de cheveux disparaît*
67   *Dans les clartés et les frissons, ô pierreries!*
68   *J'accours; quand, à mes pieds, s'entrejoignent (meurtries*
69   *De la langueur goûtée à ce mal d'être deux)*
70   *Des dormeuses parmi leurs seuls bras hasardeux;*
71   *Je les ravis, sans les désenlacer, et vole*
72   *À ce massif, haï par l'ombrage frivole,*
73   *De roses tarissant tout parfum au soleil,*
74   *Où notre ébat au jour consumé soit pareil. »*
75   Je t'adore, courroux des vierges, ô délice
76   Farouche du sacré fardeau nu qui se glisse
77   Pour fuir ma lèvre en feu buvant, comme un éclair
78   Tressaille! la frayeur secrète de la chair:
79   Des pieds de l'inhumaine au cœur de la timide
80   Qui délaisse à la fois une innocence, humide
81   De larmes folles ou de moins tristes vapeurs.
82   *« Mon crime, c'est d'avoir, gai de vaincre ces peurs*
83   *Traîtresses, divisé la touffe échevelée*
84   *De baisers que les dieux gardaient si bien mêlée;*
85   *Car, à peine j'allais cacher un rire ardent*
86   *Sous les replis heureux d'une seule (gardant*

87   *Par un doigt simple, afin que sa candeur de plume*

88   *Se teignît à l'émoi de sa sœur qui s'allume,*

89   *La petite, naïve et ne rougissant pas:)*

90   *Que de mes bras, défaits par de vagues trépas,*

91   *Cette proie, à jamais ingrate se délivre*

92   *Sans pitié du sanglot dont j'étais encore ivre.»*

93   Tant pis! vers le bonheur d'autres m'entraîneront

94   Par leur tresse nouée aux cornes de mon front:

95   Tu sais, ma passion, que, pourpre et déjà mûre,

96   Chaque grenade éclate et d'abeilles murmure;

97   Et notre sang, épris de qui le va saisir,

98   Coule pour tout l'essaim éternel du désir.

99   À l'heure où ce bois d'or et de cendres se teinte

100   Une fête s'exalte en la feuillée éteinte:

101   Etna! C'est parmi toi visité de Vénus

102   Sur ta lave posant tes talons ingénus,

103   Quand tonne une somme triste ou s'épuise la flamme.

104   Je tiens la reine!

          O sûr châtiment . . .

             Non, mais l'âme

105   De paroles vacante et ce corps alourdi

106   Tard succombent au fier silence de midi:

107   Sans plus il faut dormir en l'oubli du blasphème,

108   Sur le sable altéré gisant et comme j'aime

109   Ouvrir ma bouche à l'astre efficace des vins!

110   Couple, adieu; je vais voir l'ombre que tu devins.

Considering the Arcadian flavor of "L'Après-midi d'un faune" and the Symbolist orientation of Mallarmé's thinking, it is not hard to find echoes of the arabesque reverberating throughout the poem.[21] Readers will surely be struck by the ornamental character of Mallarmé's writing: not only is the language extremely florid, but it unfolds in a serpentine manner, constantly weaving back on itself, just like Baudelaire's "Le Thyrse." Joris-Karl Huysmans was clearly impressed and offered the following description of "L'Après-midi d'un faune" near the end of *À Rebours*: "In this extraordinary poem, new and surprising images occurred in almost every line when the poet came to describe the longings and regrets of the goat-footed god, standing on the edge of the swamp and looking at the clumps of rushes that still retained an ephemeral impression of the rounded forms of the naiads who had rested there."[22] Above all, Mallarmé exploited the principle of the arabesque to challenge poetic conventions: "I want [Faun] to be very new and very beautiful, and yet dramatic; above all, it has to be more rhythmical than lyric verse."[23]

One way in which Mallarmé created this new poetic language was by manipulating the basic elements of French prosody. Take, for example, the principle of end rhyme. Although Mallarmé arranged the line into rhyming couplets, he delighted in weaving his end rhymes into the body of the adjacent lines.[24] A single illustration will suffice.

10   Figurent un souhait de tes sens fabuleux!

11   Faune, l'illusion s'échappe des yeux bleus

12   Et froids, comme une source en pleurs, de la plus chaste:

In this case, "fabuleux" at the end of line 10 rhymes with "yeux" and "bleus" in line 11 and with "pleurs" in line 12. Notice, too, the alliterations "figurant," "fabuleux," "Faune," and "froids" in lines 10–11 and "pleurs" and "plus" in line 12. Graham Robb also notes that Mallarmé was fond of visual rhymes in which the phonemes not only sound the same but are spelled the same as well.[25] Line 1, for example, ends "Si clair" whereas line 2 ends "l'air."

Mallarmé was no less radical in his handling of the alexandrine. The predominant meter in French poetry of the early modern and modern periods, alexandrines consist of twelve-syllable lines that typically divide into groups of six or three syllables. Although he continued to use alexandrines throughout "L'Après-midi d'un faune," Mallarmé often obscured them "with multiple enjambments and by an unignorable use of assonance and alliteration."[26] To distance himself even further from poetic convention, he grouped the lines irregularly into six stanzas: lines 1–22 (stanza 1); lines 23–37 (stanza 2); lines 38–51 (stanza 3); lines 52–61 (stanza 4); lines 62–92 (stanza 3); and lines 93–110 (stanza 6).[27] The results are stunning: as Mallarmé explained to Jules Huret, the poem makes "a sort of running pianistic commentary upon the fully preserved and dignified alexandrine—a sort of musical accompaniment which the poet composes himself, so that the official verse will appear only on the really important occasions."[28]

At the same time, *L'Après-midi d'un faune* demonstrates the subtle ways in which the arabesque allowed Mallarmé to develop surface details for global purposes. Huysmans offered a particularly beautiful example from the end of stanza 2. Having noted that the poem unfolds "in mysterious and tender verse," he cited the following "bestial, frenzied cry" from the faun:

35   Alors m'éveillerais-je à la ferveur première.
36   Droit et seul, sous un flot antique de lumière,
37   Lys! Et l'un vous tous pour ingénuité.

According to him, the reference to lilies at the start of line 37 initially seems like an insignificant detail. However, by carrying the word over from line 36 and ending line 37 with the noun "ingénuité" (or innocence), Huysmans suggested that the allusion to "something tall, white, and rigid" reveals "in an allegorical manner and in a single word of passion, the effervescence, the momentary excitement of the virgin faun, maddened with desire by the sight of the nymphs."[29] In short, Mallarmé used the word *Lys!* to symbolize the motivation of the entire poem.

Besides disguising the poem's form and exploiting the significance of seemingly inconsequential details, Mallarmé invoked another feature of the arabesque—namely, blending the real with the unreal. An obvious way in which he does so is by contrasting sections expressing the faun's inner desires with those retelling the events of that particular afternoon. To highlight the faun's recollections of what might have occurred, Mallarmé capitalized two words: *CONTEZ*, or retell (stanza 2, line 26), and *SOUVENIRS*, or memories (stanza 5, line 62). The fact that the reader is never sure whether the nymphs ever existed or whether they are figments of the faun's imagination resonates with Mallarmé's general principle that to name is to destroy and to suggest is to create.[30] In his words, "Monuments, the sea, or the human face, in their natural fullness, conserve a property differently attractive than the veiling any description can offer—say, evocation, or, I know, *allusion* or *suggestion*."[31]

While much of *L'Après-midi d'un faune* remains elusive, Mallarmé did use other aspects of the arabesque to create unity and continuity. One of the most important is surely his emphasis on line. This particular idea manifests itself most explicitly in the faun's flute melody and recalls with the title of Mallarmé's second version of the poem *Improvisation d'un Faun* (1875).[32] Mallarmé introduced the image at the end of stanza 1 in lines 14–22: while dreaming, the faun describes how the afternoon air is motionless save for the vibrations created by his flute. In line 30 (stanza 2), Mallarmé was more specific: he recalled how the faun played "a slow prelude." When the faun returns to his reverie (stanza 3), he is even more effusive, comparing the tune to the dream itself.

45   Rêve, dans un solo long que nous amusions
46   La beauté d'alentour par des confusions
47   Fausses entre elle-même et notre chant crédule;
48   Et de faire aussi haut que l'amour se module
49   Évanouir du songe ordinaire de dos
50   Ou de flanc pur suivis avec mes regards clos,
51   Une sonore, vaine et monotone ligne.

By linking the faun's dream to music, Mallarmé reinforced his claim that the sensation of music can be created by words alone and that it can be composed poetically "with such pre-meditated care and sensitivity that the reader's emotional response would be accompanied at every point by an enlarged understanding."[33]

The faun's flute melody is not, however, the only theme running through *L'Après-midi d'un faune*: on the contrary, this refrain is embellished with other layers of imagery. The resulting counterpoint is so complex that Paul Valéry once described the poem as "a sort of literary fugue in which themes are intermingled with prodigious artistry; all the resources of poetics are used to support a triple development of images and ideas."[34] For example, besides focusing on the faun's memories and flute melody, Mallarmé also highlighted the faun's sensuality: "his whole being is a texture of vibrant sensuality; and though the nymphs have vanished, his hot desire sees in the air about him the memory of their inviting flesh."[35] He also explored another theme: the faun's attempt to explain the nymphs and their disappearance.[36] Were they a dream or reality? In stanza 1, for example, Mallarmé introduced the themes of sensuality (lines 1–2), the dream (lines 3–10), and the flute melody (lines 14–22); in stanza 2 he shifted to the idea of memory (lines 26–31) before returning to the faun's sensuality; in stanza 3 he dealt exclusively with the faun's flute melody (lines 37–51); in stanza 4 he focused on the faun's sensuality (lines 52–61); in stanza 5 he combined references to the faun's memory of the nymphs (lines 62–74 and 82–92) with further allusions to his sensuality (lines 75–81); and in stanza 6 he lingered on the faun's sensuality, alluding to the concept of memory (lines 94–96).[37] The complex counterpoint of themes creates an elaborate literary arabesque in which, as Robb puts it, "one spiral reveals the relative position of all others."[38]

Why was Mallarmé so intent on infusing *L'Après-midi d'un faune* with the spirit of the arabesque? There are perhaps two answers to this question. One is that he wanted to convey the complex emotional state of the faun. Since traditional versions of the myth do not allow the faun to consummate his relationship with the nymphs, the poem conveys in particularly evocative terms his sexual desires as well as his sexual frustrations, both of which are part and parcel of the human condition. The reference to lava flowing from Mount Etna in lines 101–2 implies that the faun most likely pleasured himself. This interpretation helps to explain the final moments in Nijinsky's notorious choreography. Another is that Mallarmé wanted to excite, even titillate the reader: "Great art here consists in showing through impeccable possession of all the faculties that we are in the heights of ecstasy, without revealing how we reached those summits."[39] That being said, Mallarmé insisted that great poetry is always mysterious and that it is comprehensible only to other poets or to those who look at the words and verse with a poet's eye: "What a deep study of sound and color, of music and painting, our thought must make (however beautiful it may have been originally) if it is to be poetic!"[40]

Just as Mallarmé's poem does not offer a literal retelling of Pan's encounter with Syrinx, so Debussy's score does not literally "translate" this text into music; as he mentioned to Henri Gauthier-Villars (October 10, 1895), Debussy wanted to re-create "the dream left over at the bottom of the faun's flute."[41] Not surprisingly, he used arabesques in various ways to re-create this dream state. One way in which Debussy did so was by building his piece around an ornate flute theme, which, following Mallarmé, unfolds as "un solo long . . . une sonore, vaine et monotone ligne."[42] Example 4.1 shows that this primary line or *Hauptstimme* features twelve statements of the main flute theme, half of which start on C♯ in m. 1 (ex. 4.1a), m. 11 (ex. 4.1b), m. 21 (ex. 4.1c), m. 26 (ex. 4.1d), m. 94 (ex. 4.1e), and m. 100 (ex. 4.1f), and half of which start on other notes: A in m. 23 (ex. 4.1g), G in m. 31 (ex. 4.1h), B♭ in m. 34 (ex. 4.1i), E in m. 79 (ex. 4.1j), E♭ in m. 86 (ex. 4.1k), and G♯ in m. 107 (ex. 4.1l). Not only are these statements extremely ornate, but they are also decorated and extended in different ways. The simplest version appears at the start of the movement and is shown in example 4.1a. In mm. 1–2 the melody oscillates between

Example 4.1 Debussy, *Prélude à L'Après-midi d'un faune*

Example 4.1a Main theme starting on C♯, mm. 1–4

Example 4.1b Main theme starting on C♯, mm. 11–17

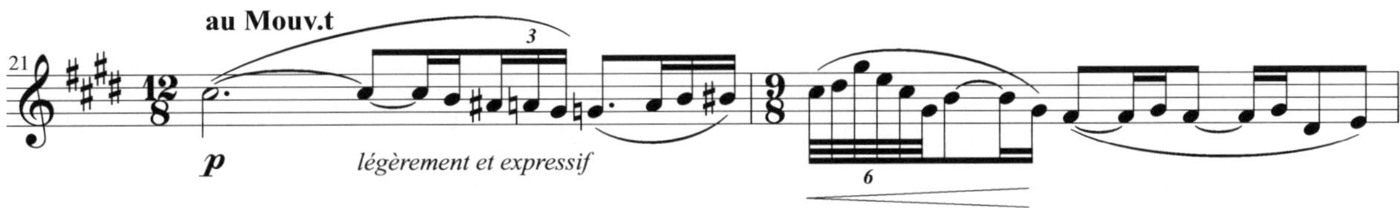

Example 4.1c Main theme starting on C♯, mm. 21–22

Example 4.1d Main theme starting on C♯, mm. 26–27

Example 4.1e Main theme starting on C♯, mm. 94–95

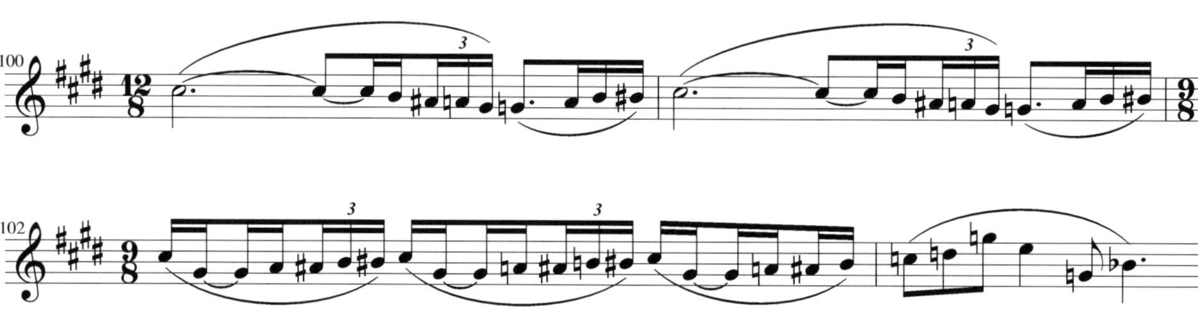

Example 4.1f Main theme starting on C♯, mm. 100–103

Example 4.1g Main theme starting on A♮, mm. 23–25

Example 4.1h Main theme starting on G♮, m. 31

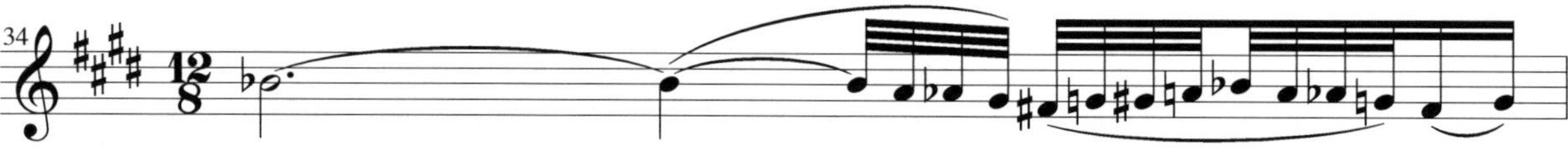

Example 4.1i Main theme starting on B♭, m. 34

Example 4.1j Main theme starting on E♮, mm. 79–83

Example 4.1k Main theme starting on E♭, mm. 86–90

Example 4.1l Main theme starting on G♯, mm. 107–9

C♯ and G, returning to C♯ by means of the chromatic pattern B–B♯–C♯. In mm. 3–4, the melody winds its way circuitously from C♯ through B to A♯. Example 4.1b shows that after beginning just like the first statement, the second one transfers the goal tone A♯ up an octave via a stepwise ascent G♯–A–A♯ in mm. 16–17. The most elaborate statements of the main theme are found in mm. 26–27 (ex. 4.1d) and mm. 100–103 (ex. 4.1f); their complex diminutions, constant rise and fall, and meandering profile convey the dreamlike fantasies that occupy the young faun while he lounges on a rock playing his flute. The serpentine line, which keeps doubling back on itself, recalls the image of the thyrsus and echoes the arabesque qualities of Mallarmé's verse.

Besides illustrating the arabesque's ornamental character, the *Prélude à L'Après-midi d'un faune* demonstrates its contrapuntal implications as well. To begin with, the opening flute theme is the quintessential polyphonic melody. As shown in examples 4.2a–4.2b, mm. 1–13 establish the global tonic of E major by means of an auxiliary cadence progression—VII^7/V–V^{9}7–I—in which the essential soprano voice descends by step C♯–B–A♯ in mm. 1–4 and from C♯ to B in mm. 11–13.[43] It is clear from examples 4.2a–4.2b that the melodic span C♯–G in mm. 1–2 arises from a stepwise motion between the soprano and the alto voices. The alto G then ascends by a half step to G♯ in m. 3 to support B in the soprano. When the soprano descends to A♯ in m. 4, the alto voice G♯ is transferred down an octave to initiate a chromatic neighbor motion G♯–A–G♯ in mm. 4–13. This neighbor motion supports a string of parallel thirds in the middle register: E/ C♯–F/D–F♯/D–F♯/D♯–G♯/E.

Recalling the polyphonic structure of the thyrsus, the main flute theme sometimes appears over tonic and dominant pedals (see ex. 4.3). One such pedal occurs in mm. 20–27 (see ex. 4.3a). Although the bass line articulates the progression I–V–I, the tenor voice projects the string of intervals 8–♭7–6–♭6–5 that J. S. Bach typically associated with tonic pedal tones. Example 4.3b

Example 4.2 The opening flute theme as a polyphonic melody

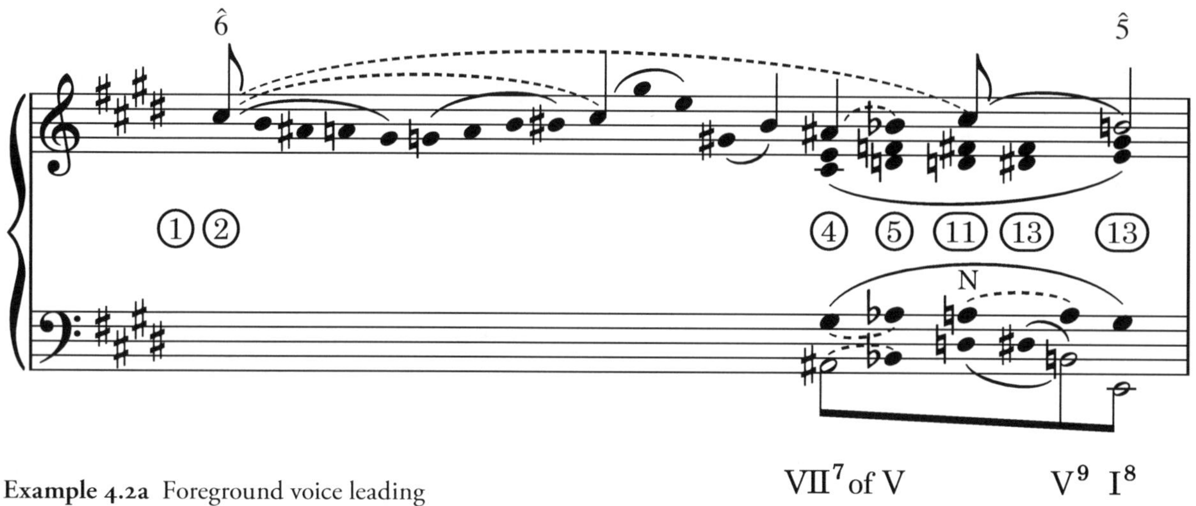

Example 4.2a Foreground voice leading

Example 4.2b Middleground voice leading

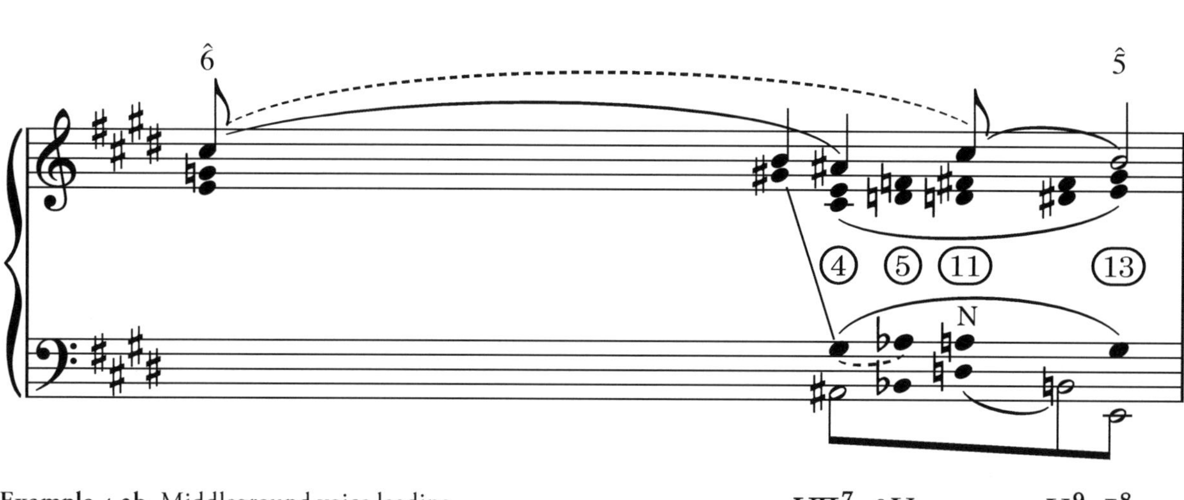

shows how the same pattern returns in the expanded reprise in the A′ section in the same octave in mm. 79–106. This time the line descends 8–♮7–♭7–♮6 in the treble clef (mm. 79–96) and continues ♭6–♮6–♭6–♮6–5–4–3 in the bass clef. Examples 4.3c–4.3e then show how dominant pedals occur at three strategic moments in the *Prélude* à *L'Après-midi d'un faune*. The first appears in mm. 28–30 and sets up the arrival in B major at the end of the opening A section. As shown in example 4.3c, the dominant of B is supported by two nested versions of the stepwise pattern mentioned earlier. One extends across the whole passage and descends (8)–♭7–6–♭6–5 in the bass clef; the other begins in m. 29 and descends 8–♮7–(♭7)–6–5. The second dominant pedal, given in example 4.3d, underpins the whole-tone episode (mm. 30–37). This time, however, the pattern is modified chromatically: 5–♭6–♮6–♮7–(8)–♭7. Last, example 4.3e shows a four-bar dominant pedal that prepares the arrival on D♭ in m. 55: the pedal tone A♭ supports versions of the descending pattern 8–♮7–♭7–6–5 in mm. 51–53 and 8–♮7–6–5 in m. 54.

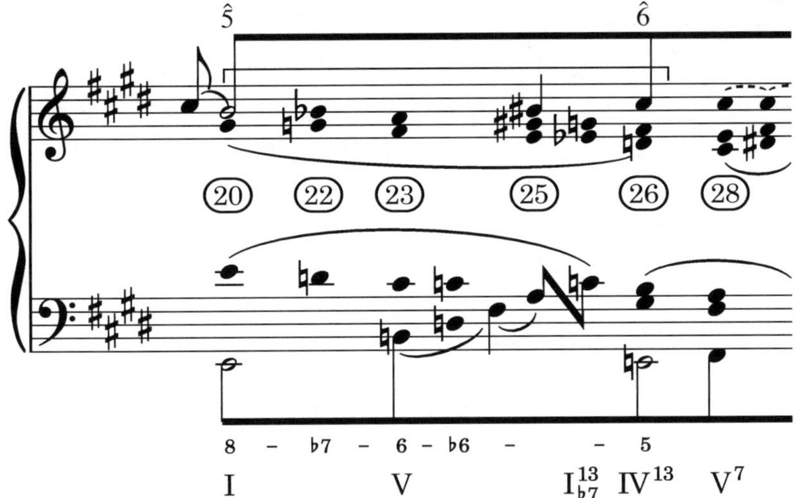

Example 4.3a Mm. 20–27/28

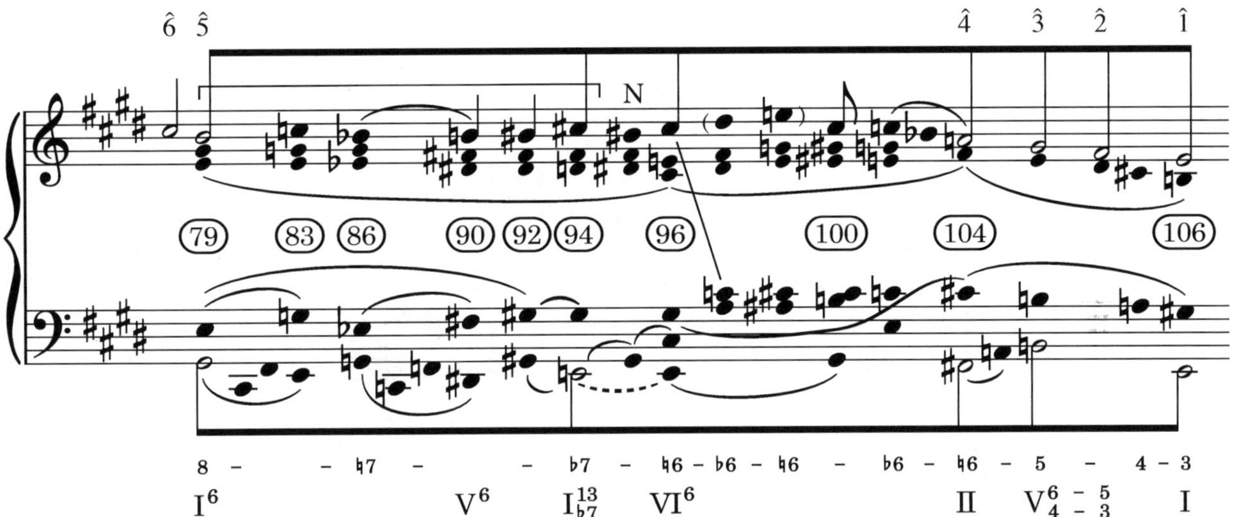

Example 4.3b Mm. 79–106

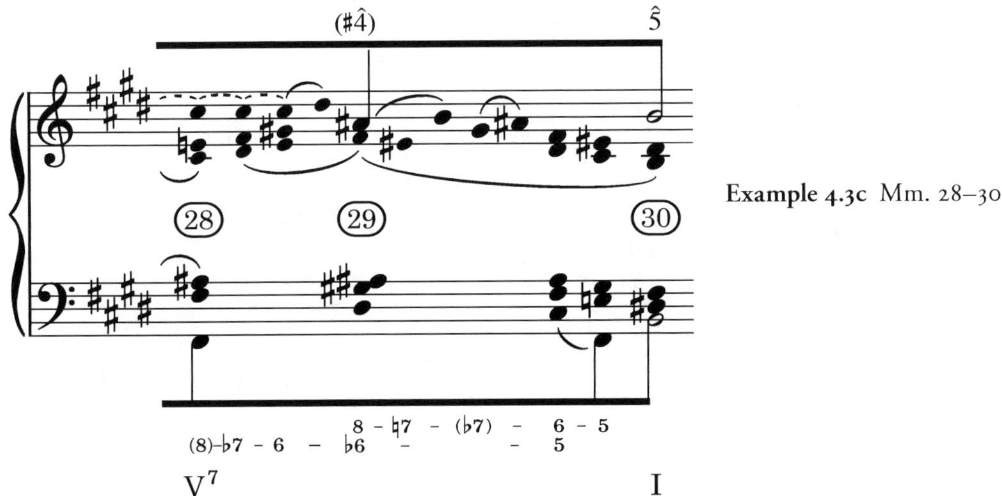

Example 4.3c Mm. 28–30

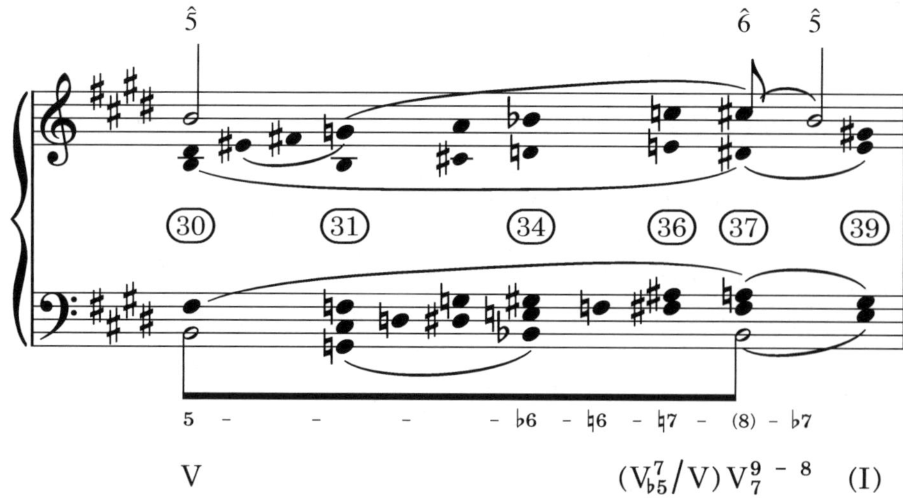

Example 4.3d Mm. 30–37/39

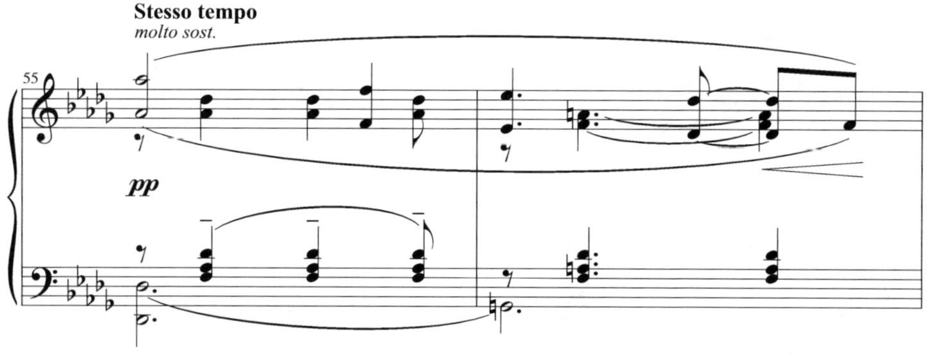

Example 4.3e Mm. 51–55/56

Just as several different layers of imagery run through Mallarmé's verse, so several different themes run through Debussy's score. The most important of these gestures is given in example 4.4a and appears three times in the secondary key of D♭/C♯ major: mm. 55–62, 63–74, and 74–78. Debussy associates this B theme with the main flute theme by a network of other subordinate gestures that intertwine as the movement unfolds. Example 4.4b shows the first of these, a short pentatonic figure that initially appears at the start of the short transition section in m. 37–54. As demonstrated in example 4.4c, this figure seems to derive from a flowing motive that appears in m. 28 to prepare the cadence in B major in mm. 29–30. Next, example 4.4d shows how the pentatonic motive from the transition (ex. 4.4b) is extended by a syncopated motive and example 4.4e how this motive is immediately combined contrapuntally with a fragment of the main flute theme. Example 4.4f then demonstrates that the first statement of the B theme (mm. 55–62) culminates with a return of the flowing motive from example 4.4c. Although the flowing motive also appears at the end of the second statement of the contrasting B theme, it does so after a recollection of

Example 4.4 Secondary themes in the *Prélude à L'Après-midi d'un faune*

Example 4.4a B theme

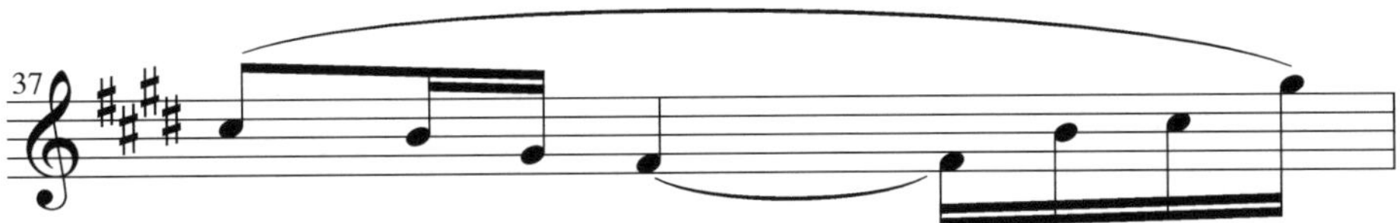

Example 4.4b Pentatonic motive from the transition

Example 4.4c Flowing motive

Example 4.4d Syncopated motive

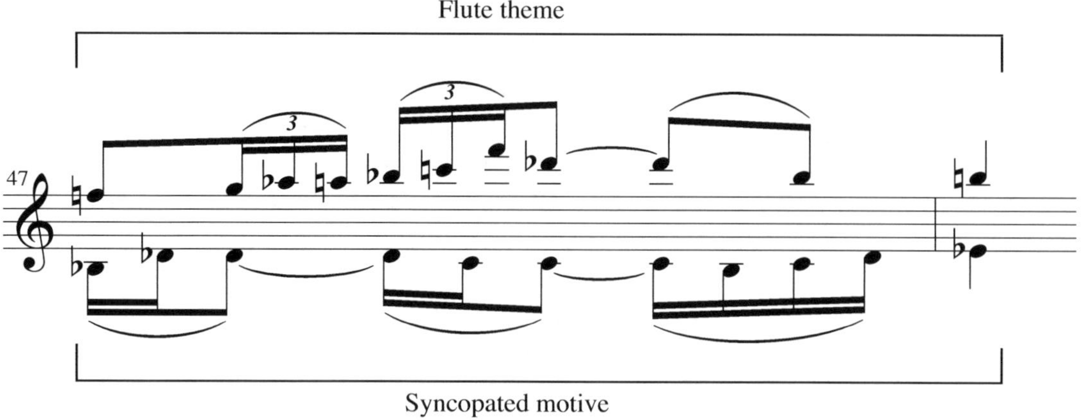

Example 4.4e Flute theme and syncopated motive

Example 4.4f B theme and flowing motive

Example 4.4g B theme, syncopated motive, and flowing motive

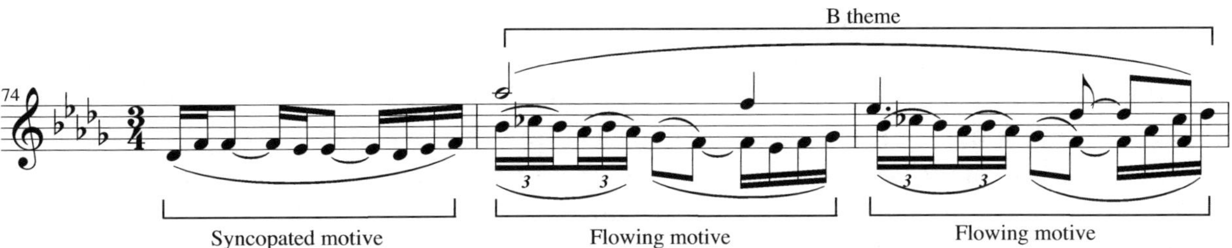

Example 4.4h B theme, syncopated motive, and flowing motive

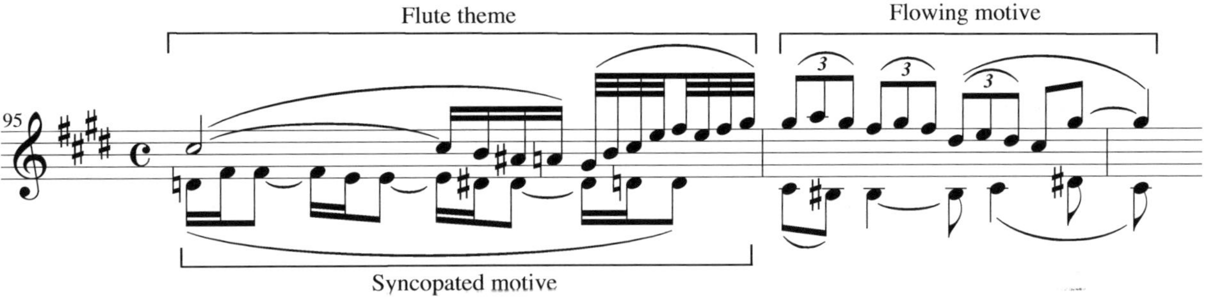

Example 4.4i Flute theme, syncopated motive, and flowing motive

the syncopated motive (see ex. 4.4g). The contrasting section in D♭/C♯ major ends with a brief codetta in which the syncopated and flowing motives both appear beside the B theme (see ex. 4.4h). Similarly, when the flute theme finally returns on C♯ in m. 94, it subsequently appears in counterpoint with the syncopated and flowing motives. This moment in the score is given in example 4.4i and, just like the passages in examples 4.2 and 4.3, it underscores the contrapuntal implications of the arabesque and even recalls Valéry's claim that Mallarmé's poem is "a sort of literary fugue."

Another characteristic of the arabesque described by Schlegel and amplified by Poe and Baudelaire is the idea that surface details should generate larger spans. Once again, the *Prélude* à *L'Après-midi d'un faune* contains several examples of this phenomenon. Example 4.5 shows how some of these involve the rising sixteenth-note pattern B–B♯–C♯. As shown in example 4.5a, this three-note gesture originally comes to the fore in mm. 1–2 as part of the rising span G–A–B–B♯–C♯. Example 4.5b then suggests how it reappears in augmentation in eighth notes B–B♯–C♯ to set up a return of the main flute theme in mm. 20–21. Next, example 4.5c shows how the transition section (mm. 37–55) articulates the same gesture sometimes spelled enharmonically both locally (e.g., in mm. 48–50 and 54–55) and globally (e.g., in mm. 37–46 and 37–55). The latter are perfect examples of what Schenker referred to as concealed repetitions. Examples 4.5d–4.5e show two more concealed repetitions of the pattern B–B♯–C♯. In example 4.5d, for instance, the essential soprano voice projects this pattern over a tonic harmony in mm. 20–26. The goal tone C♯ then serves as an upper neighbor tone to B and marks the modulation to the dominant in m. 30. Example 4.5e then suggests that mm. 79–104 present an enlarged repetition of the same general voice-leading pattern: the essential soprano projects the rising pattern B–B♯–C♯ across mm. 79–94 and the goal tone C♯ again functions melodically as an incomplete upper neighbor.

Whereas mm. 28–30 cadence in the dominant, mm. 103–6 cadence unequivocally in the global tonic E with a stepwise descent A–G♯–F♯–E in the soprano. To underscore the parallels between mm. 20–30 and mm. 79–106, examples 4.5f–4.5g show that two cadences in mm. 28–30 and mm. 103–6 rhyme musically: both passages include the same melodic figures, labeled X and Y.

It was noted in the introduction that Symbolist authors often use two distinct strategies to convey the fantastic in literature: by merging "reality by irreality" and by inserting alternate texts within the body of the main text. Debussy's *Prélude à L'Après-midi d'un faune* includes at least two examples of the latter. As shown in examples 4.6a and 4.6b, the harmonic structure of the B theme (mm. 55–63) recalls that of the opening of Debussy's song "L'Ombre des arbres" (mm. 1–11), which was published in *Ariettes oubliées* and written between 1885 and 1888.[44] Both passages unexpectedly start with the tonic chord D♭/C♯ vacillating with a dominant seventh on G, and both end with an equally startling progression from an augmented sixth chord D–F♯–A–B♯ resolving back to the tonic D♭/C♯. Examples 4.6c and 4.6d then show how the perfect authentic

Example 4.5 Details of consequence

Example 4.5a Rising motive, mm. 1–2

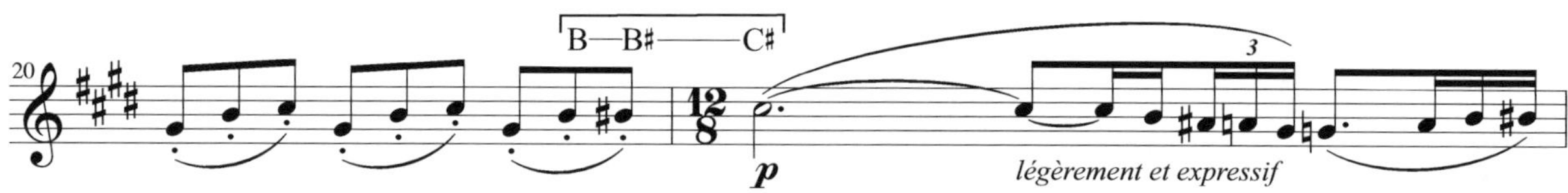

Example 4.5b Rising motive, mm. 20–21

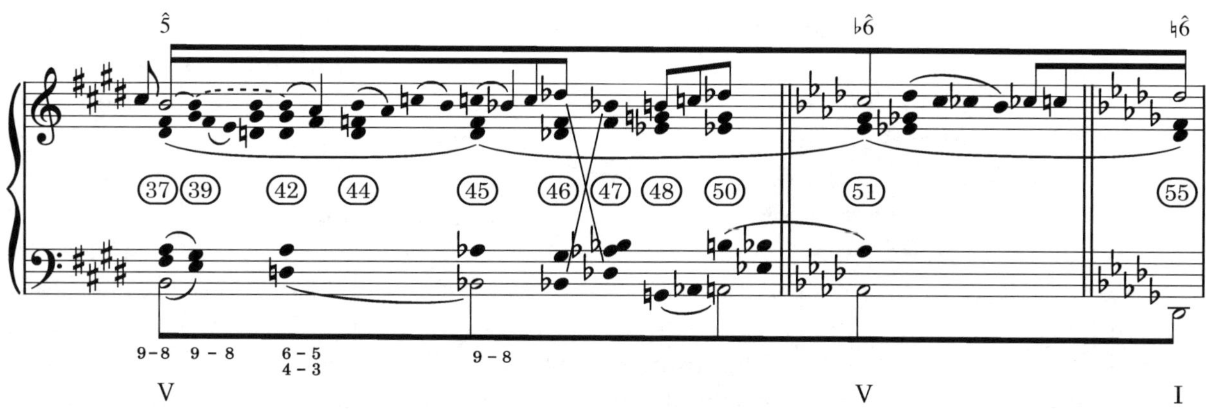

Example 4.5c Rising motive, mm. 37–55

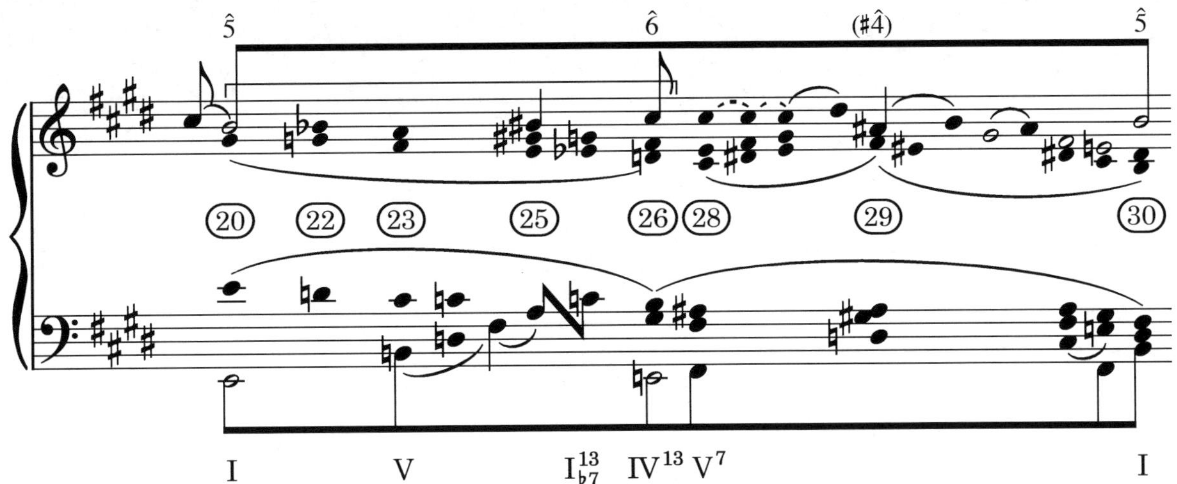

Example 4.5d Rising motive, mm. 20–30

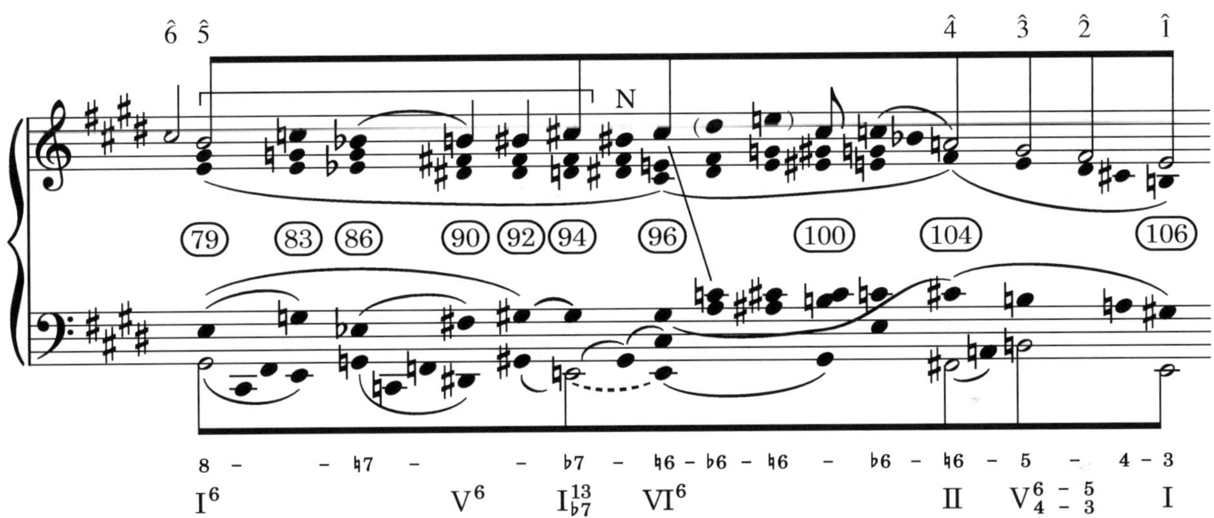

Example 4.5e Rising motive, mm. 79–106

Example 4.5f Cadental pattern, mm. 28–30

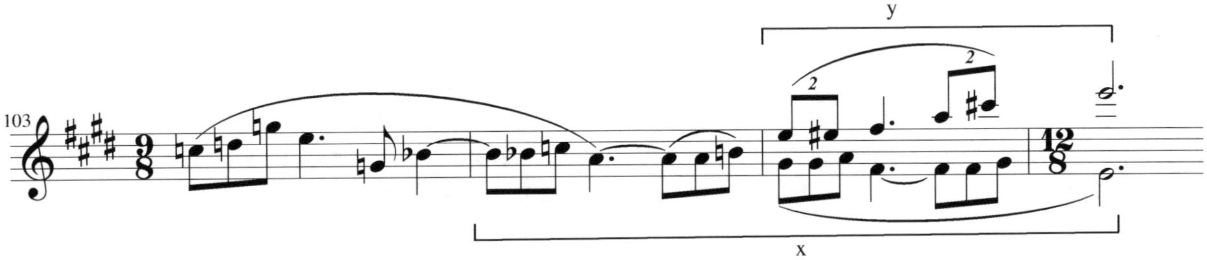

Example 4.5g Cadental pattern, mm. 103–6

Example 4.6 Premonitions of *Prélude à L'Après-midi d'un faune* in "L'Ombre des arbres" and "La Morte des amants"

Example 4.6a *Prélude à L'Après-midi d'un faune*, mm. 55–63

Example 4.6b "L'ombre des arbres," mm. 1–11/12

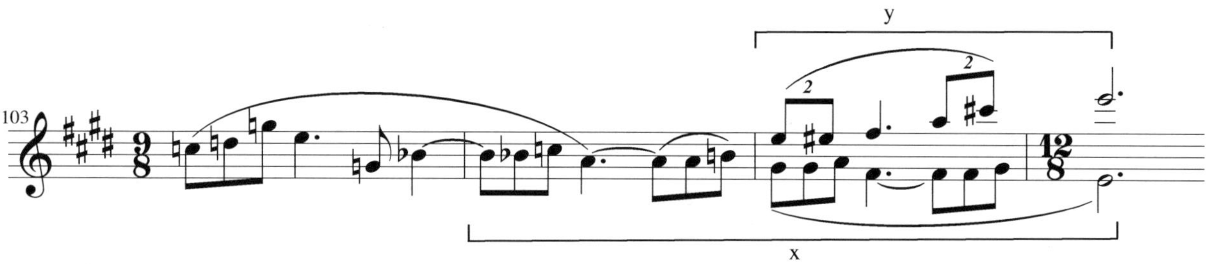

Example 4.6c *Prélude à L'Après-midi d'un faune*, mm. 103–6

Example 4.6d "La Morte des amants," mm. 20–24

cadence of mm. 103–6 of the *Prélude à L'Après-midi d'un faune* recycle a similar cadence in mm. 20–24 of Debussy's setting of "La Morte des amants," which was published in his *Cinq poèmes de Baudelaire* and written between 1887 and 1889.[45] Katherine Bergeron has even noted that the climax of "La Morte des amants" recalls the "Good Friday" cadence from act 3 of *Parsifal*, far and away Debussy's favorite Wagnerian music drama.[46]

Finally, it is important to remember that Debussy primarily used arabesques for expressive purposes to enhance the emotional power of Mallarmé's poem. One obvious way in which he did so was by using arabesques to disguise the work's tonal orientation. Consider, for a moment, the opening of the movement. Although the piece centers on E major, the tonic is not established in a typical manner. On the contrary, not only is the opening progression abstruse to say the least, but the decisive progression V^9_7–I appears in m. 13 on a weak beat of the bar in the middle of the second statement of the main theme. When the tonic chord returns on the downbeat of m. 21 to mark the third statement of the theme, it is not approached by a clear functional progression. Another way in which Debussy achieved his goal was by disguising the formal structure of the music. For one thing, it is unclear whether the opening statement of the flute theme is an integral part of the opening A section or whether it serves as an introduction. Certainly, the flute theme flows seamlessly into the movement as a whole. And yet, as shown in examples 4.7a–4.7b, the striking half-diminished seventh sonority A♯–C♯–E–G♯ in mm. 4 and 7 returns in mm. 108 and 109 of the coda, where it seems to stand outside the main body of the movement.

To heighten the allusive quality of Mallarmé's text, Debussy enhanced his setting with a number of "detours, expansions, [and] interpolations."[47] A particularly good example of such an excursion is the short episode in mm. 30–37 (see ex. 4.8). The episode stands out on several counts. Motivically, it presents two transposed versions of the main flute theme—one starting on G in m. 31 and the other starting on B♭ in m. 34. Both of these were shown in examples 4.1g–4.1h. Harmonically, the passage is remarkable because it connects the perfect authentic cadence in B in mm. 29–30 with a clear dominant sonority in m. 37 by means of whole-tone harmonies: those in mm. 31–33 use the collection G–A–B–C♯–D♯–E♯ and those in mm. 34–36 use the collection

Example 4.7 Opening and ending

Example 4.7a *Prélude à L'Après-midi d'un faune*, mm. 1–6

Example 4.7b *Prélude à L'Après-midi d'un faune*, mm. 107–10

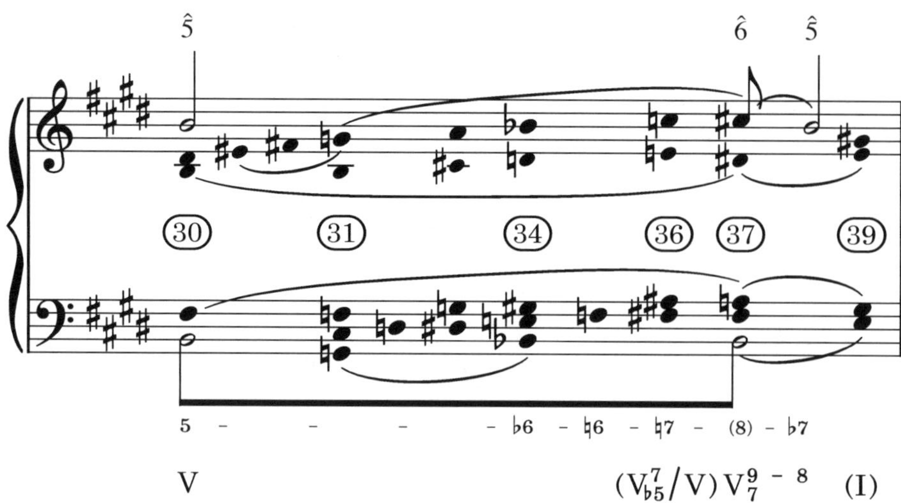

Example 4.8 Whole-tone episode, mm. 30–37

B♭–C–D–E–G♭–A♭. The function of this episode is clear: it provides a means of delaying the forward momentum of the movement, a fleeting moment of repose before the movement embarks on a modulation from the dominant as defined by the cadence in mm. 29–30 to the submediant C♯/D♭ major as defined by the authentic cadence in mm. 54–55. The intricate motivic and tonal structure of this modulation has already been explained in example 4.5c. It is also worth noting, however, that Debussy disguised the structure of the reprise by returning to the tonic E major in m. 79 but delaying the reprise of the main theme on C♯ until m. 94. As noted earlier, the voice-leading structure of mm. 79–106 is a recomposed expansion of mm. 20–26.

Given the narrative implications of the *Prélude à L'Après-midi d'un faune*, it is perhaps not so surprising that Mallarmé's poem and Debussy's score both were intended for the theater. Indeed, it was noted earlier that Mallarmé described the first version of his poem from 1865 as "pure theatre" and that he decided to collaborate with Debussy in 1890–91 on a musical work entitled *Prélude, Interludes et Paraphrase finale pour L'Après-midi d'un faune*. Mallarmé's interest in the stage is also evident in several essays that he "scribbled at the theater" including three specifically about dance.[48] Though brief, the latter are particularly noteworthy because they demonstrate that Mallarmé regarded dance as "poetry, par excellence, and theater" and revered the dancer above all other forms of the poet.[49] He was especially enamored of the American dancer Loïe Fuller who starred at the Folies Bergère in the 1890s, where she popularized the "serpentine dance" and emulated the styles of Japanese dancers such as Sada Yacco.[50] In the words of Bradford Cook, "[Mallarmé] imagined her inscribing the geometrical beauty of her steps on the nothingness of air or shooting the magic words and numbers of no book to the receiving heavens."[51] And yet, Mary Lewis Shaw insists that dance differs from poetry or prose because it is "more economical," "corporeal," and "not actually written."[52] To quote Mallarmé, "*The dancer is not a woman dancing*, for these juxtaposed reasons: that *she is not a woman*, but a metaphor summing up one of the elementary aspects of our form: knife, goblet, flower, etc., and that *she is not dancing*, but suggesting, through the miracle of bends and leaps, a kind of corporeal writing, what it would take pages of prose, dialogue, and description to express, if it were transcribed: a poem independent of any scribal apparatus."[53] The dancer's text is therefore "a poem that paradoxically is never inscribed—that is, fixed or permanently recorded as is the poem on the page."[54] In short, dancers "complicate with all kinds of vaporous spins the enchantments of Dance, *in which the dancer's body appears solely as the rhythm everything depends on but is hidden by what it makes possible.*"[55]

As it turns out, Mallarmé's desire to stage *L'Après-midi d'un faune* eventually came to pass a decade after his death when, in the spring of 1912, Vaslav Nijinsky choreographed Debussy's score for Diaghilev's *Ballets Russes*. Premiered on May 29, 1912, at the Théâtre du Châtelet, the production caused a scandal; Parisian audiences were offended by the graphic nature of Nijinsky's movements, especially the sight of him seeming to masturbate in the final measures.[56] Gaston Calmette conveyed the outrage in a vitriolic review splashed across the front page of *Le Figaro*: "Anyone who mentions the words 'art' and 'imagination' in the same breath as this production must be laughing at us. This is neither a pretty pastoral nor a work of profound meaning. We are shown a lecherous faun, whose movements are filthy and bestial in their eroticism, and whose gestures are as crude as they are indecent. That is all. And the over-explicit miming of this misshapen beast, loathsome when seen full on, but even more loathsome in profile, was greeted with the booing it deserved. Decent people will never accept such animal realism."[57] Although Calmette may have found Nijinsky's movements obscene, they were clearly not without precedent: as mentioned earlier, the original poem strongly suggests that the faun felt compelled to pleasure himself at the end of the afternoon. This idea is, in fact, entirely consistent with the misogynist overtones and sense of ennui that infects so much Symbolist art.

Debussy's reaction to Nijinsky's ballet was no more enthusiastic than Calmette's, as he made clear in an interview for *La Tribuna* from February 23, 1914: "*L'Après-midi d'un faune* as a Russian ballet was a grievous disappointment to me. . . . I will spare you a description of the terror I felt at the dress rehearsal, when I saw the Nymphs and the Faune were moving across the stage like marionettes, or rather like figures cut from pasteboard, always presenting themselves frontally, with stiff angular gestures, stylized on some grotesque archaic model."[58] And yet, Nijinsky's choreography did have an important result: it reminded audiences of the radical nature of Mallarmé's poem, especially as regards matters of sexuality and social decency, and the revolutionary nature of Debussy's music, especially with respect to its consummate use of arabesques. As it unfolds, the *Prélude à L'Après-midi d'un faune* demonstrates just how much Debussy's understanding of the arabesque had expanded in the years after finishing *Rondel chinois*, *Séguidille*, *Les elfes*, and *Le Matelot qui tombe à l'eau*, and the *Deux Arabesques*. The conceptual and technical distance that he crossed between these early works and the *Prélude* is indeed enormous, so much so that it prompted Pierre Boulez to declare, "Just as modern poetry surely took root in certain of Baudelaire's poems, so one is justified in saying that modern music was awakened by *L'Après-midi d'un faune.*"[59]

Notes

1. Claude Debussy, *Correspondance (1872–1918)*, ed. François Lesure and Denis Herlin, annotated by François Lesure, Denis Herlin, and Georges Liébert (Paris: Gallimard, 2005), 228; Claude Debussy, *Debussy Letters*, ed. François Lesure and Roger Nichols, trans. Roger Nichols (Cambridge, MA: Harvard University Press, 1987), 75.

2. Camille Mauclair (a.k.a Séverin Faust) painted a vivid picture of the premiere and of Mallarmé's *mardis* in chapter 3 of his novel *Le Soleil des morts* (Paris: P. Ollendorff, 1898). For a translation, see Rosemary Hamilton Yeoland, *A Translation from French into English of Camille Mauclair's Le Soleil Des Mort / Sun of the Dead* (Lewiston, NY: Edwin Mellen, 2015), 105–27, esp. 115–20. As Yeoland points out, Mauclair's description compares the

uproar caused by Debussy's music to that of the premiere of Wagner's *Tannhäuser* in Paris in 1861. This scandal provided a backdrop to Charles Baudelaire's essay "Richard Wagner et *Tannhäuser* à Paris," in *Charles Baudelaire: Œuvres Complètes*, vol. II, ed. Claude Pichois, Bibliothèque de la Pléiade (Paris: Gallimard, 1976), 779–815; Baudelaire, "Richard Wagner and *Tannhäuser* in Paris," in *The Painter in Modern Life*, ed. and trans. by Jonathan Mayne (London: Phaidon, 2001), 111–46. See also Susan Youens, "Le Soleil des Morts: A 'Fin-de-siècle' Portrait Gallery," *19th-Century Music* 11, no. 1, Special Issue: Resolutions II (Summer 1987): 43–58.

3. Rosemary Lloyd, "Debussy, Mallarmé, and 'Les Mardis,'" in *Debussy and His World*, ed. Jane Fulcher (Princeton, NJ: Princeton University Press, 2001), 255.

4. Bradford Cook, trans., *Mallarmé: Selected Prose Poems, Essays, & Letters* (Baltimore: Johns Hopkins Press, 1956), 86.

5. A. R. Chisholm, *Mallarmé's L'Après-Midi d'un Faune: An Exegetical and Critical Study* (Melbourne: Melbourne University Press, 1958), 10.

6. See Jean-Michel Nectoux, "Portrait of the Artist as a Faun," in *Afternoon of a Faun: Mallarmé, Debussy, Nijinsky*, ed. Jean-Michel Nectoux (New York: Vendome, 1987), 8; and Gordon Millan, *A Throw of the Dice. The Life of Stéphane Mallarmé* (London: Secker & Warburg, 1994), 282.

7. See Nectoux, "Portrait of the Artist as a Faun," 8.

8. Millan, *A Throw of the Dice*, 35–36.

9. Stéphane Mallarmé, *Le Corbeau* (Paris: R. Lescide, 1875); Mallarmé, *Poèmes de Edgar Poe* (Brussels: Deman, 1888; Paris: Vanier, 1889) and Mallarmé, *Stéphane Mallarmé: Œuvres Complètes*, vol. II, ed. Bertrand Marchal, Bibliothèque de la Pléiade (Paris: Gallimard, 2003), 727–820; Mallarmé, "Le Tombeau d'Edgar Poe," *in Stéphane Mallarmé: Œuvres Complètes*, vol. I, ed. Bertrand Marchal, Bibliothèque de la Pléiade (Paris: Gallimard, 1998), 38. Debussy's friend Gabriel Mourey translated the rest of Poe's poems: see *Edgar Poe. Poésies complètes* (Paris: C. Dalou, 1889).

10. Millan, *A Throw of the Dice*, 129.

11. Stéphane Mallarmé, "Sur l'evolution littéraire," in *Œuvres Complètes*, vol. II, ed. Bertrand Marchal, Bibliothèque de la Pléiade (Paris: Gallimard, 2003), 700; Edgar Allan Poe, "Philosophy of Composition," *Graham's American Monthly Magazine of Literature and Art* 28, no. 4 (1846): 163–67.

12. Stéphane Mallarmé, "Plainte d'autumne," in *Œuvres Complètes*, vol. I, 443–44; Mallarmé, "Autumn Lament," trans. Barbara Johnson, *Divagations* (Cambridge, MA: Harvard University Press, 2007), 13–14; Mallarmé, "La Musiques et les Lettres," (1895), in *Œuvres Complètes*, II:62–77; Mallarmé, "Music and Letters," in *Divagations*, 173–98; Mallarmé, "Crise en verse," in *Œuvres Complètes*, II:204–13; Mallarmé, "Crisis of Verse," in *Divagations*, 201–11.

13. Stéphane Mallarmé, "Le Tombeau de Charles Baudelaire," in *Œuvres Complètes*, I:38–39.

14. Théodore de Wyzéwa, "La Musique descriptive," *La Revue Wagnérienne* I/3 (April 8, 1885): 74–77; Jennifer Day, trans., "Descriptive Music," in *Music in European Thought 1851–1912*, ed. Bojan Bujić, Cambridge Readings in the Literature of Music (Cambridge: Cambridge University Press, 1988), 249.

15. Théodore de Wyzéwa, "Notes sur la peinture wagnérienne et le salon de 1886," *La Revue Wagnérienne* II/4 (May 8, 1886): 113; Henri Dorra, trans., "Notes on Wagnerian Painting," in *Symbolist Art Theories*, ed. Henri Dorra (Berkeley: University of California Press, 1994), 147–49.

16. Stéphane Mallarmé, "Richard Wagner, rêverie d'un poète français," *La Revue Wagnérienne* I/7 (August 8, 1885), in *Œuvres Complètes*, II:156; Barbara Johnson, trans., "Richard Wagner. The Reverie of a French Poet," in *Divagations*, 110.

17. Anthony Zielonka, "'L'Après-midi d'un faune': Towards the Total Work of Art," *L'Esprit Créateur* 40, no. 3, Re-casting Mallarmé / Rejouer Mallarmé (Fall 2000): 14–24.

18. Stéphane Mallarmé, "Quant au livre," in *Œuvres Complètes*, II:226; Barbara Johnson, trans., "About the Book," in *Divagations*, 228–229. For the differences between Baudelaire's response to Wagner and Mallarmé's, see Mary Breatnach, "Baudelaire, Wagner, Mallarmé: Romantic Aesthetics and the Word-Tone Dichotomy," in *Word and Music Studies* (Amsterdam: Rodopi, 2003), 4:69–83.

19. See René Ghil, *Traité du verbe* (Paris: Giraud, 1886), 28 and Stéphane Mallarmé, *Selected Letters of Stéphane Mallarmé*, ed. and trans. Rosemary Lloyd (Chicago: University of Chicago Press, 1988), 140–41.

20. Chisholm, *Mallarmé's L'Après-Midi d'un Faune*, 11–12.

21. Chisholm, *Mallarmé's L'Après-Midi d'un Faune*, 10. For a discussion of the Arcadian features of the poem, see Berman, "'Prelude to the Afternoon of a Faun' and 'Jeux': Debussy's Summer Rites," *19th-Century Music* 3, no.

3 (1980): 225–38; and David J. Code, "Hearing Debussy Reading Mallarmé: Music *après Wagner* in the *Prélude à l'après-midi d'un faune,*" *Journal of the American Musicological Society* 53, no. 3 (2001): 493–554.

22. Joris-Karl Huysmans, *À Rebours* (Paris: Garnier-Flammarion, 1978), 220–21; Huysmans, *Against Nature,* trans. Robert Baldick (Harmondsworth: Penguin, 1959), 197.

23. Cook, *Mallarmé,* 86.

24. Graham Robb, *Unlocking Mallarmé* (New Haven, CT: Yale University Press, 1996), 36.

25. Robb, *Unlocking Mallarmé,* 35.

26. Robb, *Unlocking Mallarmé,* 14.

27. Chisholm, *Mallarmé's L'Après-Midi d'un Faune,* 13–15.

28. Mallarmé, "Sur l'evolution littéraire," in *Œuvres Complètes,* II:701; Mallarmé, "The Evolution of Literature" (1891), in Cook, *Mallarmé,* 22.

29. Huysmans, *À Rebours,* 220–21; Huysmans, *Against Nature,* 197.

30. Arthur Symonds, *The Symbolist Movement in Literature* (London: Dutton, 1899/1919), 71.

31. Mallarmé, "La Musique et les Lettres (1894)," in *Œuvres Complètes,* II:65 [55–77]; Mallarmé, "Music and Literature (1894)," in *Divagations,* trans. Barbara Johnson (Cambridge, MA: Harvard University Press, 2007), 184.

32. Chisholm, *Mallarmé's L'Après-Midi d'un Faune,* 10.

33. Heath Lees, *Mallarmé and Wagner: Music and Poetic Language* (Aldershot, VT: Ashgate, 2007), xiv.

34. Paul Valéry, *Écrits divers sur Stephane Mallarmé* (Paris: Gallimard, 1950), 86. Robb, *Unlocking Mallarmé,* xiii. See also Code, "Hearing Debussy Reading Mallarmé: Music *après Wagner* in the *Prélude à l'après-midi d'un faune,*" 503.

35. Chisholm, *Mallarmé's L'Après-Midi d'un Faune,* 13.

36. Chisholm, *Mallarmé's L'Après-Midi d'un Faune,* 13.

37. Chisholm, *Mallarmé's L'Après-Midi d'un Faune,* 14–15.

38. Robb, *Unlocking Mallarmé,* xiii.

39. Mallarmé letter to Henri Cazalis (April 25, 1864), in *Œuvres Complètes,* I:657; Cook, *Mallarmé,* 82.

40. Cook, *Mallarmé,* 86–87. For a discussion of this point, see Robb, *Unlocking Mallarmé,* 15.

41. Debussy, *Correspondance,* 278; Debussy, *Debussy Letters,* 84.

42. The following discussion recycles the formal and voice-leading analyses presented in Brown, "Tonality and Form in Debussy's *Prélude à L'Après-midi d'un faune,*" *Music Theory Spectrum* 15 (1993): 127–43.

43. For a different interpretation of the harmonic structure of the opening, see James Hepokoski, "Formulaic Openings in Debussy," *19th-Century Music* 8, no. 1 (Summer 1984): 44–59, esp. 56. Unfortunately, Hepokoski not only ignores the VII–V progression in mm. 11–13 but also underestimates the significance of the stepwise voice leading of the upper parts.

44. Matthew Brown, *Debussy Redux: The Impact of His Music on Popular Culture* (Bloomington: Indiana University Press, 2012), 125–26.

45. See Matthew Brown, *Explaining Tonality: Schenkerian Theory and Beyond* (Rochester, NY: University of Rochester Press, 2005), 192–202.

46. Katherine Bergeron, "The Echo, the Cry, the Death of Lovers," *19th-Century Music* 18, no. 2 (1994): 145–48.

47. Schenker, *Der freie Satz,* 18; Schenker, *Free Composition,* 5.

48. See Stéphane Mallarmé, "Crayonné au Théâtre: Ballets," "Crayonné au Théâtre: Autres études de danse: Les fonds dans le ballet," and "Crayonné au Théâtre: 'Le seul il le fallait fluie comme *l'enchanteur,*'" in *Œuvres Complètes,* II:170–74, 174–76, 177–78; Stéphane Mallarmé, "Scribbled at the Theater: Ballets" and "Scribbled at the Theater: Another Study of Dance: The Fundamentals of Ballet According to a Recent Indication," and "Scribbled at the Theater: 'The Only One Would Have To Be as Fluid,'" in *Divagations,* trans. Barbara Johnson (Cambridge, MA: Harvard University Press, 2007), 129–34, 135–37, and 138–39. For the impact of these papers, see Frank Kermode, "Poet and Dancer Before Diaghilev," (1958–1961), in *Puzzles and Epiphanies* (London: Routledge & Kegan Paul, 1962), 1–28; and Lisa Bixenstine Safford, "Mallarmé's Influence on Degas's Aesthetic of Dance in his Late Period," *Nineteenth-Century French Studies* 21, nos. 3–4 (Spring–Summer 1993): 419–33. For a recent discussion of Degas, Fuller, and the arabesque, see Juliet Bellow, "Drawing a Line with Body," in *Arabesque without End: Across Music and the Arts, from Faust to Shahrazad,* ed. Anne Leonard (New York: Routledge, 2022), 173–202, esp. 187–96.

49. Mallarmé, "Crayonné au Théâtre," in *Œuvres Complètes,* II:163; "Scribbled at the Theater," in *Divagations,* 120.

50. Mallarmé discussed Loïe Fuller in his essays "Crayonné au Théâtre: Ballets" and "Crayonné au Théâtre: Autres études de danse: Les fonds dans le ballet." As regards Fuller and the "serpentine dance," see M. Griffith, "Loie Fuller—The Inventor of the Serpentine Dance," *Strand Magazine* 7 (January 1894): 540–45. The Lumière Brothers filmed Fuller's serpentine dance in 1896: see https://www.youtube.com/watch?v=8zkXb4aWVZs. For a general discussion of Fuller, see Davinia Caddy, "Making Moves in Reception Studies: Music, Listening, and Loie Fuller," in *Musicology and Dance: Historical and Critical Perspectives*, ed. Davinia Caddy and Maribeth Clark (Cambridge: Cambridge University Press, 2020), 91–117. For the connections between Fuller and Yacco, see Elizabeth Emery, "Appropriating Japonisme at the 1900 Exposition: Sada Yacco, Loie Fuller, and the 'Geishas' of Le Panorama du Tour du Monde," *Dix-Neuf. Journal of the Society of Dix-Neuviémistes* 24, nos. 2–3 (2020): 221–44. For the impact of Sada Yacco on Western culture, see Nicola Saravese, *Eurasian Theatre: Drama and Performance between East and West from Classical Antiquity to the Present*, trans. Richard Fowler, revised and ed. Vicki Ann Cremona (Holstebro: ICARUS, 2010), 292–364. Sarah Gutsche-Miller discusses Debussy's familiarity with Loie Fuller in her essay "Debussy's noctambule and Parisian Popular Culture," in *Debussy in Context*, ed. Simon Trezise (Cambridge: Cambridge University Press, 2024), 196–200.

51. Cook, "Introduction," in *Mallarmé*, xviii.

52. Mallarmé, "Crayonné au Théâtre," in *Œuvres Complètes*, II:163; Mallarmé, "Scribbled at the Theater," 120. Mary Lewis Shaw, "Apprehending the Idea through Poetry and Dance," *Dance Research Journal* 20, no. 1 (Summer 1988): 3.

53. Mallarmé, "Ballets," in *Œuvres Complètes*, II:171; Mallarmé, "Ballets," in *Divagations*, 130.

54. Shaw, "Apprehending the Idea," 3.

55. Mallarmé, "Le seul il le fallait fluie comme l'enchanteur," in *Œuvres Complètes*, II:177; Mallarmé, "The Only One Would Have to Be as Fluid," in *Divagations*, 138.

56. For the subversive aspects of Nijinsky's choreography, see David J. Code, "Nijinsky, Modernism, Repression: The Faun Ballet—Once Again—Under Analysis," in *Musicology and Dance: Historical and Critical Perspectives*, ed. Davinia Caddy and Maribeth Clark (Cambridge: Cambridge University Press, 2020), 207–30.

57. Gaston Calmette, *Le Figaro*, May 30, 1912; Richard Buckle, *Nijinsky* (New York: Simon and Schuster, 1971), 242.

58. Stephanie Jordan, "Debussy, the Dance, and the Faune," in *Debussy in Performance*, ed. James Briscoe (New Haven, CT: Yale University Press, 1999), 120. For details of Nijinsky's choreography, see Nectoux, ed., *Afternoon of a Faun*, esp. 18–27; and Ann Hutchinson Guest, ed., *Nijinsky's Faune Restored*, Language of Dance Series No. 3 (Philadelphia: Gordon and Breach, 1991). Nectoux reproduces still photographs of the dancers and sets taken by Adolphe De Meyer, Karl Struss, and the Studio Waléry; see Nectoux, ed., *Afternoon of a Faun*, 65–95. Christian Comte has used these photographs to recreate Nijinsky's choreography on the computer. For a discussion of Comte's recreation, see Joan Acocella, "The Faun," *New Yorker*, June 29, 2009, https://www.newyorker.com/magazine/2009/06/29/the-faun.

59. Pierre Boulez, Notes to CBS Record 32 11 0056, quoted in Glenn Watkins, *Soundings* (New York: Schirmer, 1988), 7.

III. Part and Whole

5

❦

"A Premeditated Design"

WHEN SYMBOLISTS INVOKED the concept of the arabesque, they did so because it was central to their aesthetic agenda; they regarded ornamentation as the sine qua non of all art and, in Schlegel's words, arabesques as "the oldest and most original form" of ornamentation.[1] But Symbolist artists didn't sanction ornamentation for its own sake: in typically Aristotelian fashion, they insisted that ornaments should be added for specific reasons and have a direct impact on a work's global architecture. Baudelaire said it best when describing the intricate structure of Poe's stories: "throughout the whole composition not a single word must be allowed to intrude which is not also an intention and which does not aim, directly or indirectly, at completing a premeditated design."[2] As mentioned in the introduction, Debussy endorsed the same viewpoint. In a letter to Ernest Chausson dated October 23, 1893, for example, he left no doubt about his hatred for superfluous development and superficial decoration: "Sometimes the frame is so ornate, we don't realize the poverty of the central idea. And here I forbear to mention the occasions when magnificent inner parts adorn ideas like sixpenny dolls! It would be more profitable, I feel, to go about things the other way round, that's to say, find the perfect expression for an idea and add only as much decoration as is absolutely necessary."[3] And he reiterated the same point in a letter to Raoul Bardac dated February 24, 1906: "You know how little love I have for developmental padding. It's seen long service at the hands of the masters and it's time we started to replace it by a more rigorous selection of ideas; the line needs to take more account of the value of those ideas on the orchestral and ornamental front and, above all, the ideas must breathe. So often they're overwhelmed by the richness or the banality of the frame."[4]

Widely known for its elaborate surface structure and complex motivic profile, the *Quatuor à cordes* (1892–93) offers a perfect opportunity to see how Debussy set about achieving these objectives.[5] Roger Parker, for example, has compared the work's ornate passage work to the "Forest

Murmurs" from Wagner's opera *Siegfried*.[6] The comparison is indeed apt: though the two works do not sound much alike, the "Forest Murmurs" was very highly regarded in Symbolist circles and was singled out by Jules Laforgue in his essay "Impressionism" (1883) and Théodor de Wyzéwa in his paper "La Musique descriptive" (*La Revue Wagnérienne*, 1885).[7] In particular, Laforgue compared the complex brushwork of Monet and Pissarro—"the thousand little dancing strokes in every direction like straws of color"—to the complex symphonic texture of Wagner's score that no longer sounds as "an isolated melody" but becomes "the great voice of the forest."[8] Following in the same vein, David Code has compared the highly decorated arabesques of the first movement to those found in paintings by Maurice Denis and Paul Signac.[9] Others, however, have found precedents for Debussy's sophisticated thematic techniques in Edvard Grieg's Quartet in G minor, Op. 27 and César Franck's Quartet in D major. Gerald Abraham, for example, has suggested that Debussy and Grieg built their scores "almost entirely" from a motto containing the same notes, G–F–D.[10] And Elliott Carter has claimed that Debussy's "use of motivic cells, of sequences, of cyclic repetitions—a few motives incessantly expanded, modified, carried over from one movement to another" is typical of Franck, as are his "patterned rhythms, clear-cut phraseology, and simple crescendo techniques."[11] According to him, "The work's most outstanding features are its harmonic freedom and powerful lyric impulse, which immediately put it above almost any of the string quartets of the time."[12]

And yet, Debussy's *Quatuor à cordes* has, however, proven deceptively difficult to understand formally. Opinions have diverged enormously. For his part, Parker has insisted that, despite its highly decorated surface, ingenious motivic working, and harmonic freedom, the work's formal plan is utterly conventional: "The first movement is in an obvious sonata form, with a standard-issue second [theme], a development section and obvious recapitulation; then there's a lively, Beethovenian Scherzo movement, full of inventive pizzicato effects; then a long, slow, melody-rich third movement; and lastly a finale that even gestures towards that of Beethoven's Ninth Symphony in its recitative-like opening and recollections of past movements."[13] Meanwhile, Paul Dukas found the music far more obscure. Although he marveled at how the piece uses "a single theme . . . as the basis of all the movements" and how its material is "clear and clearly drawn," Dukas conceded that the work took "a great liberty" in its formal layout.[14] And, on hearing the work's second performance by the Quatuor Ysaÿe in Brussels on March 1, 1894, Maurice Kufferath found the piece utterly unintelligible: "There is in this quartet in four movements an assemblage of sonorities sometimes charming, sometimes irritating. It is not every day, or commonplace; on the contrary, it is very distinguished, but one does not know how to take hold of it. A hallucination more than a dream. Is it a work? Can one say? Is it music? Perhaps, but in the manner that the canvases of the neo-Japanese of Montmartre and the Belgian suburb may be called painting."[15] Debussy himself was most disappointed by the reaction of Ernest Chausson, writing to him on February 5, 1894: "I should also say that I was really upset for several days by what you said about my quartet, as I felt that after all it only increased your partiality for *certain things* which I would rather it encouraged you to forget. Anyway, I'll write another one which will be for you, in all seriousness for you, and I'll try and bring some nobility to my forms. I'd like to have enough influence with you to be able to grumble at you and tell you you're heading in the wrong direction!"[16]

Although the formal structure of the first movement has been described on numerous occasions in the past, one reading has been largely overlooked, one that challenges the views of Parker and Code and sheds new light on the movement's significance within the quartet as a whole. That reading treats the first movement as a monothematic sonata form. To support this claim and demonstrate Debussy's ongoing fascination with the arabesque, this chapter opens with a detailed analysis of the first movement, focusing special attention on the significance of the movement's motto. The discussion then considers the movement's formal structure and the problems of establishing the identities of the second key area and the second theme. Using Schenkerian analysis, it confirms that E♭ is indeed the second key area and that it is established by a variant of the first theme. Next, the chapter describes Debussy's use of the motto in the three remaining movements of the *Quatuor à cordes*; among other things, it suggests that Debussy's decision to cast the first movement as a monothematic sonata form anticipates his use of the motto in the finale. To underscore the arabesque nature of the work, the chapter ends with some remarks about the work's second performance in Brussels on March 1, 1894. These remarks expand on Code's salient observations about the ornamental character of Debussy's music and its connections to the work of artists working in other domains, such as Maurice Denis and Paul Signac.

Since the opening G–F–D motto guides the structure of the entire work, let's begin by examining its decisive presentation at the start of the first movement. As shown in example 5.1a, the

Example 5.1 Motto from Debussy, *Quatuor à cordes*, mvt. 1

Example 5.1a Motto in G minor, mm. 1–3

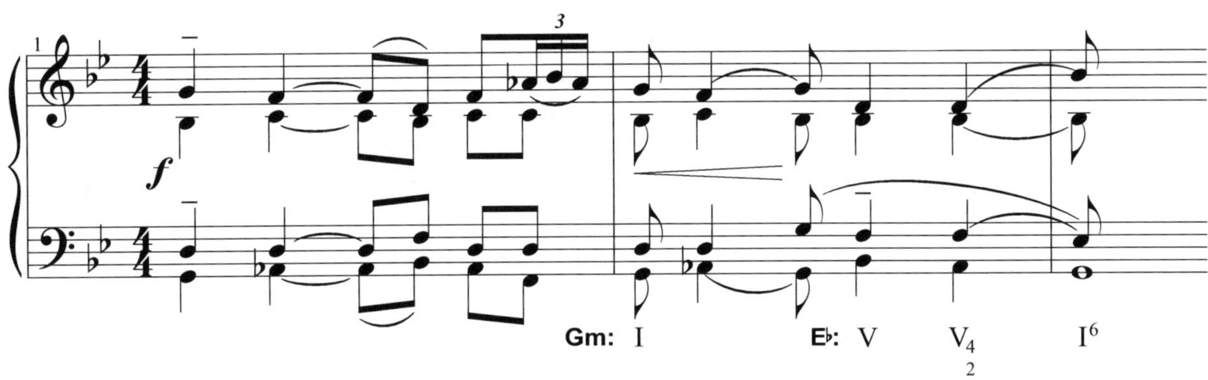

Example 5.1b Hypothetical version that shifts from G minor to E♭ major

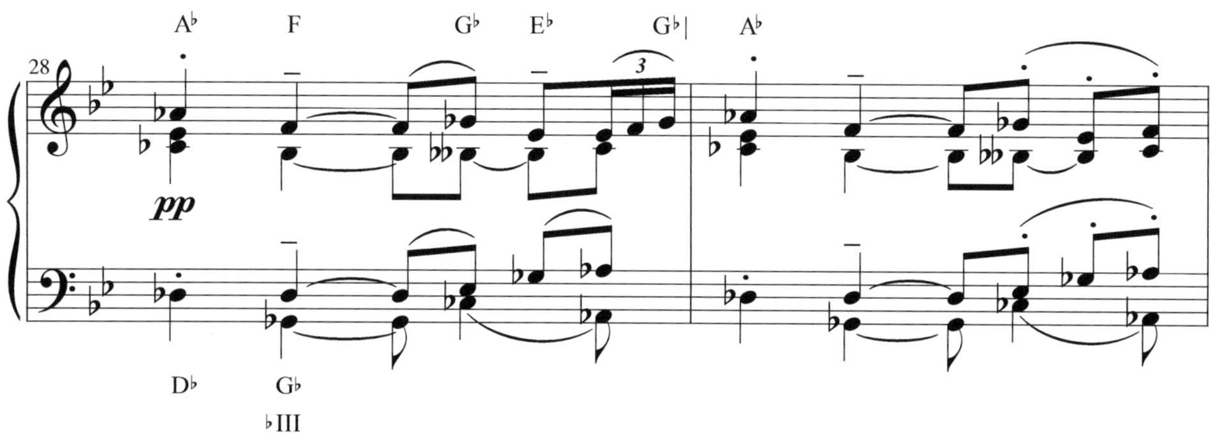

Example 5.1c Motto in E♭ major, mm. 26–29

gesture actually appears twice in the first violin, being extended in m. 1 by the rising third F–A♭ and in mm. 2–3 by the rising sixth D–B♭. Both versions are syncopated, though in different ways: in m. 1, G and F appear on the beat and D appears off the beat and in m. 2, G and D appear on the beat and F off the beat. Notice how the A♭ at the end of m. 1 is elaborated by its upper neighbor B♭. More remarkably still, the first violin part is mirrored in the cello: the melodic patterns G–F–D–F–A♭ (m. 1) and G–F–G–D–D–B♭ (m. 2) are inverted in the bass as G–A♭–B♭–A♭–F (m. 1) and G–A♭–G–B♭–A♭–G (m. 2). Some commentators have suggested that Debussy's prominent use of the note A♭ gives the passage a distinctive Phrygian flavor; but the addition of F♯ in the viola part on the last beat of m. 2 creates an augmented sixth A♭–F♯–C–D that tonicizes G on the downbeat of m. 3.[17] As will become clear, the interplay between the half-diminished seventh D–F–A♭–C, the augmented-sixth D–F♯–A♭–C, and the dominant seventh D–F♯–A–C becomes very important later in the composition. Example 5.1b suggests that by placing A♭ close to the B♭ triads in mm. 1 and 2 the latter might function as V of E♭. This is precisely what happens when the motto returns at pitch in E♭ major/minor starting in m. 26 and again in m. 30 (see ex. 5.1c–5.1d).

Example 5.1d Motto in E♭ major, mm. 30–33

Besides predicting future harmonic events, the motto also determines the movement's other themes, the most prominent of which are cataloged in example 5.2.[18] Example 5.2a shows how the main theme (mm. 1–5) spins out the motto by transforming it intervallically and by transferring it up an octave. Next, example 5.2b demonstrates how the first subordinate theme in mm. 13–14 ends with a variant of the motto A–G–D but starts with a string of eighth notes G–F–G–A–G that recall the neighbor pattern A♭–B♭–A♭–G in mm. 1–2. The connections to mm. 1–2 also extend to the lower voices; the relentless barrage of sixteenth notes in mm. 13–22 includes countless upper neighbors like those from the end of m. 1. Examples 5.2c and 5.2d then show how the basic shape of the motto in mm. 34–38, G♭–F♭–D♭–(B♭), is filled out with passing tones F–E♭–D♭ and D♭–C♭–B♭ to create the second subordinate theme G♭–F–E♭–D♭–C♭–B♭ in mm. 39–43. Notice how the pattern F♭–D♭–F♭ in m. 36 anticipates the pattern B♭–D♭–C♭ in m. 39 and how the accompaniment again develops the upper neighbor figure from m. 1. The neighbor pattern in mm. 1–2 also spawns the third subordinate theme in mm. 51–52; as shown in example 5.2e, this new theme oscillates around E and even includes a variant of the three-note figure G–F♯–D

Example 5.2a First theme, mm. 1–5

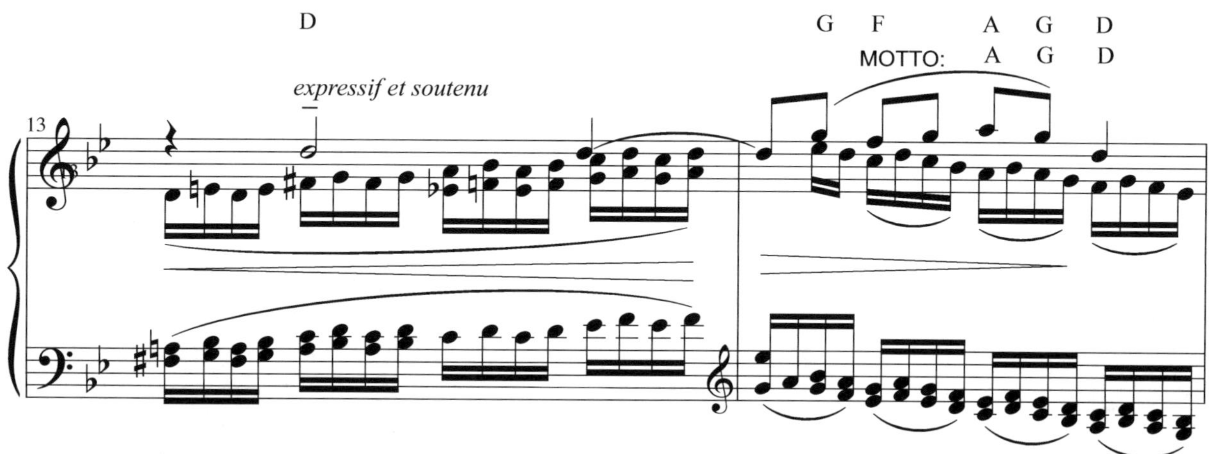

Example 5.2b First subordinate theme, mm. 13–14

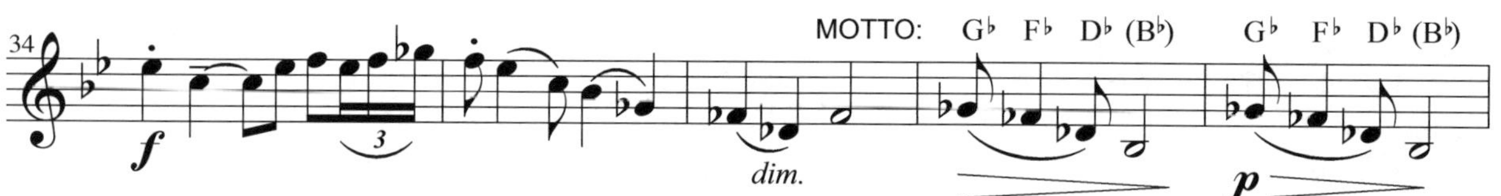

Above, **Example 5.2c** Variant of the first theme in E♭ major/minor, mm. 34–38

Facing top, **Example 5.2d** Second subordinate theme in E♭ major/minor, mm. 39–43

Facing middle, **Example 5.2e** Third subordinate theme, mm. 51–52

Facing bottom, **Example 5.2f** Fourth subordinate theme, mm. 63–64 and mm. 69–70

39
p
3 3 3 3
3 3 3 3

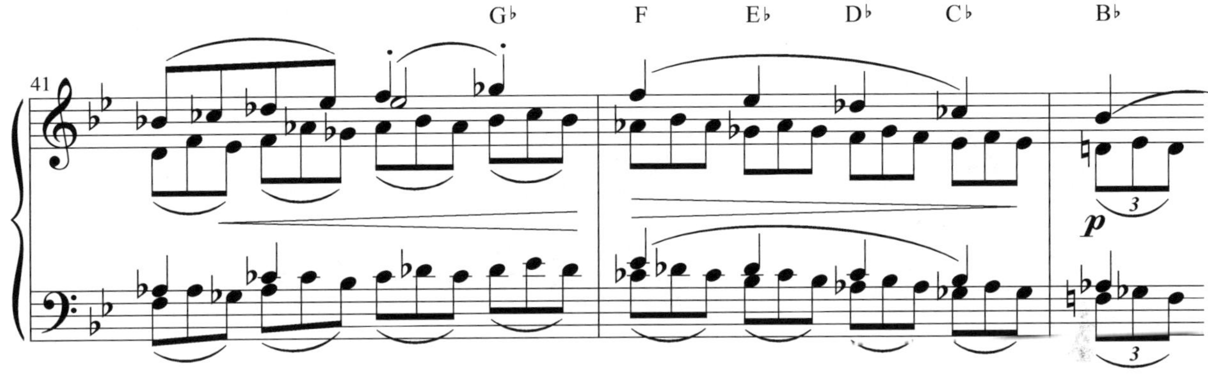
Gb F Eb Db Cb Bb
41
p
3
3

E F# E E F# E
MOTTO: G F# D
p en augmentant peu à peu

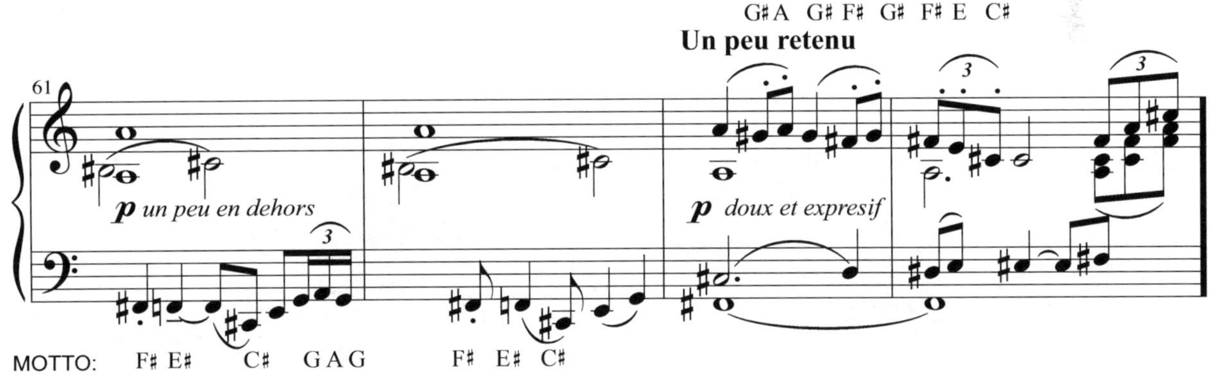
G#A G# F# G# F# E C#
Un peu retenu
61
p un peu en dehors
p doux et expresif
3
3
MOTTO: F# E# C# GAG F# E# C#

Bb A Bb A GA GF D
Un peu retenu
doux
3 3
1er Mouvt
67
p
p
3
MOTTO: G F# D F# Ab Bb Ab G F# D F# Ab

in m. 52. Finally, example 5.2f shows how statements of the motto in mm. 61–62 and 67–68 give rise to the fourth subordinate theme in mm. 63–64 and 69–70: the three-note figure F♯–E♯–C♯ in mm. 61–62 foreshadows the three-note figure F♯–E–C♯ in m. 64, and the upper neighbor patterns G♯–A–G♯ and F♯–G♯–F♯ in m. 63 recall G–A–G in m. 61.

Whereas example 5.2 demonstrates how the motto percolates through the main and subordinate themes, example 5.3a shows how mm. 1–12 transform the motto into a beautiful arabesque. It does so by transposing the motto up a third in mm. 3–4, shifting it up an octave in mm. 5–6, developing material from m. 2 in mm. 7–10, and ending with a variant of the motto F–G–D in

Example 5.3 Debussy, *Quatuor à cordes* mvt. 1, mm. 1–13

Example 5.3a Melodic arabesque, mm. 1–12

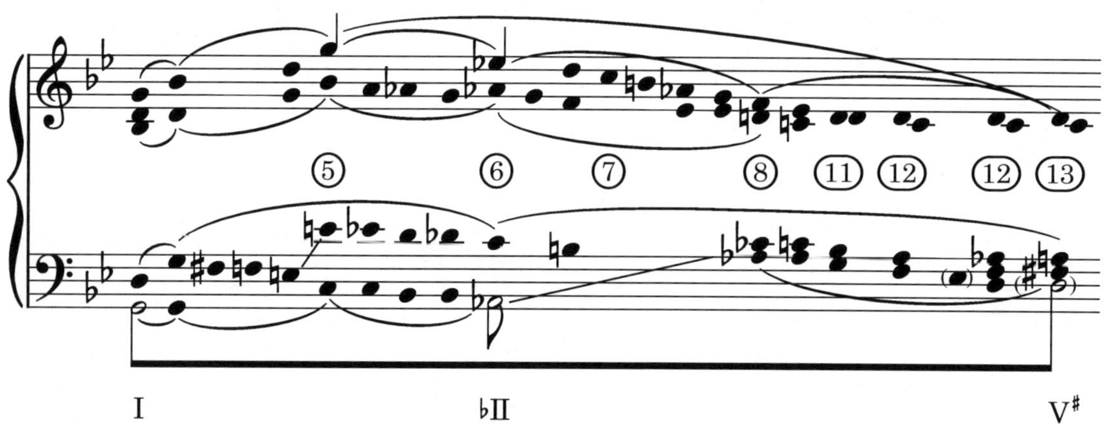

Example 5.3b Essential voice leading in mm. 1–13

mm. 10–12. When presented in succession, these gestures project a long stepwise line that descends from a high G in m. 5 through E♭ and D in mm. 6–7 and F in m. 8, to a low D in mm. 11–12. The voice-leading sketch in example 5.3b suggests that this line is accompanied by parallel scales in the other instruments: the second violin tracks the first violin's arabesque in descending parallel sixths starting on B♭ in m. 5 and descending parallel thirds starting on E♭ in m. 7. The viola projects an even longer scale that grows out of the descending pattern G–F♯–F–E in mm. 3–4 and that continues down from E through E♭, D, D♭, and C to B in mm. 5–6 and from B through B♭ to A♭ in mm. 6–12. Like those found in the *Première Arabesque*, the *Prélude à L'Après-midi d'un faune*, this scale is harmonized in several ways: in mm. 3–4 it appears over a tonic pedal and in mm. 4–6 within a sequential pattern whose essential bass line descends from C through B♭ to A♭.[19] Having prolonged A♭ as a pedal tone, the cello inserts variants of the syncopated figure F–F–G–D as part of a half-diminished seventh on the dominant D–F–A♭–C.

The arabesque quality of Debussy's writing is even more apparent in mm. 13–26, where the motto is transformed and decorated with layers of sixteenth-note filigree. To begin with, the passage is dominated by the first subordinate theme from mm. 13–14 (see ex. 5.4a). This gesture is stated in the first violins in G minor as D–G–F–G–A–G–D in mm. 13–14 and 15–16, and the cello in E♭ major as B♭–E♭–D–E♭–F–E♭–B♭ in mm. 17–18 and 19–20. The cello continues by repeating and transposing the final three notes: F–E♭–B♭; D–C–G; D–D♭–C. Example 5.4b then shows how the sixteenth-note accompaniment projects a stepwise chain of parallel thirds and sixths, which start in m. 13 and continue until m. 22. Example 5.4c then shows how mm. 12–26 modulate from G minor to E♭ and, as anticipated, replaces A in mm. 13–16 with A♭ in mm. 17–22. This modulation evolves from the stepwise bass descent in mm. 1–12: the bass line transfers the low D in m. 12 up an octave in m. 13 and then makes its way down by step from D through C, B♭, A♭, G and F, to E♭. Example 5.4c also indicates that the upper voices proceed

Example 5.4 Debussy, *Quatuor à cordes*, mvt. 1, mm. 13–26

Example 5.4a Transformation of the first theme, mm. 13–26

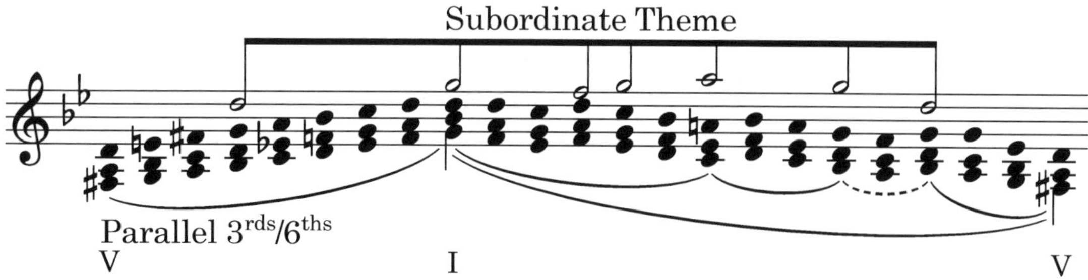

Example 5.4b Surface voice leading, mm. 13–15

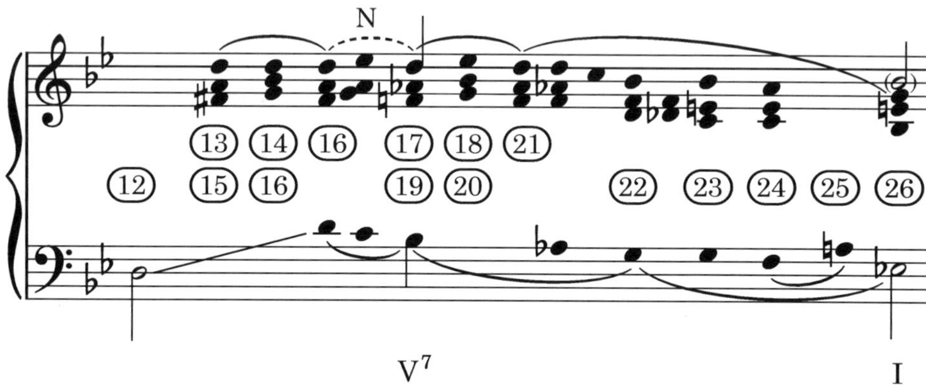

Example 5.4c Essential voice leading, mm. 13–26

in parallel thirds and sixths with the arabesque melody spiraling down D–C–B♭–A♭–G. In mm. 23–25, however, the neighbor figure that dominated mm. 13–22 gives way to a chromatic scale segment D–D♭–C–B–B♭–A–A♭–G that resembles the pattern G–F♯–F–E in m. 3.

Once E♭ has been stabilized, mm. 26–75 follow a similar course to mm. 1–26. Indeed, as shown in example 5.5a, the passage begins in mm. 26–38 by repeating the motto twice on G (mm. 26–27 and 30–31) and once transposed up a half step to A♭ (mm. 28–29). The theme is also fragmented and sequenced in mm. 32–38: on B♭ in m. 32; on C in m. 33; on E♭ in m. 34; and extended with variants on F–E♭–C in m. 35, and on G♭–F♭–D♭ in mm. 37 and 38. Harmonically, mm. 26–38 are especially complex and, as Laurence Berman has rightly noted, "cannot be completely understood until the arrival of the dominant of E♭ in measure 39."[20] Example 5.5b even suggests that the tonic E♭ in m. 26 connects to an inverted dominant sonority on the downbeat of m. 39 by means of a stepwise descent in the bass: E♭ (m. 26), D (m. 33), C (m. 34), B♭ (m. 37), an implied A♭ (m. 38), G♭ (m. 38), F (m. 39).

Just as mm. 26–38 mirror mm. 1–12 by repeating, transposing, and developing the motto, so mm. 39–75 mimic mm. 13–26 by developing the other subordinate themes mentioned earlier: the second subordinate theme enters on B♭ in mm. 39–42 and 43–46 (see ex. 5.6a); the third enters on E in m. 51 and appears sequentially on G in m. 53 and B in m. 55 (see ex. 5.6b); and, the fourth appears in mm. 63 and 69 (see ex. 5.6c). Besides presenting a rich array of melodic material, mm. 39–75 also modulate from E♭ (mm. 39–75) to D minor (m. 75). Example 5.6d interprets this passage contrapuntally. After prolonging the dominant in E♭ in mm. 39–46, the music veers off in a

Example 5.5 Debussy, *Quatuor à cordes*, mvt. 1, mm. 26–75

Example 5.5a Return of the first theme in E♭, mm. 26–38

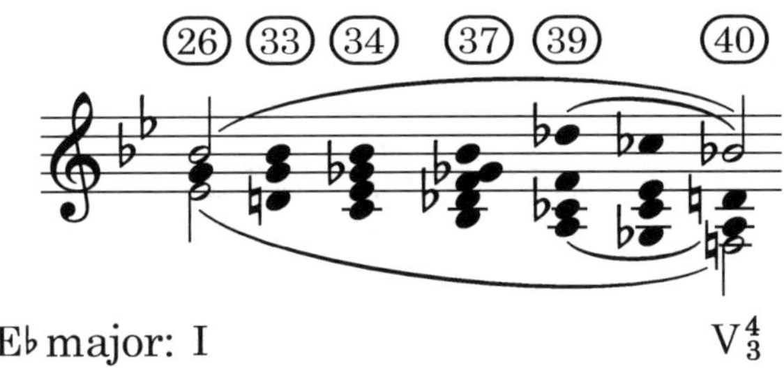

E♭ major: I   V$^4_3$

Example 5.5b Essential voice leading, mm. 26–40

new direction when the bass slides down from F to E in m. 48. Just a few measures later in m. 55, the bass lands on F♯ for snippets of the motto and the last subordinate theme in mm. 61–66 and mm. 67–74. These lead to an emphatic return of the motto in m. 75 and a decisive cadence in D minor in m. 76. Notice how the voice-leading sketch in example 5.6d highlights the sequential basis of the entire passage. From a notational perspective, it is also worth noting that the arrival in D minor is marked by a change in key signature from two flats to one and is even labeled "1re Mvt" in both the autograph *F-Pn*, Ms 1004 and first edition (Durand, 1894).

Having outlined the basic thematic and tonal geography of mm. 1–75, it is now appropriate to see how these measures guide the form of the entire movement. If, as Parker suggests, "the first movement is in an obvious sonata form," then the immediate issue is to classify the formal function of the main and subordinate themes mentioned above. Since the motto clearly articulates the first theme and key G minor, we are left to decide which of the subordinate themes and key areas serve as the second theme and second key and which, if any, serves as closing material. This decision is by no means easy to make. Some, such as Lockspeiser and Goubault, claim that the

Example 5.6 Debussy, *Quatuor à cordes*, mvt. 1, mm. 39–75

Example 5.6a Second subordinate theme, mm. 39–42 (cf. ex. 5.2d)

Example 5.6b Third subordinate theme, mm. 51–60 (cf. ex. 5.2e)

Example 5.6c Motto and fourth subordinate themes, mm. 61–75/76 (cf. ex. 5.2f)

Example 5.6d Essential voice leading, mm. 48–75/76

most likely candidate for the second theme is the fourth subordinate theme from mm. 63–64 and 69–74.[21] Although the appearance of this gesture is indeed striking, there are several problems with interpreting it in this way. For one thing, the theme appears alongside statements of the motto in mm. 61–62 and mm. 67–68. For another, it does not articulate a stable second key area: on the contrary, it appears within a sequential passage, II–V in E major (mm. 63–66) and II–V in F major (mm. 67–74). And, most troubling of all, the fourth subordinate theme enters far too late in the exposition: indeed, whereas second themes and second key areas normally appear roughly a third of the way through the exposition, this one enters just before the end. Code tried to correct this imbalance by treating the second subordinate theme (mm. 39–43) as the second theme, the third subordinate theme (mm. 51–52) as the closing material, and the fourth subordinate theme (mm. 63–74) as part of the development section.[22] But this analysis still comes up short because it introduces the second theme thirteen bars after the arrival of the second key and because this gesture is never to be heard again. This latter point is especially important because Code is forced to concede that the recapitulation does not serve as a form of tonal/thematic reconciliation but as "a non-dialectical summation."[23] In other words, the movement doesn't really have what it takes to be a traditional sonata form, a view that is endorsed by Paul Griffiths as well.[24] François De Médicis offers another interesting possibility: although he treats the return of the main theme in m. 26 as part of the start of the second group, he suggests that the entry of the fourth subordinate theme in m. 63 appears as part of the development section.[25] The disadvantages with this reading are it implies that the sonata principle is satisfied by a theme that does not appear in the exposition but in the development and that it downplays the significance of the marking "1er Mvt" in the autograph and first edition in m. 75.

As shown in table 5.1, the preceding problems can be resolved by treating the movement as a monothematic sonata in which the opening motto serves as the first theme and its return in m. 26 as the second theme. According to this scheme, which was first proposed nearly a century ago by Albert Bertelin, the exposition subdivides into five units that are more or less equal in size: mm. 1–12 present the main in G minor, thereby treating it as the first theme; mm. 13–25 use the first subordinate theme as a transition that modulates from G to E♭; mm. 26–38 use a variant of the main theme as the second theme in E♭ major/minor; mm. 39–60 introduce the second and third subordinate themes as part of the second group; finally, mm. 61–74 treat the fourth subordinate theme as the closing material, combining it with reminiscences of the motto.[26] The regularly periodic nature of this scheme, which continues through the rest of the movement, may have been what Carter had in mind when he referred to its "clear-cut phraseology."[27] The advantages of this reading are threefold. For one thing, it introduces the second theme much earlier in the

Table 5.1. First movement of Debussy's *Quatuor à cordes* as a monothematic sonata form

Exposition		Recapitulation	
1st theme	G minor, m. 1	1st theme	G minor, m. 138
Transition	G minor–E♭, m. 13	Aug. 1st theme	m. 149
(= 1st subordinate theme)			
2nd subject	E♭ major/minor, m. 26		
2nd subordinate theme	E♭ minor, m. 39		
Closing material	F♯, m. 61	Closing material	V/G minor, m. 161
(= 4th subordinate theme)		2nd/1st theme	m. 175
		Aug. 1st theme	mm. 181–98

Development	
1st theme	D minor, m. 75
Closing material	m. 88, m. 97, m. 111
Retransition	mm. 118–38
1st theme	m. 120, m. 126
Closing material	m. 133

exposition than the reading offered by Lockspeiser and Goubault. This move reflects the general principle that expositions typically spend much less time in the first key area than in the second and that both key areas are normally well defined. For another, Debussy's decision to articulate the second key area with a statement of the motto underscores the central role that this gesture plays in the entire movement: not only does it generate the various subordinate themes, but it also controls the movement's major points of tonal articulation—namely, the start of the exposition (m. 1), the second key area (m. 26), the start of the development (m. 75), and the start of the recapitulation (m. 138). And, above all, the analysis outlined in table 5.1 stands out because it suggests that the sonata principle might in fact be satisfied by the return of the closing material in the recapitulation. To explain this process in more detail, it is worth taking a close look at the latter portions of the movement, especially as regards their handling of the motto, the first theme, and the closing material.

Code was surely right to regard mm. 75–138 as "the most traditionally 'developmental' section that Debussy ever wrote."[28] In much the same manner as mm. 1–12, the passage begins by working out the motto in mm. 75–78, though it does so obscurely in the dominant key of D minor (see ex. 5.7). The first violin spins it out in a long arabesque that winds its way down from a high F through E and D to C in m. 83, A and G to F in m. 84, F through E and D to C in m. 85; and C through B♭ and A to G in mm. 86–87. As shown in example 5.8, the direction of the piece suddenly changes in m. 88: the descending pattern C–B♭–A–G from mm. 86–87 (ex. 5.8a) is transformed rhythmically into the closing material (ex. 5.8b). Examples 5.8c–5.8f then show how the closing material returns on G in mm. 92–96 (ex. 5.8c), on D♯ in mm. 97–100 (ex. 5.8d), B in mm. (103)/107–10 (ex. 5.8e), and F in mm. 111–14 (ex. 5.8f). The parallel tenths A/F–G/E–F/D lead in m. 118 to the same half-diminished seventh on D that occurred at the end of the opening paragraph mm. 1–12. The arrival on the dominant in m. 118 marks the start of the retransition. The passage follows a similar course to mm. 75–118: it begins by developing

Example 5.7 Development of the motto and first theme in Debussy's *Quatuor à cordes*, mvt. 1, mm. 75–91

Example 5.8 Development of closing material/fourth subordinate theme in the first movement of Debussy's *Quatuor à cordes*, mm. 88–117

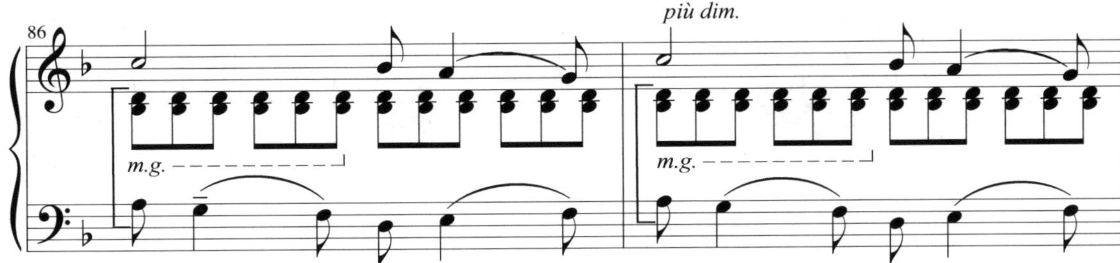

Example 5.8a Motto C–B–A–G, mm. 86–87

Example 5.8b Closing material, mm. 88–91

Example 5.8c Closing material, mm. 92–96

Example 5.8d Closing material, mm. 97–100

Above, **Example 5.8e** Closing material, mm. 103/107–10

Facing top, **Example 5.8f** Closing material, mm. 111–14

Facing middle, **Example 5.8g** Start of retransition and return of motto, mm. 118–21

Facing bottom, **Example 5.8h** Closing material, mm. 133–37

En serrant le Mouv^t
Retenu

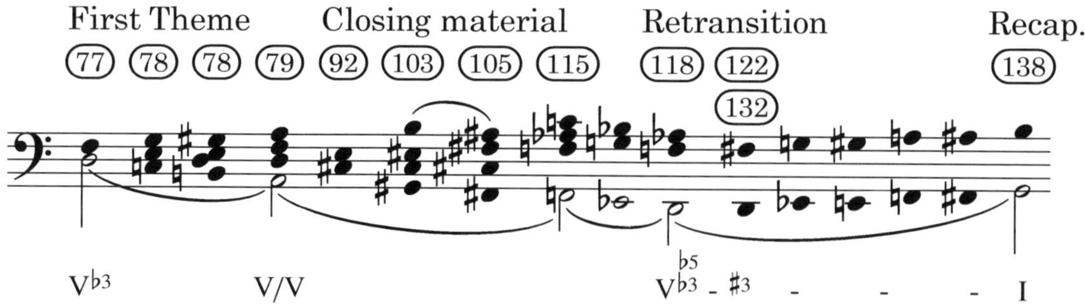

Example 5.9 Essential voice leading in Debussy's *Quatuor à cordes*, mvt. 1, mm. 76/77–138

the motto (see ex. 5.8g) and ends by recalling the closing material (see ex. 5.8h). The parallels between the two passages are particularly striking in mm. 133–38, where the contrasting theme returns on G and is supported by an ascending chromatic scale from A in the bass. Example 5.9 shows that the complete section is built from stepwise strings set in parallel thirds and sixths: in mm. 75–118, the bass line descends an octave D–C–B–A–G♯–F♯–F–E♭–D, and in mm. 118–38, it ascends a fourth D–E♭–E–F–F♯–G.

Just as the start of the development is marked by a change in key signature from two flats to one and by the label "1ʳᵉ Mvt," so the beginning of the recapitulation is indicated by a return to the work's original key signature of two flats and the label "1ʳᵉ Mvt." What follows is utterly predictable if the piece is regarded as a monothematic sonata form. Since monothematic sonata forms establish the first and second key areas by means of the first theme, they usually rely on the recapitulation of some other theme to satisfy what Edward Cone famously referred to as the sonata principle. According to Cone, this principle demands that "important statements made in a key other than the tonic must either be re-stated in the tonic or brought into closer relation to the tonic before the movement ends."[29] The closing material is a likely candidate for this role and is the one picked by Debussy in this movement. Debussy's desire to subject his themes to a process of continuous development is already apparent when the motto returns as part of the first theme at the start of the recapitulation in m. 138. As shown in example 5.10a, the first theme is not only rescored but also reharmonized so that the chromatic descent G–F♯–F–E–E♭–D–D♭–C buried in the inner voices in mm. 3–5 is placed center stage, descending from G through F♯, F, and E to D in mm. 140–41, from C♯ through C, B, B♭, and A♭ in m. 142, and then from G through F, E, and E♭ to D♭ in mm. 143–45. The bass line then doubles back on itself in m. 145 and ascends through D, E♭, and E, to F in 145–48 (see ex. 5.10b). This passage sets up the recapitulation of the closing material over a ten-measure dominant pedal starting in m. 161 (see ex. 5.10c). After recalling the final six measures of the retransition, mm. 171–74 return to the tonic G minor via an ascending chromatic scale from D (ex. 5.10d). Examples 5.10e and 5.10f then show how the return of the tonic is marked by a statement of the closing material in mm. 175–78 and by reiterating the descending pattern D–C–B♭–G in mm. 179–82. The *Quatuor à cordes* ends with further statements of the motto G–F–D starting in m. 183 (see ex. 5.10g) and m. 187 (see ex. 5.10h). One suspects that Debussy had some inkling of how the first movement would end while he was composing the exposition; his decision to reveal the connections between the motto and the closing material was, to paraphrase Baudelaire, entirely premeditated.

Example **5.10a** First theme, mm. 138–45

Example **5.10b** First theme, mm. 145–48

Example 5.10c Closing material, mm. 161–65

Example 5.10d Closing material, mm. 171–74

Example 5.10e Closing material, mm. 175–78

Example 5.10f First theme, mm. 179–82

Example 5.10g First theme, mm. 183–84

Example 5.10h First theme, mm. 187–91

While Debussy's handling of the motto is stunning in the first movement, it is no less masterful in the three other movements. For convenience, example 5.11 shows some of the many new guises in which it appears in the second, third, and fourth movements.[30] Having given the original version in G minor as a point of reference in example 5.11a and other versions in the first movement in examples 5.11b–5.11c, examples 5.11d–5.11j show how the motto is transformed in the second movement. Example 5.11d presents a version in G major that is used as an ostinato in the opening section, starting in mm. 3–4. Examples 5.11e–5.11f then show an augmentation of the motto in E♭ major starting in mm. 56–60 and a recollection of the ostinato version starting in mm. 86–90. Next, examples 5.11g–5.11h show two other versions in E♭ minor starting in mm. 111–14 and on the dominant of E major starting in mm. 124–29. Examples 5.11i–5.11j then show how the second movement ends with recollections of the motto in G major and in other transpositions. Although allusions to the motto are perhaps less obvious in the third movement of the *Quatuor à cordes*, they can be found at various points in the score. For example, echoes of the theme can be heard in the movement's main theme in D♭ major: as shown in examples 5.11k–5.11l the patterns F–E♭–D♭–B♭♭ in m. 7 and C–B♭–G♮–A♭ in mm. 11–12 resemble the pattern G–F–D–F from the motto. The secondary motive from the middle of the movement, given in examples 5.11m–5.11o, also recalls the triplet turn figure at the end of m. 1. Example 5.11p shows the return of the main theme in the waning bars of the movement. Finally, the motto resurfaces in countless guises in the fourth movement starting in mm. 1–2 (example 5.11q) and as the main theme in mm. 3–4 (see example 5.11r). Examples 5.11s–5.11t then show reminiscences of the ostinato version from the second movement, and examples 5.11u–5.11w recall the augmented version in E major from the middle of the same movement. Most remarkably of all, example 5.11x shows how the motto is juxtaposed with the finale's main theme in mm. 252–57; example 5.11y how it eventually takes over entirely in mm. 326–29; and example 5.11z how the motto is distilled down to just three notes in the final measures of the score. Though these passages clearly hark back to the end of

Example 5.11 Transformations of the motto

Example 5.11a First movement, mm. 1–4

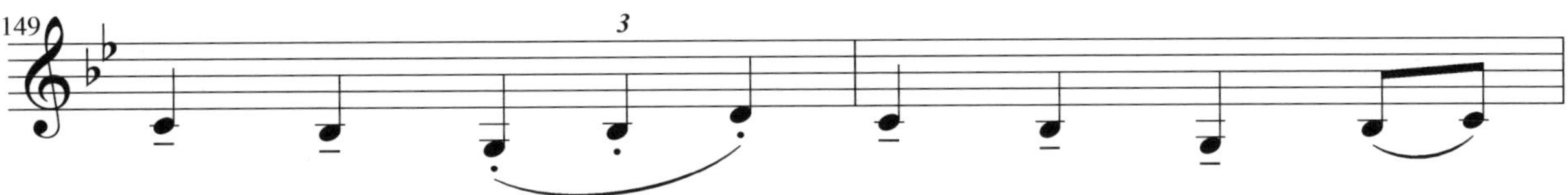

Example 5.11b First movement, mm. 149–50

Example 5.11c First movement, mm. 190–91

Example 5.11d Second movement, mm. 3–4

Example 5.11e Second movement, mm. 56–60/62

Example 5.11f Second movement, mm. 86–88

Example 5.11g Second movement, mm. 111–14

Example 5.11h Second movement, mm. 124–29

Example 5.11i Second movement, mm. 148–51

Example 5.11j Second movement, mm. 160–61

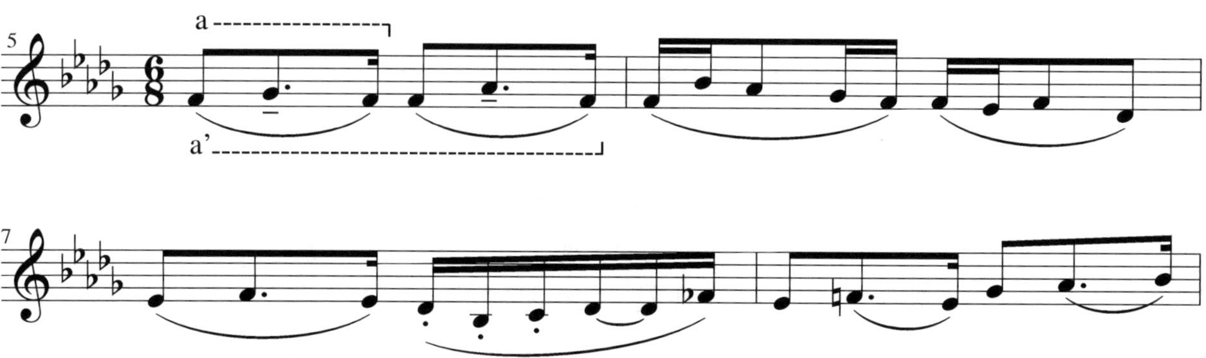

Example 5.11k Third movement, mm. 5–8

Example 5.11l Third movement, mm. 9–14

Example 5.11m Third movement, mm. 28–31

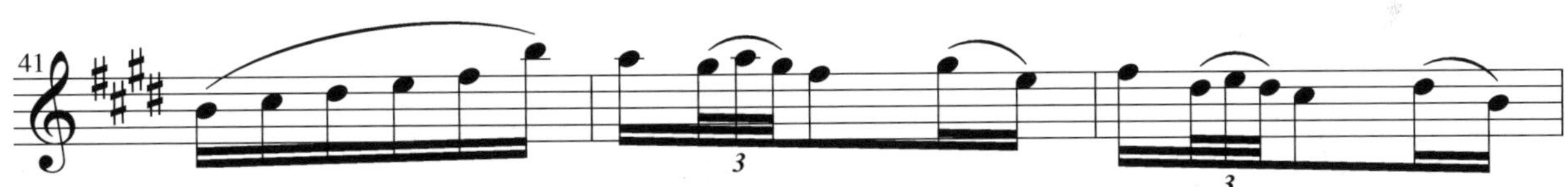

Example 5.11n Third movement, mm. 41–43

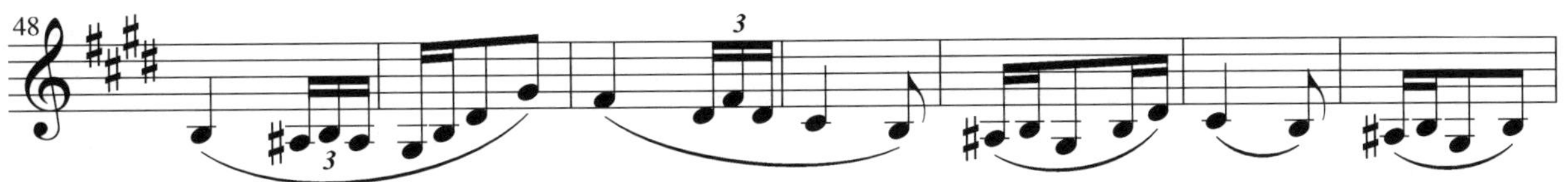

Example 5.11o Third movement, mm. 48–54

Example 5.11p Third movement, mm. 111–17

Example 5.11q Fourth movement, mm. 1–2

Example 5.11r Fourth movement, mm. 3–4

Example 5.11s Fourth movement, m. 15

Example 5.11t Fourth movement, mm. 31–32

Example 5.11u Fourth movement, mm. 125–32

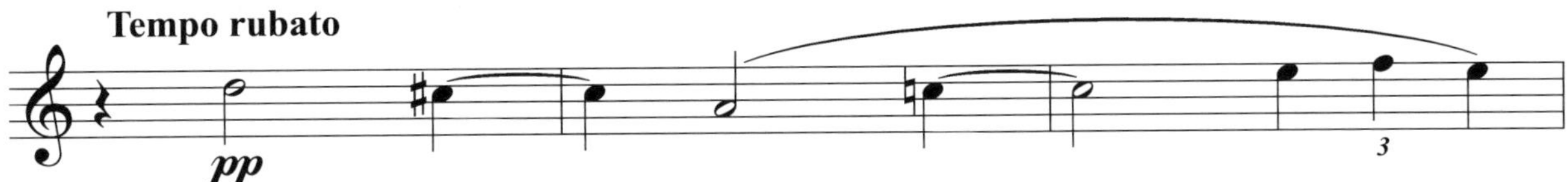

Example 5.11v Fourth movement, mm. 141–43

Example 5.11w Fourth movement, mm. 181–95

Example 5.11x Fourth movement, mm. 252–57

Example 5.11y Fourth movement, mm. 326–29

Example 5.11z Fourth movement, m. 349

the first movement (e.g., ex. 5.11b–5.11c), they all appear in G major rather than G minor. This change in mode marks the final stage in a process of motivic transformation that began all the way back in the opening when Debussy decided to cast the first movement as a monothematic sonata form. Yet again, it underscores Baudelaire's idea that nothing should intrude "which is not also an intention and which does not aim, directly or indirectly, at completing a premeditated design."[31]

The preceding discussion has focused on the decorative nature of Debussy's *Quatuor à cordes* and on how the first movement uses the three-note motto to generate an intricate array of musical arabesques. To paraphrase Baudelaire, it shows how Debussy made every detail count. Although the analysis differs in many ways from the one presented by David Code, it does not contradict Code's claim that Debussy's string writing bears strong similarities to the designs found in paintings by Denis and Signac. By way of conclusion, let us delve more deeply into the implications of this idea. From the outset, it is important to stress that Code based his observations on the fact that the second performance of Debussy's *Quatuor à cordes* occurred in Brussels on March 1, 1894, as part of "a month-long exhibition of avant-garde painting and decorative art" under the name La Libre Esthétique.[32] That event, which was part of the first ever concert devoted entirely to Debussy's music, also included performances of *Proses lyriques* and *La Damoiselle élue* (see fig.

PREMIER CONCERT DU QUATUOR YSAYE

MM. Eugène YSAYE, CRICKBOOM, VAN HOUT ET J. JACOB,
avec le concours de M. Henri MERCK, violoncelliste

Vendredi 23 février 1894, à 2 heures et demie.

1. Quintette à deux basses en *ré majeur* (op. 163) . F. SCHUBERT.
   Allegro ma non troppo. — Adagio. — Scherzo. — Andante sostenuto. — Allegretto.

2. Quatuor pour deux violons, alto et violoncelle (op. 35) . . . . VINCENT D'INDY.
   I. *Lent et soutenu; modérément animé.* — II. *Lent et calme.* — III. *Assez modéré; assez vite.* — IV. *Assez lent et déclamé; vif et joyeusement animé.*

3. Quatuor (n° 11, op. 95) . . . . BEETHOVEN.
   Allegro con brio. — Allegretto ma non troppo. — Allegro assai vivace ma serioso. — Larghetto expressivo; allegretto agitato.

DEUXIÈME CONCERT DU QUATUOR YSAYE

AVEC LE GRACIEUX CONCOURS DE
Mme T. ROGER, cantatrice de la Société nationale de musique de Paris, de Mlle LAURE CALLEMIEN, du Choral mixte fondé par MM. L. Soubre et Carpay, et des solistes des Concerts du Conservatoire de Bruxelles.

Jeudi 1ᵉʳ mars 1894, à 2 heures précises.

ŒUVRES DE M. CLAUDE-A. DEBUSSY (PREMIÈRE AUDITION)

1. Quatuor en *sol mineur* pour deux violons, alto et violoncelle (op. 10).
   I. — *Animé et très décidé.* — II. *Assez vif et bien rythmé.* — III. *Doucement expressif.* — IV. *Très modéré; très mouvementé et avec passion.*

2. *Proses lyriques.*
   a) *De fleurs.* — b) *De soir.*
   Chantées par Mme T. ROGER et accompagnées par l'auteur.

3. *La Damoiselle élue*, pour soli, chœurs et orchestre, d'après D.-G. ROSSETTI (traduction de G. Sarrazin).
   Solistes : La Damoiselle élue . . . . Mlle T. ROGER.
   Une Récitante . . . . . . Mlle L. CALLEMIEN.

Piano Pleyel.

N. B. — L'orchestre se composait de 51 musiciens, tous solistes ou chefs de pupitres des Concerts du Conservatoire.

TROISIÈME CONCERT DU QUATUOR YSAYE

Vendredi 18 mars 1894, à 2 heures précises

1. Quatuor à cordes en *ré majeur* . . . . CÉSAR FRANCK.
   I. *Poco lento; allegro.* — II. *Scherzo vivace.* — III. *Larghetto.* — IV. *Allegro molto.*

2. *Sarabande, Gigue* et *Chaconne* extraites de la Suite en *ré mineur* pour violon seul . . . . J.-S. BACH.

3. XIV° Quatuor à cordes (op. 131) . . . . . . BEETHOVEN.
   Les divisions qui composent ce quatuor s'enchaînent sans interruption.

QUATRIÈME CONCERT DU QUATUOR YSAYE

AVEC LE GRACIEUX CONCOURS DE
MM. Auguste PIERRET, pianiste, et Alfred MARCHOT, violon solo au Théâtre de la Monnaie.

Mardi 27 mars 1894, à 2 heures précises.

1. Quatuor n° 8 (op. 59) . . . . BEETHOVEN.
   I. *Allegro.* — II. *Molto adagio.* — III. *Allegretto.* — IV. *Presto.*

2. a) *Portraits de musiciens* . . . . ⎫
   G. *Fauré.*
   V. *d'Indy; E. Chausson; V. d'Indy.*
   C. *Franck.*
                    P. DE BRÉVILLE.
   b) Fantaisie pour piano . . . . ⎭
   Introduction. — Fugue. — Finale.

3. Concert en *ré majeur* (op. 21) pour violon, piano et quatuor à cordes . . . . ERNEST CHAUSSON
   I. *Décidé.* — II. *Sicilienne.* — III. *Grave.* — IV. *Finale.*

Piano Pleyel.

Figure 5.1a Concert series by the Quatuor Ysaÿe at the salon of "Le Libre Esthetique" (1894), Maus, *Trente Années de Lutte pour L'Art*, 174–75

5.1a). The program was meant to feature performances of the *Cinq poèmes de Baudelaire* and an early version of the *Prélude à L'après-midi d'un faune*, but these did not come to pass.[33]

Code was, of course, entirely correct to suggest that the inclusion of Debussy's music at an exhibition of avant-garde painting and decorative art reveals much about the rich aesthetic cross currents occurring in Paris and Brussels in the early 1890s and about Debussy's particular response to them. As shown in figure 5.1b and emphasized by Code, the exhibition included works representing the most significant trends and artists of the period: pointillism (e.g., Paul Signac, Théo van Rysselberghe); Impressionism (e.g., Camille Pissarro, Pierre-Auguste Renoir, Alfred Sisley, and Berthe Morisot); Japonisme (e.g., Paul Gauguin, Henri de Toulouse-Lautrec); Les Nabis (e.g., Maurice Denis, Aristide Maillol, Paul Ranson); Symbolism (e.g., Odilon Redon, Pierre Puvis de Chavannes, James Ensor, Fernand Khnopff, and Jan Toorop); social activists (e.g., Eugène Laermans and Constantin Meunier); and British arts and crafts/aestheticism (e.g., William Morris and Aubrey Beardsley).[34] Code also noted that arabesques featured prominently in the work of these artists, especially that of Maurice Denis, who designed the cover for the first edition of Debussy's *La Damoiselle élue*, a work based on a text by the British Pre-Raphaelite Dante Gabriel Rossetti.[35] And Code rightly drew attention to Denis's vision of a new kind of art based on "expression by means of the harmony of forms and colors, and by means of the material employed," rather than "expression by means of the subject."[36]

EXPOSANTS :

C. R. Ashbee, Jean Baffier, Albert Bartholomé, Aubrey Beardsley, Albert Besnard, Mlle Anna Boch, D. Cameron, François-Rupert Carabin, Eugène Carrière, Guillaume Charlier, Alexandre Charpentier, Jules Chéret, Mlle Camille Claudel, Emile Claus, Arthur Craco, Henry Cros, Dalpayrat et Lesbros, Mlle Louise Danse, William Degouve de Nuncques, Auguste Delaherche, Maurice Denis, Louis-Henri Devillez, Auguste Donnay, Charles Doudelet, Paul Dubois, James Ensor, Fernand Dubois, Georges Frampton A. R. A., Jean Gaspar, Paul Gauguin, Victor Gilsoul, Emile Grasset, L. Welden Hawkins, A. J. Heymans, Henri-Gabriel Ibels, Selwyn Image, Fernand Khnopff, Eugène Laermans, Georges Lemmen, Henri Lerolle, Auguste Levêque, Alexandre Lunois, Aristide Maillol, Elkin Mattews et John Lane, Xavier Mellery, Charles Meunier, Constantin Meunier, Marius Michel, Comte R. de Montesquiou-Fézensac, Mme Berthe Morisot, William Morris, Emile Motte, J. R. Murray, J. P. Niederkorn, Hermann Paul, Camille Pissarro, Georges Pissarro, Lucien Pissarro, Pierre Puvis de Chavannes, Paul Ranson, Odilon Redon, Auguste Renoir, Henri Rivière, Charles Samuel, Georges Sauter, Georges Serrurier, Paul Signac, Alfred Sisley, Charles Storm de s'Gravesande, Max Stremel, Heywood Sumner, Fritz Thaulow, Fernand Thesmar, Jan Toorop, Henri de Toulouse-Lautrec, Edouard Tourteau, Charles Vanderstappen, Théo Van Rysselberghe, Thomas Vinçotte, Guillaume Vogels, Hector Wallaert, Georges Fr. Watts, R. A., Christopher-W. Whall, *le Café-Concert, l'Escarmouche, l'Estampe originale, la Royale.*

CONFÉRENCES :

Henri de Régnier : *le Bosquet de Psyché.*
Carton de Wiart : *Léon Bloy.*
Henry Van de Velde : *L'Art futur.*
Edmond Picard : *Dialégomènes artistiques* (en deux séances).
Papus : *La Femme.*

Figure 5.1b Artists and lecturers featured at the salon of "Le Libre Esthetique" (1894), Maus, *Trente Années de Lutte pour L'Art*, 173

Code's remarks can, however, be amplified in a couple of ways. To begin with, although the list of names given in figure 5.1b demonstrates the rich aesthetic environment that existed in Paris and Brussels in 1894, it doesn't make clear that Debussy knew many of these individuals personally.[37] Besides Denis, the names of Camille Claudel, Paul Gauguin, Odilon Redon, Henri Lerolle, Ernest Chausson, and Henri de Régnier spring to mind. As mentioned in chapter 3, Debussy probably met Claudel through her brother Paul in the early 1890s at Mallarmé's *mardis,* and as noted in chapter 4, he was involved with a fundraiser for Gauguin in February 1891 at Paul Fort's Théâtre d'Art. It is also clear that Debussy and Redon met on numerous occasions in the early 1890s at Bailly's La Librarie de L'Arte Indépendent and at the homes of Mallarmé, Chausson, Jacques-Émile Blanche, and Jean de Tinan.[38] Debussy had even more contact with Henri Lerolle and his brother-in-law Ernest Chausson. A gifted artist and musician, Lerolle provided financial support to Denis, Degas, and Renoir. In his biography of Lerolle, Denis even transcribed three letters from Debussy to Lerolle from the period 1894–95, as well as letters to Lerolle from Pierre Puvis de Chavannes and Edgar Degas.[39] Chausson, who had known Debussy since his return from Rome in 1887, became his "big brother," giving him advice and even money.[40] In March 1894, however, their relationship collapsed when Debussy broke off his engagement to Thérèse Roger and it was discovered that he had been living with his girlfriend Gaby Dupont the whole time.[41] Roger had, in fact, sung *La Damoiselle élue* and two of the *Proses lyriques* ("De fleurs" and "De soir") at the concert in Brussels.[42] Chausson was outraged by Debussy's infidelity and immediately turned his back on him; Lerolle was less draconian and maintained contact with Debussy until 1898–99.[43] A friend of Mallarmé and Louÿs, Henri de Régnier had known Debussy since 1890 or so and served as an intermediary with Maeterlinck when Debussy tried to secure authorization for setting *Pelléas et Mélisande* to music.[44] Around the same time, de Régnier advised Debussy when he was writing his own texts for *Prose Lyriques*.[45] De Régnier regularly sent Debussy copies of his books until his separation from Lily in 1904 and was one the few literary types to attend Debussy's funeral in 1918.[46]

Another way in which Code's observations can be amplified is by widening the scope of the discussion to include literary interpretations of the arabesque; this move is particularly relevant both because Denis had close relations with many Symbolist writers and because de Régnier delivered a lecture about Symbolist literature and art at La Libre Esthétique. In the first case, Gerard Vaughan has noted Denis's close affiliations to authors such as Édouard Dujardin, Stéphane Mallarmé, Adolphe Retté, Auguste Germain, and André Gide and that he was a frequent visitor to literary enclaves such as the Librarie de L'Arte Indépendent, the Café Voltaire, the more theatrically and journalistically Café Gutenberg, and, perhaps most importantly, Mallarmé's *mardis*.[47] Additionally, Vaughan has highlighted Denis's debts to Baudelaire. To cite an obvious case in point, Denis's claim that artistic expression should rely on the harmony of forms and colors clearly recalls Baudelaire's notion of *correspondances*. In "Définition du Néo-Traditionnisme," for example, Denis specifically alludes to Baudelaire's account of the topic in "Richard Wagner et *Tannhäuser* à Paris": "And lighting, and air! The blue arabesques, from the luxuriant background, accompany with an invasive and caressing rhythm, the orange motif, like the seduction of the violins in the opening of Tannhäuser."[48] And Denis was surely inspired by Baudelaire's essay "Salon de 1846" and its discussion of the synesthetic effects of Delacroix's paintings.[49]

In the second case, de Régnier's lecture "Le Bosquet de Psyché," or "Psyche's Arbor," stands out as one of the most evocative accounts of Symbolist aesthetics published in the early 1890s. Delivered at the Cercle Artistique et Littéraire de Bruxelles on February 16, 1894, La Libre Esthétique on February 20, 1894, and the Société libre d'Émulation de Liège on February 21, 1894, the lecture is particularly noteworthy for mentioning a wide array of French and Belgian authors, including Auguste Villiers de l'Isle-Adam, Paul Verlaine, Stéphane Mallarmé, Francis Vielé-Griffin, Maurice Maeterlinck, Émile Verhaeren, Albert Giraud, and Iwan Gilkin.[50] Nevertheless, like so many Symbolists before him, de Régnier's primary source of inspiration was Poe, especially his poem "Ulalume" (1847).[51] Almost rivaling "The Raven" in popularity, "Ulalume" presents a dialogue between a speaker and his soul, which he calls "Psyche," en route to his dead lover's tomb.[52] According to de Régnier, Poe captured the speaker's state of melancholia through his careful use of richly decorated literary arabesques: "They descend into their consciousness and decipher its intimate cryptography and its sophisticated arabesques; they care more about knowing themselves than imagining themselves, so I suppose that for them the walls of the inner recess are decorated above all with portraits and mirrors." De Régnier's evocative descriptions of Poe's verse recall those offered by Baudelaire in his essays "Edgar Allan Poe: Sa Vie et Ses Ouvrages" and "Notes Nouvelles sur Edgar Poe" and remind us that, in his opinion, Poe always endeavored to make every word count: "throughout the whole composition not a single word must be allowed to intrude which is not also an intention and which does not aim, directly or indirectly, at completing a premeditated design."[53]

Notes

1. Theisen, "Early Romantic Poetics of Complex Form," 305 and Schlegel, *Dialogue on Poetry and Literary Aphorisms*, 86.

2. Charles Baudelaire, "Notes Nouvelles sur Edgar Poe," in *Charles Baudelaire: Œuvres Complètes*, vol. II, ed. Claude Pichois, Bibliothèque de la Pléiade (Paris: Gallimard, 1976), 329; Baudelaire, "Further Notes on Edgar Poe," in *The Painter in Modern Life and Other Essays*, ed. and trans. Jonathan Mayne (London: Phaidon, 2001), 103.

3. Claude Debussy, *Correspondance (1872–1918)*, ed. François Lesure and Denis Herlin, annotated by François Lesure, Denis Herlin, and Georges Liébert (Paris: Gallimard, 2005), 167; and Claude Debussy, *Debussy Letters*, ed. François Lesure and Roger Nichols, trans. Roger Nichols (Cambridge, MA: Harvard University Press, 1987), 58.

4. Debussy, *Correspondance*, 941; and Debussy, *Letters*, 166.

5. For the chronology of Debussy's *Quatuor à cordes*, see Denis Herlin, "L'esquisses du quatuor à cordes," *Cahiers Debussy* 14 (1990): 23–54; and Peter Bloom, "Foreword," in Claude Debussy, *Trio for piano, violin and cello, Nocturne et Scherzo for cello and piano, Quatuor à cordes*, ed. Peter Bloom, Œuvres Complètes Série III Musique de Chambre, vol. 1 (Paris: Durand, 2015), XXXI–XLVI. For analyses of the work, see Albert Bertelin, *Traité de composition musicale*, vol. 2 (Paris: Editions de la Schola Cantorum, 1931), 203–13; Léon Vallas, *Claude Debussy: His Life and Works*, trans. Maire and Grace O'Brien (Oxford: Oxford University Press, 1933; repr. New York: Dover, 1973), 90–99; Elliott Carter, "The Three Late Sonatas of Debussy," in *Elliott Carter: Collected Essays and Lectures, 1937–1995*, ed. Jonathan W. Bernard (Rochester, NY: University of Rochester Press, 1997), 127–29; Edward Lockspeiser, *Debussy* (London: Dent, 1963), 164–74; Laurence David Berman, "The Evolution of Tonal Thinking in works of Claude Debussy," PhD diss., Harvard University, 1965, 97–123; Eugene N. Wilson, "Form and Texture in the Chamber Music of Debussy and Ravel," PhD diss., University of Washington, 1968, 93–101; Christian Goubault, *Claude Debussy* (Paris: Champion, 1986), 216–19; Teresa Marie Davidian, "Debussy's Sonata Forms," PhD diss., University of Chicago, 1988; Richard S. Parks, *The Music of Claude Debussy* (New Haven, CT: Yale University Press, 1989), 10–14; Annie K. Yih, "Analysing Debussy: Tonality, Motivic Sets, and the Referential Pitch-Specific Collection," *Music Analysis* 19, no. 2 (2000): 203–29; Jean-Philippe Guye, Philippe Gouttenoire, and Éric Demange, "Le quatuor de Debussy: recherches analytiques et esthétiques," *Analyse Musicale* 37 (2000): 32–60; Michel Fischer, "Le quatuor à cordes en sol mineur de Claude Debussy: de la contraction formelle à la polyvalence de l'idée génératrice," *Musurgia* 8 (2001): 33–68; Matthew Brown, *Debussy's 'Ibéria': Studies in Genesis and Structure* (Oxford: Oxford University Press, 2003), 151–56; Marianne Wheeldon, "Debussy and La Sonata Cyclique," *Journal of Musicology* 22 (2005): 644–79; David J. Code, "Debussy's Quartet in the Brussels Salon of 'La Libre Esthétique,'" *19th-Century Music* 30, no. 3 (2007): 257–87; Michel Strasser, "Grieg, the Société Nationale, and the Origins of Debussy's String Quartet," in *Berlioz and Debussy: Sources, Contexts, and Legacies*, ed. Barbara L. Kelly and Kerry Murphy (Aldershot: Ashgate, 2007), 103–15; Roger Parker, "Debussy, String Quartet in G minor, Op. 10," Gresham College Lecture, January 29, 2008, https://www.gresham.ac.uk/lectures-and-events/debussy-quartet-in-g-minor-op-10; Marianne Wheeldon, "Debussy's String Quartet," in *Intimate Voices: The Twentieth-Century String Quartet*, vol. 1: *Debussy to Villa-Lobos*, ed. Evan Jones, Eastman Studies in Music, vol. 70 (Rochester, NY: University of Rochester Press, 2009), 3–26; François De Médicis, *La Maturation Artistique de Debussy dans son Contexte Historique*, Speculum Musicae XXXVIII (Turnhout: Brepols, 2020), 436–541.

6. See Parker, "Debussy, String Quartet in G minor, Op. 10."

7. Jules Laforgue, "Impressionnisme," in Jules Laforgue, *Œuvres Complètes*, Vol. III, ed. Jean-Louis Debauve, Mireille Donin-Orsini, Daniel Grojnowski, and Pierre Olivier Walzer, in collaboration with Maryke de Courten and Michèle Hannoosh (Lausanne: L'Age d'Homme, 2000), 329–36; Laforgue, "Impressionism," in Linda Nochlin, *Impressionism and Post- Impressionism 1874–1904*, Sources & Documents in the History of Art Series

(Englewood Cliffs, NJ: Prentice-Hall, 1966), 14–20; Théodor de Wyzéwa, "La Musique descriptive," *La Revue Wagnérienne* 1, no. 3 (April 8, 1885): 74–77; Théodor de Wyzéwa, "Descriptive Music," in *Music in European Thought 1851–1912*, ed. Bojan Bujić, Cambridge Readings in the Literature of Music (Cambridge: Cambridge University Press, 1988), 247–50. For important insights about Debussy and Impressionism, see Richard Langham Smith, "Debussy's Impressionism Interrogated," in *Debussy in Context*, ed. Simon Trezise (Cambridge: Cambridge University Press, 2024), 59–68.

8. Laforgue, "Impressionnisme," in *Œuvres Complètes*, 331; Laforgue, "Impressionism," in *Art in Theory 1815–1900*, 938.

9. Code, "Debussy's Quartet," 283–87.

10. Gerald Abraham, "Preface," in *Grieg: A Symposium* (Norman: University of Oklahoma Press, 1950), 8 [7–9].

11. Carter, "Three Late Sonatas," 127. Wheeldon also focuses on the influence of Franck; see Wheeldon, "Debussy and La Sonata Cyclique."

12. Carter, "Three Late Sonatas," 127.

13. Parker, "Debussy, String Quartet in G minor, Op. 10," Gresham College Lecture, January 29, 2008.

14. Paul Dukas, "Debussy's Quartet (May, 1894)," in Claude Debussy, *Prelude to "The Afternoon of a Faun,"* ed. William Austin, Norton Critical Score (New York: Norton, 1970), 153.

15. Maurice Kufferath, *Guide Musical*, March 4, 1894, reprinted in Michel Stockhem, *Eugène Ysaÿe et la Musique de Chambre* (Liège: Pierre Mardaga, 1990), 116.

16. Debussy, *Correspondance*, 192; Debussy, *Letters*, 65.

17. Code, "Debussy's Quartet," 268–81.

18. Bertelin presents a similar list of themes in his *Traité de composition musicale*, 2:206.

19. For the connections between sequences and scales, see Matthew Brown, *Explaining Tonality: Schenkerian Theory and Beyond* (Rochester, NY: University of Rochester Press, 2005), 99–139.

20. Berman, "Evolution of Tonal Thinking," 104–5. Whereas Bertelin and Davidian also interpret the passage in E♭ major, Parks analyzes it in G; see Parks, *Music of Claude Debussy*, 10–14.

21. See Lockspeiser, *Debussy*, 166; Goubault, *Claude Debussy*, 217.

22. Code, "Debussy's Quartet," 270–75.

23. Code, "Debussy's Quartet," 278. Bertelin and Davidian also suggest that the development section begins with the return of the motto in m. 61.

24. To quote Griffiths, "The gestures towards orthodox sonata form—most notably the decisive recapitulation of the first theme—come near impotence, standing as conventional signposts in music which is taking routes of a different kind." Paul Griffiths, *The String Quartet* (New York: Thames and Hudson, 1983), 146.

25. De Médicis, *La Maturation Artistique*, 442.

26. Bertelin, *Traité de composition musicale*, 2:206. Davidian offers a similar interpretation, "Debussy's Sonata Forms," mm. 120–28.

27. Carter, "Three Late Sonatas," 127. The idea of using the first theme as closing material is certainly not without precedent; see the first movement of Beethoven's Piano Sonata in E major, Op. 14, no. 1.

28. Code, "Debussy's Quartet," 275.

29. Edward T. Cone, *Musical Form and Musical Performance* (New York: Norton, 1968), 77. For a critique of Cone, see James Hepokoski, "Beyond the Sonata Principle," *Journal of the American Musicological Society* 55, no. 1 (2002): 92–95. It is worth noting that instead of citing Cone directly, Hepokoski mainly relies on incomplete glosses by Ethan Haimo and James Webster. None of these authors address the main shortcoming with Hepokoski's position—namely, that it is one thing to label the various themes and points of articulation in a sonata form movement and quite another to explain why the different themes belong together in a single coherent movement. Hepokoski's model does not explain why a particular second or closing theme belongs in the same exposition as a given first theme. As a result, it does not explain why such a relationship might be clarified when the second or closing themes return transposed in the recapitulation.

30. Example 5.11 is adapted from Bertelin, *Traité de composition musicale*, 2:203–5.

31. Baudelaire, "Notes Nouvelles sur Edgar Poe," 329; Baudelaire, "Further Notes on Edgar Poe," 103.

32. Code, "Debussy's Quartet," 258.

33. The latter is mentioned in announcements for the Brussels concert in several newspapers; see Vallas, *Claude Debussy*, 97. See also François Lesure, *Claude Debussy* (Paris: Klincksieck, 1994), 146–47; François Lesure, *Claude*

Debussy: A Critical Biography, ed. and trans. Marie Rolf, Eastman Studies in Music 159 (Rochester, NY: University of Rochester Press, 2019), 120–21.

34. Code, "Debussy's Quartet," 258–60.

35. Code, "Debussy's Quartet," 283–87.

36. Maurice Denis, "Ils ont préféré dans leurs oeuvres l'expression par le décor, par l'harmonie des formes et des couleurs, par la matière employée, à l'expression par le sujet." From "Préface de la IXe Exposition des Peintres Impressionistes et Symbolistes," in Maurice Denis, *Théories, 1890–1910: Du Symbolisme et de Gauguin vers un Nouvel Ordre Classique*, 3rd ed. (Paris: Bibliothèque de L'Occident, 1913), 27. See also Code, "Debussy's Quartet," 283–84.

37. Madeleine Octave Maus, *Trente Années de Lutte pour L'Art: Les XX et La Libre Esthétique, 1884–1914*, rev. ed. (Brussels: Éditions Lebeer Hossmann, 1980), 173 and 174–75.

38. Debussy, *Correspondance*, 2280.

39. Denis, *Henry Lerolle et Ses Amis* (Paris: Duranton, 1932), 29–33 and 33–34. The second letter from Debussy dates from June 20, 1895, not 1894.

40. Lesure, *Claude Debussy*, 94; François Lesure, *Claude Debussy: A Critical Biography*, Eastman Studies in Music 159, ed. and trans. Marie Rolf (Rochester, NY: University of Rochester Press, 2019), 74. See also Roger Nichols, *Debussy Remembered* (London: Faber, 1992), 43.

41. See Lesure, *Claude Debussy*, 147–53; Lesure, *Claude Debussy: A Critical Biography*, Eastman Studies in Music 159, ed. and trans. Marie Rolf (Rochester, NY: University of Rochester Press, 2019), 121–25.

42. See Lesure, *Claude Debussy*, 147; Lesure, *Claude Debussy: A Critical Biography*, 121.

43. Debussy, *Correspondance*, 2209.

44. See Lesure, *Claude Debussy*, 117; Lesure, *Claude Debussy: A Critical Biography*, 91. Nichols, *Debussy Remembered*, 64.

45. Nichols, *Debussy Remembered*, 64.

46. Debussy, *Correspondance*, 2280.

47. Gerard Vaughan, "Maurice Denis and the Sense of Music," *Oxford Art Journal* 7, no. 1 Correspondences (1984): 38–48.

48. Denis, "Définition du Néo-Traditionnisme," in *Théories, 1890–1910*, 13.

49. Vaughan, "Maurice Denis," 39.

50. See Henri de Régnier, *Le Bosquet de Psyché* (Brussels: Paul Lacomplez, 1894).

51. Mallarmé's translation apparently dates from 1862. See Jean-Louis Curtis, "Préface," in Edgar Allan Poe, *Les Poèmes d'Edgar Poe. Traduction de Stéphane Mallarmé*, ed. Jean-Louis Curtis (Paris: Gallimard, 1982), 25. The translation appears on pages 53–56.

52. The poem apparently replicates the plot of Elizabeth Oakes Smith's "The Summons Answered," in which a reveler arrives unwittingly at his wife's tomb. See Eliza Richards, "'The Poetess' and Poe's Performance of the Feminine," in *Critical Insights: The Poetry of Edgar Allan Poe*, ed. Steven Frye (Pasadena, CA: Salem, 2011), 271.

53. Baudelaire, "Notes Nouvelles sur Edgar Poe," in *Œuvres Complètes*, II:329; Baudelaire, "Further Notes on Edgar Poe," 103.

6

La Mer and the Case of the Missing Fanfares

AMONG THE MOST important conclusions to be drawn from chapter 5 is that, for Debussy and other Symbolists, details mattered. Adamant that ornamentation is essential to art, they presumed that it should always be aesthetically motivated and serve some larger purpose within the work as a whole. Baudelaire underscored this idea by praising Poe's writing for the ways in which it avoided elements that "do not aim directly or indirectly, at completing a premeditated design."[1] Debussy likewise had a visceral hatred for "superfluous development, or useless ornament" and urged composers to "find the perfect expression for an idea and add only as much decoration as is absolutely necessary."[2] It turns out that Schenker was of the same mind; he maintained that there should be an organic relationship between a work's local details and its global form. This prompted him to develop the concept of concealed repetitions, noting that, by enlarging distinctive voice-leading patterns, they open the door to "organic connections" between distant points in a piece.[3]

And yet, such claims raise a number of interesting questions. If details do indeed matter and contribute in specific ways to a work's overall design, then what happens if composers decide to rewrite a particular passage or remove particular details? Do such changes mean that the particular details in the original did not matter after all or that the work's premeditated design was at best a rough approximation? In the case of so-called cyclic compositions, does that design apply to individual movements or to the entire work as a single unified whole?

Although these questions might seem overly abstract, they nonetheless have concrete ramifications for editors, performers, and analysts: editors must decide which version of the score to take as their primary source; performers must decide which version of the score to play and record; and analysts must decide which version of the score to use in their interpretations. These decisions may not be easy to make and may force the editor, the performer, and the analyst to reconsider their underlying philological goals and artistic values. In Debussy's case, they may make us rethink whether his claims about rejecting "superfluous development, or useless ornament" were actually achievable and not simply empty rhetoric.

This chapter considers one famous and controversial detail: a succession of short brass fanfares from "Dialogue du vent et de la mer," the third movement of *La Mer*. The fanfares are rightly famous because they appear in some editions and recordings but not in others, prompting pointed responses on both sides. Marie Rolf, for example, is in favor of removing them on the grounds that they are unrelated to "other thematic material in the movement." Meanwhile, Simon Trezise has suggested that their removal is tantamount to aesthetic vandalism—"we might cite the Mona Lisa without her smile, Notre Dame minus its flying buttresses, Beethoven's Ninth without a bass soloist, and numerous other analogies."[4]

This chapter reconsiders the case of the missing fanfares. As regards their removal, the chapter begins by suggesting that the fanfares first appeared quite late in the genesis of *La Mer* and were removed incrementally after the score was published. The middle portion of the chapter then considers the editorial and analytical implications of Debussy's indecision. On the one hand, it underscores the difference between editions that aim to preserve a composer's final version and those that reconstruct a composer's original vision of the piece. This section pits the editors of the Œuvres Complètes de Claude Debussy, who elect to endorse *Die Fassung der letzter Hand*, against

Example 6.1 Brass fanfares in mm. 237–44 of "Dialogue du vent et de la mer" (*La Mer*, III)

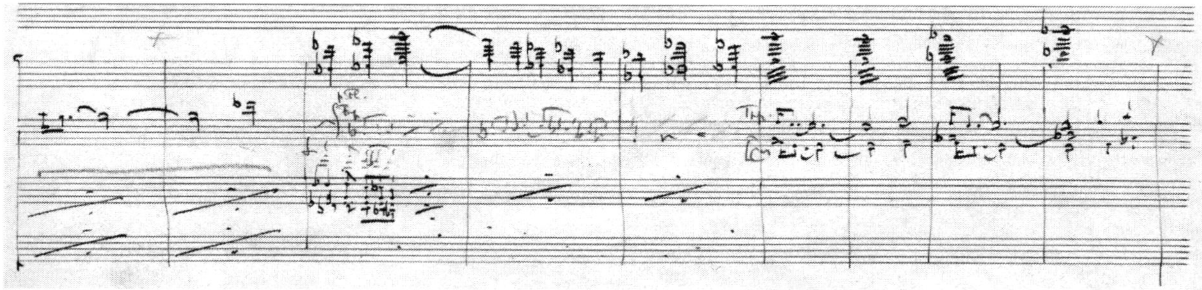

Example 6.1a Debussy, short-score draft (US: R, Sibley Music Library), fol. 19

Example 6.1b Debussy, short-score draft (US: R, Sibley Music Library), fol. 20

Example 6.1c Debussy, transcription for piano, four-hand (Paris: Durand, 1905), mm. 237–44

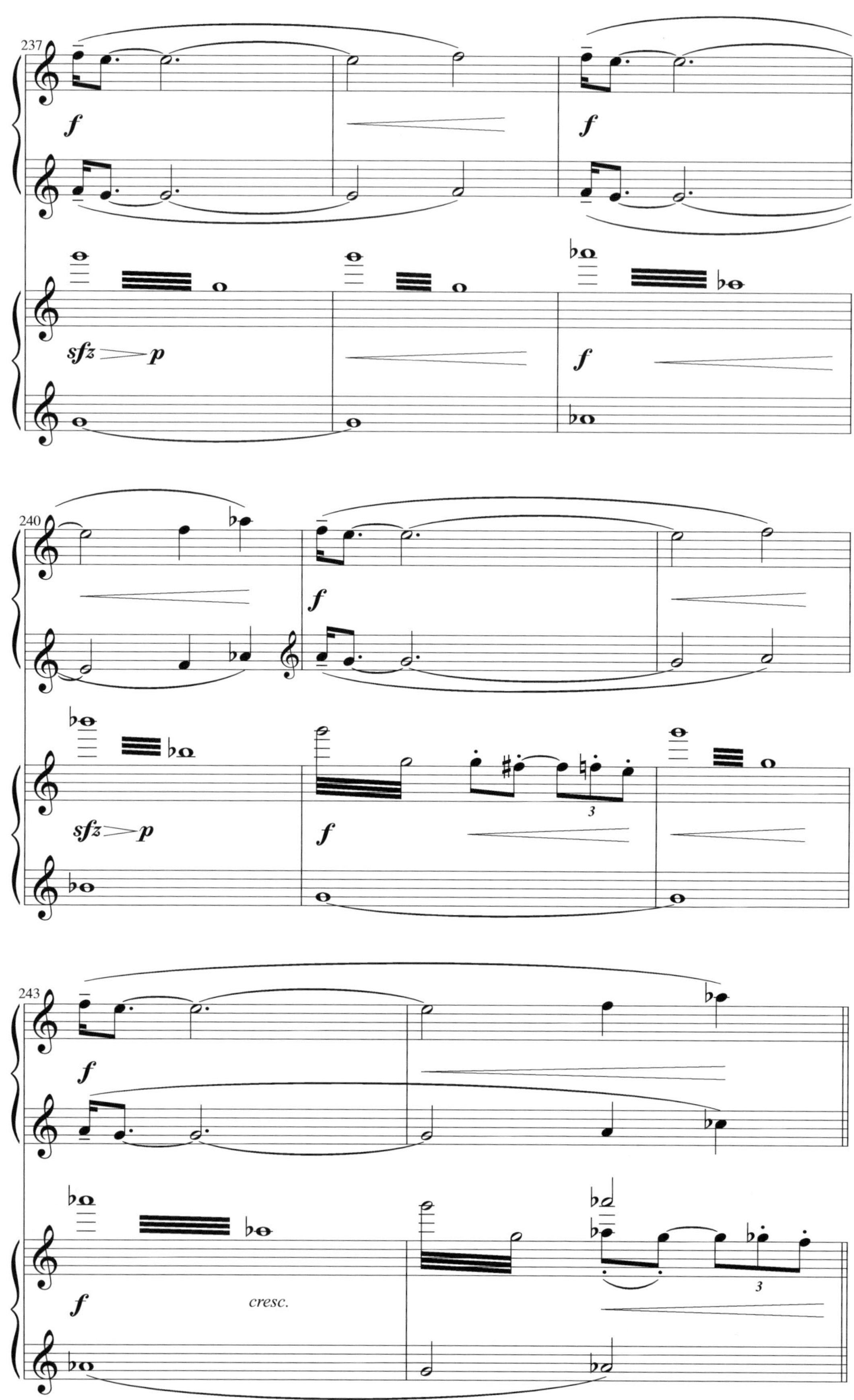

Example 6.1d Caplet, transcription for two pianos (Paris: Durand, 1909)

164

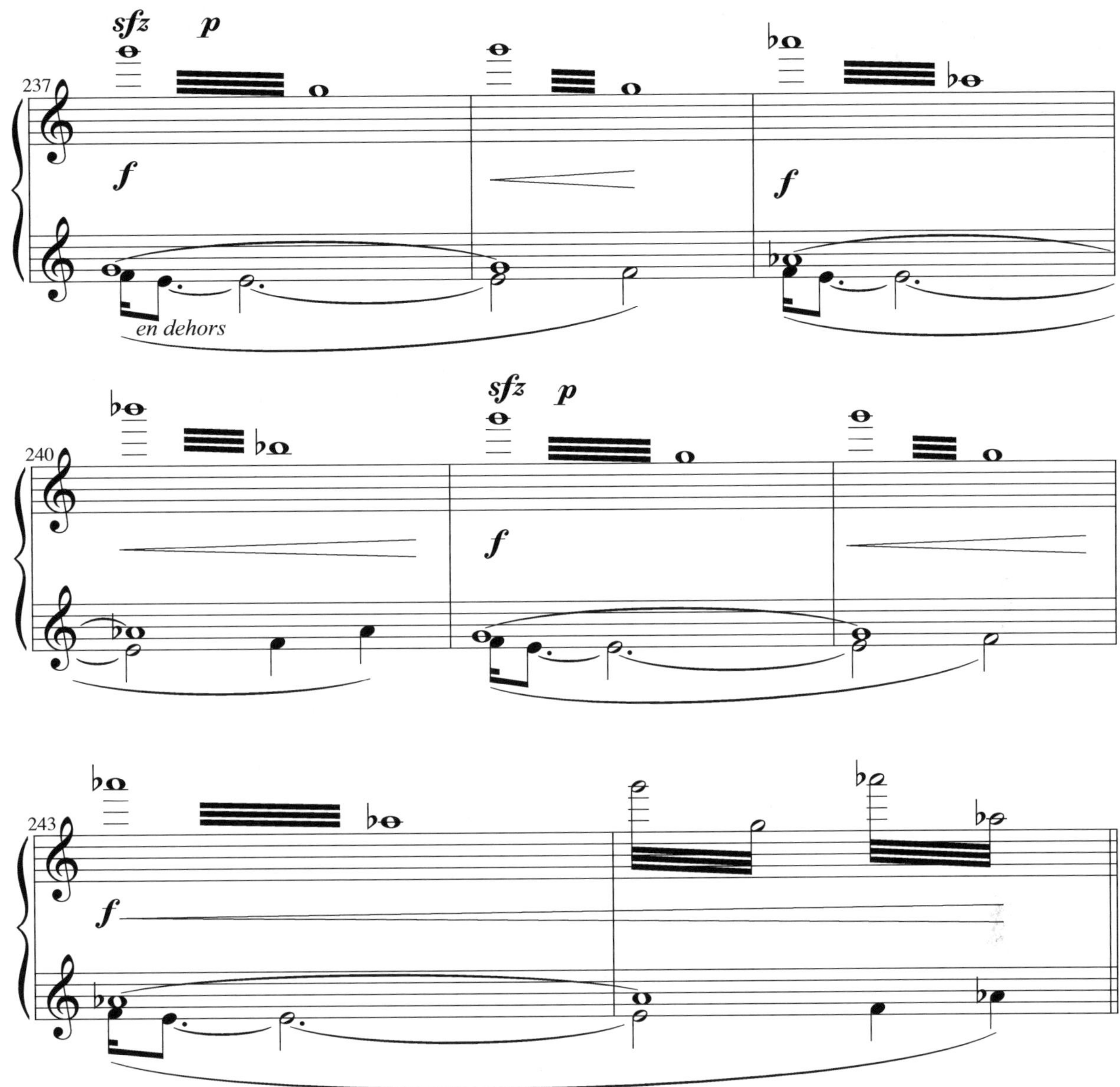

Example 6.1e Debussy, second edition (Paris: Durand, 1909)

Heinrich Schenker, who was an early advocate of so-called Urtext editions. The chapter ends by considering the analytical significance of the fanfares to the design of "Dialogue du vent et de la mer" as well as that of *La Mer* as a whole. It concludes that the fanfares should not be dismissed as "superfluous development, or useless ornament." Details do indeed matter.

To understand why the case of the missing fanfares has become so controversial, it is helpful to start by sketching their role in the composition history of "Dialogue du vent et de la mer." For convenience, the basic facts are given in example 6.1. Example 6.1a begins by showing that the fanfares are missing from Debussy's short-score draft (US: R, Sibley Music Library). They are, however, present in his autograph (F-Pn MS 967), Durand's first edition of the score (Paris: Durand, 1905), and, as shown in example 6.1b, the version for piano four-hands (Paris: Durand, 1905), where they appear four times in counterpoint to the iambic pattern F–E–F, F–E–F–A♭ (mm. 237–38, 239–40, 241–42, and 244). Starting in 1908, however, Debussy apparently had a change of heart: as shown in example 6.1c, he also urged André Caplet to partially remove them from his two-piano transcription (Paris: Durand, 1909).[5] Finally, example 6.1d demonstrates how the two residual statements in Caplet's transcription were completely expunged from Durand's second edition (Paris: Durand, 1909). Although no one knows for sure why Debussy dumped the fanfares altogether, it is widely supposed that they were cut because he was accused of plagiarizing them from Puccini's *Manon Lescaut*. This charge was apparently made after Debussy conducted *La Mer* in Rome and was reported to Ernest Ansermet and others by Arturo Toscanini.[6]

Given that Durand published several versions of *La Mer*, some with the fanfares and some without, it should come as no surprise that opinions have differed widely about how to perform "Dialogue du vent et de la mer." Some conductors, notably Pierre Monteux, Ernest Ansermet, Charles Münch, Herbert von Karajan, Dimitri Mitropoulos, and Charles Dutoit, have included the fanfares, thereby favoring Debussy's first edition of the score. Others, however, such as Piero Coppola, Désiré-Émile Inghelbrecht, Guido Cantelli, Leonard Bernstein, and Pierre Boulez, have excluded them, thereby promoting Debussy's later view of the piece.[7] Editors have been equally divided. Douglas Woodfull-Harris, for instance, has chosen to keep the fanfares, albeit notating them in small notes, whereas Max Pommer, Marie Rolf, and Peter Jost have removed them entirely.[8] In defending his decision, Woodfull-Harris brushes aside the charge of plagiarism by pointing out that Debussy performed *La Mer* in Rome after the fanfares had been excised, that Ansermet regarded their removal as a regrettable "misunderstanding," and that most early recordings include all of them, with the most notable exception being the one by Toscanini.[9] Whatever the merits of this decision, it is ultimately based on hearsay rather than on concrete philological evidence.

From an editorial perspective, the case of the fanfares is noteworthy because it reminds us that musical compositions generally pass through several distinct phases in their progress from a composer's desk to the concert hall. The first "private" phase encompasses all the preliminary steps that composers take in trying to come up with a complete version of their score. In the case of *La Mer*, the initial steps are preserved in Debussy's sketches, his drafts, and his final version in the autograph manuscript.[10] The second "public" phase encompasses all the refinements made to score after the work has been handed off to the publisher. These revisions might be made by the original composer or someone else involved in the publication process. Of course, the distinction between "private" and "public" is by no means hard and fast. Sometimes composers seek the advice of others while they are still putting together their scores: Debussy is known, for example, to have played nascent versions of his compositions for close friends. And sometimes composers change their minds while a work is in the process of publication; Debussy is also known to have worked with Caplet and Durand's editorial staff when preparing the first edition. Such modifications generally divide into two main types: those that correct errors that were overlooked when the original edition was prepared and proofread and those that rework passages that the composer subsequently deemed inadequate for one reason or another.[11]

In the case of *La Mer*, the private phase seems to have lasted about two years: Debussy originally conceived the piece in the summer of 1903 and, after much sketching and drafting, completed it on March 5, 1905, copying this date on the final page of his autograph.[12] *La Mer* then entered its public phase when the first edition was published by Durand and premiered by Camille Chevillard and the Orchestre Lamoureux on October 15, 1905. The work soon reached larger audiences: Karl Muck conducted it in Boston and New York in March 1907. According to Douglas Woodfull-Harris, the fanfares were definitely performed at the premiere and most likely in Boston and New York as well.[13] Sometime later, Debussy started to revise his score: among other things, he partially removed the fanfares from the two-piano version as well as from the scores used at the performances in Paris and London in 1908.[14] Further refinements occurred over the next years, prompting Durand to issue a second edition in 1909. This edition completely removes any trace of the fanfares and clearly falls under the rubric of a reworking rather than an error.[15] But that is not all: Debussy continued to make adjustments long after Durand had published the second edition.

Given Debussy's incessant tinkering, editors of *La Mer* face an interesting dilemma: do they reconstruct Debussy's final vision of the piece, or do they reconstruct the version he originally shared with Durand and the public in 1905? Many editors pick the first option and, as a result, favor corrected copies of the second edition (1909) that omit the four fanfares from "Dialogue du vent et de la mer." Marie Rolf's edition of *La Mer* for the Œuvres Complètes de Claude Debussy is just such a score.[16] Although there is nothing wrong with Rolf's decision to endorse *Die Fassung der letzter Hand*, it does raise some interesting technical issues. Since Rolf presents *La Mer* as Debussy conceived of it after 1909 and not as he imagined it in 1905, the reader is left to ponder whether the changes improve the original score or whether they represent a new vision of the music. This issue is tricky because Rolf downplays the distinction between errors and reworkings in her notes. More perplexing still, however, Rolf had no way of knowing for sure whether she actually had access to Debussy's last version of *La Mer*. Indeed, as David Grayson rightly notes, "One of an editor's greatest fears is that a new primary source will surface after the edition has gone to press."[17] Alas, this is precisely what happened; Woodfull-Harris recently unearthed a previously unknown score that Debussy gave to his wife, Emma, in 1913 with the inscription "*de ma petite mienne / Ton Claude Debussy / Avril 1913.*" This copy, which was unknown to Rolf, contains many annotations by Debussy.[18] And, of course, it is quite possible that other scores might yet see the light of day.

At the other extreme, some editors are interested in re-creating the version that the composer originally made public; they generally like to base their editions on the composer's own autographs. Heinrich Schenker was just such an editor. Regarded as the "forefather of the Wiener Urtext Edition," he recommended that editors re-create the composer's original intentions for a work and that they confine their emendations to correcting blatant errors and obvious inconsistencies.[19] He championed such views on the grounds that composers' manuscripts often contain important insights about "the principles of art, the creation of musical coherence, the individual style of notation, etc." Seen from Schenker's perspective, any Urtext edition of *La Mer* should properly include the brass fanfares since they all appear in F-Pn MS 967.[20] That being said, Schenker's approach raises issues of its own. What does the editor do if the autograph is lost, destroyed, or simply unavailable? What happens if the document is inaccurate or illegible? And what if it is hard to distinguish between errors and variants? In situations where the autograph is available, free of errors, and easy to decipher, it makes more sense to publish a facsimile rather than re-create the entire document: indeed, the process of typesetting the music is likely to introduce new errors into the text. This was precisely the solution Schenker adopted in his edition of Beethoven's Piano Sonata Op. 27 no. 2: he elected to publish a color facsimile of the original autograph with extensive commentary.[21] But facsimile editions may be prohibitively expensive to produce, especially for stage works where set and costume designs are also part of the mix. Given the complexities of these issues, it remains an open question whether preparing definitive scores of a work like *La Mer* is ultimately "an unobtainable ideal."[22]

Besides posing difficulties for the editor, the case of the missing fanfares raises interesting issues for the analyst.[23] These issues are particularly interesting because they remind us that the task of editing a score is interrelated with that of understanding the work's structure; how editors understand the structure of a piece depends on what texts they decide to use; how editors pick their source texts depends on how they understand the work's structure. Such understanding is particularly important in trying to determine whether an anomalous reading should be treated as an error or a reworking. Such determinations clearly change from one composer to the next: successions of parallel perfect 8^{ves} and 5^{ths} would be considered erroneous in a work by Palestrina but not necessarily in one by Debussy. Although no one has suggested that Debussy made an error when he originally included the fanfares in "Dialogue du vent et de la mer," the controversial nature of their removal seems to cry out for some sort of analytical defense. If editors include the fanfares, thereby overriding Debussy's decision to cut them from the second edition, then they have an obligation to explain why the score sounds better with them than without them. If, however, editors exclude the fanfares, thereby overriding Debussy's original decision to include them in his autograph, then they have an obligation to explain why Debussy ultimately found them superfluous.

As it turns out, current editions of *La Mer* make little or no effort to offer such a defense. Jost, for example, says nothing whatsoever about the impact of removing the fanfares from his edition. Rolf, meanwhile, decided to cut them because she found a "disparity between [the fanfares] and other thematic material in the movement."[24] To muddy the waters, she notes that the material is absent from Debussy's short-score draft (US: R, Sibley Music Library), a fact that is ultimately irrelevant to the task of re-creating Debussy's final version of the score. And, although Woodfull-Harris includes the fanfares because Ansermet considered them "essential to the structure of the movement and necessary as a transition to the final section of the work," he doesn't spell out what Ansermet actually had in mind.[25] Of the four editions mentioned above, the only one that includes any analytical commentary is the one prepared by Pommer; unfortunately, however, this commentary glosses over the matter of the fanfares.[26]

This lack of analytical support stands in stark contrast to the elaborate analytical remarks that Schenker provided in his so-called annotated editions (or *Erläuterungsausgaben*).[27] Indeed, these editions brim with instructions on how to perform the piece as well as with analytical insights about how to interpret the work's musical structure. It is no coincidence, for example, that Schenker used his Urtext edition of Beethoven's Piano Sonata Op. 101 (1920) as a pretext for introducing the concept of an Urlinie in his commentary and including some of his earliest experiments in graphic analysis.[28] His reasons for doing so were clear: for him, Urtexte reconstruct what the composer actually wrote, whereas Ursätze explain the thought processes guiding those actions.[29] Schenker even believed that a composer's original orthography can shed light on these issues: when commenting on the autograph of Beethoven's Piano Sonata Op. 109, he suggested that Beethoven stemmed the right-hand part downward in mm. 70–71 in order to clarify that it actually articulates a middle voice.[30]

As regards *La Mer*, the need to support editorial decisions with analytical evidence hasn't gone unnoticed. In his review of Rolf's edition, Trezise rejects her claim about the irrelevancy of the fanfares: "the reverse is true, for the fanfares are a rhythmically distilled version of a descending chromatic figure heard repeatedly from m. 219 and adumbrated many times before."[31] It is also clear that they set up the final statements of the movement's main theme in mm. 245–57. But do Trezise's observations put the matter to rest? Given that *La Mer* is one of Debussy's most intricate experiments in cyclic compositions, it seems likely that there is more to say about the significance of the fanfares within the context of "Dialogue du vent et de la mer" and within *La Mer* as a whole. To that end, let us take a close look at the formal structure of the entire movement, focusing special attention on the relationship between the main theme and the fanfares and, above all, the descending chromatic motive mentioned by Trezise.

When thinking about the formal structure of "Dialogue du vent et de la mer," it is important to remember that the movement recycles three prominent gestures from the first movement, "De l'aube à midi sur la mer." These gestures, which are shown in example 6.2, include a short iambic figure (see ex. 6.2a–6.2b), a "Melancholy call" (see ex. 6.2c–6.2d), and a stately chorale (see ex. 6.2e–6.2g).[32] These three gestures are interwoven with a new arabesque theme (see ex. 6.3a) whose prominent descending half step A♮–G♯ recalls the final cadence of *Pelléas et Mélisande* (ex.

Example 6.2 Cyclic gestures in *La Mer* iambic figure

Example 6.2a "De l'aube à midi sur la mer," mm. 6–9

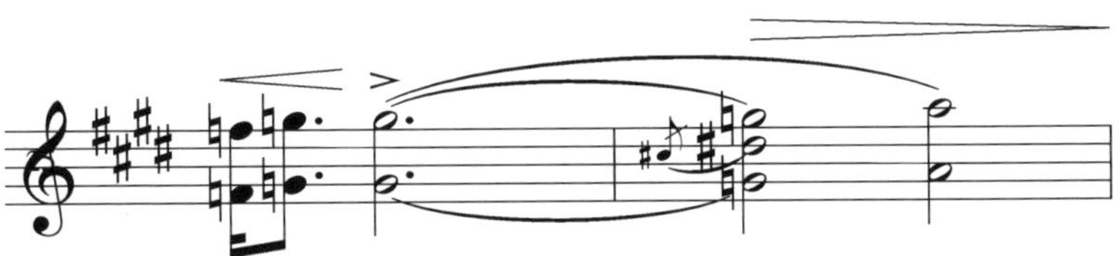

Example 6.2b "Dialogue du vent et de la mer," mm. 25–26 "Melancholy call"

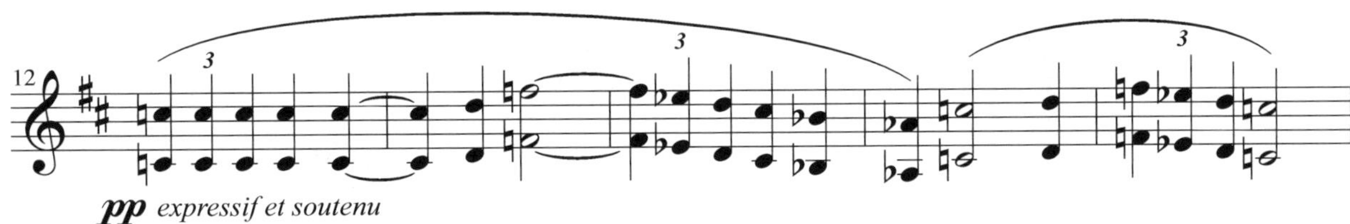

Example 6.2c "De l'aube à midi sur la mer," mm. 12–16

Example 6.2d "Dialogue du vent et de la mer," mm. 31–35 chorale

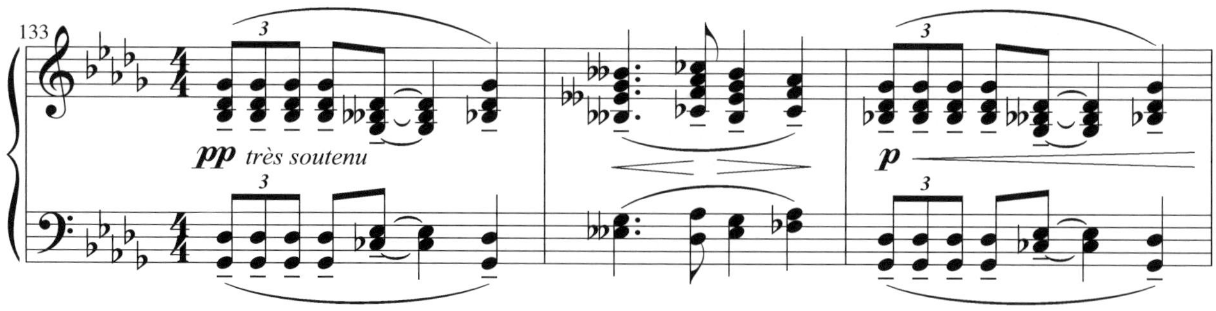

Example 6.2e "De l'aube à midi sur la mer," mm. 133–36

Example 6.2f "Dialogue du vent et de la mer," mm. 139–42

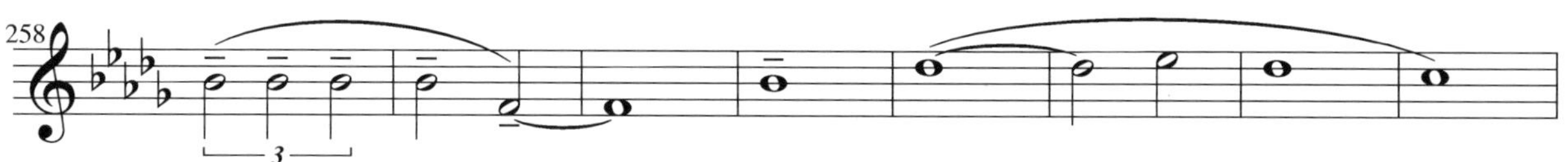

Example 6.2g "Dialogue du vent et de la mer," mm. 258–65

6.3b).[33] Table 6.1 then shows how these four gestures are arranged to create a sort of rondo form. According to this scheme, the iambic pattern and soaring theme from "De l'aube à midi sur la mer" appear in the introduction, episodes 1 and 2, and coda with the chorale entering in episodes 1 and 2 and just before the coda; whereas the arabesque theme dominates refrains 1, 2, and 3.[34] Table 6.1 also plots the basic tonal plan of the movement. It suggests that the introduction, episode 1, and episode 2 are tonally unstable and often feature prominent whole-tone harmonies,

Table 6.1. Formal divisions of "Dialogue du vent et de la mer"

Mm. 1–55	Introduction	Cyclic material	Whole tone
Mm. 56–94	Refrain 1	Arabesque theme	C# minor
Mm. 94–156	Episode 1	Cyclic material	Whole tone
Mm. 157–210	Refrain 2	Arabesque theme	Db major
Mm. 211–44	Episode 2	Cyclic material	Whole tone
Mm. 245–57	Refrain 3	Arabesque theme	C# minor/Db major
Mm. 258–69	Interpolation	Chorale	VI of Db major
Mm. 270–92	Coda	Cyclic material	Db major

Example 6.3 Thematic connections between "Dialogue du vent et de la mer" and *Pelléas et Mélisande*

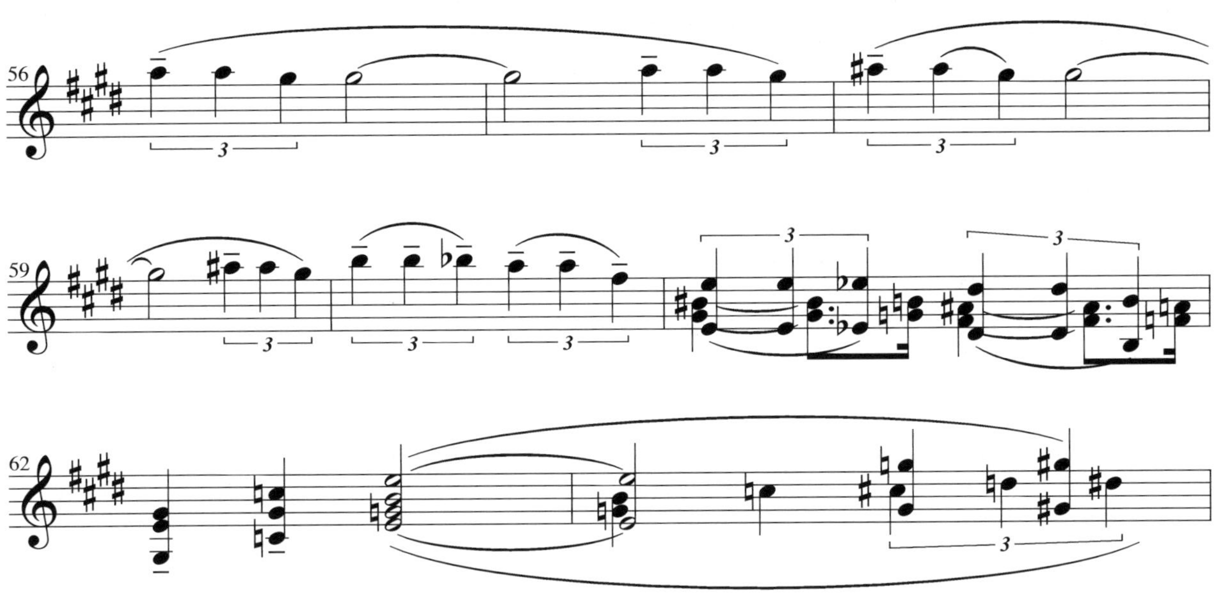

Example 6.3a New arabesque theme in "Dialogue du vent et de la mer," mm. 56–63

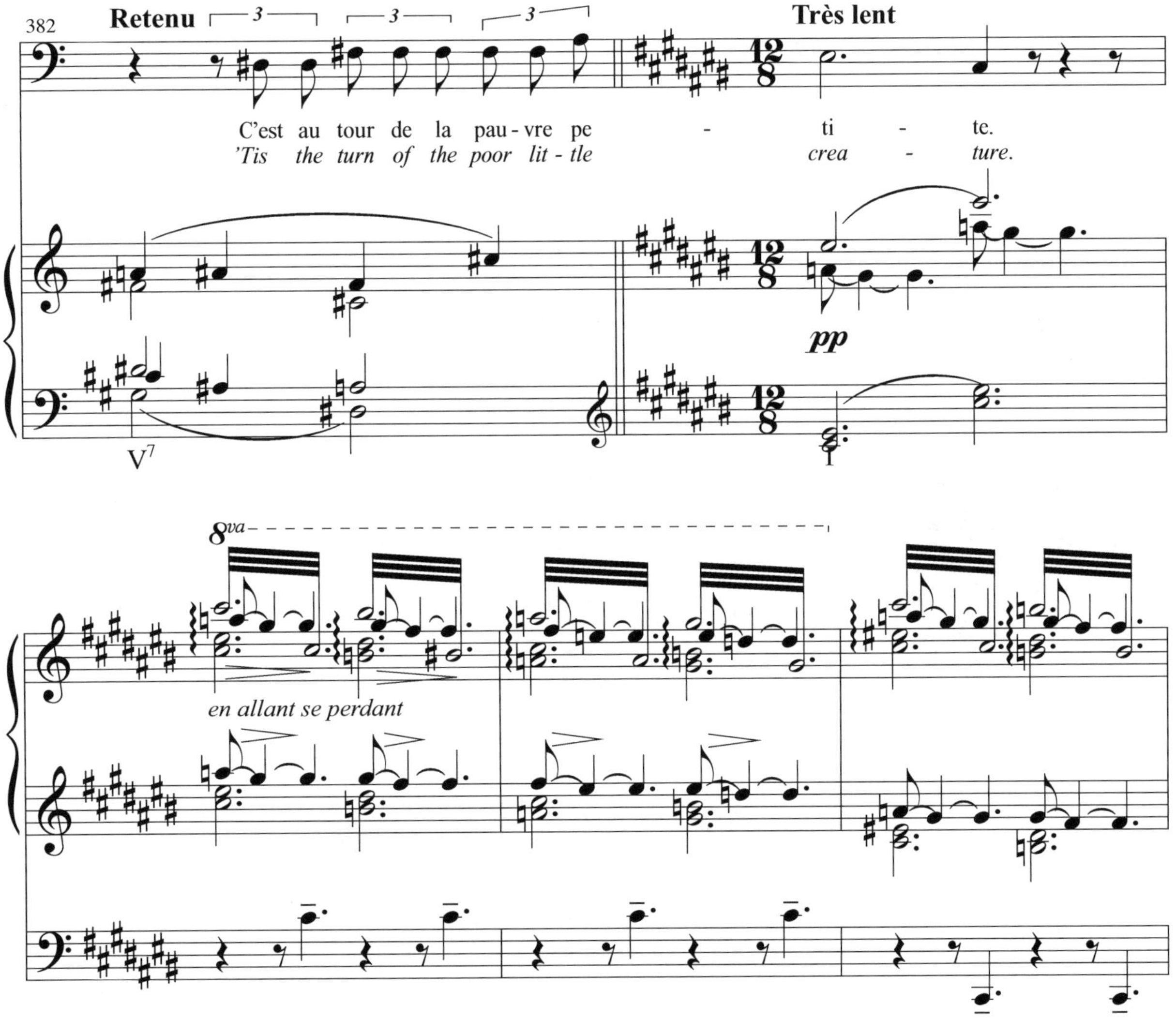

Example 6.3b Final cadence in *Pelléas et Mélisande*, act 5, mm. 382–86

Example 6.4a Refrain 1, mm. 56–61 and 65–70

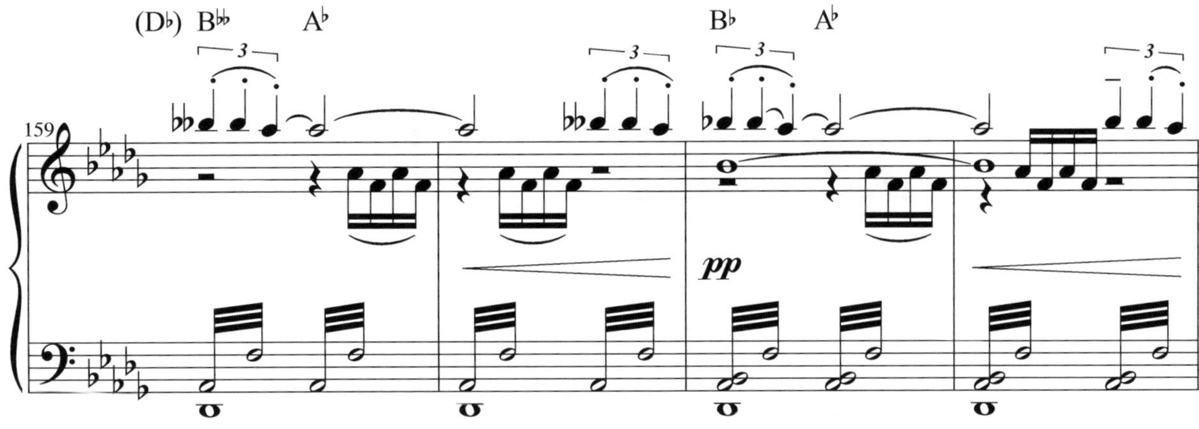

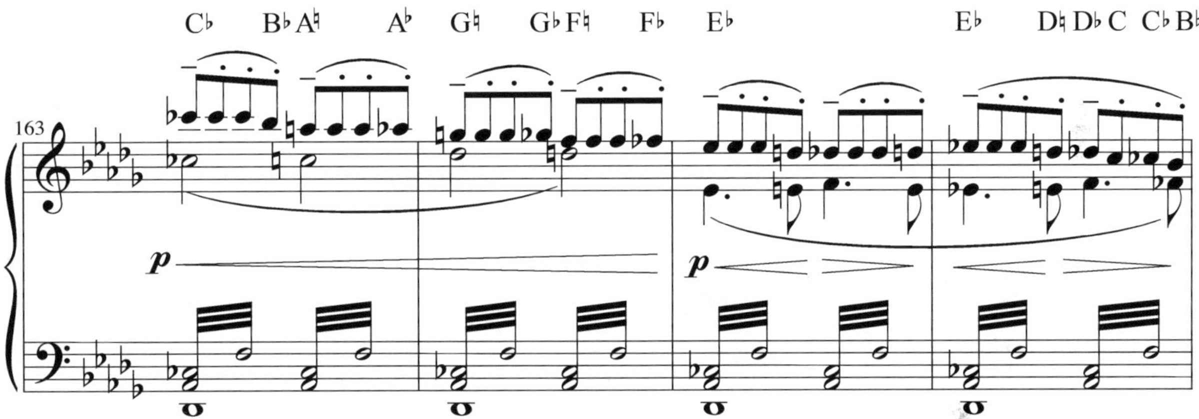

Example 6.4b Refrain 2, mm. 159–66

whereas the refrains are tonally stable and articulate the primary keys of C♯ minor/D♭ major. It is worth noting, however, that the plan given in table 6.1 treats the entry of the chorale near the end as an interpolation, a claim will be explained in detail later in this chapter.

Since the arabesque theme plays such an important role in refrains 1, 2, and 3, example 6.4 charts their main appearances. In the case of refrain 1, the arabesque theme appears twice in C♯ minor, in mm. 56 and 65 (ex. 6.4a). Both begin by decorating the primary tone G♯, first with a upper neighbor tone A♮ (mm. 56–57 and mm. 65–66) and then by its chromatic variant A♯ (mm. 58–59 and mm. 67–68). The melody then leaps up from G♯ to B♮, before spiraling down chromatically down through B♭, A♮, an implied G♯, F♯ to E♯ (mm. 61 and 70). The bass line is equally chromatic. At the surface, it includes a four-note figure C♯–D♮–D♯/E♭–E– in the lower strings. This figure recalls a six-note ostinato pattern F♯–G♮–G♯–A–D–A in the cellos and basses at the start of the introduction. On a larger scale, however, the bass line projects a stepwise chromatic scale that ascends from C♯ in m. 59/68 through D♮, D♯, E, E♯, F♯, G♯, A♯, B, and B♯ to C♯ in m. 61/70. Whereas both statements of the arabesque theme begin in the same way, they diverge near the end. The first statement continues to descend by step, shifting E♯ in m. 61 through E, D♯,

Example 6.4c Refrain 2, mm. 195–202

Example 6.4d Refrain 3, mm. 245–50

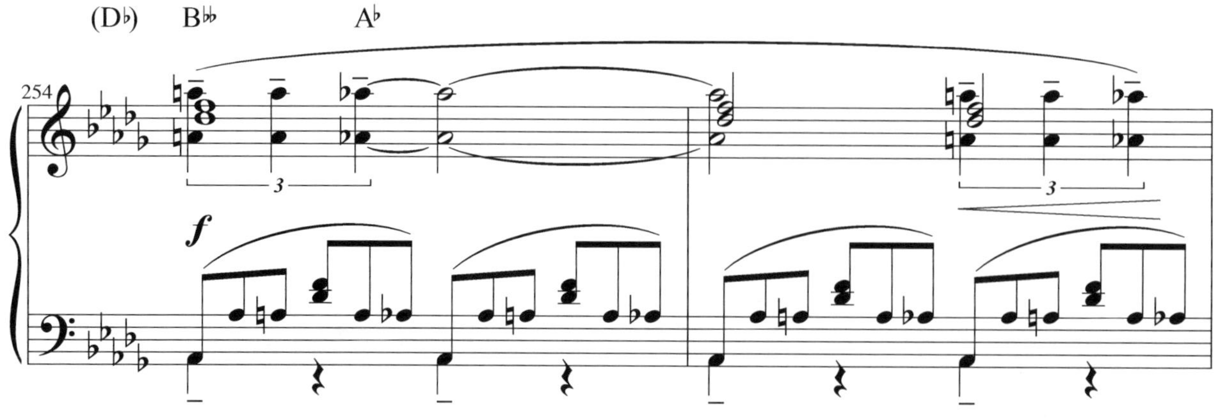

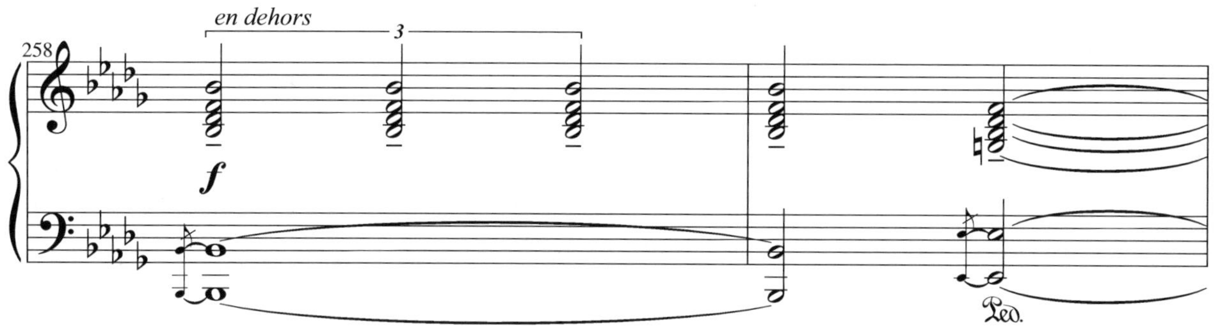

Example 6.4e Refrain 3, mm. 254–57 and chorale, mm. 258–59

and D♮ in m. 62 to C♮ in m. 63. It then changes direction returning to G♯ at the end of m. 65. The second statement, however, ascends from F♮ through G♮ to G♯ for an inversion of the iambic figure in m. 72. This figure occurs over a long pedal tone A♮ in the bass and incessant repetitions of the four-note pattern D–B–C♮–C♯–D in the middle register.

Whereas refrain 1 presents the arabesque theme twice in the local key of C♯ minor, refrain 2 presents it three times in the local key of D♭ major. Example 6.4b shows that this new version follows the original version by elaborating the primary note A♭ with upper neighbor tones B♭♭ and B♭ and then by leaping up to B♮ and descending from C♭ (=B♮), through B♭, A♮, A♭ (=G♯). Unlike refrain 1, the statements in refrain 2 continue their downward path from G♮ through G♭, F♮, F♭, E♭, D♮, D♭, C♮, and C♭, to B♭. All this happens over a tonic pedal D♭. The first statement (mm. 159–166) continues its descent from B♭ through A♭, and G♮ to E and G♭, F♮ in m. 170. The second statement (mm. 171–78) begins like the first but follows a slightly different course starting in mm. 178–79 by descending from B♭ to A♮ and then from A♮ through A♭ and G♮ to E in mm. 181–82. And the third statement (mm. 195–202), which is given in example 6.4c, continues down from C♭ and B♭ in m. 202 through A♮, A♭, G, and G♭ to F in m. 203. Material from mm. 179–86 is then repeated in mm. 203–10.

Finally, examples 6.4d–6.4e show how refrain 3 recalls the arabesque theme. Once again, the gesture appears twice: the first statement recalls the original version of the theme from refrain 1 (mm. 245–53 = mm. 56–64) over a dominant pedal in C♯ minor, whereas the second statement presents an abbreviated version (mm. 254–57 = mm. 56–59) over a dominant pedal in D♭ major. Before the latter is completed, however, the arabesque theme is interrupted by a recollection of the chorale from "De l'aube à midi sur la mer" starting in B♭ (mm. 258–69). This recollection delays the return of the global tonic D♭ major; as mentioned earlier with regard to table 6.1, it occurs at the start of the coda and extends for the remainder of the movement (mm. 270–92).

It is clear from example 6.4 that the arabesque theme is extended in all three refrains by adding descending chromatic lines to the end. Similar chromatic lines appear elsewhere in the movement. Examples 6.5a–6.5b show, for instance, how the bass line descends chromatically E♮, E♭, D♮, C♯ in mm. 82–83 and A♮, A♭, G♮, F♯ in 92–93. An even more prominent case occurs in mm. 118–30 (see ex. 6.5c). This passage begins, in fact, with a string of parallel triads that descends chromatically from E♮ through E♭, D♮, C♯, C♮, and B♮ to B♭ in mm. 118–21 for a statement of the iambic pattern F♯–G♯–B♭ and from E♮ through E♭, D♮, C♯, C♮, B♮, B♭, A♮, G♯, G♮, F♯, F♮, E♮, D♯, D♮, C♯, C♮, and B♮ to B♭ in mm. 123–30 for an abbreviated version of the iambic pattern F♯–G♯.

Having described how the arabesque theme is extended with descending chromatic lines and how those lines are foreshadowed elsewhere in the movement, it is now time to return to the fanfares, which appear at the end of episode 2 just before the start of refrain 3. Example 6.6 lists the main events of episode 2. It opens on a half-diminished seventh B♭, D♭, F♭, A♭ articulated by the distinctive triplet rhythm long, short, short, short, short (see ex. 6.6a). This rhythmic pattern recalls the extension of the arabesque theme from mm. 203–10 (see ex. 6.6b). Starting in m. 219, the texture is dominated by a five-note ostinato E♮, E♭, D♮, D♭, C♮ (see ex. 6.6c); this pattern, which mainly appears in the first bassoons not only derives from the four-note pattern C♯–D♮–D♯–E shown earlier in example 6.4a, but also perpetuates the triplet rhythm long, short, short, short, short that ended refrain 2. The ostinato is relentless, repeating thirty-six times in different transpositions in mm. 219–36. It is also accompanied by the iambic pattern in mm. 221–24 (see ex. 6.6c) and augmentations of the soaring theme in mm. 225–29 (see ex. 6.6d) and again in mm. 234–36. Finally, example 6.6e gives the fanfares as they appear in mm. 237–44.

Example 6.5 Chromatic descending patterns

Example 6.5a Refrain 1, mm. 82–83

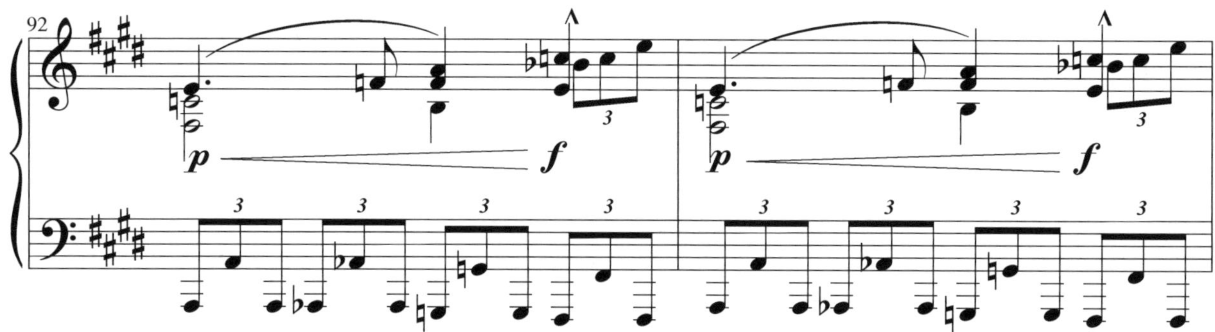

Above, **Example 6.5b** Refrain 1, mm. 92–93

Facing, **Example 6.5c** Episode, mm. 118–30/32

It shows that the gesture is a variant of the rhythmic pattern long, short, short, short, short that is anticipated in refrain 2, highlighted at the start of episode 2, and reinforced in the five-note ostinato pattern. In other words, Trezise is entirely correct to reject Rolf's claim that the fanfares can be removed because of their "disparity" with "other thematic material in the movement" and to insist that they continue to develop a descending chromatic figure "heard repeatedly from m. 219 and adumbrated many times before."[35]

Example 6.7 suggests, however, that there is even more to be said about the descending chromatic figure mentioned by Trezise and cataloged in example 6.5. To begin with, example 6.7a shows how the very first statement of the soaring theme in mm. 11–17 of "De l'aube à midi sur la mer" is prepared by a bass pattern B–A–G♯–F♯ in m. 11 and supported by similar patterns B–A–A♭–G♭–F♯ in mm. 12–14 and G♭–G♭–F♭–E♭–E♭–D♭ in mm. 15–17. Later, in mm. 59–62, a new chromatic motive enters in the oboes and flutes with the same overall profile as the fanfares (see ex. 6.7b). While the descending chromatic figure resurfaces elsewhere in the opening movement, "De l'aube à midi sur la mer," it becomes more prominent in the second movement, "Jeux de vagues." In the case of example 6.7c, mm. 5–8 present a diminution of the pattern C♯, C♮, B♮, B♭, A♮ with the rhythm long, short, short, short, short. Similarly, examples 6.7d–6.7e show two other melodic patterns that include variants of the descending chromatic figure: A♯, A♮, G♮, F♯

Example 6.6 Episode 2

Example 6.6a Mm. 211–16/18

in m. 62 (see ex. 6.7d); F♯, E♯, D♯, D♮ in m. 68 (see ex. 6.7e). Finally, example 6.7f shows how the same pattern returns in refrain 2 from "Dialogue du vent et de la mer": it resurfaces as F♮, E♮, E♭, D♮, C♯ in m. 206 and as C♯, C♮, B♮, B♭, A♮ in m. 210. In short, not only does the descending chromatic figure embedded in the brass fanfares derive from earlier motifs in "Dialogue du vent et de la mer" as Trezise suggests, but it is also foreshadowed in the two preceding movements, "De l'aube à midi sur la mer" and "Jeux de vagues."[36] Since "Jeux de vagues" does not include any obvious statements of the "Melancholy call" or the chorale, removing the fanfares therefore threatens to undermine its cyclic connections with "Dialogue du vent et de la mer." To make matters worse, removing the fanfares from the climax leaves a blank space in the surface structure of the finale, something that theorists such as Eugène Grasset abhorred: "Just as it is a fault to decorate plain surfaces if they are of a material very rich in itself, such as certain marbles or

Example 6.6b Mm. 203–10 (refrain 2)

Example 6.6c Mm. 219–24

woods already displaying great contrasts and variations in color, so it is also a fault to leave long sections empty when the material has no tonal variations of its own."[37]

Although the preceding discussion has argued in favor of keeping the brass fanfares because they enhance the cyclic structure of *La Mer*, it is still important to speculate about why Debussy elected to remove them between 1905 and 1909. The obvious answer to this question lies in the fact that the fanfares are foreground details, albeit significant ones, that elaborate the middle ground voice leading of episode 2: removing them does not, therefore, compromise the passage's tonal and contrapuntal underpinnings. The voice-leading sketch in example 6.8a explains this

Example 6.6d Mm. 225–30

basic framework by providing an overview of the final portion of refrain 2 (mm. 195–210), episode 2 (mm. 211–44), refrain 3 (mm. 245–57), the return of the chorale (mm. 258–69), and the coda (mm. 270–92). The sketch suggests that the passage consists of a large arpeggiation of D♭ major/ minor, with D♭ being affirmed in refrain 2, F♭ entering at the start of episode 2, A♭ in refrain 3, and D♭ returning at the start of the coda. The arpeggiation from D♭ through F♭ to A♭ in the bass supports an ascending chain of parallel 3rds that ascends an octave from A♭/F♮ in refrain 2 to A♭/F♮ at the end of episode 2. This chain of parallel 3rds is accompanied by a stepwise descent in the bass from F♭, through E♭, D♮, C♮, B♭, A♮, to A♭. The brass fanfares decorate the final phase of

Example 6.6e Mm. 237–44

Example 6.7 Chromatic descending patterns in "De l'aube à midi sur la mer" and "Jeux de vagues"

Example 6.7a "De l'aube à midi sur la mer," mm. 11–17

Example 6.7b "De l'aube à midi sur la mer," mm. 59–62

Example 6.7c "Jeux de vagues," mm. 5–8

Example 6.7d "Jeux de vagues," mm. 62–65

Example 6.7e "Jeux de vagues," mm. 68–71

this ascent when the thirds rise G♮/E♭, G♮/E♮, A♭/F♮, A♭/F♭. The arpeggiation from A♭ to D♭ in the bass supports a stepwise descent in the upper voice from A♭ through G♭(=F♯), F♮, and E♭ to D♭.

Besides showing how the tonic D♭ major/minor is projected across the latter half of the movement, example 6.8a also offers an alternative interpretation of the chorale's return in mm. 258–69; instead of treating the passage as part of the coda, as suggested by Roy Howat and Boyd Pomeroy, the voice-leading sketch treats the passage as an interpolation that delays the return of the tonic until m. 270.[38] Interpolations of this sort are not uncommon in tonal music, as Schenker made clear at the start of his treatise *Der freie Satz*: "In the art of music, as in life, motion toward the goal encounters obstacles, reverses, disappointments, and involves great distances, detours, expansions, interpolations, and, in short, retardations of all kinds."[39] These sidetracks are, of course, essential features of arabesques, moresques, and grotesques; they recall the complex designs reproduced in chapter 1. Debussy was especially fond of interpolations and parenthetical passages; in "La sérénade interrompue" (*Préludes*, Bk. 1), for example, he interrupts the piece with the main theme from "Le matin d'un jour de fête" (*Ibéria*, mvt 3).[40] This passage and its extra-musical implications will be discussed in more detail in chapter 12. Treating the chorale in this way is significant because it suggests that this material is fundamentally different from the other cyclic elements, especially the iambic pattern and "Melancholy call." Indeed, whereas those other gestures are woven throughout-the fabric of "Dialogue du vent et de la mer," the chorale stands apart from its surroundings and always sounds otherworldly. This is also true of the two previous recollections in episode 1, mm. 133–36 and 139–42. In this sense, it is notable that Pomeroy does not include these reminiscences in his voice-leading sketch of episode 1, thereby suggesting that he, too, sees them as being in some sense "outside" the main structure of the passage (see ex. 6.8b).[41]

Example 6.7f "Dialogue du vent et de la mer," mm. 203–10

Example 6.8 Formal and motivic details in "Dialogue du vent et de la mer"

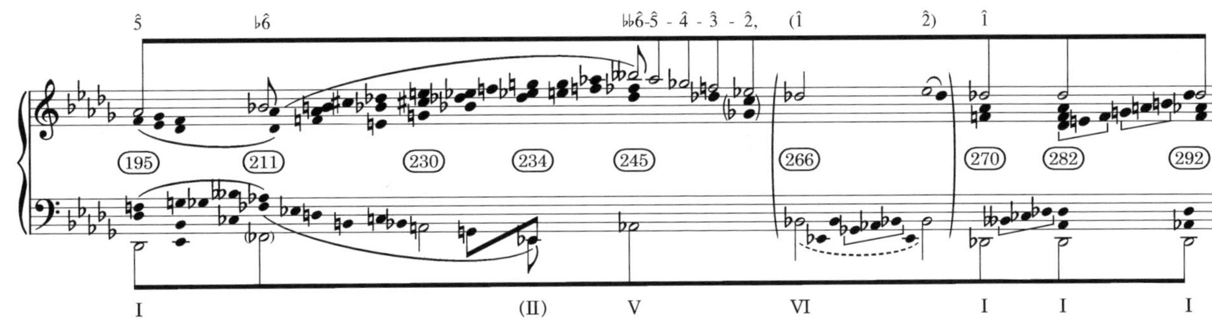

Example 6.8a Voice-leading sketch of "Dialogue du vent et de la mer," mm. 195–292

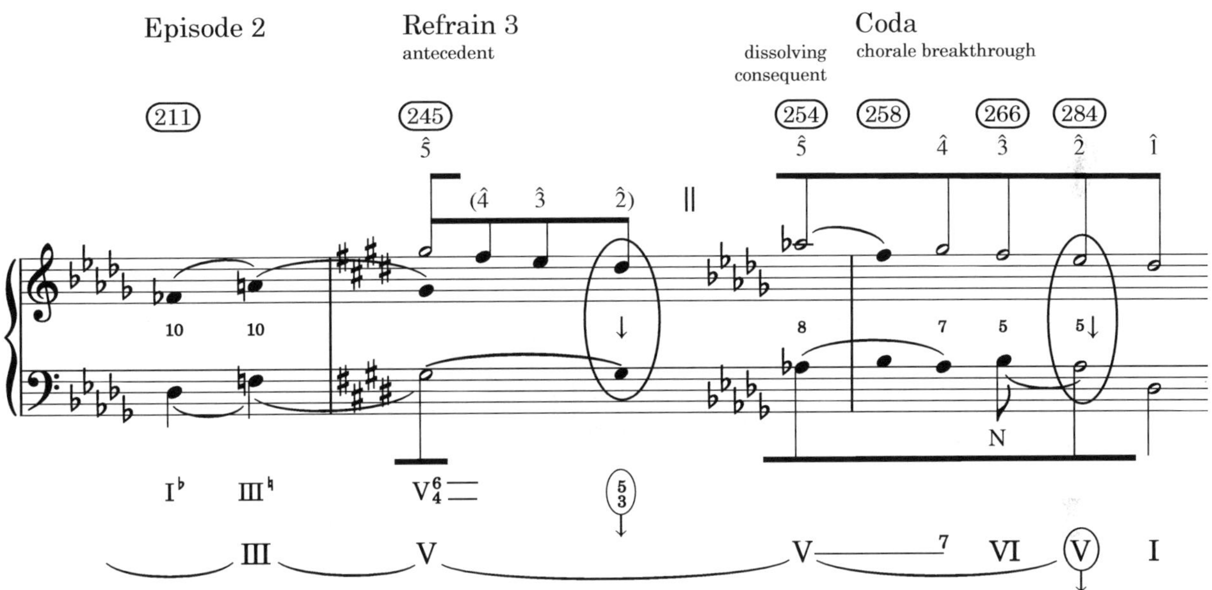

Example 6.8b Pomeroy, voice-leading analysis of "Dialogue du vent et de la mer," mm. 211–84

Such suspicions become even stronger when the score of *D'un cahier d'esquisses* is thrown into the mix. This work, which Debussy wrote at the same time as *La Mer*, was originally destined for a set of three piano pieces that would also include *Masques* and *L'Isle Joyeuse*.[42] But this plan did not come to fruition, and *D'un cahier d'esquisses* was published individually in *Paris Illustré* in 1904. As Cummins has noted, the title should be taken literally; the work is a grotesque assembled from fragments of other works from the period 1903–4. Those include *Masques*, *L'Isle Joyeuse*, "Reflets dans l'eau" (*Images*, sér. 1), and, more importantly for the present discussion, *La Mer*.[43] Indeed, examples 6.8c–6.8d show that *D'un cahier d'esquisses*, which is also in D♭ major, contains a clear reference to the chorale from the end of "Dialogue du vent et de la mer." In particular, the root

Example 6.8c *D'un cahier d'esquisses*, mm. 14–22

Example 6.8d "Dialogue du vent et de la mer," mm. 265–70

Example 6.8e "Melancholy call" from *La Mer*

Example 6.8f Sketch for *La chute de la maison Usher*

position chords on A♭, B♭, followed by the ninth chord on E♭ and the root triad on B♭ in mm. 15–17 of *D'un cahier d'esquisses*, specifically recall mm. 265–69 from "Dialogue du vent et de la mer."

One final point. The idea that the chorale is foreshadowed in *D'un cahier d'esquisses* resonates not only with the fact that Debussy subtitled *La Mer* "Trois esquisses symphonique," but also with Mallarmé's dictum that writers "ought to record in symbolic terms, the impressions made by objects and events rather than the objects and events themselves."[44] Debussy may well have had this idea in mind when he responded to Pierre Lalo's negative reaction to *La Mer* and wrote on October 25, 1905, ten days after the work's premiere.

> You say—keeping your unkindest cut for the last—'that you do not see or smell the sea throughout these three sketches'! That's a large claim and I don't know who is going to evaluate it for us. . . . I love the sea and I've listened to it with the passionate respect that it deserves. If I've been inaccurate in taking down what it dictated to me, that is no concern of yours or mine. You must admit, not all ears hear in the same way. The heart of the matter is that you love and defend traditions which, for me, no longer exist or, at least, exist only as representative of an epoch in which they were not all as fine and valuable as people make out; the dust of the past is not always respectable.[45]

But this is by no means the only sign of *La Mer*'s debts to Symbolist ideology. Marie Rolf has suggested that the original title of the first movement—"Mer belle aux île sanguinaires"—may have been inspired by a short story of the same name by Camille Mauclair published in the *Echo de Paris illustré* in 1893.[46] Mauclair, who was a staunch advocate of Impressionism and Symbolism and cofounded the avant-garde Théâtre de l'Œuvre with Aurelian Lugné-Poe, apparently based his story on a weather report for the Corsican Islands printed in *Le Temps* that Debussy also read.[47] Peter Cogman has, however, challenged this view, arguing instead that the composer was more likely inspired by the catchphrase of another Symbolist poet, his friend Pierre Louÿs.[48] The phrase apparently captured Debussy's imagination because Louÿs sent him a copy of his *Sanguines* in 1903 while he was composing *La Mer*. And, by a strange twist of fate, Trezise has noted that the "Melancholy call" heard in "Dialogue du vent et de la mer" (see ex. 6.8e) bears a striking similarity to a sketch of material for the final portion of Debussy's unfinished opera *La chute de la maison Usher* (see ex. 6.8f).[49] In sum, this chapter has shown that, although the case of the missing fanfares poses the reader with a wide range of editorial, analytical, and historical issues, those issues intersect with the concept of the arabesque in many interesting ways. Most obviously, it has confirmed the idea advanced by Baudelaire, Debussy, and Schenker that details matter. In particular, the discussion has shown how the fanfares have important consequences not only to the surface design of "Dialogue du vent et de la mer" but also to the cyclic structure of *La Mer* as a whole. Moreover, the arabesque provided a way to describe the ornamental character of the finale's main theme and the disjunct ways in which it delays the final climactic statement of the chorale from "De l'aube à midi sur la mer." The otherworldly nature of this climax and the allusions to material designed for Debussy's unfinished opera *La chute de la maison Usher* offer further signs of the subtle ways in which Debussy was haunted by the spirits of Poe and Baudelaire.

Notes

1. Charles Baudelaire, "Notes Nouvelles sur Edgar Poe," *Œuvres Complètes*, vol. II, 329; Baudelaire, "Further Notes on Edgar Poe," in *The Painter in Modern Life and Other Essays*, 103.

2. Gabriel Mourey, "Memories of Claude Debussy," *Musical News and Herald*, June 11, 1921, 747–48; Nichols, *Debussy Remembered*, 31 and Lesure and Herlin, ed., Debussy, *Correspondance*, 167. See also Debussy's letter to Raoul Bardac (February 24, 1906); Lesure and Herlin, ed., Debussy, *Correspondance*, 940–42.

3. Heinrich Schenker, *Der freie Satz*, Neue musikalische Theorien und Phantasien, vol. 3 (Vienna: Universal, 1935), §308, 213; Heinrich Schenker, *Free Composition* (New York: Longman, 1979), 131–32.

4. Simon Trezise, "Review: *La Mer* by Claude Debussy and Marie Rolf," *Notes* 2nd series 56, no. 3 (2000): 783.

5. For the philological status of Caplet's transcriptions, see Matthew Brown, *Debussy Redux: The Impact of His Music on Popular Culture* (Bloomington: Indiana University Press, 2012), 70–73.

6. See Douglas Woodfull-Harris, "Introduction," in Claude Debussy, *La Mer*, ed. Douglas Woodfull-Harris (Barenreiter: Kassel, 2014), V–VI.

7. Woodfull-Harris, "Introduction," V–VI.

8. Claude Debussy, *La Mer*, ed. Max Pommer (Leipzig: Peters, 1971), XX–XXI. Claude Debussy, *La Mer*, ed. Marie Rolf, Œuvres Complètes de Claude Debussy, Sér. V, vol. 5 (Paris: Durand, ca. 1997); Claude Debussy, *La Mer*, ed. Peter Jost (Wiesbaden: Breitkopf & Härtel, 2006); Claude Debussy, *La Mer*, ed. Douglas Woodfull-Harris (Barenreiter: Kassel, 2014). For those who have purchased or rented scores without the fanfares, it is now possible to download engraved versions of the missing material to paste into their parts: http://www.orchestralibrary .com/Nieweg%20Charts/Debussy-LaMer1905BrassInserts.pdf.

9. Woodfull-Harris, "Introduction," IV–V.

10. Alan Tyson introduced the distinction between "private" and "public" phases in his essay "Sketches and Autographs," in *The Beethoven Companion*, ed., Denis Arnold and Nigel Fortune (London: Faber, 1971), 443–58.

11. For the distinction between errors and variants, see David Grayson, "Editing Debussy: Issues *en blanc et noir*," *19th-Century Music* 13, no. 3 (1990): 245–48.

12. For the basic chronology of *La Mer*, see Rolf, "Foreword," in *La Mer*, *Œuvres Complètes*, XV–XVI.

13. See Woodfull-Harris, "Introduction," IV.

14. See Woodfull-Harris, "Introduction," IV.

15. Besides removing the brass fanfares from mm. 237–44 of "Dialogue du vent et de la mer," the 1909 edition compresses "two bars into one" in m. 83 of "De l'aube à midi sur la mer" and replaces "the cornets' high crotchet triplets" in mm. 237–44 of "Dialogue du vent et de la mer." See Simon Trezise, *La Mer*, Cambridge Music Handbook (Cambridge: Cambridge University Press, 1994), 29.

16. Roy Howat, "The New Debussy Edition: Approaches and Techniques," *Studies in Music* 19 (1985): 95; and Grayson, "Editing Debussy," 243.

17. Grayson, "Editing Debussy," 256.

18. See Woodfull-Harris, ed., *La Mer* (Barenreiter: Kassel, 2014), 145.

19. Wiener Urtext Edition, homepage, https://wiener-urtext.com/en/wiener-urtext-edition (accessed October 28, 2023).

20. Schenker, *Der freie Satz*, 23–24; Schenker, *Free Composition*, 7.

21. L. Van Beethoven, *Sonate Op. 27, Nr. 2*, facsimile with commentary by Heinrich Schenker (Vienna: Universal, 1921).

22. Trezise, "Review: *La Mer*," 783.

23. Trezise, "Review: *La Mer*," 783.

24. Debussy, *La Mer*, ed. Marie Rolf, 238.

25. See Woodfull-Harris, *La Mer*, V.

26. Debussy, *La Mer*, ed. Max Pommer (Leipzig: Peters, 1971), XIX–XXII.

27. For general discussions of Schenker's *Erläuterungsausgabe*, see William Drabkin, "The New *Erläuterungsausgabe*," *Perspectives of New Music* 12, no. 1/2 (1973–4): 319–30; Ian Bent, "'That Bright New Light': Schenker, Universal Edition, and the Origins of the Erläuterung Series, 1901–1910," *Journal of the American Musicological Society* 58, no. 1 (2005): 69–138; and Nicholas Marston, "Schenker's Concept of a Beethoven Sonata Edition," in *Essays from the Fourth International Schenker Symposium*, vol. 2, ed. Poundie Burstein, Lynne Rogers, Karen and M. Bottge. (Heidesheim: G. Olms, 2013), 91–101. For a general discussion of Schenker's approach to editing, see Matthew Brown, "Review: John Rothgeb ed. and trans., *Beethoven: The Last Piano Sonatas: Edited, with Analytic Commentary, by Heinrich Schenker*," *Theory and Practice* 41 (2017): 213–28; and Robert W. Wason and Matthew Brown, *Heinrich Schenker's Conception of Harmony* (Rochester, NY: University of Rochester Press, 2020), 299–308.

28. William Pastille, "The Development of the *Ursatz* in Schenker's Published Works," in *Trends in Schenkerian Research*, ed. Allen Cadwallader (New York: Schirmer, 1990), 71–85. Schenker anticipated the term *Urlinie* before WWI when he referred to *Urideen* in *Harmonielehre* and to *Urformen* and melodic fluency in *Kontrapunkt 1*.

29. See Cristina Urchueguía, "Wie kam die 'Urlinie' in den 'Urtext'? Aporien musikalischer Schrift im Denken Heinrich Schenkers," *Schweizer Jahrbuch Für Musikwissenschaft* Neue Folge 32 (2012): 237–52. For the cognitive implications of Schenker's ideas, see John Sloboda, *The Musical Mind: The Cognitive Psychology of Music* (Oxford: Oxford Press, 1985).

30. Brown, "Review: John Rothgeb," 217. Grayson rightly notes that Debussy's orthography is also very suggestive; see Grayson, "Editing Debussy," 248–49.

31. Trezise, "Review: *La Mer*," 784.

32. See Trezise, *La Mer*, 54.

33. Jean Barraqué, *Debussy* (Paris: Seuil, 1962), 147–54; David Cox, *Debussy Orchestral Music*, BBC Music Guide (Seattle: University of Washington Press, 1974), 24–32; Debussy, *La Mer*, ed. Max Pommer, XX–XXI; Roy Howat, *Debussy in Proportion: A Musical Analysis* (Cambridge: Cambridge University Press, 1983), 93–109; Christian Goubault, *Claude Debussy* (Paris: Champion, 1986), 152–53; Siglind Bruhn, *Debussy's Instrumental Music in Its Cultural Context*, Studies in 20th-Century Music: Dimension and Diversity (Hillsdale, NY: Pendragon, 2019), 91–98; Laurence Berman, "The Evolution of Tonal Thinking in the Works of Claude Debussy," PhD diss., Harvard University, 1965, 217 and 233–42. See also Boyd Pomeroy, "A Force of Nature: Debussy and the Chromatically Displaced Dominant," in *Explorations in Schenkerian Analysis*, ed. David Beach and Su Yin Mak, Eastman Studies in Music (Rochester, NY: University of Rochester Press, 2016), 303–27.

34. This plan is basically the one given by Debussy, *La Mer*, ed. Max Pommer, XX–XXI; Goubault, *Claude Debussy*, 152–53; and Pomeroy, "A Force of Nature." The only significant difference is that, unlike Goubault and Pommer, Pomeroy ends refrain 1 in m. 71.

35. Trezise, "Review: *La Mer*," 784.

36. Trezise, *La Mer*, 52.

37. Eugène Grasset, *Méthode de Composition Ornementale*, vol. 2, Éléments courbes (Paris: Librairie Centrale des Beaux-Arts, ca. 1900), 160; Jean Pierrot, *The Decadent Imagination 1880–1900*, trans. Derek Coltman (Chicago: University of Chicago Press, 1981), 231.

38. Howat, *Debussy in Proportion*, 94; Pomeroy, "A Force of Nature," 310–11.

39. Schenker, *Der freie Satz*, 18; Schenker, *Free Composition*, 5.

40. See Matthew Brown, "Tonality and Form in Debussy's *Prélude à L'Après-midi d'un faune*," *Music Theory Spectrum* 15 (1993): 142.

41. Pomeroy's treatment of the dominant toward the end of episode 1 (ex. 15.4) is theoretically possible but most unlikely in view of its dissonant and therefore unstable nature.

42. Roy Howat, "En route for 'L'île joyeuse': The Restoration of a Triptych," *Cahiers Debussy* 19 (1995): 37–52.

43. Linda Cummins, *Debussy and the Fragment* (Amsterdam: Rodopi, 2006), 124–27.

44. Brian Stableford, "Introduction," in Adolphe Retté, *Misty Thule*, trans. Brian Stableford (Print of Demand: Snuggly Books, 2018), 7.

45. Debussy, *Correspondance*, 928; Debussy, *Letters*, 163–64.

46. For the original title, see Debussy's letters to Durand and André Messager from September 12, 1903; Debussy, *Correspondance*, 779–80; Debussy, *Letters*, 141.

47. Rolf, "Foreword," in *La Mer, Œuvres Complètes*, XVI. See also Marie Rolf, "Mauclair and Debussy: The Decade from 'Mer Belle aux île Sanguinaires' to *La Mer*," *Cahiers Debussy* 11 (1987): 9–23.

48. Peter Cogman, "Claude Debussy, Pierre Louÿs, and the îles sanguinaires," *French Studies Bulletin* 26, no. 97 (2005): 7–9.

49. Trezise, *La Mer*, 41–43.

7

Bitten by the Tarantella
Debussy and Self-Generating Form

Although debussy's modernist leanings clearly made him critical of the Musical Establishment, the preceding chapters have nonetheless shown how he specifically linked the concept of the arabesque to the music of J. S. Bach and the ornamental character of its melodic lines. Bach's music had, of course, been widely revered in France since the early nineteenth century and, as mentioned in chapter 2, played a central role in Debussy's music education both in his piano lessons with Antoinette Mauté and in his studies of performance and composition at the Paris Conservatoire.[1] His admiration for Bach did not wane in later years; on hearing one of Bach's motets in 1914, he proclaimed that the vocal writing was "unsurpassed."[2] And yet, Debussy's involvement with Bach's music took an unexpected turn in April 1915, when he signed a contract with Durand to edit several volumes of his forebear's chamber works for the company's Édition Classique. Undertaken after the outbreak of WWI and the French government's ban on the sale of works by German publishing houses, the Édition Classique presented new versions of canonical pieces: editions of Mozart's piano music by Camille Saint-Saëns, Schumann's piano music by Gabriel Fauré, Chopin's piano music by Claude Debussy, Mendelssohn's piano works by Maurice Ravel, Mendelssohn's chamber music by Albert Roussel, Beethoven's piano sonatas and violin sonatas by Paul Dukas, and Haydn's violin sonatas by Florent Schmitt.[3] Bach's music featured prominently in the series: the *Well-Tempered Clavier* and many other keyboard works were edited by Gabriel Fauré; the sonatas for solo violin by Paul Lamaître; the French and English Suites, Partitas, *Italian Concerto*, and *Chromatic Fantasy and Fugue* by Maurice Emanuel; the suites for solo cello by Fernand Pollain (1918); the *Passacaglia in C minor* for solo piano by Jean Roger-Ducasse; and the *Notebook of Anna Magdalena Bach* by Lucien Garban.[4]

For a fee of one thousand francs, Debussy was commissioned to edit Bach's six sonatas for violin and keyboard (BWV 1014–1019), three sonatas for viola da gamba and keyboard (BWV

1027–1029), six sonatas for flute (BWV 1030–1035), and a pair of trio sonatas (BWV 1032 and 1038).[5] Although the gamba sonatas were ready in the fall of 1915, with Louis Fournier editing the cello part, the accompanied violin sonatas were another matter entirely and were delayed by events beyond Debussy's control. Following an unsuccessful round of cancer surgery in December 1915, Debussy "started a new treatment" only to endure "sixty days" of medical torture.[6] The pain was so severe that he was forced to take morphine and remain in his Parisian home for much of 1916: "Without realizing it, I've spent a full six months now contemplating my misery; it's too long for someone who hasn't the time to lose any more. Will I ever again know what it is to be well? I don't dare to think so and I'd much rather have a sudden end than this pursuit of health in which, so far, the disease is always one step ahead of me."[7] At the same time, the war entered a new phase: France and her Allies were bogged down at Verdun (February–December 1916) and the Somme (July–November 1916), and Parisians were threatened by artillery and aerial attacks. Debussy's precarious financial situation made a bad situation even worse.[8] It was so dire in the early months of 1917 that he composed his short piano piece *Les soirs illuminés par l'ardeur du charbon* in order to reimburse his coal merchant Monsieur Tronquin.[9] All the while, Debussy kept working on his Bach editions, completing his version of the accompanied violin sonatas on April 15, 1915, with the first three being published in May 1917 and the second three in September.[10] Narcisse Augustin Lefort edited the violin part.

Besides providing some much-needed income, the latter project also spurred him on to compose several sonatas of his own. Those works were to be scored for six diverse sets of instruments and cast "in the ancient mould with none of the grandiloquence of modern sonatas."[11] Some of these sonatas were scored for combinations preferred by Bach—the *Sonate pour violoncelle et piano* and the *Sonate pour violon et piano* (1916–17)—but others were to have been written for more radical groups—one for *Sonate pour flûte, alto, et harpe*, one for oboe, horn, and harpsichord, one for trumpet, bassoon, and clarinet, and a final one for trumpet, clarinet, bassoon, oboe, horn, harpsichord, violin, flute, viola, harp, cello, piano, and double bass.[12] According to Durand, Debussy decided to write a sonata for trumpet after hearing Saint-Saëns's Septet for trumpet, two violins, viola, cello, double bass, and piano at the Concerts Durand in 1915.[13] Debussy subsequently composed his *Sonate pour violoncelle et piano* and *Sonate pour flûte, alto, et harpe* in the summer and fall of 1915 and his *Sonate pour violon et piano* in the fall of 1916 and spring of 1917. Alas, he never finished the other sonatas.

Since Debussy's three late sonatas share the same highly decorated melodic style as Bach's chamber works, it leaves us to wonder whether the former were influenced by the latter: do Debussy's elaborate arabesques rely on the same principles of ornamentation as Bach's finely wrought melodies? To answer this question, the following chapter focuses on Debussy's use of arabesque in one specific movement: the "Neapolitan" finale of his *Sonate pour violon et piano*.[14] The discussion begins by describing the complex compositional history of the final movement. It then analyzes the intricate cellular structure of the movement's main theme and demonstrates how this gesture resembles not only that of a traditional tarantella but also the main theme from the finale of Bach's sonata for violin and keyboard in G major, BWV 1019, one of the works that Debussy edited for Durand. Having considered several connections between the finale and the rest of the *Sonate pour violon et piano*, the chapter ends by speculating about what Debussy meant when he claimed that the late sonatas were to be cast "in the ancient mould" and why Debussy's appreciation for Bach's music remained so strong at the end of his life.

Given the intense pressure that Debussy faced from 1916 to 1917, it should come as no surprise that he had a hard time finishing the *Sonate pour violon et piano*: the process took over a year from the day Debussy signed his contract with Durand (February 5, 1916) to the day he performed the work's premiere (May 5, 1917).[15] The "terrible finale" gave him the most headaches and, as Delécluse has shown, prompted him to create at least three alternative versions before coming up with the definitive score.[16] In a letter to Durand from October 17, 1916, Debussy explained how he had particular difficulty weaving the movement's main theme into the fabric of the sonata as a whole: "Going for a walk recently at Cap Ferrat, I found the 'cellular' idea for the finale of the Violin Sonata. . . . Unfortunately, the first two movements don't want to have anything to do with it. . . . Knowing myself as I do, I am certainly not going to force them to put up with an awkward neighbour."[17] Debussy was still stuck at the start of the New Year. On February 23, 1917, he wrote apologetically to Durand, "You were right to be sorry I abandoned the 'Neapolitan' finale; after having great hopes of its replacement, I've come back to it—with some changes. It's one of a thousand little personal tragedies which occur without so much noise as the fall of a rose-petal and without disturbing the universe. So in a few days you'll see Naples again . . . and you won't die."[18] He made similar excuses through March 1917.[19] But on May 7, 1917, Debussy announced to Godet that the score was finally ready: "I've at last finished the sonata for violin and piano. . . . By one of those very human contradictions it's full of happiness and uproar. In future don't be taken in by works that seem to fly through the air; they've often been wallowing in the shadows of a gloomy brain. Such is the finale of this same sonata. It goes through the most curious contortions before ending up with a simple idea which turns back on itself like a [snake] biting its own tail—an amusement whose attraction I take leave to doubt."[20]

In the meantime, Debussy had already approached Gaston Poulet about performing the work's premiere. Poulet was apparently nervous, as Debussy noted in a letter to Durand from April 14, 1917: "Saw G. Poulet this morning. . . . I showed the draft of the finale—he trembled!"[21] Poulet's reaction, which apparently gave Debussy "goosebumps," is surprising because Poulet was one of the most accomplished French violinists of his day and known to Debussy since before the war. Pierre Monteux had hired the twenty-year-old violinist to lead the orchestra for the premiere of *Jeux* (and *Le Sacre de Printemps*) at the Théâtre des Champs-Elysées on May 15, 1913.[22] On June 19, 1913, Poulet played at a "Gala Debussy" hosted by the esteemed critic Émile Vuillermoz at the Comédie des Champs-Elysées, and the following year he founded the Quatuor Poulet with Henri Giraud playing second violin, Albert Leguillard viola, and Louis Ruyssen cello.[23] Although Poulet was called up for military service, he was discharged for health reasons and was able to resume his career as a chamber musician. On February 10, 1917, Poulet's group performed Debussy's *Quatuor à cordes* at La salle Gaveau in Paris, and, to prepare for another on March 17, they even rehearsed at Debussy's house, with Poulet's wife, Jeanne (a.k.a. Jeanne Evrard), playing second violin. Debussy was quick to compliment his young colleague: "I greatly appreciate your beautiful talent and it assures me of some good times."[24] He was especially impressed by Poulet's wife and sent her a short note quoting a passage from his quartet along with the following comments: "These two measures become admirable under the bow of Madame G. Poulet! The author keeps for her an affectionate gratitude and assures his respectful devotion. Claude Debussy. June 1917."[25]

Whatever doubts Poulet may have had about the *Sonate pour violon et piano*, they had clearly evaporated by the next spring; on May 5, 1917, he performed the premiere at the Salle Gaveau with Debussy at the keyboard. This performance was given as part of a fundraiser for blind soldiers

("Pour le foyer du soldat aveugle"); Debussy and Rose Féart also performed the composer's *Trois Chansons de François Villon, Chansons de Bilitis,* and *Noël des enfants*.[26] Debussy teamed up with Poulet later in the year to give repeat performances in the south of France on September 11 and 14, 1917, in order to raise money for victims of the Somme ("L'Œuvres de la Sommes dévastée").[27] The audience was so impressed by the second of these performances that they demanded an encore of the second movement. Out of respect for "the unity of composition," Debussy and Poulet played the entire sonata for a second time![28]

Turning to the score itself, Debussy gave the finale of the *Sonate pour violon et piano* its Neapolitan character by casting the movement as a tarantella, a dance long associated with the cities of Taranto and Naples. As suggested in figure 7.1, the tarantella was originally danced as a "method of curing those stung" by a wolf spider (*Lycosa tarantula*).[29] It is typically fast and written in compound duple or quadruple meter. The steps were notoriously disjunct and angular, something that seems entirely appropriate given Debussy's desire to convey "happiness and uproar" in a time of extreme stress.[30] He may well have been inspired to do so from reading Poe and from playing Chopin and Liszt.[31] Whatever the case, example 7.1 compares the main theme of Debussy's finale as it appears in mm. 29–34, 67–72, and 146–51, with two typical tarantellas, one by Sebastian Bach Mills (ex. 7.1b) and another by Giuseppe Galimberti (ex. 7.1c). Example 7.1d then shows how Debussy's tarantella theme resembles the Ronde theme from tableau I of *La Boîte à joujoux*:

Figure 7.1 An eighteenth-century depiction of the tarantella adorned by arabesques

Example 7.1 Tarantella themes

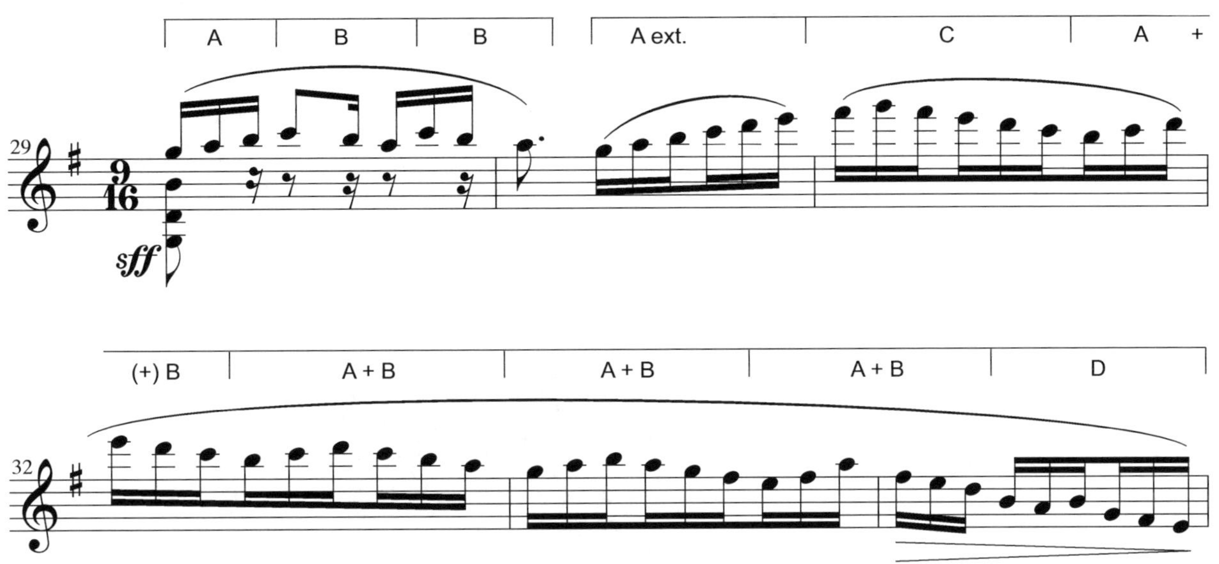

Example 7.1a Debussy, *Sonate pour violon et piano*, Finale, mm. 29–34, 67–72, 146–51

Example 7.1b Sebastian Bach Mills, Tarantelle No. 2, Op. 20 (Leipzig: Schuberth & Co., 1868)

Example 7.1c Giuseppe Galimberti, *Tarantella Napoletana*, Op. 519 (Milan: Ricordi, ca. 1890)

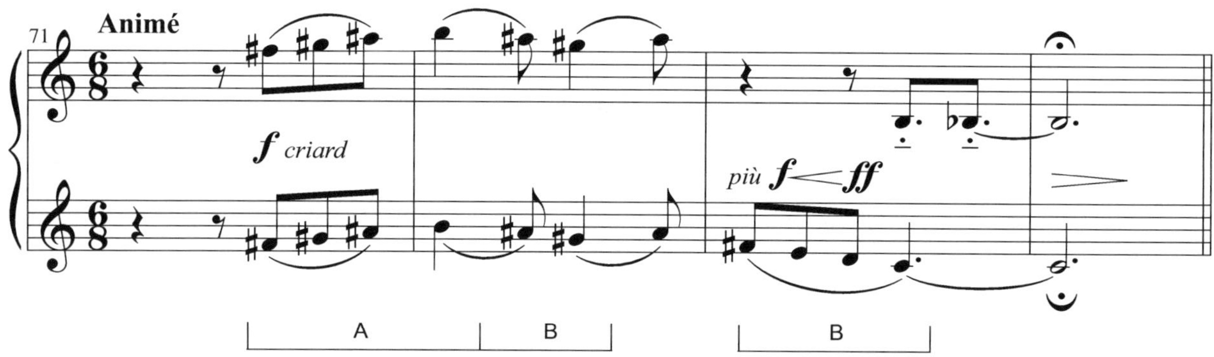

Example 7.1d Debussy, Ronde theme, *La Boîte à joujoux*, tableau I, mm. 71–74

as will become clear in chapter 9, this theme dates from 1913, just three years before Debussy composed the *Sonate pour violon et piano*.[32]

Example 7.1a also highlights the "cellular" nature of Debussy's melody: it suggests that the highly decorated tune is built from at least four discrete motivic cells: Cell A features the rising fourth G–A–B–C, Cell B the descending third C–B–A, Cell C a longer pattern starting with an upper neighbor F♯–G–F♯–E–D–C, and Cell D starts with a lower neighbor pattern B–A–B and ends with a stepwise descent G–F♯–E. Examples 7.1b–7.1c demonstrate that some of the same cells appear in the tarantella themes composed by Sebastien Bach Mills and Giuseppe Galimberti. More to the point, however, example 7.1e indicates that they can also be found in the main theme of the finale to Bach's sonata for violin and keyboard in G major, BWV 1019, a work that Debussy was commissioned to edit for Durand.[33] In mm. 9–13, for example, the right hand of the keyboard presents six repetitions of a motive that begins with an upper neighbor pattern just

Example 7.1e Bach, Sonata for violin and keyboard in G major, BWV 1019, 5th mvt., mm. 9–16

like Cell C, followed by an inverted scale pattern similar to the extended version of Cell A. The latter are echoed in the violin part in mm. 12–13. And in mm. 14–16, the left and right hands of the keyboard present melodic diminutions that recall the rising fourth associated with Cell A, the descending third with Cell B, and an extended version of Cell A. These melodic diminutions are treated sequentially, spiraling around and eventually leading back to a perfect authentic cadence in G on the downbeat of m. 31. The finale ends with an exact reprise of mm. 1–31 in mm. 89–119.

Although Debussy states the tarantella theme three times in the form given in example 7.1a, he extended it in different ways each time around. These differences highlight the arabesque nature of the score and are illustrated in example 7.2. The first statement, for example, continues with a string of broken fifths E–B and A–E, followed by repetitions of B–A–G (Cell B) in the violin starting in m. 38 and 40 (see ex. 7.2a) and again in the piano starting in m. 51. The latter leads directly to the return of the tarantella theme in m. 67. On this occasion, however, the theme dissolves into successive repetitions of the lower neighbor figure F♯–E–F♯ (mm. 73–75) followed by recollections of Cell C, with its characteristic upper neighbor pattern, and Cell A, with its distinctive rising fourth (see ex. 7.2b). This pattern appears in counterpoint with the broken fifths and Cell D in the piano part (mm. 73–75). Finally, the third repetition of the tarantella theme, which appears in mm. 146–51, slides effortlessly into repetitions of Cell D in mm. 152–59 and an extended melodic inversion of Cell A in m. 160 (see ex. 7.2c). The fact that the passages in example

Example 7.2 Continuations of the tarantella theme

Example 7.2a Debussy, *Sonate pour violon et piano*, Finale, mm. 37–48

Example 7.2b Debussy, *Sonate pour violon et piano*, Finale, mm. 73–81

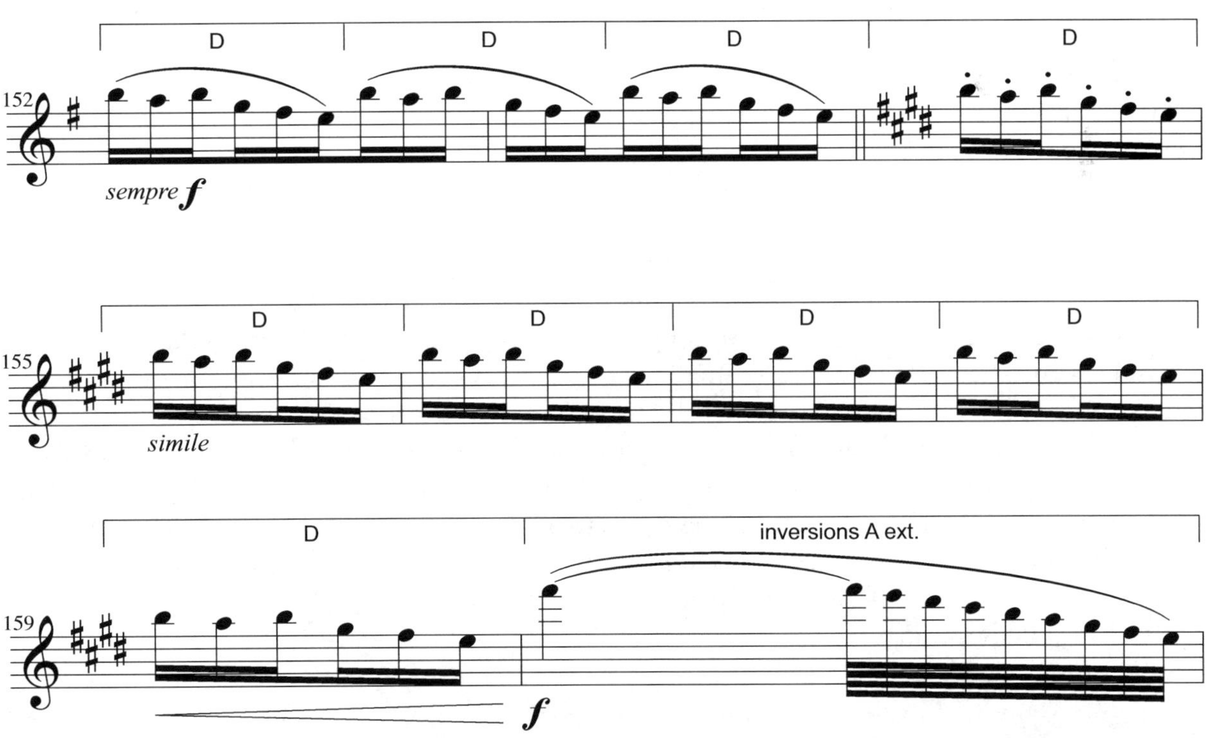

Example 7.2c Debussy, *Sonate pour violon et piano*, Finale, mm. 152–60

7.2 constantly repeat one or two cells almost verbatim confirms Elliott Carter's observation that in his later sonatas, Debussy avoided "the usual methods of development by repeating phrases almost identically."[34] According to him, "the accumulation of short melodic fragments" makes the lines sound continuous until that sense of continuity is suddenly broken by the intrusion of a "new [and] unexpected figure."[35] Though Carter doesn't say so, his description sounds a lot like a definition of an arabesque and the blueprint for a self-generating form.

Compared to the motivic procedures shown in example 7.2, those in example 7.3 are considerably more abstruse; they are perfect instances of the curious contortions that Debussy mentioned to Robert Godet in his letter from May 7, 1917. First up, example 7.3a shows a truncated version of the tarantella theme from mm. 116–31. This reworking stands out on at least two counts. To begin with, the substitution of B♭ for B♮ allows the theme to appear within the local context of B♭ major, something that is confirmed by the trills and B♭ major scales in mm. 124–27. This chromatic variant of the tarantella theme is particularly striking because it returns near the end of the movement: as shown in example 7.3b, mm. 191–94 culminate in chromatic variants of Cell A supported by root position triads on E♭ and A♭. Incidentally, the return of the tarantella theme in mm. 116–131 jumps out rhythmically: whereas the versions in mm. 29–34, 67–72, and 146–51 are vibrant and decisive, the new one sounds languid and almost improvisational. Examples 7.3c–7.3d then show how the deceleration in tempo anticipates two augmented statements of Cells A and B in mm. 154–60 and 163–69. Significantly, these augmentations in the right hand of the piano are accompanied by incessant repetitions of Cell D in the violin. Although he is hardly remembered for his interest in learned counterpoint, Debussy often showed off his contrapuntal prowess in his mature compositions: in August 1915, for example, he mentioned to Durand that he had included a similar case of motivic augmentation in the second movement of *En blanc et noir* (mm. 145–46).[36] It is surely no coincidence that Debussy also wrote the latter while editing Bach's chamber music.

Finally, example 7.4 shows how the finale ends with the tarantella theme turning back on itself just "like a snake biting its own tail." To begin with, mm. 176–78 present an abbreviated version of the tarantella theme akin to the one mentioned earlier in mm. 116–31 (see ex. 7.4a). This segment leads to a longer version in mm. 178–84 that, unlike example 7.1a, omits the last two statements of Cells A+B and Cell D. Example 7.4b shows that the same sequence of cells reappears in mm. 184–91: mm. 184–86 present the abbreviated theme (Cells A, B, B) from mm. 176–78, whereas mm. 186–91 recall the longer version from mm. 178–84 (Cells A, B, B, A ext., C, A+B, A+B). The latter leads to chromatic variants of Cell A (mm. 191–94), a trill on high A (mm. 196–99 and 200–203), and eventually to a diatonic version of Cell A (mm. 199 and 203). This passage is given in example 7.4c. The latter is, of course, the same cell that marked the start of the tarantella theme in mm. 29–34, 67–72, and 146–51. In other words, mm. 176–207 bring the listener back full circle; the final arabesque returns to whence it came. This is precisely what Bach accomplished in the finale of his sonata BWV 1019 when he brought back the material from mm. 1–31 in mm. 89–119. Once again, it seems that Debussy was inspired by the arabesque qualities of Bach's music.

In focusing on the "cellular" nature of the tarantella theme, it is important to remember that when Debussy originally came up with it in October 1917, he was concerned that "the first two movements don't want to have anything to do with it."[37] Such concerns beg the question: how, in fact, did Debussy connect these movements to their "awkward neighbor"? On reflection, several answers spring to mind. Perhaps the most obvious way was for Debussy to include explicit

Example 7.3 Contortions of the tarantella theme

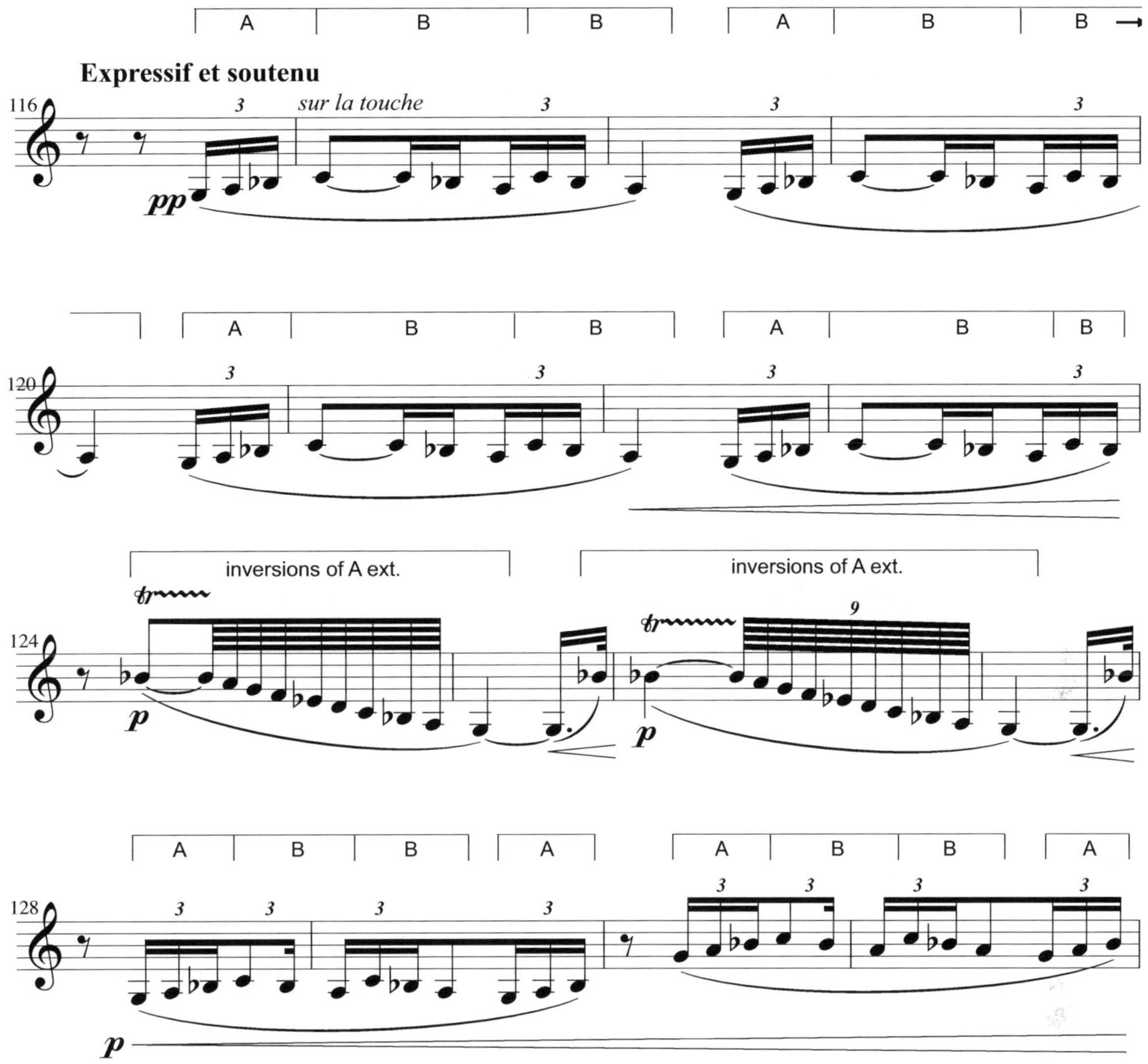

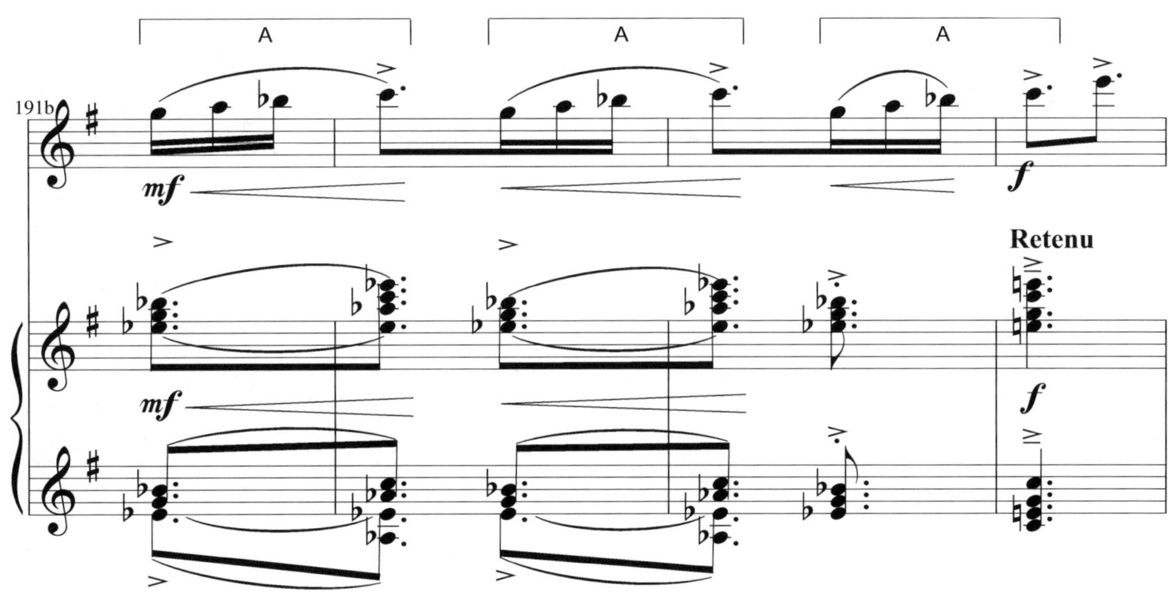

Example 7.3a Debussy, *Sonate pour violon et piano*, Finale, mm. 116–31

Example 7.3b Debussy, *Sonate pour violon et piano*, Finale, mm. 191–94

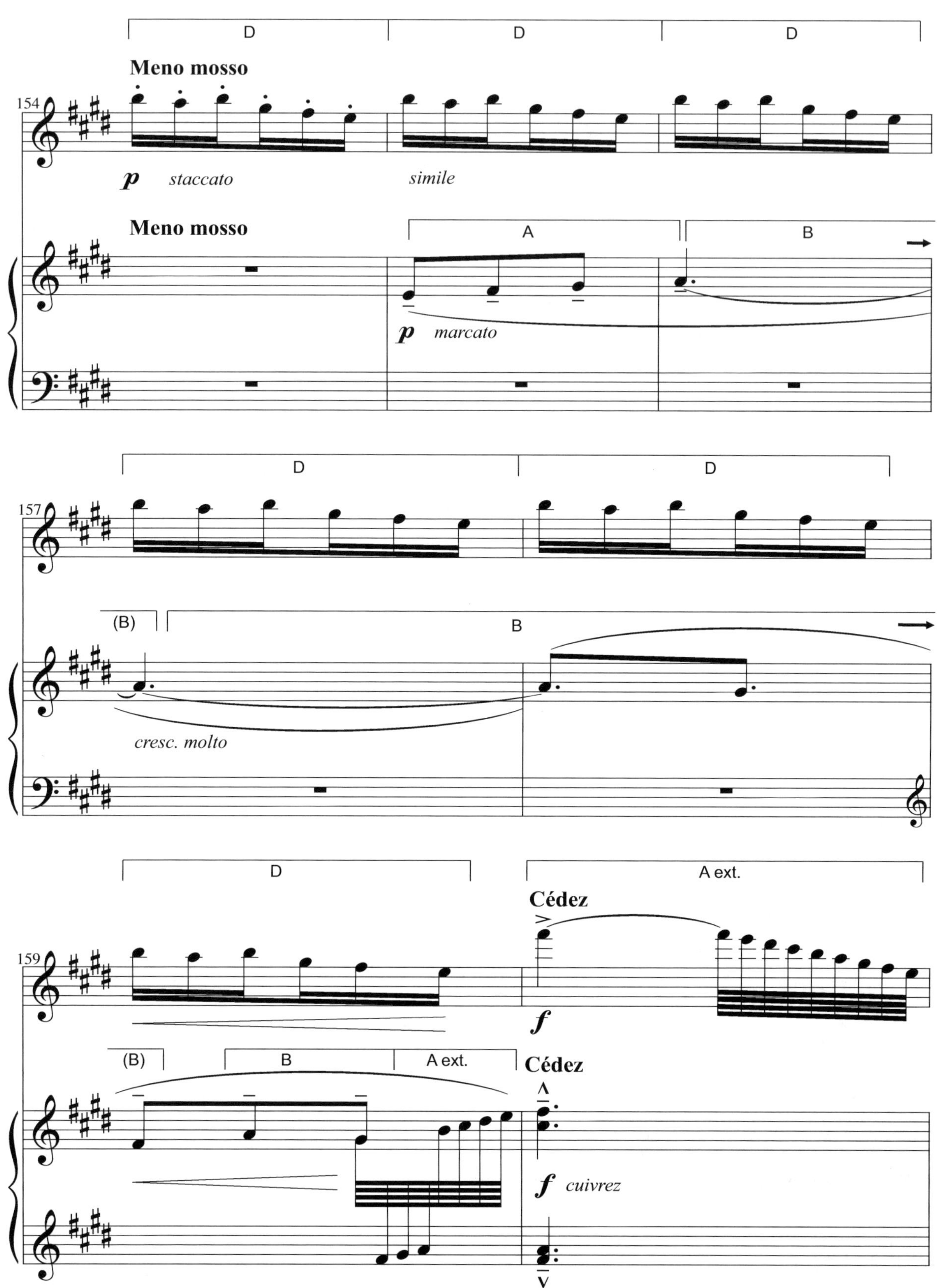

Example 7.3c Debussy, *Sonate pour violon et piano*, Finale, mm. 154–60

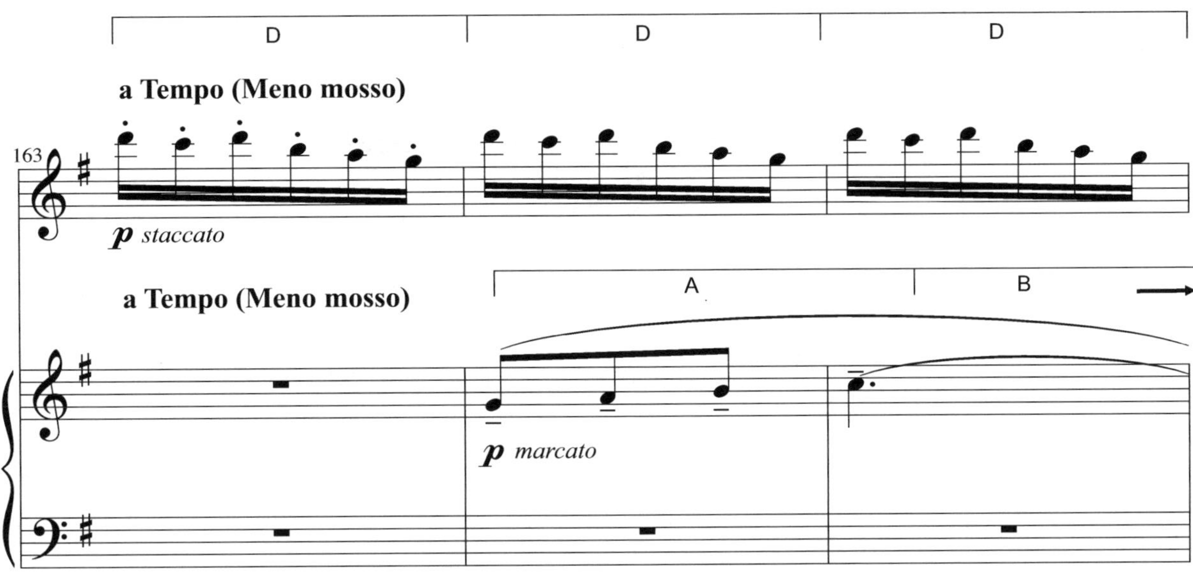

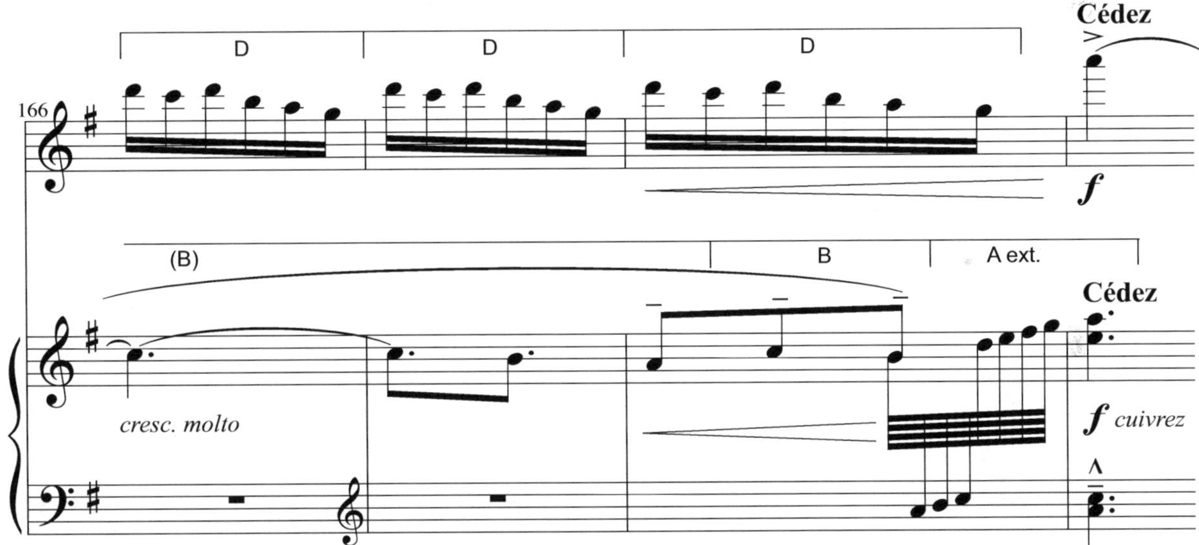

Example 7.3d Debussy, *Sonate pour violon et piano*, Finale, mm. 163–69

statements of material from the first and second movements at strategic points in the finale. This is, in fact, precisely the strategy Debussy employed at the start of the third movement. Example 7.5, for instance, shows how mm. 1–28 of the finale recycles prominent themes both from the first and the second movements. To begin with, examples 7.5a–7.5c show how the finale begins with a recollection of a subordinate theme from mm. 72–78 and 101–7 of the second movement. Notice how the rhythmic profile of the theme is changed: the pattern of straight eighth notes in the finale (ex. 7.5a) stands in contrast to the dotted rhythms of the Intermède (ex. 7.5b–7.5c). Significantly, the new version of the theme introduced at the start of the finale returns in the piano

Example 7.4 Debussy, *Sonate pour violon et piano*, Finale, mm. 176–84

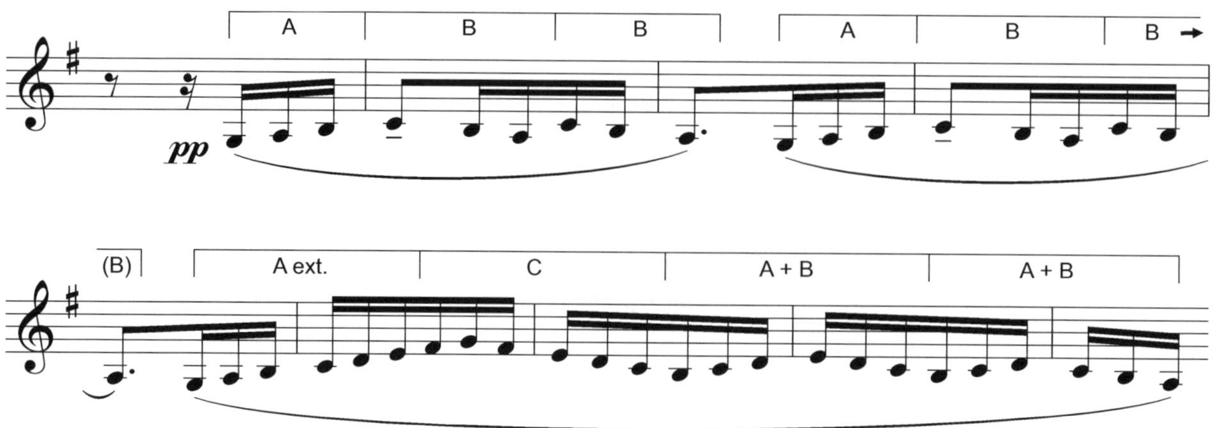

Example 7.4a Tarantella theme, mm. 176–84

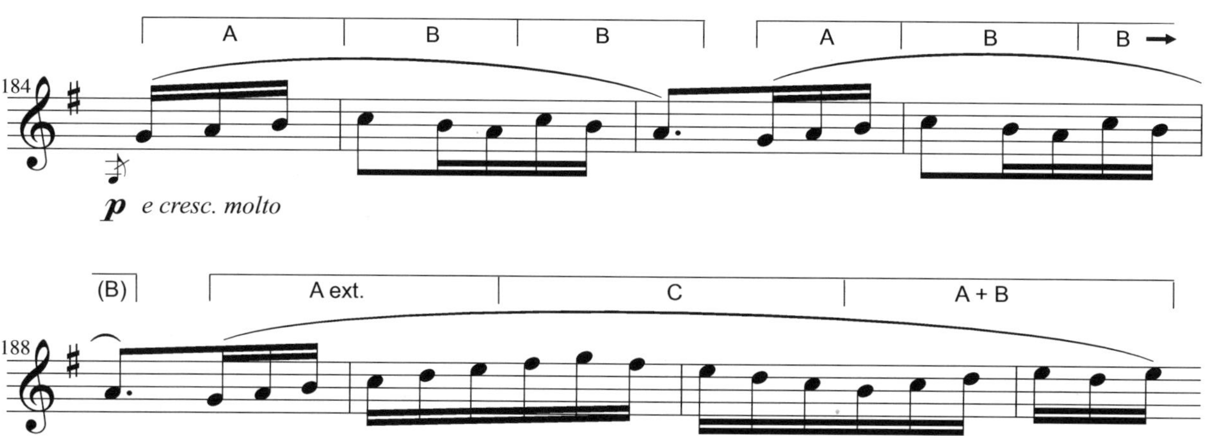

Example 7.4b Tarantella theme, mm. 184–91

part much later in the movement in mm. 100–108 (see ex. 7.5d). Having recalled material from the second movement, examples 7.5e–7.5f show how the opening section of the finale subsequently brings back the main theme from the first movement. Once again, the theme is transformed rhythmically: whereas the notes of the theme appeared on the beat in the first movement, they are syncopated in the finale. The harmonic structure of the theme is also changed considerably, something that will be discussed more later in this chapter.

While thematic cross-references like those in example 7.5 provided an important means for connecting the first and second movements of the *Sonate pour violon et piano* to their "awkward neighbor," they are by no means the only one: as mentioned earlier, Carter suggested Debussy also did so by creating a network of so-called hidden motives: "For if Debussy avoids the usual methods of development by repeating phrases almost identically, he emulates these methods in a play of hidden motives that appear in phrases of contrasting character."[38] Example 7.6 tries to demonstrate what Carter may have in mind. For convenience, examples 7.6a–7.6b recall the

Example 7.4c Tarantella theme, mm. 191–207

diatonic and chromatic versions of the tarantella theme as they appear in the finale. Next, example 7.6c shows how the chromatic version of Cell A, with its characteristic stepwise ascent G–A–B♭–C, is foreshadowed in the final measures of the first movement: after repeated G five times in mm. 238–39, the violin reinforces G with its upper neighbor A♭ in mm. 240–41, another chromatic variant of Cell A (G–A♭–B♭–C) in mm. 242–43, and two extended versions of this pattern (G–A♭–B♭–C–D♭ and G–A♭–B♭–C–D♭–E♭) in mm. 244–45 and 246–47. The simple arabesques lead to repetitions of Cell C (G–A♭–G–F–E♭ and D♭–E♭–D♭–C–B♭–A♭) in mm. 248–49 and 250–51. It is also worth noting that the prominent use of A♭ (♭) and D♭ (♭) and the intense almost improvised nature of line almost sounds like *cante jondo*, one of the most emotionally charged forms of Spanish music that Debussy had already explored in pieces such as "La Puerta del Vino" (*Préludes*, Bk. 2).[39] Examples 7.6d–7.6e then show how Cell C is immediately absorbed into the opening arabesque at the beginning and ending of the second movement. Last, example 7.6f demonstrates how Cell C appears in mm. 24–28 of the finale before the entry of the tarantella theme in m. 29. Once again, the recurrence of Cell C provides a way of transitioning smoothly and unobtrusively from one movement to the next and illustrates Carter's notion of a hidden motive in the clearest of terms. There are even augmentations of Cell C in the bass line C–A–G–D at mm. 23–24, 25–26, and 27–29.

Example 7.5 Cyclic themes in Debussy, *Sonate pour violon et piano*

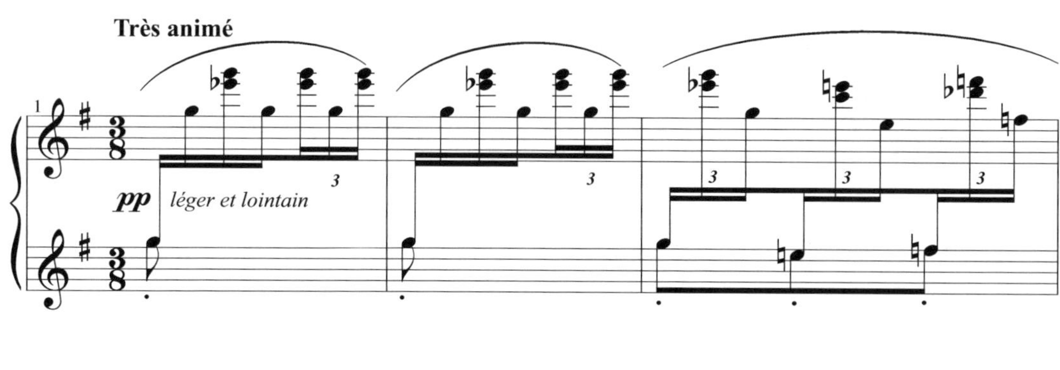

Example 7.5a Debussy, *Sonate pour violon et piano*, Finale, mm. 1–5

Example 7.5b Debussy, *Sonate pour violon et piano*, Intermède, mm. 72–78

Example 7.5c Debussy, *Sonate pour violon et piano*, Intermède, mm. 101–7

Above, **Example 7.5d** Debussy, *Sonate pour violon et piano,* Finale, mm. 100–108

Facing, **Example 7.5e** Debussy, *Sonate pour violon et piano,* Finale, mm. 9–22

Meno mosso (poco)
sur la touche
pp dolce sostenuto
Meno mosso (poco)
pp
pp
pp
pp
213

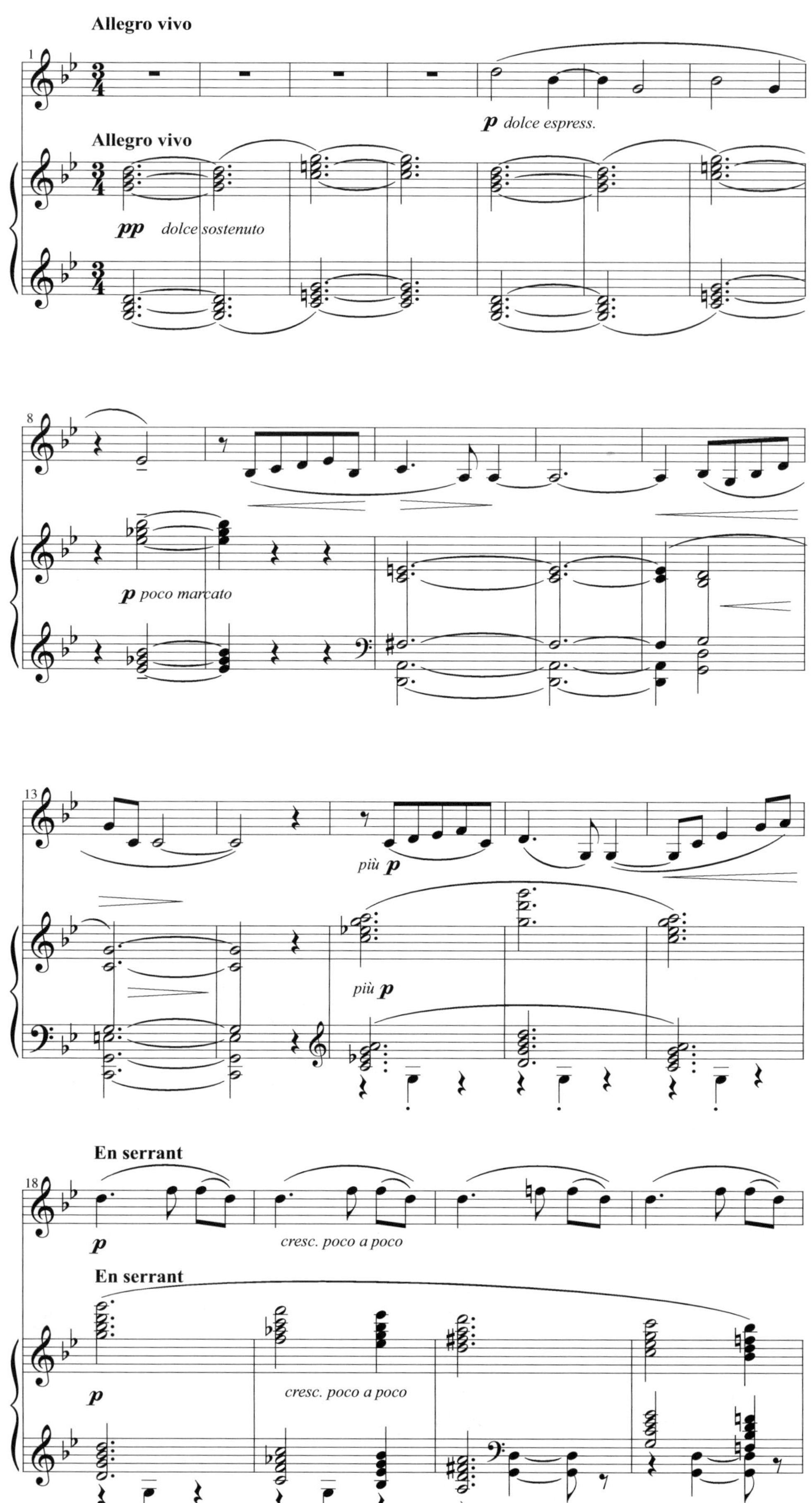

Example 7.5f Debussy, *Sonate pour violon et piano*, first movement, mm. 1–21

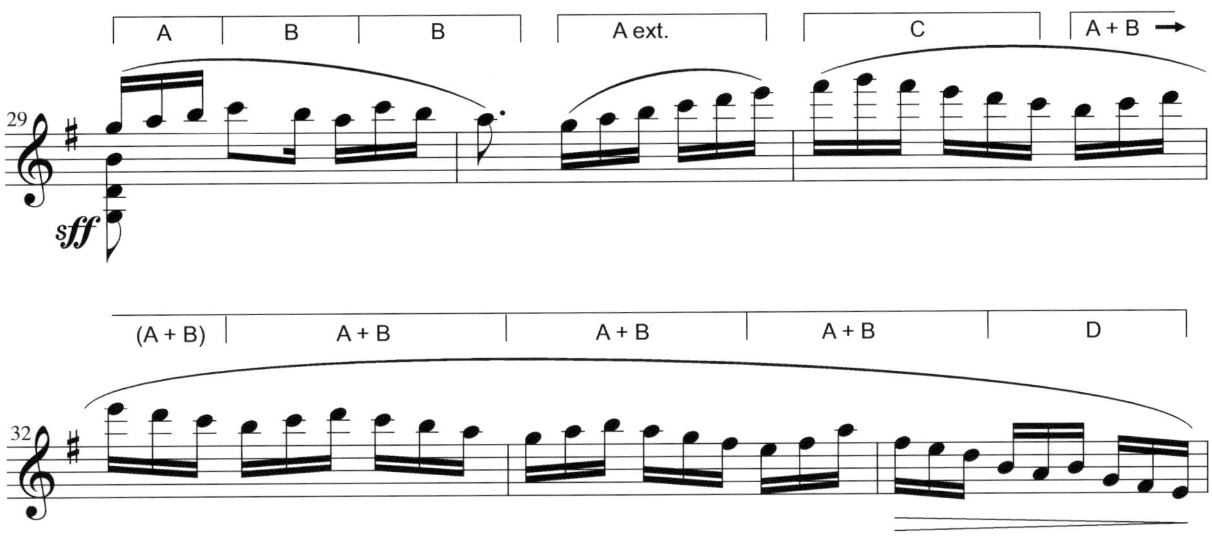

Example 7.6a Debussy, *Sonate pour violon et piano*, Finale, mm. 29–34, 67–72, 146–51

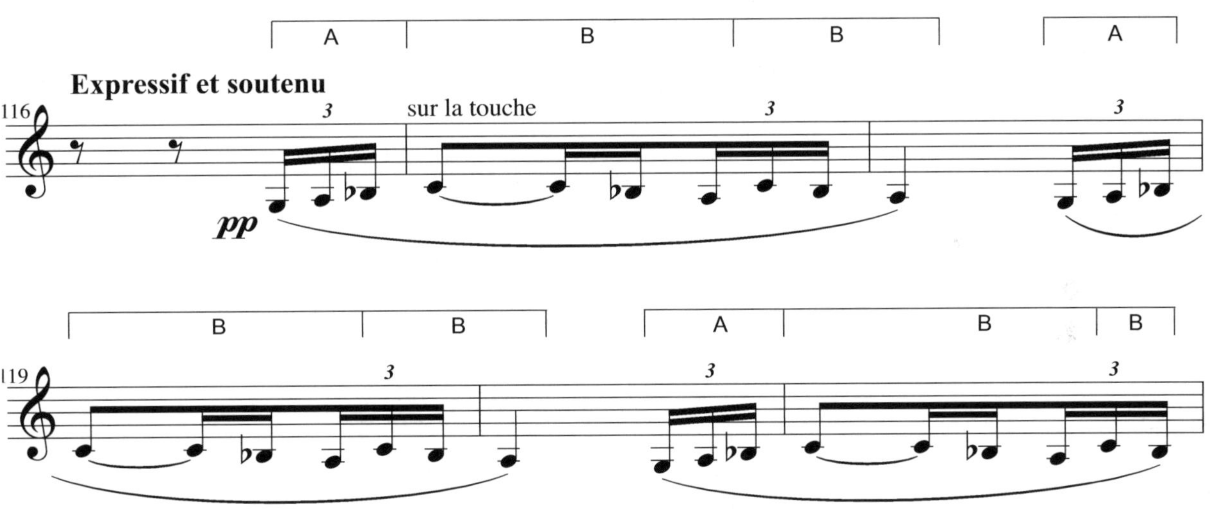

Example 7.6b Debussy, *Sonate pour violon et piano*, Finale, mm. 116–21

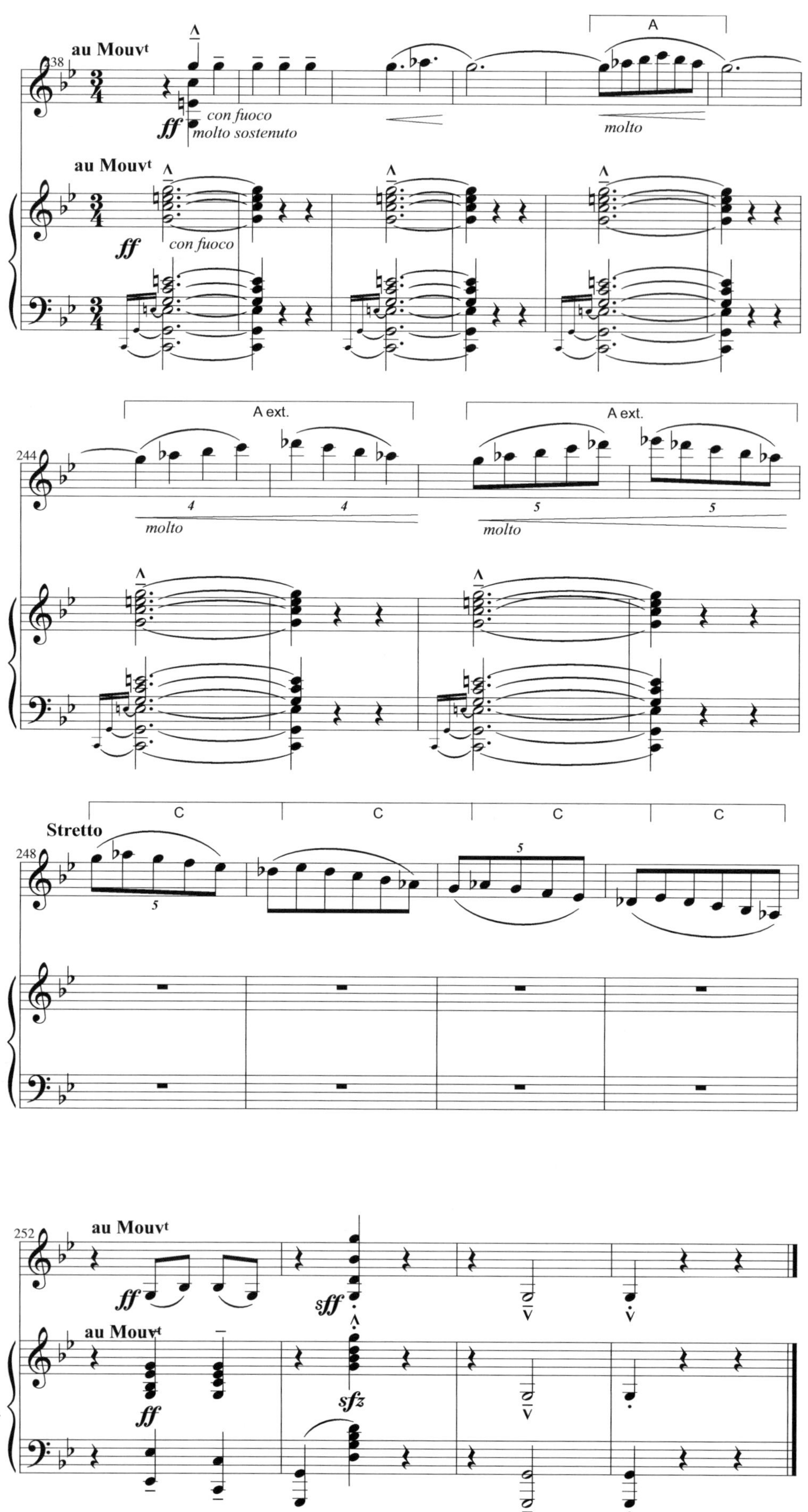

Example 7.6c Debussy, *Sonate pour violon et piano*, first movement, mm. 238–55

Example 7.6d Debussy, *Sonate pour violon et piano*, Intermède, mm. 1–16

217

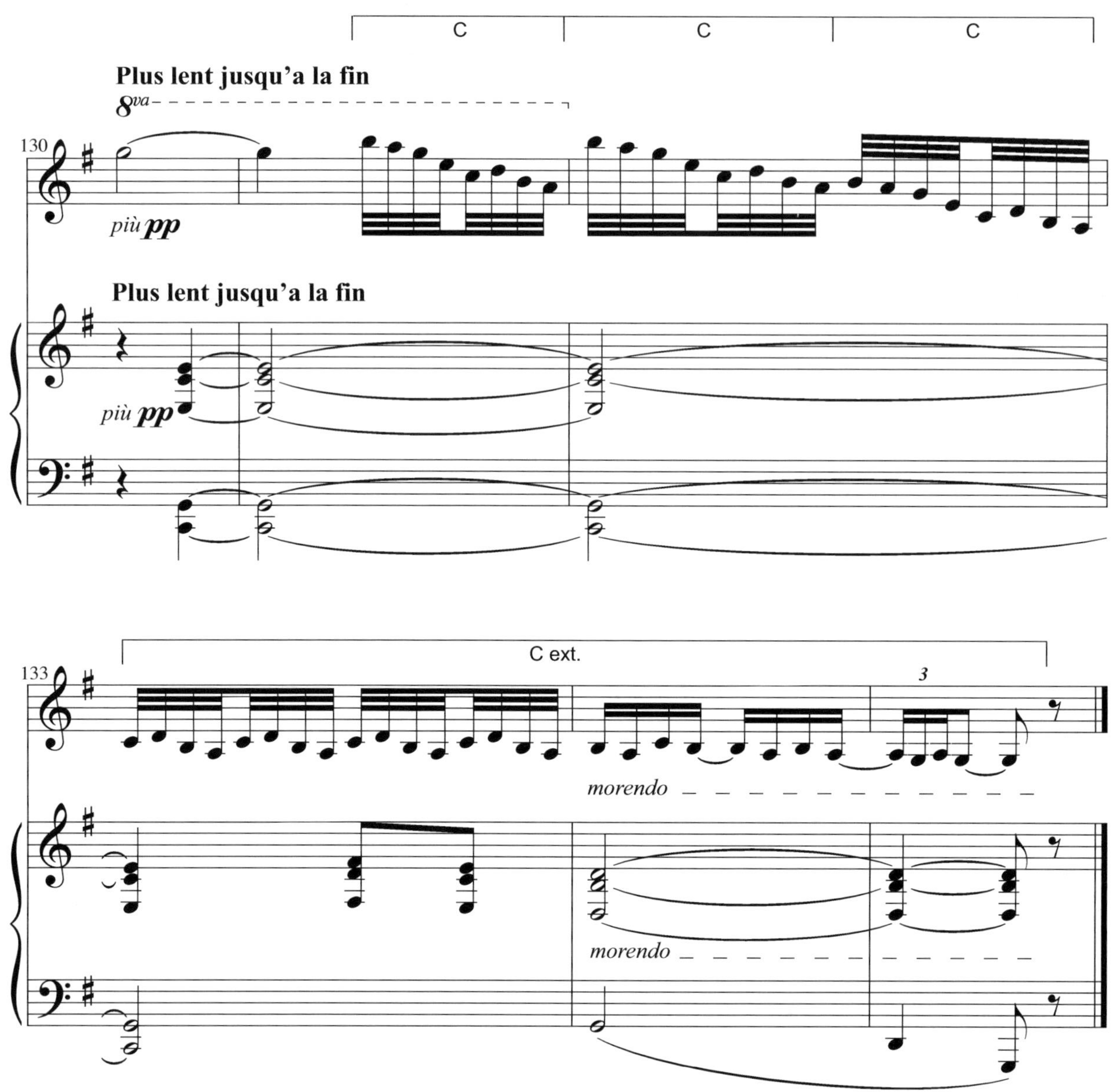

Example 7.6e Debussy, *Sonate pour violon et piano*, Intermède, mm. 130–35

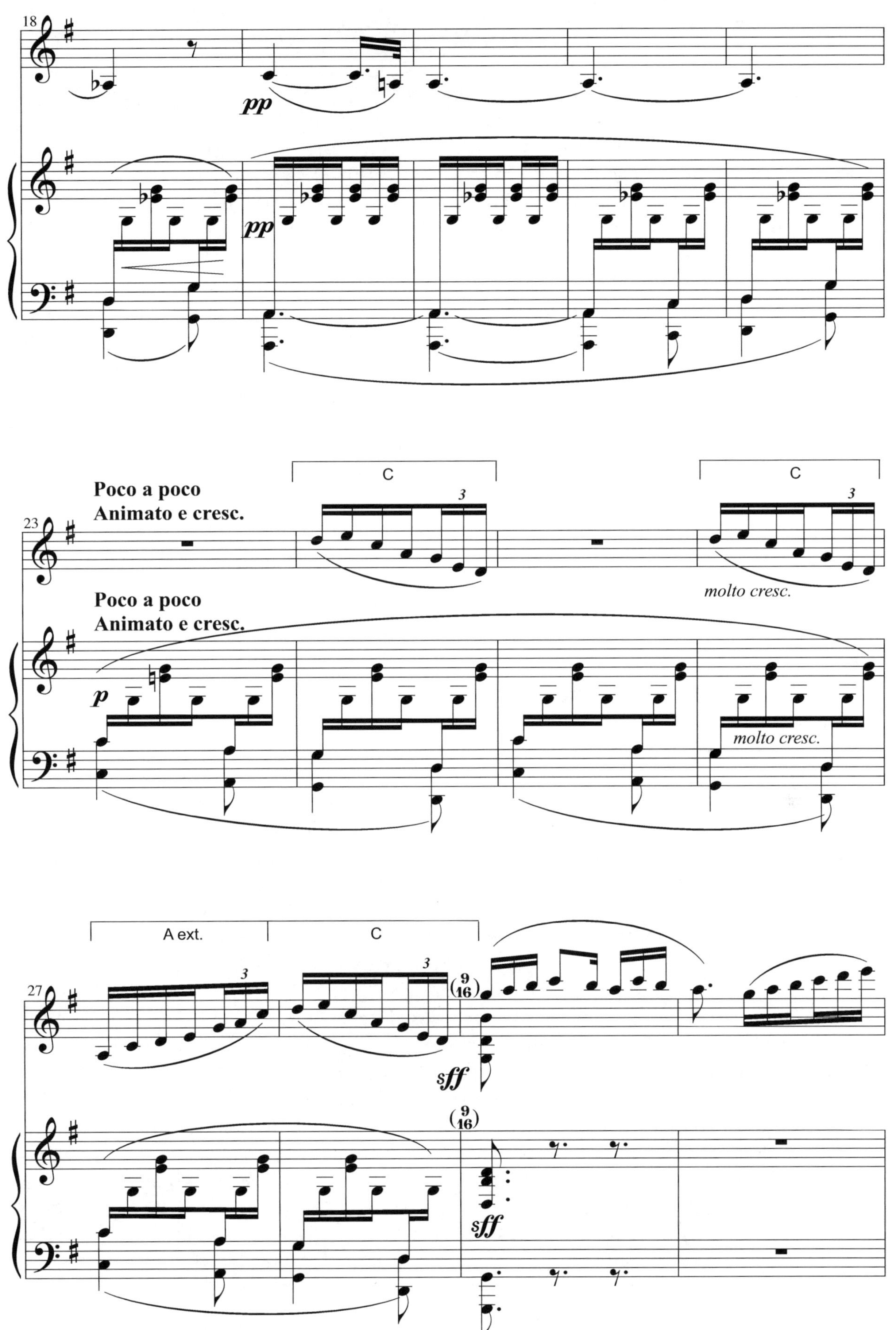

Example 7.6f Debussy, *Sonate pour violon et piano*, Finale, mm. 18–36

Just as the three movements of the *Sonate pour violon et piano* are bound together by their use of cyclic themes and hidden motives, so they are also linked by their dependence on recurring harmonic and contrapuntal patterns. One such pattern appears at the end of the finale. Having arrived on a clear dominant sonority in m. 171, the movement ends with an extremely unusual progression in the tonic G major. As shown in example 7.7a, the tarantella theme returns in m. 172 on a tonic chord, whose authority is weakened by the addition of its flattened seventh F♮, a move that is extremely common in codas from works by J. S. Bach.[40] This sonority first leads to a striking E♭ major sonority (♭VI) in mm. 191–93 and then to an equally startling C major (IV♮) in m. 194. The arrival on C is followed by a long trill on A in m. 196 and a descending pattern C–A–G–E–C in the bass, both of which imply a II^7 harmony. The falling fifth A–D in the violin in mm. 204–5 suggests a dominant harmony even though the leading tone F♯ is absent, and the statement of Cell A in the piano obscures the root of the chord. Nevertheless, the final tonic G returns emphatically in mm. 206–7. It is surely no coincidence that the same harmonic progression and bass patterns appear at the start of the finale in mm. 12–29 (see ex. 7.7b). While G major emerges as the tonic in m. 29, the movement actually begins with a first inversion triad on E♭ sonority. This sonority is especially clear in m. 12, where the return of the main theme from the first movement articulates the pattern B♭–C–D–E♭–B♭ over another pedal tone G. The music then arrives abruptly on a C major triad in m. 18 for repetitions of Cell C in the violin and the descending pattern C–A–D–G in the bass. Once again, the leap from D to G in the bass from mm. 28–29 might suggest an authentic cadence, but the leading tone is nowhere to be found. The parallels between this passage and the end of the movement are indeed striking and underscore Debussy's image of a snake biting its own tail.

More remarkably still, the same harmonic progression also pervades the first and second movements. This much is clear from example 7.8. To begin with, example 7.8a shows how the main theme of the first movement opens by alternating between G minor triads (I♭) and C major triads (IV♮) and then shifts to an E♭ minor triad (♭VI^b) before returning to G minor via the dominant seventh chord in mm. 10–12. Example 7.8b then shows how the similar harmonic patterns return at the end of the first movement (mm. 224–55). The passage begins with a return to the tonic G minor, though once again its function is undermined by the addition of the flattened seventh F♮. Having spun out the tonic with the bass pattern D–F–C, a transposed version of C–A–G from the finale, the first movement lands emphatically on a glorious C major sonority in m. 238. Instead of restoring the tonic by means of an authentic cadence V–I, the piece ends with the progression E♭ (♭VI)–C (IV♭)–G (I♭). As before, the music scrupulously avoids the leading tone F♯. Example 7.8c then shows how the string of chords—C major, E♭ minor, D^9, and G—also serve as a model for mm. 84–146 of the first movement. Having closed the opening section in G minor in mm. 56–63 the middle section begins in E major/minor in m. 84 with statements of two new motives that push the music first toward C major in m. 106 for a statement of the first new motive and then to E♭ minor in m. 128 and the dominant D starting in m. 140 for a statement of the second new motive. Just like the opening, G♭ in m. 128 is reinterpreted enharmonically as F♯ in m. 140 and eventually resolves onto the tonic G in m. 146. Finally, example 7.9 shows an analogous progression at the end of the second movement. In this case, the violin part in mm. 127–29 clearly outlines members of an E♭ major triad, whereas mm. 130–33 shift to a sustained C major triad in the piano, followed by a tonic G in mm. 134–35. As in the other movements, there is no concluding V–I cadence at the end: the bass does descend D–G, but there is no leading tone in the upper voices.

Example 7.7a Debussy, *Sonate pour violon et piano*, Finale, mm. 171–78 and 186–207

Example 7.7b Debussy, *Sonate pour violon et piano*, Finale, mm. 12–26

Example 7.8 The first movement of Debussy's *Sonate pour violon et piano*

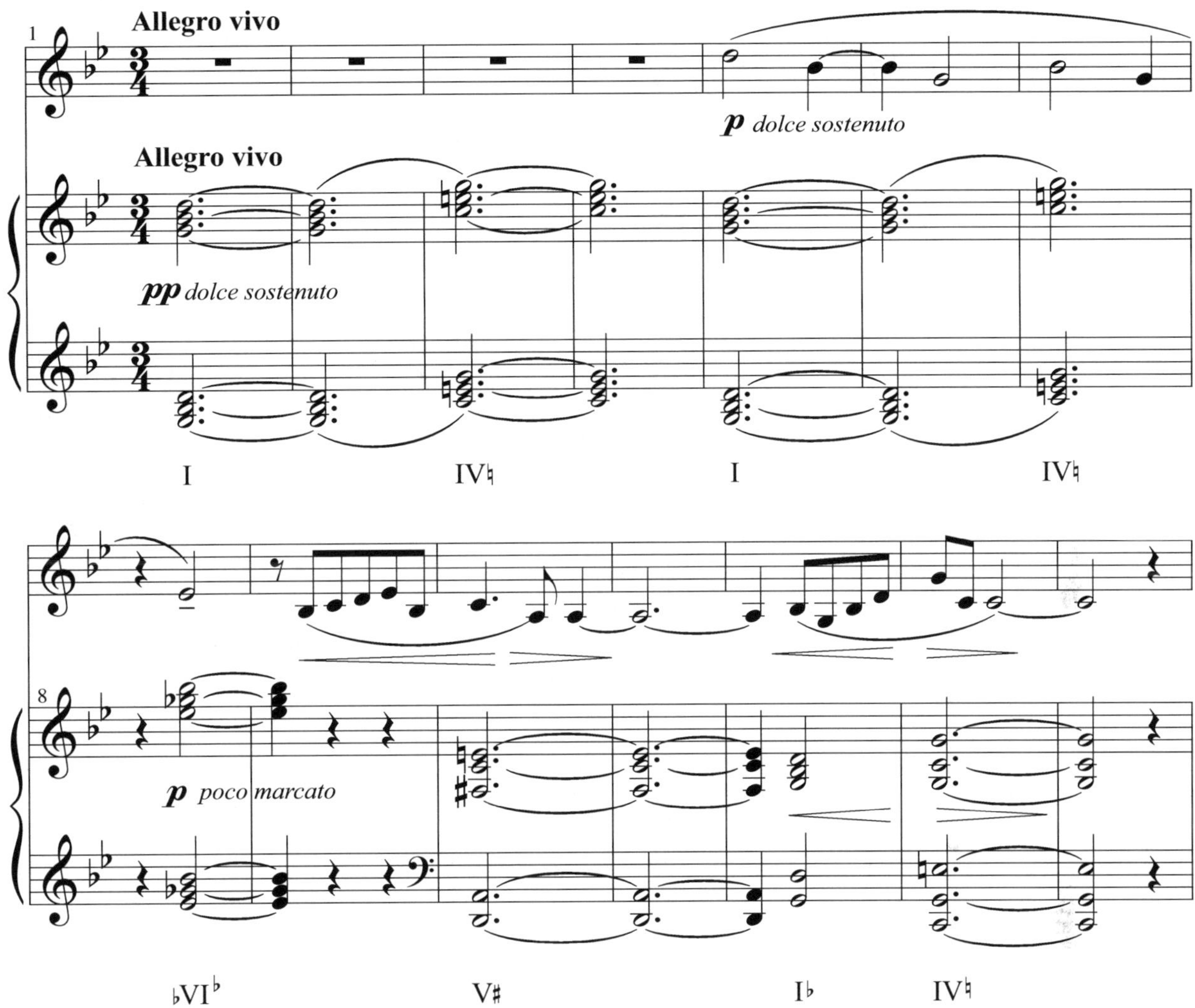

Example 7.8a Debussy, *Sonate pour violon et piano*, first movement, mm. 1–14

Example 7.8b Debussy, *Sonate pour violon et piano*, first movement, mm. 224–47

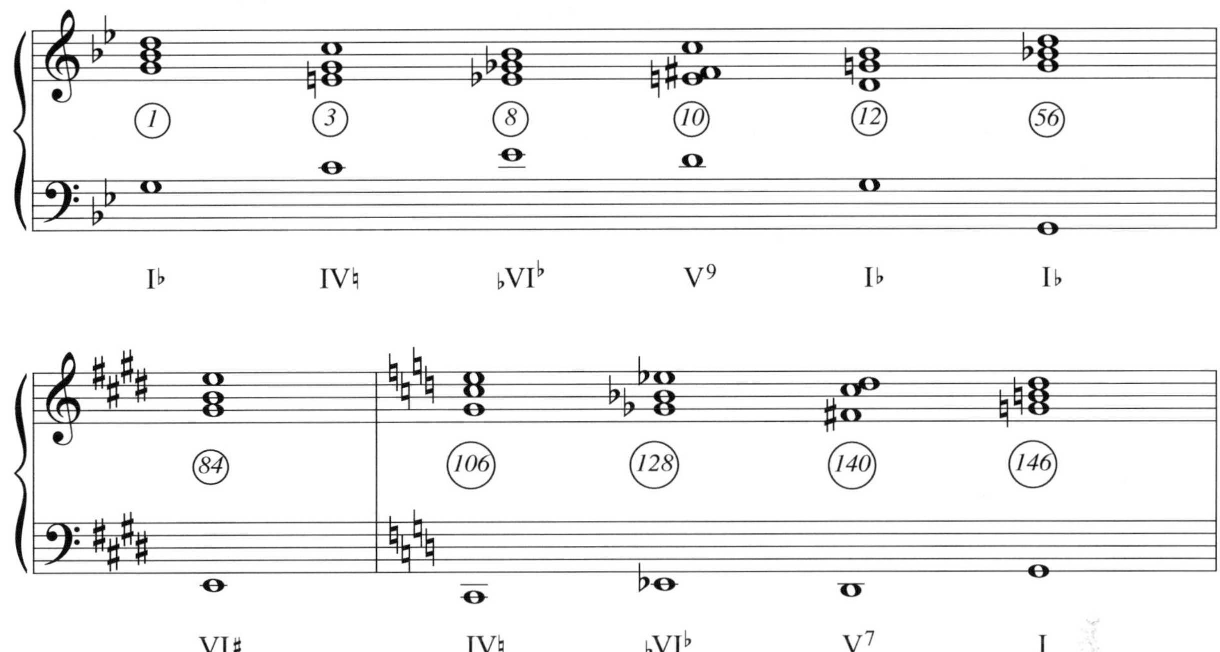

Example 7.8c Tonal structure of Debussy, *Sonate pour violon et piano*, first movement

One last point about the ending of the finale: in the same letter in which Debussy described how the music turned back on itself like a snake biting its own tail, he also claimed that the work was anything but somber and hopeless. On the contrary, he claimed that "by one of those very human contradictions it's full of happiness and uproar."[41] Debussy added: "In [the] future don't be taken in by works that seem to fly through the air; they've often been wallowing in the shadows of a gloomy brain. Such is the finale of this same sonata."[42] The optimistic ending of the finale does indeed stand in stark contrast to the desolate ending of the first movement. As mentioned, the first movement ends with a particularly gloomy passage that seems to conjure up the sounds of *cante jondo*: this impression is created by the passage's prominent use of A♭ (♭$\hat{2}$) and D♭ (♭$\hat{5}$) and its quasi-improvised character. At the other extreme, the Neapolitan finale ends with one of the most ebullient passages Debussy ever composed: A♭ (♭$\hat{2}$) and D♭ (♭$\hat{5}$) are replaced by A ($\hat{2}$) and D ($\hat{5}$) and the tonic G is transformed from minor to major. It is a remarkable testimony to "what an invalid can write in time of war."[43]

Taken as a whole, the preceding discussion has underscored the fact that details certainly mattered to Debussy: he relied on them both to unify individual movements and to bind together different movements into a single coherent whole. As Carter noted seventy-five years ago, "[Debussy's] formal methods spring from two different sources, the Franckian cyclical method employed in the *Quatuor à cordes* and the method of continuous development used by the Baroque composers of which he was so fond. Unlike many composers of the nineteenth century, he did not treat the seventeenth and eighteenth centuries as a source of neoclassic stylization—as did, for instance, Tchaikovsky in his *Mozartiana* or Wagner in *Die Meistersinger*—but more like Chopin and Schumann, both of whom were deeply influenced by Bach. His works abound in the concept of continuous development."[44] He added, "The cuts in continuity are contrasted and sometimes

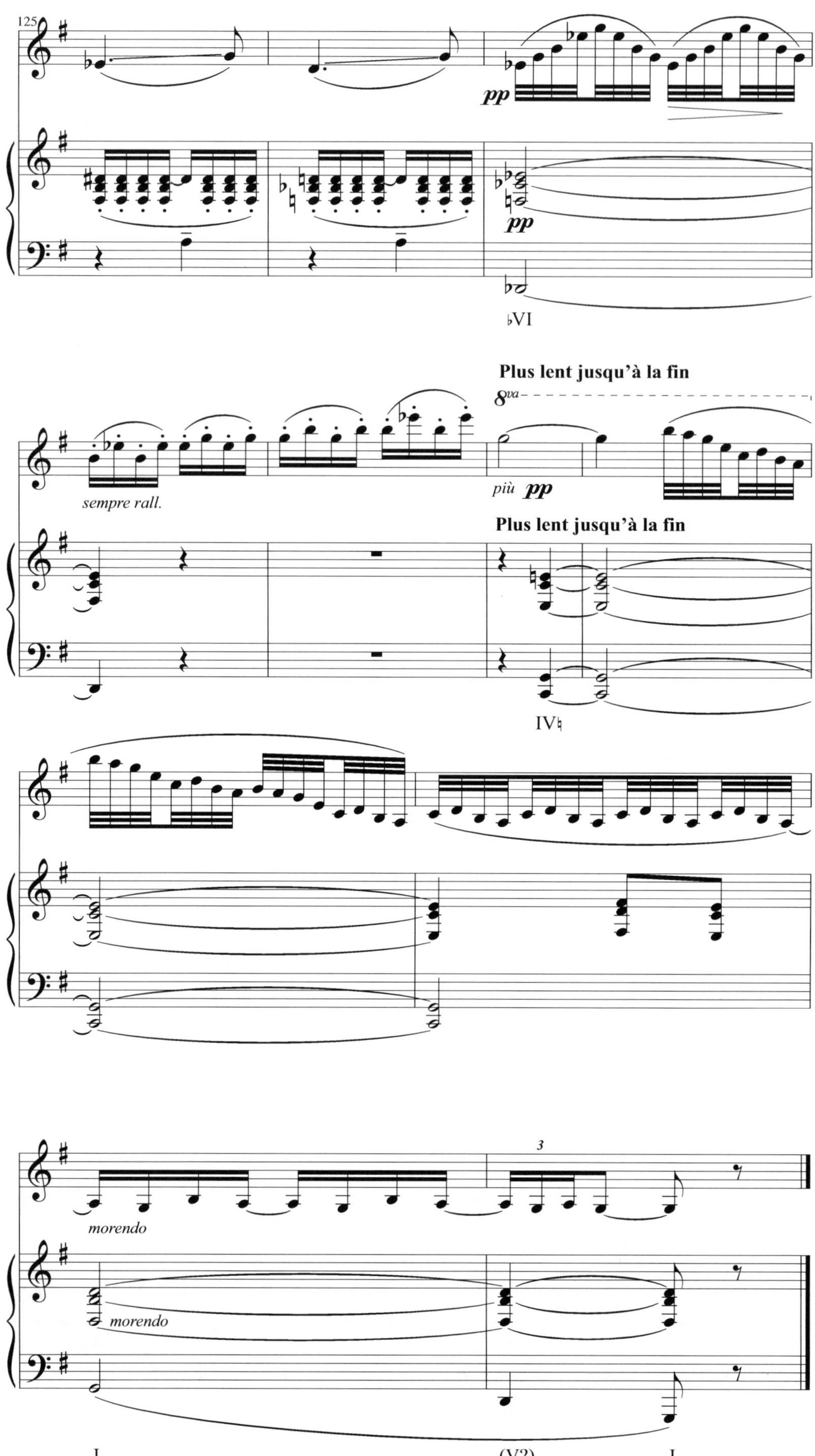

Example 7.9 Debussy, *Sonate pour violon et piano*, Intermède, mm. 125–35

provide a diverting cross current which follows its own continuous development." Once again, this all resonates with traditional notions of the arabesque, especially with Hogarth's serpentine lines and Schlegel's self-generating forms.

Nevertheless, associating Debussy's music with that of Bach doesn't simply shed light on the motivic structure of the *Sonate pour violon et piano*: it also helps to answer other important questions concerning the work's fluid formal plan. What did Debussy have in mind when he entitled the piece "sonata" and claimed it was cast "in the ancient mould"? Did he mean to suggest that the movements were constructed according to traditional schemes associated with late-eighteenth and nineteenth-century sonatas, especially some version of sonata form? Or did he do so in the more general seventeenth- and early eighteenth-century sense to indicate that the works were to be performed by instruments rather than voices as in cantatas?

Although Teresa Davidian has rightly noted that the *Sonate pour violon et piano* does not conform "completely to conventional sonata form," several writers have nonetheless found residues of the model running through the first movement.[45] Certainly there is no doubt that the movement's main theme in G minor, first heard in mm. 1–14 and shown in example 7.5f, returns in G minor in mm. 146/150–62 and again starting in m. 196. There is also no doubt that the movement ends in G minor with material derived from the main theme and with the *cante jondo* gesture shown in example 7.6c. It is less obvious, however, how to interpret the function of the various subordinate themes and secondary key areas within the context of a sonata form. The two most likely candidates—the third motive D–F–D in mm. 18–22 and the stepwise pattern Gb–Ab–Gb in mm. 133–39—are both problematic: the former because it occurs too early while the music still lies within the orbit of the first key; the latter because it enters too late in the movement and too close to the reprise. These are much the same problems that we encountered in analyzing the first movement of the *Quatuor à cordes*.

Rather than treat the first movement of the *Sonate pour violon et piano* as a modified sonata form, it seems more reasonable to see it as a sonata in the baroque sense found in Bach's six sonatas for violin and keyboard (BWV 1014–19), three sonatas for viola da gamba and keyboard (BWV 1027–29), and six sonatas for flute (BWV 1030–35) and his trio sonatas (BWV 1032 and 1038). Such movements invariably bring back the opening material in the tonic key in some varied form at the movement's end, but they do not follow the predictable scheme of so-called sonata forms. On the contrary, table 7.1a suggests that the first movement of Debussy's *Sonate*

Table 7.1. Formal layout of Debussy, *Sonate pour violon et piano*, first movement

a. Debussy, *Sonate pour violon et piano*, first movement

Opening Section mm. 1–63

Middle Section mm. 64–145 [C (mm. 106–27), Eb (mm. 128–39), D (mm. 140–45)]

Varied Reprise mm. 146–195

Coda mm. 195–255

b. Bach, Sonata in E major for Violin and Keyboard (BWV 1016), first movement

Opening Section mm. 1–5

Middle Section mm. 6–19 and 20–25

Varied Reprise mm. 25–31

Coda mm. 31–34

pour violon et piano has four main sections: an opening section (mm. 1–63) based on the main theme; a middle section (mm. 64–145) that presents new gestures in C (mm. 106–27), E♭ (mm. 128–39), and D (mm. 140–45); a varied reprise (mm. 146–95); and a coda (mm. 195–255). Table 7.1b shows that this scheme closely resembles those used by Bach, such as in the first movement of his Sonata in E major for Violin and Keyboard (BWV 1016). Given Debussy's reluctance to embrace traditional sonata form, his comments about Chopin seem strangely prophetic: "Chopin's nervous disposition let him down when it came to the endurance of writing a sonata form. But he did make some finely wrought 'sketches,' and it is at least agreed that he invented new ways of handling the form, not to mention the marvellous music he achieved in doing so. He was a man with abundant imagination, and he would flit from idea to idea without a one hundred percent commission on the transaction—which is what some of our more celebrated masters do."[46]

Some will doubtless be tempted to see Debussy's return to the music of Bach as an anomaly, an aberration in the composer's otherwise staunchly modernist agenda. Richard Taruskin is a good case in point. Indeed, when discussing Debussy's editorial projects, he noted, "Counterpoint as such was a thing of the academy, from which (after he'd been through the mill with honors) Debussy retained a horror of technical routine that lasted and grew to his dying day. Not even Bach was spared toward the end. In the last year of his life, Debussy accepted a commission from his publisher, Durand, to edit the six sonatas for violin and the three for viola da gamba with harpsichord. 'Never correct J. S. Bach's accompanied violin sonatas on a rainy Sunday!' he wrote back to Durand."[47] Taruskin added, "In fact [Debussy] was full of contempt for the materials of his art. They were to be transcended, not 'mastered.' He set no store by métier. Facility nauseated him, his own above all; and that is what kept him from being prolific."[48] Never one to let facts get in the way of a good yarn, Taruskin clearly had a superficial understanding both of Debussy's compositional methods and of his debts to the past, especially to Bach. Though Debussy was certainly critical of how counterpoint was taught in the academy, he was by no means critical of polyphonic music per se. Consider, for a moment, his observations about the works of Palestrina and Lasso in a letter to Eugène Vasnier (November 24, 1885): "I'm truly amazed at the effects they can get simply from a vast knowledge of counterpoint. I expect you think of counterpoint as the most forbidding article in the whole of music. But in their hands, it becomes something wonderful, adding an extraordinary depth to the meaning of words. And every now and then the melodic lines unroll and expand, reminding you of the illuminations in ancient missals."[49]

Debussy's admiration for Bach's contrapuntal prowess was no less overt; as mentioned in the introduction, he not only associated the concept of the arabesque with Bach's instrumental music but also marveled at how its fusion of polyphonic lines "stirs our emotions."[50] More significantly, perhaps, art critic Jed Perl has suggested that deliberate references to and reinterpretations of the past are part and parcel of avant-garde aesthetics: "The backwards glance is almost always a critical element in the avant-garde enterprise. The avant-garde rejection of current assumptions, standards, and prejudices is driven by root causes and primary sources—by a desire to reject the present not in favor of some amorphous future but in favor of first principles."[51] For Debussy, Stravinsky, Schoenberg, Webern, and countless other early twentieth-century composers, the return to first principles meant reacquainting themselves with the music of Bach. Schoenberg said it best when he noted that the originality and novelty of Bach's work "seems the more astonishing to us the more we study his music" and "still escapes the observation of the experts."[52] According to him, Bach didn't simply write "new music," he wrote "eternal music" that is never out of date, thereby showing composers how to invent "musical figures that can be used to accompany themselves," making it possible to produce "everything from one thing" by "relating figures by transformation."[53] Schoenberg would doubtless have agreed with Debussy when he claimed that Bach was the "father of us all."[54]

Notes

1. Antoine Hennion and Joël-Marie Fauquet, *La grandeur de Bach: L'amour de la musique en France au XIXe siècle* (Paris: Fayard, 2000); Antoine Hennion and Joël-Marie Fauquet, "Authority as Performance: The Love of Bach in Nineteenth Century France," *Poetics* 29 (2001): 75–88.

2. Claude Debussy, "Pour la Musique," *SIM* (March 1, 1914), in *Monsieur Croche et autres écrits*, ed. François Lesure (Paris: Gallimard, 1987), 263; Claude Debussy, "For the Cause of Music," in *Debussy on Music*, ed. François Lesure and trans. Richard Langham Smith (New York: Knopf, 1977), 314–15; and Claude Debussy, "A la Société nationale," *Gil Blas* (February 23, 1903), in *Monsieur Croche*, 104; Claude Debussy, "At the Société Nationale," in *Debussy on Music*, 126. Debussy again listed Bach among his favorite composers a month later in April 1914; see Debussy, "An Appreciation of Modern Music," *Etude Magazine* (June 1914), in Debussy, *Debussy on Music*, 317.

3. Barbara L. Kelly, Deborah Mawer, Rachel Moore, and Graham Sadler, "Introduction," in *Accenting the Classics: Editing European Music in France, 1915–1925*, ed. D. Mawer, B. L. Kelly, R. Moore, and G. Sadler (Woodbridge: Boydell and Brewer, 2023), 1. As regards Debussy's edition of Chopin's piano music, see Barbara L. Kelly, "Debussy's Homage to Chopin: As Editor, Performer, and Composer," in *Accenting the Classics*, 219–52.

4. Deborah Mawer, "Accenting Bach: An Editorial Trajectory from Fauré to Roger-Ducasse," in *Accenting the Classics*, 153–88, esp. 155–56.

5. See Debussy's letter to Durand (June 30, 1915) in Claude Debussy, *Correspondance (1872–1918)*, ed. François Lesure and Denis Herlin, annotated by François Lesure, Denis Herlin, and Georges Liébert (Paris: Gallimard, 2005), 1904fn2; and Herlin, "An Artist High and Low, or Debussy and Money," in *Rethinking Debussy*, ed. Elliot Antokoletz and Marianne Wheeldon, trans. Vincent Giroud (New York: Oxford University Press, 2011), 195.

6. See Debussy's letter to Robert Godet, February 5, 1916. Debussy, *Correspondance*, 1972; Claude Debussy, *Debussy Letters*, ed. François Lesure and Roger Nichols, trans. Roger Nichols (Cambridge, MA: Harvard University Press, 1987), 315.

7. See Debussy's letter to Victor Segalen, June 5, 1916. Debussy, *Correspondance*, 1999; Debussy, *Letters*, 315.

8. The courts ordered him to pay outstanding alimony payments to his first wife, Lily Texier, in July 1916.

9. Denis Herlin, "*Les soirs illuminés par l'ardeur du charbon*: de Baudelaire à Debussy," in *Claude Debussy—Portraits et Études* (Hildesheim: Georg Olms, 2023), 497–504.

10. See Debussy's letter to Durand, April 15, 1917. Debussy, *Correspondance*, 2099; Debussy, *Letters*, 323; and Mawer, "Accenting Bach," 156.

11. See Debussy's letter to Bernardo Molinari, October 6, 1915. Debussy, *Correspondance*, 1943; Debussy, *Letters*, 303–304.

12. There have been several attempts to imagine what these other sonatas might have sounded like. Kenneth Cooper published a hypothetical version of Debussy's sonata for oboe, horn, and harpsichord; see Kenneth Cooper, arr., *Debussy's Sonata 'No. 4' for oboe, horn, and harpsichord* (New York: International Music, 2011). This "reconstruction" actually reworks three existing pieces by Debussy: the "prelude" from *La Boîte à joujoux*; "Pour les notes répétées," *Études*, Bk. 2; and "Movement" (*Images*, Bk. 1). A decade earlier, Minako Tokuyama, Theo Loevendie, and Jacques Hétu wrote their own versions of the three projected sonatas; see Tokuyama, *Sonata Japanese for Oboe, Horn, and Harpsichord* (1998); Loevendie, *Golliwog's Other Dances* for trumpet, bassoon, and clarinet (1998); and Hétu, *Sonata for 13 Instruments* (1996). Most recently, Robert Orledge has completed Debussy's fourth projected sonata for oboe, horn, and harpsichord. His reconstruction was premiered in March 2018: https://www.robertorledge.co.uk/performances, accessed July 27, 2021.

13. Jacques Durand, *Quelques souvenirs d'un éditeur de musique*, vol. 2 (Paris: Durand, 1924/1925), 77; Roger Nichols, *Debussy Remembered* (London: Faber, 1992), 242.

14. For Debussy's melodic writing in the sonatas, see Elliott Carter, "The Three Late Sonatas of Debussy," in Elliott Carter, *Collected Essays and Lectures, 1937–1995*, ed. Jonathan W. Bernard, (Rochester, NY: University of Rochester Press, 1997), 129–31; Christian Goubault, *Claude Debussy* (Paris: Champion, 1986), 220–29; Wheeldon, "Debussy and La Sonate cyclique," *Journal of Musicology* 22 (2005): 644–79; François Delécluse, "Dans l'atelier de Claude Debussy. Processus créateur et méthodes de composition dans les esquisses des dernières oeuvres, 1915–1917," PhD diss., Université Jean Monnet, Saint-Étienne, 2018; and Siglind Bruhn, *Debussy's Instrumental Music in Its Cultural Context*, Studies in 20th-Century Music: Dimension and Diversity (Hillsdale, NY: Pendragon, 2019), 245–58.

15. For Debussy's contract, see Debussy, *Correspondance*, 1973–74.

16. See Debussy's letter to Durand, February 1917, Debussy, *Correspondance*, 2080; and Delécluse, "Dans l'atelier de Claude Debussy," 548–82. For another perspective, see Denis François Rauss, "*Ce terrible finale*. Les sources manuscrites de la sonate pour violon et piano de Claude Debussy et la genèse du troisième mouvement," *Cahiers Debussy* 2 (1978): 30–62.

17. Debussy, *Correspondance,* 2037; Debussy, *Letters*, 319.

18. Debussy, *Correspondance,* 2078; Debussy, *Letters*, 323.

19. See Debussy's letters to Durand, March 4, 21, 22, and 26; Debussy, *Correspondance*, 2082, 2089, 2091, 2091.

20. Debussy, *Correspondance*, 2106; Debussy, *Letters*, 324–25.

21. Debussy, *Correspondance*, 2099.

22. See Debussy's letter to Durand dated April 15, 1917; Debussy, *Correspondance*, 2099–100.

23. See Debussy's letter to André Caplet dated June 23, 1913; Debussy, *Correspondance*, 1630–31; Debussy, *Letters*, 274–76.

24. See Debussy's letter to Gaston Poulet dated March 14, 1917; Debussy, *Correspondance*, 2085–86.

25. A color photograph of the note has been posted by Kotte Autographs Roßhaupten, Germany, https://www.abebooks.com/servlet/SearchResults?kn=debussy%2C%20poulet%2C%20quartet&sts=t&cm_sp=SearchF-_-topnav-_-Results, accessed January 11, 2023.

26. To quote from Debussy's letter to Paul Dukas (May 19, 1917), "The Sonata for Violin and Piano was first completed and then performed in a benefit concert for blind soldiers—that's the best part of my story—by Gaston Poulet, who looks like a Gypsy, although he was born quietly in Paris." Debussy, *Correspondance*, 2111. See also Marianne Wheeldon, *Debussy's Late Style* (Bloomington: Indiana University Press, 2009), 16.

27. For details, see Wheeldon, *Debussy's Late Style*, 14–18.

28. See Debussy's letter to Durand dated September 12, 1917; Debussy, *Correspondance*, 2149.

29. This engraving comes from Charles Middleton's *A New and Complete System of Geography*, 2 vols. (London: Henry Rhodes, 1777, 1778).

30. Debussy, letter to Robert Godet (May 7, 1917); Debussy, *Correspondance*, 2106; Debussy, *Letters*, 324.

31. Poe's story "The Gold Bug" (1843) opens with the following epigram: "What ho! What ho! This fellow is dancing mad. He has been bitten by the tarantula." Having translated the story as "Le Scarabée d'or" in 1848, Baudelaire included it in his Edgar Poe, *Histoires extraordinaires* (Paris: Michel Lévy Frères, 1856). See Edgar Allan Poe, *Edgar Allan Poe, Œuvres en prose*, trans. Charles Baudelaire, Bibliothèque de la Pléiade, ed. Y.-G. Le Dantec (Paris: Gallimard, 1951), 65–103. Debussy would surely have known Chopin's Tarantelle in A♭ major, Op. 43, Piano Sonata No. 3, Op. 58, the Cello Sonata, Op. 65 (finale), and the tarantella from Liszt's *Années de pèlerinage II*.

32. Many years earlier, Debussy composed *Tarantelle styrienne* (1890, revised ca. 1901). Code has suggested that the main theme of "Fêtes" (*Nocturnes*) resembles that of a tarantella; see David J. Code, "Debussy, Discourse, Time," *Musical Quarterly* 100, nos. 3/4 (2017): 340–98.

33. The origins of Bach's theme are unclear, but Albert Schweitzer and others have suggested that it also appears in the soprano aria "Phoebus eilt mit schnellen Pferden" from *Weichet nur, betrübte Schatten*, BWV 202, a secular wedding cantata that seems to date from ca. 1714–18. Bach is not known to have composed a tarantella; Luca Purchiaroni has suggested that echoes can be heard in the "Gigue" from Bach's *English Suite* in A minor, BWV 807. See https://www.youtube.com/watch?v=Llo6Cr1Nvuo, accessed October 30, 2023.

34. Carter, "Three Late Sonatas of Debussy," 131.

35. Carter, "Three Late Sonatas of Debussy," 130.

36. Debussy, *Correspondance*, 1916; Debussy, *Letters*, 299. For a discussion of this point and of Debussy's fascination with learned counterpoint, see Matthew Brown, "Follow the Leader: Debussy's Contrapuntal Games," in

Debussy's Resonance, ed. François de Médicis and Steven Huebner (Rochester, NY: University of Rochester Press, 2018), 395–418.

37. Debussy, *Correspondance*, 2037; Debussy, *Letters*, 319.

38. Carter, "Three Late Sonatas of Debussy," 131.

39. See Brian Wise, "A Look Back 100 Years Later on Debussy's Violin Sonata—the Last Piece He Wrote before His Death," *String Magazine*, March 14, 2018, https://stringsmagazine.com/a-look-back-100-years-later-on -debussys-violin-sonata-the-last-piece-he-wrote-before-his-death.

40. Mark Anson Cartwright, "Elision and the Embellished Final Cadence in J. S. Bach's Preludes," *Music Analysis* 26/3 (2007): 267–88.

41. Debussy, *Correspondance*, 2106; Debussy, *Letters*, 324.

42. Debussy, *Correspondance*, 2106; Debussy, *Letters*, 324.

43. Debussy, *Correspondance*, 2117; Debussy, *Letters*, 327.

44. Carter, "Three Late Sonatas of Debussy," 129.

45. Teresa Davidian, "Debussy's Sonata Forms," PhD diss., University of Chicago, 1988, 186. See also Raymond Roy Park, "The Late Style of Claude Debussy," PhD diss., University of Michigan, 1967; Eugene N. Wilson, "Form and Texture in the Chamber Music of Debussy and Ravel," PhD diss., University of Washington, 1968; and Wilfred Mellers, "The Final Works of Claude Debussy or Pierrot fâché avec la lune," *Music and Letters* 20, no. 2 (1939): 168–76.

46. Debussy, "L'Entretien avec M. Croche," *La Revue blanche*, July 1, 1901; Claude Debussy, "Conversation with M. Croche," in *Monsieur Croche et autres écrits* ed. François Lesure (Paris: Gallimard, 1987), 51; and Claude Debussy, *Debussy on Music*, ed. François Lesure and trans. Richard Langham Smith (New York: Knopf, 1977), 47.

47. Richard Taruskin, "The First Modernist," in *The Danger of Music and Other Anti-Utopian Essays* (Berkeley: University of California Press, 2009), 198 [195–201].

48. Taruskin, "First Modernist," 198.

49. Debussy, *Correspondance*, 44–45; and Debussy, *Letters*, 14.

50. Debussy, "Vendredi Saint," in *Monsieur Croche*, 33–34; Debussy, "Good Friday," in *Debussy on Music*, 26–27.

51. Jed Perl, "The Art of Pleasure," *New York Review of Books* 64, no. 20 (2017), https://www.nybooks.com /articles/2017/12/21/renoir-art-of-pleasure.

52. Arnold Schoenberg, "New Music, Outmoded Music, Style and Idea," in *Style and Idea*, ed. Leonard Stein, trans. Leo Black, 60th Anniversary ed. (Berkeley: University of California Press, 2010), 117–18.

53. Schoenberg, "National Music (2)," in *Style and Idea*, 173.

54. Debussy, "A la Société nationale," in *Monsieur Croche*, 104; Debussy, "A la Société Nationale," in *Debussy on Music*, 126.

IV. Borrowing and Self-Generation

8

Pelléas et Mélisande, Arabesques, and Texts within Texts

THE PRECEDING CHAPTERS treated arabesques as forms of ornament and endorsed the idea
that they are contrapuntal in nature and prone to create self-generating forms. And yet, it is clear
from Debussy's review of Ysaÿe's Good Friday concert that arabesques are something more: they
also guide a work's expressive power and extra-musical meaning. Debussy was adamant that arabesques "stir our emotions" and "fill [our] imaginations with images"; these claims clearly resonate
with Baudelaire's concept of *correspondances*, Mallarmé's belief in the musicality of poetry, and
Wagner's concepts of *Versmelodie* and the *Gesamtkunstwerk*.[1] Debussy also associated arabesques
with the notion of "free fantasy," something that reverberated with the Symbolist predilection
for mixing diverse literary genres (e.g., letters, poetry, prose, confessions, etc.), combining the
real with the unreal, texts within texts, and promoting the mise en abyme. The latter are readily
apparent in works such as *L'Après-midi d'un faune*, which interweaves Mallarmé's account of what
happened that sultry afternoon with the faun's dream of what might have happened, and "The
Fall of the House of Usher," which interleafs Poe original story with passages from his previously
published poem "The Haunted Palace" and Launcelot Canning's fictional story "Mad Trist."

This chapter sets out to show how Debussy cultivated these aspects of the arabesque in his
opera *Pelléas et Mélisande* by fusing elements from diverse genres, juxtaposing aspects of the
real and the unreal, and including texts within texts and mise en abyme. The discussion begins
with Maeterlinck's libretto and explains how it combines elements from several literary genres
and texts. In particular, it focuses on four scenes where those elements are introduced to create a
strong sense of fantasy: the final scene of act 1, in which Pelléas first encounters Mélisande walking Geneviève along the cliffs one stormy evening; the grotto scene from act 2, in which Pelléas
escorts Mélisande to a cave by the sea; the vault scene from act 3, in which Golaud threatens

Pelléas in the caverns beneath the castle; and finally, the sheep scene from act 4, in which Yniold meets a shepherd leading his flock to slaughter. The chapter then considers Debussy's setting of Maeterlinck's drama. Having described the score's elaborate compositional history and Wagnerian influences, it reconsiders the four scenes mentioned above and the ways in which Debussy's music reinforces the fantastic elements of the play. By quoting material from other works, such as earlier songs and future orchestral pieces, Debussy highlighted two central features of the literary arabesque: the text within a text and the mise en abyme.

Born in Ghent in 1862 and a lawyer by training, Maeterlinck caught the literary bug in the mid-1880s after spending seven months in Paris ostensibly to study the French legal system. Instead of spending hours poring over arcane statutes and prior rulings, he passed his time in the company of leading Symbolist authors, including Auguste Villiers de l'Isle-Adam, Paul Verlaine, and Stéphane Mallarmé.[2] They encouraged him to devote himself to writing and inspired him to publish *Serres chaudes*, a collection of poems from 1889.[3] Maeterlinck's early notebooks reveal that by this time he was already familiar with the writings of Schlegel, E. T. A. Hoffmann, Poe, Baudelaire, Wagner, and many other authors mentioned in chapter 1.[4] Poe's influence was especially profound and cultivated in him "an inner sense of mystery, and a passion for all that lies beyond life."[5] Maeterlinck even wrote his own fantastic stories on occult, supernatural, and paranormal themes, just like those in Poe's *Tales of the Grotesque and Arabesque*. One such story—*Onirology* (1889)—"is a pioneering exploration of the hidden meaning of dreams, repressed memories, and the pre-Freudian unconscious" that specifically uses the theater "as a metaphor for the dream."[6] Not long after, Maeterlinck developed this last point by writing a string of Symbolist plays starting with *La Princesse Maleine* (1889), a Shakespearean reworking of the German fairy story "Jungfrau Maleen."[7] He wrote his next play—*Pelléas et Mélisande*—just a few years later; this second drama was immediately published in Brussels by Paul Lacomblez (May 1892) and premiered in Paris at the Théâtre de l'Œuvres (May 1893) under the direction of Aurélien Lugné-Poe.

Part myth or fable, part gothic horror story, part Shakespearean tragedy, and part social critique, Maeterlinck's play *Pelléas et Mélisande* combines elements from numerous sources and genres: Dante's *Paolo e Francesca*, Wagner's *Tristan und Isolde*, Tennyson's "Pelleas and Ettarre" (*Idylls of the King*), and Poe's "Annabel Lee" as well as the legend of King Arthur, Queen Guinevere, and Sir Lancelot.[8] Since it is set during the Black Death, *Pelléas et Mélisande* specifically recalls Shakespeare's *Romeo and Juliet* and Poe's "The Masque of the Red Death."[9] The individual characters have equally diverse origins. Smith, for example, has traced Pelléas back to Tennyson, Mélisande to the mythological siren Melusine, and Golaud to the Medieval story of *Geneviève de Brabant*.[10] Tennyson's poem "The Marriage of Geraint" (*Idylls of the King*) even mentions that Enid's father is named Yniold. As regards the play's mood, Smith has connected its melancholy sensuality to the works of Edward Burne-Jones, Walter Crane, and other Pre-Raphaelite artists, something that is apparent from Jessie Marion King's arabesque depiction of act 3, scene 2 from the play (see fig. 8.1).[11]

As regards the plot of *Pelléas et Mélisande*, Maeterlinck apparently adapted it from a novella entitled "A Ladie Falslie Accused" by the Italian Renaissance author Matteo Bandello (ca. 1480–1561).[12] The story, which was translated into French by Pierre Boaistuau and François de Belleforest, appeared in William Painter's anthology *The Palace of Pleasure* (1566–67), an English translation of 101 stories written by the likes of Herodotus, Plutarch, Livy, Tacitus, Boccaccio, Straparola, Margaret of Navarre, Matteo Bandello, Bannelier, and others. Since Maeterlinck probably didn't know Painter's original or Joseph Haslewood's version from 1813, he most likely

Figure 8.1 Jessie Marion King, *Pelléas et Mélisande* (1901)

consulted Joseph Jacobs's revised edition of 1890. That version, which was dedicated to Burne-Jones, would have piqued his curiosity for a couple of reasons.[13] One was Jacobs's fascination with fairy tales: over the course of his career, he compiled numerous collections, such as *English Fairy Tales* (1890), *Celtic Fairy Tales* (1892), *More English Fairy Tales* (1894), and *More Celtic Fairy Tales* (1894). Another was Maeterlinck's love of Shakespeare; he was surely aware that *The Palace of Pleasure* contained models for several of the bard's plays, including *Romeo and Juliet*, *All's Well That Ends Well*, and *Timon of Athens*.[14]

In reworking Bandello's "A Ladie Falslie Accused," Maeterlinck situated *Pelléas et Mélisande* in Allemonde, a mythical kingdom gripped by a deadly pandemic. When the curtain opens, the servants can be seen scrubbing the steps outside the castle to wash away the plague's deadly germs. King Arkel's wife is dead; Golaud's father/Geneviève's first husband is dead; Golaud's first wife/Yniold's mother is dead; Pelléas's father/Geneviève's second husband is dying, and his friend Marcellus is on his deathbed; and Mélisande has escaped the clutches of a notorious serial killer. Given the peculiarities of the royal family tree, it is unclear whether the previous deaths stemmed from natural causes or whether, like "The Fall of the House of Usher," the family is cursed by a recurring pattern of violence and incest.[15] When Arkel warns at the end that Mélisande's newborn baby faces the same fate as its mother, Maeterlinck implied that this cycle of mutual destruction would continue for the foreseeable future.[16]

Since he believed at the time that human actions are determined by fate, Maeterlinck intimated that Golaud, Mélisande, and Pelléas were all shaped by past events and inherent flaws in their characters. Potentially violent and prone to jealousy, Golaud was scarred by the death of his first wife; he has been left to bring up his young son Yniold on his own, sometimes abusing him (act 3, scene 5). Arkel has urged him to marry Princess Ursula for political reasons, but Golaud picks Mélisande instead. As for Mélisande, she clearly recognizes that men find her attractive, but she has difficulty finding her perfect match; in his play *Ariane et Barbe-Bleue*, Maeterlinck portrayed her as an abused wife of Bluebeard. Once Mélisande realizes that Golaud is jealous and violent, she deliberately lies about the whereabouts of her wedding ring (act 2, scene 2) and confesses to Pelléas that she only lies to Golaud (act 4, scene 4). Meanwhile, Pelléas is immature and incapable of accepting his familial responsibilities. Golaud is clearly aware of Pelléas's shortcomings: when talking to Mélisande about Pelléas in act 2, scene 2, Golaud described his half brother as "a little strange" and "young." Arkel also recognizes Pelléas's failings. When the young prince admits that he wants to leave Allemonde to visit his sick friend Marcellus (act 1, scene 3), Arkel chides him: "It would be well to wait awhile, nevertheless. . . . Is not your father here, overhead, more dangerously ill, perhaps, than your friend . . . Are you able to choose between father and friend?" The same lack of loyalty explains why he falls in love with his half brother's wife.

Set against this volatile backdrop, Maeterlinck cast *Pelléas et Mélisande* as a macabre love triangle. The triangle is set up in act 1. Golaud, who is heir to the throne of Allemonde, encounters Mélisande while hunting in the forest (act 1, scene 2). She has dropped her crown in a well. Golaud questions her, but she discloses nothing about her past. They marry and return to his ancestral home to meet his grandfather, Arkel, his mother, Geneviève, his half brother Pelléas, and his son Yniold. Pelléas is planning to visit his sick friend Marcellus (act 1, scene 3) but delays his departure when he encounters Mélisande (act 1, scene 4). The triangle starts to unravel in acts 2, 3, and 4. Mélisande drops her wedding ring in Blindman's Well (act 2, scene 1). She lies about the ring (act 2, scene 2), and Golaud demands that she recover it with Pelléas (act 2, scene 3). When Golaud notices that Pelléas and Mélisande are spending time together, he becomes jealous and warns them to stop meeting; he threatens Pelléas in the castle vaults (act 3, scene 2) and abuses Mélisande in front of Arkel (act 4, scene 2). The triangle disintegrates completely at the end of act 4. Pelléas and Mélisande meet one last time outside the castle (act 4, scene 4). Golaud discovers them and stabs Pelléas with the sword that Mélisande had found earlier on his prayer stool. When Pelléas collapses beside Blindman's Well, Mélisande betrays him. She has been wounded by Golaud, and she flees into the forest. Golaud chases her, after unsuccessfully trying to kill himself. Finally, act 5 shows Mélisande on her deathbed, having given birth to a baby girl. Golaud is at her bedside, a confused and broken man.

As regards the arabesque and the fantastic, Maeterlinck includes several examples of a text within a text. The most obvious are surely Golaud's letter, which Geneviève reads near the start of act 1, and Mélisande's song "Mes longs cheveux descendent," which she sings at the start of act 3. Both appear only in the play, the song was not reprinted as an independent text in Maeterlinck's collection *Douze Chansons* (Paris: P. V. Stock, 1896) or reprinted in *Quinze Chansons* (Brussels: Paul Lacomblez, 1912). Another less obvious example is the final scene of act 1. Just as Mélisande and Geneviève are taking an evening stroll along the cliffs, Pelléas scrambles up the rocks to warn everyone that a storm is brewing. The three characters look out to sea and notice a large ship departing guided by light from a distant lighthouse. Mélisande foretells that the ship will flounder in the tempest. After Geneviève has departed, Pelléas tells Mélisande that he might leave tomorrow. Those familiar with Poe's work will immediately spot parallels with "A Descent into the Maelstrom" (1841). Cast as a text within a text, Poe's story describes two men walking along a rocky path overlooking the sea. A white-haired fisherman has brought the narrator to the lofty crag to recount a traumatic event he experienced three years earlier. It occurred one evening while he was fishing with his brothers. Their boat was driven off course in a violent storm and engulfed in a massive whirlpool: one brother died when the masts of the boat were torn off; the other went insane. Although the man survived, he was "broken . . . up body and soul," and his hair turned from black to white. By recalling the creepy location of Poe's story, the final scene of act 1 warns of the impending disaster facing Pelléas and Mélisande. This possibility is conveyed by Louis Roger in his haunting painting *À Brouie* (see fig. 8.2). A ship has gone down: debris is strewn across a rocky shore, bodies are scattered everywhere, and crows are feasting on the corpses.

The principle of the text within a text also shapes the final scene of act 2, in which Pelléas escorts Mélisande to a grotto by the sea. This eerie scene is precipitated by the fact that Mélisande lies about her wedding ring, claiming to have dropped it in the grotto while collecting shells with Yniold. Golaud is furious and orders her to search for it before the tide comes in. Pelléas accompanies Mélisande on her mission. The sun has already set, and the scene is pitch black when they arrive. But as they wind their way down the narrow trail, the grotto is flooded with moonlight, revealing three beggars asleep in the corner. Pelléas explains that they are victims of the plague and recommends that they return another day. For fans of Poe, the image of bodies lying in a grotto by the sea clearly recalls "Annabel Lee." First published in 1849, this well-known poem describes the narrator's love for a beautiful maiden named Annabel Lee. They meet many years before in a kingdom by the sea. Their love is so intense that it makes the angels jealous. When she dies one chilly night, the narrator assumes that the angels have taken her life. She is buried in a tomb beside the sea. And yet his love for her never fades; every night, he lies down beside her still body.[17] By invoking Poe's poem and referring to the three beggars, the final scene of act 2 again foreshadows the demise of the three protagonists. Its placement at the end of act 2 seems to echo the clifftop scene at the end of act 1.

Figure 8.2 Louis Roger, *À Brouie* (ca. 1907?)

An even more obvious appropriation of Poe's work occurs in act 3. Golaud has just caught Pelléas flirting with Mélisande outside the castle (act 3, scene 1). Although he initially dismisses their incident as child's play, Golaud becomes increasingly suspicious of his half brother and his influence over Mélisande, who is pregnant and vulnerable. To force Pelléas into changing his ways, Golaud leads him down into the vaults beneath the castle and orders him to peer down into a deep cavern below. When Pelléas complains that the cavern "smell[s] of tombs," Golaud mentions that the stench sometimes infects the whole castle and that the cavern should be walled up. Golaud adds, "Have you noticed the crevices in the walls and in the pillars of the vaults? There is some hidden, unsuspected work; and the whole castle will be engulfed one night if no care be taken."[18] The references to Poe's "The Fall of the House of Usher" are unmistakable: the crevices in the walls recall the zigzag crack in Roderick's ancestral home, and the image of the entire castle being engulfed recalls that of the "deep black lake" swallowing up the building at the end of the story. The images of rocks and water again hark back to the final scenes of acts 1 and 2; like them, the vault scene foreshadows that Golaud will murder Pelléas.

Act 4, scene 3 provides yet another example of a text within a text. Yniold is near the fountain one evening, trying to recover a golden ball from beneath a rock. He hears a flock of sheep and is concerned that they have suddenly stopped bleating. The shepherd explains that they have gone silent because they have turned onto a path that doesn't lead back to their sheepfold. When the shepherd won't say where the sheep will sleep, Yniold goes off to ask someone else. That person is presumably Golaud because Pelléas and Mélisande are about to meet one another outside the castle. Although this scene initially seems like a non sequitur, it alludes to the story of Absolom from the Old Testament, in which Absolom murders his half brother Amnon during a feast celebrating the shearing of Absolom's sheep at Baal-hazor because he believes that Amnon has raped their sister Tamar.[19] The allusions are set up earlier in *Pelléas et Mélisande*. Just as Absolom died when his mule ran into a tree and his hair was caught in the branches, so Golaud and his horse run into a tree at precisely the same time that Mélisande drops her wedding ring into the well (act 2, scenes 1–2). And earlier in act 4, scene 2, Golaud drags Mélisande by the hair, screaming, "Ah! Ah! Your long hair serves some purpose after all! . . . Absalom! Absalom!" Yniold's encounter with the shepherd thus serves as the quintessential mise en abyme: fate has led Pelléas and Mélisande to their deaths, and it is hardly by chance that Golaud discovers their whereabouts from his son.

Having shown how the four scenes create a literary arabesque by fusing together elements from the gothic horror story, the Romantic poem, and even the Bible, let us now turn our attention to Debussy's score, describing briefly how it was composed and how it conveys the elements of the fantastic in each of the four scenes outlined above. No one knows for sure how Debussy initially encountered Maeterlinck, but it seems likely that he did so through their mutual friend Villiers de l'Isle-Adam, whom Debussy had met in March 1889. The two men became personally acquainted when Debussy approached Maeterlinck about setting *La Princesse Maleine*.[20] Although nothing came of this particular project, Debussy soon became fascinated by *Pelléas et Mélisande*, not only purchasing a copy early in 1893 but also attending the premiere in the company of Stéphane Mallarmé, Théodore Duret, Henri de Régnier, and James McNeill Whistler.[21] This was around the same time that he was completing his *Prose Lyriques* for voice and piano. He was clearly impressed with the play and, through the intervention of Henri de Régnier, visited Ghent to ask Maeterlinck for permission to treat it operatically. Maeterlinck gave his blessing on August 8, 1893, and Debussy immediately mapped out the climactic scene when Golaud stalks Pelléas and Mélisande outside the castle and murders Pelléas (act 4, scene 4). As shown in table 8.1, Debussy

Table 8.1. Comparison of Maeterlinck's play and Debussy's opera

Maeterlinck	Locale/Characters	Debussy	Chronology of Draft
act 1, scene 1	The castle gates Servants	Cut	
act 1, scene 2	Forest Golaud, Mélisande	act 1, scene 1	Dec. 1893–Feb. 1894
act 1, scene 3	Inside the castle Geneviève, Arkel, Pelléas	act 1, scene 2	Dec. 1893–Feb. 1894
act 1, scene 4	Outside the castle Geneviève, Mélisande, Pelléas	act 1, scene 3	Dec. 1893–Feb. 1894
act 2, scene 1	On the grounds by Blindman's Well Pelléas, Mélisande	act 2, scene 1	June–Aug. 1895
act 2, scene 2	Room in the castle Golaud, Mélisande	act 2, scene 2	June–Aug. 1895
act 2, scene 3	Grotto near the sea Pelléas, Mélisande	act 2, scene 3	June–Aug. 1895
act 2, scene 4	Room in the castle Arkel, Pelléas	Cut	
act 3, scene 1	Room in the castle Pelléas, Mélisande, Yniold, Golaud	Cut	
act 3, scene 2	Tower of the castle Mélisande, Pelléas, Golaud	act 3, scene 1	May–June/July 1894
act 3, scene 3	Castle vaults Golaud, Pelléas	act 3, scene 2	July–Aug. 1894
act 3, scene 4	Outside castle vaults Pelléas, Golaud	act 3, scene 3	Aug. 1894
act 3, scene 5	Outside the castle Golaud, Yniold	act 3, scene 4	Aug. 1894
act 4, scene 1	Inside the castle[1] Pelléas, Mélisande	act 4, scene 1	Jan.–Feb. 1895?
act 4, scene 2	Room in castle Arkel, Mélisande, Golaud	act 4, scene 2	Jan.–Feb. 1895?
act 4, scene 3	Castle terrace[2] Yniold, Shepherd	act 4, scene 3	Aug. 1894
act 4, scene 4	Park by Blindman's Well Pelléas, Mélisande, Golaud	act 4, scene 4	Sept.–Oct. 1893, May 1895
act 5, scene 1	Lower hall of castle Servants	Cut	
act 5, scene 2	Room in castle Arkel, Mélisande, Golaud, Doctor	act 5	April–June 1895

1. Originally "A corridor in the castle" but changed to share the décor with scene 2. The change simplified set changes and explains why Debussy only had to expand the central interlude in this act.

2. Originally "Castle terrace" but changed to share the décor with scene 4. Scene 3 was not performed during the first season but was reinstated in the second.

completed the first draft in September and October 1893. His immediate goal was apparently to set Maeterlinck's original play as faithfully as possible: David Grayson rightly notes that the earliest known sketch for act 4, scene 4 contains virtually every word written by Maeterlinck.[22]

The original play appealed to Debussy on many counts. For one thing, it satisfied his desire to find a dreamlike text that "only hints at what is to be said," one that evokes "no place, nor time" and conveys "a picture executed in grey."[23] It is surely no coincidence that Debussy was concurrently working with Mallarmé on his *Prélude à L'Après-midi d'un faune*. For another, the protagonists conveyed the inner feelings of real people: "Despite its atmosphere of dreams [*Pelléas*] contains much more humanity than those so-called documents of real life."[24] And Debussy was clearly attracted to the play's arabesque qualities, even describing certain scenes as if they belonged to one of Poe's gothic tales. On August 28, 1894, for example, he admitted to Henri Lerolle that he found Golaud's harsh interrogation of Yniold (act 3, scene 4) horrific: "It's terrifying, the music's got to be profound and absolutely accurate! There's a 'petit père' that gives me nightmares."[25]

But Debussy soon realized that the text needed to be changed, and he discussed the matter with Maeterlinck on a visit to Ghent in November 1893.[26] There is no record of what the two men said, but Debussy subsequently cut four entire scenes (see table 8.1): act 1, scene 1 with servants outside the castle gates; act 2, scene 4 with Arkel and Pelléas inside the castle; act 3, scene 1 with Pelléas, Mélisande, Yniold, and Golaud inside the castle; and act 5, scene 1 with the servants in the lower hall of the castle.[27] Having sketched act 4, scene 4 in September and October 1893, Debussy spent the next two years drafting the rest of the opera. Table 8.1 also shows that he finished the other scenes out of order, starting with act 1, scenes 1–3 in December 1893–February 1894 and ending with act 2, scenes 1–3 in June–August 1895.[28] Debussy continued to fuss with the draft over the next few years, but he focused much of his energy on arranging stage performances with Pierre Larochelle's Théâtre Libre and Lugné-Poe's Théâtre de l'Œuvre. Unfortunately, both events fell through, as did performances at the Comte de Montesquiou's Pavillon des Muses and the Théâtre de la Monnaie in Brussels.[29] In 1900, however, the Opéra-Comique expressed interest, and Debussy set about completing the piano/vocal score. Plans were temporarily put on hold after the death of Debussy's patron, Georges Hartmann, but the premiere was eventually scheduled for the spring of 1902.

With that performance looming on the horizon, Debussy made further revisions in the summer of 1901.[30] Since Maeterlinck's longtime partner Georgette Leblanc was being considered for the role of Mélisande, the playwright gave Debussy his most recent revisions, even those from the 1902 edition.[31] Except for act 1, scene 1 and act 3, scene 1, most of the scenes were trimmed to one degree or another.[32] Act 3, scenes 2 and 3 were particularly heavily cut. In Maeterlinck's play, the vault scene stands out because Golaud threatens Pelléas and because, as noted earlier, it specifically recalls Poe's "The Fall of the House of Usher." And yet, Debussy excised the most explicit allusion to Poe—namely, that the vaults had "the smell of tombs," that the walls were littered with strange crevices, and the strange aura that might engulf the entire castle one night "if no care be taken." Once rehearsals began, Debussy made further cuts. A casting decision prompted him to modify Pelléas's part so that it would fit a *baryton Martin* rather than a tenor range.[33] To facilitate changes of scenery, he expanded the interludes in acts 1 and 2 and one in act 4.[34] As shown in table 8.2, the first performance eventually took place on April 30, 1902. During the public dress rehearsal on April 28, 1902, Henry Roujon, director of fine arts, found Golaud's interrogation of his young son Yniold (act 3, scene 4) unacceptable and forced Debussy to remove the offending passages.[35] He made other small cuts in response to audience reactions.[36] Despite further delays, Debussy's

Table 8.2. First production of Debussy's *Pelléas et Mélisande*

Premiere	Paris, Théâtre Nationale de L'Opéra-Comique, April 30, 1902
Cast	Golaud, Hector Dufranne
	Mélisande, Mary Garden
	Pelléas, Jean Périer
	Arkel, Félix Vieuille
	Geneviève, Jeanne Gerville-Réache
	Yniold, Blondin
	doctor, M. Viguié
Scenery	Lucien Jusseaume (act 1, scene 1, act 2, scenes 1–2, act 3, scenes 2 and 4, act 4, scenes 1, 3 [scene was cut during the first season], and 4, and act 5) and Eugène Ronsin (act 1, scenes 2–3, act 2, scene 3, act 3, scenes 1 and 3, and act 4, scene 2)
Costumes	Charles Bianchini
Producer	Albert Carré
Conductor	André Messager
First edition	Paris, Fromont, vocal score, 1902 [lacks extended interludes], orchestral score 1904
Rev. edition	Paris, Durand, orchestral score, 1905, piano version of extended interludes arranged by Samazeuilh, 1905, vocal score, 1907 [includes extended interludes, but lacks 15 mm. from act 3, scene 4]
Excerpts	Paris, Durand, vocal [Récit. Geneviève "La Lettre" (act 1, scene 2); "Duo à la fontaine," Pelléas, Mélisande (act 2, scene 1); Récit Pelléas "Les cheveux" (act 3, scene 1); Récit Arkel et Mélisande (act 4, scene 2)], 1905–1908; piano ["Duo à la fontaine" (act 2, scene 1); "Les cheveux" (act 3, scene 1); and "La mort de Pelléas" (act 4, scene 4)], arranged by Léon Roques, 1906
Piano solo	Paris, Durand, arranged by Léon Roques, 1907
Critical edition	Paris, Durand-Costallat, edited by David Grayson, Œuvres Complètes de Claude Debussy Sér. 6, Vol. 2, 2010

operatic version of *Pelléas et Mélisande* received its premiere at the Théâtre de l'Opéra-Comique on April 30, 1902: as shown in table 8.2, it was produced by Albert Carré and conducted by André Messager, with Jean Périer starring as Pelléas, Mary Garden as Mélisande, Hector Dufranne as Golaud, Félix Vieuille as Arkel, Mme. Gerville-Réache as Geneviève, Blondin as Yniold, and M. Viguié as the doctor.

When thinking about Debussy's score, it is worth remembering that *Pelléas et Mélisande* was as much a response to Wagner as it was to Maeterlinck; listeners have found countless allusions to Wagner's operas, some more believable than others.[37] And yet, although Debussy clearly wanted to capture the intimate connections between text and music suggested by Wagner in "Music of the Future" (1861) and Baudelaire in "Richard Wagner et *Tannhäuser* à Paris," he could not ignore the fact that the form and mood of Maeterlinck's text called for a radically new type of musical setting. The differences are, indeed, profound: whereas Wagner's libretti are usually written in verse and based on his version of *Stabreim*, Maeterlinck's play is in prose and features few extended speeches. And, whereas Wagner emphasized the idea of *Die unendliche Melodien* and quasi-symphonic orchestral accompaniments, Debussy favored melodic lines based on short melodic/rhythmic cells supported by more delicate instrumental writing. Though both composers use leitmotifs, Debussy picked gestures that are usually less assertive than those preferred by Wagner and often consist of brief rhythmic cells or simple melodic patterns.[38] Indeed, as Marie Rolf has demonstrated in the context of act 4, scene 4, Debussy liked to arrange these simple patterns in succession to create arabesque-like structures.[39] Given their brevity and plasticity, his leitmotifs usually "hint at, rather than declare, the emotions and events depicted on stage."[40]

To illustrate these ideas, example 8.1a presents a representative passage from the opening of act 2, scene 1, in which Mélisande meets Pelléas and drops her wedding ring down Blindman's Well. The passage begins with a statement of Pelléas's leitmotif in the flutes, followed by a descending figure A–G♯–F♯–E–D♯–C♯ in the flutes and clarinets (mm. 2–3). These gestures are echoed by a lush dominant ninth chord in E major with amorous connotations.[41] Those connotations are all the more striking because Debussy highlighted the moment by including a musical text within a text: it recalls the opening measures of his early song "C'est l'extase" (*Ariettes oubliées*, ca. 1887). As shown in example 8.1b, both passages present the same dominant ninth sonority and descending figure. The interconnections are reinforced a few bars later: the syncopated rhythms in mm. 15–16

Example 8.1 Debussy, *Pelléas et Mélisande* and "C'est l'extase," *Ariettes oubliées*

Example 8.1a *Pelléas et Mélisande*, act 2, scene 1, mm. 1–6

Example 8.1b Debussy, "C'est l'extase," mm. 1–10

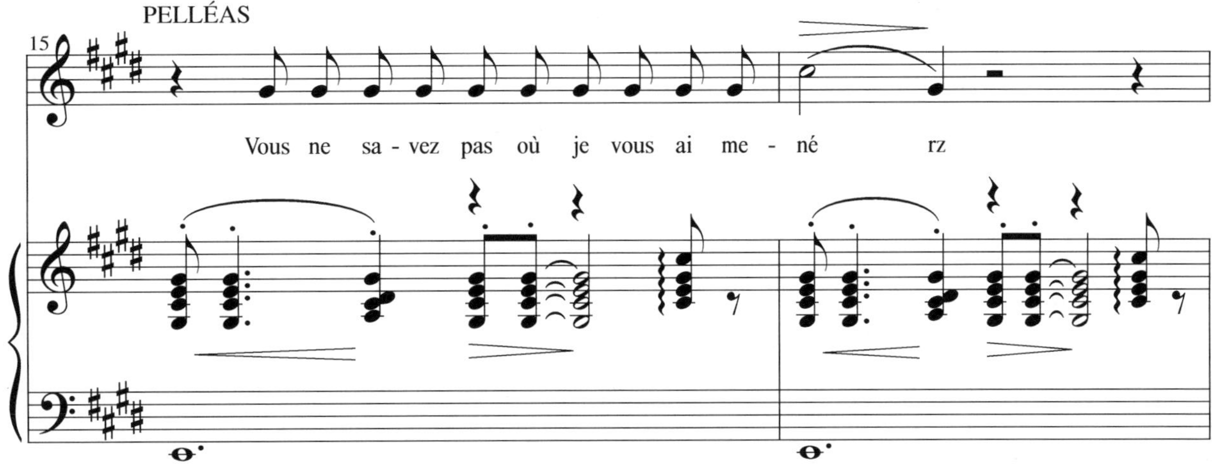

Example 8.1c *Pelléas et Mélisande,* act 2, scene 1, mm. 15–16

Example 8.1d Debussy, "C'est l'extase," mm. 11–15

of the opera (ex. 8.1c) resemble those heard starting in m. 11 of "C'est l'extase" (ex. 8.1d).[42] These cross-references are a perfect example of a text within a text and hence of a literary arabesque.

Debussy adopted similar compositional strategies in the final scene of act 1, when Pelléas meets Mélisande for the first time on the cliffs and predicts that the ship on which she came to Allemonde will sink in the impending storm. When setting this scene to music, Debussy followed a strategy he had employed since the start of the opera: he set the general mood of the scene by introducing a primary leitmotif and establishing a principal key; to advance the narrative, he developed this leitmotif melodically and contrapuntally with other melodic cells. As shown in example 8.2, act 1, scene 3 uses Mélisande's leitmotif as its primary motive and F♯ major as its principal key. First introduced at the opening of the opera, Mélisande's motive appears numerous times as the scene unfolds, often starting on different notes. As is normally the case in *Pelléas et Mélisande* and most Wagnerian music dramas, those statements are in the orchestral accompaniment rather than in the vocal parts. Examples 8.2a–8.2b also show that Mélisande's motive appears in counterpoint with an oscillating figure reminiscent of wavelike patterns from his orchestral work "Sirènes" (*Nocturnes* [mvt. 3]), another piece occupying Debussy in the 1890s and stylistically related to *Pelléas et Mélisande* (see ex. 8.2c).[43] Act 1, scene 3 also contains several other important gestures. Pelléas's arrival is marked by a statement of his leitmotif in what appears to be the dominant of E major (see ex. 8.2d). Not long after, Golaud's presence can be felt through several recollections of the so-called fate motive, starting with the one given in example 8.2e. Examples 8.2f–8.2g then show two passages in which this gesture appears in counterpoint with or in proximity to Mélisande's motive and the oscillating figure.

Besides illustrating the subtle ways in which Debussy hinted at the emotions and events depicted onstage, the musical details shown in examples 8.2a–8.2g stand out because they provide musical clues to what will happen in the future, thereby underscoring the Symbolist mantra that details matter. The connections between the oscillating motive in act 1, scene 3 (ex. 8.2b) and

Example 8.2 Debussy, *Pelléas et Mélisande*, act 1, scene 3

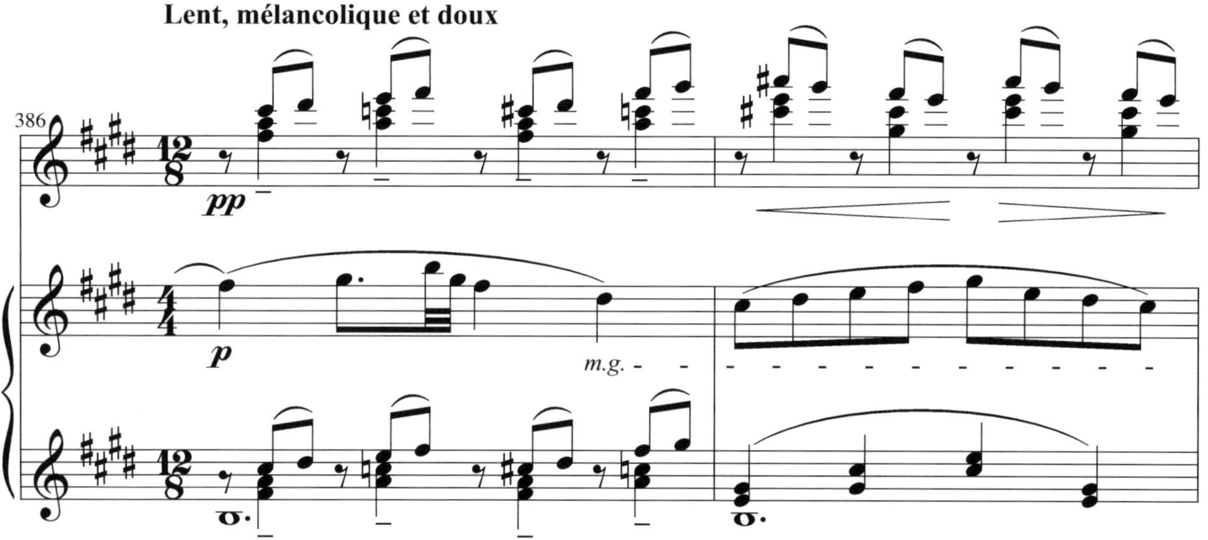

Example 8.2a Mélisande's motive, mm. 386–87

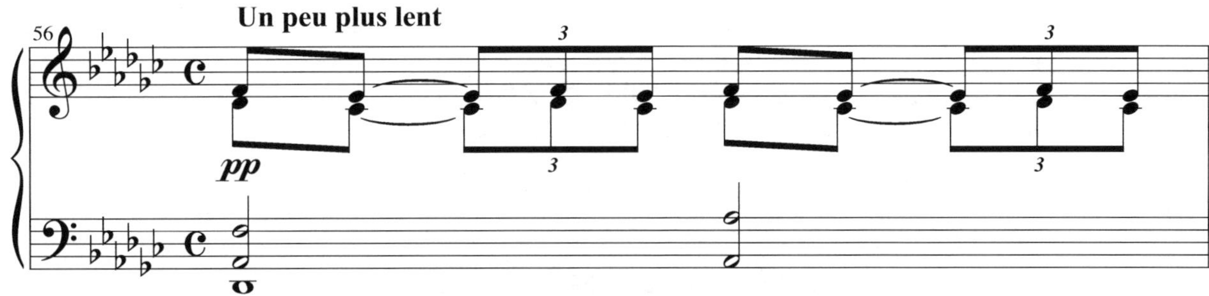

Example 8.2b Mélisande's motive, mm. 403–5

Example 8.2c Oscillating figure from Debussy, "Sirènes," *Nocturnes*, m. 56

Example 8.2d Pelléas's motive, mm. 416–17

Example 8.2e Golaud's motive (fate), mm. 424–25

the gesture from "Sirènes" (ex. 8.2c) not only underscore the fact that both works evoke similar locations—namely, cliffs overlooking the sea—but also predict that Mélisande will metaphorically lead Pelléas down a path to self-destruction. Similarly, the passage in example 8.2f stands out because the motives accompany the sound of sailors singing, an effect that clearly recalls act 1, scene 5 of *Tristan und Isolde*, when Isolde (with Brangäne at her side) and Tristan have drunk the love potion and are interrupted by the sound of the sailors announcing their arrival in port. The passage given in example 8.2g is equally important because it underscores the significance of F♯ major as a tonal center. Above all, it will return in act 4, scene 4 when Mélisande meets Pelléas for the last time and admits that she has loved him since the first time they met on top of the cliffs in act 1, scene 3. The passage in question is shown in example 8.2h.

Example 8.2f Mélisande's motive in counterpoint with Golaud's motive, the oscillating figure, and the sailor's chorus, mm. 443–44

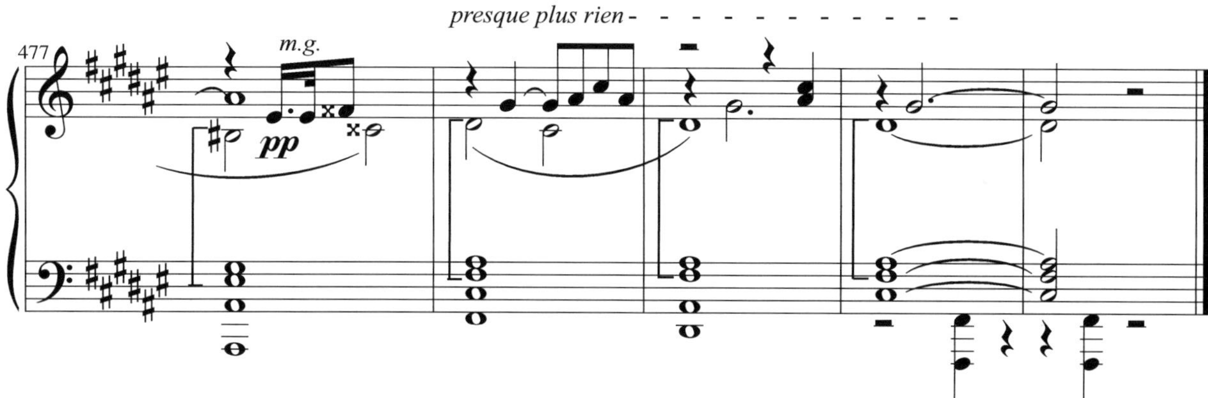

Example 8.2g The oscillating figure, Mélisande's motive and Golaud's motive, mm. 475–81

Example 8.2h Debussy, *Pelléas et Mélisande*, act 4, scene 4, mm. 627–35

Example 8.3 Debussy, *Pelléas et Mélisande*, act 2, scene 3

Example 8.3a Mm. 410–12

Much the same can be said of the grotto scene (act 2, scene 3). Since the scene takes place at night near the sea in a location not dissimilar to that of act 1, scene 3, it is hardly surprising that Debussy's setting is awash with statements of the oscillating figure. Pelléas and Mélisande's trip to the grotto was precipitated, of course, by her deliberate decision to lie to Golaud about the whereabouts of her wedding ring and motivated by a desire for her "to enlighten herself."[44] In this context, the oscillating figure seems to convey "the mystery of the night," a silence so intense that one can hear "a blade of grass disturbed from its sleep" and the sea telling "its grievances to the moon."[45] As shown in example 8.3, the first half of the scene presents several different transpositions of the original theme, including those starting on C (ex. 8.3a), C♯ (ex. 8.3b), and A over a pedal tone F (ex. 8.3c). They even support statements of Golaud's fate motive (ex. 8.3d). The

Example 8.3b Mm. 428–31

oscillating figure finally appears in augmentation and is transformed into a whole-tone scale that descends by step from D♮, through C♮, B♭, and A♭, to G♭ (see ex. 8.3e). The arrival on G♭ coincides with a crucial moment in the drama; the clouds above suddenly clear and allow moonlight to stream through the roof of the grotto. Musically, the moment is highlighted by a new version of Golaud's fate motive that culminates in the descending pattern F♮–E♭–D♭–C–B♭–A♭–B♭ (see ex. 8.3f). The latter seems to foreshadow Pelléas's declaration of love in act 4, scene 4. Example 8.3g then shows that this new version of Golaud's fate motive will return at the end of the entire scene. In mentioning Pelléas's declaration of love in act 4, scene 4, it is worth noting that the final version of this material at the climax of the scene bears a striking similarity to the end of "De rêve," the first of Debussy's *Proses lyriques*.[46] This song, which Debussy composed in 1892, a few

Example 8.3c Mm. 440–41

months before sketching the first version of act 4, scene 4, ends with a string of block chords.[47] Example 8.3h shows a string of descending block chords in quarter notes over a pedal tone B (mm. 82–88) followed by an undulating string of eighth notes and triplets over another pedal tone F♯ (mm. 82–88). A similar pattern occurs at the climax of act 4, scene 4: as shown in example 8.i, the passages include a succession of quarter-note block chords over pedal tones B (mm. 812–15) and C (mm. 816–19) and an undulating string of eighth-note quintuplets and quarter notes over pedal tones E–A♭ and C (mm. 820–25).

Whereas the first half of the grotto scene features the original version of the oscillating figure, the second half shifts to an augmented version derived from the passage in example 8.3e. This augmented version, which is anticipated in act 2, scene 2, mm. 330–31 when Mélisande tells Golaud that she knows the whereabouts of her wedding ring, is given in example 8.4a and casts a melancholy shadow over the remainder of the scene. The change in mood is entirely appropriate: when the clouds clear, Pelléas and Mélisande can see three beggars huddled in the corner of the

Example 8.3d Mm. 442–44

grotto. The sight of the beggars is important because it reminds us that Allemonde is gripped by a deadly plague and warns us that Pelléas, Mélisande, and Golaud also face a tragic future. Examples 8.4b–8.4c then suggest that the augmented version of the oscillating figure not only recalls a passage from Mussorgsky's song "The Noisy Festival Day Is Ended" from the cycle *Sunless* (1874) but also resembles the main theme from Debussy's orchestral work "Nuages" (*Nocturnes*, mvt. 1).[48] But which passage by Debussy came first? Was it the music for the grotto scene or the opening of "Nuages"? Although Debussy published *Pelléas et Mélisande* after "Nuages," his earliest known sketches for the grotto scene (ex. 8.4d) date from June to August 17, 1895, several years before the definitive version of "Nuages."[49] Either way, such musical cross-references illustrate the fusion of genres and principles of intertextuality that are so much a part of Schlegel's views about the arabesque and the fantastic.

Above, **Example 8.3e** Mm. 445–49

Facing top, **Example 8.3f** Mm. 449–50

Facing bottom, **Example 8.3g** Mm. 474–79

PELLÉAS
449
Oh!
Oh!
Doux et calme
pp
450
voi - ci la clar - té!..
see here comes the light!
474
477

Example 8.3h Debussy, "De rêve," *Proses lyriques*, mm. 81–91

Example 8.3i Debussy, *Pelléas et Mélisande*, act 4, scene 4, mm. 821–30

Example 8.4 Debussy, *Pelléas et Mélisande*, act 2, scene 3

Example 8.4a Mm. 453–54

Example 8.4b Mussorgsky, "The noisy festival day is ended," *Sunless*, mm. 15–17

Example 8.4c Debussy, "Nuages," *Nocturnes*, mm. 1–2

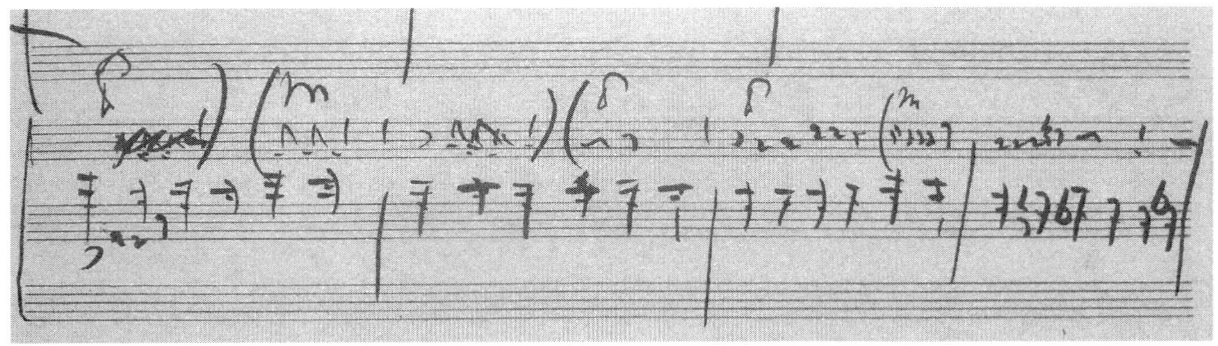

Example 8.4d Sketch for act 2, scene 3, Meyer Manuscript F-Pn Ms. 20631 (ca. June–August 17, 1895)

Regarding act 3, scene 2, Debussy found this episode particularly menacing, as he made clear in a letter to Henri Lerolle from August 28, 1894: "I've finished the vault scene. It's full of impalpable terror and mysterious enough to make the most well-balanced listener giddy. The climb from the vaults is done too, full of sunshine but a sunshine reflecting our mother, the sea. I hope it'll make an attractive scene; anyway, you'll see for yourself—the last thing I want to do is influence you."[50] In setting the scene to music, Debussy highlighted the seriousness of the warning by including Golaud's revenge motive just before the start (see ex. 8.5a). This motive will feature prominently at the climax of act 4, scene 4, when Golaud follows through with his threat and murders his half brother. Example 8.5a also shows how the scene actually begins with the introduction of a new quarter-note motive C–D–G–C–D–F. Examples 8.5b–8.5c then show Debussy created the sinister mood of the scene by adding whole-tone scales in the bass and the oscillating figure from act 1, scene 3 and act 2, scene 3. Example 8.5d then shows how the new quarter-note motive is transformed into the rising pattern E–F♯–A♯–C–E–F♯ at the scene's end. This motive is then inverted as the descending pattern E–C–A–F♯–E–C–A at the start of act 3, scene 3 (see ex. 8.5e). Debussy's draft for act 3, scene 3 shows how the scene originally contained allusions to his *Nocturnes* for orchestra: example 8.5f shows another version of the oscillating motive from "Sirènes" (see ex. 8.2c) and example 8.5g gives an allusion to an ascending sixteen-note pattern B–C–D–E that resembles the pattern C♯–D–E–F from mm. 5–6 of "Nuages" (see ex. 8.5h).[51]

Example 8.5 Debussy, *Pelléas et Mélisande*, act 3, scene 2

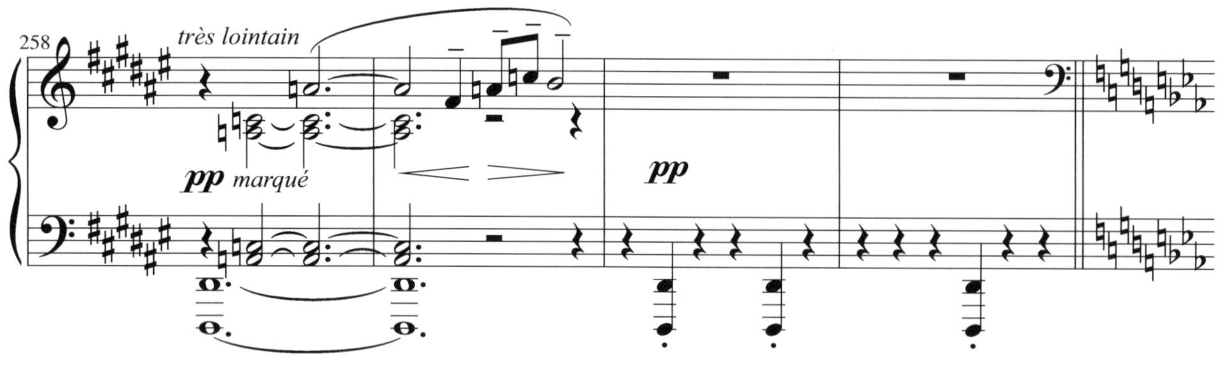

Act III, Scene 2

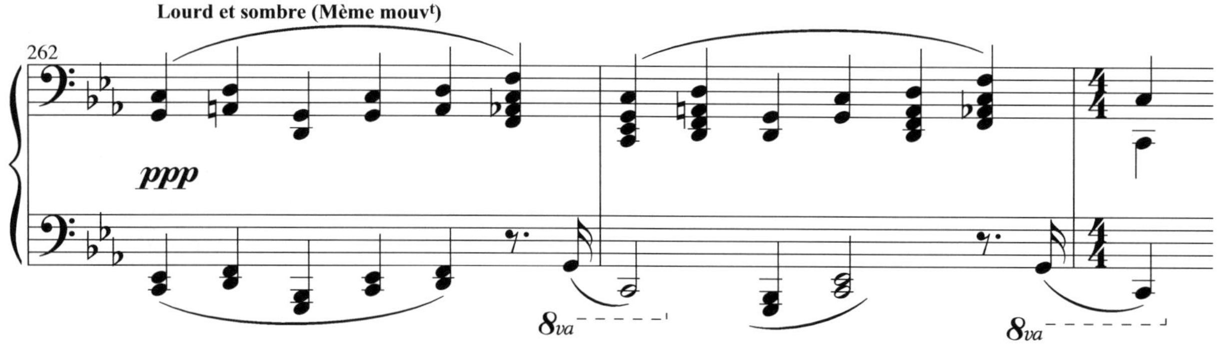

Example 8.5a Mm. 258–64

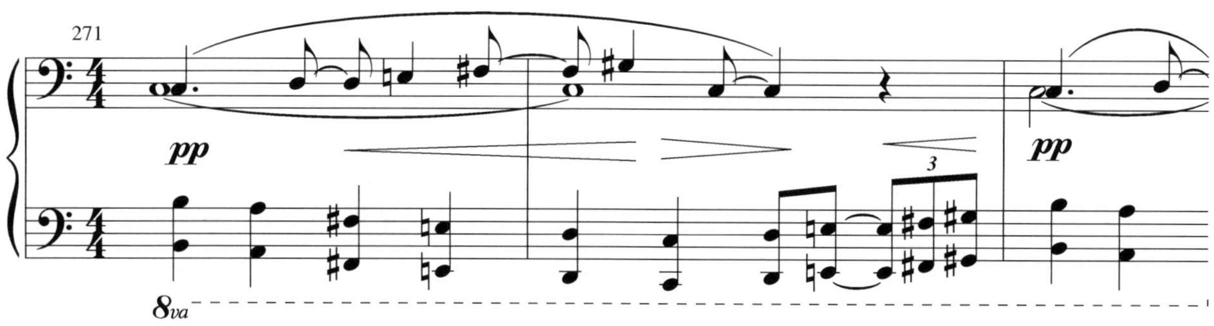

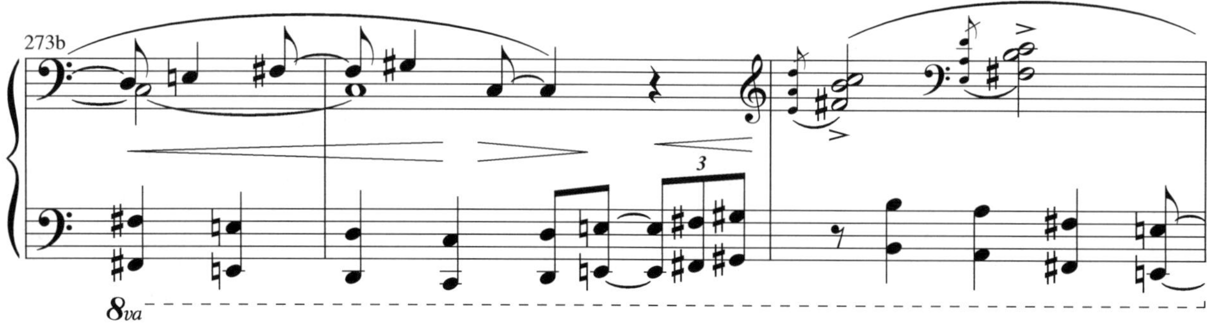

Example 8.5b Mm. 271–75

Example 8.5c Mm. 292–96

Example 8.5d Mm. 318–23

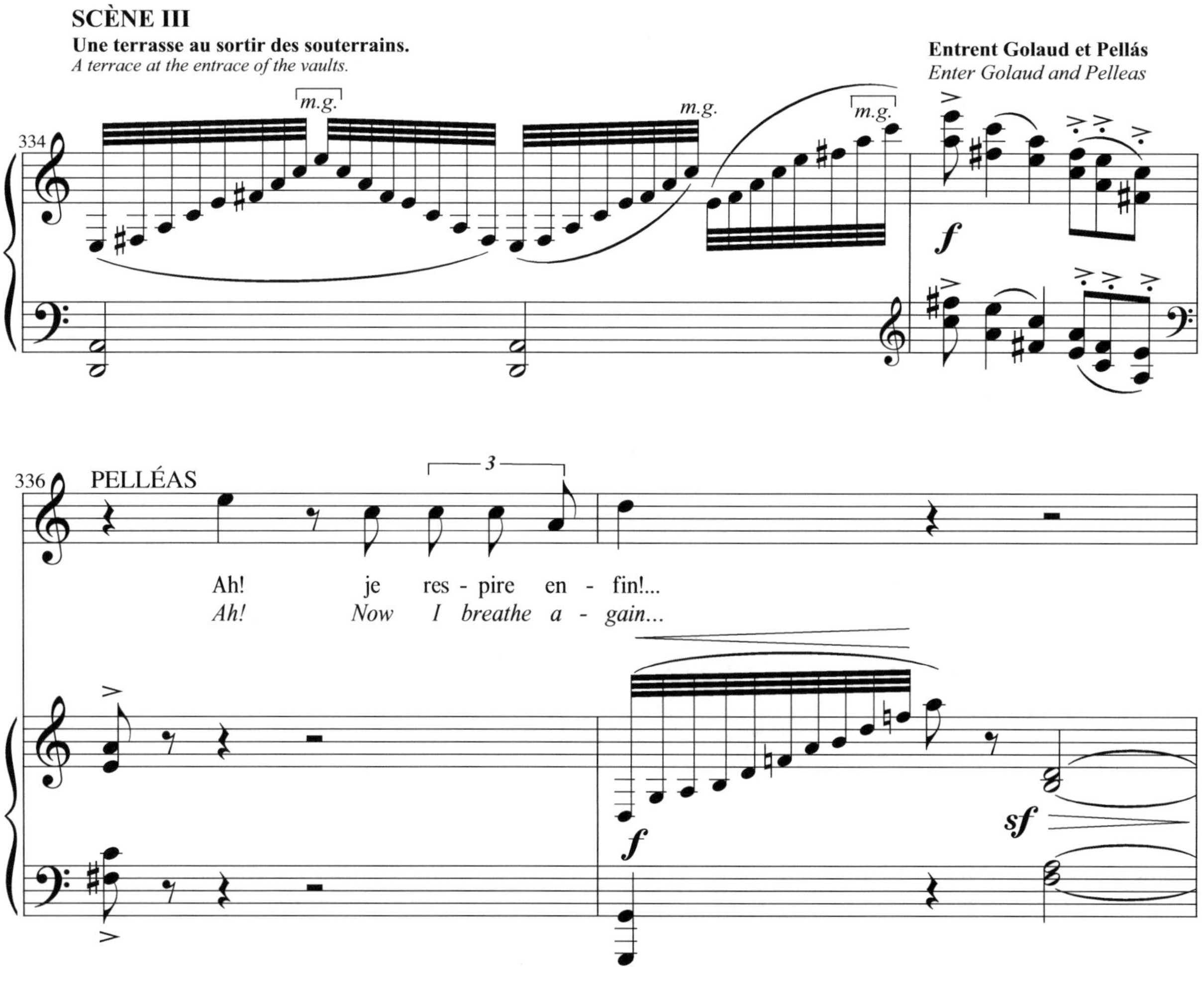

Example 8.5e Mm. 334–37

Example 8.5f Sketch for act 3, scene 3, Frederick R. Koch Foundation Collection, US-NYpm, m. 11

Example 8.5g Sketch for act 3, scene 3, Frederick R. Koch Foundation Collection, US-NYpm, m. 14

Example 8.5h Debussy, "Nuages," *Nocturnes*, mm. 5–6

When Debussy updated Lerolle about *Pelléas et Mélisande* in August 1894, he didn't simply mention act 3, scene 3, in which Golaud threatens Pelléas in the castle vaults, and act 3, scene 4, in which Golaud interrogates and abuses Yniold; he also cited act 4, scene 3, the mise en abyme in which Yniold tries to recover his golden ball from under a rock and encounters a shepherd leading his flock to slaughter. According to Debussy, his goal was to convey Yniold's innocence and trusting nature: "Here I've tried to get across something at least of the compassion of a child who sees a sheep mainly as a sort of toy he can't touch and also as the object of pity no longer felt by those who are only anxious for a comfortable life."[52] Like act 2, scene 3, Debussy's musical setting divides into two distinct parts. On the surface, at least, the first part has a playful upbeat quality, which is conveyed in various ways: by a syncopated pedal E and angular chords (ex. 8.6a), a string

Example 8.6 Debussy, *Pelléas et Mélisande*, act 4, scene 3

Example 8.6a Mm. 403–6

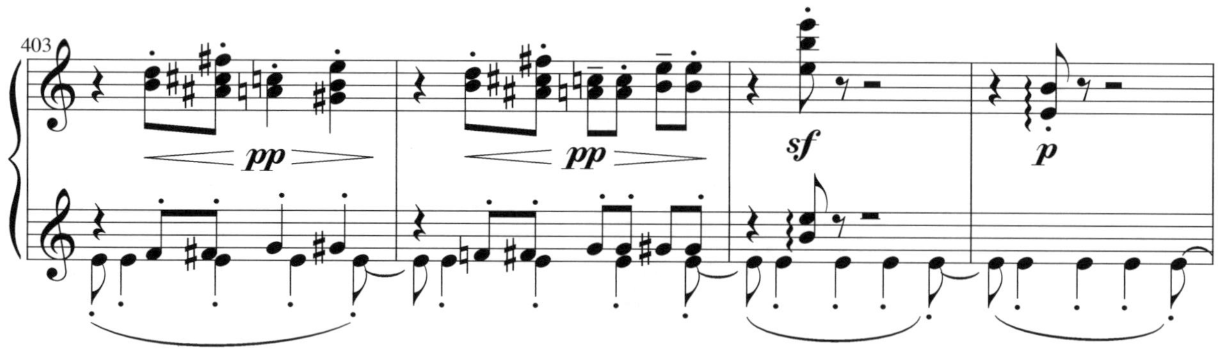

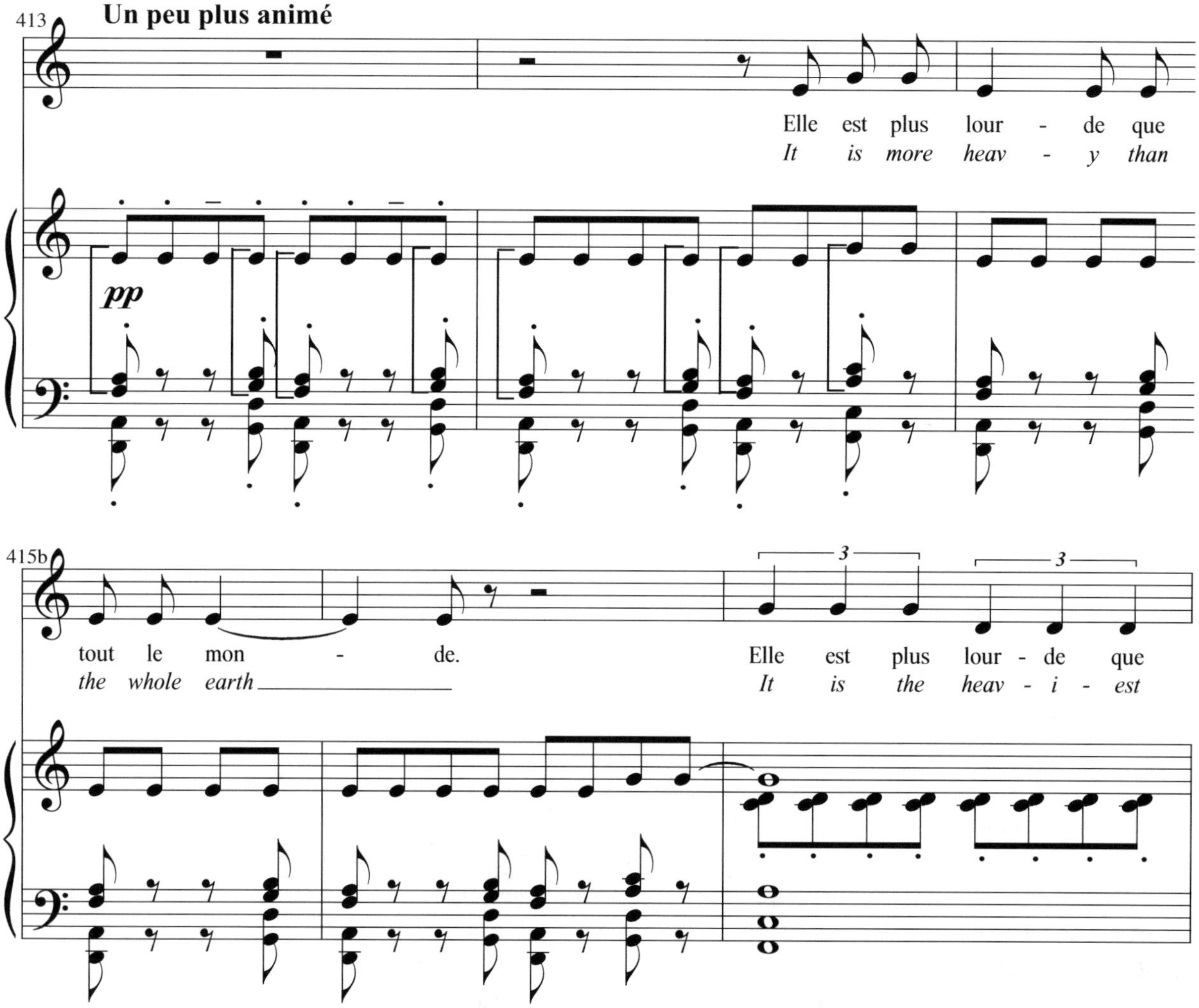

Example 8.6b Mm. 413–17

Example 8.6c Mm. 421–28

Example 8.6d Mm. 429–33

Above, **Example 8.6e** Mm. 390–98

Facing top, **Example 8.6f** Mm. 437–41

Facing bottom, **Example 8.6g** Mm. 503–6

repeated eighth note E and offbeat chords (ex. 8.6b), a simple canon (ex. 8.6c), and a succession of syncopated chords (ex. 8.6d). The canonic passage is particularly evocative and occurs at the point when Yniold attempts to roll over a large rock to retrieve his ball.[53] Meanwhile, the mood of the second part is, however, far more serious. The shift in tone is not, however, entirely unexpected. Indeed, as shown in example 8.6e, the inclusion of Golaud's fate motive and descending scale patterns before the start of the scene create a sinister backdrop to the entire proceedings. The parallels between act 2, scene 3 and act 4, scene 3 become more apparent when, as shown in example 8.6f, the repeated eighth note E and offbeat chords from example 8.6b give way to the oscillating figure to accompany the sound of sheep bleating. Just like the earlier scene, the oscillating figure subsequently appears in augmentation (see ex. 8.6g) and eventually dissolves into a descending scale when Pelléas eventually appears at the start of act 4, scene 4 (see ex. 8.6h–8.6j).

On entend au loin les bèlements d'un troupeau.
Distant bleating of sheep is heard.
437
sf
pp
440 YNIOLD
m.g.
Oh!
Oh!
oh!
oh!
f
m.g.
m.g.
503
sont dé - jà trop loin...
gone too far a - way...
3
3
3
3
505
Ils ne font plus de bruit...
They're mak - ing no more noise...
pp
271

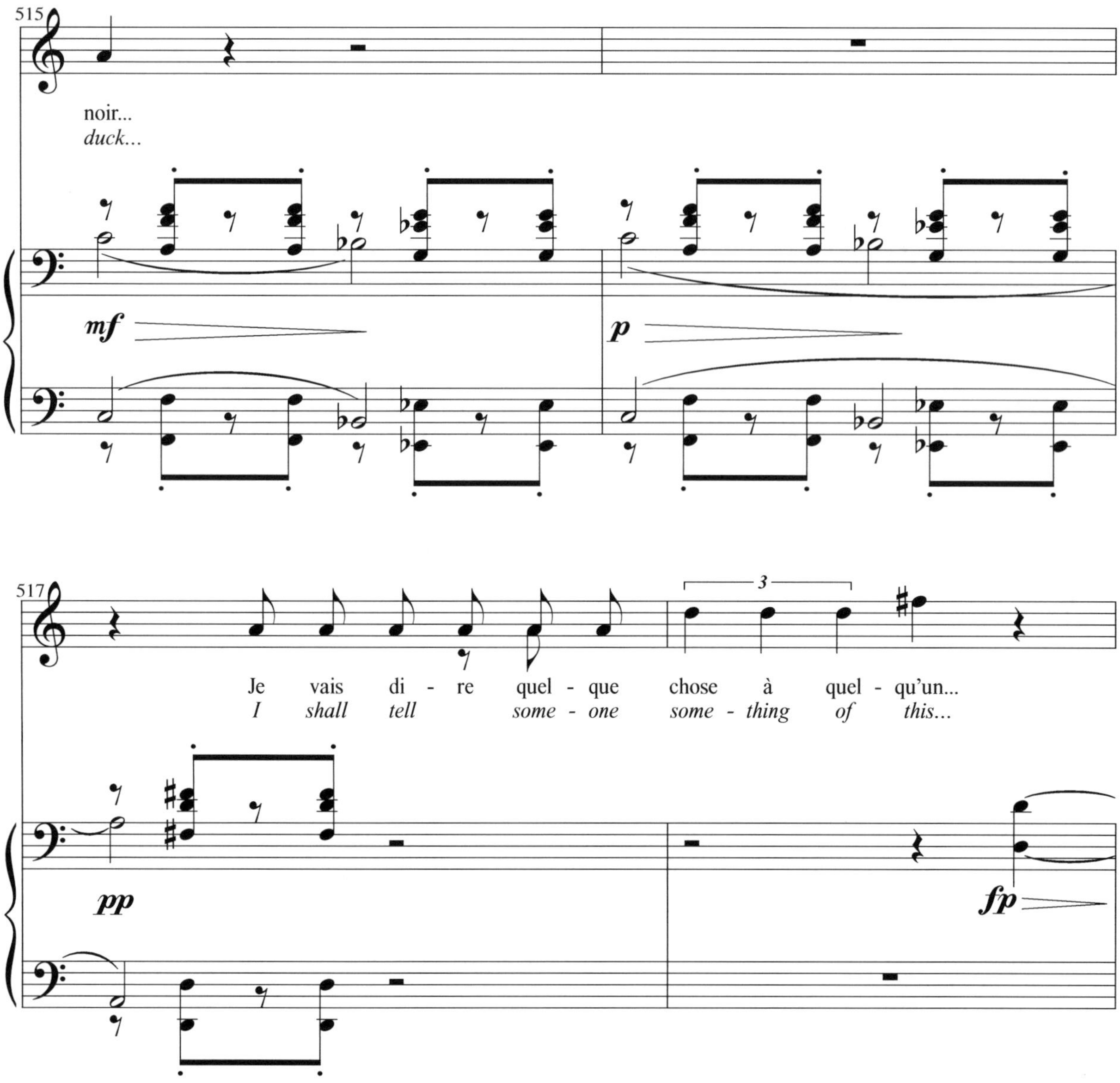

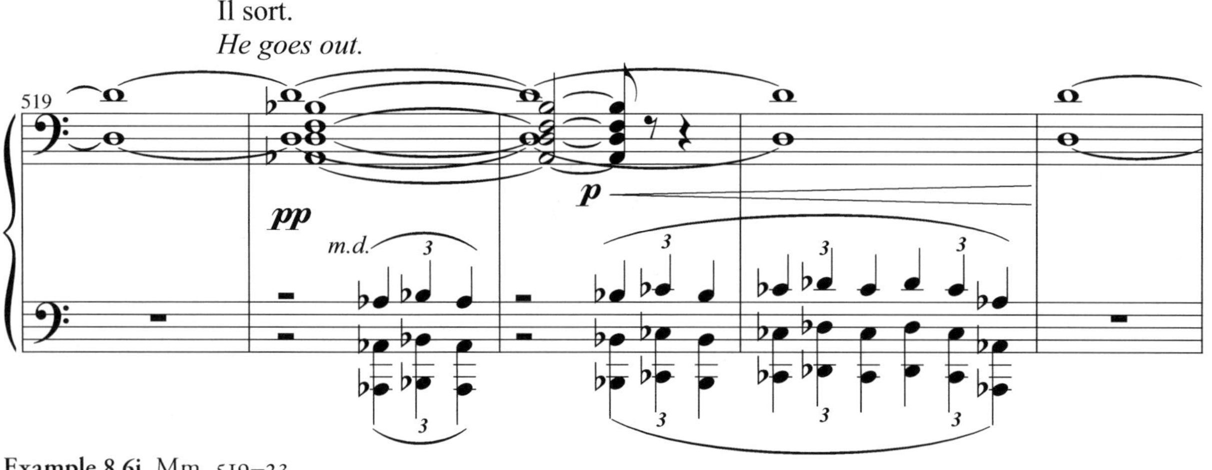

Example 8.6h Mm. 515–18

Example 8.6i Mm. 519–23

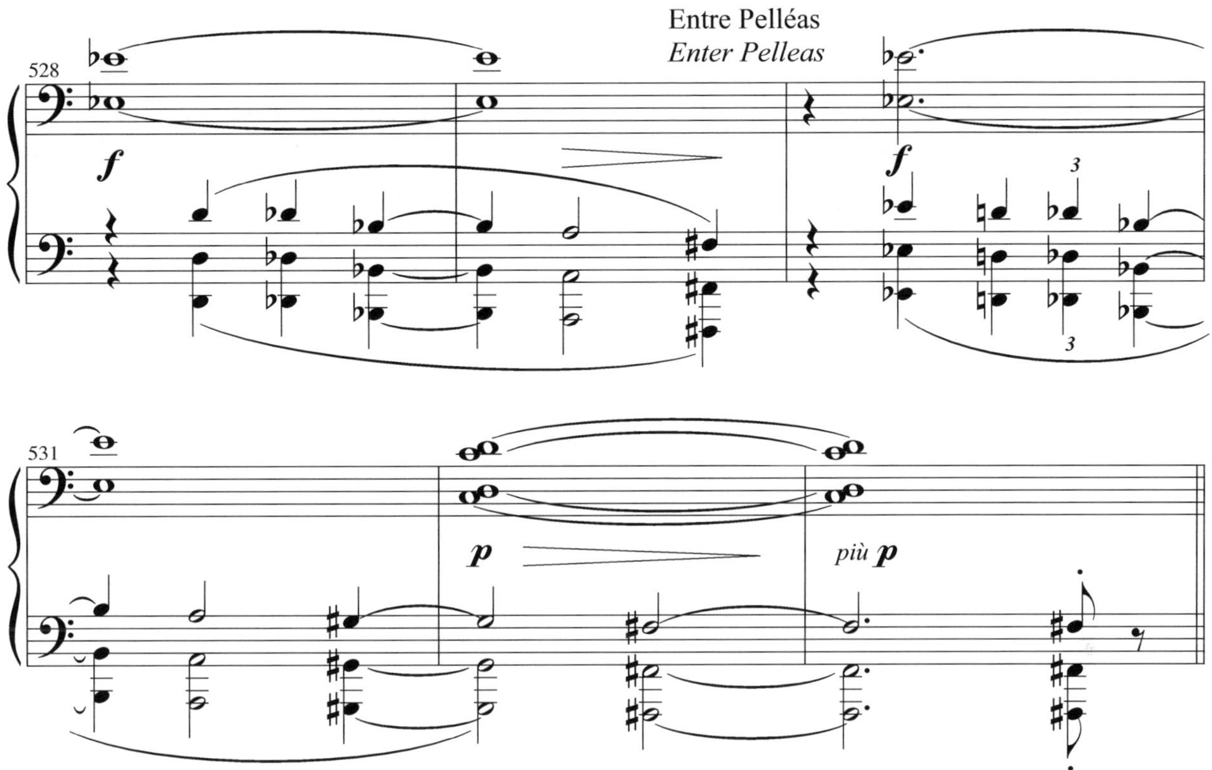

Example 8.6j Mm. 528–33

This chapter has interrogated Debussy's claim that arabesques are not simply forms of ornament: they also shape a work's expressive power and extra-musical meaning. In particular, it has focused on the notion that literary conceptions of the arabesque often fuse together different genres, thereby interweaving the real with the unreal, promoting the use of texts within a text and mises en abyme. These ideas, which can all be traced back to the writings of Schlegel, are especially prominent in the writings of Poe: Maeterlinck captured this idea of infusing *Pelléas et Mélisande* with images drawn from gothic horror stories such as "A Descent into the Maelstrom," "The Fall of the House of Usher," and "The Masque of the Red Death"; Romantic poems such as "Annabel Lee"; and biblical references such as Samuel II, chapters 13–18. The libretto's numerous allusions to other preexistent texts are mirrored by Debussy's penchant for reworking music from other works and even works by other composers. The list ranges from allusions to Mussorgsky's song "The Noisy Festival Day Is Ended" and Wagner's *Tristan und Isolde* to hints of "Nuages" and "Sirènes" from Debussy's *Nocturnes* for orchestra and songs such as "C'est l'extase" from his collection *Ariettes oubliées* and "De rêve," the first of his *Proses lyriques*. Fusing genres in this way allowed Debussy to connect the concept of the fantastic with that of the arabesque, thereby stirring the listener's emotions and filling the imagination with memorable but potentially disturbing images.

Notes

1. Claude Debussy, "Vendredi Saint—Le neuvième Symphonie," in *Monsieur Croche et autres écrits*, ed. François Lesure (Paris: Gallimard, 1987), 33–34; and Debussy, "Good Friday—The Ninth Symphony," in *Debussy on Music*, ed. François Lesure and trans. Richard Langham Smith (New York: Knopf, 1977), 26–27.

2. See Jethro Bithell, *Life and Writings of Maurice Maeterlinck* (London: Walter Scott, 1913). Villiers de l'Isle-Adam subsequently visited Maeterlinck in Ghent in March 1888, as did Mallarmé in February 1890. See W. D. Halls, *Maurice Maeterlinck: A Study of His Life and Thought* (Oxford: Oxford University Press, 1960), 17 and 22.

3. Maurice Maeterlinck, *Serres chaudes* (Paris: Léon Vanier, 1889). See Richard Howard, "Translator's Note," in Maurice Maeterlinck, *Hothouses*, trans. Richard Howard (Princeton, NJ: Princeton University Press, 2003), vii. Patrick McGuinness, *Maurice Maeterlinck and the Making of Modern Theatre* (Oxford: Oxford University Press, 2000), 13–47.

4. Maurice Maeterlinck, *Carnets de Travail (1881–1890)*, ed. and annotated by Fabrice van de Kerckhove, Archives du Future (Brussels: AMI Editions, 2002).

5. Quoted in Pierrot, *The Decadent Imagination 1880–1900*, trans. Derek Coltman (Chicago: University of Chicago Press, 1981), 32–33. Fluent in English, Maeterlinck read the original versions of Poe. See Richard Langham Smith, "The Play and Its Playwright," in *Pelléas et Mélisande*, Cambridge Opera Handbooks, ed. Roger Nichols and Richard Langham Smith (Cambridge: Cambridge University Press, 1989), 3.

6. Daniel Geroud, "An Opening on the Unknown and Unknowable," 7. For a translation, see *A Maeterlinck Reader*, ed. and trans. David Willinger and Daniel Gerould (New York: Peter Lang, 2011), 273–86.

7. Geroud, "An Opening," 7.

8. Bettina Knapp, *Maurice Maeterlinck* (Boston, MA: Twayne, 1975), 67–76; and Smith, "The Play and Its Playwright," 1–29, esp. 13–14.

9. For references to the Black Death in *Romeo and Juliet*, see the exchange between Eugene Stelzig and Stephen Greenblatt, "Letters," *New York Review of Books* 68, no. 6 (April 8, 2021): 62.

10. Smith, "The Play and Its Playwright," 14–18.

11. Smith, "The Play and Its Playwright," 4–5, 8, and 15. Charles Holme, *Modern Pen Drawings: European and American* (London: Offices of Studio, 1901), 83.

12. For details, see Matthew Brown, "On the Literary Origins of Maeterlinck's *Pelléas et Mélisande*," *Cahiers Debussy* 39 (2015): 5–17. Patrick F. Mahony, *Maurice Maeterlinck: Mystic and Dramatist* (Washington, DC: Institute for the Study of Man, 1979), 77.

13. For the book's complex publication history, see William Painter, *The Palace of Pleasure*, ed. Joseph Jacobs (London: David Nutt, 1890; repr., New York: Dover, 1966), xlv–lii.

14. Painter's *The Palace of Pleasure* was a source of plots for other Elizabethan playwrights such as Webster, Beaumont and Fletcher, Massinger, Marston, and Shirley. See Brown, "On the Literary Origins," 10.

15. For a discussion of Arkel's family tree, see Roger Nichols, "Synopsis," in *Pelléas et Mélisande*, 65. There are hints of incest in Poe's own life, as mentioned in chapter 1.

16. Maurice Maeterlinck, *Pelléas et Mélisande*, act 5, scene 2.

17. See Knapp, *Maurice Maeterlinck*, 69–70; and Smith, "The Play and Its Playwright," 13.

18. Debussy cut this section of dialogue from the opera.

19. The story appears in Samuel II, chapters 13–18. For the significance of sheepshearing, see Jeffrey C. Geoghegan, "Israelite Sheepshearing and David's Rise to Power," *Biblica* 87, no. 1 (2006): 55–63. For Poe's references to Samuel II, chapters 13–18, see William Mentzel Forrest, *Biblical Allusions in Poe* (New York: Macmillan, 1928), 47–51, 55–67, 101–29, 155, 174, 187, and 198. Forrest also claims that Poe's tales and poems draw heavily on rhetorical strategies used in the Bible and even on general themes, especially mysticism, the uncanny, death, and melancholy.

20. See Jean Marie Matthias Philippe Auguste Villiers de l'Isle-Adam, *The Scaffold and Other Cruel Tales*, ed. Brian Stableford (London: Black Coat, 2004), 7; François Lesure, *Claude Debussy* (Paris: Klincksieck, 1994), 117; Léon Vallas, *Claude Debussy et son temps*, 2nd ed. (Paris: Albin Michel, 1958), 140; and Robert Orledge, *Debussy and the Theatre* (Cambridge: Cambridge University Press, 1982), 45–46.

21. Gordon Millan, *A Throw of the Dice. The Life of Stéphane Mallarmé* (London: Secker & Warburg, 1994), 289.

22. See David Grayson, "The Libretto of Debussy's *Pelléas et Mélisande*," *Music and Letters* 66, no. 1 (1985): 37.

23. Sylvie Douche, "Transcription littérale du carnet de notes de Maurice Emmanuel au sujet des échanges de Debussy-Guiraud (1889–1890)," in *Pelléas et Mélisande cent ans après: études et documents*, ed. Christophe Branger, Sylvie Douche, and Denis Herlin (Lyon: Symétrie, 2012), 285; Lockspeiser, *Debussy: His Life and Mind*, vol. 1, *1862–1902*, 2nd ed. (Cambridge: Cambridge University Press, 1978), Appendix B, 205.

24. Claude Debussy, "Pourquoi j'ai écrit *Pelléas*," (April 1902), in *Monsieur Croche et autres écrits*, ed. François Lesure (Paris: Gallimard, 1987), 63; Claude Debussy, "Pourquoi j'ai écrit *Pelléas*," in *Debussy on Music*, ed. François Lesure and trans. Richard Langham Smith (New York: Knopf, 1977), 75.

25. Claude Debussy, *Correspondance (1872–1918)*, ed. François Lesure and Denis Herlin, annotated by François Lesure, Denis Herlin, and Georges Liébert (Paris: Gallimard, 2005), 220; Claude Debussy, *Debussy Letters*, ed. François Lesure and Roger Nichols, trans. Roger Nichols (Cambridge, MA: Harvard University Press, 1987), 73. For interesting insights about the sadistic aspects of act 3, scene 3 and its allusions to Poe, see François De Médicis, *La Maturation Artistique de Debussy dans son Contexte Historique*, Speculum Musicae XXXVIII (Turnhout: Brepols, 2020), 652–64.

26. David Grayson, "Foreword," in *Pelléas et Mélisande*, ed. David Grayson, Œuvres Complètes de Claude Debussy. Série VI Œuvres lyriques, vol. 2 (Paris: Durand-Costallat, 2010), xvii.

27. David Grayson, "The opera: genesis and libretto," in *Pelléas et Mélisande*, Cambridge Opera Handbooks, ed. Roger Nichols and Richard Langham Smith (Cambridge: Cambridge University Press, 1989), 34.

28. Grayson, "The opera: genesis and libretto," 41.

29. Grayson, "Foreword," xviii.

30. Grayson, "Foreword," xviii–xix.

31. Grayson, "Libretto," 34–35 and 44.

32. Grayson, "Opera," 37.

33. Grayson, "Foreword," xix.

34. Grayson, "Foreword," xix.

35. Grayson, "Libretto," 47.

36. Grayson, "Libretto," 48.

37. See, for example, Robin Holloway, *Debussy and Wagner* (London: Eulenberg, 1979), 60–142; and Carolyn Abbate, "*Tristan* in the Composition of *Pelléas*," *19th-Century Music* 5, no. 2 (1981): 117–41.

38. See Déirdre Donnellon, "Debussy as Musician and Critic," in *The Cambridge Companion to Debussy*, ed. Simon Trezise (Cambridge: Cambridge University Press, 2003), 47.

39. Marie Rolf, "Symbolism as Compositional Agent in Act IV, Scene 4 of Debussy's *Pelleas et Melisande*," in *Berlioz and Debussy: Sources, Contexts, and Legacies*, ed. Barbara L. Kelly and Kerry Murphy (Aldershot: Ashgate, 2007), 117–48.

40. Donnellon, "Debussy as Musician and Critic," 47.

41. Smith, "Motives and Symbols," in Nichols and Smith, *Pelléas et Mélisande*, 95–96.

42. Gervais described a similar passage of quasi-recitative from act 1, scene 2; see Françoise Gervais, "La notion d'arabesque chez Debussy," *La Revue musicale* 241 (1958): 12.

43. To quote Pierre Boulez, "If you take the *Nocturnes*, they are very close to the style of *Pelléas*, as are certain passages in *La Mer*, for example the sun at noon (1st movement) and the exit from the underground (act 3, scene 3)." Pierre Boulez, "Préface, Entretien Pierre Boulez," in *Pelléas et Mélisande cent and après: études et documents*, Palazzetto Bru Zane, Centre de musique contemporaine Française, ed. Jean-Christophe Branger, Sylvie Douche, and Denis Herlin (Lyon: Symétrie, 2013), 1.

44. See Debussy's letter to Henry Lerolle (August 17, 1895). Debussy, *Correspondance*, 268.

45. Debussy, *Correspondance*, 268.

46. For interesting insights about the connections between act 3, scene 3, Debussy's song "De Soir" (*Proses lyriques*), and Rimsky-Korsakov's *Snegourochka*, see De Médicis, *La Maturation Artistique de Debussy*, 696–722.

47. See Denis Herlin, "From Debussy's Studio: The Little-Known Autograph of *De rêve*, the First of the *Proses lyriques* (1892)," trans. Peter Bloom, *Notes* 71, no. 1 (September 2014): 9–34.

48. Léon Vallas, *Claude Debussy. His Life and Works*, trans. Maire and Grace O'Brien (Oxford: Oxford University Press, 1933), 113. Vallas notes that Stravinsky used a similar gesture at the start of his opera *Le Rossignol* (1908–14). For Mussorgsky's influence on Debussy, see Vallas, *Claude Debussy. His Life and Works*, 61–62; and Edward Lockspeiser, "Musorgsky and Debussy," *Musical Quarterly* 23, no. 4 (1937): 421–27.

49. David Grayson, *The Genesis of* Pelléas et Mélisande (Ann Arbor, MI: UMI, 1986), 134, and "The Opera: Genesis and Sources," in *Pelléas et Mélisande*, Cambridge Opera Handbooks, ed. Roger Nichols and Richard Langham Smith (Cambridge: Cambridge University Press, 1989), 37 [30–61]. See also Linda Cummins, *Debussy and the Fragment* (Amsterdam: Rodopi, 2006), 143–50.

50. See Debussy, letter to Henri Lerolle (August 28, 1894); Debussy, *Correspondance*, 220; Debussy, *Letters*, 73. According to Grayson, Debussy composed the preliminary version of act 3, scene 2 in July and August 1894. See Grayson, "Opera," 37.

51. David Grayson, "Waiting for Golaud: the Concept of Time in *Pelléas*," in *Debussy Studies*, ed. Richard Langham Smith (Cambridge: Cambridge University Press, 1997), 40.

52. Debussy, *Correspondance*, 220; Debussy, *Letters*, 73.

53. Louis Laloy specifically mentions this canon in his essay "La Musique de l'Avenir," *Le Mercure de France*, December 1, 1908, 419–34; "The Music of the Future," trans. Louise Liebich, in *Music through Sources and Documents*, ed. Ruth Halle Brown (Englewood Cliffs, NJ: Prentice-Hall, 1979), 318.

9

Fake Beards and False Mustaches

A STRIKING FEATURE OF arabesques, moresques, and grotesques is their capacity to absorb disparate elements within a single overall design. Those elements might include everything from interlocking geometric shapes and floral patterns, as in arabesques and moresques, to complex images of plants, animals, and even people, as in grotesques. As shown in figures 9.1a–9.1b, the latter may even include overt representations of particular scenes or narratives. Both designs allude to hunting. The first does so by offering a snapshot of Diana, goddess of the hunt, surrounded by acanthus leaves, birds, and a stag. Meanwhile, the second conveys a hunt in progress: the images convey hunters and hounds as they stalk their prey, in this case, a boar, a fox, a duck, and a deer. Figure 9.1b seems inherently dynamic because individual images are connected through a process known as *enchaînement*. The same process can be seen in figure 9.1c: these eighteenth-century "headers" depict a hunt not unlike those in figure 9.1b. *Enchaînement* can likewise be seen in countless non-Western designs: figure 9.1d shows a leaf from the Kennicott Bible (ca. 1476, copied by Moses Ibn Zabarah) in which foxes and hounds chase rabbits around the page, and figure 9.1e shows the title page from Yōshū Chikanobu's "Chiyoda no on-omote" (1897), in which a flock of cranes encircles two panels of text.

It turns out that narrative grotesques like those in figures 9.1b–9.1e were extremely common in the eighteenth and nineteenth centuries; their popularity coincided with the proliferation of comic books, illustrated books, magazines, chapbooks, and the like. Many are frivolous in tone. Figure 9.1f, for example, shows Walter Crane's illustration "The Hunt Is Up" from *Pan Pipes*, a collection of popular songs and poems with music by Theo Marzials. Here the huntsmen and their hounds pursue a majestic stag around the borders of the page. Next, figure 9.1g shows a page from Claude Terrasse's *Petit Solfège illustré*.[1] In a touching display of whimsy, Pierre Bonnard illustrated

Figure 9.1a Martin Riester and Charles Ernest Clerget, motifs ornamentation, ca. 1850

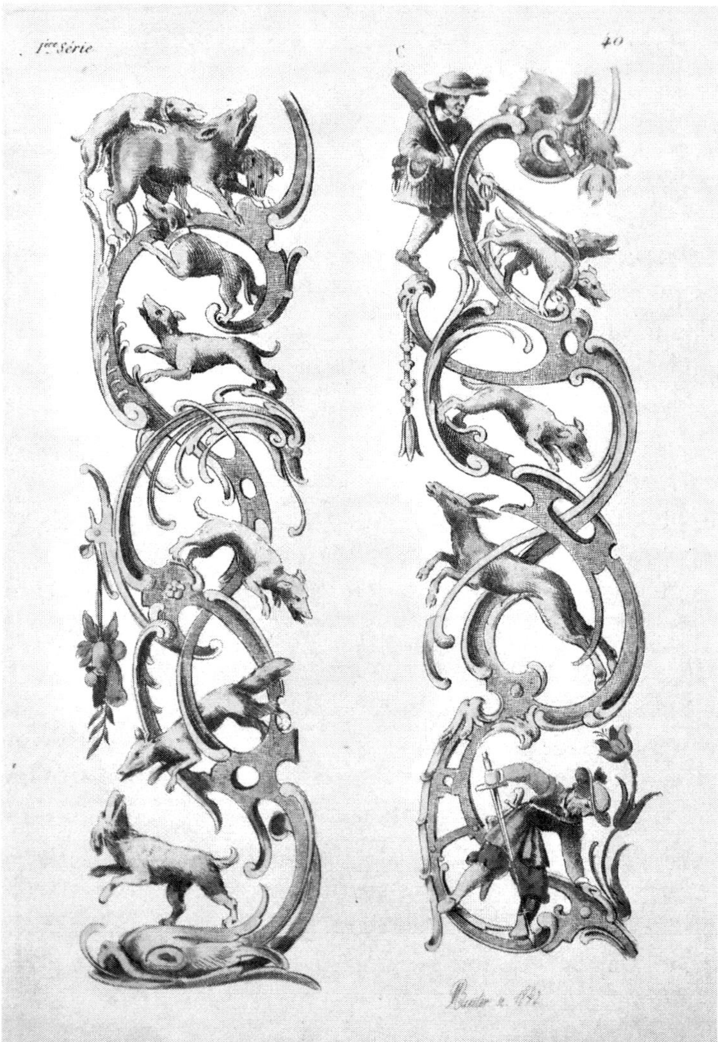

Figure 9.1b Anonymous grotesque, ca. 1850

Above, **Figure 9.1c** Eighteenth-century engraved "headers" depicting hunting scenes

Left, **Figure 9.1d** Kennicott Bible: GB-Ob, fol. 7 (ca. 1476)

Figure 9.1e Yōshū Chikanobu, title page of "Chiyoda no on-omote," woodblock print (1897)

Terrasse's account of syncopation with images of two dogs chasing one another. Bonnard, like Crane before him, used his charming design to convey the rough-and-tumble antics of the two furry friends.[2] But some narrative grotesques were utterly serious in tone and served as visual analogs to Poe's celebrated *Tales of the Grotesque and Arabesque*. Take, for example, the etching "L'hiver à Paris" by French artist Félix Buhot (see fig. 9.1h). Notice how the central image of a side street in Montmartre is framed with an arabesque border built from sequential images of a horse dying. These images reveal the grim reality of city life conjured up by Poe in "The Man of the Crowd" (1840) and Baudelaire in "Une Charogne" from *Les Fleurs du Mal*.[3]

The idea that grotesques have the capacity to enchain diverse elements dramatically is particularly relevant to this project because it sheds light on one of Debussy's most attractive scores: *La Boîte à joujoux*. Composed in 1913 in collaboration with artist André Hellé, the score is nothing but a "mosaic . . . filled with old tunes" and rich in "innuendo, ellipses, and the distribution of silence."[4] This "Aladdin's cave" of material includes an array of popular tunes, military bugle calls, classical war horses, and contemporary work and even some of Debussy's own compositions.[5] The list of children's and popular songs is especially long: "Do, do, l'enfant do," "Pan! Qu'est-ce qu'est là? C'est Polichinelle," "Il était une bergère," "Jean-Pierre, tiens-toi bien; tu vas tomber

Figure 9.1f Walter Crane and Theo Marzials, *Pan Pipes* (London: George Routledge, 1883)

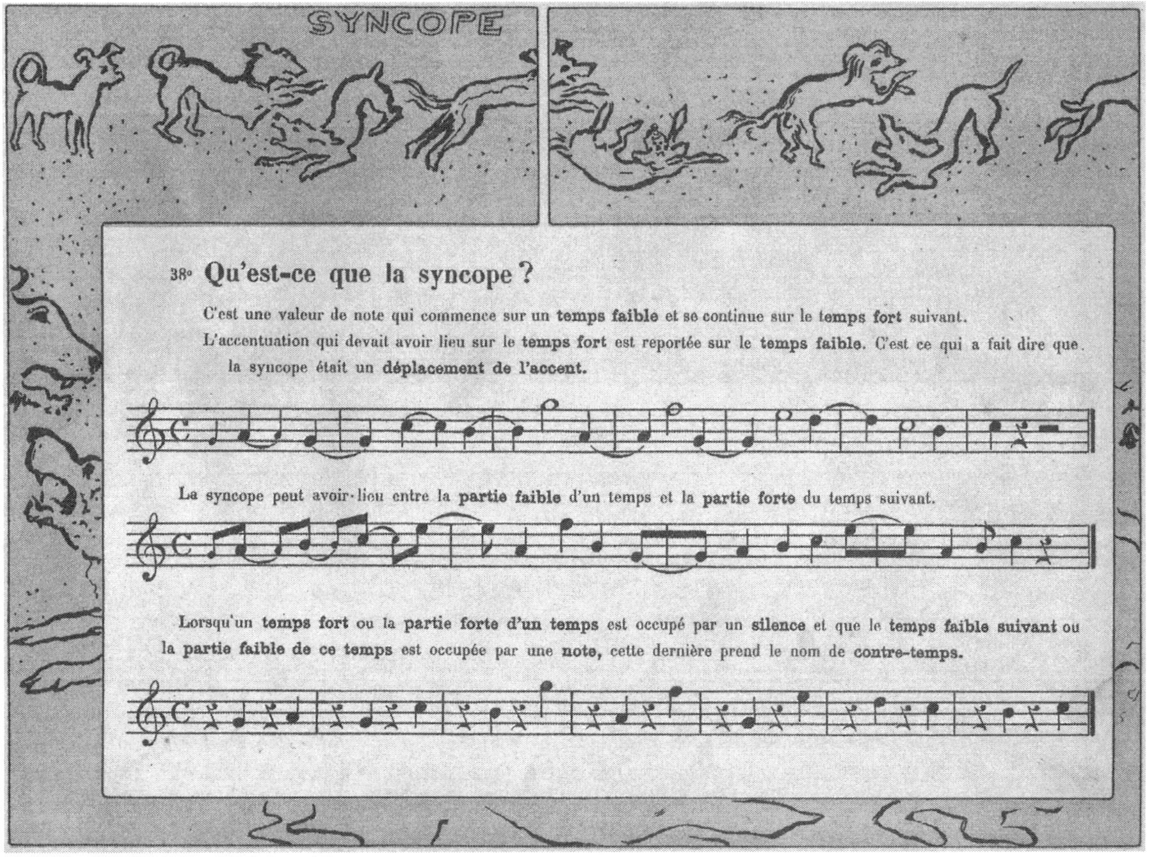

Figure 9.1g Claude Terrasse and Pierre Bonnard, *Petit Solfège illustré* (Paris, 1893)

Figure 9.1h Félix Buhot, "L'hiver à Paris," etching, 1879

sur le derrière," and "Fanfan La Tulipe." The disparate nature of the score is even reflected in the physical structure of the first edition: pages of music are interleaved with drawings by Hellé (see fig. 9.2). As shown in figure 9.3, the print even identifies the leitmotifs for the ballet's most prominent characters, the doll, polichinelle, the soldier, and the red rose.

But *La Boîte à joujoux* also reflects other strains of Symbolist thought. When Hellé first came up with the idea of creating a "ballet for puppets" in 1912, he explained his rationale as follows: "Toy boxes are, in effect, kinds of cities in which toys live like people. Or maybe cities are only toy boxes in which people live like toys."[6] By likening the behavior of toys in toy boxes to that of people in cities, Hellé not only recalled Jacques's famous line from Shakespeare's *As You Like It*—"All the world's a stage, and all the men and women merely players"—but also one of Baudelaire's essays: "Morale du joujou" (1853).[7] This fascinating essay describes how, in the hands of a child, toys become "actors in the great drama of life, reduced in size by the camera obscura of their little brains."[8] But this great drama always ends tragically. To quote Patrick Langley: "At first, the child experiences a strange intensity of presence: their inanimate 'actors' have the spark of life. Later, children feel a deep sense of frustration, to the point of blind rage, at their toys' inertia. Where are their souls? The 'little brat' is consumed by an 'overriding desire' to know. She scratches, shakes, hurls, smashes and even destroys her toy, baffled by its stubborn refusal to awaken to life."[9] To understand how such ideas shed light on the structure of *La Boîte à joujoux*,

Figure 9.2 André Hellé, *La Boîte à joujoux* (Paris: Durand, 1913)

Figure 9.2a Tableau II, page 32/33

Figure 9.2b Tableau III, page 30/31

Figure 9.2c Tableau III, page 42/43

Figure 9.2d Tableau IV, page 46/47

let's begin by reconsidering the role potpourri played in nineteenth-century music making and examine how they might have impacted Debussy while he composed this fascinating score. The discussion ends by reflecting on Baudelaire's comments about the aesthetic and psychological significance of toys.

Debussy was not, of course, the first composer to compose works that combine preexistent melodies with newly composed tunes: on the contrary, potpourris, quodlibets, and medleys can be found as far back as the thirteenth century and were especially popular in the fifteenth and sixteenth centuries.[10] Although some of them were utterly serious in tone, many were deliberately comical, as Wolfgang Schmeltzl made clear in his *Guter, seltzamer und künstreicher teutscher Gesang* (Nürnberg: 1544): "[The quodlibet's] origin has to be traced back to a primitive, almost childlike joy in simple numbers, in colorful combinations and linguistic rhythms, in the

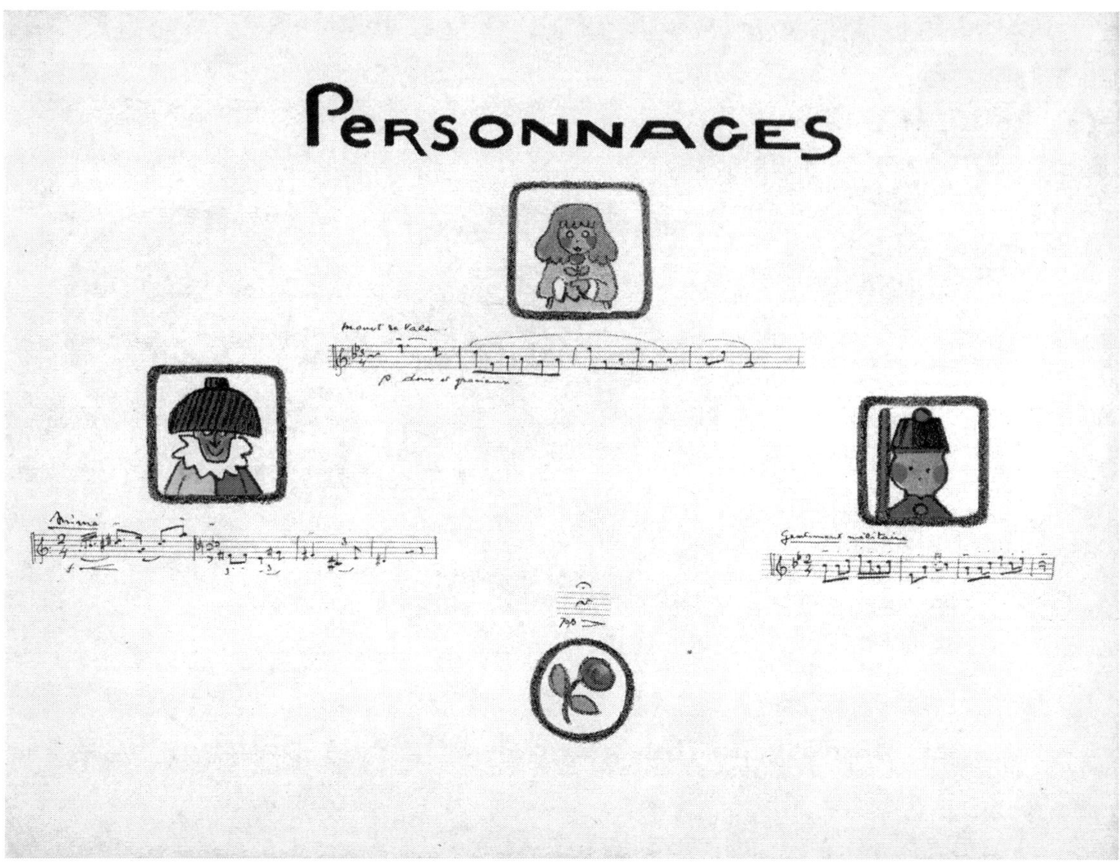

Figure 9.3 Main leitmotivs in Debussy's *La Boîte à joujoux*

elementary joy of playing, which is deeply rooted in every person despite all 'artistic demands,' and how it always occurs in special situations and moods to break through again."[11] They were also popular during the nineteenth and early twentieth centuries: publishers often printed potpourris, quodlibets, and medleys based on themes from famous ballets, operas, and symphonies, some focusing on material from a single ballet, opera, or symphony and others presenting a smorgasbord of top ten hits.[12] The scores were arranged for piano solo, piano duet, or other combinations of chamber instruments and were intended for players of every ability. A good case in point is Emmanuel Chabrier's *Souvenirs de Munich*. Composed in 1885–86 after Chabrier had visited Munich to hear *Tristan und Isolde* (1879), the piano duet contains five Wagnerian quadrilles: *Le Pantalon* (*Trousers*); *L'été* (*Summer*); *La Poule* (*The Hen*); *La Pastourelle* (*The Shepherd Girl*); and *Finale*. In the words of Francis Poulenc, they dress up Wagner's leitmotivs with "false beards and fake moustaches."[13] A few years later, Gabriel Fauré and André Messager completed a similar set of quadrilles entitled *Souvenirs de Bayreuth* (1888). They decided to parody themes from Wagner's *Der Ring der Nibelungen*: the first lampoons the Ride of the Valkyries (*Die Walküre*), the second the Tarnhelm motive (*Das Rheingold*), the third Siegmund's love song (*Die Walküre*), the fourth the magic fire music (*Die Walküre*), and the fifth Siegfried's call and the Rhine maiden's song (*Götterdämmerung*). Example 9.1 gives the opening of Quadrille 1.

Example 9.1 Quadrille 1, Gabriel Fauré and André Messager, *Souvenirs de Bayreuth* (1888)

When creating potpourris, composers often took the same steps that performers used to improvise keyboard fantasies.[14] In his *Systematische Anleitung zum Fantasieren auf dem Pianoforte* (1829), for example, Carl Czerny described how pianists might improvise six basic types of keyboard fantasy, the last of which calls for them to combine motives from several operas, ballets, popular songs, and so on without favoring any one over any other.[15] According to Czerny, there are two basic ways of accomplishing this task.[16] The first involves taking material from works by different composers and developing it successively in independent sections. To illustrate what he had in mind, Czerny presents a potpourri with sections based on themes from Bach's B♭ minor fugue *WTC II*, the "Harmonious Blacksmith" from Handel's Suite No. 5 in E major, Haydn's Symphony No. 99 in E♭ major, Mozart's "Non più andrai" from the first act of *Le nozze di Figaro*, Beethoven's *Fidelio* Overture, Op. 72b, and two unidentified works by Gluck and Cherubini. The second strategy involves taking ideas from diverse sources and developing them simultaneously. Example 9.2 shows how this might be done. This potpourri starts with a march theme in C major, which it then imitates canonically and inverts at the octave (ex. 9.2a). Next, it combines the march theme with other themes: one from Mozart's "Bacchuslied" from *Die Entführung aus dem Serail* (ex. 9.2b), the patriotic song "Rule Britannia," the French folk song "Marlborough s'en va-t-en guerre," Papageno's aria "Mädchen oder Weibchen" from act 2 of *Die Zauberflöte*, and an original tune by Czerny himself.

Judging from the success of Czerny's treatise and the large number of potpourris that he produced, the art of improvising keyboard fantasies remained popular in Europe throughout the nineteenth century. By 1900, it was even associated with other genres, especially the shadow play (or *ombre chinoise*).[17] A good case in point is *La Tentation de Saint Antoine*. Based on Gustave Flaubert's famous novel (1874), this two-act show was first presented at Le Chat Noir in Montmartre on December 28, 1887. It featured forty tableaux with backgrounds painted by Henri Rivière and puppets designed by Caran d'Ache, among others. The musical accompaniment was originally improvised by Albert Tinchant (1860–92) and Georges Fragerolle (1855–1920).[18] As shown in example 9.3, it consisted of original melodies by Tinchant (ex. 9.3a) and Fragerolle (ex. 9.3b), interspersed with arrangements of popular tunes such as "Choeur des Montagnards" (ex. 9.3c), and melodies from famous classical pieces such as Haydn's "Venite adoramus" (ex. 9.3d), Schumann's "Traumerei" from *Kinderszenen*, Op. 15 (ex. 9.3e), Gounod's *Faust* (ex. 9.3f), Massanet's *Marche héroïque de Szabady* (ex. 9.3g), and Wagner's *Das Walkyre* (ex. 9.3h). Figure 9.4a gives Henri Rivière's adjoining illustration "Les Deux Scandinaves: Odin et les Walkyres." This illustration jumps out because it recalls magic lantern slides from the same period: figure 9.4b shows one such slide depicting death on a pale horse made from a famous image by Gustave Doré (1868). Given the close links between shadow plays, magic lantern shows, pantomimes, and early movies, there is every reason to suppose that these improvised potpourris performed by Tinchant and Fragerolle for *La Tentation de Saint Antoine* served as models for pianists when, starting in December 1895, they were hired to accompany "silent films."[19] Erno Rapée and others even produced anthologies of musical excerpts to create "the necessary bridge between the screen and the audience."[20] The excerpts were indexed in terms of their mood or the scenes they were intended to depict. For example, Rapée recommended playing Schumann's "Traumerei" at moments of calm, Massanet's "Andante molto sostenuto" (from the overture to *Phèdre*) for gruesome events, Mendelssohn's "Wedding March" for marriages, and Wagner's "Spinning Song" (from *Der Fliegende Holländer*) for scenes involving the railroad. He also quoted an array of military bugle calls and a selection of folk songs from all corners of the globe.

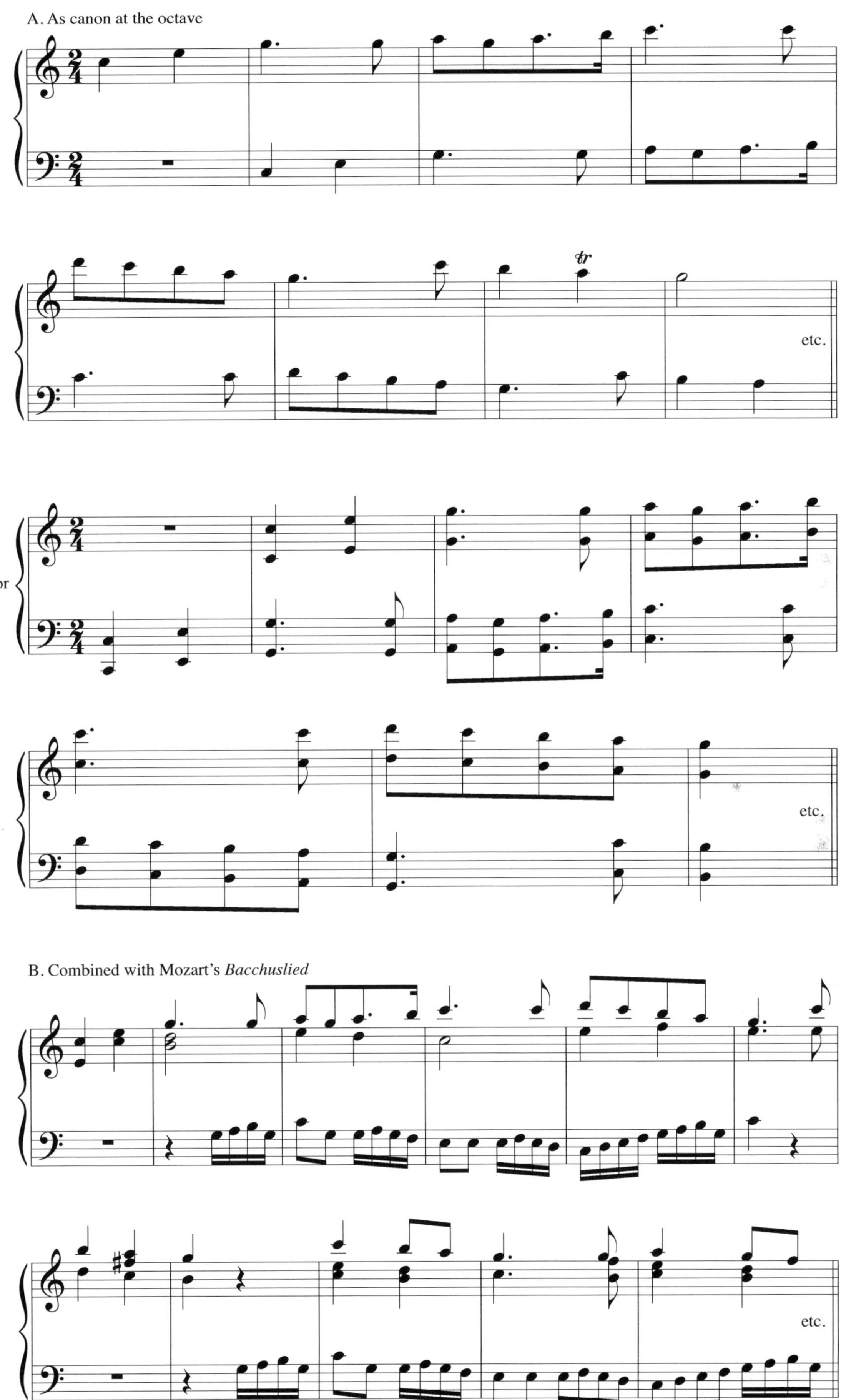

Example 9.2 Czerny's strategy for improvising potpourri by combining themes by different composers   287

Example 9.3 Albert Tinchant and Georges Fragerolle, *La Tentation de Saint Antoine*

Example 9.3a Melody by Albert Tinchant

Example 9.3b Melody by Georges Fragerolle

Example 9.3c Melody of folk song "Choeur des Montagnards"

Example 9.3d Melody from Haydn, "Venite adoramus"

Example 9.3e Melody from Schumann, "Traumerei," *Kinderszenen*, Op. 15

Example 9.3f Melody from Gounod, *Faust*

Example 9.3g Melody from Massanet, *Marche héroïque de Szabady*

Example 9.3h Melody from Wagner, *Das Walkyre*

Figure 9.4 Shadow plays and magic lantern slides

Figure 9.4a Henri Rivière's illustration of "Les Deux Scandinaves: Odin et les Walkyres"

The fact that many shadow plays were accompanied by potpourris illuminates the present discussion in several ways. For starters, Debussy is known to have experienced them firsthand at Le Chat Noir during the late 1880s and 1890s. Camille Benoît, for example, reported to Paul Dukas (May 12, 1892) that he had seen Debussy in Le Chat Noir "at the table in front of Paul Robert, by the big open window of the Chat Noir"; and Maurice Donnay remembers seeing him conduct "a frenetic chorus" of a song at the cabaret.[21] Rosemary Lloyd has suggested that Debussy's connections with the cabaret may have stemmed from his associations with Paul Verlaine and his family: Verlaine's sonnet "Langeur" appeared in Le Chat Noir's weekly magazine on May 26, 1883; his mother-in-law, Antoinette Mauté, was Debussy's first piano teacher; and his stepbrother Charles de Sivry was a regular pianist at the venue.[22] Another reason is that Debussy originally conceived of *La Boîte à joujoux* as "a pantomime" similar to the "Christmas and New Year albums" that he created each year "to amuse children."[23] Although there is no way to know the contents

Figure 9.4b Magic lantern slide based on Gustave Doré, "Death on a pale horse" (ca. 1890)

of those albums, Debussy had wowed his friends with his improvisational skills since his student days at the Paris Conservatoire: there is every reason to suppose that he displayed those talents in his holiday albums.[24] Moreover, Orledge has found direct connections between the music of *La Boîte à joujoux* and one of Debussy's Christmas gifts to his wife, Emma: "the arpeggio motif of the soldier as transformed in the second tableau recurs almost exactly to end the *Noël pour 1914* written for Emma some fifteen months after the second tableau."[25]

It is also important to remember, however, that there is nothing surprising about Debussy's decision to quote nursery rhymes and folk songs in *La Boîte à joujoux*; on the contrary, similar quotations can be found in many of his other compositions. For example, Debussy quoted the melody for "Do, do, l'enfant do," which enters near the start of *La Boîte à joujoux*, in "Jardins sous la pluie" (*Estampes* [1903]) and again in *Rondes de printemps* (*Images* for orchestra [1903–9]). In addition, both of these pieces recall the children's song "Nous n'irons plus au bois," as does his early song *La Belle au bois dormant* (ca. 1890) and his piano piece "Quelques aspects de 'Nous n'irons plus au bois'" (*Images oubliées* [1894]). There is every reason, therefore, to suppose that Debussy's holiday albums featured potpourris of nursery rhymes, folk songs, and classical themes along the lines of *La Boîte à joujoux*. And just like the potpourris used to accompany *La Tentation de Saint Antoine* and other shadow plays, the score for *La Boîte à joujoux* was published in oblong format with the music on the left (verso) and a snapshot from the scene on the right (recto).[26] Durand even published three excerpts from *La Boîte à joujoux* in 1914—"Danse de la Poupée," "Ronde," and "Polka Finale"—as well as a suite transcribed for piano à 4 by Léon Roques and arranged for chamber ensemble by Henri Mouton.[27]

Eugène Marsnan also reminds us that by resembling a "mosaic . . . filled with old tunes," *La Boîte à joujoux* has similarities with that of *Petrouchka*, which Stravinsky completed a couple of years earlier and which Debussy knew extremely well. The point is well taken: Orledge has found echoes of Stravinsky's ballet at the opening, especially in mm. 45–48, and "the final joyous polka danced by the doll's children."[28] Meanwhile Lekić finds parallels between Debussy's toy-box motive and the opening bassoon solo from *Le Sacre du Printemps*, and the transition to the fourth tableau of *La Boîte à joujoux* and the "Dance of the Adolescents."[29] Marsnan's use of the term *mosaic* is especially telling because it is widely used in Stravinsky circles: Richard Taruskin has suggested that the term recalls the Russian concept of *drabnost* (or splinteredness), and Mark McFarland has traced Stravinsky's use of the concept to the opening scene of *Petrouchka*.[30] The term *collage* applies equally well and resonates with recent developments in cubism by artists such as Pablo Picasso, Georges Braque, and Juan Gris.[31]

But how exactly did Debussy manage to weave his potpourri of preexistent tunes into a single coherent narrative? To answer this question, it is helpful to consider the prélude to *La Boîte à joujoux*. As shown in example 9.4 and table 9.1, the passage is the quintessential musical grotesque. It depicts a toy shop at night: a large toy box is in the foreground; Harlequin, Pierrot, Polichinelle, and three dolls are asleep by a wall. Musically, Debussy establishes the eerie nocturnal setting of the excerpt by means of a leitmotiv specifically associated with the toybox (see ex. 9.4a): this gesture, which vaguely resembles the opening of Stravinsky's *Le Sacre du Printemps*, appears at the opening (mm. 1–3) and the end (mm. 49–54) and at regular points in between (mm. 11–15, 21–24, 37–39, and 45–47). These statements, which form a continuous thread, are interspersed with those of other motives: a chromatic motive (ex. 9.4b); a motive derived from Mussorgsky's *Pictures at an Exhibition* (ex. 9.4c); a leitmotiv associated with the doll (ex. 9.4d); one derived from the opening of Satie's *Fantasie-Valse* (ex. 9.4e); a pattern reminiscent of "Jimbo's Lullaby" from

Example 9.4 Main motives in the prélude, *La Boîte à joujoux*

Example 9.4a Toybox motive, mm. 1–3

Example 9.4b Chromatic motive, mm. 7–10

Example 9.4c Mussorgsky, "Promenade," *Pictures at an Exhibition*, mm. 15–20

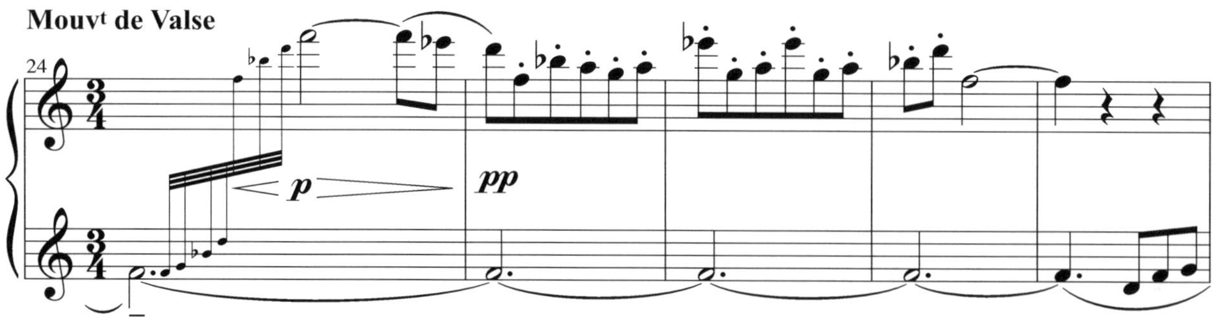

Example 9.4d Doll's motive, mm. 24–28

Example 9.4e Satie, *Fantasie-Valse*, mm. 1–4

Example 9.4f "Jimbo's Lullaby," *Children's Corner*, mm. 38–39

Debussy's piano work *Children's Corner* (ex. 9.4f); the nursery rhyme "Do, do, l'enfant do" (ex. 9.4g); a leitmotiv associated with the soldier (ex. 9.4h); and a motive associated with Polichinelle's grimace combined with the toybox motive (ex. 9.4i).[32] Table 9.1 then shows that, by returning throughout the entire prélude, the Toybox motive recalls the stylized acanthus leaf forming the border in figure 9.1b; by breaking up the flow of the toybox motive, it also suggests that the array of other motives resemble the huntsmen, hounds, deer, fox, and boar in figure 9.1b.

The main goal of tableau I is to introduce the three characters of the drama: the doll, the soldier, and the villainous Polichinelle.[33] They all wake up when one of the dolls turns on a light. A wooden soldier pops his head out of the toybox and emerges along with other figures—an elephant, an English soldier, a minstrel, a policeman, a sailor, and so on. They all take turns dancing, as do Harlequin and Polichinelle. The first doll then dances a waltz, during which she drops a red

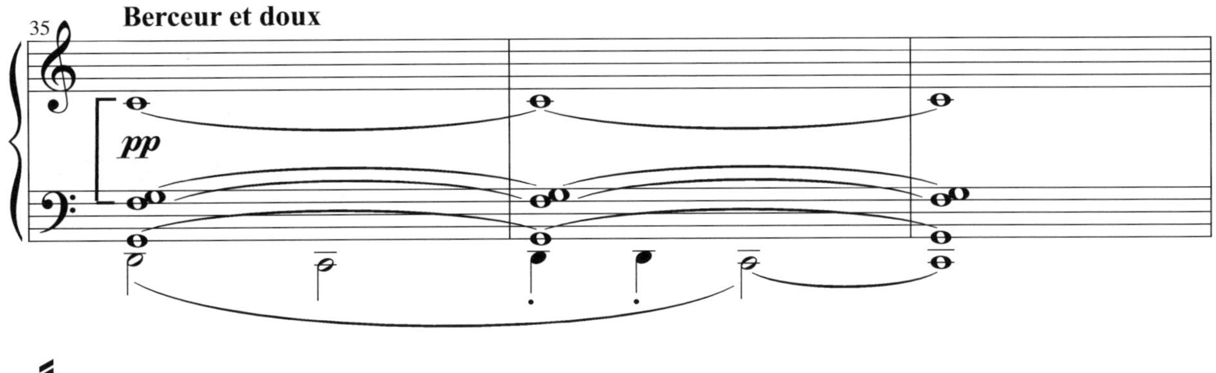

Example 9.4g "Do, do, l'enfant do," mm. 35–37 and 39–41

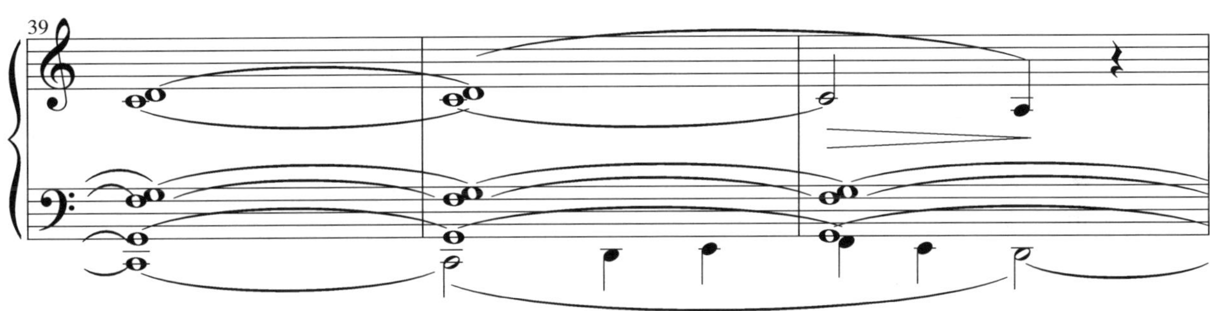

Example 9.4h Soldier's motive, mm. 39–43

Example 9.4i Polichinelle's grimace and Toybox motive, mm. 45–46

Table 9.1. The Prélude as a grotesque or potpourri

Toybox motive, mm. 1–3	
	Chromatic motive, mm. 7–10
Toybox motive, mm. 11–15	
	Mussorgsky, *Pictures at an Exhibition*, mm. 15–20
Toybox motive, mm. 21–24	
	Doll's motive, mm. 24–28
	Chromatic motive, mm. 29–34
	"Jimbo's Lullaby," mm. 33–34
	"Do, do, l'enfant do," mm. 35–37
Toybox motive, mm. 37–39	
	Soldier's motive, mm. 39–40
	"Do, do, l'enfant do," mm. 40–41
	Soldier's motive, mm. 42–45
Toybox motive, mm. 45–47	
	Polichinelle's grimace, mm. 45–46
	Soldier's motive, m. 47
	Doll's motive, mm. 47–48
	Polichinelle's grimace, mm. 49–46
Toybox motive, mm. 49–54	

rose near the soldier.[34] The soldier picks it up and kisses her. The other toys mock him, and after the first doll has finished her dance, Harlequin, Pierrot, Polichinelle, and two other dolls dance an elaborate round. From a musical perspective, tableau I follows a similar plan to the prélude. Globally, it is framed by statements of a primary motive, in this case one associated with the final round dance. This theme, which first appears when the doll turns on a phonograph, undulates by step in much the same way as the tarantella theme from the finale of Debussy's *Sonate pour violon et piano* (see ex. 9.5a–9.5b). When it returns for the round dance, the motive is supported by an ostinato pattern that recalls Debussy's piano piece *Rêverie* (see ex. 9.5c–9.5d). Tableau I ends with two final reminiscences of the motive, the first of which is shown in example 9.5e.

To convey the moment-to-moment action of the ballet, Debussy introduces a succession of subordinate motives associated with various toys. These include Polichinelle's motive (ex. 9.5f: mm. 88–91, 152–58, 159–61, 207–18, 234–44), the soldier's motive (mm. 132–33, 467–69), and the doll's motive (mm. 296–384, 457–64, 560–63) as well as material that alludes to works either by other composers or by Debussy himself. For starters, the new motive presented in mm. 92–99, 134, 146–47 resembles mm. 67–82 of Liszt's Mephisto Waltz (see ex. 9.5g–9.5h): as Lekić notes, the image of the doll dragging the other toys into the scene recalls that of Mephistopheles urging Faust to join a village wedding feast.[35] Similarly, the entrance of the elephant in mm. 139–45 recalls the exotic arabesques over long pedal tones heard at the end of scene 2 of Debussy's ballet *Khamma* (see ex. 9.5i–9.5j). And, examples 9.5k–9.5l show how Debussy marked the appearance of the English soldier in mm. 180–87 of *La Boîte à joujoux* with a transposed version of the main theme from *Le Petit Nègre* fused with a hint of the "Golliwog's Cakewalk" (*Children's Corner*).[36] From a historical perspective, the reference to the phonograph at the start of the scene

Example 9.5 Main motives in the tableau I: "Le Magasin de jouets," *La Boîte à joujoux*

Example 9.5a Debussy, Ronde theme, *La Boîte à joujoux*, tableau I, mm. 72–75

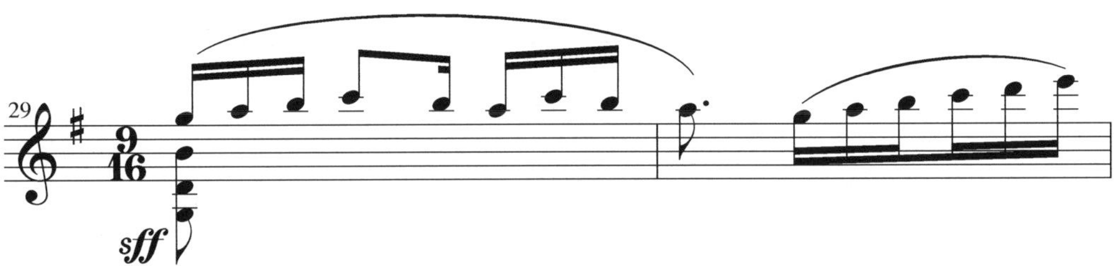

Example 9.5b Debussy, "Tarantella" motive, *Sonate pour violon et piano*, Finale, mm. 29–30

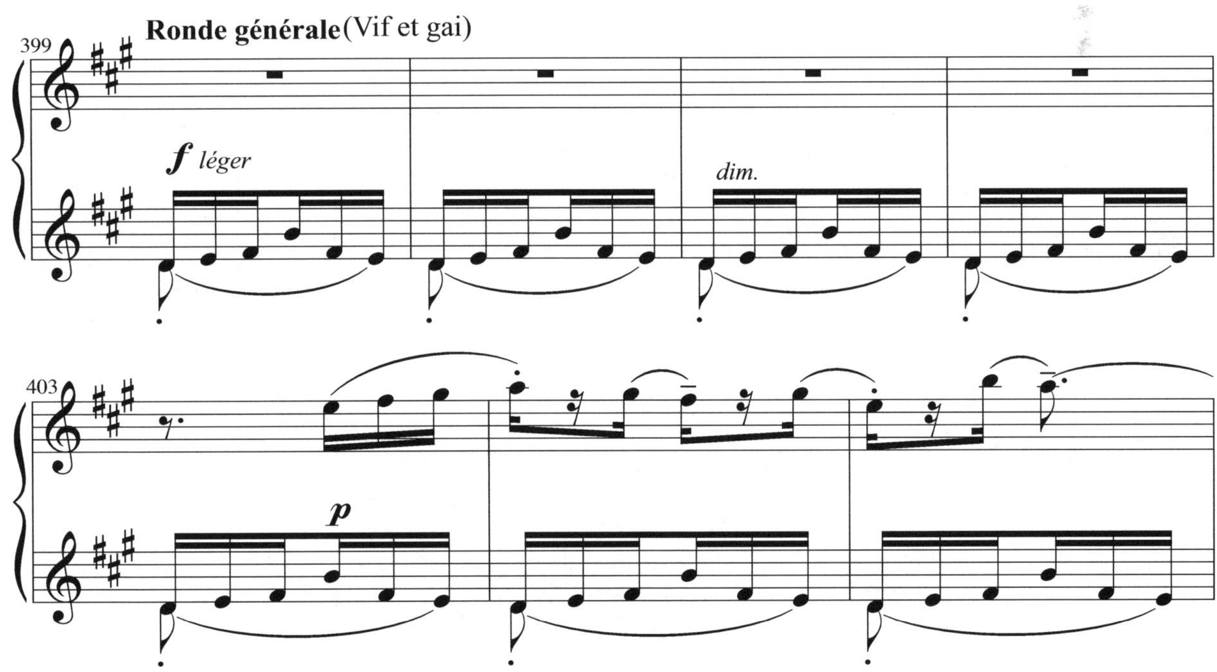

Example 9.5c Debussy, Ronde theme, *La Boîte à joujoux*, tableau I, mm. 399–405

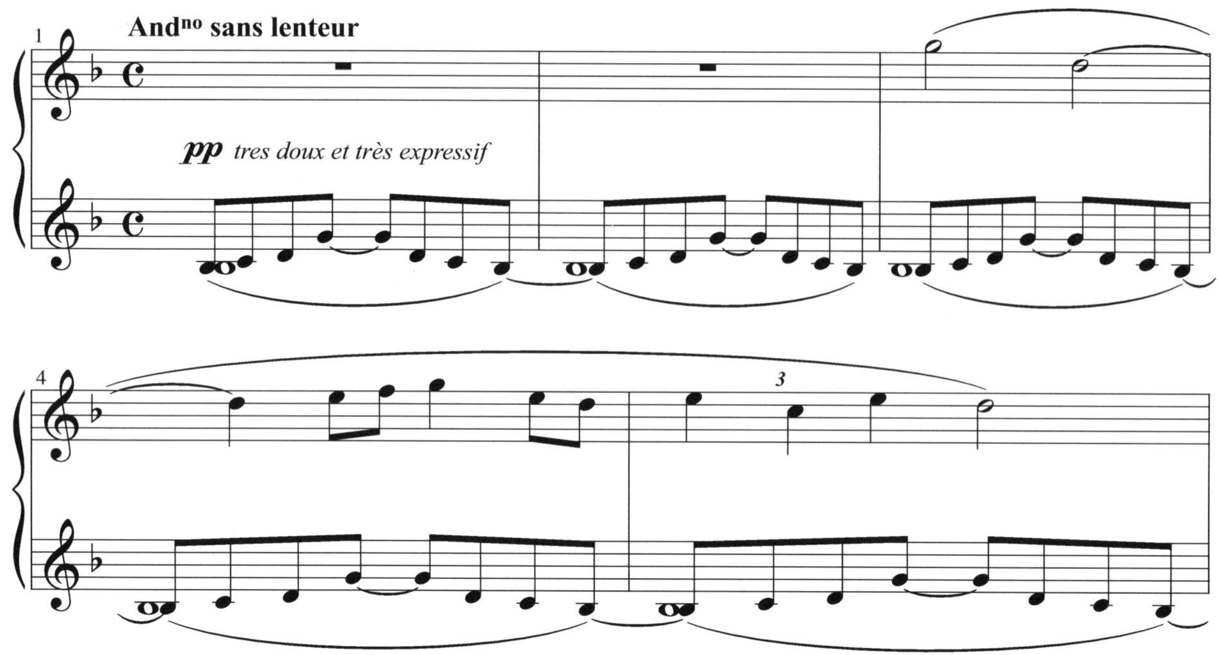

Example 9.5d Debussy, *Rêverie*, mm. 1–5

Example 9.5e Debussy, Ronde theme, *La Boîte à joujoux*, tableau I, mm. 595–97

Example 9.5f Debussy, Polichinelle's motive, *La Boîte à joujoux*, tableau I, mm. 88–91

Example 9.5g Debussy, *La Boîte à joujoux*, tableau I, mm. 92–99

Example 9.5h Liszt, *Mephisto Waltz*, mm. 67–82

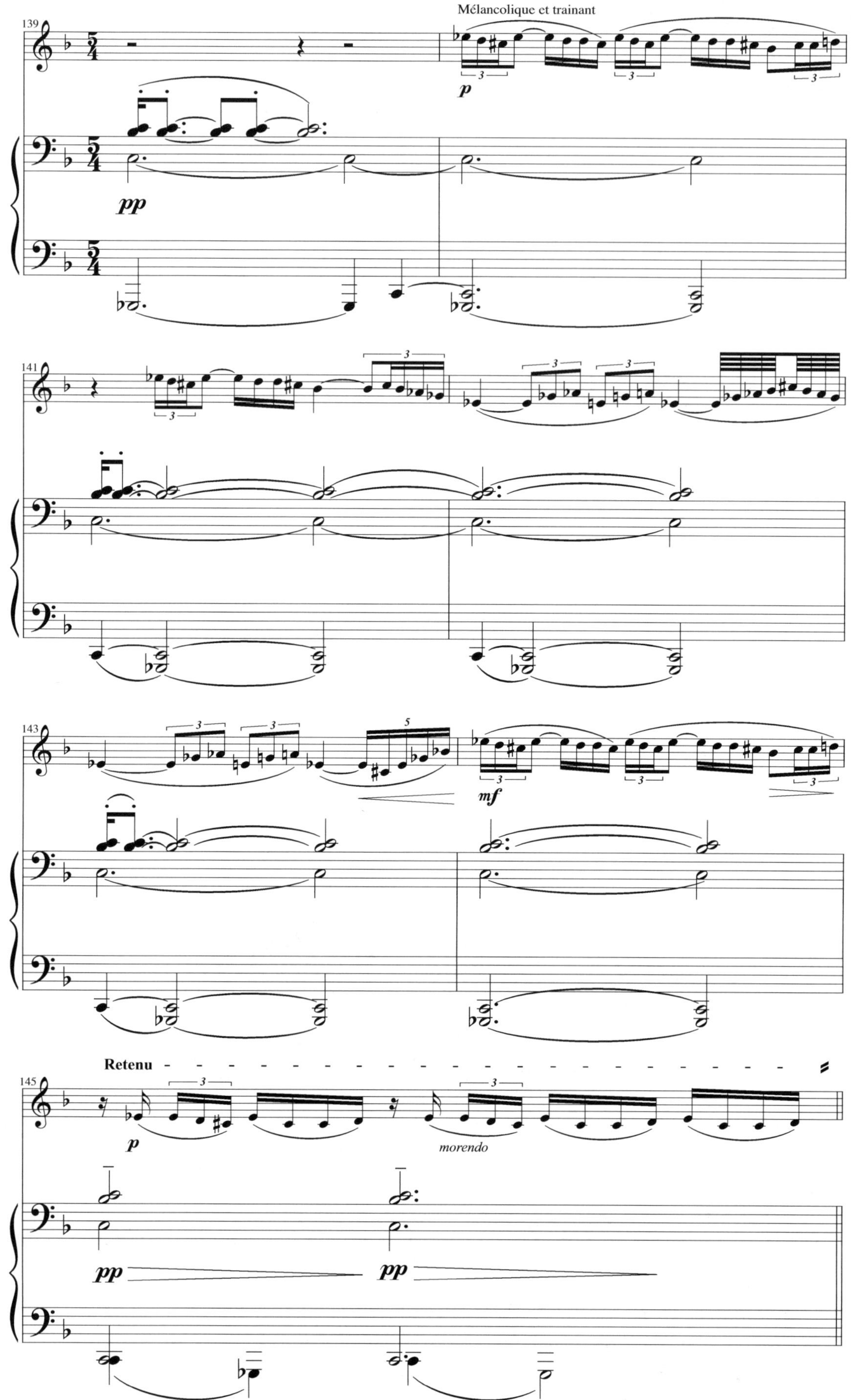

Example 9.5i Debussy, *La Boîte à joujoux*, tableau I, mm. 139–45

Example 9.5j Debussy, *Khamma*, mm. 314–25

Example 9.5k Debussy, *La Boîte à joujoux*, tableau I, mm. 180–87

Example 9.5l Debussy, *Le Petit Nègre*, mm. 1–8

is particularly ironic: while working on *La Boîte à joujoux*, Debussy made a second batch of six piano rolls with Welte-Mignon.[37]

Whereas tableau I introduces the characters and leitmotivs of the doll, the soldier, and Polichinelle, tableau II focuses on their interrelationships. Polichinelle is flirting with the doll even though the soldier is in love with her. She lets Polichinelle kiss her; she even asks for a wedding ring, but he refuses. When the soldier's regiment arrives, Polichinelle assembles a force of his own. The two armies engage; the soldier is wounded and lies between two trees, clutching the red rose to his heart. Once again, Polichinelle mocks him and rebuffs the doll. But she takes pity on the soldier and brings him back to life. Following the model used for the prélude and tableau I, Debussy conveyed the action in tableau II by presenting a potpourri of different material. As shown in example 9.6, the scene is framed and delineated by statements of Polichinelle's motive. Example 9.6a shows the original presentation of the leitmotiv in mm. 88–91 of tableau I, where it has the character of a simple fanfare. At the start of tableau II, however, the motive is slow and mysterious, its syncopated rhythms giving it a nervous quality (see ex. 9.6b). When Polichinelle arrives (ex. 9.6c), his motive conveys the sarcastic nature of his character. Sarcasm turns into belligerence when the two armies eventually withdraw. Example 9.6d shows various rhythmic transformations of his motive; these are punctuated by a descending pattern to accompany his grimace (cf., mm. 44–45 and 51–54 of the prélude) and by statements of the doll's motive when he picks up the soldier's flower. Tableau II ends with two other transformations of Polichinelle's motive: the one in mm. 225–28 recalls the slow mysterious version from mm. 1–4 (see ex. 9.6e) while the other in mm. 262–68 recalls the motive's first appearance in tableau I (see ex. 9.6f).

While Polichinelle's motive saturates tableau II, other themes appear for specific dramatic effects. Lekić suggests, for example, that Polichinelle's attempts to woo the doll recall music from Debussy's piano piece "Serenade for the Doll," *Children's Corner* (see ex. 9.6g–9.h). Meanwhile, the arrival of the soldier's regiment is marked by the theme "Gloire immortelles de nos aïeux" from act 4 of Gounod's *Faust* (see ex. 9.6i–9.6j). To convey the sound of the troops marching, examples 9.6k–9.6l show Debussy recycled material from the start of "Le matin d'un jour de fête" (*Ibéria*, mvt. 3). And it is hard to disagree with Lekić when she claims that mm. 99–153 sound like passages from Stravinsky's *Petrouchka*, a work Debussy had already alluded to in mm. 205–20 of tableau I (see ex. 9.6m–9.6n).[38]

Tableau III opens ominously: the doll is alone with the soldier, who has one arm in a sling and a red rose in the other. They stand in front of a dilapidated sheepfold with a "for sale" sign. A passing shepherd sells the doll two sheep and a passing poulterer two geese. The soldier and the doll kiss each other; they are in love and are eventually married. To convey the soldier's change in fortune, Debussy's setting frames the scene with statements of the nursery rhyme "Il était une bergère" in mm. 1–6 and 16–21. Whereas those statements are in B minor (see ex. 9.7a–9.7b), the tune returns in B major in mm. 137–42 and 143–48 (see ex. 9.7c). The somber mood of the opening is further reinforced by the appearance of several other themes including a variant of Polichinelle's leitmotiv in mm. 7–10, 11–15, and 23–27 (see ex. 9.7d) and a pentatonic lament in mm. 16–41 and 127–36 that recalls "Pour invoquer Pan, dieu du vent d'été," the opening movement of Debussy's *Six épigraphes antique* (see ex. 9.7e–9.7f).[39] In Caplet's orchestration, the lament is performed by the *cor anglais*, thereby recalling "Die alte Weise" from act 3 of *Tristan und Isolde*. The shepherd's lament leads directly to parodies of "Il vecchio castello" from Mussorgsky's *Pictures at an Exhibition* (see ex. 9.7g–9.7h) and of Mendelessohn's "Wedding March" from *A Midsummer Night's Dream* when the soldier is finally united with the doll (see ex. 9.7i).

Example 9.6a Debussy, Polichinelle's motive, *La Boîte à joujoux*, tableau I, mm. 88–91

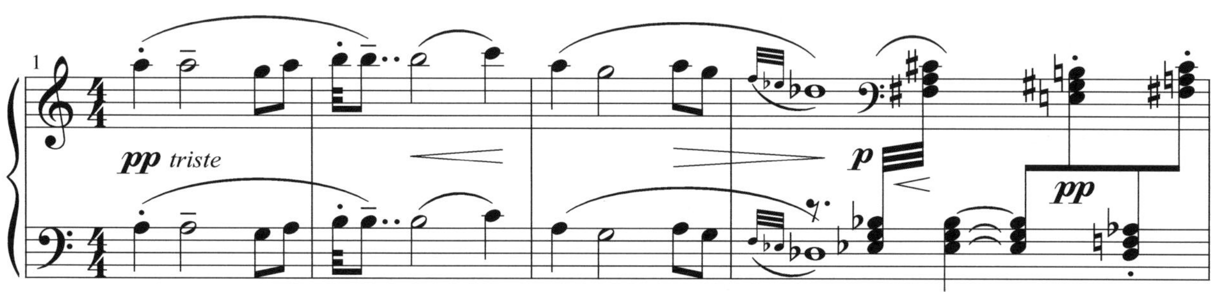

Example 9.6b Debussy, Polichinelle's motive, *La Boîte à joujoux*, tableau II, mm. 1–4

Example 9.6c Debussy, Polichinelle's motive, *La Boîte à joujoux*, tableau II, mm. 15–22

Example 9.6d Debussy, Polichinelle's motive, *La Boîte à joujoux*, tableau II, mm. 171–93

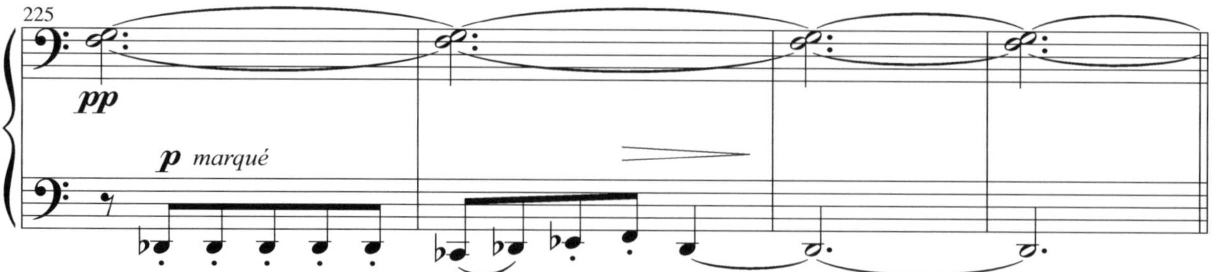

Example 9.6e Debussy, Polichinelle's motive, *La Boîte à joujoux*, tableau II, mm. 225–28

Example 9.6f Debussy, Polichinelle's motive, *La Boîte à joujoux*, tableau II, mm. 262–68

Example 9.6g Debussy, *La Boîte à joujoux*, tableau II, mm. 36–43

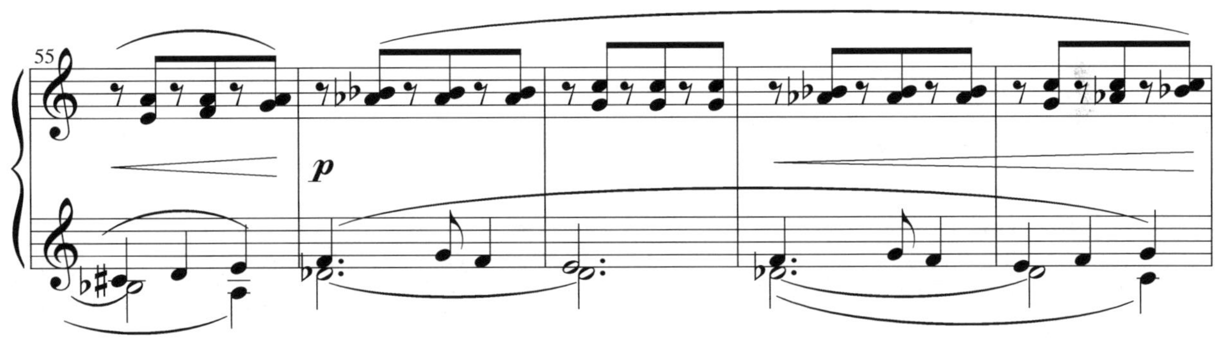

Example 9.6h Debussy, "Serenade for the doll," *Children's Corner*, mm. 55–59

Example 9.6i Debussy, *La Boîte à joujoux*, tableau II, mm. 73–85

Example 9.6j Gounod, "Gloire immortelles de nos aïeux," *Faust*, act 4

Example 9.6k Debussy, *La Boîte à joujoux*, tableau II, mm. 78–83

Example 9.61 Debussy, "Le matin d'un jour de fête," *Ibéria*, mvt. 3, mm. 1–4

Example 9.6m Debussy, Polichinelle's motive, *La Boîte à joujoux*, tableau II, mm. 99–106

Example 9.6n Debussy, Polichinelle's motive, *La Boîte à joujoux*, tableau I, mm. 203–18

Example 9.7 Main motives in tableau III: "La bergerie à vendre," *La Boîte à joujoux*

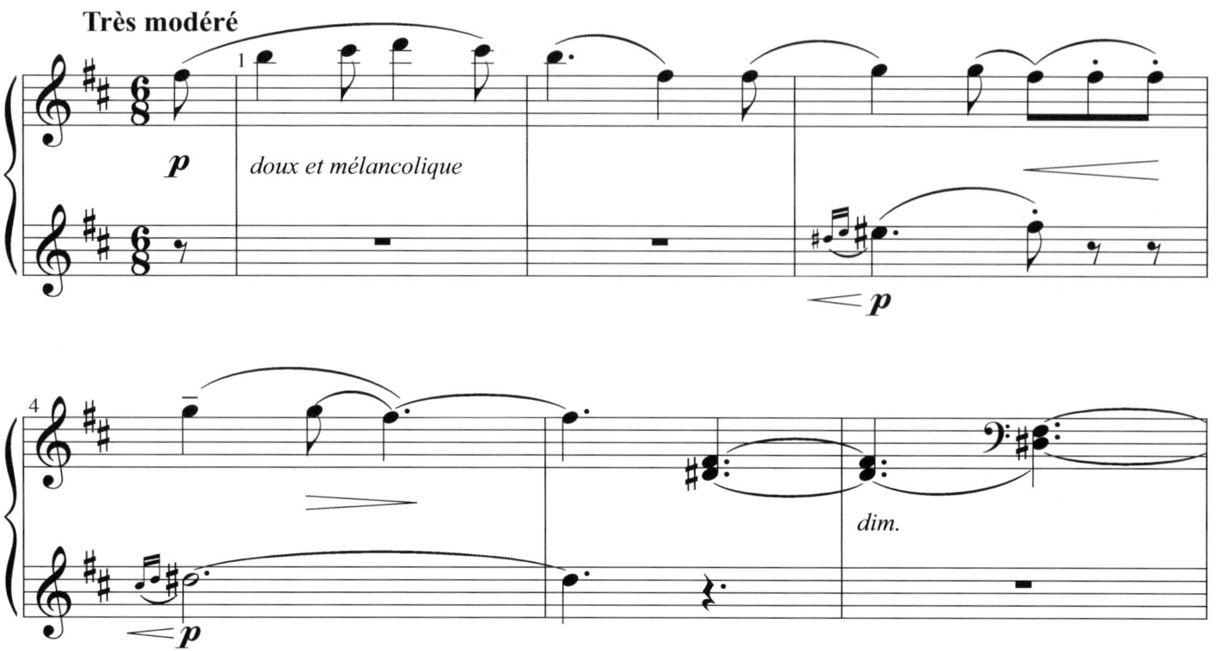

Example 9.7a "Il était une bergère," *La Boîte à joujoux*, tableau III, mm. 1–6

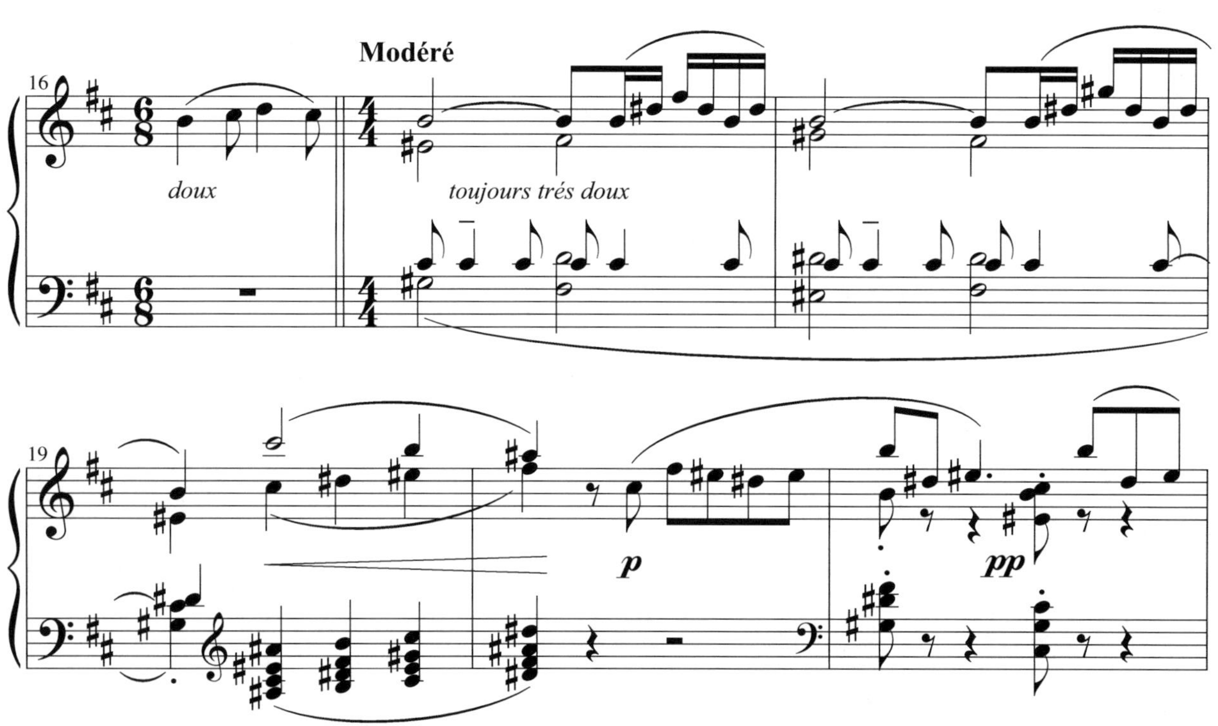

Example 9.7b "Il était une bergère," *La Boîte à joujoux*, tableau III, mm. 16–21

Example 9.7c "Il était une bergère," *La Boîte à joujoux*, tableau III, mm. 137–48

Example 9.7d Debussy, Polichinelle's motive, *La Boîte à joujoux*, tableau III, mm. 7–10

Example 9.7e Shepherd's Lament, *La Boîte à joujoux*, tableau III, mm. 26–30

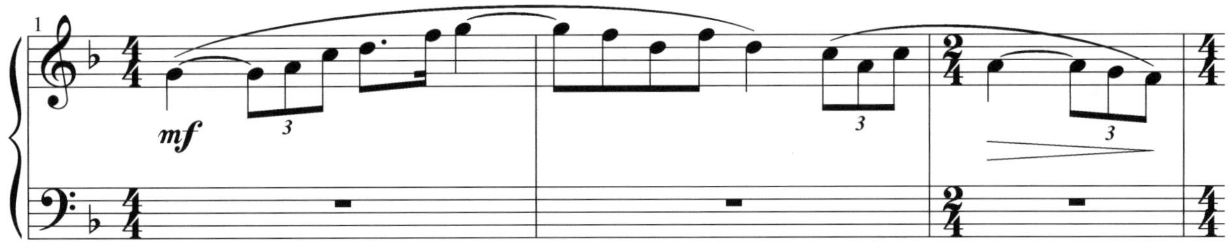

Example 9.7f Debussy, "Pour invoquer Pan, dieu du vent d'été," *Six épigraphes antique*, mm. 1–6

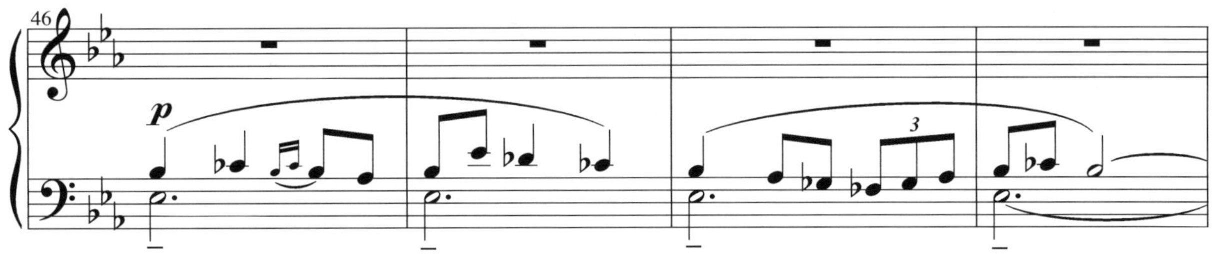

Example 9.7g Debussy, *La Boîte à joujoux*, tableau III, mm. 42–49

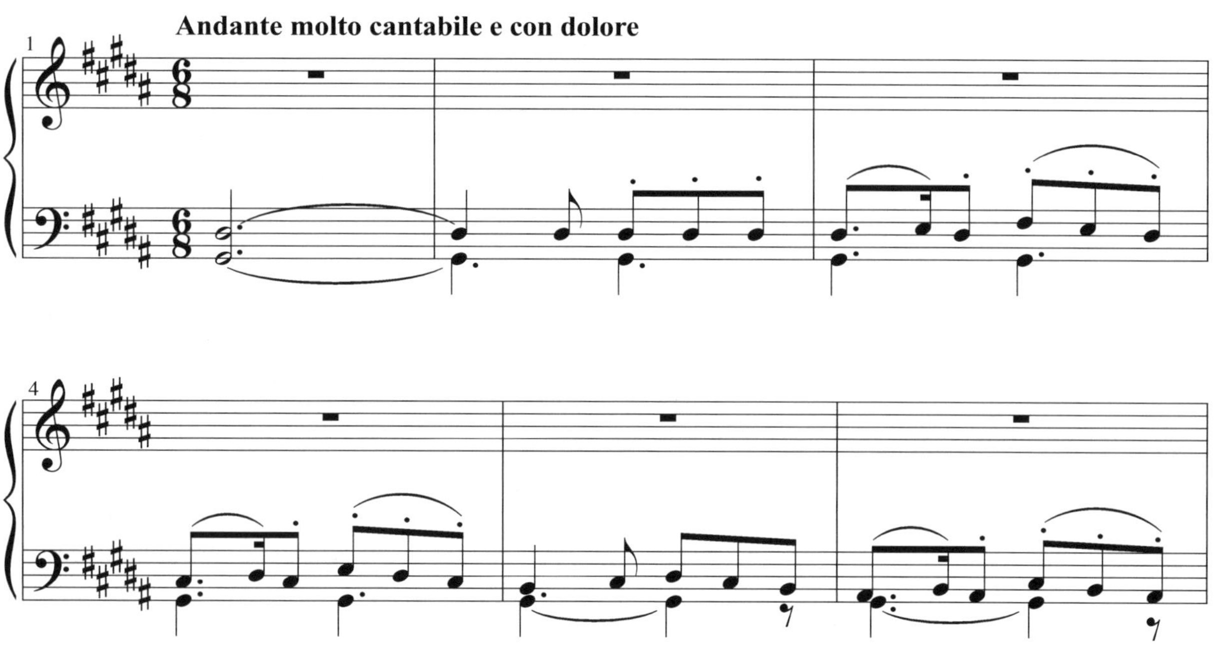

Example 9.7h Mussorgsky, "Il vecchio castello," *Pictures at an Exhibition*, mm. 1–6

Example 9.7i Mendelssohn, "Wedding March," *La Boîte à joujoux*, tableau III, mm. 154–62

Tableau IV, which takes place twenty years later, merges seamlessly with tableau III. The soldier and the doll have made their fortune and are standing outside a comfortable chalet with their brood of five children. The soldier is sporting a white beard and leaning on a safe; she is ruddy cheeked and chubbier than before. Polichinelle has faced retribution and is forced to wear a placard that reads "The Law." The children dance a lively polka before the lights go out and the scene returns to the toy shop at night. The music recalls material associated with the three main protagonists: Polichinelle by statements of the nursery rhyme "Pan! Qu'est-ce qu'est là? C'est Polichinelle" in mm. 163–67, a tune that was first heard in mm. 217–20 of tableau I (see ex. 9.8a–9.8b); the soldier by versions of his motive in mm. 169–76; and the doll by recollections of her motive in mm. 176–80. The children's polka quotes several more nursery rhymes: "Jean-Pierre, tiens-toi bien; tu vas tomber sur le derrière" in mm. 181–95 (see ex. 9.8c) and "Fanfan La Tulipe" in mm. 196–227 (see ex. 9.8d).[40] After a measure of complete silence, the epilogue follows a similar plan to the prélude. Example 9.9 and table 9.2 indicate that the passage is a potpourri built from alternating statements of the Toybox motive (ex. 9.9a) with recollections of Polichinelle's motive (ex. 9.9b) and the soldier's motive (ex. 9.9c). The epilogue closes with strains of a simple

Example 9.8 Main motives in tableau IV: "Après fortune fait," *La Boîte à joujoux*

Example 9.8a "Pan! Qu'est-ce qu'est là? C'est Polichinelle," *La Boîte à joujoux*, tableau IV, mm. 163–67

Example 9.8b "Pan! Qu'est-ce qu'est là? C'est Polichinelle," *La Boîte à joujoux*, tableau I, mm. 215–19

Example 9.8c "Jean-Pierre, tiends-toi bienl tu vas tomber sur le derrière," *La Boîte à joujoux*, tableau IV, mm. 181–84

Example 9.8d "Fantin la tulipe," *La Boîte à joujoux*, tableau IV, mm. 196–204

Table 9.2. The epilogue as a grotesque or potpourri

Toybox motive, mm. 5–6	
	Polichinelle's motive, mm. 7–8
Toybox motive, mm. 9–12	
	Soldier's motive, m. 13
	Soldier's motive, m. 15
	Farewell Call, mm. 15–16

Example 9.9 Main motives in the "Epilogue," *La Boîte à joujoux*

Example 9.9a Toybox motive, mm. 5–6

Example 9.9b Polichinelle's motive, mm. 7–8

Example 9.9c Soldier's motive, m. 13

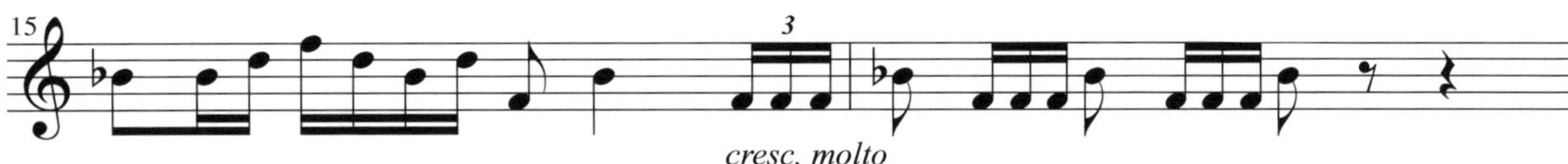

Example 9.9d Farewell Call, mm. 15–16

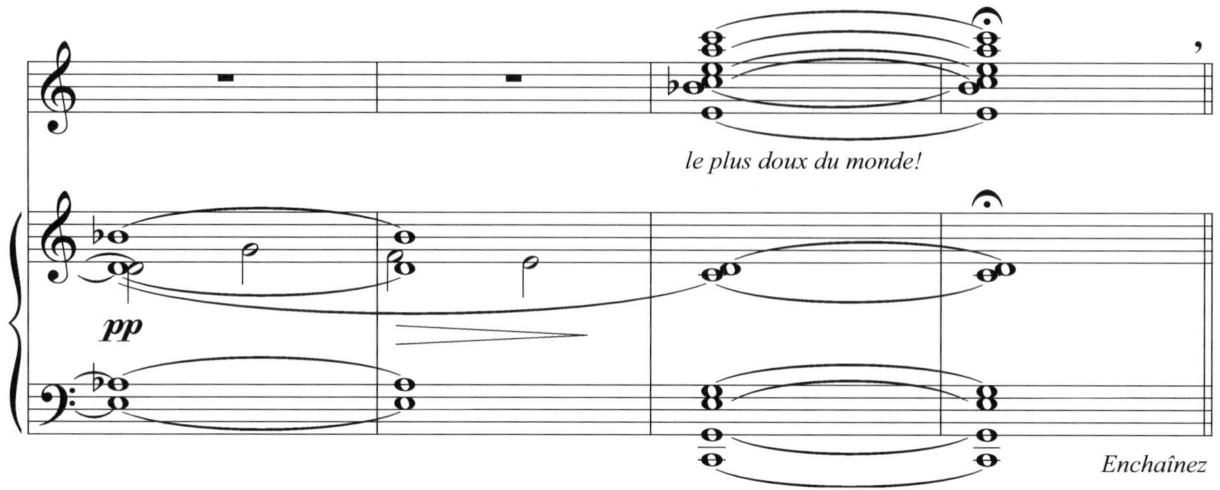

Example 9.10a Final cadence at the end of the prelude

Example 9.10b Final cadence at the end of the epilogue

bugle known as "Farewell Call" (ex. 9.9d). Examples 9.10a–9.10b then show the strong similarities between the cadences that end both passages: both approach the tonic C major with sonorities that include the notes A♭ and D. It also underscores, yet again, Debussy's penchant for grotesques.

The preceding discussion has shown that Debussy's score for *La Boîte à joujoux* is a quasi-improvised potpourri or musical grotesque just like those that Tinchant, Fragerolle, Satie, and others performed at shadow plays during the later 1880s and 1890s and, as revealed in books such as Rapée's *Motion Picture Moods For Pianists and Organists* (1924), those used to accompany screenings of silent movies in the 1890s–1920s.[41] This point is particularly interesting because Debussy is known to have had a strong affinity for the cinema. For example, in response to a screening of *L'agonie de Byzance*, a thirty-minute feature film directed by Louis Feuillade, at the luxurious Gaumont Palace Theater on October 24, 1913, Debussy enthused about the musical accompaniment provided by Léon Moreau and Henry Février.

> There remains but one way of reviving the taste for symphonic composition among our contemporaries: to apply cinematic treatments to pure music (*"appliquons à la musique pure traitement du cinématographe"*). It is film—the Ariadne's thread—that will show us the way out of this disquieting labyrinth. M. Léon Moreau and Henry Février have just supplied proof of this with great success. Those hordes of listeners who find themselves bored stiff by a performance of a Bach *Passion*, or even Beethoven's *Missa Solemnis*, would find themselves brought to attention if the screen were to take pity on their distress.[42]

Just as audiences found many "silent films" endlessly entertaining, so audiences found the score of *La Boîte à joujoux* extremely endearing. After watching a performance of *La Boîte à joujoux* by Les Ballets Suédois on February 17, 1921, one reviewer declared, "Hearing melodies that I was familiar with both from the folk-tune genre as well as the high art genre was refreshing, and made me remember back to the past. From the very beginning of the piece, *Le Sacre du Printemps* comes to mind in the flute melody. At the entrance of the Soldier, 'Golliwog's Cakewalk' is heard. Some other familiar tunes include a theme from Gounod's *Faust*, Mendelssohn's *Wedding March*, even a few French folk tunes. All of these allusions, and neither [vulgar] nor [tending to] vulgarity. How charming!"[43] Enthusiasm for the piece was apparently widespread: Durand's illustrated piano score sold extremely well and, according to Orledge, was Debussy's last "real success."[44] Sales of the music were no doubt buoyed by the fact that Hellé reused designs from *La Boîte à joujoux* in other children's books and even toys of the period.[45]

And yet, there are several signs that Hellé and Debussy may have had more serious motives for creating *La Boîte à joujoux*, motives that might be traced back to Baudelaire's "Morale du joujou." As noted earlier, this remarkable essay explores the special role that toys play in shaping peoples' feelings about the world around them, especially their attitudes toward art and themselves. It leaves no doubt about the lure of toys: "There is in a great toy store an extraordinary gaiety which makes it preferable to the finest bourgeois apartment. Is not the whole of life to be found there in miniature, and in forms far more colourful, pristine and polished than the real thing? There you may find gardens, theatres, beautiful costumes, eyes as clear as diamonds, cheeks kindled with rouge, charming lacework, carriages, stables, drunkards, charlatans, bankers, actors, punchinellos like fireworks, kitchens, and of course entire armies, in perfect discipline, complete with cavalry and artillery."[46] The essay also distinguishes between genuine play, which provides evidence of a child's capacity for abstraction and imaginative power, and games that merely imitate adult behavior, such as "little girls who play at grown-ups" (i.e., homemaking) and "children who play at war" (i.e., war mongering).[47] And it suggests that toys provide children with their "earliest

Above and facing page, **Figure 9.5** Performance of *La Boîte à joujoux* by marionettes at the
Teatro Visconti Modrone in Milan, March 1915

324

VINGT ANS APRES

initiation to art" and that their subsequent encounters with art as adults seldom give them "the same feelings of warmth . . . the same enthusiasms . . . the same convictions."[48] Simply put, toys help to shape a person's basic aesthetic orientation: children given toy theaters by their parents are likely to regard the theater as "the most delicious form of Beauty."[49]

As children grow up, however, they develop an insatiable desire to *see the soul* of their toys" in order to find out if, like them, their playthings are real.[50] That impulse can be overwhelming: "When this desire has implanted itself in the child's cerebral marrow, it fills his fingers and nails with an extraordinary agility and strength. The child twists and turns his toy, scratches it, shakes it, bumps it against the walls, throws it on the ground. From time to time he makes it re-start its mechanical motions, sometimes in the opposite direction." Then comes the inevitable: the toy's "marvellous life comes to a stop."[51] When the child finally opens up the toy, however, she or he faces grim reality: "But *where is the soul?*"[52] This discovery marks "the beginning of melancholy and gloom."[53] In other words, playing with toys not only guides a person's aesthetic compass but also makes them appreciate the gaps that inevitably arise between their own views of the world, the views of other people, and reality itself. This is much the same moral that Baudelaire offered in his perverse tale "Les Dons de fées," in which fairies give people gifts but not necessarily the ones they want. To quote one disillusioned fairy, "How do you like this conceited little Frenchman who wants to understand everything? He received the best of all [presents] for his son, and yet he dares to question me and dispute the indisputable."[54]

Baudelaire's influence on Debussy was no less palpable. One sign comes from Debussy's inaugural essay as music editor for *La Revue blanche*. Published on April 1, 1901, this essay begins by echoing Baudelaire's claim that people often lose their feeling of warmth, enthusiasm, and conviction for art when they grow up:

> Grownups tend to forget that as children they were forbidden to open the insides of their dolls—a crime of high treason against the cause of mystery. . . . And yet they still insist on poking their aesthetic noses into things that don't concern them! Without their dolls to break open, they still try to explain things, dismantle them, and quite heartlessly kill all their mystery. I suppose it *is* more convenient to know how things work: at least it gives us something to chat about. But, my God! Some of them we can excuse because of their complete ignorance, but others—the more spiteful of them—give rein to their malice: they have to cling frantically to their own pitiful mediocrity, and these latter have a faithful flock of followers.[55]

Another comes from a description of *La Boîte à joujoux* in which Debussy subscribed to his predecessor's view that toys become "actors in the great drama of life": "The plot? Oh, very simple: a cardboard soldier falls in love with a doll, he tries to show off to her, but she betrays him with *Polichinelle*. The soldier learns of this, and terrible things begin to happen: there is a battle between [the] wooden soldiers and the *Polichinelles*. In short, the soldier in love with the beautiful doll is gravely wounded in the battle, the doll nurses him and . . . they all live happily ever."[56] The idea that toys are in some sense alive is one that clearly stems from Baudelaire and his reference to "the living toy."[57]

But what about the soul of toys? Debussy's views seem to reflect those of his onetime collaborator Maurice Maeterlinck, as he indicated in a letter to Durand from September 27, 1913: "The third tableau is going slowly. The soul of a doll is more mysterious than even Maeterlinck imagines; it doesn't easily tolerate the kind of humbug so many human souls put up with."[58] Debussy's claim about the mysteriousness of the soul is entirely apropos given Maeterlinck's portrayal of Mélisande in his play *Pelléas et Mélisande* and his desire to replace normal actors with "a shadow, a reflection" or "by a being who would have all the appearances of life without being so."[59] Debussy would doubtless have enjoyed the performance by marionettes at Milan's Teatro Visconti di Modrone in March 1915 (see fig. 9.5).[60] For Maeterlinck and Debussy, it is simply a mistake to assume that people are more *alive* than puppets or dolls. This pessimistic message is one that resonates perfectly with Baudelaire's gloomy image of modern city life Buhot's poignant street scene from Montmartre. It is something that will become even more apparent in the following chapter.

Notes

1. Claude Terrasse and Pierre Bonnard, *Petit Solfège illustré* (Paris: Ancienne Maison Quantin, Librairies-imprimeries réunies, 1893).

2. In his humorous score *Le morceau de l'accordeur* (Paris: Société d'Éditions Musicales, 1912), Claude Terrasse added the following verse by Franc-Nohain: "Do, sol, ré, la, ré, la, mi, si/Et moi aussi, et moi aussi/J'aurai pu être un Debussy." As it happens, Pierre Bonnard would later produce designs for the Ballets Suédois's production of Debussy's *Jeux* in 1920; for illustrations, see Pierre Tugal Tansman, *Les Ballets Suédois dans l'art contemporain* (Paris: Éditions du Trianon, 1931).

3. Charles Baudelaire, "Une Charogne," *Les Fleurs du mal*, in *Charles Baudelaire: Œuvres Complètes*, vol. I, ed. Claude Pichois, Bibliothèque de la Pléiade (Paris: Gallimard, 1975), 31–32.

4. E[ugène] Marsnan, "Champs-Elysées: Nouvelle saison des Ballets Suédois: ODEON; La Paix," *Paris-Journal*, February 20, 1921; Dansmuseert Svenska Baletten, Pressurklipp Bok 2 and cited by Simon Morrison, "Debussy's Toy Stories," *Journal of Musicology* 30, no. 3 (Summer 2013): 426.

5. Robert Orledge, "Another Look inside Debussy's 'Toybox,'" *Musical Times* 117, no. 1606 (1976): 988 [987–89]. See also Orledge, "Debussy's Musical Gifts to Emma Bardac," *Musical Quarterly* 60, no. 4 (1974): 544–56; Orledge, *Debussy and the Theatre* (Cambridge: Cambridge University Press, 1982), 177–85. Mirna Lekić, "Secrets of a Toy-Box: A Study of Claude Debussy's *La Boîte à joujoux*," DMA diss., City University of New York, 2014.

6. See Denis Herlin, "André Hellé et La Boîte à joujoux: interview, conférence et texte intégrale de *L'Histoire d'une Boîte à joujoux*," *Cahiers Debussy* 30 (2006): 108; and Morrison, "Debussy's Toy Stories," 426.

7. Baudelaire, "Morale du joujou," in *Œuvres Complètes*, I:581–87; Baudelaire, "A Philosophy of Toys," in *The Painter of Modern Life*, ed. and trans. Jonathan Mayne (London: Phaidon, 2001), 197–204. Like Poe and Wagner, Baudelaire was a big fan of Shakespeare's work, especially *Hamlet*; see Max I. Baym, "Baudelaire and Shakespeare," *Shakespeare Association Bulletin* 15, no. 3 (July 1940): 131–48; Burton R. Pollin, "Shakespeare in the Works of Edgar Allan Poe," *Studies in the American Renaissance* 9 (1985): 157–86; and Margaret Inwood, *The Influence of Shakespeare on Richard Wagner* (Lewiston, NY: Edwin Mellen, 1999).

8. Baudelaire, "Morale du joujou," in *Œuvres Complètes*, I:582–83; Baudelaire, "A Philosophy of Toys," in *Painter of Modern Life*, 198.

9. Patrick Langley, "Master of Puppets," *Freize*, September 16, 2017, https://www.frieze.com/article/master-puppets (accessed July 11, 2025).

10. Maria Rika Maniates, "Quodlibet Revisum," *Acta Musicoligica* 38, no. 2/4 (1966): 169–78.

11. Maniates, "Quodlibet Revisum," 170, 171.

12. Till Gerrit Waidelich, "Das Opern-Potpourri: Musikalisches Kaleidoskop, ars combinatoria oder musikimmanente Pornographie?," in *Jenseits der Bühne: Bearbeitungs- und Rezeptionsformen der Oper im 19. und 20. Jahrhundert. Symposium der IMS Konferenz Zürich 2007*, ed. Hans-Joachim Hinrichsen and K. Pietschmann, Schweizer Beiträge zur Musikforschung 15 (Bärenreiter: Kassel, 2010), 128–38.

13. Francis Poulenc, *Emmanuel Chabrier* (Paris: La Palatine, 1961), 101; Francis Poulenc, *Emmanuel Chabrier*, trans. Cynthia Jolly (London: Denis Dobson, 1981), 57.

14. Steven Vande Moortele discusses the idea that opera and ballet overtures are often potpourris in his book *The Romantic Overture and Musical Form from Rossini to Wagner* (Cambridge: Cambridge University Press, 2007), 75–107.

15. Carl Czerny, *Systematische Anleitung zum Fantasieren auf dem Pianoforte*, Op. 200 (Vienna: Diabelli, 1829), esp. 86–106; Carl Czerny, *A Systematic Introduction to Improvisation on the Pianoforte*, ed. and trans. Alice L. Mitchell (New York: Longman, 1983), esp. 86–106.

16. Czerny, *Systematische Anleitung zum Fantasieren*, 4; Czerny, *A Systematic Introduction to Improvisation*, 3.

17. For information about shadow plays at Le Chat Noir, see Paul Jeanne, *Les Théâtre d'Ombres à Montmartre de 1887–1923* (Paris: Les Éditions des Presses Modernes au Palais-Royal, 1937); Steven Moore Whiting, "Music on Montmartre," in *The Spirit of Montmartre: Cabarets, Humor, and the Avant-Garde, 1875–1905*, ed. Phillip Dennis Cate and Mary Shaw (New Brunswick, NJ: Rutgers University Press, 1996), 159–97; and Madhuri Murkherjee, "When the Saints Go Marching In: Popular Performances of *La Tentation de Sainte Antoine* and *St Geneviève de Paris* at the Chat Noir Shadow Theater," in *Medieval Saints in Late Nineteenth-Century French Culture*, ed. Elizabeth Emery and Laurie Postelwate (Jefferson, NC: McFarland, 2004), 25–44; Emilio Sala, "Hearing the Shadows at the Chat Noir's Pre-cinematic Theatre," in *The Oxford Handbook of Cinematic Listening*, ed. Carlo Cenciarelli (Oxford: Oxford University Press, 2021), 42–67.

18. *La Tentation de Sainte-Antoine*, illustrated by Henri Rivière, music by Albert Tinchant and Georges Fragerolle (Paris: E. Plon, Nourrit et Cie, s.d. [1888]). See Whiting, "Music on Montmartre," 184–88.

19. Films were first shown publicly in Paris at the Salon Indien du Grand Café on December 28, 1895. For the influence of pantomimes on early film, see Carlo Piccardi, "Pierrot at the Cinema: The Musical Common Denominator from Pantomime to Film, Part I," trans. Gillian Anderson and Lauren Cregor with the help of Lidia Bagnoli, *Music and the Moving Image* 1, no. 2 (Summer 2008): 37–52; "Pierrot at the Cinema: The Musical Common Denominator from Pantomime to Film, Part II," trans. Gillian Anderson and Lauren Cregor with the help of Lidia Bagnoli, *Music and the Moving Image* 2, no. 2 (Summer 2009): 7–23; and "Pierrot at the Cinema: The Musical Common Denominator from Pantomime to Film, Part III," trans. Gillian Anderson and Lauren Cregor with the help of Lidia Bagnoli, *Music and the Moving Image* 6, no.1 (Spring 2013): 4–54.

20. Erno Rapée, "Foreword and Instructions for the Use of this Manual," in *Motion Picture Moods for Pianists and Organists* (New York: Schirmer, 1924), iii. For other guides to accompanying early films, see George W. Tyacke, *Playing to Motion Pictures* (London: Kinematograph Weekly, 1914); and Edith Lang and George West, *Musical Accompaniment of Moving Pictures* (Boston: Boston Music Company, 1920).

21. François Lesure, "Debussy et le Chat Noir," *Cahiers Debussy* 23 (1999): 37 [35–43]; and François Lesure, *Claude Debussy* (Paris: Klincksieck, 1994), 93. See also Sarah Gutsche-Miller, "Debussy's Noctambule and Parisian Popular Culture," in *Debussy in Context*, ed. Simon Trezise (Cambridge: Cambridge University Press, 2024), 196–200.

22. Rosemary Lloyd, *Mallarmé: The Poet and His Circle* (Ithaca, NY: Cornell University Press, 1999), 154.

23. Claude Debussy, "Claude Debussy nous dit ses projets Théâtre," *Comœdia* (February 1, 1914), in *Monsieur Croche et autres écrits*, ed. François Lesure (Paris: Gallimard, 1987), 329–30; Claude Debussy, "Claude Debussy Tells Us of His Theatrical Projets," in *Debussy on Music*, ed. François Lesure and trans. Richard Langham Smith (New York: Knopf, 1977), 311–12.

24. See Paul Vidal, "Souvenirs d'Achille Debussy," *Revue Musicale* 7 (1926): 10–16; Roger Nichols, *Debussy Remembered* (London: Faber, 1992), 6, 8; Sylvie Douche, "Transcription littérale du carnet de notes de Maurice Emmanuel au sujet des échanges de Debussy-Guiraud (1889–1890)," in *Pelléas et Mélisande cent ans après: études et documents*, ed. Jean-Christophe Branger, Sylvie Douche, and Denis Herlin, Palazzetto Bru Zane, Centre de musique contemporaine Française (Lyon: Symétrie, 2013), 285; Lockspeiser, *Debussy. His Life and Mind*, vol. 1, *1862–1902*, 2nd ed. (Cambridge: Cambridge University Press, 1978), Appendix B, 208.

25. Orledge, *Debussy and the Theatre*, 182 [177–85].

26. By a strange coincidence, Auguste, 4e comte Gilbert de Voisins, approached Debussy in July 1897 about composing his own score for *La Tentation de Saint Antoine*, but he never replied. See Orledge, *Debussy and the Theatre*, 265.

27. These scores have the following plate numbers: "Danse de la Poupée" (D&F: 9040); "Ronde" (D&F: 9041); "Polka Finale" (D&F: 9082); suite version for piano by Léon Roques (D&F: 9082); suite version for piano trio with optional parts for clarinet and double bass by Henri Mouton (D&F: 9044). Roques also made transcriptions of "Danse de la Poupée" for violin and piano and for flute and piano.

28. Orledge, "Another Look," 989.

29. Lekić, "Secrets of a Toy-Box," 73–77.

30. Richard Taruskin, *Stravinsky and the Russian Traditions* (Berkeley: University of California Press, 1996), 1451. Edward Cone, "Stravinsky: The Progress of a Method," *Perspectives of New Music* 1, no. 1 (1962): 18–26. Mark McFarland, "Debussy and Stravinsky: Another Look into Their Musical Relationship," *Cahiers Debussy* 24 (2000): 79–112; and Mark McFarland, "Debussy: The Origins of a Method," *Journal of Music Theory* 48, no. 4 (2004): 295–323.

31. Elizabeth Cowling, "Feminine/Masculine: The Collages of Picasso, Braque, and Gris. How did Cubist Artists Use Collage to Probe the Relationship between the Sexes?," *The Met*, November 8, 2022, https://www.metmuseum.org/perspectives/articles/2022/11/feminine-masculine-cubist-collage#:~:text=Inanimate%20objects%20dominated%20the%20imagery,combination%20of%20things%20and%20text.

32. For the connections to Mussorgsky, see José Ednardo Martins, "La Vision de L'univers Enfantin chez Moussorgsky et Debussy," *Cahiers Debussy* 9 (1985): 3–16.

33. There is, however, some confusion about the number of sections in the ballet: Debussy's autograph (F-Pn 2138) and the piano score lists a prélude, three tableaux, and an epilogue; Hellé's illustrated table of contents for the piano score lists four tableaux; and an advertisement on the back of Durand's edition of the "Polka Finale" describes piece as "ballet enfantin en 5 tableaux."

34. For the symbolic significance of the red rose, see Orledge, *Debussy and the Theatre*, 126.

35. Lekić, "Secrets of a Toy-Box," 40–41. Lekić also claims that the Harlequin's theme resembles one from Schumann's *Carnival*; Lekić, "Secrets of a Toy-Box," 28.

36. Lekić, "Secrets of a Toy-Box," 45–46. See also Ann McKinley, "Debussy and American Minstrelsy," *Black Perspective in Music* 14, no. 3 (Autumn 1986): 249–58.

37. These rolls include WM 2733 (*Children's Corner*); WM 2734 (*D'un cahier d'esquisses*); WM 2735 ("La Soirée dans Grenade" [*Estampes*]); WM 2736 (*La Plus que lente*); WM 2738 ("Danseuses de Delphes," "La Cathédrale engloutie," "La Danse de Puck" [*Préludes*, Bk. 1]); WM 2739 ("Le Vent dans la plaine," "Minstrels" [*Préludes*, Bk. 2]).

38. Lekić, "Secrets of a Toy-Box," 73–77, esp. 76–77.

39. Although Debussy completed *Six épigraphes antique* just after *La Boîte à joujoux* in 1914, he originally wrote the music in 1901 to accompany a set of staged poems written by his friend Pierre Louÿs. The poems come from a volume of 143 poems and 3 epitaphs entitled *Les Chansons de Bilitis* (Paris: Librairie De L'art Indépendant, 1895). Louÿs claimed to have translated these poems from manuscripts found in the tomb of a sixth-century BC Greek poetess named Bilitis, but he had actually fabricated them himself.

40. The polka might be derived from Émile Spencer's "La jambe en bois" and from the English nursery rhyme "One, two, three, four, five / once I caught a fish alive." See Morrison, "Debussy's Toy Stories," 430.

41. Erno Rapée, *Motion Picture Moods for Pianists and Organists* (New York: Schirmer, 1924).

42. Debussy, "Concert Colonne—Société des nouveaux concerts," in *Monsieur Croche*, 248; Debussy, *Debussy on Music*, 298. The controversial nature of Debussy's phrase "apply cinematic treatments to pure music" ("*appliquons à la musique pure traitement du cinématographe*") will be discussed in chapter 12.

43. Concert Review 17 February 1921: *La Boîte à Joujoux*. https://musicalgeography.org/concert-review-17-february-1921-la-boite-a-joujoux (accessed July 11, 2025).

44. Robert Orledge, "Debussy, Durand et Cie," in *The Business of Music*, ed. Michael Talbot (Liverpool: University of Liverpool Press, 2002), 149–50.

45. See André Hellé, *Grosses bêtes & petites bêtes* (Paris: Tolmer & Cie, 1912); André Hellé, *French Toys* (Paris: Éditions De L'Avenir Féminin, 1915); and https://parisbreakfasts.blogspot.com/2013/02/musee-du-jouets-andre-helle.html.

46. Baudelaire, "Morale du joujou," in *Œuvres Complètes*, I:582; Baudelaire, "A Philosophy of Toys," in *Painter of Modern Life*, 198.

47. Baudelaire, "Morale du joujou," in *Œuvres Complètes*, I:583; Baudelaire, "A Philosophy of Toys," in *Painter of Modern Life*, 198–99.

48. Baudelaire, "Morale du joujou," in *Œuvres Complètes*, I:583; Baudelaire, "A Philosophy of Toys," in *Painter of Modern Life*, 199.

49. Baudelaire, "Morale du joujou," in *Œuvres Complètes*, I:585; Baudelaire, "A Philosophy of Toys," in *Painter of Modern Life*, 201.

50. Baudelaire, "Morale du joujou," in *Œuvres Complètes*, I:586; Baudelaire, "A Philosophy of Toys," in *Painter of Modern Life*, 202.

51. Baudelaire, "Morale du joujou," in *Œuvres Complètes*, I:587; Baudelaire, "A Philosophy of Toys," in *Painter of Modern Life*, 202.

52. Baudelaire, "Morale du joujou," in *Œuvres Complètes*, I:587; Baudelaire, "A Philosophy of Toys," in *Painter of Modern Life*, 203.

53. Baudelaire, "Morale du joujou," in *Œuvres Complètes*, I:587; Baudelaire, "A Philosophy of Toys," in *Painter of Modern Life*, 203.

54. Charles Baudelaire, "Les Dons de fées," *Le Spleen de Paris* XX, in *Œuvres Complètes*, I:305–7; Gretchen Schultz and Lewis Seifert, *Fairy Tales for the Disillusioned* (Princeton, NJ: Princeton University Press, 2016), 5. Is this an allusion to Poe's short story "Why the Little Frenchman Wears His Hand in a Sling"?

55. Claude Debussy, "Le 'Faust' de Schumann.–Ouverture pour 'L Roi Lear,' D'A. Savard.–Le Troisième Acte de 'Siegfried'.—Une Symphonie de Witkowski," *La Revue blanche* (April 1, 1901), in *Monsieur Croche*, 23; Debussy, *Debussy on Music*, 13.

56. Claude Debussy, "Claude Debussy nous dit ses projets Théâtre," *Comoedia* (February 1, 1914), in *Monsieur Croche*, 329–30; Debussy, *Debussy on Music*, 311–12.

57. Baudelaire, "Morale du joujou," in *Œuvres Complètes*, I:585; Baudelaire, "A Philosophy of Toys," in *Painter of Modern Life*, 201.

58. Debussy, *Correspondance*, 1667; Debussy, *Letters*, 278–79.

59. Union Internationale de la Marionette, "Maurice Maeterlinck," *World Encyclopedia of Puppetry*, accessed October 20, 2022, https://wepa.unima.org/en/maurice-maeterlinck.

60. Morrison, "Debussy's Toy Stories," 434.

10

Jeux

Poetry as Dance

It should be clear from the preceding chapters that while Debussy and other Symbolists acknowledged the ornamental character of arabesques, moresques, and grotesques, they nonetheless accepted that those concepts have wider aesthetic and even social implications. Chapter 8 claimed, for example, that by fusing different literary and musical genres in the manner of Poe's *Tales of the Grotesque and Arabesque*, Maeterlinck and Debussy imbued *Pelléas et Mélisande* with a sense of fantasy that mirrored the disturbing undertones of the opera's narrative. Next, chapter 9 showed how Debussy exploited the capacity for grotesques to absorb diverse elements to articulate the scenario of his ballet *La Boîte à joujoux*; although the work looks like a children's pantomime, similar to the ones he performed for his family during the Christmas holidays, it also offers a critique of bourgeois values; in the manner of Baudelaire's "Morale du joujou," it leaves the audience wondering whether city folk are barely more "alive" than children's puppets. This chapter then extends these ideas by suggesting that Debussy's next ballet—*Jeux*—used the arabesque to challenge traditional social values and familiar images of Paris "as a playground," a hub of public entertainment, the "City of Light."[1]

Of all Debussy's mature compositions, few embody the concept of the arabesque more clearly than his score for the ballet *Jeux*. Commissioned by Diaghilev for his Ballets Russes and completed by Debussy in 1912–13, the piece is widely regarded as one of the composer's most innovative works and a monument to musical modernism. The ballet was not, however, widely appreciated by audiences of the time, who found it extremely hard to fathom. The absurdity of the scenario was laid bare in a contemporary review written by the satirical author Swift and reproduced in figure 10.1: "Summer sports: many readers ask us about the rules of Russian tennis which will be all the rage, this season, in all country estates. They can be summed up as follows: the game is played at night, surrounded by baskets of flowers illuminated by flood lamps; it calls for just

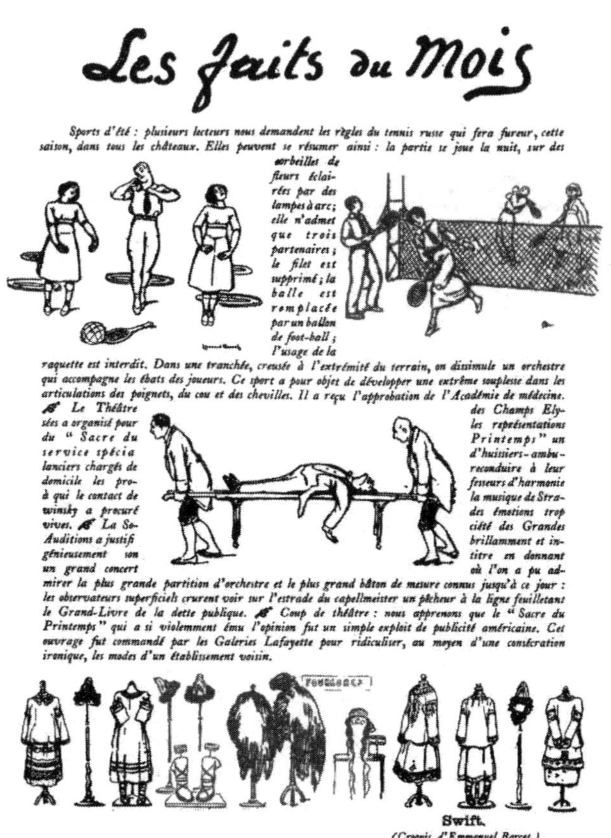

Figure 10.1 Satirical response to *Jeux*, *Revue musicale S.I.M.* 9, no. 6 (June 15, 1913)

three participants; the net is discarded; the [regular] ball is replaced by a soccer ball; the use of racquet is prohibited. In a trench, dug at the end of the land, a concealed orchestra accompanies the antics of the players."[2] Swift suggested that the purpose of this sport was "to develop extreme flexibility in the joints of the wrists, neck, and ankles [and] has received approval from the Academy of Medicine."

Overshadowed by the success of Stravinsky's *Le Sacre du printemps*, which appeared on the same program, *Jeux* was largely ignored in the 1920s and 1930s and was not rehabilitated until the 1950s, when it was championed by Pierre Boulez, Karlheinz Stockhausen, Herbert Eimert, György Ligeti, and other members of the Darmstadt School.[3] Since then, several scholars have discussed the work in detail, often commenting directly or indirectly on its use of arabesques. Robin Holloway, for example, has drawn attention to the ornamental character of Debussy's writing, comparing it with that of act 2 of Wagner's *Parsifal*, especially those passages "concerned with enticements, voluptuousness, and magic."[4] Eimert has focused on the self-generating or "vegetative" nature of *Jeux*'s form, deriving most, if not all, of the work's motives from the main *scherzando* motive (see fig. 10.2). Eimert's elaborate table of motives attempts "to cast light on the associative motivic coherence of the melodic shapes in the piece: is one to call them this, or to refer to ornaments, arabesques, motives and themes."[5] Boulez has likewise claimed that the music sounds "braided," without any clear hierarchy in the organization of the sections.[6] Echoing the analysis of *La Boîte à joujoux* given in chapter 9, Jann Pasler has traced the arabesque qualities of Debussy's music back to the disparate/disjunct nature of its material: "In *Jeux*, 'arabesque'

Figure 10.2 Herbert Eimert's analysis of motives in *Jeux* (*Die Reihe*, 1961), 15

might apply to the play or *jeu* between the various sections of music. Each section develops its own vector, its own force of contrasting shape and direction, which needs resolution or balance. Between many of the sections, there is a free alternation between different rhythms, harmonies, melodies, and instrumental combinations."[7] At the same time, Holloway, Pasler, and Berman have described the extra-musical significance of Debussy's arabesques: they have found parallels between the sensuality of the score and the sexually charged nature of the choreography, which has been painstakingly reconstructed by Millicent Hodson.[8] And Arnold Whittall has charted the underlying drama of Debussy's score to its large-scale tonal structure, something that is also reiterated by Berman and most recently by Mark McFarland.[9]

And yet, certain details suggest that more can still be said about the arabesque qualities of *Jeux* and their Symbolist origins. One is Holloway's observation that the score is a complex mosaic "in which all kinds of valse movements rush tantalizingly past."[10] Besides implying that the music is mostly written in triple meter, usually a nimble 3/8, this simple point stands out for several reasons. For one thing, it offers a helpful reminder that waltzes were usually performed in sequential strings: for example, Johann Strauss's *An der schönen blauen Donau* consists of an introduction, five discrete dances, and a coda that recalls the introduction.[11] For another, it recalls Eugène Marsnan's description of *La Boîte à joujoux* and, in so doing, raises the possibility that *Jeux* might have interconnections with other waltz-based compositions, such as "The Flower Maiden's Dance" from Wagner's *Parsifal*, and two of Debussy's most famous compositions, *L'Isle joyeuse* and "Jeux de vagues" (*La Mer*, mvt. 2). Holloway's observation also prompts us to reconsider the score's cryptic subtitle "Poème dansé." The idea that dance is a form of poetry was almost baked into Symbolist aesthetics: it is one that Mallarmé actively promoted (see chap. 4) and that Baudelaire implicitly endorsed through his concept of *correspondances* (see chap. 1). Last, Debussy suggested on more than one occasion that he found the plot of *Jeux* inherently alarming. Writing to Stravinsky on November 7, 1912, for example, he noted, "Please believe me, *Jeux* is better. For one thing, it's shorter; and for another it's a convenient way of expressing the 'horrors' that take place between the three participants."[12] And in a statement for *Le Matin* (May 15, 1913), Debussy suggested that there was something "slightly wicked" ("un peu méchant") about the ballet's mysterious nocturnal setting.[13] Why did Stravinsky and Debussy find Nijinsky's story disturbing or, to paraphrase Baudelaire, "mal"?

To address these issues, the following chapter begins by describing Baudelaire's views about dance as he expressed them in his published and unpublished writings. It focuses on the connections he found both between dance and the arabesque, especially its links to the fantastic, and between dance and the anxieties of modern city life. In particular, it discusses Baudelaire's poem "Harmonie du soir," which Debussy included in his collection *Cinq poèmes de Baudelaire* (1887–89). Next, the spotlight shifts to *Jeux*, to Nijinsky's choreography, and to Debussy's involvement in the project. The chapter will then offer a detailed analysis of the score, highlighting the ways in which Debussy embodies the principles of the arabesque, through its highly ornamented melodic writing, complex contrapuntal textures, self-generating forms, and allusions to other waltz compositions. The discussion ends with some final comments about the significance of the work's enigmatic subtitle, "Poème dansé."

Although there is nothing very remarkable about associating the arabesque with dance—the arabesque is, after all, a specific position in classical ballet—Baudelaire had other connections in mind when he linked the one with the other. Indeed, as Suzanne F. Braswell has shown, dance played a very special role in his aesthetic agenda.[14] Like Poe before him, Baudelaire clearly had a penchant for dance, so much so that his writings teem with references to dancing, especially waltzing.[15] Braswell, for example, cites numerous works that explicitly refer to dance: the verse poems "Le Serpent qui danse," "Harmonie du soir," and "Danse macabre"; the essay *Les Paradis artificiels* (1853), the prose poem "Le Thyrse" (1863), scenes from his novella *La Fanfarlo* (1847), and several passages in his *Journals Intimes*.

Given their polyphonic nature, Baudelaire believed that arabesques set the imagination into motion in much the same way that music inspires people to crisscross a dance floor. It is a belief that he expressed explicitly in the second stanza of "Le Thyrse": "The baton is your will: erect, firm, unshakeable; the flowers are the wanderings of your fancy around it: the feminine element encircling the masculine with her illusive dance. Straight line and arabesque—intention and expression—the rigidity of the will and the suppleness of the word—a variety of means united for a single purpose—the all-powerful and indivisible amalgam that is genius—what analyst will have the detestable courage to divide or to separate you?"[16] And just as Poe described the poetry of words as "the rhythmical creation of beauty," so Baudelaire claimed that these rhythms can even move the soul: "Which of us has never imagined, in his more ambitious moments, the miracle of a poetic prose, musical though rhythmless and rhymeless, flexible yet strong enough to identify with the lyrical impulses of the soul, to the ebbs and flows of revery, the pangs of conscience?"[17]

Or, to quote *Les Paradis artificiels*, "The idea of beauty must naturally occupy a significant place in the spiritual temperament that I have imagined. The harmony, [balance of the lines,] eurythmy of movements appear to the dreamer as necessities, as duties not only in relation to all beings in creation but also to himself . . . and the dreamer finds that he is endowed with a marvelous aptitude for understanding the immortal, universal rhythm immortal."[18]

According to Braswell, Baudelaire demonstrated such harmony, balance, and eurythmy to perfection in his poem "Harmonie du soir" (*Les Fleurs du Mal*). This remarkable poem, whose text is given in figure 10.3, explores the poet's recollections of past love. Those memories bring back feelings both of pleasure, as illustrated by the image of a perfumed flower gently swaying in the evening air, and of sorrow, as conveyed by the quivering sounds of a violin and the fluid motions of a melancholy waltz. The poem conveys the mobility of the flower, the dancers, and the poet's own feelings by casting the text in the form of a pantoum: the second and fourth lines of one stanza become the first and third lines of the next. The subtle repetition of lines from one stanza to the next illustrates Schlegel's claim that arabesques are self-generating forms: "transitions [are] unrecognizable, or at least not as stressed as breaks, for every position in the ornament is simultaneously that of another."[19] Braswell suggests that the lines "gradually form an interlacing structure through which rhythmic repetition creates a layering effect that is both visible and sonorous" and that this is encapsulated "in Baudelaire's metonymic use of the waltz."[20] As she explains: "the allusion to the waltz announces the undulating effects instantiated by the movement of the verses and the rhythmic patterns they trace across the fixed space constituted by the four stanzas of the poem."[21] Braswell likewise shows how an interplay between feminine and masculine end rhymes conjures up images of several couples interweaving across the ballroom: "in the first quatrain, the couplet formed by [lines] 2 and 4 is of course subsumed into an *embrassé* pattern (abba). But owing to the movement that occurs across the first and second quatrains, the repeated [lines] become an independent and moving crossed-rhyme couplet (ba), whose meaning and color change by association with the next feminine-masculine couplet with which it is matched in the second quatrain."[22]

Baudelaire, "Harmonie du soir" (*Les Fleurs du Mal*)

Voici venir les temps où vibrant sur sa tige
Chaque fleur s'évapore ainsi qu'un encensoir;
Les sons et les parfums tournent dans l'air du soir;
Valse mélancolique et langoureux vertige!

Chaque fleur s'évapore ainsi qu'un encensoir;
Le violon frémit comme un coeur qu'on afflige;
Valse mélancolique et langoureux vertige!
Le ciel est triste et beau comme un grand reposoir.

Le violon frémit comme un coeur qu'on afflige,
Un coeur tendre, qui hait le néant vaste et noir!
Le ciel est triste et beau comme un grand reposoir;
Le soleil s'est noyé dans son sang qui se fige.

Un coeur tendre, qui hait le néant vaste et noir,
Du passé lumineux recueille tout vestige!
Le soleil s'est noyé dans son sang qui se fige . . .
Ton souvenir en moi luit comme un ostensoir!

"Harmonie du soir" also explores the nature of human memory. Drawing on Baudelaire's concept of correspondance, Braswell explains how memories may be triggered in a Proustian manner by stimulating different senses: "With the synesthetic effects of turning sounds and perfumes ('Les sons et les parfums tournent dans l'air du soir'), and the brushing contact of whirling skirts suggested by the fricative consonants [/v/ and /f/] and amplified by the allusion to the waltz, it is as if Baudelaire were creating a performative space that surrounded the reader with the sights, movements, sounds, and scents associated with the experience of the waltz."[23] Moreover, Baudelaire's poem "affirms the power of a certain kind of poetic experience to achieve what memory [of a strictly cerebral order] alone cannot." According to Braswell, it relies instead on a type of embodied memory that the poet "seeks to awaken through sensory and kinaesthetic experience."[24] It is precisely such embodied memory that prompted Baudelaire to declare, "Dance is poetry with arms and legs, it is matter, graceful and terrible, lively, embellished by movement."[25] This claim foreshdows Mallarmé's suggestion that dance is "poetry, par excellence, and theater" because "poetry is everywhere in language, so long as there is rhythm."[26]

Baudelaire's views about the connections between poetry and dance also reflect his wider views about the dynamic yet disturbing aspects of the modern metropolis. In works such as *Les Fleurs du mal*, Baudelaire painted a dismal picture of contemporary Paris with its grim rows of factory chimneys, drab houses, and vacant lots. One of his most shocking poems, "Une Charogne," describes a carcass rotting in the street; flies are buzzing around its belly, and maggots are devouring its decomposing flesh.[27] Baudelaire went further to discuss the shocking aspects of modern society usually suppressed by the bourgeoisie: prostitution, drug addiction, poverty, disease, homelessness, and so forth. Through their "obsession with blood, torture, and poisoning," his works often display an underlying streak of violence.[28] As Scott Shinabarger has noted, the "previously censored, or simply devalorized aspects of human existence" were all part of what Baudelaire meant by the term "*le mal*."[29]

At the same time, Baudelaire examined the shocking impact the contemporary urban landscape had on the human psyche. Above all, he focused on the nameless people, or flâneurs, who crowded the streets but were too horrified to interact with one another. He studied their expressions of anxiety, indifference, and melancholia. According to him, the sheer volume of people and rapidity of city life overloaded the senses of each inhabitant, prompting them to distance themselves emotionally from one another. By the turn of the twentieth century, Georg Simmel suggested that the desire for isolation was in effect a "protective mechanism" that people developed in order to survive in the modern metropolis.[30] Taking a cue from Simmel, Walter Benjamin "singled out the experience of the flâneur as representative of the modern subject."[31] Indeed, according to Benjamin, "Baudelaire placed the shock experience at the very center of his artistic work."[32] Drawing an analogy with shock therapy, he suggested that "the acceptance of shocks is facilitated by training in coping with stimuli, and, if need be, dreams as well as recollections may be enlisted."[33] In other words, "man's need to expose himself to shock effects is his adjustment to the dangers threatening him."[34]

Vexed by feelings of alienation and ennui, Baudelaire believed that flâneurs are inherently restless; they are constantly searching for the modern in the guise of "the ephemeral, the fugitive, the contingent."[35] Christopher Prendergast has even suggested that the fugitive behavior of the flâneur and the jagged rhythms of urban life compelled Baudelaire to rethink his notion of poetic harmony in order for him to stay poetically in the metropolis.[36] Among other things, this helps to explain Baudelaire's fondness for prose poems, noting in "À Arsene Houssaye" that their origins can be traced back to "our experience of the life of great cities, the confluence and inter-actions of the countless relationships within them."[37] And, according to Shinabargar, such ideas account for the disruptive and violent nature of Baudelaire's diction, that is, "through the physical expression—in the articulated sounds imposed by the text—of precisely those 'evil' sublimated drives."[38] Braswell concurs, suggesting that the recurring image of dance evokes the "writhing movements of a body in pain" and "the ruptures associated with urban life during Baudelaire's lifetime."[39] It is also an idea that resonates with Mallarmé's views about dance: "Dance, capable of translating, in the perfection of its rendition, the fleeting and the sudden up to the Idea—such a vision comprehends all, absolutely all, of the spectacle of the future."[40]

In many ways, *Jeux* epitomizes Baudelaire's thinking both about the role of the fantastic in the arabesque and about the ways in which arabesques and grotesques convey the anxieties of modern city life. The plot, which is decidedly modern, was apparently developed by Nijinsky and Léon Bakst during a visit to London in 1912, while they were having tea with Lady Ottaline Morrell at her home in Bedford Square.[41] Nijinsky and Bakst were apparently enthralled by the fact that some London squares contained gated tennis courts in which local residents, dressed in white outfits, enjoyed playing against the backdrop of "dreaming garden trees."[42] It is a scene lifted straight from Baudelaire: two flâneurs watching three young people play tennis behind iron railings. For his part, Nijinsky was adamant that the choreography would capture the disjunct aspects of modern city life: "The man that I see foremost on the stage is a contemporary man. I imagine the costume, the plastic poses, the movement that would be representative of our time. . . . By attentively studying polo, golf, tennis, I have become convinced that sports are not only a healthy pastime, but also create their plastic beauty."[43]

Besides being set firmly in the present, *Jeux* gave Nijinsky a pretext for bringing the art of cho-reography into the modern age. One way in which he did so was by downplaying the significance of familiar balletic forms within the scenario. To quote Jacques-Émil Blanche: "There [were] no *corps de ballet*, no ensembles, no variations, no *pas de deux*, only boys and girls in flannels and rhythmic movements."[44] Instead, the ballet strings together a number of dances with short con-nective sections: an opening dance for the two girls, one for the first girl and the young man, another for the second girl and the young man, and a final one for all three dancers.[45] Nijinsky likewise revolutionized ballet by requiring the dancers to perform new steps. Diaghilev, for exam-ple, reported that the dance was originally conceived as a "Scherzo-valse" for three male dancers performing on pointe![46] Furthermore, Lynn Garafola notes that the performers "only danced on three-quarter pointe; their feet were in parallel, their fingers clenched, and their arms held stiffly in half-circles, so that the ballet seemed to build on an abstraction of line and curve, not unlike the images of the era's cubists."[47] Nijinsky's only significant concession to the past was that he rejected Diaghilev's idea that the ballet might feature a ménage à trois between a man and two boys. For Nijinsky, that was too modern, even for Parisian audiences in 1913.[48]

When Diaghilev and Nijinsky approached Debussy about setting *Jeux* to music, the latter had already worked with the Ballets Russes on two occasions: *Masques et bergamasques* (1909–10) and the *Prélude à L'Après-midi d'un faune* (1910–12). But Debussy was unimpressed with the new project; he described the ballet's subject as "idiotic" and detested everything about Nijinsky's choreography. But he was in no position to turn down Diaghilev's offer of ten thousand francs for the piano score and ten thousand francs for the full score.[49] The fee was so tempting that it encouraged Debussy to complete the project on time and quite possibly write the unsigned program notes for the work's first concert performance at the Théâtre de Châtelet on March 1,

1914.[50] Finances aside, Debussy may also have taken on the project because of his long-standing interest in the waltz. That interest dates at least back to the mid-1880s, when he first set Baudelaire's "Harmonie du soir" to music. Over the next few years, Debussy wrote a short piano piece entitled *Valse Romantique* (1890–91) and acquired a small statue entitled *La Valse* by the gifted Camille Claudel.[51] *Valse Romantique* was followed by *Hommage à Haydn* in 1909, *La Plus que lente* in 1910, *Page d'album* in 1915, and "Pour les octaves" (*Études*, Bk. 1, 1915). It is also clear that the text of "Harmonie du soir" left an indelible mark on his psyche; not only did he use individual lines from the poem as titles for pieces—for example, "Les Sons et les parfums tournent dans l'air du soir" (*Préludes*, Bk. 1) and *Les Soirs illuminés par l'ardeur du charbon* (1917)—but he also parodied them at the start of his essay "Music in the Open Air" (*La Revue blanche*, June 1, 1901).[52] More remarkably still, Debussy included sections of waltz in three large-scale works: *L'Isle joyeuse* (1904), "Jeux de vagues" (*La Mer*, 1903–5), and *La Boîte à joujoux* (1913).[53]

To understand how Debussy's previous encounters with the waltz might have influenced him while completing the score to *Jeux*, it is helpful to analyze the piece according to the interpretation outlined in the anonymous program notes mentioned above. As shown in example 10.1a, the piece begins with a Prélude. The notes mention that the passage is "short, very slow, soft and dreamy" and that it includes a pedal tone B in the violins and a string of chords derived from a whole-tone scale. The music changes character in m. 9 with the appearance of a short chromatic motive over a pedal tone A (ex. 10.1b): this gesture is in 3/8 and marked *scherzando* ($\downarrow$. = 72). The motive is subsequently developed in mm. 9–42, only to be interrupted by the return of music from the

Example 10.1 Motivic structure of *Jeux*

Example 10.1a Prélude, mm. 1–8

Example 10.1b *Scherzando* motives in *Jeux*, mm. 9–12, mm. 49–50, and mm. 118–21

Prélude in mm. 43–46. Next, example 10.1b shows the entry of another *scherzando* motive over a C♯ pedal; this entry occurs in mm. 49–50, just after the curtain has risen and the action begins. It also shows how the new motive eventually dissolves into a variant of the first over pedal tone A major in mm. 118–21: a tennis ball falls onstage and is accompanied by a loud C major chord (see ex. 10.1c). A young man leaps across the stage only to disappear behind some trees; his abrupt movements are accompanied by brief flashes of melody and a trill A–B♭ over a pedal B♭ (see ex. 10.1d). The arrival of the two young girls is marked by a new motive that oscillates around A and B♭ over lush chords and a long pedal F♯ (see ex. 10.1e).[54] As they nervously search for somewhere to exchange confidences, their motive is reharmonized over an E♭ pedal (see ex. 10.1f). This

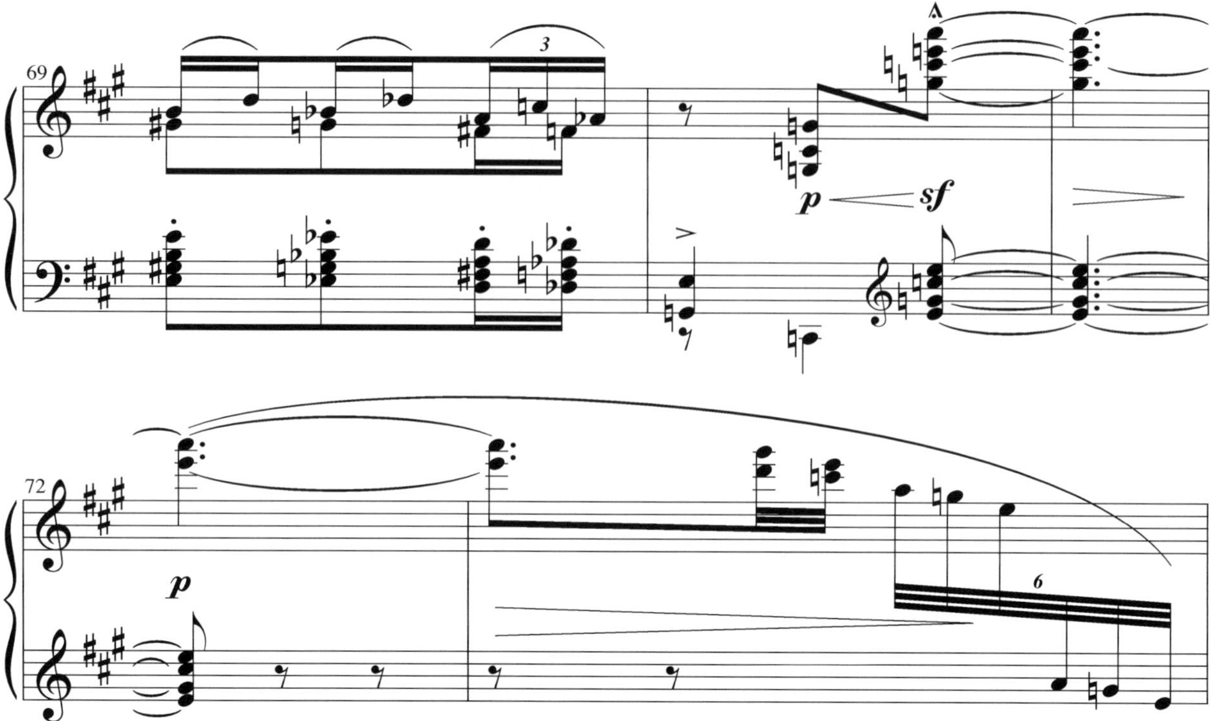

Example 10.1c A tennis ball falls onstage, *Jeux*, mm. 69–73

Example 10.1d A young man leaps across the stage and disappears, *Jeux*, mm. 74–83

Example 10.1e Two young girls enter, *Jeux*, mm. 84–93

Example 10.1f The girls search for a place to exchange confidences, *Jeux,* mm. 100–105

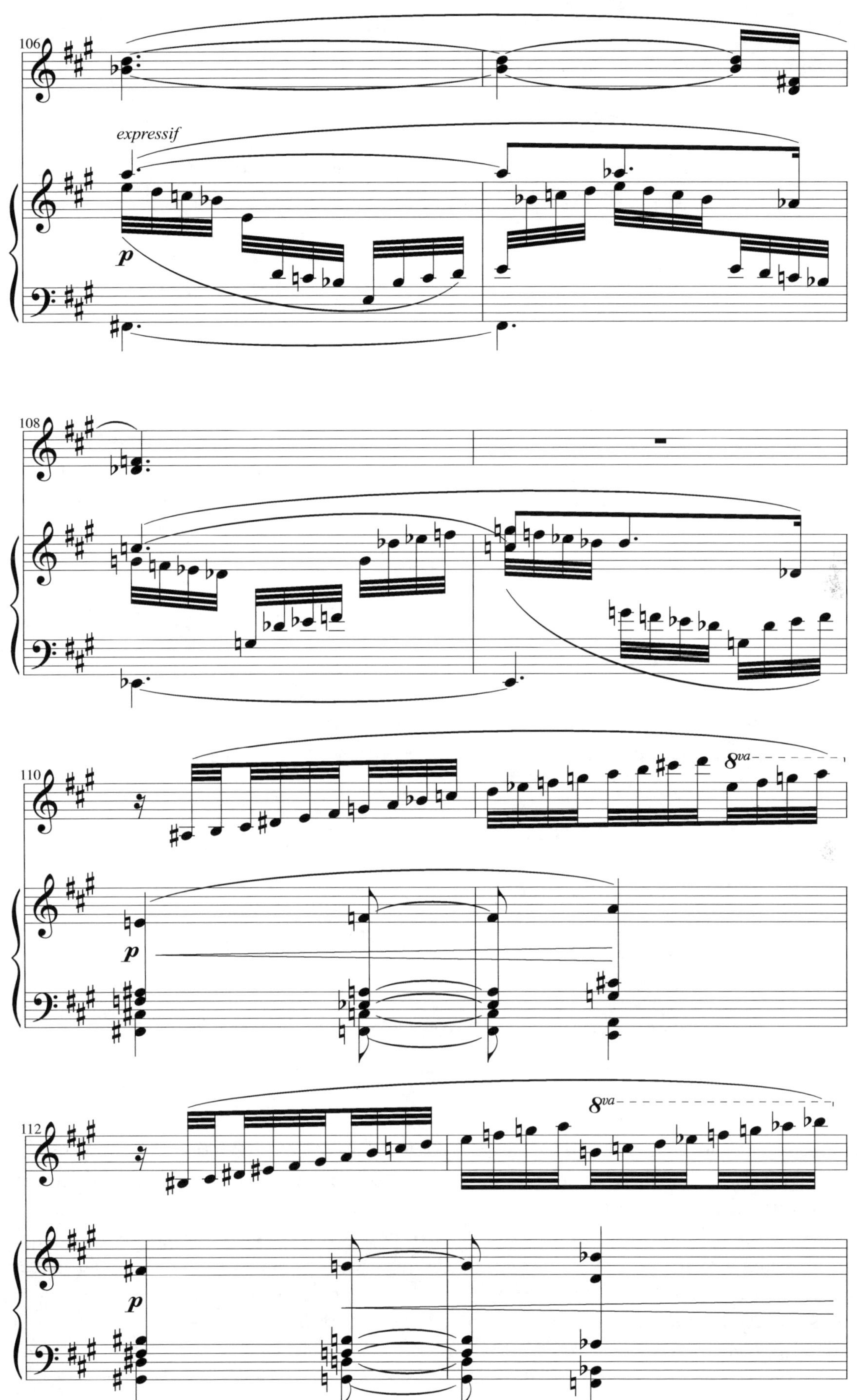

Example 10.1g Their search continues, *Jeux*, mm. 106–13

Example 10.1h Ending material based on the second *scherzando* motive, *Jeux*, mm. 128–37

material eventually morphs into yet another new gesture (see ex. 10.1g). After returning to the second *scherzando* motive in A major (mm. 118–21), the section ends with a shift from the tonic A to the dominant of E (see ex. 10.1h).

Even from this simple overview, it is possible to offer some general observations about the organization of Debussy's score. First, the *scherzando* motive is ornamental in character and a perfect example of a musical arabesque. By presenting it over fixed pedal tones, Debussy specifically recalls the structure of Baudelaire's beloved thyrsus. As shown in example 10.2a, two of the most important pedal tones are E and A, and they help to orient the opening sections

Example 10.2a *Scherzando* motives in *Jeux*, mm. 61–64 and mm. 118–21

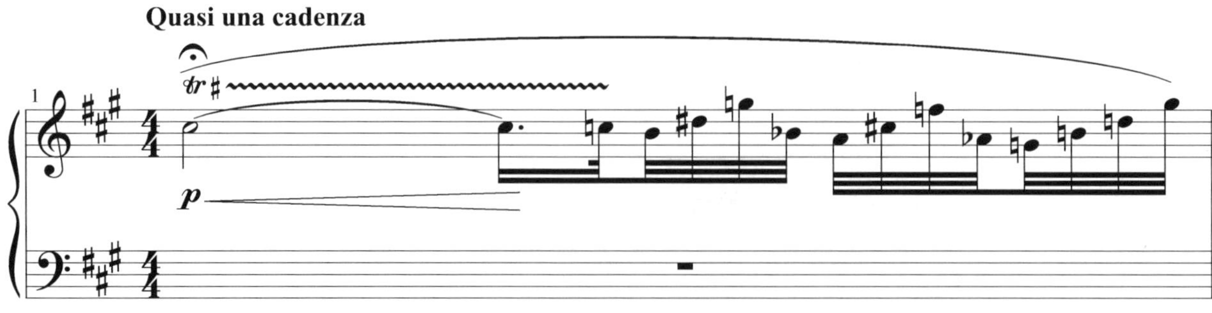

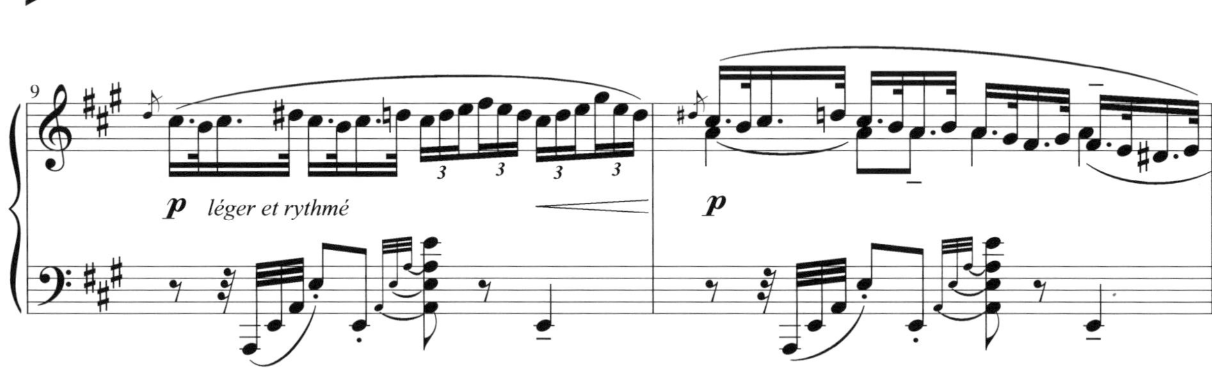

Above, **Example 10.2b** *Scherzando* motives in *L'Isle joyeuse*, m. 1 and mm. 9–10

Facing top, **Example 10.2c** *Scherzando* motives in "Jeux de vagues" (*La Mer*, II), mm. 5–6 and 92–95/97

Facing bottom, **Example 10.2d** Debussy, *Jeux*, mm. 84–93

around the central tonic A: not only does the *scherzando* motive first appear over a pedal tone A, but it subsequently tonicizes A by means of a local V–I progression in mm. 61–64 and again in mm. 118–21 (see ex. 10.2a). That being said, the manner in which the tonic is projected across the section is unconventional and disjunct: traditional functional progressions are few and far between. Second, the *scherzando* motive spawns a string of secondary gestures that serve to accompany moment by moment the erratic action on stage. Significantly, these secondary motives have the same undulating character as the original *scherzando* motive and seem to grow out of one another in the self-generated manner suggested by Schlegel and demonstrated by Eimert in figure 10.2. Third, the original *scherzando* motive is closely related to themes found in other works associated with the waltz.[55] Examples 10.2a–10.2b, for example, show how the chromatic pattern G♮–A♯–F♯–A♮–F♮–A♭–E♮–D♯ from the *scherzando* motive resembles the chromatic figure C♯–C♮–B♮–D♯–B♭–A♮–C♯–A♭–G♮–B♮ from the opening of *L'Isle joyeuse* and the prominent tritone A–D♯ in the second version of the *scherzando* motive recalls the main theme of *L'Isle joyeuse*. Similarly, example 10.2c show how the same figure recurs in the chromatic pattern C♯–C♮–B♮–B♭–A♮ from mm. 5–6 of "Jeux de vagues" (*La Mer*, II) and the main theme of this movement as it appears when it outlines the pitches A–D♯ in mm. 92–95/96 and 100–105. Finally, the new melody for the entry of the young girls and given in examples 10.2d and 10.2e calls to mind a theme from mm.

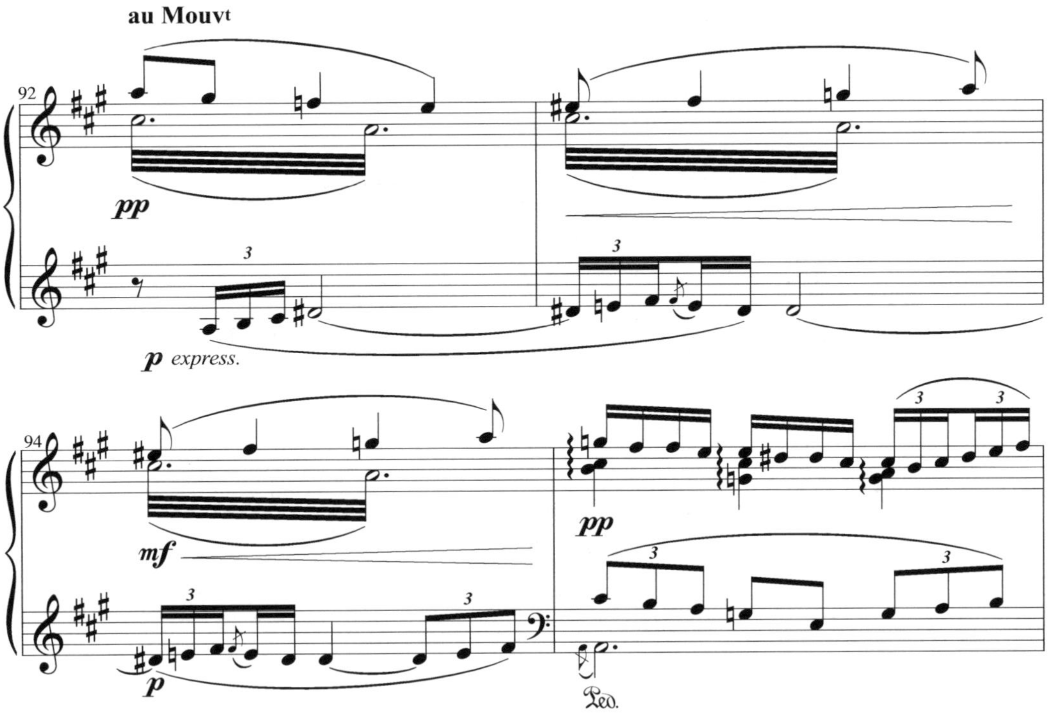

au Mouvt
pp
p express.
mf
pp
p
Ped.
Du fond, à gauche, apparaissent deux jeunes filles craintives et curieuses.
au Mouvt
pp
pp
pp
sfp

Example 10.2e Debussy, *Jeux*, mm. 100–105

Example 10.2f Wagner, "The Flower Maiden Dance," *Parsifal*, act 2, scene 2, mm. 587–95

587–95 of the "The Flower Maiden's Dance" from act 2, scene 2 *Parsifal* (see ex. 10.2f).[56] This nod to Wagner is not entirely unexpected given the fact that Debussy discussed his debts to *Parsifal* while he was composing *Jeux*, and, though oblique, it gives the score an aura of the fantastic.[57] The elaborate filigree in the accompaniment only reinforces the sense of arabesque, as does the return of the pattern from mm. 591–95 at the end of the ballet for the triple kiss.

Once the scene is set and the three characters are introduced, the main part of *Jeux* is built around four set pieces, each of which contains allusions to the waltz. The first one involves the two girls, who dance individually and together.[58] Given the passage's erotic undertones, Hodson labels this particular set piece as "Women's Secrets."[59] As shown in example 10.3, the passage is marked by the introduction of a new theme that has the same undulating profile as the scherzando. The theme appears over pedal tones: E for the solo dances (see ex. 10.3a–10.3b) and D♯ for the duet (see ex. 10.3c). The tonic E is clearly articulated by a progression from V–I in mm. 155–57 at the point in which the second girl begins her dance. Though cast in 3/8, the syncopated nature of the melody doesn't make it sound very waltz-like in mm. 138–73. Things change, however, with the entry of a new motive in m. 174: example 10.3d indicates that not only does this new gesture, which descends from G♮ through F♯ and F♮ to E, appear twice in mm. 174–81 and mm. 186–94, separated by a recurrence of the *scherzando* motive in mm. 182–85, but it also projects the triple meter and duple hypermeter that we expect from a waltz. Notice, too, that it recalls a similar waltz theme from "Jeux de vagues": example 10.3e shows that this latter theme is cast in 6/8 rather than

Example 10.3 First set piece between the two girls

Example 10.3a Debussy, *Jeux*, mm. 138–41

Example 10.3b Debussy, *Jeux*, mm. 146–50

Example 10.3c Debussy, *Jeux*, mm. 166–71

3/8, but it, too, descends by step from G♮, though this time through F♯ and E♮ to D. Once again, the metric and hypermetric structure of this passage is indicative of a waltz.

The amorous encounter between the two girls comes to an abrupt end in m. 193, when they hear leaves rustling nearby and spot the young man spying on them through the bushes. They want to run away, but he gently brings them back. He then persuades the first girl to dance with him and even kisses her.[60] Example 10.4a shows that, like its predecessor, the second set piece is marked by a new motive. Although this material is again cast in triple meter arranged into two- and four-bar groups, it doesn't flow continuously in the manner we might expect from a waltz. Starting in m. 264, however, the groove shifts and allows for a magnificent waltz theme to emerge in the local tonic of F♯, which is tonicized by a resolution of its leading tone E♯–F♯ in mm. 262–63 and a V–I progression in mm. 273–74. Example 10.4b shows that this theme has the undulating character of an arabesque, F♯–G♮–B♭, F♯–G♮–B♭, B♭–G♮–A♭, G♮–E♮–F♮, E♮–C♯–D♮, E♮–C♯–D♮, and is decorated with extremely elaborate filigree in the flutes and clarinets. The metric and hypermetric structure of the waltz is reinforced by the bass motion, which clearly articulates regular two- and four-bar groupings.

Example 10.3d Debussy, *Jeux*, mm. 174–81, 186–94

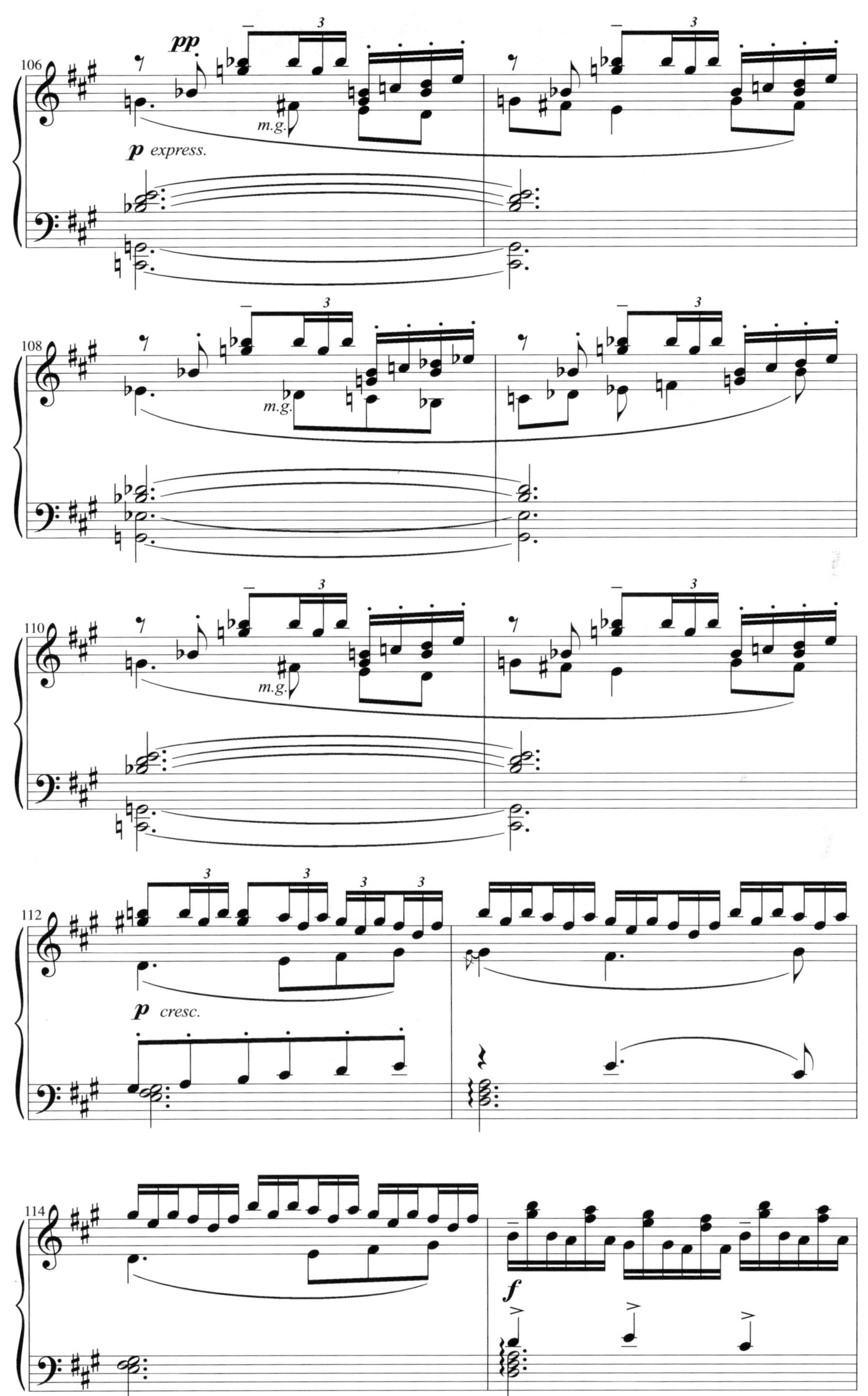

Example 10.3e Debussy, "Jeux de vagues," mm. 106–15

353

Example 10.4 Second set piece between the first girl and the young man

Example 10.4a Debussy, *Jeux*, mm. 219–37

Example 10.4b Debussy, *Jeux*, mm. 264–67/68

The third set piece appears after a short dance in duple meter in which the second girl mocks her friend and the young man. Unlike its predecessors, this set piece is explicitly marked "Mouvement de Valse (moins vif que le 3/8 initial)" in both the piano and orchestral scores.[61] The dance is framed by statements of a new motive C–D♭–E♭–F–G♭–A♭–B♭♭–A♭–G♭–F♮–E♭–D♭–C (see ex. 10.5a) and a variant that rises C–D♮–E♭–F–G♮–A♭–B♭ (see ex. 10.5b). Although the former returns in the final waltz starting in m. 566, latter dominates the third set piece: having been introduced in mm. 357–64, it returns in mm. 395–400 (see ex. 10.5c) and again in mm. 420–34 (see ex. 10.5d). Examples 10.5b–10.5d also indicate that this theme highlights a progression from II–V in the local tonic of E♭ major. In examples 10.5b–10.5c, this progression shifts deceptively onto ♭VI, the latter being respelled enharmonically. But in example 10.5d, the music swells up to a glorious climax in mm. 419–28: instead of resolving immediately, the melodic line adds an elaborate cadenza that spirals its way down from a high B♭ to cadence in E♭ minor (enharmonically respelled as D♯ minor) in m. 441 (see ex. 10.5e).[62] Mark DeVoto has rightly observed that this arabesque resembles similar passages in *Gigues* (*Images* sér. 3, 1912), *Khamma* (1912), *Syrinx* (1913), and other pieces by Debussy. Examples 10.5f–10.5g suggest that it also resembles the *Zaubermotiv* from Wagner's *Parsifal*, a serpentine gesture associated with Klingsor's enchanted garden (ex. 10.5f) and Kundry's magic sleep (ex. 10.5g). This allusion is quite in keeping with the mysterious, herbaceous, nocturnal setting of *Jeux*.

The final set piece begins when, feeling abandoned, the first girl motions to leave. But the second girl holds her back and persuades her to stay. The two of them begin to dance with the young man. The three characters dance faster and faster until, in a moment of pure ecstasy, they embrace in a triple kiss.[63] The dance is framed by statements of the *scherzando* motive, which returns in its original form transposed down a half step to D in m. 455 (see ex. 10.6a). The main motive from the third set piece then returns on C in m. 566 (see ex. 10.6b). The latter is especially memorable because it recalls the waltz theme from *L'Isle joyeuse* (see ex. 10.6c). Finally, an abbreviated version of the scherzando motive appears in augmentation starting on G♯ in m. 677 for the triple kiss (see ex. 10.6d). Notice how this gesture is fused with a descending pattern B–C♯–B–A♯–B–A♯ in m. 680 and F♯–G♯–F♯–E♯–F♯–E♯–D♯ in mm. 684–85 that recalls mm. 591–95 from "The Flower Maiden's Dance" from Wagner's *Parsifal*, cited earlier in example 10.2e. Meanwhile, the various statements of the scherzando motive are broken up by yet another waltz theme that enters over an extremely long pedal tone A♭ in m. 535 (see ex. 10.6e); this pedal is reminiscent of the long pedal G♯ that supports the waltz theme at the climax of "Jeux de vagues" (ex. 10.6f). The ballet ends in much the same way that it began.[64] While the three dancers embrace one another, another stray tennis ball falls onto the scene, and they all run away. The orchestra brings back a string of whole-tone chords from the opening prelude and, after a few furtive glissandi, articulates a clear cadence on the original tonic A major (see ex. 10.6g). The rhetorical impact of the passage is much the same as that of the epilogue from *La Boîte à joujoux*; it returns to the eerie sounds of the night that the audience heard before the curtain was first raised.

In focusing on Nijinsky's four Scherzo-valses and on the self-generating nature of Debussy's melodic material, this chapter has underscored the episodic and quasi-improvisational nature of his score. Just as *La Boîte à joujoux* creates a mosaic out of snatches of familiar themes, so *Jeux* unfolds organically through continuous transformations of the *scherzando* motive and subtle allusions to other waltz-based compositions, such as *L'Isle joyeuse*, "Jeux de vagues," and the "Flower Maiden's Dance." This process is not unlike those found in the improvisational works by Bach and described by Czerny in his treatise on improvising keyboard fantasies, mentioned in the previous

Example 10.5a Debussy, *Jeux*, mm. 331–41

Example 10.5b Debussy, *Jeux*, mm. 357–64

Example 10.5c Debussy, *Jeux*, mm. 395–402

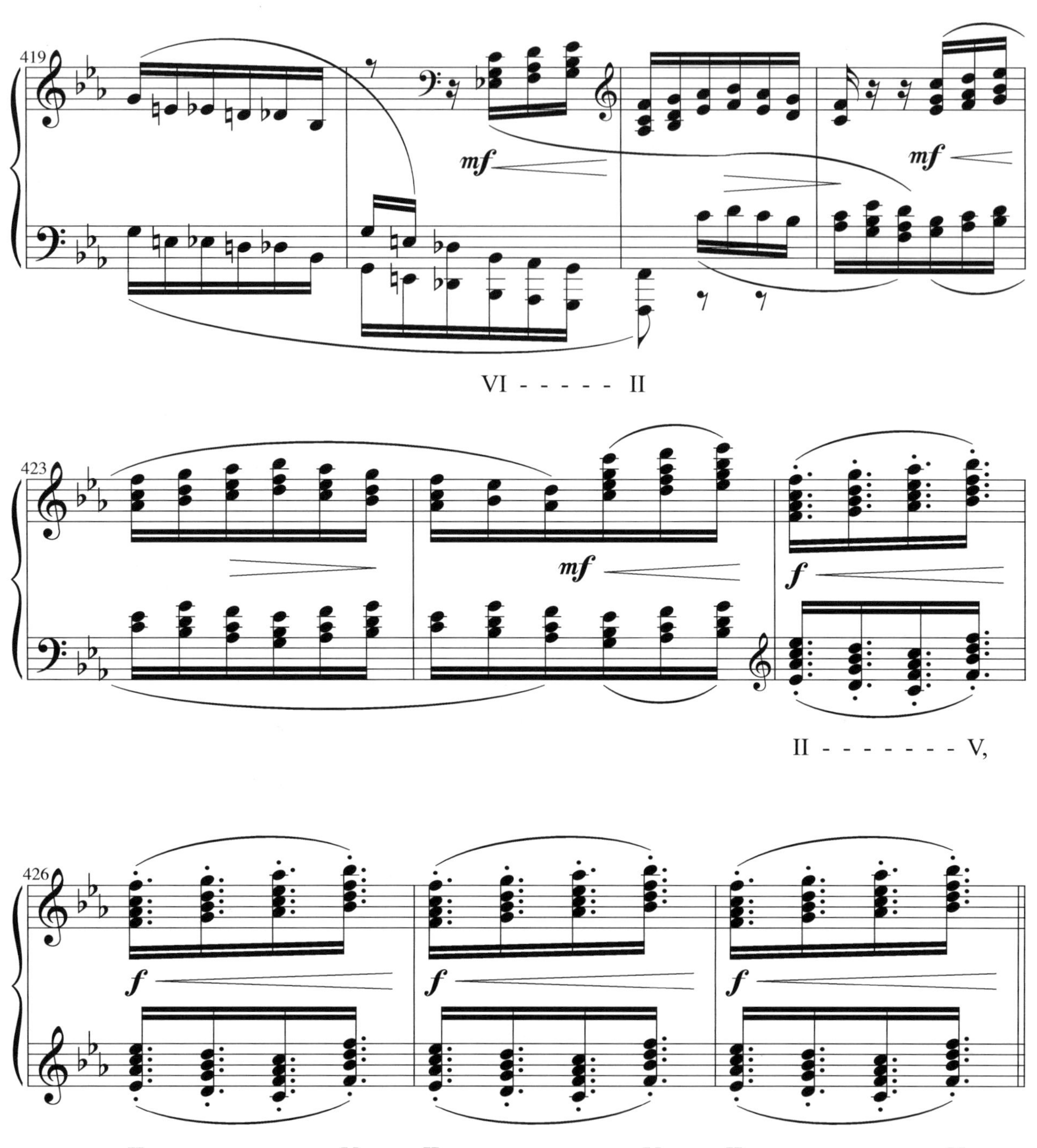

Example 10.5e Debussy, *Jeux*, mm. 429–41

Example 10.5f Wagner, *Parsifal*, act 2, mm. 28–31

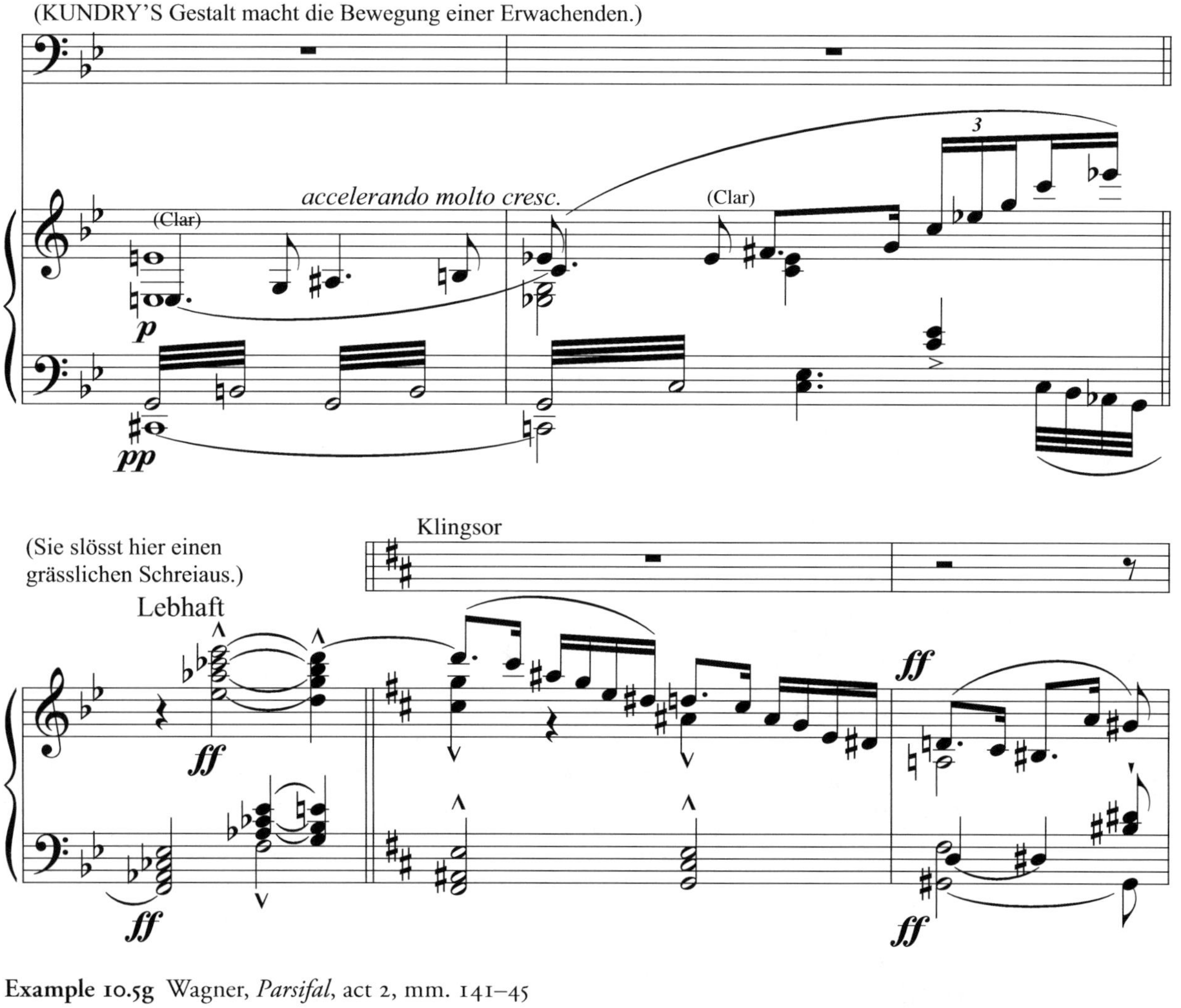

Example 10.5g Wagner, *Parsifal*, act 2, mm. 141–45

Example 10.6a Debussy, *Jeux*, mm. 455–64

chapter. According to Czerny, improvisers must always balance the desire to constantly vary their material with the need to make their improvisations sound coherent: "Indeed, especially when great natural ability and much skill are involved, fantasy-like improvisation frequently consists in an almost subconscious and dreamlike playing motion in the fingers, which make it only so much the better,—just as the orator does not think through each word or phrase in advance. Nevertheless, the performer must always just have the presence of mind (especially when he has to develop a given theme) to adhere constantly to his plan, and to surrender neither to rhapsodic incomprehensible tediousness nor to an overabundantly broad spinning out."[65] For his part,

Example 10.6b Debussy, *Jeux*, mm. 565–82

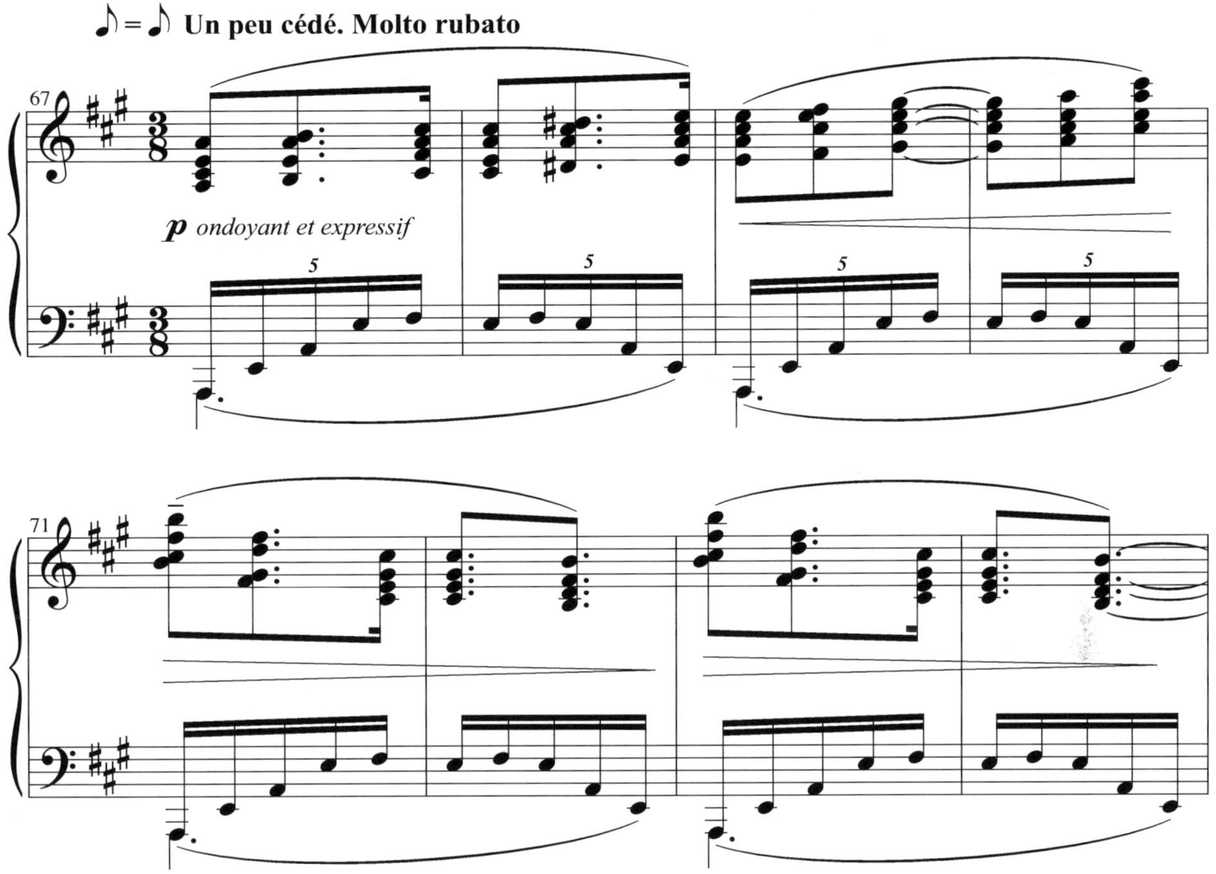

Example 10.6c Debussy, *L'Isle joyeuse*, mm. 67–74

Debussy worked extremely hard to unify the disparate elements of *Jeux*, as he made clear in a letter to Gabriel Pierné (March 5, 1914) on the eve of the first concert performance: "I also felt the various episodes lacked homogeneity! The link between them may be subtle but it exists, surely? You know that as well as I do."[66]

But this chapter has also demonstrated that the disjunct surface structure of Debussy's score for *Jeux* was motivated by a desire to capture the moment-to-moment actions and feelings of the individual dancers. Indeed, as John McGinnis has pointed out, "Nijinsky sought to portray emotion through movement, and Debussy, playing his collaborative part, fulfilled this ideal through the disparate rhythms and harmonies based on the emotional juxtapositions of Nijinsky's story."[67] Sometimes those feelings are frivolous and fanciful, but at other times they are disruptive and even disturbing. The juxtaposition of one with the other is striking and clearly resonates with the ephemeral, fugitive, and contingent aspects of life in Baudelaire's modern metropolis. They call to mind the jagged rhythms of poems like "Harmonie du soir," rhythms that Mallarmé, Braswell, Prendergast, and Shinabarger associate with the fractiousness of contemporary city life. It is for this reason that Debussy wrote of the "horrors" that take place between the three protagonists and described the ballet's mysterious nocturnal setting as "slightly wicked." It is also why Wassily Kandinsky heard in Debussy's music "the suffering and tortured nerves of the present time" and why *Jeux*—the quintessential grotesque—bears the subtitle "Poème dansé."[68]

Example 10.6d Debussy, *Jeux*, mm. 677–85

Example 10.6e Debussy, *Jeux*, mm. 535–50

express.

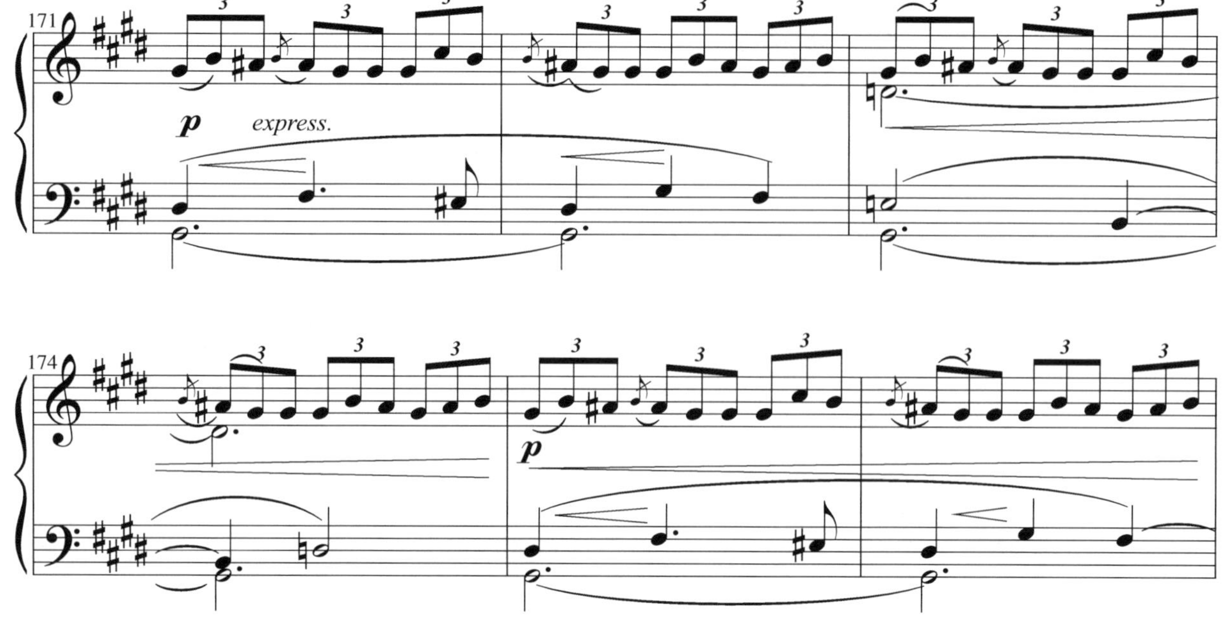

Example 10.6f Debussy, "Jeux de vagues," *La Mer*, mm. 171–76

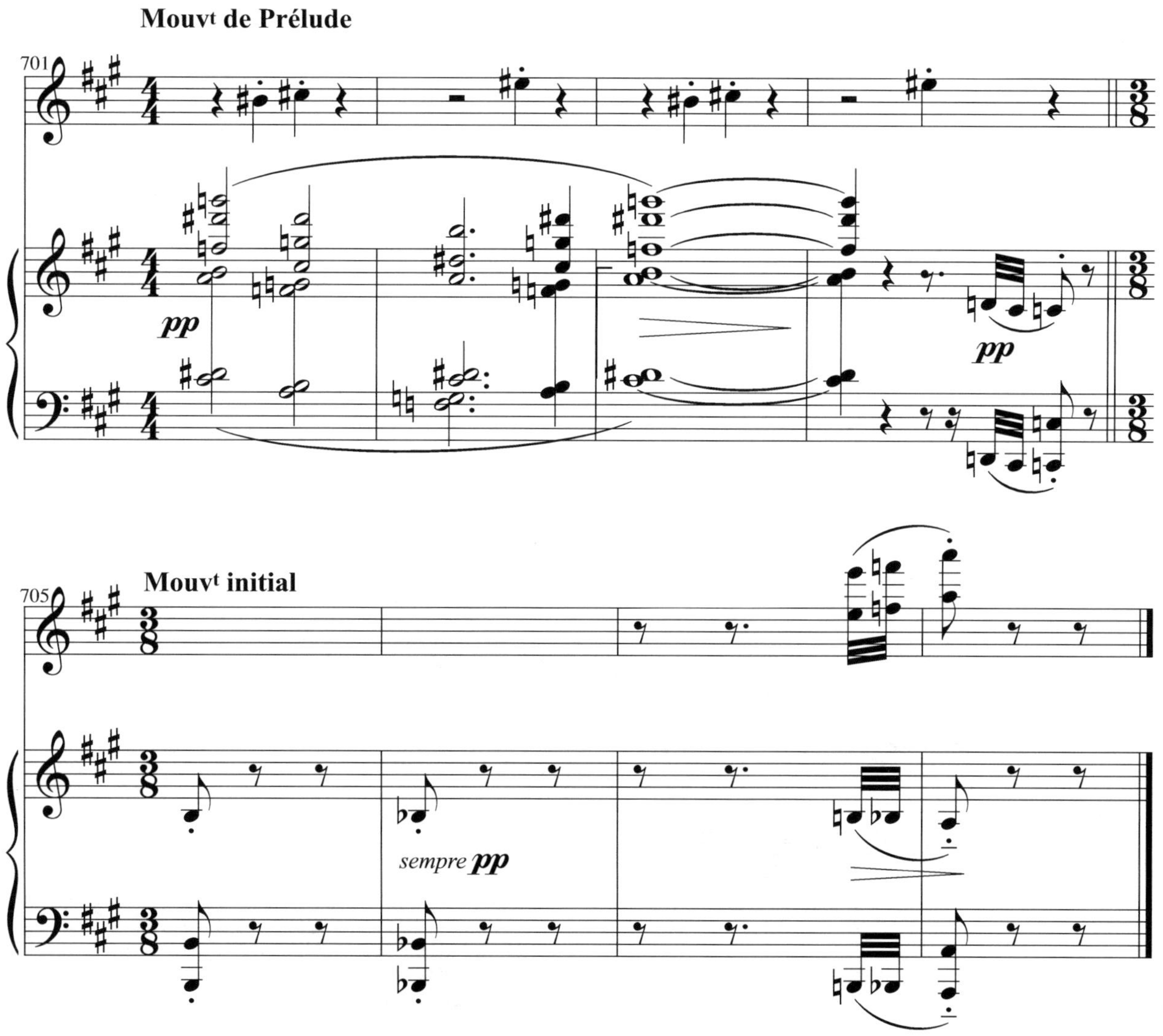

Mouvt de Prélude
Mouvt initial
sempre pp

Example 10.6g Debussy, *Jeux*, mm. 701–9

Notes

1. Christopher Prendergast, *Writing the City: Paris and the Nineteenth Century* (Oxford: Blackwell, 1992), 150. For a survey of public entertainment in Paris in the nineteenth century, see Charles Rearick, *Pleasures of the Belle Epoque: Entertainment and Festivity in Turn of the Century France* (New Haven: Yale University Press, 1985). Paris acquired its reputation as *La Ville-Lumière* in the mid-seventeenth century when Gabriel Nicolas de la Reynie, Louis XIV's lieutenant general of police, tried to make the city safer by hiring more police and installing more lanterns on almost every street. Residents were asked to light their windows with candles and oil lamps. For a general discussion of Debussy and Paris, see Martin Guerpin, "Paris, the City," in *Debussy in Context*, ed. Simon Trezise (Cambridge: Cambridge University Press, 2024), 3–15.

2. Swift, "Les faits du mois," *Revue musicale S.I.M.* 9, no. 6 (June 15, 1913): 69. For a serious response, see Émile Vuillermoz, "La Saison Russe au Théâtre des Champs Élysées," *Revue musicale S.I.M.* 9, no. 6 (June 15, 1913): 49–51.

3. Herbert Eimert, "Debussy's *Jeux*," trans. Leo Black, *Die Reihe* 5 (1961): 3–20; Karlheinz Stockhausen, "Von Webern zu Debussy, Bemerkungen zur statistischen Form," *Texte zur electronischen und instrumentalen Musik* (Cologne: DuMont, 1963), 75–85; Pierre Boulez, *Stocktakings from an Apprenticeship*, ed. Paule Tilevenin, trans. Stephen Walsh (Oxford: Clarendon, 1991); Jean Barraqué, *Debussy* (Paris: Seuil, 1962), 166–69. For a summary of their views, see Claudia Maurer Zenck, "Form- und Farbenspiele: Debussys 'Jeux,'" *Archiv für Musikwissenschaft* 33 (1976): 28–47; and Marianne Wheeldon, "Interpreting Discontinuity in the Late Works of Debussy," *Current Musicology* 77 (2004): 97–115.

4. Robin Holloway, *Debussy and Wagner* (London: Eulenberg, 1979), 160–94, esp. 167.

5. Eimert, "Debussy's *Jeux*," 9.

6. Boulez, *Stocktakings*, XX.

7. Jann Pasler, "Debussy, 'Jeux': Playing with Time and Form," *19th-Century Music* 6, no.1 (1982): 64 [60–75].

8. Laurence Berman, "'Prelude to the Afternoon of a Faun' and 'Jeux': Debussy's Summer Rites," *19th-Century Music* 3, no. 3 (1980): 225–38. Millicent Hodson, *Nijinsky's Bloomsbury Ballet. Reconstruction of the Dance and Design for* Jeux, The Wendy Hilton Dance & Music Series No. 12 (Hillsdale, NY: Pendragon, 1996), 1. See also John McGinness, "Vaslav Nijinsky's Notes for 'Jeux,'" *Musical Quarterly* 88, no. 4 (Winter 2005): 574–75.

9. Arnold Whittall, "Tonality and the Whole-Tone Scale in the Music of Debussy," *Music Review* 36, no. 4 (1975): 261–71, esp. 270–71; Mark McFarland, "The Games of *Jeux*," in *Debussy's Resonance*, ed. François de Médicis and Steven Huebner (Rochester, NY: University of Rochester Press, 2018), 476–510.

10. Holloway, *Debussy and Wagner*, 168.

11. Schenker famously sketched the first and third waltzes of *An der schönen blauen Donau* in *Der freie Satz*, fig. 43 for (a) and 152.3.

12. Claude Debussy, *Correspondance (1872–1918)*, ed. François Lesure and Denis Herlin, annotated by François Lesure, Denis Herlin, and Georges Liébert (Paris: Gallimard, 2005), 1555; and Claude Debussy, *Debussy Letters*, ed. François Lesure and Roger Nichols, trans. Roger Nichols (Cambridge, MA: Harvard University Press, 1987), 265.

13. Debussy, "*Jeux*," *Le Matin* (May 15, 1913), in *Monsieur Croche et autres écrits*, ed. François Lesure (Paris: Gallimard, 1987), 243; and Claude Debussy, *Debussy on Music*, ed. François Lesure and trans. Richard Langham Smith (New York: Knopf, 1977), 291 (I have changed the translation slightly).

14. Suzanne F. Braswell, "An Aesthetics of Movement: Baudelaire, Poetic Renewal, and the Invitation of Dance," *French Forum* 31, no. 3 (Fall 2006): 23–43. See also Amanda Lee, "The Romantic Ballet and the Nineteenth-Century Poetic Imagination," *Dance Chronicle* 39, no. 1 Dance and Literature, Part II (2016): 32–55.

15. As regards Poe's interest in dance, see Burton R. Pollin, "Poe and the Dance," *Studies in the American Renaissance* (Boston: G. K. Hall, 1980), 169–82. Building on May Garretson Evans' book *Music and Edgar Allan Poe* (Baltimore: Johns Hopkins University Press, 1939), Pollin has discussed Poe's interest in music at length; see Burton R. Pollin, "Music and Edgar Allan Poe: A Second Annotated Check List," *Poe Studies* (1971–1985) 15, no. 1 (1982): 7–13; Burton R. Pollin, "More Music and Edgar Allan Poe: A Third Annotated Check List," *Poe Studies/Dark Romanticism* 25, no. 1–2 (1993): 41–58; Burton R. Pollin, "Music and Edgar Allan Poe: A Fourth Annotated Checklist," *Poe Studies* 36, nos. 1–2 (2003): 77–100.

16. Baudelaire, "Le Thyrse," in *Charles Baudelaire: OEuvres Complètes*, vol. I, ed. Claude Pichois, Bibliothèque de la Pléiade (Paris: Gallimard, 1975), 336; Baudelaire, "The Wand," 145.

17. See Edgar Allan Poe, "The Poetic Principle," in *Edgar Allan Poe: Poetry, Tales, and Selected Essays*, ed. Patrick F. Quinn and G. R. Thompson (New York: Library of America, 1996), 1438; and Charles Baudelaire, "À Arsènne Houssaye," *Le Spleen de Paris*, in *Œuvres Complètes*, I:275–76; Baudelaire, "To Arsènne Houssaye," in *The Poems in Prose and La Fanfarlo*, ed. and trans. Francis Scarfe (London: Anvil Press Poetry, 1989), 24–25.

18. Baudelaire, "Le Poème du hachisch," *Les Paradis artificiels*, in *Œuvres Complètes*, I:432; Baudelaire, "The Poem of Hashish," *Artificial Paradises*, trans. Stacy Diamond (New York: Carol, 1996), 65.

19. Niklas Lubmann, *Die Kunst der Gesellschaft* (Frankfurt a.m.: Suhrkamp, 1995), 195; and Niklas Lubmann, *Art as a Social System*, trans. Eva M. Knodt (Redwood City, CA: Stanford University Press, 2000), 120, cited by Bianca Theisen, "Early Romantic Poetics of Complex Form," *Studies in Romanticism* 42, no. 3 (Fall 2003): 311.

20. Braswell, "Aesthetics of Movement," 34.

21. Braswell, "Aesthetics of Movement," 34.

22. Braswell, "Aesthetics of Movement," 35.

23. Braswell, "Aesthetics of Movement," 36.

24. Braswell, "Aesthetics of Movement," 36.

25. Baudelaire, *La Fanfarlo*, 284, https://archive.org/details/lafanfarlooobauduoft/page/n11/mode/2up.

26. Stéphane Mallarmé, "Crayonné au Théâtre," in *Stéphane Mallarmé: Œuvres Complètes*, vol. II, ed. Bertrand Marchal, Bibliothèque de la Pléiade (Paris: Gallimard, 2003), 163; Stéphane Mallarmé, "Scribbled at the Theater," *Divagations*, trans. Barbara Johnson (Cambridge, MA: Harvard University Press, 2007), 120; and Stéphane Mallarmé, "Sur l'evolution littéraire," in *Œuvres Complètes*, II:698; Bradford Cook, trans., *Mallarmé: Selected Prose Poems, Essays, & Letters* (Baltimore: Johns Hopkins University Press, 1956), 19.

27. Baudelaire, "Une Charogne," in *Oeuvres Complètes*, I:31–32.

28. Scott Shinabargar, "La Diction du Mal: Baudelaire," in *The Revolting Body of Poetry*, Chiasma 36 (Leiden: Brill Rodopi, 2016), 34.

29. Shinabargar, "La Diction du Mal," 33.

30. See Georg Simmel, "Die Großstädte und das Geistesleben," *Jahrbuch der Gehe-Stiftung* 9 (1903), 185–206; Georg Simmel, "The Metropolis and Mental Life" (1903), in *The Sociology of Georg Simmel*, ed. and trans. K. Wolff (New York: Free Press, 1964), 409–24.

31. Marit Grøtta, *Baudelaire's Media Aesthetics: The Gaze of the Flâneur and Nineteenth-Century Media* (London: Bloomsbury 2015), 5. See Walter Benjamin, "The *Flâneur*," in *Charles Baudelaire. A Lyric Poet in the Era of High Capitalism*, trans. Harry Zohn (London: New Left Books/Verso, 1973/1997), 33–66.

32. Walter Benjamin, "Über einige Motive bei Baudelaire," in *Illuminationen. Ausgewählte Schriften 1* (Frankfurt am Main: Suhrkamp, 1955), 193; Walter Benjamin, "On Some Motifs in Baudelaire," in *Illuminations: Essays and Reflections*, ed. Hannah Arendt and trans. Harry Zohn (New York: Harcourt, Brace, and World, 1968), 163. See also Ulrich Baer, *Remnants of Song: Trauma and the Experience of Modernity in Charles Baudelaire and Paul Celan* (Redwood City, CA; Stanford University Press, 2000).

33. Benjamin, "Über einige Motive bei Baudelaire," in *Illuminationen*, 192; Benjamin, "On Some Motifs in Baudelaire," in *Illuminations*, 162.

34. Benjamin, "Das Kunstwerk im Zeithalter seiner technischen Reproduzierbarkeit," in *Illuminationen*, 165fn29; Benjamin, "The Work of Art in the Age of Mechanical Reproduction," in *Illuminations*, 250fn19.

35. Baudelaire, "Le Peintre de la vie moderne: IV Modernité," in *Œuvres Complètes*, II:695; Baudelaire, "The Painter in Modern Life: IV Modernity," in *The Painter in Modern Life and Other Essays*, ed. and trans. Jonathan Mayne (London: Phaidon, 2001), 13.

36. Prendergast, *Writing the City*, 131.

37. Baudelaire, "A Arsènne Houssaye," *Le Spleen de Paris*, in *Œuvres Complètes*, I:275–76; Baudelaire, "To Arsènne Houssaye," in *Poems in Prose and La Fanfarlo*, 25.

38. Shinabargar, "La Diction du Mal," 34.

39. Braswell, "Aesthetics of Movement," 27.

40. Stéphane Mallarmé, "Richard Wagner, rêverie d'un poète français," *La Revue Wagnérienne* I/7 (August 8, 1885), in *Œuvres Complètes*, II:153–54; Stéphane Mallarmé, "Richard Wagner. The Reverie of a French Poet," in *Divagations*, 107–8.

41. François Lesure, *Claude Debussy* (Paris: Klincksieck, 1994), 353; François Lesure, *Claude Debussy: A Critical Biography*, Eastman Studies in Music 159, ed. and trans. Marie Rolf (Rochester, NY: University of Rochester Press, 2019), 289.

42. This sentence is paraphrased from Lesure, *Claude Debussy*, 353.

43. Hector Cahusac, *Le Figaro*, May 15, 1913; see Hodson, *Nijinsky's Bloomsbury Ballet*, 1.

44. Jacques-Émile Blanche also mentioned that the scene originally included a group of dancers depicting a fountain and that the tennis match was interrupted by an airplane crash. Neither of these appears in the final version. See Richard Buckle, *Nijinsky* (New York: Simon and Schuster, 1971), 260.

45. For helpful discussions of the form of *Jeux*, see Jann Pasler, "Debussy, 'Jeux': Playing with Time and Form," *19th-Century Music* 6, no.1 (1982): 66–67, Table 2; and Hodson, *Nijinsky's Bloomsbury Ballet*.

46. Bronislava Nijinska, *Early Memoirs*, trans. and ed. Irina Nijinska and Jean Rawlinson (Durham, NC: Duke University Press,1992), 468. Bronislava was originally slated to dance in *Jeux* with her brother and Tamar Karsavina but was replaced, after she became pregnant, by Ludmilla Schollar. She gave birth to her daughter Irina on November 20, 1913. Nijinska, *Early Memoirs*, 465.

47. Lynn Garafola, *La Nijinska: Choreographer of the Modern* (New York: Oxford University Press, 2022), 15–16.

48. To quote Nijinsky, "Diaghilev wanted to make love to two boys at the same time. . . . In the ballet, the two girls represent the two boys, and the young man is Diaghilev. I changed the characters, as love between three men could not be represented on the stage." Vaslav Nijinsky, *The Diary of Vaslav Nijinsky*, ed. Romola Nijinsky (Berkeley: University of California Press, 1968), 140–41.

49. For the historical background to *Jeux*, see Orledge, *Debussy and the Theatre*, 162–76; and Claude Debussy, *Jeux. Poème dansé*, ed. Pierre Boulez and Myriam Chimènes, in Œuvres Complètes de Claude Debussy, Série V Œuvres de orchestre, vol. 8 (Paris: Durand-Costallat, 1988), XV–XVIII. Debussy expressed his dislike of Nijinsky's choreography in a letter to Godet dated June 9, 1913. Having referred to "Nijinsky's perverse genius" and his quasi-mathematical Dalcrozian approach, he declared, "The man adds up demisemiquavers with his feet, checks the result with his arms and then, suddenly struck with paralysis all down one side, glares at the music as it goes past. I gather it's called 'the stylization of gesture' . . . It's awful!" Debussy, *Correspondance*, 1619; Debussy, *Letters*, 272.

50. As regards these program notes and their authorship, see Barraqué, *Debussy*, 166–69; and Pasler, "Debussy, 'Jeux,'" 60.

51. See Odile Ayral-Clause, *Camille Claudel: A Life* (New York: Abrams, 2002), 106–7; Robert Godet, "En marge de la marge," *La Revue musicale* 7 (May 1, 1926), 71–72; Roger Nichols, *Debussy Remembered* (London: Faber, 1992), 37; Nectoux, *Harmonie en bleu et or. Debussy, la musique et les arts* (Paris: Fayard, 2005), 168–75 and 189.

52. See Debussy, "La Musique en plein air," *La Revue blanche*, June 1, 1901, in *Monsieur Croche*, 46; Debussy, "Music in the Open Air," in *Debussy on Music*, 40.

53. For discussions of the waltz sections in *L'Isle Joyeuse* and "Jeux de vagues," see Matthew Brown, "Composing with Prototypes: Charting Debussy's *L'Isle joyeuse*," *Intégral* 16 (2004/2005): 151–88; and Matthew Brown, "Debussy Today," in *Debussy in Context*, ed. Trezise, 299–310.

54. The rich texture, lush harmonies, and sensual mood of this passage recall those of mm. 44–47 from "Ondine" (*Préludes*, Bk. 2).

55. See also Berman, "Debussy's Summer Rites," 225–38.

56. See Thomas Grey, "The 'Splendid and Shameful Art': Dancing in and around the Wagnerian *Gesamtkunstwerk*," in *Musicology and Dance. Historical and Critical Perspectives*, ed. Davinia Caddy and Maribeth Clark (Cambridge: Cambridge University Press, 2020), 121–50, esp. 135–38.

57. In a letter to Caplet (August 25, 1912), Debussy announced not only that he had finished *Jeux* but also that, following Wagner's example in *Parsifal*, he tried to make his score sound like an "orchestra without feet" and give it "an orchestral color which seems to be lit from behind." Debussy, *Correspondance*, 1540; Debussy, *Letters*, 262. For the general impact of *Parsifal* on *Jeux*, see Holloway, *Debussy and Wagner*, esp. 160–94. Although he does not discuss the connections between mm. 84–93 and 100–105 of *Jeux* and mm. 587–95 of "The Flower Maiden's Dance," he does mention those between the triple kiss at m. 680 and mm. 684–85 and mm. 591–95 of Wagner's score and also mentions that the latter is also connected to the character of Kundry; see Holloway, *Debussy and Wagner*, 189–91.

58. To quote Debussy's alleged program note, "Elle se mettent à danser l'une après l'autre." For additional comments, see Hodson, *Nijinsky's Bloomsbury Ballet*, 75–96.

59. See Hodson, *Nijinsky's Bloomsbury Ballet*, 86–96.

60. See Hodson, *Nijinsky's Bloomsbury Ballet*, 96–139, esp. 118–31.

61. See Hodson, *Nijinsky's Bloomsbury Ballet*, 140–82.

62. Mark DeVoto, *Debussy and the Veil of Tonality: Essays on his Music*, Dimension and Diversity No. 4 (Hillsdale, NY: Pendragon, 2004), 57–59.

63. See Hodson, *Nijinsky's Bloomsbury Ballet*, 183–224.

64. See Hodson, *Nijinsky's Bloomsbury Ballet*, 225–29.

65. Carl Czerny, *Systematische Anleitung zum Fantasieren auf dem Pianoforte*, Op. 200 (Vienna: Diabelli, 1836), 36; Carl Czerny, *A Systematic Introduction to Improvisation on the Pianoforte* (New York: Longman, 1983), 43.

66. Debussy, *Correspondance*, 1783; Debussy, *Letters*, 288.

67. McGinness, "Vaslav Nijinsky's Notes for 'Jeux,'" 574–75.

68. Wassily Kandinsky, *Concerning the Spiritual in Art* (1912), trans. M. T. H. Sadler (New York: Dover, 1977), 16.

V. Emotions and Images

11

"Les miroirs ternis"

Central to symbolist thinking was the idea that arabesques are not simply a form of ornamentation: they also provide artists with a means for stirring the emotions. The previous chapter showed, for example, how Baudelaire's literary arabesques in "Harmonie du soir" express the anxieties of modern city life, how Nijinsky's choreographic arabesques in *Jeux* represent "a contemporary man" living in such a metropolis, and how Debussy's musical arabesques convey the slight wickedness that people often feel in urban environments at night. This chapter develops these thoughts by showing how Baudelaire, Verlaine, Mallarmé, Huysmans, and other Symbolists used the metaphor of a distorted reflection to express their underlying feelings of melancholy and ennui. The process of distortion was achieved poetically by viewing the arabesque through a tarnished mirror or similar device, thereby giving the reflection an aura of the supernatural.[1] Having connected tarnished mirrors to feelings of melancholia and ennui, this chapter discusses three particular poems in which those images predominate and which Debussy subsequently set to music: Baudelaire's "La Morte des amants" (*Les Fleurs du mal*), Verlaine's "L'Ombre des arbres" (*Romances sans paroles*), and Mallarmé's "Soupir" (*Poésies*). The musical analyses, which rely heavily on Schenkerian theory, demonstrate how Debussy's songs conveyed these feelings by concluding with a distorted recollection of some earlier musical material. Significantly, this material invariably takes the form of a highly decorated arabesque. The chapter ends by describing how Debussy's own sense of melancholy and ennui intensified toward the end of his life, thereby confirming Kandinsky's astute observation that one hears in Debussy's music "the suffering and tortured nerves" experienced by so many people in the years leading up to the outbreak of WWI.[2]

There is something of a consensus among historians that a dark cloud hung over Europe at the turn of the twentieth century. Margaret Stoljar captures this idea with particular clarity: "The fin de siècle, however, is a time when the complacency of the Second Empire and the Wilhelminian age gives way to a disturbed self-questioning, forefront of consciousness in the arts that strain of cultural pessimism, personal doubt, and philosophical scepticism which had been present all along followed Schopenhauer, Kierkegaard, and Nietzsche. It brings, too, a fresh contemplation of the nature of the individual psyche, its fragility and imperfection. There is new poignancy in the ineluctable passing of youth, and a desperate desire to capture time in exquisite objects and decorations."[3] Symbolists responded to the situation by evoking images of tarnished mirrors and rippled pools. The choice of images was not, however, new: on the contrary, they had long been associated with melancholia and ennui.[4] This much is clear from the *Encyclopédie, ou dictionnaire raisoné des sciences, des arts et des métiers collectifs* (Paris: 1765), which claimed that people suffering from melancholia "see objects only indistinctly, as if in a tarnished mirror or through cloudy water."[5] Following Hippocrates's theory of the bodily humors (black bile, yellow bile, phlegm, and blood), physicians of the period believed that patients feel melancholy because their spleen produces too much black bile.[6] Mirrors made of polished black obsidian (so-called scrying mirrors) and black glass (so-called Claude glass) supposedly allowed viewers to foretell what might happen in the future.[7] As suggested in chapter 1, such forms of mirroring play a central role in "The Fall of the House of Usher": the demise of Roderick and Madeline is symbolized by the sinister reflection of their ancestral home in the dark waters of the lake.[8]

Not surprisingly, such images cast a powerful shadow over Baudelaire: melancholy and ennui were, in the words of Jean Starobinski, "the poet's most intimate companions."[9] Take, for example, the following lines from "Epigraph for a Condemned Book," a poem from the fourth section of Baudelaire's celebrated collection *Les Fleurs du Mal*:

> Quiet and bucolic reader,
> Upright man, sober and naive,
> Throw away this book, saturnine,
> Orgiac and melancholy.

Or those from the first poem "Au Lecture," in which Baudelaire introduces "the grotesque and repellent figure of ennui":

> There is one more ugly, more wicked, more filthy!
> Although he makes neither great gestures nor great cries,
> He would willingly make of the earth a shambles
> And, in a yawn, swallow the world;
> He is Ennui!—His eye watery as though with tears,
> He dreams of scaffolds as he smokes his hookah pipe.
> You know him reader, that refined monster,
> Hypocritical reader,—my fellow,—my brother!

It is hardly a coincidence that these lines prepare the reader for a group of poems that Baudelaire placed under the heading "Spleen et Idéal."

References to melancholy, ennui, and ancillary concepts abound in Baudelaire's letters and diaries. On December 30, 1857, for example, Baudelaire described his anxieties to his mother, Caroline Aupick: "Certainly, I have much to complain about myself, and I am stunned and alarmed at this state. Do I need a move, I don't know. Is it physical sickness, which diminishes the spirit and the will, or is it the spiritual cowardice that tires my body, I do not know."[10] He explained his feelings of dismay, disillusionment, and anhedonia: "But what I feel is an immense discouragement, an unbearable feeling of isolation, a perpetual fear of vague misfortune, a complete distrust of my strength, a total absence of desires, an inability to find any amusement whatsoever." The publication of *Les Fleurs du Mal* provided little relief: "The bizarre success of my book and the furor it caused interested me for a while, and then I relapsed." On the contrary, it merely fed his sense of melancholy and ennui: "You see, my dear mother, this is a fairly serious state of mind for a man whose profession is to produce and dress up fictions. I keep asking myself: what use it this? what use is that? This is the true spirit of spleen.—No doubt, remembering that I have already suffered analogous states and that, I got up, I will be inclined not to be too alarmed; but I also do not remember having ever fallen so low and dragged myself into [a state of] ennui for so long."

According to Roger Pearson, Baudelaire folded the idea of melancholia into his definitions of beauty and modernity.[11] In the *Fusées*, for example, Baudelaire claimed that beauty "is something both ardent and sorrowful, something a bit vague, lending itself to endless conjecture."[12] He illustrated his point by referring to the face of a beautiful woman: "one that provokes dreams which simultaneously—if confusedly—involve sensuality and sorrow; one that conveys an idea of melancholy, lassitude, even satiety—or else the contrary idea, that is an ardor, a desire for life, ever crowded out by surges of bitterness, products as it were of deprivation or despair. Mystery and regret are also characteristics of Beauty."[13] According to him, the voluptuousness of those features makes them more "provocatively attractive" and "generally . . . melancholy" than the features of a handsome man.[14] And yet, the man's face may still be ardent and sorrowful: "spiritual longings, ambitions darkly swallowed—sometimes the idea of a power that lies there growling, unemployed—sometimes the idea of vengeful imperviousness (for the ideal type of Dandy is not to be neglected here)—and sometimes too the idea of mystery (one of the most interesting characteristics of Beauty—and finally (gathering my courage to admit just how modern I feel in matters aesthetic), *Misfortune*."[15] For Baudelaire, joy was "merely one of its most vulgar ornaments" and melancholy "its illustrious companion": wondering whether his brain was "a witch's mirror," he concluded that all forms of Beauty include *Misfortune*.[16] This latter idea resonates with his more general claim that the beautiful is bizarre: "If something is not slightly deformed, it strikes us as lacking feeling—from which it follows that irregularity, that is to say, the unexpected, the elements of surprise and astonishment are an essential portion and characteristic of beauty."[17] And it is implicit in Baudelaire's attitudes to vernacular and non-Western art, as well as in the concept of "le jolie-laide."

Baudelaire even went so far as to suggest that "the most perfect type of manly Beauty is *Satan*," at least as represented by the sense of Milton's *Paradise Lost*.[18] Baudelaire based this claim on the connections he saw between melancholy and the irremediable "tragedy" of human desire and between beauty and misfortune. According to Pearson, Milton's Satan "is the angel who resisted, who knew the joy of heaven but wanted more, wanted to *know* more. This is the Satan who revolted against God and was banished from heaven, Satan as Lucifer, the angel of light who was cast into outer darkness, and a Satan whose 'beauté virile' thus derives from 'des besoins spirituels,' 'des ambitions [ténébreusement] refoulées,' 'l'idées d'une pouissance grondante, et sans emploi.' In short, this is the Satan who for Baudelaire epitomizes modern melancholy, or what had to be known since Chateaubriand as the *mal du siècle*."[19]

It is also clear that Baudelaire associated male beauty with melancholia and with the dandy. For him, Dandyism as "an institution beyond the law, itself has rigorous laws which all its subjects must strictly obey, whatever their natural impetuosity and independence of character."[20]

The dandy should have "no other calling than but to cultivate the idea of beauty in their persons, to satisfy their passions, to feel, and to think."[21] He should constantly strive for the sublime and "live and sleep before a mirror."[22] And yet the dandy is in a perpetual state of melancholy and ennui: "Dandyism is a sunset; like the declining daystar, it is glorious, but without heat and full of melancholy."[23] The idea that mirrors create anxiety about the loss of beauty or youth is a familiar one in Symbolist art and is manifest most explicitly in *The Picture of Dorian Gray*. First written in 1890 and expanded in 1891, Oscar Wilde's masterpiece replaced the tarnished mirror with a portrait of a person that ages while its subject remains perpetually young: "The questioning of time in introspective writing or painting commonly, perhaps inevitably, leads to contemplation of mortality, and many uses of the mirror motif are concerned with a fresh awareness of death."[24]

The self-centeredness of Baudelaire's dandy and Wilde's Dorian Gray stand out because they remind us that tarnished mirrors and distorted reflections have been fixtures of Western culture through countless myths, such as the story of Echo and Narcissus. As retold by Ovid, Echo is one of many nymphs visited by Jupiter; Jupiter's wife, Juno, punishes Echo by allowing her to speak only the last words she hears.[25] Narcissus is the son of Liriope who is destined to live a long life provided he does not discover himself. The two characters meet one day, and Echo falls in love with him. When he calls out to her, Echo simply repeats his words. When she tries to embrace him, he rejects her, and she rushes off. Distraught, she wastes away: her bones turn into rocks; her voice remains in the mountains and caves. The gods decree that since Narcissus has denied his love to everyone, he should be deprived of anything he loves. Sometime later, Narcissus is hunting in the forest and bends down to drink from a pool. When he sees a reflection in the water, he falls in love—with himself! Unable to capture his reflection, he stays by the pool and wastes away just like Echo. When she eventually returns, Echo repeats Narcissus's last farewell to his reflection. Like Dorian Gray's portrait, Narcissus's reflection is both seductive and destructive: seductive because it prompts him to fall in love with himself; destructive because it ultimately leads to his death.

Given the melancholy tone of Ovid's story, references to Narcissus surface regularly in Symbolist writings from the decades around 1900: the list includes Mallarmé's monumental poem *Hérodiade* (1864–98), Jean Moréas's short story "Narcissus" (1891), Paul Valéry's poem "Narcisse Parle" (1891), André Gide's *Le Traité du Narcisse* (1891), Camille Mauclair's poem "Narcisse" (1892), and Henri de Régnier's poem "L'Allusion à Narcisse" (1897).[26] The myth of Narcissus also attracted attention from Sigmund Freud and other pioneers of psychoanalysis. In his influential essay *Zur Einführung des Narzißmus* (1914), for example, Freud used Ovid's story to suggest that self-love might not be as abnormal as many believed.[27] During the oral stage of psychosexual development, Freud proposed that children are highly egocentric and believe they are the center of the world. As they grow up, however, those beliefs are transformed, and children become less self-absorbed; extreme self-love is replaced by love for others. Nevertheless, Freud acknowledged that some level of narcissism, what he referred to as primary narcissism, is required for normal human development and is not detrimental to a person's mental health. Three years after the publication of *Zur Einführung des Narzißmus*, Freud's essay "Trauer und Melancholie" (1916/1917) introduced the concept of secondary narcissism to explain the distinction between mourning and melancholy.[28] Freud insisted that mourning and melancholy denote two quite different responses to losing a love object: whereas the former involves conscious acceptance of the loss and, though difficult, is entirely natural, the latter mostly occurs unconsciously because the loss is hard to identify or incomprehensible. According to him, mourning is healthy, but melancholy is pathological.

Although it is unclear why Debussy set Baudelaire's "La Morte des amants," Verlaine's "L'Ombre des arbres," and Mallarmé's "Soupir," he may have been inspired by the fact that Joris-Karl Huysmans mentioned each of them in his infamous novel *À Rebours*. First published in 1884, the book focuses on the life of Duc Jean Floressas des Esseintes.[29] Des Esseintes is the quintessential dandy: "the modern man *par excellence*, tortured by that vague longing for an elusive ideal which we used to call the *mal du siècle*; torn between desire and satiety, hope and disillusionment; painfully conscious that his pleasures are finite, his needs infinite."[30] His escapist tendencies are manifest in his love of books such as De Quincey's *Confessions of an English Opium Eater* and Baudelaire's *Les Fleurs du Mal*.[31] Des Esseintes particularly revered the latter's "solid, sinewy style" and "power to define in curiously healthy terms the most fugitive and ephemeral of the unhealthy conditions of weary spirits and melancholy souls."[32] His admiration for "La Morte des amants" was so great that he displayed an ornate vellum copy over the fireplace in his library.[33] Also a fan of Verlaine's *Fêtes galantes*, *La Bonne chanson*, *Romances sans paroles*, and *Sagesse*, des Esseintes delighted in the way these texts hint "at certain strange spiritual aspirations, of whispering certain thoughts, of murmuring certain confessions so softly, so quietly, so haltingly that the ear that caught them was left hesitating, and passed on to the soul a languor made all the more pronounced by the vagueness of these words that were guessed rather than heard."[34] This description echoes the wistful final stanza of "L'Ombre des arbres": "And how this pallid landscape reflected your pallor, O voyager, and how sadly your drowned expectations wept among the high branches."[35] And des Esseintes marveled at Mallarmé's ability to "knot ideas" together "with an adhesive style, a unique, hermetic language, contracted phrases, [and] elliptical constructions" and create verses that are "soothing as a melancholy incantation, an intoxicating melody."[36] This is true of extended works such as *L'Après-midi d'un faune* as well as brief poems such as "Soupir."[37] In short, des Esseintes was attracted both to the arabesque features of their writing and the feelings of melancholia and ennui they engendered.

It turns out that "La Morte des amants" is one of five poems from *Les Fleurs du mal* that Debussy set to music in his *Cinq poèmes de Baudelaire*. He composed the collection over a two-year period from 1887 to 1889: he completed "La Morte des amants" in 1887, "Le Balcon" in January 1888, and "Harmonie du soir," "Le Jet d'eau," and "Recueillement" in 1889.[38] Melancholy and ennui cast their shadows over each of these poems, with the first poem coming from a set of six that Baudelaire grouped under the heading "La Morte" and the remaining five from a much longer section entitled "Spleen et Idéal." Once Debussy had completed each song, Gaston Choisnel arranged to have the entire set published by subscription and, starting in February 1890, distributed by Edmund Bailly at his bookstore, the Librairie de l'Art Indépendent.[39] Bailly's tiny shop on the rue de la Chaussée d'Antin was a remarkable institution: specializing in Symbolist and esoteric literature, it was a favorite haunt of avant-garde writers and artists such as Mallarmé, Verlaine, and Huysmans.[40] But Bailly didn't simply sell books—he also published them: his catalog included Gide's *Le Traité du Narcisse*, Oscar Wilde's *Salomé* (1893), and his own esoteric texts such as *Le Son dans la Nature* (1900), *Le Chant des Voyelles comme Invocation des Dieux Planétaires* (1912), and his musical setting of Mallarmé's "Apparition" (1894).[41]

Debussy began to frequent the Librairie de l'Art Indépendent as soon as it opened its doors in 1889. A few years later, in 1893, he persuaded Bailly to publish the piano/vocal score of *La Damoiselle élue* with a decorative cover by Maurice Denis and, in 1894, unsuccessfully negotiated with him about publishing the *Prose lyriques*.[42] During his visits to the Librairie de l'Art

Figure 11.1 Henry Colas frontispiece, Jules Bois, *Les noces de Sathan: drame ésotérique* (Paris: Chamuel Éditeur, 1892)

Indépendent, Debussy may have met Jules Bois, whose books on hermeticism and the occult were sold at Bailly's store alongside Rosicrucian works of Joséphin Péladan.[43] Bois's fascination with satanism resonated not only with Huysmans, who explored occult themes in his novel *Là-bas* (Paris: Tresse & Stock, 1891) and wrote a preface to Bois's *Le Satanisme et la Magie* (1895), but also with Debussy, who considered contributing incidental music for a production of Bois's *Les noces de Sathan* at the Théâtre d'Application in March 1892. Figure 11.1 shows Henry Colas's arabesque frontispiece for Chamuel's edition of the play.[44] Bois's interest in tarot also rubbed off on Debussy as will become clear later.[45]

Turning to the score of "La Morte des amants," one is immediately struck by the careful ways in which Debussy projected the structure as well as the meaning of Baudelaire's text.[46] Take, for example, his setting of the opening two quatrains. As shown in figure 11.2, the poem conveys the image of two lovers, comparing the human soul to a mirror ("Dans nos deux esprits, ces miroirs jumeaux") and the heart to an enormous flame ("Nos deux coeurs seront deux vastes flambeaux"). Debussy's setting re-creates this intimate scene by introducing two motives (see example 11.1): an arpeggiated gesture D♭–B♭–D♭–B♭–C♭–E♭–D♮ (see ex. 11.1a, Motive X) and a sinuous chromatic pattern D♭–E♭♭–E♭–F♭–F♮ (see ex. 11.1b, Motive Y). The former is especially striking because it recalls the beautiful arabesque that opens "Clair de lune" (*Suite bergamasque*); this arabesque, which he completed just a few years later, is shown in example 11.1c. And when interwoven with the chromatic pattern, it calls to mind the staff and the vines of a thyrsus. The first quatrain also establishes the global tonic of the song: G♭ major. As shown in example 11.1d, the passage begins with a progression from V–I in mm. 1–5, followed by an authentic cadence in G♭ in mm. 7–8. The music then shifts back to the dominant D♭ major in mm. 9–12. Example 11.1e

Example 11.1 Main motives in Debussy, "La Morte des amants" (*Cinq poèmes de Baudelaire*)

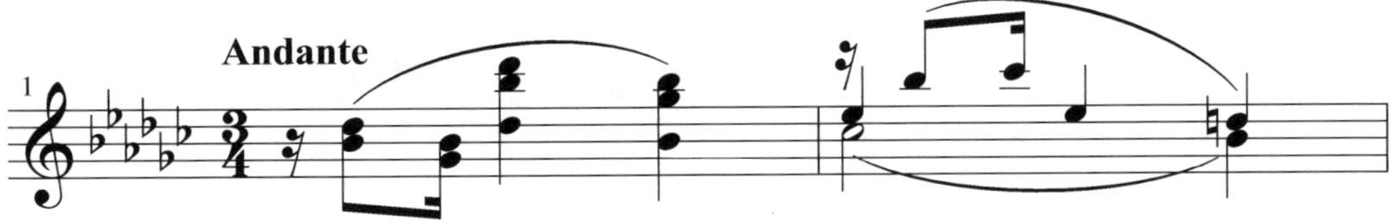

Example 11.1a Debussy, "La Morte des amants," motive X, mm. 1–2

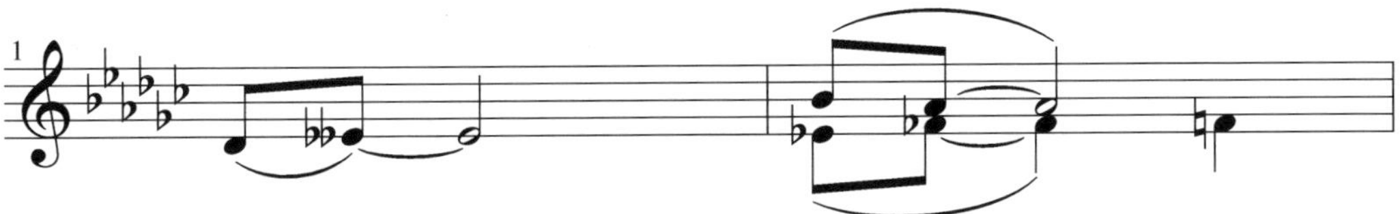

Example 11.1b Debussy, "La Morte des amants," motive Y, mm. 1–2

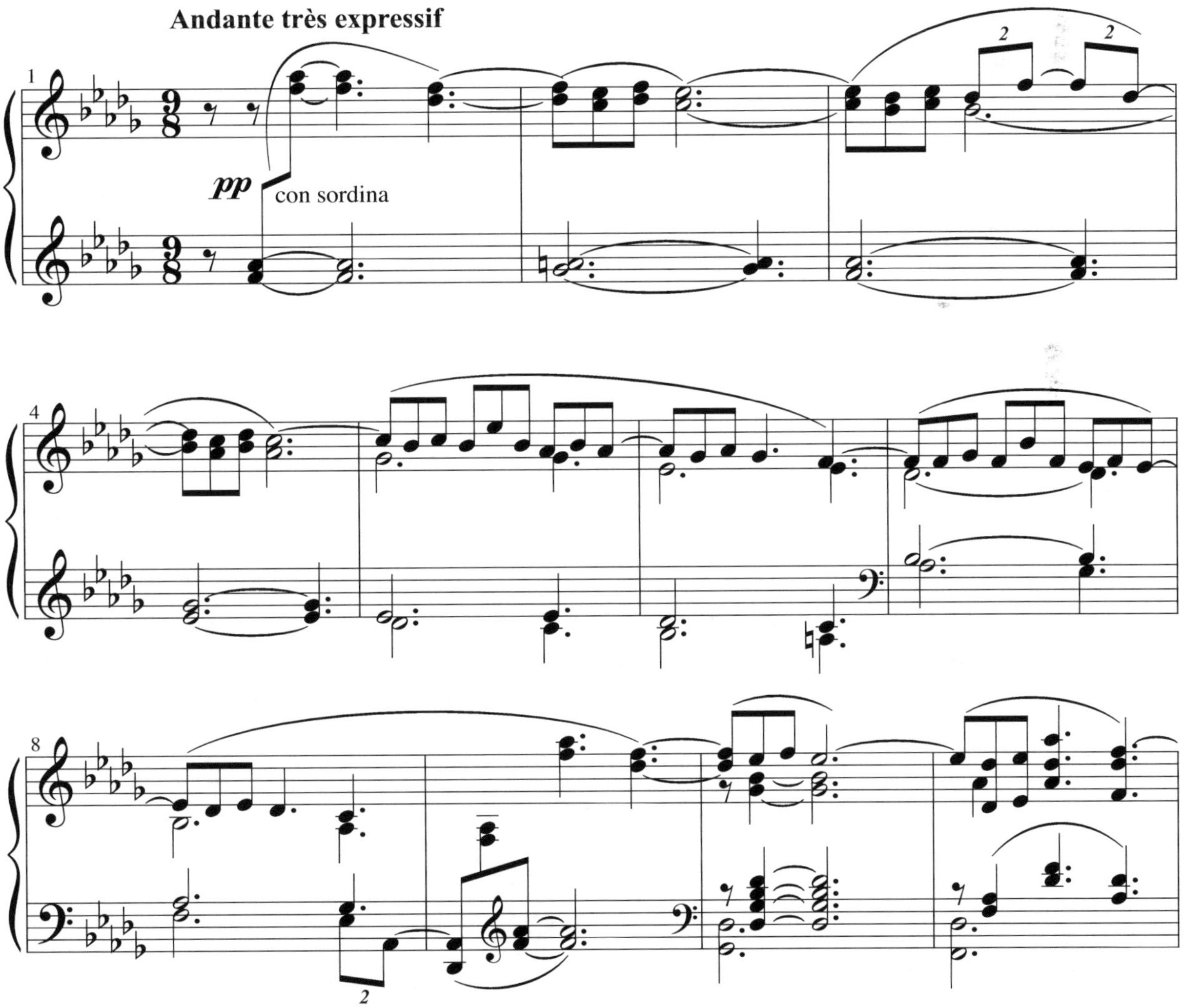

Example 11.1c Debussy, "Clair de lune," *Suite bergamasque*, mm. 1–11

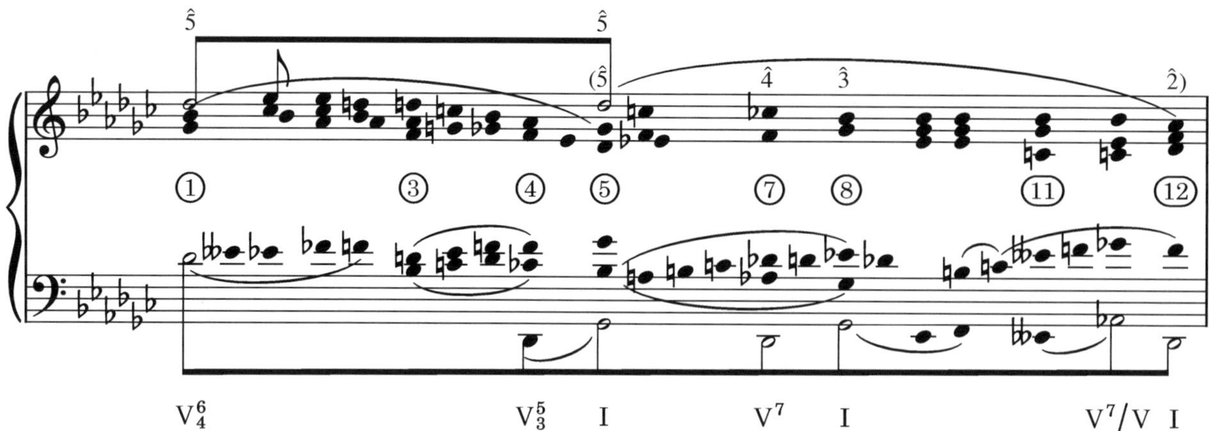

Example 11.1d Tonal structure of quatrain 1, Debussy, "La Morte des amants" (*Cinq poèmes de Baudelaire*)

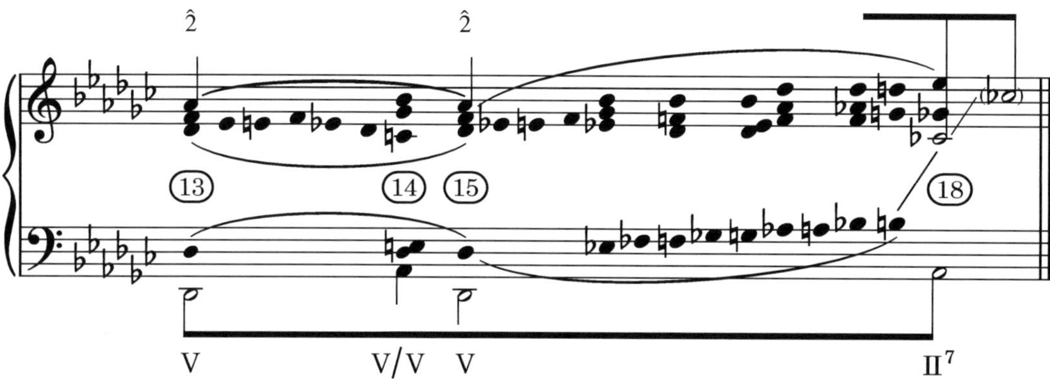

Example 11.1e Tonal structure of quatrain 2, Debussy, "La Morte des amants" (*Cinq poèmes de Baudelaire*)

then demonstrates how the second quatrain hovers around D♭, the dominant of G♭, landing on a predominant seventh A♭–C♭–E♭–G♭ in m. 18 to set up another potential cadence in G♭ in mm. 19–20. This harmonic skeleton is elaborated melodically by variants of the arpeggiated gesture and ascending chromatic lines that seem to invert Motive Y. Significantly, these measures not only recall the arabesque quality of the opening measures but also expand them in the process. Instead of reaffirming G♭ major in mm. 19–20, however, the dominant seventh A♭–C♭–E♭–G♭ in m. 18 is enharmonically respelled as G♯–B–E♮–F♯, thereby setting a perfect authentic cadence in E major near the start of the sestet in mm. 22–23.

Charles Baudelaire, "La Mort des amants," *Les Fleurs du mal*, CXXI

Nous aurons des lits pleins d'odeurs légères,
Des divans profonds comme des tombeaux,
Et d'étranges fleurs sur des étagères,
Écloses pour nous sous des cieux plus beaux.

Usant à l'envi leurs chaleurs dernières,
Nos deux coeurs seront deux vastes flambeaux,
Qui réfléchiront leurs doubles lumières
Dans nos deux esprits, ces miroirs jumeaux.

Un soir fait de rose et de bleu mystique,
Nous échangerons un éclair unique,
Comme un long sanglot tout chargé d'adieux;
Et plus tard un Ange, entr'ouvrant les portes,
Viendra ranimer, fidèle et joyeux,
Les miroirs ternis et les flammes mortes.

In contrast to the first and second quatrains, the final sestet suggests that sexual pleasure, however intense it may be, is always fleeting and can only be recaptured in the future through interactions with a new lover, which Baudelaire refers to as an Angel: "Et plus tard un Ange, entr'ouvrant les portes, Viendra ranimer, fidèle et Joyeux, Les miroirs ternis et les flammes mortes." Debussy's setting of these lines is remarkable on several counts. First, to highlight the poem's reference to the spark of passion between the two lovers and the ensuing farewell, the music turns suddenly from G♭ major to E major in m. 19 (see ex. 11.2a) and includes material that alludes

Example 11.2 Motivic allusions in Debussy, "La Morte des amants"

Example 11.2a Debussy, "La Morte des amants," mm. 19–23

Example 11.2b Debussy, *Prélude à L'Après-midi d'un faune*, mm. 103–6

Example 11.2c Wagner, "Good Friday Cadence," *Parsifal*, act 3

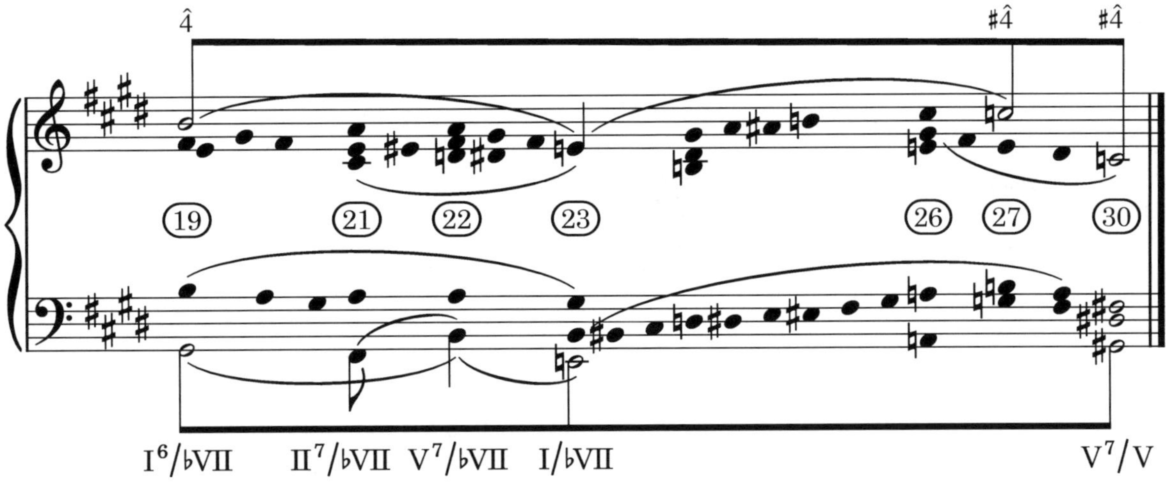

Example 11.2d Tonal structure of "La Morte des amants," mm. 19–30

to the *Prélude à L'Après-midi d'un faune* (see ex. 11.2b) and Wagner's *Parsifal* (see ex. 11.2c). As shown in example 11.2d, m. 29 culminates in another version of the dominant seventh from m. 18, this time respelled enharmonically as G♯–C♮–D♯–F♯. Second, the appearance of the Angel and the promise of future liaisons is marked by a return of the arpeggiated gesture, a sudden shift to C major, and by another allusion to the dominant seventh in m. 38, this time restored to its original notation A♭–C♭–E♭–G♭ (see ex. 11.3a). The latter sonority sets off the final line of the poem in which the lovers realize that their own relationship is over: tarnished mirrors and extinguished flames (see ex. 11.3b). Third, although the music finally returns to its global tonic G♭ major, it does so by mirroring the rising chromatic lines of the first and second quatrains with descending chromatic lines and by reversing the large-scale progression from G♭ (mm. 7–8) to D♭ (mm. 12–13) to A♭ (m. 18) with a progression from A♭ (m. 41) through D♭ (mm. 43–44) to G♭ (mm. 45–48). This process of reflection and distortion is shown in example 11.3c. The song ends with a tonic pedal over which the upper voices echo the opening statements of the arpeggiated gesture (Motive X) and the chromatic pattern (Motive Y).

Two years before completing "La Morte des amants," Debussy set another poem tinged with melancholia and ennui: Verlaine's "L'Ombre des arbres."[47] The song is one of six *Ariettes oubliées* that he wrote for Mme de Vasnier. As mentioned in chapter 3, Debussy had been in love with her and had given her a collection of thirteen songs, the so-called *Receuil Vasnier*, before leaving for his Prix de Rome in 1885. By the time he returned to Paris in 1887, however, their relationship had waned: Marcel Dietschy has suggested that Debussy's dedication of the *Ariettes oubilées* to her should be interpreted as a melancholy farewell rather than a declaration of love. The songs themselves actually come from two different collections mentioned by Huysmans: five come from *Romances sans paroles* (1874)—"C'est l'extase," "Il pleure dans mon cœur," and "L'Ombre des arbres" belonging to a subsection entitled "Ariettes oubliées" and "Green" and "Spleen" to one entitled "Aquarelles"; and the sixth—"Chevaux des bois"—comes from another collection, *Sagesse* (1881), though an early version of the poem does appear in *Romances sans Paroles*. It seems that Debussy composed "L'Ombre des arbres" and "Chevaux des bois" first in January 1885,

Above, **Example 11.3a** Debussy, "La Morte des amants," mm. 30–38

Facing top, **Example 11.3b** Debussy, "La Morte des amants," mm. 39–48

Facing bottom, **Example 11.3c** Tonal structure of "La Morte des amants," mm. 30–48

molto espress.
mp
39
dèle et jo - yeux, Les mi -
m.g. 8va
mp molto espress.
42
roirs ter - nìs et les flam - mes mor - tes.
8va
p
più p
45
morendo e rit.
m.d. pp
m.d. pp
m.d. pp
m.d. ppp
#4̂ #4̂ 4̂ 3̂ 2̂ 1̂
cover tone
(30) (34) (38) (41) (42) (45) (48)
V/V II7 V6/4 5/3 I

then "Green" in January 1886, "C'est l'extase" and "Il pleure dans mon cœur" in March 1887, and finally "Spleen" in January 1888. The set was published a month later in six installments by the widow of Étienne Girod, and Debussy performed two of the songs with Maurice Bagès on February 2, 1889, at the Société nationale de musique. A decade or so later, Debussy revised the songs and arranged for Fromont to publish them in one volume in 1903.

Like several other poems in *Romances sans paroles*, Verlaine's "L'Ombre des arbres" is prefaced by lines from another writer, in this case from a letter by Cyrano de Bergerac.[48] The epigram describes a nightingale looking down from the branch of an oak tree onto a stream. The bird thinks it has fallen in and fears it may drown. Verlaine's poem echoes the same mood and sentiments. The text divides into two sentences, each of which contains two pairs of rhyming couplets. The first pair describes a nocturnal landscape in which turtle doves lament the death of another as the shadow of the trees dissolves into the mists lingering over a stream. The trees may be the subject of the couplets, but Verlaine focuses on their shadowy reflections, which seem to dissolve into the water. Next, the second pair of couplets compare the melancholy of the doves to that of a traveler whose hopes for the future have likewise been drowned. The traveler feels empty and alone and, like the nightingale in the epigram, sees himself reflected in the murky landscape where the river and the trees merge into one.

Paul Verlaine, "L'Ombre des arbres," *Romances sans paroles*

Le rossignol qui du haut d'une
branche se regarde dedans, croit
être tombé dans la rivière. Il est
au sommet d'un chêne et toute fois
il a peur de se noyer.
          Cyrano de Bergerac

L'ombre des arbres dans la rivière embrumée
Meurt comme de la fumée
Tandis qu'en l'air, parmi les ramures réelles,
Se plaignent les tourterelles.
Combien, ô voyageur, ce paysage blême
Te mira blême toi-même,
Et que tristes pleuraient dans les hautes feuillées
Tes espérances noyées!

It is clear that Debussy's setting of "L'Ombre des arbres" mirrors the poem's two-part plan, the second part being a distorted reflection of the first. Simply put, mm. 1–10 set the first pair of couplets and mm. 11–31 the second pair. Both passages open with the same material: a quarter-note pattern A♯–B♮–E♯ presented in octaves in mm. 1–2 (ex. 11.4a) and a sinuous chromatic gesture in triplet and duplet eighth notes E♭–B–E♭–B–D♮ in m. 2 (ex. 11.4b). Harmonically, these measures articulate two triads a tritone apart, C♯⁷ in m. 1 and G♮⁷ in m. 2 (see ex. 11.4c). After repeating both measures, the music then shifts via an E♮⁷ sonority in m. 5 to a minor dominant G♯ in m. 6 and m. 8 for a repetition of the quarter-note pattern A♯–B♮–E♯. This progression supports an overall stepwise descent E♯–E♮–D♯ in the vocal part across mm. 1–8. At this point, the two units part company and the reflections become distorted. In mm. 9–11 the stepwise pattern E♯–E♮–D♯ continues its downward trajectory D♮–C♯–B♯–C♯ in the right hand of the piano. This pattern is

Example 11.4a Debussy, "L'Ombre des arbres," quarter-note pattern, m. 1

Example 11.4b Debussy, "L'Ombre des arbres," eighth-note figure, m. 2

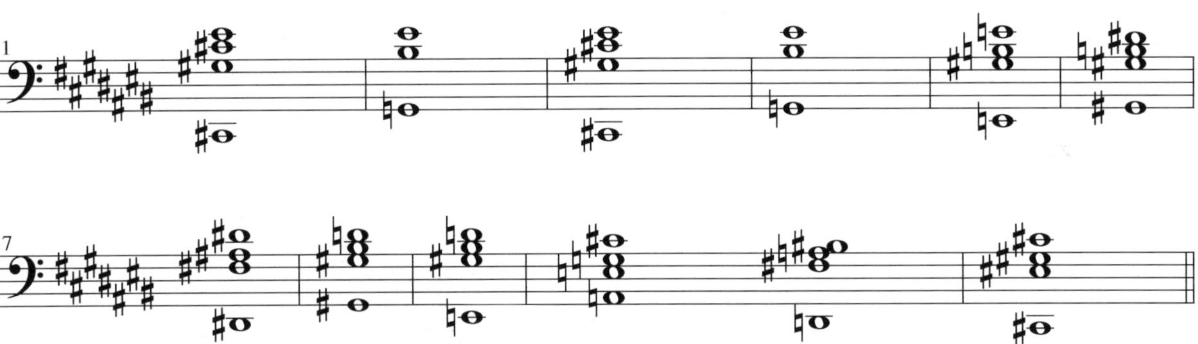

Example 11.4c Tonal structure of "L'Ombre des arbres," mm. 1–11/12

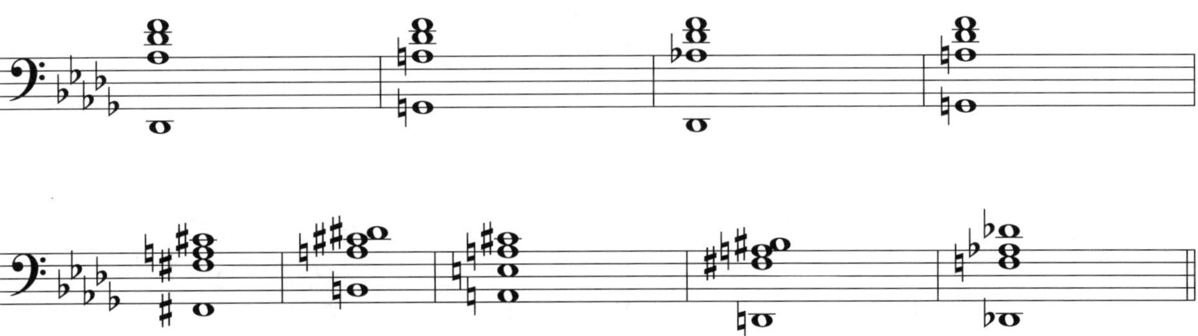

Example 11.4d Tonal structure of *Prélude à L'Après-midi d'un faune*, mm. 55–63

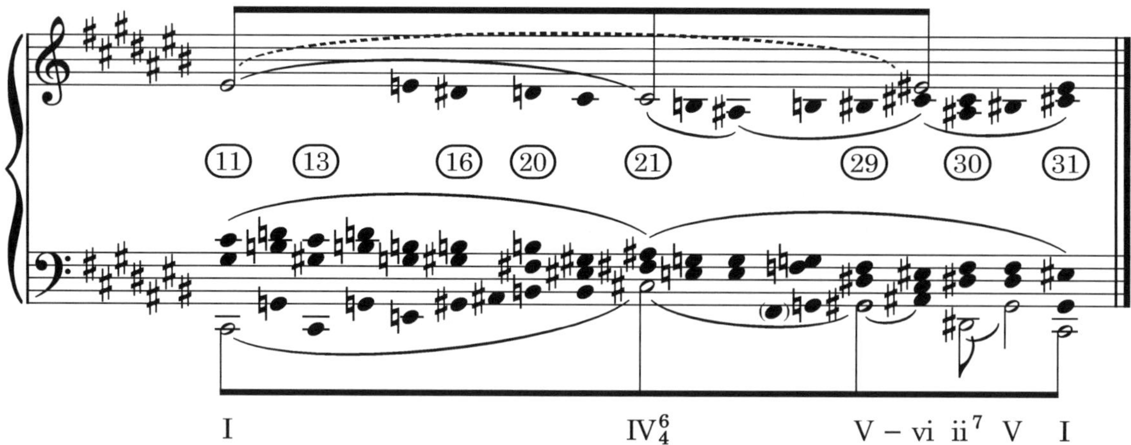

Example 11.4e Tonal structure of "L'Ombre des arbres," mm. 11–31

supported by a progression E♭^{7}–A♭^{7}–D♭^{7}–C♯, in which D♭^{7} functions as an augmented sixth chord and tonicizes C♯ on the down beat of m. 11. Example 11.4d shows that this progression anticipates a similar one in mm. 55–63 of the *Prélude à L'Après-midi d'un faune*. Having repeated mm. 1–6 as mm. 11–16 and projected the same stepwise descent from E♯ through E♮ to D♯, the melody for the second pair of couplets continues its downward trajectory albeit in a more serpentine manner (see ex. 11.4e). It starts by descending from D♯ in m. 16 through D♮ in m. 20 to C♯ in mm. 20–21. This pattern is reinforced by an arrival on F♯6/4 in m. 21 and again in m. 23. Once on C♯ in the right hand of the piano, the stepwise pattern shifts down through B to A♯ in mm. 24–26 to set up a return of the quarter-note pattern A♯–B♮–E♯ from m. 1 over the G♮^{7} from m. 2 in mm. 27–28. The global tonic C♯ is restored over dominant harmonies in mm. 29 and 30, with the leading tone B♯ resolving up to C♯ in m. 29. Notice how the final cadence A♯–D♯–(G♯)–C♯ is a distorted reflection of the progression A–D–C♯ in mm. 10–11 and how the final cadence in mm. 29–31 is covered by an octave E♯ in the right hand of the piano.

The final work on our list is Debussy's setting of Mallarmé's "Soupir," which he included in his *Trois poèmes de Stéphane Mallarmé* (1913). Although this is one of the last songs that Debussy ever composed, his interest in Mallarmé's work began in the early 1880s when he composed a version of "Apparition." As mentioned in chapter 4, the two men finally met around 1890 and attended Mallarmé's celebrated *mardis* off and on through most of the decade until the poet died in 1898. Spurred by the publication of Albert Thibaudet's *La Poésie de Stéphane Mallarmé* (1911) and the third edition of Mallarmé's *Poésies* (1913), Debussy decided to set a group of three poems to music—"Soupir," "Placet futile," and "Éventail."[49] Although Mallarmé's family had already given Ravel permission to set "Soupir" and "Placet futile," they also gave their approval to Debussy, who dedicated his three songs to the memory of the poet and in gratitude to his daughter Geneviève (Madame E. Bennoit). Debussy completed the songs between April and August 1913.

Written in 1864 and published in *Le Parnasse contemporain* on May 12, 1866, "Soupir" is one of many "mirror-poems" that Mallarmé completed during the 1860s and 1870s.[50] "Soupir," reproduced below, consists of ten lines of text, all of which are alexandrines, that divide into two groups of five lines each. Lines 1–5 describe how the poet's soul is uplifted when he looks up, first toward his former lover's brow ("vers ton front"), then toward her angelic eye ("vers le ciel errant de ton oeil angélique"), and then toward the sky ("vers l'Azur"). By delaying the appearance of the only inflected verb, "monte" (rises), until the start of line 4 and by running lines 2–4 together, Mallarmé re-creates the sensation of someone breathing deeply as they gaze upward. Lines 6–10 then describe how the poet looks down to see the blue sky reflected on the surface of stagnant pools ("l'eau morte"), on which autumn winds have strewn dead leaves ("la fauve agonie des feuilles") and gouged a deep ripple ("creuse un froid sillon"). Indeed, by repeating the phrase "vers l'Azur!" from the end of line 5 at the beginning of line 6, by contrasting the image of the blue sky with that of the stagnant pools, and by comparing the lover's russet freckles (line 2) with the tawny leaves on the pool (lines 8–9), Mallarmé suggests that the second half of the poem is a distorted reflection of the first. He confirms this possibility by running lines 6–9 together, thereby capturing the sensation of someone exhaling or sighing. The melancholy tone of these lines is mitigated slightly by the image of a long ray of yellow sun glistening across the surface of the pools ("Se traîner le soleil jaune d'un long rayon").

Stéphane Mallarmé, "Soupir," *Poésies*

Mon âme vers ton front où rêve, ô calme sœur,
Un automne jonché de taches de rousseur,
Et vers le ciel errant de ton œil angélique
Monte, comme dans un jardin mélancolique,
Fidèle, un blanc jet d'eau soupire vers l'Azur !
—Vers l'azur attendri d'octobre pâle et pur
Qui mire aux grands bassins sa langueur infinie
Et laisse, sur l'eau morte où la fauve agonie
Des feuilles erre au vent et creuse un froid sillon,
Se trainer le soleil jaune dun long rayon.

When setting "Soupir" to music, Debussy decided to open the song with an introduction for the piano: this passage presents two main motives: a rising pattern E♭–B♭, F–C, B♭–F, which appears in mm. 1–2, 4, and 5–6, and a falling pattern F–C–B♭–E♭, which appears in mm. 2 and 3 (see ex. 11.5a).[51] Although the contour of the former is a mirror image of the latter, the reflection is not exact: whereas the first two notes of the rising pattern E♭–B♭ are reversed at the end of the falling pattern as B♭–E♭, the third and fourth notes of the rising pattern F–C are not reversed at the start of the descending pattern as C–F. This difference is further accentuated rhythmically: the rising pattern appears as triplet eighth notes in m. 1, as duplet eighth notes in m. 2, and as quarter notes in m. 3. When the rising motive eventually returns at the end of the song, it seems to recall the triplet eighth notes from m. 1 over the tonic A♭ from m. 4 and mm. 5–6 (see ex. 11.5b). For the record, the autograph (F–Pn 1028) replaces the rising and falling patterns in mm. 1–3 with a chain of parallel triads (see ex. 11.5c).

Example 11.6 then shows how Debussy's setting of lines 1–5 is reflected in his setting of lines 6–10 (mm. 18–31). In both cases, the vocal arabesques feature undulating patterns that oscillate between A♭ and E♭ or F. The song opens with two such patterns for lines 1–5: in mm. 6–9, the voice ends by rising from A♭ to E♭ before falling back to A♭ (ex. 11.6a), and in mm. 10–11, it rises from A♭ to F before descending chromatically from F through E, D♯, C♯, and B to G♯. Lines 6–11 follow a similar plan: as shown, examples 11.6c and 11.6d, mm. 18–20 and mm. 21–23, both ascend from G♭ to F before descending back to A♭. Further parallels can be found between mm. 13–15 and mm. 23–26: both vocal parts intone the repeated tone D (see ex. 11.6e–11.6f). And

Example 11.5a Debussy, "Soupir," mm. 1–6

Example 11.5b Debussy, "Soupir," mm. 30–31

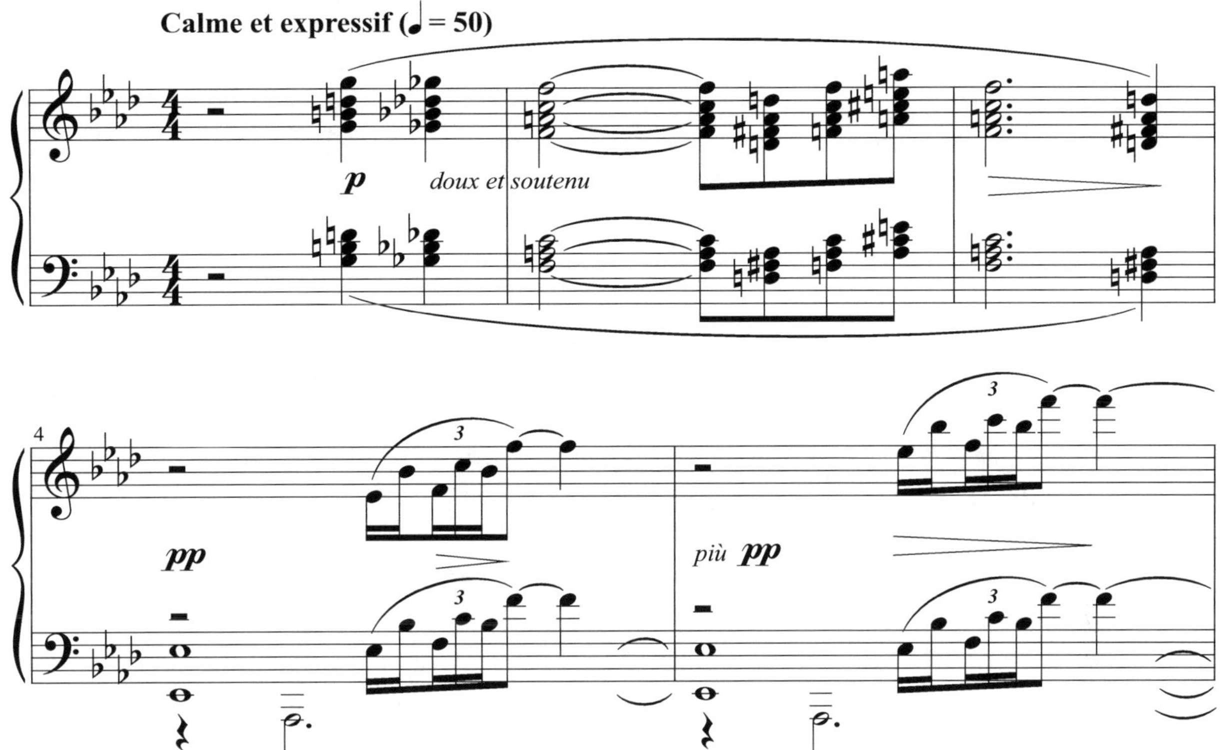

Example 11.5c Debussy, "Soupir," Autograph F-Pn 1028

both halves culminate in an affirmation of A♭ as the global tonic of the song. The voice-leading analysis in example 11.7a shows that the first half ends with an oblique authentic cadence V⁷–I in mm. 13–17, with D♭ and B♭ resolving down by step to C and A♭, and G♮ resolving up to A♭. Instead of supporting these lines with E♭ in the bass, they are harmonized with C major chords in mm. 15 and 16. Example 11.7b then shows how mm. 6–11 are recomposed in mm. 18–22. And example 11.7c demonstrates how the implied cadence V⁷–I in mm. 13–17 is reworked in mm. 29–31: the upper and lower leading tones G and B♭ again resolve onto A♭, the seventh D♭ resolves down to C, and the bass descends E♭–A♭. This time, however, the cadence is enhanced by a final recollection of the rising pattern E♭–B♭, F–C, B♭–F.

The sketches in example 11.7b also suggests other complex ways in which the voice-leading structure of mm. 6–17 differs from that of mm. 18–31. In mm. 6–12, for example, the parallel lines of the upper voices are supported by a stepwise descent in the tenor from C through C♭, B♭, A♭, and implied tones G♭ and F♭ to E♭, whereas in mm. 18–31, those upper voices are supported by an ascending tenor voice E♭, F, G, A♭, B♭, B, C, to D. When the recitative-like passage from mm. 13–15 returns in m. 24–26, the repeated tone D♯ is accompanied in the bass with inversions of the descending fifth E♭–A♭: A♭–D♮ and A♭–D♭ in mm. 24–25, and C–G in mm. 26 (see ex. 11.8a). The resulting ostinato not only conveys the sound of dead leaves being blown across rippled water but also recalls similar passages from two piano works from 1913, the same year as "Soupir." In particular, example 11.8b shows a similar whole-tone ostinato D♮–G♯ from mm.

Example 11.6a Debussy, "Soupir," mm. 6–9

Example 11.6b Debussy, "Soupir," mm. 10–11

Example 11.6c Debussy, "Soupir," mm. 18–20

Example 11.6d Debussy, "Soupir," mm. 21–23

Example 11.6e Debussy, "Soupir," mm. 13–15

Example 11.6f Debussy, "Soupir," mm. 24–27

Example 11.7 Voice-leading analysis of Debussy, "Soupir"

Example 11.7a Debussy, "Soupir," mm. 6–17

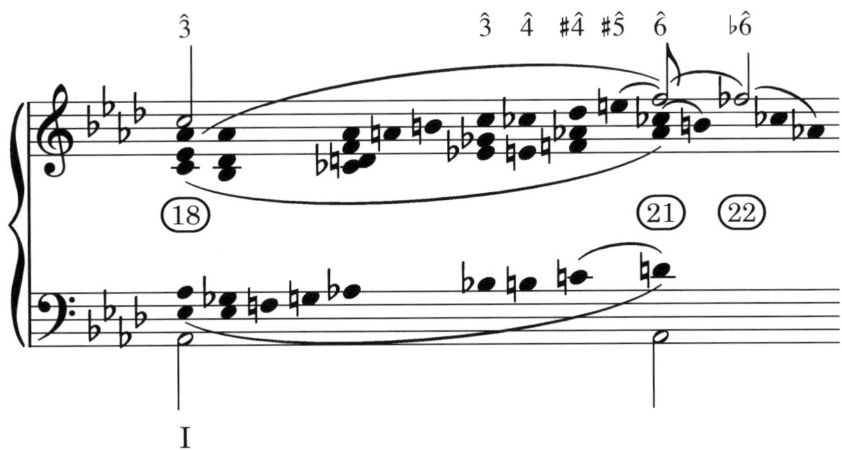

Example 11.7b Voice-leading analysis of Debussy, "Soupir," mm. 18–22

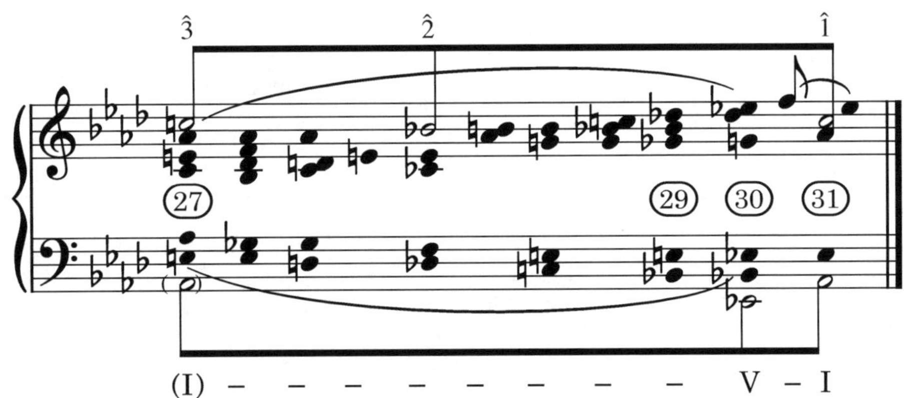

Example 11.7c Voice-leading analysis of Debussy, "Soupir," mm. 27–31

19–24 of "Feuilles mortes" (*Préludes*, Bk. 2), and example 11.8c gives an analogous ostinato B♮–E♭ starting in m. 32 of "Ondine" (*Préludes*, Bk. 2). In the case of example 11.8c, the repeated melodic tone B♮ in mm. 34–35 of "Ondine" recalls the repeated tone D in mm. 24–27 of "Soupir" as well as the main theme of "La terrasse des audiences du clair de lune" (*Préludes*, Bk. 2). The ostinato pattern in example 11.8a is important from a formal perspective because the ostinato pattern leads to the final portion of "Soupir"; here the melodic pattern C, D♭, E♭, F from m. 10 ("de taches de rousseur") is augmented in mm. 28–31 to convey the long ray of sun sparkling on the water ("Se traîner le soleil jaune d'un long rayon"). "Soupir" ends by reworking the cadence from mm. 15–17 in mm. 30–31.

Example 11.8 Motivic allusions in Debussy, "Soupir"

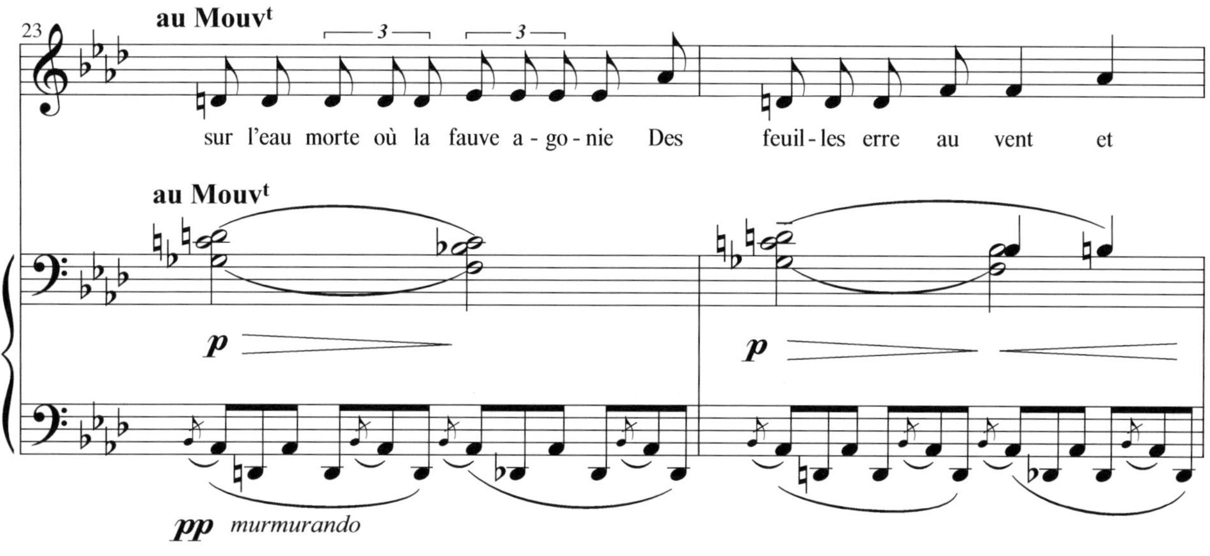

Example 11.8a Debussy, "Soupir," mm. 23–26

Example 11.8b Debussy, "Feuilles mortes," *Préludes*, Bk. 2 (1913), mm. 19–24

The preceding discussion has shown how Debussy's setting of "Soupir" highlights the fact that it is a "mirror-poem," with lines 6–10 serving as a *distorted* reflection of lines 1–5. In the case of the text, lines 1–5 describe the poet's upward glances, first to his former lover's brow, then to her eyes, and then to the sky. Lines 6–10 then depict the sound of the autumn winds blowing dead leaves across rippled water with a long ray of sun sparkling across the surface. In the case of the music, the symmetry of the text is conveyed by the rise and fall of the two main motives and globally by allowing the melody to ascend repeatedly from A♭ or G♭ to F before descending to E♭–E♮ and by balancing the upward trajectory of the melody in the first part with the downward trend of the bass in the second part. And yet, Debussy's score also captures the menacing and melancholy atmosphere of lines 6–10 by including the ostinato patterns in mm. 24–27: the repeated D in the melody, whole-tone harmonies, disorienting rhythms, and bare textures stand in sharp contrast

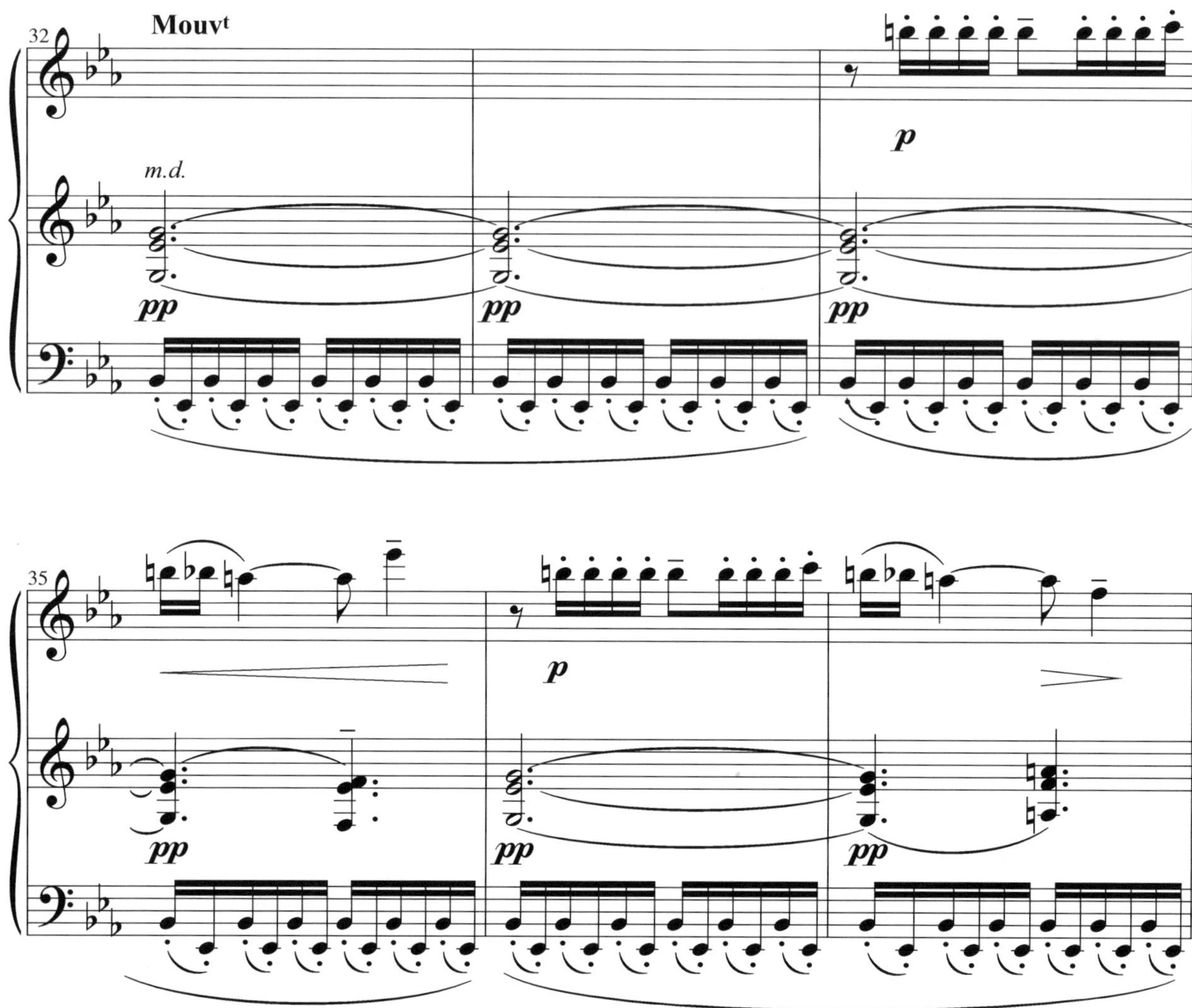

Example 11.8c Debussy, "Ondine," *Préludes*, Bk. 2 (1913), mm. 32–37

to the lush sonorities of mm. 18–23 and mm. 28–31. "Soupir" may end with a final recollection of the rising pattern from mm. 1–6, but that reminiscence is tinged with sadness and belongs firmly in the past.

When thinking about the subtle ways in which Debussy conveyed the idea of the tarnished mirror musically in "Soupir," it is surely no coincidence that he composed the song at a time when he was overcome by his own feelings of melancholia and ennui. They had been festering for several years. On July 8, 1910, he confided to Durand:

Those around me persist in not understanding that I have never been able to live in a real world of people and things. And that is why I have this irrefutable need to escape and become involved in adventures which seem inexplicable because they involve a man no one recognizes. And perhaps that is what is best in me! Besides, an artist by definition is a man accustomed to dreams and who lives with phantoms. . . . How could it be expected that this same person would be able to follow in his daily life the strict observance of traditions—laws and other barriers erected by a hypocritical and cowardly world.[52]

They erupted yet again soon after the premiere of the *Trois poèmes de Stéphane Mallarmé* in January 1914. On July 14, 1914, Debussy mentioned to Godet that a recent accident had the most tiresome consequences: "Flu; shingles, which attacks the nerves frightfully; in the end, for four and a half months I've done precisely nothing! Naturally these things cause miserable domestic worries and times when one can hardly see any way out but suicide."[53] He continued, "For a long time—it has to be admitted—I've felt lost, and terribly diminished! Ah! The 'magician' ('le magician') you loved in me, where is he? All he is now is a builder of gloomy towers ('tours morose'), who will soon break his back in a final pirouette devoid of beauty."[54] Debussy's references to the magician and gloomy tower conjure up images of tarot cards in which the magician is usually thought to represent energy, creativity, and personal desires, and the tower to represent imprisonment from which the subject must escape (see fig. 11.5a–11.5b).[55] Just like Baudelaire, melancholia and ennui were Debussy's "most intimate companions"; their presence would only become more conspicuous in later years, when the outbreak of WWI, the death of his mother, and the decline in his health prompted him, once again, to contemplate suicide.

Figure 11.2a Tarot card representing the magician by Patricia Colman Smith for the Rider-Waite Tarot deck

Figure 11.2b Tarot card representing the tower by Patricia Colman Smith for the Rider-Waite Tarot deck. Smith Waite Centennial Tarot™, c. 2015, used with permission of U.S. Games Systems, Inc., Stamford, CT 06902. All rights reserved.

Notes

1. For Baudelaire's interest in esotericism and the occult, see Jon Leaver, "'Sorcellerie évocatoire': Magic and Memory in Baudelaire and Eliphas Lévi," *Symposium: A Quarterly Journal in Modern Literatures* 66, no. 3 (2012): 139–49.

2. Wassily Kandinsky, *Concerning the Spiritual in Art* (1912), trans. M. T. H. Sadler (New York: Dover, 1977), 16.

3. Margaret Stoljar, "Mirror and Self in Symbolist and Post-Symbolist Poetry," *Modern Language Review* 85, no. 2 (1990): 362.

4. Stoljar, "Mirror and Self," 364–66.

5. Patrick Dandrey, "Encyclopédisme mélancolique, ou d'un 'miroir terni,'" in *Anthologie de l'humeur noir. Écrits sur la mélancolie d'Hippocrate à l'Encyclopédie* (Paris: Gallimard, 2005), 749.

6. https://www.nlm.nih.gov/exhibition/shakespeare-and-the-four-humors/index.html. For a comprehensive overview of melancholy from ancient times to the twentieth century, see Jennifer Radden, ed., *The Nature of Melancholy from Aristotle to Kristeva* (Oxford: Oxford University Press, 2000). See also Emily Brady and Arto Haapala, "Melancholy as an Aesthetic Emotion," Contemporary Aesthetics, vol. 1 (2003), https://quod.lib.umich.edu/c/ca/7523862.0001.006?view=text;rgn=main (accessed July 11, 2025).

7. See Rosemary Ellen Guiley, *The Art of Black-Mirror Scrying* (New Milford, CT: Visionary Living, 2014); and Arnaud Maillet, *The Claude Glass: Use and Meaning of the Black Mirror in Western Art*, trans. Jeff Fort (New York: Zone Books, 2009).

8. See also Ya-Ju Yang, "The House as Mirrors in Edgar Allan Poe's 'The Fall of the House of Usher,'" Official Proceedings of the Asian Conference on Arts and Humanities, Osaka, Japan, 2013, https://papers.iafor.org/wp-content/uploads/papers/acah2013/ACAH2013_0239.pdf (accessed November 6, 2023).

9. Jean Starobinski, "Melancholy in the Mirror: Three Readings of Baudelaire," trans. Charlotte Mandell, *Hyperion* 5 (2010): 118. See also Maurie Z. Schroder, *ICARUS: The Image of the Artist in French Romanticism* (Cambridge, MA: Harvard University Press, 1961), 181–216; Ross Chambers, *The Writings of Melancholy: Modes of Opposition in Early French Modernism*, trans. Mary Seidman Trouille (Chicago: University of Chicago Press, 1993), esp. 115–74; Kevin Godbout, "Saturnine Constellations: Melancholy in Literary History and in the Works of Baudelaire and Benjamin," PhD diss., University of Western Ontario, 2016; Piotr Śniedziewski, *The Melancholic Gaze*, trans. Dwight Williams (Berlin: Peter Lang, 2018), 151–70.

10. Louis-Adolphe Chabouille, ed., *Lettres inédites [à sa mère] de Charles Baudelaire* (Paris: Calmann-Levy, 1891), 150, 213–14, https://gallica.bnf.fr/ark:/12148/bpt6k15222415.image.

11. Roger Pearson, *Beauty of Baudelaire: The Poet as Alternative Lawgiver* (Oxford: Oxford University Press, 2021), 108–12, esp. 108.

12. Charles Baudelaire, "Fusées: X," in *Charles Baudelaire: Œuvres Complètes*, vol. I, ed. Claude Pichois, Bibliothèque de la Pléiade (Paris: Gallimard, 1976), 657; Baudelaire, "Flares: 16," in *Late Fragments. Flares, My Heart Laid Bare, Prose Poems, Belgium Disrobed*, ed. and trans. Richard Sieburth (New Haven, CT: Yale University Press), 2022, 90.

13. Baudelaire, "Fusées: X," in *Œuvres Complètes*, I:657; Baudelaire, "Flares: 16," in *Late Fragments*, 90.

14. Baudelaire, "Fusées: X," in *Œuvres Complètes*, I:657; Baudelaire, "Flares: 16," in *Late Fragments*, 90.

15. Baudelaire, "Fusées: X," in *Œuvres Complètes*, I:657; Baudelaire, "Flares: 16," in *Late Fragments*, 90–91.

16. Baudelaire, "Fusées: X," in *Œuvres Complètes*, I:657–58; Baudelaire, "Flares: 16," in *Late Fragments*, 91.

17. Baudelaire, "Fusées: VIII," in *Œuvres Complètes*, I:657–58; Baudelaire, "Flares: 12," in *Late Fragments*, 89.

18. Baudelaire, "Fusées: X," in *Œuvres Complètes*, I:658; Baudelaire, "Flares: 16," in *Late Fragments*, 91.

19. Pearson, *Beauty of Baudelaire*, 112.

20. Baudelaire, "Le Peintre de la vie moderne: IX Le Dandy," in *Œuvres Complètes*, 709; Baudelaire, "The Painter in Modern Life: IX The Dandy," in *The Painter in Modern Life and Other Essays*, ed. and trans. Jonathan Mayne (London: Phaidon, 2001), 26.

21. Baudelaire, "Le Peintre de la vie moderne: IX Le Dandy," in *Œuvres Complètes*, 709–10; Baudelaire, "The Painter in Modern Life: IX The Dandy," in *Painter in Modern Life*, 27.

22. Baudelaire, "Mon cœur mis à nu: III," in *Œuvres Complètes*, I:678; Baudelaire, "My Heart Laid Bare: 5," in *Late Fragments*, 113.

23. Baudelaire, "Le Peintre de la vie moderne: IX Le Dandy," in *Œuvres Complètes*, I:712; Baudelaire, "The Painter in Modern Life: IX The Dandy," in *Painter in Modern Life*, 29.

24. Stoljar, "Mirror and Self," 368.

25. Ovid, *Metamorphosis*, Oxford World Classics, trans. A. D. Melville with an introduction and notes by E. J. Kenney (Oxford: Oxford University Press, 1986), Bk. 3.337, 61–66.

26. Niclas Johansson, *The Narcissus Theme from* Fin de Siècle *to Psychoanalysis* (Frankfurt am Main: Peter Lang, 2017), 93–151.

27. Sigmund Freud, *Zur Einführung des Narzißmus* (Leipzig: Internationaler Pyschoanalytischer, 1914).

28. Sigmund Freud, "Trauer und Melancholie," *Internationale Zeitschrift für ärztliche Psychoanalyse* 4, no. 6 (1916/1917): 288–301.

29. See Philippe Jullian, *Prince of Aesthetes: Count Robert de Montesquiou 1855–1921* (New York: Viking, 1967). The character of des Esseintes also recalls that of Samuel Cramer, the hero of Baudelaire's novella *La Fanfarlo*. The book apparently fictionalized Baudelaire's own love affair with Jeanne Duval.

30. Baldick, "Introduction," in Joris-Karl Huysmans, *Against Nature*, trans. Robert Baldick (Harmondsworth: Penguin, 1959), 13.

31. Joris-Karl Huysmans, *À Rebours* (Paris: Garnier-Flammarion, 1978), 127–28; Joris-Karl Huysmans, *Against Nature*, trans. Robert Baldick (Harmondsworth: Penguin, 1959), 90.

32. Huysmans, *À Rebours*, 178; Huysmans, *Against Nature*, 148.

33. Huysmans, *À Rebours*, 75; Huysmans, *Against Nature*, 31.

34. Huysmans, *À Rebours*, 211; Huysmans, *Against Nature*, 186.

35. Huysmans, *À Rebours*, 211; Huysmans, *Against Nature*, 186.

36. Huysmans, *À Rebours*, 220 and 221–22; Huysmans, *Against Nature*, 196 and 198.

37. Mallarmé reciprocated by dedicating his poem "Prose" to des Esseintes.

38. For general discussions of "Le Balcon" and "La Morte des amants," see François De Médicis, *La Maturation Artistique de Debussy dans son Contexte Historique*, Speculum Musicae XXXVIII (Turnhout: Brepols, 2020), 309–57.

39. Claude Debussy, *Correspondance (1872–1918)*, ed. François Lesure and Denis Herlin, annotated by François Lesure, Denis Herlin, and Georges Liébert (Paris: Gallimard, 2005), 117; Claude Debussy, *Debussy Letters*, ed. François Lesure and Roger Nichols, trans. Roger Nichols (Cambridge, MA: Harvard University Press, 1987), 42. An organist and arranger, Gaston Choisnel (1857–1921) was the cousin of Debussy's future publisher Jacques Durand. When Durand officially took over his father's publishing house in 1909, he made Choisnel a partner.

40. See Denis Herlin, "À la librairie de l'Art indépendent: l'univers symboliste de Debussy," in *Claude Debussy— Portraits et Études* (Hildesheim: Georg Olms, 2023), 17–47.

41. For Bailly's occult activities, see Joscelyn Godwin, *Music and the Occult: French Musical Philosophies, 1750–1950* (Rochester, NY: University of Rochester Press, 1995), 151–77.

42. Debussy, *Correspondance*, 117; Debussy, *Letters*, 42.

43. For occult influences on Debussy, see Tobias Churton, *Occult Paris: The Lost Magic of the Belle Époque* (Rochester, VT: Inner Traditions, 2016); Roy Howat, *Debussy in Proportion: A Musical Analysis* (Cambridge: Cambridge University Press, 1983), 167–71; David Paul Goldman, "Esotericism as a Determinant of Debussy's Harmonic Language," *Musical Quarterly* 75, no. 2 (Summer 1991): 130–47; Pasler, "Revisiting Debussy's Relationships with Otherness: Difference, Vibrations, and the Occult," *Music & Letters* 101, no. 2 (2020): 321–42; and Annegret Fauser, "Crosscurrents in Debussy's Creative World," in *Debussy in Context*, ed. Simon Trezise (Cambridge: Cambridge University Press, 2024), 107–9.

44. Jules Bois, *Le Satanisme et la Magie. Avec une Étude de J.-K. Huysmans* (Paris, Léron Chailley, 1895). Originally appearing in *La revue indépendent* (1890), *Les noces de Sathan, drame ésotérique* was republished with illustrations by Henry Colas (Paris: Chamuel Éditeur, 1892). For Debussy's involvement with *Les noces de Sathan*, see Orledge, *Debussy and the Theatre*, 46–47 and 308.

45. https://traditionaltarot.wordpress.com/2023/01/14/jules-bois-an-unpublished-tarot-book-and-deck/ (accessed July 11, 2025).

46. Baudelaire, "La Morte des amants," *Les Fleurs du mal*, CXXI, in *Œuvres Complètes*, I:126. For other accounts of Debussy's song, see Katherine Bergeron, "The Echo, the Cry, the Death of Lovers," *19th-Century Music* 18, no. 2 (1994): 136–51; and Helen Abbott, *Parisian Intersections. Baudelaire's Legacy to Composers* (Bern: Peter Lang, 2012), 110–20.

47. Huysmans, *À Rebours*, 211; Huysmans, *Against Nature*, 186. See Paul Verlaine, "L'Ombre des arbres," in *Oeuvres poétiques complètes*, ed. Y.-G. Le Dantec and Jacques Borel, Bibliothèque de la Pléiade (Paris: Gallimard, 1962), 196.

48. Letter VII, see https://www.bacfrancais.com/commentaire/convaincre/cyrano-lettres-diverses-lettre-7 (accessed July 11, 2025).

49. Albert Thibaudet, *La Poésie de Stéphane Mallarmé* (Paris: Éditions de la nouvelle revue français, 1911); Stéphane Mallarmé, *Poésies*, 3rd ed. (Paris: Éditions de la nouvelle revue français, 1913). See also Paolo Dal Mollin and Jean-Louis Leleu, "Comment composait Debussy: les leçons d'un carnet de travail (à propos de *Soupir* et d'*Éventail*," *Cahiers Debussy* 35 (2011): 9–82.

50. Roger Pearson, *Unfolding Mallarmé: The Development of Poetic Art* (Oxford: Clarendon, 1996), 45.

51. Avo Somer, "Chromatic Third-Relations and Tonal Structure in the Songs of Debussy," *Music Theory Spectrum* 17, no. 2 (1995): 215–41; Marie Rolf, "Semantic and Structural Issues in Debussy's Mallarmé Songs," *Debussy Studies*, ed. Richard Langham Smith (Cambridge: Cambridge University Press, 1997), 179–200; Marianne Wheeldon, "Debussy's 'Soupir': An Experiment in Permutational Analysis," *Perspectives of New Music* 38, no. 2 (2000): 134–60; Julian Johnson, "Vertige!: Debussy, Mallarmé, and the Edge of Language," in *Debussy's Resonance*, ed. François de Médicis and Steven Huebner (Rochester, NY: University of Rochester Press, 2018), 366–92.

52. See Debussy's letter to Jacques Durand (July 8, 1910), *Correspondance*, 1299; Eric Frederick Jensen, *Debussy* (Oxford: Oxford University Press, 2014), 105.

53. Debussy, *Correspondance*, 1836; Stephen Walsh, *Debussy: A Painter in Sound* (London: Faber and Faber, 2014), 282.

54. Debussy, *Correspondance*, 1836; Walsh, *Painter in Sound*, 282.

55. For a history of tarot cards and Debussy's interest in them, see Rachel Pollack, *Seventy-Eight Degrees of Wisdom: A Tarot Journey to Self-Awareness*, 40th Anniversary ed. (Newburyport, MA: Red Wheel/Weiser, 2020); and Orledge, *Debussy and the Theatre*, 124–27. Debussy was especially attracted to Patricia Colman Smith's work, including her illustrations for the Rider-Waite tarot deck (1909), see Anonymous, "Pictures in Music," *The Strand Magazine* Vol. 35, No. 210 (July 1908), 648–52 and M. Irwin Macdonald, "The Fairy Faith and Pictured Music," *The Craftsman* XXIII October 1912, 20–34.

12

Debussy's Cinematic Obsessions

Symbolist artists were clearly interested in arabesques, moresques, and grotesques for a wide array of technical as well as nontechnical reasons: the concepts helped them understand the role of ornamentation in art and offered a way to explain how art functioned in the world around them. That world—the streets of the modern metropolis—was in a constant state of flux, none more so than Paris. Following a grand plan devised by Georges-Eugène Haussmann, the French capital underwent a dramatic transformation during the period of the Second Empire (1852–70): many of the city's old neighborhoods were replaced by new buildings and wide boulevards. Whatever its benefits, gentrification involved demolishing large swathes of the city, displacing countless working-class inhabitants, and encouraging the rise of suburbia.[1] Baudelaire, who witnessed much of the destruction, described his dismay in the celebrated poem "Le Cygne" (*Les Fleurs du mal*).

> Paris change! mais rien dans ma mélancolie
> N'a bougé! palais neufs, échafaudages, blocs,
> Vieux faubourgs, tout pour moi devient allégorie
> Et mes chers souvenirs sont plus lourds que des rocs.[2]

Here and elsewhere, he equated contemporary urban life with upheaval, loss, and decay and modernity with "the ephemeral, the fugitive, the contingent."[3] These ideas were embodied in the flâneurs, those nameless residents who crowded the city's streets, cafés, stores, arcades, parks, museums, art galleries, and so on. Suffering from sensory overload, flâneurs responded by insulating themselves emotionally from other inhabitants and by indulging in narcissistic acts of voyeurism. The need to be both close and distant often gave rise to feelings of melancholia and ennui and a craving for distractions, for fleeting moments of liberation in the eternal continuum, brief releases from their dull and humdrum lives.

Baudelaire's fascination with the arabesque, moresque, and grotesque and with the ephemeral, fugitive, and contingent also impacted his response to the tensions that he perceived between traditional forms of art such as poetry, plays, novels, painting, sculpture, opera, and ballet and modern forms such as the newspaper, the prose poem, the short story, photography, toys, vaudeville, and vernacular dances. That response was complex, to say the least. Although Baudelaire is widely regarded as an advocate for "pure art" and an opponent to new media technology, Marit Grøtta has found little hard evidence to support this view.[4] On the contrary, she claims that his "fury" against new media was caused by "the vulgarity inspired by [them]" and reflected a deep fascination with "everything that was new."[5] Grøtta has gone further to suggest that Baudelaire is actually the father of media studies and his figure of the flâneur was the "precursor to twentieth-century conceptions of virtual and mediated vision."[6] She supports her case by pointing to Baudelaire's interest in "scientific toys," such as kaleidoscopes and phénakistiscopes, that make static images appear to move. According to her, these "precinematic" devices confirm his belief that visual perceptions are vulnerable to manipulation and recoding, effects that were in some ways analogous to the distorted images produced by scrying mirrors and Claude glass.[7]

Since, as noted in chapter 9, Debussy adored early films, this chapter explores the idea that Baudelaire's precinematic sensibilities influenced Debussy's views about music and the cinema.[8] The discussion unfolds in three phases. First, it returns to Baudelaire's poem "Le Thyrse" and the idea that arabesques stir the emotions by filling the mind with images and by conveying a sense of movement. Next, it considers the ways in which arabesques appear in different media, taking note of Baudelaire's concept of *correspondances* and the problems of translating experiences from one medium to another. The discussion ends with a brief review of Baudelaire's interest in scientific toys and other precinematic devices. Next, the second phase examines what Debussy might have meant when he referred to music as cinematic. Having discussed some of the ways in which this description has so far been interpreted by the scholarly community, the focus shifts to the cinematic features of act 4, scene 4 of *Pelléas et Mélisande* and the climax of Poe's "The Fall of the House of Usher." The third phase then shows how the cinematic qualities of act 4, scene 4 of *Pelléas et Mélisande* resurface in many Hollywood film scores. In particular, it shows how Debussy's opera was in the back of Bernard Herrmann's mind when he composed the score for Brian DePalma's classic Hitchcockian thriller *Obsession* (Columbia, 1976).

When considering Debussy's interest in music and the cinematic, one is immediately tempted to trace its origins back through his review of Ysaÿe's Good Friday concert (1901) to Baudelaire's prose poem "Le Thryse." The connections are clear enough: just as Debussy's review insists that arabesques can "stir the emotions" and "fill the imagination with images," so Baudelaire's text proposes that the straight line and the arabesque represent "intention and expression," with the latter dancing around the former in "silent admiration."[9] Baudelaire's description is notable because it highlights the capacity for arabesques to convey a sense of motion: "The harmony, [balance of the lines], eurythmy of movements appear to the dreamer as necessities, as duties not only in relation to all beings in creation but also to himself . . . and the dreamer finds that he is endowed with a marvelous aptitude for understanding the immortal, universal rhythm."[10] Elsewhere, Baudelaire compared his love of images with the expressive power of music: "To glorify the cult of images (my great, my single, my earliest passion). To glorify vagrancy and what might be called Bohemianism, the cult of multiplied sensation, as expressed by music. Refer to Liszt here."[11]

Baudelaire's reference to Liszt is particularly telling in this regard because it recalls his celebrated essay "Richard Wagner et *Tannhäuser* à Paris," in which he quoted the first and second quatrains of his poem "Correspondances" from *Les Fleurs du mal* (1857). Indeed, the final line of the second quatrain of "Correspondances" clearly points to the idea that poetry can invoke perfumes, colors, and sounds in the mind of the reader.[12] Baudelaire elaborated this thought as follows: "True music evokes analogous ideas in different brains. However it would be by no means absurd at this point to argue *a priori*; for what would be truly surprising would be to find that sound *could not* suggest colour, that colours *could not* evoke the idea of a melody, and that sound and colour were *unsuitable* for the translation of ideas, seeing that things have always found their expression through a system of reciprocal analogy ever since the day when God uttered the world like a complex and indivisible statement."[13]

> La Nature est un temple où de vivants piliers
> Laissent parfois sortir de confuses paroles;
> L'homme y passe à travers des forêts de symboles
> Qui l'observent avec des regards familiers.
>
> Comme en longs échos qui de loin se confondent
> Dans une ténébreuse et profonde unité,
> Vaste comme la nuit et comme la clarté,
> Les parfums, les couleurs et les sons se répondent.
>
> Il est des parfums frais comme des chairs d'enfants,
> Doux comme les hautbois, verts comme les prairies,
> —Et d'autres, corrompus, riches et triomphants,
>
> Ayant l'expansion des choses infinies,
> Comme l'ambre, le musc, le benjoin et l'encens,
> Qui chantent les transports de l'esprit et des sens.

To illustrate what he had in mind, Baudelaire compared three different translations of the Prelude to Wagner's *Lohengrin*: one presented by Wagner in the program notes for performances at the Théâtre Italien on January 25 and February 1 and 8, 1860; one offered by Franz Liszt in his book *Lohengrin et Tannhäuser de Richard Wagner* (1851); and one written by the poet himself after hearing the piece in 1860. The differences are startling.

> Wagner prescribes *a host of angels bringing a holy vessel*; Liszt sees *a monument of miraculous beauty*, re-flected in a vaporous mirage. My own reverie is much less adorned with material objects; it is vaguer and more abstract. But the important thing here is to concentrate on the resemblances. Even if they had been few, they would still constitute a sufficient proof; fortunately however they are numerous and striking to excess. In all three interpretations we find a sensation of *spiritual and physical bliss*; of *isolation*; of the contemplation of *something infinitely great and infinitely beautiful*; of an *intensity of light* which rejoices *the eyes and the soul until they swoon*; and finally a sensation of *space reaching to the furthest conceivable limits*.[14]

Baudelaire added, "No musician excels as Wagner does in *painting* space and depth, both material and spiritual. . . . He possesses the art of translating, by means of the subtlest shades, all that is excessive, immense and ambitious in spiritual and natural man. One seems sometimes, when listening to this fiery and peremptory music, to recapture the dizzy perceptions of an opium-dream, painted upon a backcloth of darkness."[15]

Although Baudelaire said nothing per se about moving images, he did refer to certain "scientific toys" that create the illusion of motion from a succession of static images.[16] One such toy is the phenakistoscope, fantascope, or stroboscope.[17] Invented independently by Joseph Plateau and Simon von Stampfer in 1832, phénakistiscopes were marketed throughout Europe starting in 1833. They consisted of a sequential string of images placed at regular intervals around a cardboard disc, with small rectangular apertures at the disc's rim. When the disc is spun, the images appear to move when they are viewed in a mirror. Baudelaire offered a particularly detailed description of these devices in his essay "Morale du joujou."[18] Though he complained about their high cost, Baudelaire found them utterly delightful: "You can watch twenty dancing figures reflected in the glass—all exactly the same and executing the same movements with a fantastic precision. Each little figure has availed himself to the nineteen others."[19] Like Poe before him, Baudelaire was also fascinated by magic lantern shows, which had become all the rage in eighteenth- and nineteenth-century Europe.[20] Enterprising entrepreneurs like Paul Philidor and Étienne-Gaspard Robert (a.k.a. Robertson) famously produced so-called phantasmagoria on mysterious or supernatural themes.[21] As the nineteenth century wore on, manufacturers produced ever more complex projectors that could handle multiple slides at the same time. Projectionists responded in several ways. To begin with, they began to arrange their slides so that particular groups would end with a close-up: this approach to sequencing images became a standard strategy for creating movie montages. Projectionists also used an array of transitional effects, such as dissolves, fades, and cuts, to move from one slide to the next. They also juxtaposed images shot from different angles and even superimposed or matted images. As Emmanuelle Toulet notes, the same effects were regularly employed by early filmmakers and still form the basis of modern film editing.[22]

But to what extent did Baudelaire's claims about the connections between images and sounds shape Debussy's thoughts about the connections between music and cinema? In his seminal paper, "Debussy and the Art of the Cinema," Richard Langham Smith suggests that Baudelaire's influence was in fact very strong.[23] Indeed, just as Baudelaire claimed that his greatest and earliest passion was "to glorify the cult of images," so Debussy admitted that he loved images "almost as much as music."[24] Smith, for his part, marshals a wide array of evidence to support his views. For one thing, he describes just how often Debussy referred to the work of visual artists (e.g., Turner, Rossetti, Velázquez, Watteau, Redon, Moreau, Whistler, and Hokusai) and art critics (e.g., Baudelaire, Mourey, Thadée Natanson) in his letters and published essays. For another, he points to Debussy's penchant for describing music using visual and painterly metaphors. The following remarks by Debussy to his stepson Raoul Bardac from February 24, 1906, are typical in this regard: "Collect impressions. Don't be in a hurry to write them down. Because that's something music can do better than painting: it can centralize variations of color and light within a single picture—a truth generally ignored, obvious as it is. . . . You must even forget music entirely from time to time."[25] And Smith pays particular attention to Debussy's love of shadow plays, especially those produced at the Chat Noir in the 1880s and 1890s.

More generally, Smith has identified three conditions that allow for music to function cinematically. First, music can conjure up specific environments and moods simply through its use of sounds. This particular idea is one that Debussy spelled out in an essay published in *Gils Blas* on January 26, 1903: "For it is music alone that has the power to evoke imaginary scenes at will, to conjure up the intangible world of fantasies secretly shrouded within the mysterious poetry of the night, the thousand indistinguishable noises made by moonbeams caressing the leaves."[26] Pierre Lalo echoed these sentiments in a short essay, "Claude Debussy et l'Universe" (1932): "He is not an author who speaks to an audience, he is a spirit who evokes for himself the images with which he has been charmed. Brief and fleeting images in their ideal accuracy: they appear and pass; they have said everything, do not repent and do not insist. And to paint these images, the simplest and most delicate means; never any accumulation, complication or noise; incomparable sobriety and choice; it is made with nothing, as they say, and nothing is missing."[27]

Second, music can paint sonic portraits of individual characters. Above all, Debussy was impressed by Wagner's skills at characterization: "Nothing in the music of Wagner is more beautiful than the Prelude to act 3 of *Parsifal*, and the 'Good Friday Spell.' But Wagner's real insight into humanity comes out in the way he depicts several characters in this play."[28] In Debussy's opinion, the finest of them is Klingsor: "his hateful malice is wonderful! He knows what men are really like, and weighs up the strength of their vows to chastity on his dreadful scales. One could easily argue that this cunning magician and old offender is not only the one 'human' character but also the only 'moral' one in this play, in which many wrong-headed moralistic and religious ideas are propounded."[29]

Third, music can enchain successions of unrelated ideas, thereby allowing it to tell stories. Smith has cited a vivid example of this possibility in a letter to André Caplet after a rehearsal of *Iberia* on February 25, 1910: "You can't imagine how naturally the transition works between 'Parfums de la nuit' and 'Le Matin d'un jour de fête.' *It sounds as though it's improvised. (Ca n'a pas l'air d'être écrit).* The way it comes to life, with people and things waking up. . . . There's a man selling watermelons and urchins whistling. I see them clearly."[30] As shown in examples 12.1a–12.1b, Debussy created this effect by joining both movements together (the last measure of ex. 12.1a is marked "*enchaînez*") and by including a flashback to "Parfums de la nuit" after introducing the opening theme of "Le Matin d'un jour de fête" (see ex. 12.1b).[31] As Smith explains, "The film-like sequence of 'Ibéria' has strongly visual connotations: it moves from scene to scene, and within each movement it focuses on this idea, then that. Debussy is concerned with the logic of the senses, infinitely more complex than any notions of musical grammar, and a logic with which the cinema now had to grapple."[32] The piece is, in effect, a quintessential case of cinematic montage.

Smith's claim that Debussy created music that appears "film-like" through its "*enchaînement* of fresh ideas [or] *images*" is extremely suggestive; it not only resonates with Orledge's observation that Debussy toyed with the idea of creating a film version of *Le martyre de Saint Sébastien* but it also opens the door to analyzing Debussy's music using concepts borrowed from film theory.[33] This is precisely the strategy taken by Rebecca Leydon, who has tried to explain some of his late works in terms of familiar cinematic devices: "the dissolve, the juxtaposition of different camera angles, the direct cut, the close-up, as well as adjustments of film speed and direction, superimpositions and matted images, and double-exposure of the film."[34] Mark McFarland largely agrees with Leydon, claiming that Debussy's use of these devices was amplified by his contact with Igor Stravinsky: "The years in which Debussy was first exposed to the music of Stravinsky and began to realize the important role cinematic techniques could play in music (1911–1913) were also those in which he composed his second book of preludes for piano."[35] But others have been more skeptical. Scott Paulin, for example, has insisted that when Debussy discussed the possibility of "applying cinematic treatments to pure music" after watching *L'agonie de Byzance* on October 30, 1913, he "was actually riffing on d'Indy's notion of making films to be projected in concert."[36] Ian Pace has been equally cagey: having criticized Leydon's work as "far-fetched," he echoes Paulin's recommendation that "cinematic analogies should be used when they provide a specific form of illumination, not just as relatively exotic metaphors."[37]

And yet, though Paulin and Pace are rightly cautious about interpreting what Debussy meant by "applying cinematic treatments to pure music" and using concepts borrowed from film theory

Example 12.1 The transition between "Parfums de la nuit" and "Le Matin d'un jour de fête"

Example 12.1a "Parfums de la nuit"

to analyze music, there is still good reason to think of Debussy's music in cinematic terms. Those reasons stem in large part from his fascination with the arabesque and its power to convey images, movement, emotions, and even narratives. To riff on Smith, the concept of the arabesque provided Debussy with a means of enchaining successions of unrelated ideas, thereby allowing it to tell stories visually as well as musically. Or, to quote from Debussy's review of Ysaÿe's Good Friday performance, "Based on this conception of the ornamental, the music will impress the public as regularly as clockwork, and it will fill their imaginations with pictures."[38] Let us now

Example 12.1b "Le Matin d'un jour de fête"

see what Debussy may have had in mind by investigating the cinematic properties of act 4, scene 4 of *Pelléas et Mélisande*.

Few excerpts from *Pelléas et Mélisande* have attracted more attention than act 4, scene 4. And with good reason. Not only does this scene serve as the dramatic core of the entire opera—namely, the moment when Golaud murders Pelléas, wounds Mélisande, and destroys himself—but it was also the first one that Debussy tried to set musically. Indeed, as mentioned in chapter 8, he mapped out the first version in the summer of 1893.[39] At first, Debussy made considerable progress and

Example 12.2 The declaration of love in Debussy's *Pelléas et Mélisande*, act 4, scene 4, mm. 850–57

even announced on September 3, 1893, that he was ready to try out the scene on his old friend Ernest Chausson.[40] But a month later, on October 2, he was more circumspect: "I was premature in crying 'success!' over *Pelléas et Mélisande*. After a sleepless night (the bringer of truth?) I had to admit it wouldn't do at all. It was like a duet by Mr So-and-so, or nobody in particular, and worst of all the ghost of old Klingsor, alias R. Wagner, kept appearing in the corner of a bar, so I've torn the whole thing up."[41] In an effort to make his material sound less Wagnerian and "give the emotion of a phrase its full value," Debussy found himself using a means of expression seldom found in Wagner's work: silence.[42] He may have been inspired to do so from reading Poe's short story "Silence—A Fable" or from remembering the Sino-Japanese concept of "Ma," or negative space. Example 12.2 shows how, in contrast to the famous love duet in act 2 of *Tristan und Isolde*, Pelléas and Mélisande declare their love for each other in act 4, scene 4 without any orchestral accompaniment. But Debussy didn't exorcise the ghost of old Klingsor altogether: example 12.3 shows that he not only deliberately accompanied Mélisande's line "Je suis triste" with a Tristan chord in the orchestra (see ex. 12.3a–12.3b) but also ended the scene with a veiled allusion to the

Example 12.3 Allusions to Wagner's *Tristan und Isolde* in Debussy's *Pelléas et Mélisande*

Example 12.3a Wagner, Prelude, act 1, mm. 1–3

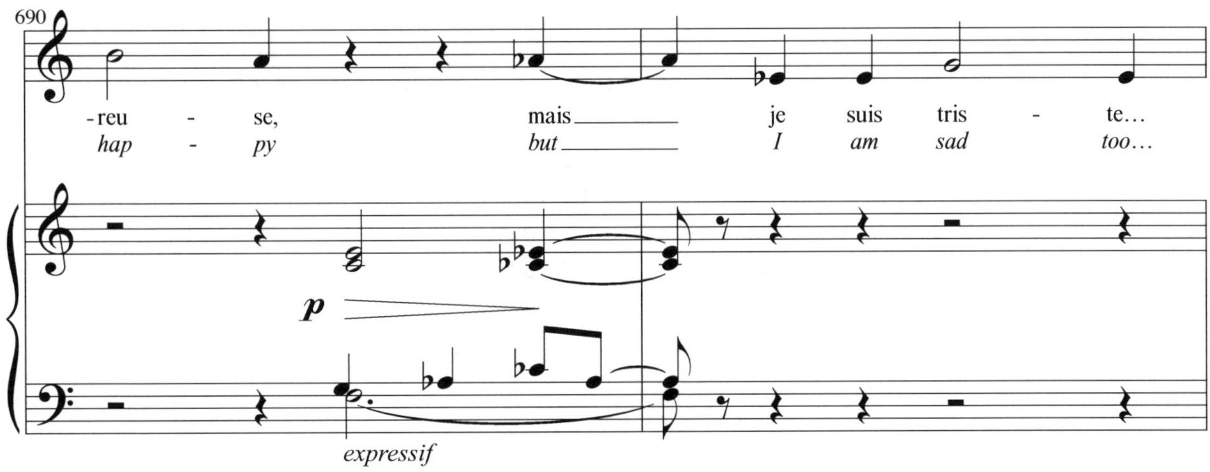

Example 12.3b Debussy, act 4, scene 4, mm. 690–91

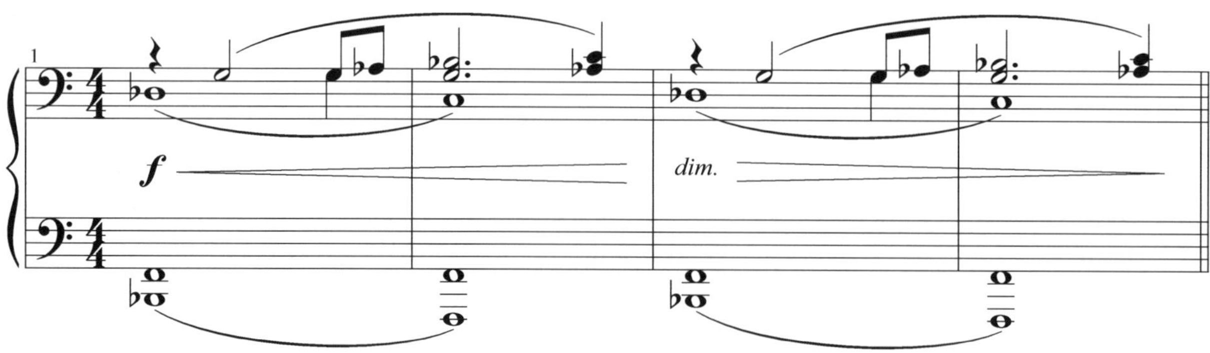

Example 12.3c Wagner, "Tristan's Delirium," from *Tristan und Isolde*, act 3, mm. 1–4

Example 12.3d Debussy, Pelléas's death, *Pelléas et Mélisande*, act 4, scene 4, mm. 850–54

opening measures of act 3 of *Tristan und Isolde*, just before Tristan dies from wounds inflicted by King Marke at the end of act 2 (see ex. 12.3c–12.3d).

Besides hiding the influence of Wagner as much as possible, Debussy faced another daunting task: he had to create a sense of suspense while Golaud stalks Pelléas and Mélisande at night outside the castle and a sense of terror when he murders him, wounds her, and attempts to commit suicide. The distinction between suspense and terror is, of course, central to gothic literature and drama and was described at length by Alfred Hitchcock, the great master of the macabre. According to him, suspense requires forewarning and attains a peak in crescendo fashion, whereas terror requires surprise and comes suddenly like a bolt of lightning.[43] To illustrate the distinction, Hitchcock described the different effects of buzz bombs and V-2 rockets on Londoners during WWII: "The buzz bomb made a noise like an outboard motor, and its chugging in the air above served notice of its impending arrival. When the motor stopped, the bomb was beginning its descent and would shortly explode. The moments between the time the motor was first heard and the final explosion were moments of *suspense*. The V-2, on the other hand, was noiseless until the moment of its explosion. Anyone who heard a V-2 explode, and lived, had experienced *terror*."[44]

In another essay entitled "Why I Am Afraid of the Dark," Hitchcock admitted that his understanding of the distinction between suspense and terror stemmed in large part from reading Poe's *Tales of the Grotesque and Arabesque*.[45] Consider, for a moment, "The Fall of the House of

Usher." As mentioned in chapter 1, Poe's story ends one stormy night when Lady Madeline escapes premature burial, kills Roderick, and precipitates the destruction of their ancestral home. Poe casts the scene as a mise en abyme in which he correlates the sounds of Lady Madeline slowly clawing her way to freedom with sounds from the story of Ethelred and the dragon as read aloud by the friend. To create suspense, however, Poe arranged the scene cyclically in a string of elaborate arabesques, each one delaying the outcome and making the drama more intense. As shown in table 12.1, the first arabesque correlates the sound of Lady Madeline splitting open her coffin with that of Ethelred smashing down the hermit's door; the second arabesque with the sound of the iron door grating against the floor with that of Ethelred fighting the dragon; and the third arabesque the sound of Lady Madeline struggling along the copper-lined corridor with that of Ethelred dropping the shield. The three arabesques take up several pages and include about thirteen hundred words. To create terror, however, Poe ends his story with an incredible bang. In about three hundred words, he describes how Lady Madeline appears dressed in white like the Angel of Death, how she collapses on and kills her twin brother (just as he had anticipated), how there is a flash of "wild light," and how the House of Usher is engulfed by the dark lake to a long, tumultuous sound resembling the cries of a thousand voices.

Table 12.2 shows how, in typical Hitchcockian fashion, the climax of act 4, scene 4 of *Pelléas et Mélisande* exhibits a similar balance between suspense and terror. To create suspense, Maeterlinck follows the same plan Poe had used for the climax of "The Fall of the House of Usher" and

Table 12.1. Cyclic structure of climax to *The Fall of the House of Usher*

Arabesque 1

| Narrator reads story. | Mentions sound of Ethelred smashing door | Hears sound of Madeline splitting coffin |

Arabesque 2

| Narrator reads story. | Mentions sound of Ethelred slaying dragon | Hears sound of Madeline opening iron door |

Arabesque 3

| Narrator reads story. | Mentions sound of Ethelred dropping shield | Hears sound of Madeline crossing copper archway |

Climax

Madeline returns from the grave like the Angel of Death and collapses on Roderick, and the house collapses into the tarn.

Table 12.2. Cycles and motives at the climax of *Pelléas et Mélisande*, act 4, scene 4

Arabesque 1

| Sound of gate | Pelléas accepts fate. | Pelléas/Mélisande swoon. |

Arabesque 2

| Sound of Golaud | Pelléas ignores warning. | Their shadows entwine. |

Arabesque 3

| Sound of Golaud | Pelléas is in denial. | Pelléas/Mélisande embrace. |

Climax

| Golaud stabs Pelléas | Mélisande flees into forest. | Pelléas dies. |

arranged the events cyclically around certain sounds.[46] The first cycle starts abruptly when Pelléas hears the castle gates closing. Mélisande realizes that they will be discovered. Eventually, Pelléas accepts his fate and embraces her. But Mélisande suddenly interrupts him at the start of the second cycle when she hears someone behind them. Pelléas ignores her as their shadows entwine. Mélisande interrupts once more at the start of the third cycle when she hears Golaud stalking them. Pelléas doesn't care and embraces her yet again. This time, however, Golaud suddenly rushes forward to slash Pelléas. His response is visceral: whereas cycles 1–3 crescendo slowly across nearly four hundred words of text, the final atrocities occur at lightning speed in just forty-four!

For his part, Debussy created a sense of suspense by highlighting the three-part structure of Maeterlinck's libretto and a sense of terror by making the final denouement as sudden and terrifying as possible. As shown in example 12.4, his setting is built around repetitions of a few short motivic cells, most of which have been present since the beginning of the opera.[47] Unlike Wagner's heroic leitmotivs, Déirdre Donnellon rightly notes that Debussy's motives are "often little more than brief rhythmic cells or oscillating intervals that hint at, rather than declare, the emotions and events depicted onstage."[48] Perhaps the most important cell is Golaud's motive: presented in its original form when the castle gates close (see ex. 12.4a), it mainly appears in a rhythmic diminution associated with his revenge (see ex. 12.4b). The next most important cells are a descending arpeggio (see ex. 12.4c) and a motive associated with Pelléas's ecstasy (see ex. 12.4d). Several other cells appear near the end of the scene: one associated with Golaud's fate (see ex. 12.4e); one with Mélisande's (see ex. 12.4f); and another with Pelléas's death (see ex. 12.4g). The latter is especially noteworthy because, as mentioned earlier, it recalls the tragic opening of

Example 12.4 Motives used at the climax of *Pelléas et Mélisande*, act 4, scene 4

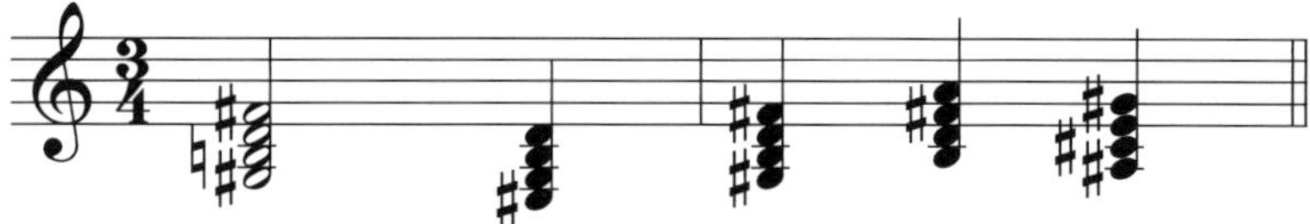

Example 12.4a Golaud/Destiny

Example 12.4b Revenge

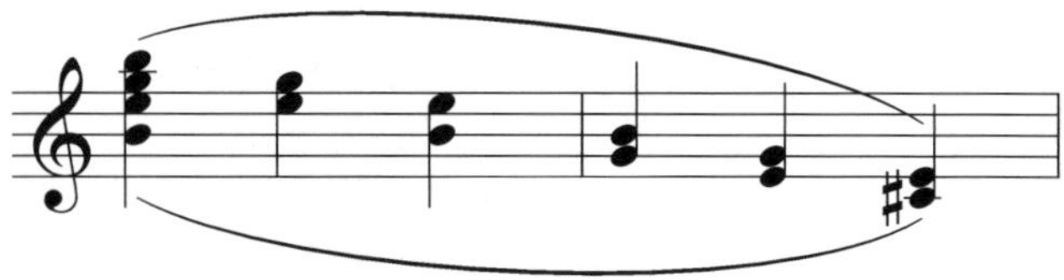

Example 12.4c Arpeggio

Example 12.4d Ecstasy

Example 12.4e Fate

Example 12.4f Mélisande

Example 12.4g Pelléas's death

Table 12.3. Cycles and motives at the climax of *Pelléas et Mélisande*, act 4, scene 4

Arabesque 1		
Sound of gate	Pelléas accepts fate.	Pelléas/Mélisande swoon.
Revenge	Arpeggio	Ecstasy
Arabesque 2		
Sound of Golaud	Pelléas ignores warning.	Their shadows entwine.
Revenge	Arpeggio	Ecstasy
Arabesque 3		
Sound of Golaud	Pelléas is in denial.	Pelléas/Mélisande embrace.
Revenge	Arpeggio	Ecstasy
[Fate, Ecstasy]	[Mélisande]	
Climax		
Golaud stabs Pelléas	Mélisande flees into forest.	Pelléas dies.
Fate	Revenge	Death/Tristan's Delirium

act 3 of *Tristan und Isolde* and because the first arabesque is preceded by a reminiscence of the Tristan chord to accompany Mélisande's comment "Je suis triste."

To underscore the significance of the motives shown in example 12.4, table 12.3 shows how they articulate the cyclic structure of the passage as a whole.[49] Golaud's revenge motive appears at or near the beginning of each constituent arabesque where it conveys Mélisande's concern that they are being hunted. When Pelléas brushes those concerns aside, the descending arpeggio appears in the high register. Each cycle then culminates with statements of the ecstasy motive: in the first and second, they help to establish a motion to C major; in the third, they set up Pelléas's murder by Golaud and his betrayal by Mélisande. Golaud's sudden appearance is marked by the fate motive and Mélisande's flight with the revenge motive. The scene culminates with a statement of Pelléas's death motive at the final plagal cadence in F minor. Remarkably, the proportions of Debussy's score match those of Maeterlinck's libretto to perfection: cycles 1–3, which include nearly 400 words of text, occupy about 130 measures (mm. 692–826) and the outcome, which includes just 44 words, encompasses only 27 measures (mm. 826–53).

Besides repeating prominent motives, Debussy also recycled certain distinctive voice-leading models. These models provided him not only with a means for creating suspense and tension in the music but also, through their parallel movement and ornamental character, to embody the principles of the arabesque as he described them in his review of Ysaÿe's Good Friday concert in 1901. The first appears at the start of cycle 1 and is shown in example 12.5 (top system). It consists of long, linear progressions that ascend in parallel thirds and/or sixths; these patterns are reminiscent of the one in mm. 6–16 of the *Première Arabesque* and sketched in example 2.12. Cycle 1 includes two such progressions: the first ascends from F/A♭ to B/D, whereas the second ascends from E/G♯ to E/G. Debussy also reworked the first model midway through cycle 2, when Pelléas sees his shadow entwined with Mélisande's. As shown in example 12.5 (second system), the linear progressions rise first over an F triad and then over whole tone chords over A♭. More significantly still, Debussy composed out the first model yet again in cycle 3 to set up Pelléas and Mélisande's final embrace. This greatly enlarged version of the model is shown in example 12.5 (third system)

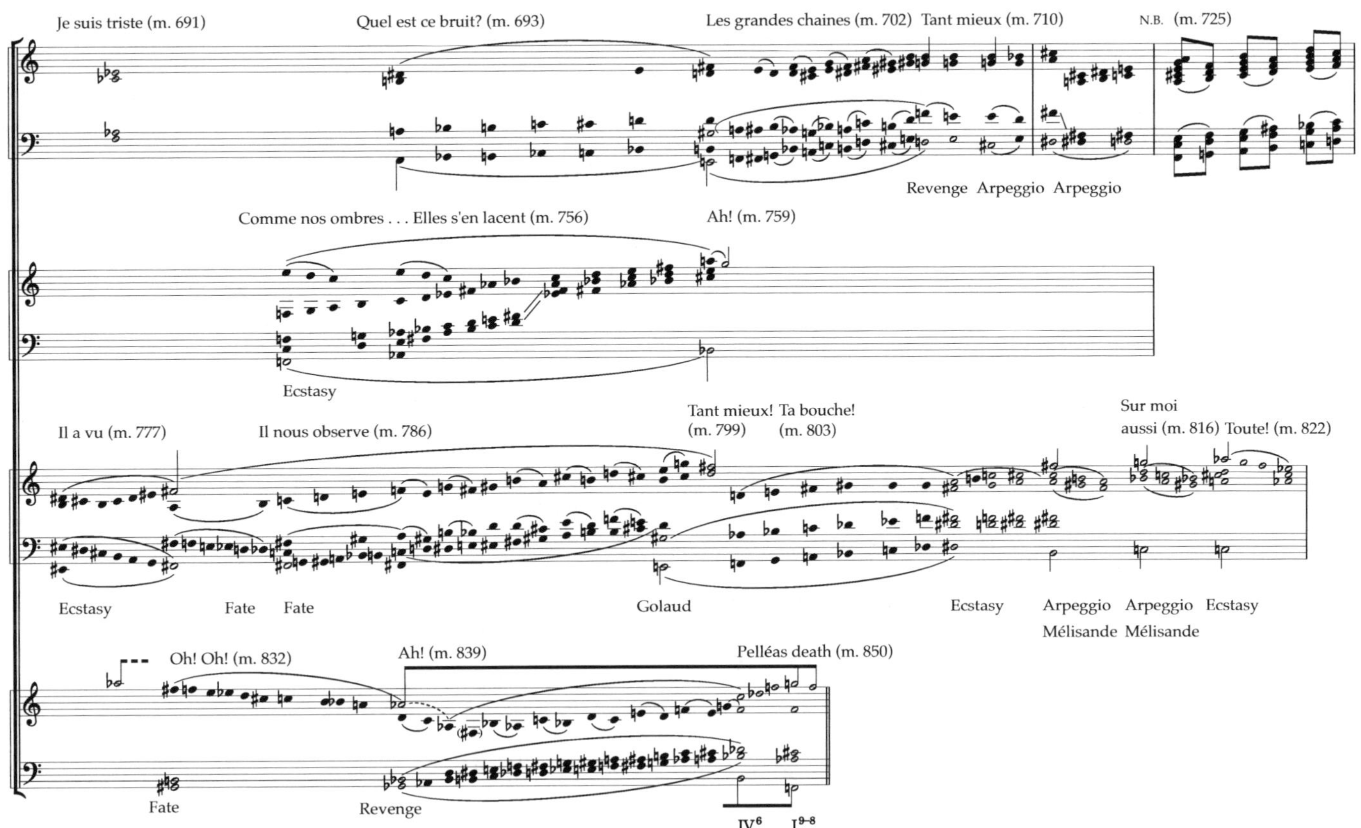

Example 12.5 Voice-leading models in the climax of *Pelléas et Mélisande*, act 4, scene 4

and, like cycle I, has two successive statements of the model. Example 12.5 (bottom system) shows the final portion of the scene when Golaud murders Pelléas and wounds Mélisande.

Whereas the first model creates suspense by ascending from one register to another and by being functionally unstable and tonally ambiguous, the other models do so by delaying the climax of the section. The second model appears near the end of cycle 1, when Pelléas listens to the sound of his own heartbeat. As shown in example 12.6 (top system), it consists of a stepwise motion in the bass from C through D, E, and F to F♯. Examples 12.6 (middle system) and 12.6 (bottom system) then show how Debussy recalls the same pattern at the start of cycles 2 and 3 when Mélisande thinks she hears Golaud creeping up. To round off cycles 1 and 2, Debussy introduces a third model (see ex. 12.7). Example 12.7 (top system) shows how, in cycle 1, this model articulates the local tonic C before rising melodically from G through A to A♯/B♭. Examples 12.7 (middle system) and 12.7 (bottom system) show the same model returns twice in cycle 2 when Pelléas once again cries out in ecstasy. Remarkably, Debussy alluded to the first model in the final moments of act 4, scene 4 (see ex. 12.5 [bottom]). Whereas the first model is originally associated with an ascending line in the bass that moves up from E♯ or F♯, Debussy transformed this gesture into a descending line in the upper register when Mélisande betrays Pelléas and flees into the forest. Not only does this descending line recall similar patterns in cycle 3, but it also releases the enormous sense of tension that has been accumulating across the cycle as a whole. To

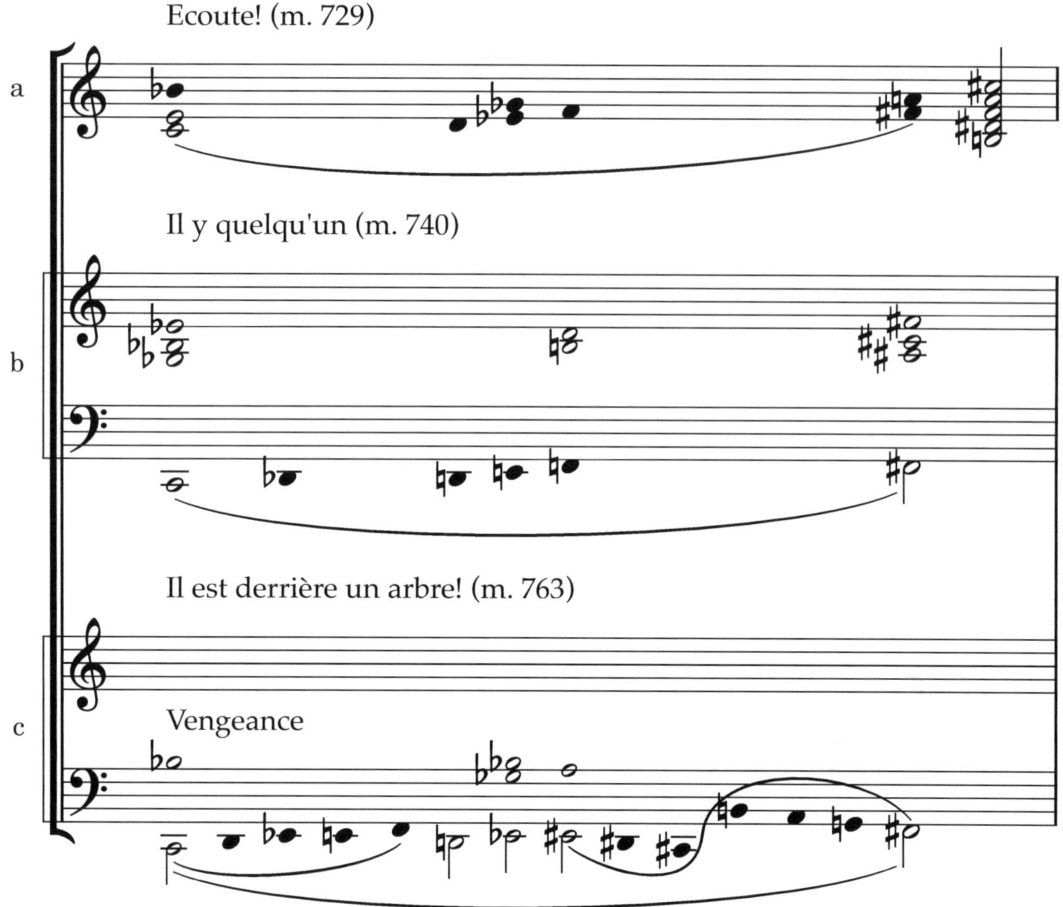

Example 12.6 Voice-leading models in the climax of *Pelléas et Mélisande*, act 4, scene 4

make Pelléas's death seem all the more frightening, Debussy sets up the terrible statement of his death motive with a final version of the first model that rises from G♭/B♭ and culminates in the heart-wrenching final cadence.

Given the gothic nature of Maeterlinck's libretto and the arabesque/grotesque qualities of Debussy's music, it is hardly surprising that act 4, scene 4 attracted the attention of one of Hollywood's most distinguished film composers: Bernard Herrmann (1911–75). Trained in music at NYU and Juilliard, Herrmann joined CBS in 1934 as a staff conductor; over the next few years, he not only championed unfamiliar works, especially by contemporary composers, but also began to compose music for radio shows. His wife, Lucille Fletcher, was a noted radio scriptwriter and, partly through her, he met Orson Welles and began to arrange scores for his celebrated radio shows. He wrote his first film score for Welles in 1941: *Citizen Kane*. Though Herrmann had an encyclopedic knowledge of classical music, he had a special affinity for the works of Debussy and included some on his album *The Impressionists: Satie, Debussy, Ravel, Fauré, Honegger* (Decca, 1970).[50] His knowledge of Debussy's music was extensive indeed. As he made clear in a talk given in Rochester, New York, in 1973, Herrmann was especially taken by the cinematic and melodramatic qualities of *Pelléas et Mélisande*, qualities that are readily apparent in act 4, scene 4.

Example 12.7 Voice-leading models in the climax of *Pelléas et Mélisande*, act 4, scene 4

[In] the early part of the 20th century Claude Debussy became fascinated by the concept of melodrama. He faced the same problem as the Greeks, but he, of course, created the form of his kind of vocal music—as evidenced in "Pelleas"—which is practically spoken drama with music. Debussy's dream was to write pure melodram[a], and he lived long enough to see some early examples of the cinema! He saw early experiments in the cinema in which an orchestra sat behind the screen and played specially composed music. He felt that this was the art of the future. Debussy said that the cinema would allow the perfect creation of poetry, vision, and dreams.[51]

He added, "If Debussy had lived long enough into the era of the sound film, who knows what he would have created. Who knows what we've lost."

Herrmann was surely thinking of Debussy two years later when he completed one of his last scores, for Brian de Palma's psychological thriller *Obsession*. Just as de Palma's film is a tribute to Hitchcock's famous suspense movie *Vertigo* (1958), so Herrmann's score is an homage to the suspenseful music of Debussy. Christopher Palmer, for example, finds signs of Debussy's influence in Herrmann's orchestration, especially his treatment of the harp and wordless women's chorus and in his use of the waltz, arguably Debussy's favorite dance.[52] Herrmann had in fact recorded an orchestrated version of Debussy's short waltz *La Plus que lent* on his aforementioned album *The Impressionists*. Meanwhile, William Wrobel claims that Herrmann was also inspired by Debussy's

Table 12.4. Basic layout of the first kidnapping scene, *Obsession*

Time	Action	Music
6:40	Michael Courtland is in his room preparing for bed.	Cell 1 (mm. 1–8)
6:54	His wife, Elizabeth, appears at the bedroom door.	
7:08	She enters the room.	Cell 2 (mm. 9–20)
7:16	They gaze at each other.	
7:24	They come together.	
7:30	They embrace.	Cell 3 (mm. 21–31)
7:40	They kiss.	
7:53	Michael reveals that he is holding a book.	Cell 4 (mm. 32–38)
7:56	They hear cries from their daughter, Amy.	
7:58	Elizabeth goes to Amy's bedroom.	
8:06	She sees a kidnapper pointing a gun at Amy.	Cell 5
8:10	Elizabeth is immediately restrained by another kidnapper.	
8:16	Michael follows.	
8:24	He opens the door.	Cell 6
8:25	The room is empty and a lamp is turned over.	Whole-tone
8:34	Michael spots something taped to the bedpost and walks over.	Half-diminished
8:40	He reads the ransom note.	Cell 7
8:54	Shot of kidnapper's house.	

use of half diminished sonorities and his "drive to use sonorous chords and colorful instruments to create *atmosphere* or generalized mood."[53]

For convenience, table 12.4 charts the basic layout of the film's first kidnapping scene. The scene features three main characters: Michael Courtland (played by Cliff Robertson), a New Orleans businessman who has just hosted a party for his wife, Elizabeth (played by Geneviève Bujold). As Michael prepares for bed, Elizabeth appears and embraces him. But when they hear cries from their daughter, Amy (played by Wanda Blackman), Elizabeth rushes to her aid. She sees a kidnapper threatening Amy at gunpoint but is immediately overpowered by another intruder. By the time Michael arrives in the room, his daughter, his wife, and the intruders are nowhere to be seen. He figures out what has happened from reading a ransom note that is taped to the bedpost.

Table 12.4 also shows how Herrmann marked each phase in the drama with its own musical cell: these cells not only mirror the immediate feelings of the characters but also capture the scene's overall change in mood from ecstasy to horror to despair. Cells 1–3 convey Michael and Elizabeth's love by means of short motives supported by lush half-diminished sevenths or extended dominant harmonies.[54] These sentiments are reinforced in cell 4 with the stepwise motive B–A–G–F♯–G–A.[55] Cell 5 conveys the terror of the kidnapping through whole-tone chords and threatening jabs on the French horns.[56] As Michael enters the room, cell 6 presents ominous whole-tone harmonies. Cell 7 captures the sense of despair he feels reading the ransom note: Herrmann recalls a two-note motive from the film's opening.[57]

Significantly, Debussy used similar strategies in act 4, scene 4 of *Pelléas et Mélisande*. To convey Pelléas's sense of desire, Debussy added the material given in example 12.8a: this music contains the same half-diminished seventh chord C–E♭–G♭–B♭ as Herrmann's cell 2. In example 12.8b, Debussy accompanied Pelléas and Mélisande's embrace with extended dominant harmonies akin to those used in Herrmann's cell 3. Example 12.8c shows how, like Herrmann's cell 4, it leads to a stepwise motive B–A–G–F♯–G–A for the moment of ecstasy. When Golaud murders Pelléas and wounds Mélisande, Debussy included string tremolos and horn jabs, just like Herrmann's cell 5 (see ex. 12.8d). The ensuing whole-tone chords are vintage Debussy. And the ominous two-note motive from Herrmann's cell 7 resembles an analogous gesture from the finale of *La Mer* (see ex. 12.8e). Using the same modus operandi as Herrmann, Debussy used the cells to convey the moment-to-moment changes in mood from ecstasy to horror to despair.

Besides conveying Michael's deep love for Elizabeth and Amy, and his shock at realizing that they have been wrenched from him, Herrmann's decision to model the kidnapping scene of *Obsession* on act 4, scene 4 of *Pelléas et Mélisande* has wider dramatic implications. To understand what they might be, it is helpful to understand how the film subsequently unfolds. Having read the ransom note, Michael contacts the police to negotiate with the kidnappers. But things go seriously wrong; there is a car chase, an enormous explosion, and the death of the kidnappers and victims. The film then jumps forward sixteen years. Michael meets Sandra in the same Florentine church where he had originally met his first wife.[58] Sandra is Elizabeth's double; he falls in love

Example 12.8 Allusions to Debussy's *Pelléas et Mélisande*, act 4, scene 4 and *La Mer*, mvt. 3 in Herrmann's *Obsession*, "Kidnap Scene"

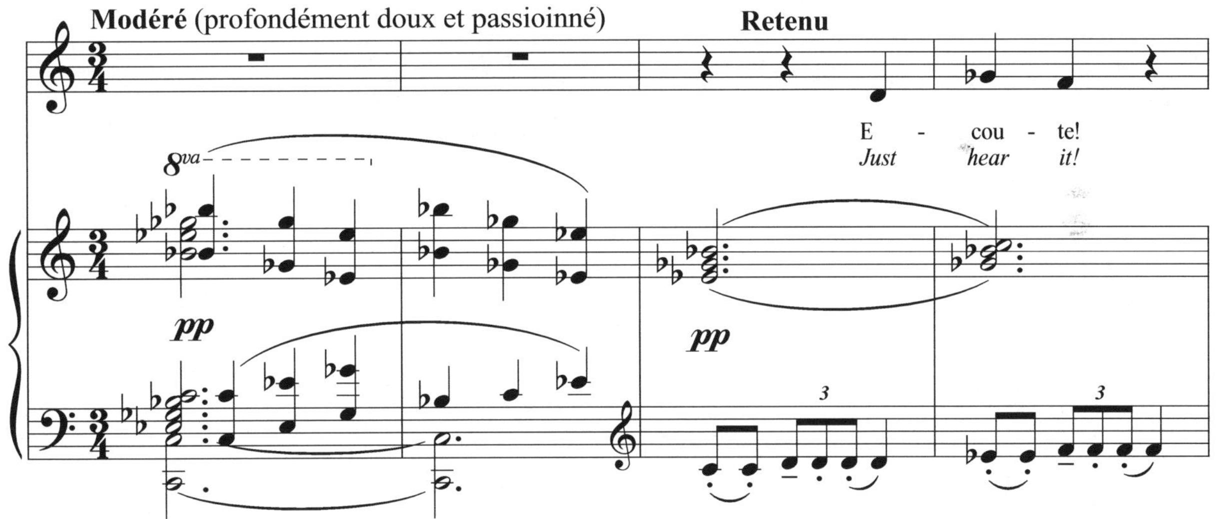

Example 12.8aa *Pelléas et Mélisande*, mm. 727–30

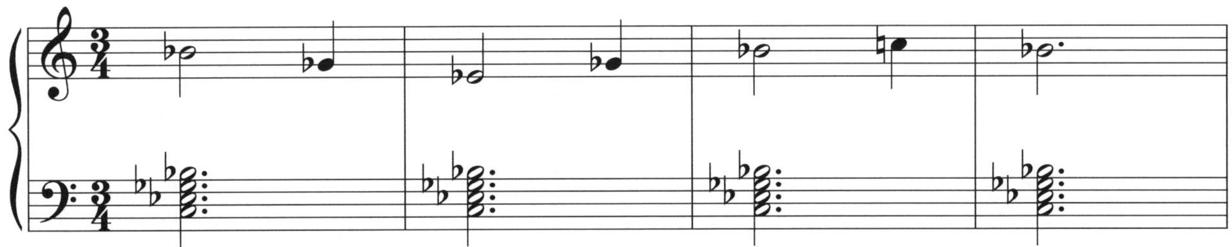

Example 12.8ab *Obsession*, cell 2

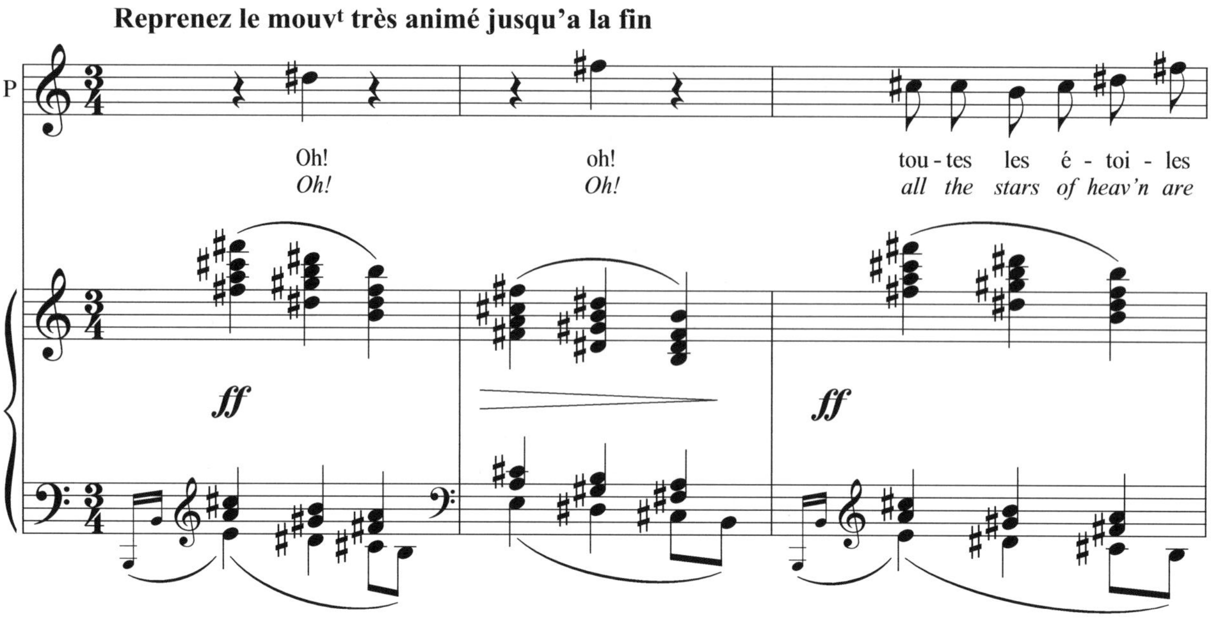

Example 12.8ba *Pelléas et Mélisande*, mm. 812–15

Example 12.8bb *Obsession*, cell 3

Example 12.8ca *Pelléas et Mélisande*, mm. 810–11

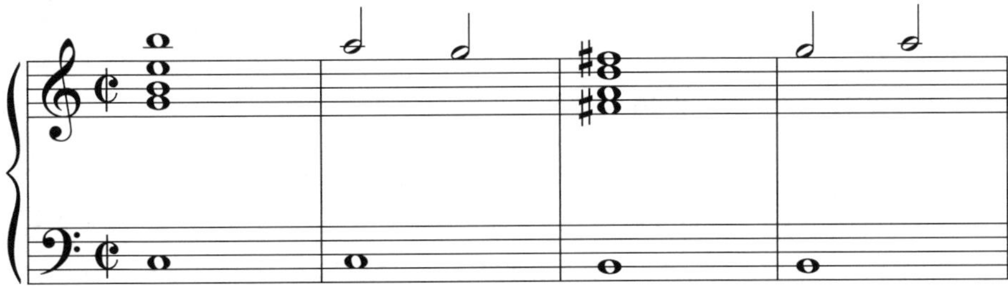

Example 12.8cb *Obsession*, cell 4

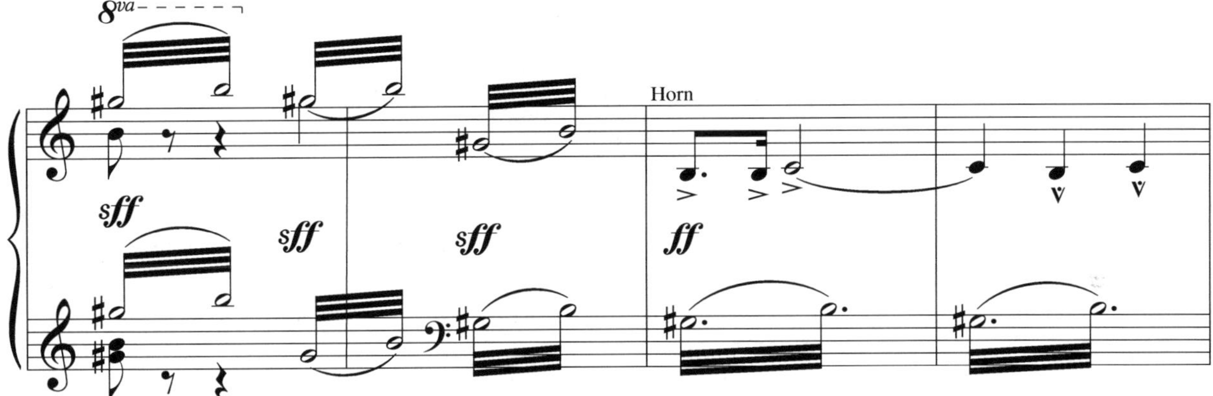

Example 12.8da *Pelléas et Mélisande*, mm. 826–29

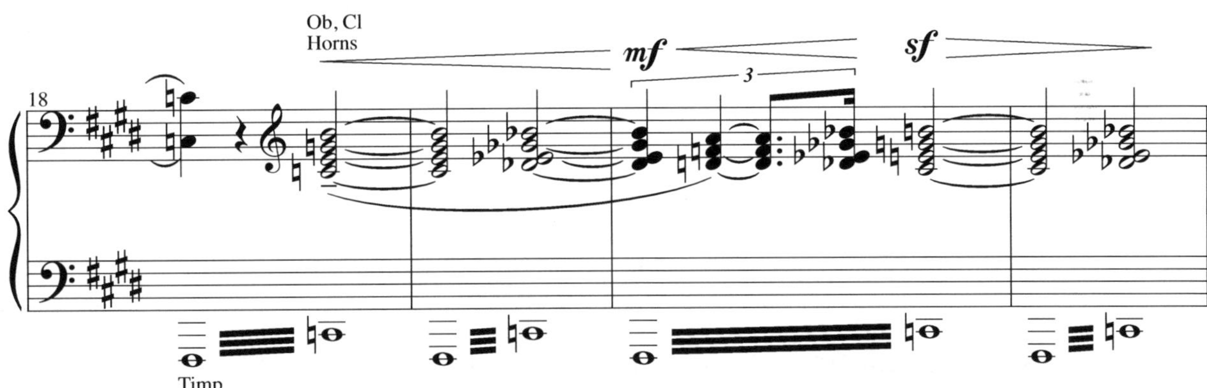

Example 12.8db *La Mer*, mvt. 3, mm. 18–21

with her. But on the eve of their marriage, Sandra is kidnapped, though she is in cahoots with Michael's business partner in a plot to ruin him financially. Michael learns of the plot and of the fact that Sandra is actually his own long-lost daughter. The film ends with Michael running to an airport terminal intending to kill the suicidal Sandra, only to embrace her instead. Michael has committed incest with his own daughter! Herrmann was well aware of the controversial nature of this plot twist; the producer and the studio were so concerned that they removed an intimate love scene between Michael and Sandra.[59] Herrmann's response was, however, far more subtle; he conveyed the idea of incest by alluding to *Pelléas et Mélisande*, a drama in which this taboo theme also plays a significant role, just like its predecessor, "The Fall of the House of Usher." Herrmann clearly had no regrets about his choice; he inscribed de Palma's personal copy of *Obsession* "with thanks for the finest film of my musical life."[60]

This chapter has shown that Baudelaire's precinematic sensibilities did indeed shape Debussy's views of the cinematic.[61] That influence stems from the fact that both men were fascinated with arabesques, moresques, and grotesques and with their capacity to convey images, movement, emotions, and even narratives. In Debussy's case, arabesques, moresques, and grotesques provided him with a means of enchaining strings of unrelated ideas, thereby articulating narratives both visually and musically. The principle of *enchaînement* is, of course, one that surfaced in several previous chapters. For example, chapter 9 demonstrated how the score for *La Boîte à joujoux* is an elaborate potpourri or collage of new and preexisting themes, similar in design to those Debussy encountered at performances of shadow plays of the 1880s and 1890s. The disjunct nature of the musical surface prompted Eugène Marsnan to describe *La Boîte à joujoux* as a "mosaic." Chapter 10 then revealed that Debussy constructed his score of *Jeux* along similar lines, thereby mirroring the angular motions of Nijinsky's choreography and the nervous disposition of the contemporary. It is surely no coincidence that Robin Holloway described Debussy's score as a complex mosaic "in which all kinds of valse movements rush tantalizingly past." And chapter 11 explained how, in his settings of "La Morte des amants," "L'Ombre des arbres," and "Soupir," Debussy created distorted reflections of the constituent arabesques in order to convey feelings of melancholy and ennui. According to Marianne Wheeldon, the fragmented structure of "Soupir" resembles that of Mallarmé's revolutionary poem *Un coup de dés jamais n'abolira le hasard*.[62] In other words, Debussy's cinematic obsessions were not some sudden response to some new artistic medium or some new technology: on the contrary, they were a natural outgrowth of his long-standing interest in arabesques, moresques, and grotesques. Debussy didn't learn how to create disjunct mosaic-like forms from watching early films; he had already started to experiment with such forms in the early 1890s while he was composing his first version of *Pelléas et Mélisande*. In short, he began to compose music cinematically long before setting foot in any movie theater.[63]

Notes

1. See Donald J. Olsen, *The City as a Work of Art. London. Paris. Vienna* (New Haven, CT: Yale University Press, 1986), esp. 35–57.

2. Charles Baudelaire, "Le Cygne," *Les Fleurs du mal*, LXXXIX, in *Charles Baudelaire: Œuvres Complètes*, vol. I, ed. Claude Pichois, Bibliothèque de la Pléiade (Paris: Gallimard, 1976), 85–86. F. P. Sturm translated this passage as follows: "Paris may change; my melancholy is fixed / New palaces, and scaffoldings, and blocks, / And suburbs old, are symbols all to me / Whose memories are as heavy as a stone." See Thomas Robert Smith, ed., *Baudelaire: His Prose and Poetry*, The Modern Library (New York: Boni and Liveright, 1919), 161.

3. Baudelaire, "Le Peintre de la vie moderne: IV Modernité," in *Charles Baudelaire: Œuvres Complètes*, Vol. II, ed. Claude Pichois. Bibliothèque de la Pléiade (Paris: Gallimard, 1976), 575–97, 695; Baudelaire, "The Painter in Modern Life: IV Modernity," in *The Painter in Modern Life and Other Essays*, ed. and trans. Jonathan Mayne (London: Phaidon, 2001), 13.

4. Marit Grøtta, *Baudelaire's Media Aesthetics: The Gaze of the Flâneur and Nineteenth-Century Media* (London: Bloomsbury 2015), 6.

5. Grøtta, *Baudelaire's Media Aesthetics*, 6.

6. Grøtta, *Baudelaire's Media Aesthetics*, 1.

7. Grøtta, "Precinematic Devices," in *Baudelaire's Media Aesthetics*, 73–102, esp. 76–77.

8. Claude Debussy, "Concert Colonne.—Société de nouveaux concerts," *SIM* (November 1, 1913), in *Monsieur Croche et autres écrits*, ed. François Lesure (Paris: Gallimard, 1987), 245–49; Claude Debussy, *Debussy on Music*, ed. François Lesure and trans. Richard Langham Smith (New York: Knopf, 1977), 295–99.

9. Debussy, "Vendredi Saint—Le neuvième Symphonie," in *Monsieur Croche*, 34; Debussy, "Good Friday—The Ninth Symphony," in *Debussy on Music*, 27; Baudelaire, "Le Thyrse," *Le Spleen de Paris*, XXXII, in *Œuvres Complètes*, I:336; Baudelaire, "The Wand," in *Vol. II: The Poems in Prose and La Fanfarol*, ed. and trans. Francis Scarfe (London: Anvil Press Poetry, 1989), 145.

10. Baudelaire, "Le Poème du hachisch," *Les Paradis artificiels*, in *Œuvres Complètes*, I:432; Baudelaire, "The Poem of Hashish," *Artificial Paradises*, trans. Stacy Diamond (New York: Carol, 1996), 65.

11. Baudelaire, "Mon cœur mis à nu," XXXVIII, in *Œuvres Complètes*, I:701; Baudelaire, "My Heart Laid Bare," in *Late Fragments. Flares, My Heart Laid Bare, Prose Poems, Belgium Disrobed*, ed. and trans. Richard Sieburth (New Haven, CT: Yale University Press, 2022), 38, 139.

12. Baudelaire, "Corréspondances" IV, in *Œuvres Complètes*, I:11.

13. Baudelaire, "Richard Wagner et *Tannhäuser* à Paris," in *Charles Baudelaire: Œuvres Complètes*, vol. II, ed. Claude Pichois, Bibliothèque de la Pléiade (Paris: Gallimard, 1976), 784; Baudelaire, "Richard Wagner and *Tannhäuser* in Paris," in *Painter in Modern Life*, 116.

14. Baudelaire, "Richard Wagner et *Tannhäuser* à Paris," in *Œuvres Complètes*, II:785; Baudelaire, "Richard Wagner and *Tannhäuser* in Paris," in *Painter in Modern Life*, 117.

15. Baudelaire, "Richard Wagner et *Tannhäuser* à Paris," in *Œuvres Complètes*, II:785; Baudelaire, "Richard Wagner and *Tannhäuser* in Paris," in *Painter in Modern Life*, 117.

16. Grøtta, *Baudelaire's Media Aesthetics*, 73–102.

17. Jonathan Mayne expresses doubt about which particular toy Baudelaire was describing; see Baudelaire, "A Philosophy of Toys," *Painter of Modern Life*, 201fn1.

18. Baudelaire, "Morale du joujou," in *Œuvres Complètes*, I:581–87, esp. 585–86; Baudelaire, "A Philosophy of Toys," *Painter of Modern Life*, 197–204, esp. 201. Stephen Prince, "Through the Looking Glass: Philosophical Toys and Digital Visual Effects," *Projections* 4, no. 2 (2010): 19–40.

19. Baudelaire, "Morale du joujou," in *Œuvres Complètes*, I:586; Baudelaire, "A Philosophy of Toys," in *Painter of Modern Life*, 201.

20. Grøtta, *Baudelaire's Media Aesthetics*, 70.

21. See Mervyn Heard, *Phantasmagoria: The Secret Life of the Magic Lantern* (Hastings: Projection Box, 2006); and Marina Warner, *Phantasmagoria: Spirit Visions, Metaphors, and Media into the Twenty-First Century* (Oxford: Oxford University Press, 2006). For the influence of phantasmagoria on Poe, see Fred Botting, "Poe's Phantasmagoreality," *Edgar Allan Poe Review* 11, no. 1 (Spring 2010): 9–21.

22. Emmanuelle Toulet, *Birth of the Motion Picture*, trans. Susan Emanuel (New York: Abrams, 1995), 112–13 and 124–26.

23. Richard Langham Smith, "Debussy and the Art of the Cinema," *Music and Letters* 54, no. 1 (1973): 61–70.

24. See Baudelaire, "Mon cœur mis à nu," in *Œuvres Complètes*, I:701; Baudelaire, "My Heart Laid Bare," 139; Baudelaire, "Fusées: IV, V," in *Œuvres Complètes*, I:652; Baudelaire, "Flares: 5 and 6," in *Late Fragments*, 139. Debussy's letter to Edgar Varèse (February 12, 1911), Claude Debussy, *Correspondance (1872–1918)*, ed. François Lesure and Denis Herlin, annotated by François Lesure, Denis Herlin, and Georges Liébert (Paris: Gallimard, 2005), 1389; Claude Debussy, *Debussy Letters*, ed. François Lesure and Roger Nichols, trans. Roger Nichols (Cambridge, MA: Harvard University Press, 1987), 237; and Smith, "Debussy and the Art of the Cinema," 61.

25. See Smith, "Debussy and the Art of the Cinema," 63; Debussy, *Correspondance*, 942; and Debussy, *Letters*, 166.

26. Debussy, "Titania," in *Monsieur Croche*, 84; Debussy, "Titania," in *Debussy on Music*, 101.

27. Pierre Lalo, "Claude Debussy et l'universe," *Programme Festival de Claude Debussy*, Théâtre des Champs-Élysées, Juin 17, 1932, 5.

28. Debussy, "*Parsifal* et la Société des Grands Auditions de France," *Gil Blas* (April 6, 1903), in *Monsieur Croche*, 143; Debussy, "*Parsifal* and the Société des Grands Auditions de France," in *Debussy on Music*, 166 [164–70].

29. Debussy, "*Parsifal* et la Société des Grands Auditions de France," in *Monsieur Croche*, 143; "*Parsifal* and the Société des Grands Auditions de France," in *Debussy on Music*, 166 [164–70].

30. Debussy, *Correspondance*, 1253; and Debussy, *Letters*, 217.

31. For the composition history of this passage and its links to "La sérénade interrompue" (*Préludes*, Bk. 1), see Matthew Brown, *Debussy's 'Ibéria': Studies in Genesis and Structure* (Oxford: Oxford University Press, 2003), 138–44. As mentioned in chapter 9, Debussy even quoted this particular passage in *La Boîte à joujoux*, tableau II.

32. See Smith, "Debussy and the Art of the Cinema," 69.

33. Robert Orledge, *Debussy and the Theatre* (Cambridge: Cambridge University Press, 1982), 233.

34. Rebecca Leydon, "Debussy's Late Style and the Devices of the Early Silent Cinema," *Music Theory Spectrum* 22, no. 2 (2001): 223.

35. Mark McFarland, "Debussy: The Origins of a Method," *Journal of Music Theory* 48, no. 2 (2004): 298.

36. See Debussy, "Concert Colonne.—Société des nouveaux concerts," in *Monsieur Croche*, 248; Debussy, *Debussy on Music*, 298; and Scott D. Paulin, "'Cinematic' Music: Analogies, Fallacies, and the Case of Debussy," *Music and the Moving Image* 3, no.1 (Spring 2010): 9–10.

37. Ian Pace, "From Jean-Luc Godard to Dennis Potter: Finnissy's cinematic and televisual inspirations," in *Critical Perspectives on Michael Finnissy: Bright Futures, Dark Pasts*, ed. Ian Pace and Nigel McBride (London: Routledge, 2019), 344 and 366 [344–72].

38. Debussy, "Vendredi Saint," *La Revue blanche* (May 1, 1901), in *Monsieur Croche*, 33–34; Debussy, "Good Friday," in *Debussy on Music*, 26–27 [26–28].

39. As regards the genesis of act 4, scene 4, see James McKay, "The Bréval Manuscript: New Interpretations," *Cahiers Debussy*, nouvelle série no. 1 (1977): 5–15; Carolyn Abbate, "*Tristan* in the Composition of *Pelléas*," *19th-Century Music* 5, no. 2 (1981): 117–41; Orledge, *Debussy and the Theatre*, 73–87; Grayson, *The Genesis of Pelléas et Mélisande* (Ann Arbor, MI: UMI, 1986), 234–61; and Grayson, "The Opera: Genesis and Sources," in *Pelléas et Mélisande*, Cambridge Opera Handbooks, ed. Roger Nichols and Richard Langham Smith (Cambridge: Cambridge University Press, 1989), 48–52.

40. Debussy, *Correspondance*, 156; Debussy, *Letters*, 52.

41. Debussy, *Correspondance*, 160–162; Debussy, *Letters*, 54 [54–57].

42. Debussy, *Correspondance*, 160–162; Debussy, *Letters*, 54 [54–57].

43. Alfred Hitchcock, "The Enjoyment of Fear," in *Hitchcock on Hitchcock: Selected Writings and Interviews*, ed. Sidney Gottlieb (Berkeley: University of California Press, 1995), 120.

44. Hitchcock, "Enjoyment of Fear," 118.

45. Hitchcock, "Why I Am Afraid of the Dark," in *Hitchcock on Hitchcock*, 143.

46. For a discussion of the cyclic structure of act 4, scene 4, see Abbate, "*Tristan* in the Composition of *Pelléas*," 117–41.

47. For discussion of the motivic content of act 4, scene 4, see Grayson, *Genesis of* Pelléas et Mélisande, 234–61; and Rolf, "Symbolism as Compositional Agent in Act IV, Scene 4 of Debussy's *Pelleas et Melisande*," in *Berlioz and Debussy: Sources, Contexts, and Legacies*, ed. Barbara L. Kelly and Kerry Murphy (Aldershot: Ashgate, 2007), 117–48. Léon Roques transcribed an excerpt from "La Mort de Pelléas" for piano (Paris: Durand, 1906). This excerpt begins a few pages earlier with Pelléas's line "On dirait que ta voix."

48. Donnellon, "Debussy as Musician and Critic," in *The Cambridge Companion to Debussy*, ed. Simon Trezise (Cambridge: Cambridge University Press, 2003), 47.

49. See Abbate, "*Tristan* in the Composition of *Pelléas*," 135ff; and Richard Langham Smith, "Tonalities of darkness and light," in *Pelléas et Mélisande*, Cambridge Opera Handbooks, ed. Roger Nichols and Richard Langham Smith (Cambridge: Cambridge University Press, 1989), 107–39.

50. Bernard Herrmann, *The Impressionists: Satie, Debussy, Ravel, Fauré, Honegger*, London Philharmonic Orchestra, Phase 4 (Decca: London, SPC 21062, 1970). The album contains orchestral versions of "Clair de lune" and *La Plus que lente* as well as Debussy's orchestrations of Satie's *Gymnopédies* No. 1 and 3 on *The Impressionists* (London: SPC 21062, 1971).

51. See Bernard Hermann, "Bernard Herrmann. Composer," in *Sound and Cinema: The Coming of Sound to American Film*, ed. Evan William Cameron (Pleasantville, NY: Redgrave, 1980), 118.

52. Christopher Palmer, *The Composer in Hollywood* (London: Marion Boyars, 1990), 271, 286, and 293.

53. William Wrobel, "Half-Diminished Seventh: The Bernard Herrmann Chord," (2002, rev. 2017), 3, 8, 16–17, https://archive.org/details/herrmann-chord-filmscorerundowns.

54. See William Wrobel, "Cue 4 'Kidnap," in "*Obsession*: Music by Bernard Herrmann" (2015), 22–26, https://archive.org/details/obsession-filmscorerundowns.

55. See Wrobel, "Cue 4 'Kidnap,'" in *"Obsession,"* 22–26.

56. See Wrobel, "Cue 33 'Papers,'" in *"Obsession,"* 100–101.

57. See Wrobel, "Cue 1 'Prelude'" in *"Obsession,"* 4–9.

58. This summary is borrowed from Steven C. Smith, *A Heart at Fire's Center: The Life and Music of Bernard Herrmann* (Berkeley: University of California Press, 2002), 341.

59. Cinephilia & Beyond, "'Obsession': When de Palma Stepped Out of Hitchcock's Shadow," accessed December 26, 2022, https://cinephiliabeyond.org/obsession-de-palma-stepped-hitchcocks-shadow.

60. Smith, *A Heart at Fire's Center*, 341.

61. Debussy, "Concert Colonne.—Société de nouveaux concerts," *SIM* (November 1, 1913), in *Monsieur Croche*, 245–49; Debussy, *Debussy on Music*, 295–99.

62. Marianne Wheeldon, "Debussy's 'Soupir': An Experiment in Permutational Analysis," *Perspectives of New Music* 38, no. 2 (2000): 134–36. See also Mallarmé, *Un coup de dés jamais n'abolira le hasard*, in *Stéphane Mallarmé: Œuvres Complètes*, vol. I, ed. Bertrand Marchal, Bibliothèque de la Pléiade (Paris: Gallimard, 1998), 365–87.

63. This observation puts a new twist on Kerman's view of Debussy's *Pelléas et Mélisande* as a sung play; see Joseph Kerman, *Opera as Drama* (Berkeley: University of California Press, 1988), 140–57. Durand even published a version of the score in which the text is included without the vocal part. This version suggests that the work might be performed as a melodrama.

13

Arabesques as Confessions

A central theme running through this book is the claim that arabesques, moresques, and grotesques provided Debussy with a means of explaining how music can stir the emotions and even recount narratives. One way they did so was by allowing him to confess his own feelings. The idea of associating arabesques with confessions was not new. Indeed, it is apparent not only in De Quincey's notorious literary arabesque *Confessions of an English Opium Eater* (1821/1822) but also in Schlegel's "Letter about the Novel" (1799–1800): "There would be true arabesques, which together with confessions . . . are the only romantic products of nature in our age."[1] For his part, Schlegel held this view because he believed that "true story is the foundation of all romantic poetry" and that "what is best in the best novels is nothing but a more or less veiled confession of the author, the profit of his experience, the quintessence of his originality." According to him, the personal experiences revealed in travelogues, private letters, and autobiographies would be appreciated more if they were read "romantically" in the same manner as a novel: "Confessions . . . mainly by way of the naïve, develop themselves into arabesques. But at best those novels rise to the arabesque only at the end, when the bankrupt merchants regain their money and credit, all those poor devils get to eat, the likeable scoundrels become honest, and the fallen women become virtuous again."[2] As a result, he regarded Jean-Jacques Rousseau's *Confessions* as "a most excellent novel" and his *Héloise* as "a very mediocre one."[3] Such claims were not, however, merely speculative on his part: on the contrary, Schlegel based the prologue of his novel *Lucinde*—"Confessions of an Improper Man"—on his own relationship with his future wife, Dorothea Veit-Schlegel. The couple had first met in 1797, two years before he finished *Lucinde,* and caused a major scandal by living together before their marriage in 1804.

Both fans of De Quincey's work, Poe and Baudelaire clearly recognized the connections between arabesques and confessions; they regularly drew on their personal experiences when creating their poetry, nonfiction, and fiction. Take, for instance, Baudelaire's "Le Joujoue du Pauvre" (*Le Spleen de Paris*).[4] This prose poem describes an incident witnessed by a flâneur while strolling around a chic Parisian neighborhood. He witnessed an encounter between a wealthy child standing behind the gate of a lavish home and an urchin passing on the street outside. Although the wealthy child owns an expensive toy, he is transfixed by what the urchin is carrying in a small box. On examining the box, the wealthy child realizes that the urchin's toy is actually a live rat. The two laugh together "as brothers, with teeth of an equal whiteness." Although "Le Joujoue du Pauvre" seems like pure fiction, Baudelaire revealed in his essay "Morale du joujou" that he was the flâneur in question and that he had observed the encounter firsthand.[5] Experts likewise believe that the narrators in many of Poe's stories recount events that stemmed from the author's own experiences. Chapter 1 provided a perfect case in point: it suggested that Roderick's possibly incestuous relationship with Madeline resonates with the fact that Poe married his thirteen-year-old first cousin Virginia Clemm.[6]

The links between arabesques and confessions also left their mark on Debussy, especially in his efforts to complete his opera *La chute de la maison Usher*. One of the main goals of this chapter is to show just how much the twists and turns of this remarkable story mirrored the ups and downs of Debussy's life between 1914 and 1917. It shows how the fate of Debussy's score was shaped in large part by two traumatic experiences that the composer had during these years: the first occurred at the start of WWI and left him unable to compose music for the latter part of 1914 and much of 1915; the second happened at the start of 1916 and left him housebound much of the following year. In a remarkable instance of life imitating art, Debussy sank into a severe depression while he was composing *La chute de la maison Usher*. As a result, he increasingly identified himself with the character of Roderick Usher and imagined himself suffering a similar downfall.

To explain why Debussy responded so viscerally to these two events, this chapter takes a close look at his life and career during the war years. It begins by suggesting that Debussy experienced a mental breakdown at the start of WWI; this breakdown occurred because the German advance in August 1914 brought back suppressed childhood memories of the Franco-Prussian War of 1870 and his father's imprisonment in the spring of 1871 after the collapse of the Paris Commune. The chapter then describes how Debussy used composition as a form of therapy in the summer of 1915 and how this process of healing allowed him to complete a string of memorable chamber compositions. Debussy experienced a second trauma early in 1916 when he realized that he would never recover from colorectal cancer, from which he had been suffering since at least 1909. Having explained the extent of these two traumatic experiences, the chapter shows how they had a direct impact on his score for *La chute de la maison Usher*. On the one hand, they help to explain why Debussy rewrote Poe's grotesque story so that it transforms the character of the doctor into a full-blown villain. On the other, they suggest how Debussy's unstable mental state, like that of Roderick Usher, manifests itself in the disjunct and disturbing character of the music, which often recalls the arabesque structures of *La Boîte à joujoux, Jeux*, and *Pelléas et Mélisande* as described in chapters 9, 10, and 12. In short, the chapter offers a perfect illustration of the link between arabesques and confessions.

When thinking about Debussy's incomplete opera *La chute de la maison Usher*, it is important to remember he had contemplated setting Poe's stories to music as far back as 1890 and that he signed a contract for two thousand francs with Giulio Gatti Casazza and the Metropolitan Opera House to premiere the scores of three new operas, *La chute de la maison Usher, Diable dans le beffroi*, and *La Légende de Tristan* on July 5, 1908.[7] Over the next few years, Debussy wrote two

Table 13.1. Debussy's wartime editions, compositions, and performances

Date	Editions, Compositions, Premieres	Performances	Aid Organization
1914			
October	Edits *Œuvres Complètes* of Chopin.[1]		
November	Writes *Berceuse héroïque* to honor the soldiers and King of Belgium.		*King Albert's Book*
1915			
24 April		Debussy (pn), Claire Croiza (sop.), "En Sourdine," "Fantoches," "Clair de lune," *Fêtes galantes*, sér. 1, and "Green" (*Ariettes oubli*ées).	Le Vêtement du blessé
Spring	Begins editing Bach chamber music.[2]		
June	Composes *Page d'Album* for piano.	Claire Croiza (sop.), Alfredo Casella (con), *Trois Ballades de François Villon* at the Théâtre national de l'Odéon organized by the Association des Concerts Pierre Monteux.	Le Vêtement du blessé
4 June		Debussy (pn), Alfredo Casella (pn), *Iberia, Images pour orchestre*.	Croix-Rouge italienne
12 July–12 October Pourville-sur-mer	Completes *En blanc et noir* for 2 pianos, *Sonate pour violoncelle et piano, Douze études* for piano, and *Sonate pour flûte, alto, et harpe*.		
24 October	Premiere of *Berceuse héroïque*.		
December	Completes *Élégy* for piano.		*Pages Inédites Sur la Femme et la Guerre*. For the orphans of the the war in France.
	Composes *Noël des enfants* for voice and piano or two voices and chorus.		
1916			
22 January		Premiere of *En blanc et noir* by Walter Rummel and Thérèse Chaigneau at the residence of the Princesse de Polignac.	L'Aide affecteuse aux musiciens
8 April		Festival Debussy at the Huygens Room.	L'Appui aux artistes
9 April		Jane Montjovet, *Noël des enfants*.	Concert des Amitiés franco-étrangères
10 December		French premiere of *Sonate* for flute, viola, and harp: Albert Manouvrier (flute), Darius Milhaud (viola), Jeanne Dalliès (chromatic harp).	
14 December		Premiere of four *Études* by Walter Rummel.	L'Aide affecteuse aux musiciens

21 December		Debussy (pn), Jane Bathori (sop.), *Noël des enfants, Le promenoir des deux amants, Chansons de Bilitis.*	Le Vêtement du prisonnier de guerre
		Debussy (pn), Roger-Ducasse (pn), *En blanc et noir.*	

1917

February–March	Writes *Les Soirs illuminés par l'ardeur du charbon* for piano to pay his coal merchant Monsieur Tronquin.		
9 March		Debussy (pn), Rose Féart (sop.), *Trois Ballades de François Villon, Fêtes galantes* (1 sér.), and *Noël des enfants.*	L'Aide affecteuse aux musiciens
17 March		Debussy (pn), Claire Croiza (sop.), *Le promenoir des deux amants,* "De grève," "De soir" (*Prose lyriques*), *Noël des enfants.*	L'Aide affecteuse aux musiciens
24 March		Debussy (pn), Claire Croiza (sop.), *Trois Ballades de François Villon, Fêtes galantes,* sér. 2, *Noël des enfants.*	Le Vêtement du blessé
		Debussy (pn), Jacques Salmon (vc), *Sonata* for cello and piano.	
April	Completes *Sonate pour violon et piano,* two weeks after his edition of Bach's chamber music.		
5 May		Debussy (pn), Gaston Poulet (vln), *Sonata* for violin and piano.	Pour le foyer du soldat aveugle
11 September Saint-Jean-de-Luz		Debussy (pn), Gaston Poulet (vln), *Sonata* for violin and piano.	L'Œuvres de la Sommes dévastée
14 September Biarritz		Debussy (pn), Gaston Poulet (vln), *Sonata* for violin and piano.	L'Œuvres de la Sommes dévastée

Unfinished Works

1916–1917	Completes draft of *Ode à La France* and, after completing a third and final libretto for *La Chute de la maison Usher,* completes short score for Scene 1 and part of Scene 2.[3]		

1918

25 March	Debussy dies at his home in Paris.		

1. That edition contained 11 volumes: Valses; Preludes and Rondos (Opp. 28, 45, 1, 5, 16); Etudes; Nocturnes; Polonaises (Opp. 26, 40, 44, 53, 61, 71); Mazurkas; Berceuse, Barcarolle, Variations, etc.; Sonatas; Scherzos and Fantaisie; Morceau de Concert; and the Concertos.

2. J. S. Bach. Six Sonatas for violin and keyboard (BWV 1014–1019), three sonatas for viola da gamba and keyboard (BWV 1027–1029), six sonatas for flute (BWV 1030–1035), and a pair of trio sonatas (BWV 1032 and 1038).

3. Marius-François Gaillard completed *Ode à La France* in 1928 and, most recently, Robert Orledge completed *La Chute de la maison Usher* in 2004.

versions of the libretto for *La chute de la maison Usher*, one in 1908–August 1909 and another in August 1909–June 1910.[8] He did not, however, produce much music. Debussy was still discussing the project in 1911–13, around the same time that he was completing *La Boîte à joujoux*, *Jeux*, and "Soupir." But things soon ground to an abrupt halt during the first years of WWI: it wasn't until late 1915 that he finally returned to *La chute de la maison Usher*. Over the next two years, Debussy finished his third libretto (October 1915–September 1917), a draft of scene 1, the start of scene 2, and "some strange sinister music for the melodrama leading towards the gory denouement."[9] But he did not reach the end. When Debussy died at his home on March 25, 1918, his manuscript lay unfinished on the desk in his study.

Why did Debussy make so little progress on *La chute de la maison Usher* in the first years of WWI? Why did the piece cause him so many headaches? Although there are many answers to these questions, it is clear that the outbreak of WWI had a massive impact on Debussy, as it did on everyone living in Northern France: it forced him to compose works that were modest in scale and to write them sporadically, completing most during a three-month stay in Pourville-sur-Mer in the summer of 1915.[10] These points are both apparent from table 13.1, a detailed catalog of Debussy's wartime activities. This catalog shows that Debussy wrote three types of music during the war: short occasional works such as *Berceuse héroïque* (1914), *Page d'Album* (1915), *Élégy* (1915), and *Les Soirs illumines par l'ardeur du charbon* (1917) for piano, *Noël des enfants* (1915) for voice and piano or two voices and chorus, and *Ode à la France* (1916–17) for chorus; multimovement piano and chamber works such as *En blanc et noir*, *Douze études*, and the three late sonatas; and the short score of *La chute de la maison Usher*. Table 13.1 also indicates that Debussy wrote next to nothing during the fall of 1914 and spring of 1915, a lot in the summer and fall of 1915, and very little from 1916 to 1918.

Debussy's decision to shift his attention away from large-scale works to shorter pieces for small instrumental combinations is not, of course, hard to explain; it was clearly a response to external pressures brought about by the conflict. Since countless professional musicians served in the French army and since the country's financial resources were mainly diverted to the war effort, there were few opportunities to program full-scale symphonic scores or elaborate stage works. And given that Paris was under constant threat of being bombarded, large public gatherings were not encouraged. Table 13.1 likewise demonstrates that Debussy wrote many pieces to raise money for victims of the war: wounded soldiers (Le Vêtement du blessé, 1915 and 1917, the Italian Red Cross, 1915); musicians' families (L'Aide affecteuse aux musiciens, 1916 and 1917); prisoners of war (Le Vêtement du prisonierre de guerre, 1916); blind soldiers (Foyer du soldat aveugle, 1917); and even specific communities that were obliterated by the fighting (L'Œuvres de la Sommes dévastée, 1917).[11]

The sporadic nature of Debussy's output is, however, another matter entirely. Certainly, there were good reasons why Debussy found it hard to compose during the first year of the conflict. Although the prospect of war had been in the air for some time, the situation exploded dramatically following the assassination of Archduke Franz Ferdinand and his wife, Sophie, on July 28, 1914. Germany declared war on France on August 3 and began a rapid advance toward the French capital. Luxembourg fell on August 2, 1914; Longwy—"the iron gate to Paris"—on August 3; and much of Belgium by the end of the first week. The onslaught was finally halted thirty miles from Paris at the Battle of the Marne (September 5–12). As German forces neared the French capital, Debussy evacuated his family to Angers, where they stayed in the Grand Hotel. But they returned to Paris in October when the situation looked more stable.

A letter from the first days of the conflict suggests, however, that there may have been deeper psychological reasons for Debussy's lack of creativity. Written to Durand on August 8, 1914, the letter reveals that the German advances had traumatized Debussy because they brought back suppressed memories of a similar invasion during the Franco-Prussian War.

> As you know, I'm quite devoid of sang-froid and even more so of the military mentality, never having had the occasion to handle a gun. Then there are my memories of 1870 which prevent me reaching a pitch of enthusiasm, as well as the anxiety of my wife who has a son and a son-in-law both in the army! As a result, my life is one of intensity and disquiet. I'm nothing more than a wretched atom hurled around by this terrible cataclysm, and what I'm doing seems to me so miserably petty! It makes me envious of Satie and his real job of defending Paris as a corporal. So if you have any work you can put my way, please think of me.[12]

Five months later, Debussy made similar revelations in another letter to Godet: "What will take a long time to remove is these false, heavy, foreign tastes that have insinuated themselves . . . into our ways of thinking, listening, even of feeling. For forty-four years we've been playing at self-effacement; even in France, the French were determined to cultivate thick-headedness and claimed to be lending some weight to our ideas!"[13]

It is not hard to see why the catastrophic events of 1870–71 left such an indelible mark on the composer's psyche.[14] Debussy was just eight years old when Prussian forces routed the French army at Sedan on September 1–2, 1870, and began to bombard Paris starting on September 19, 1870. Conditions in the city were deplorable: its residents faced shortages of food, medicine, and fuel as well as freezing temperatures. The situation went from bad to worse when the Prussian artillery resumed its bombardment in January 1871; shells rained down for twenty-three consecutive nights, killing four hundred. The French government surrendered on January 26, and Adolphe Thiers was elected president of the Third Republic. But when Thiers tried to restore order to the city, the residents rose up and claimed the city in the name of the Commune. Thiers besieged Paris yet again, killing around twenty thousand Communards between March 21 and March 28. Debussy's parents, Manuel and Victorine, were among the many working-class Parisians caught up in the upheavals. His father, who was made redundant when the war broke out, joined the Parisian National Guard in 1870 and soon rose to the rank of captain. On May 8, 1871, he led an attack on Fort d'Issy. That attack failed. Manuel was duly arrested, held at the Satory camp, and sentenced to four years imprisonment.[15] He was pardoned, however, on May 11, 1872, thanks to the intervention of Victorine.[16] Although Debussy found comfort studying the piano with Antoinette Mauté, whose son Charles had met Manuel in the Satory camp, he never discussed these events as an adult: he revealed nothing after his father's death on October 28, 1910. Indeed, it wasn't until the late 1950s that Dietschy discovered what had transpired and speculated about how it left Debussy with a sense of antipathy toward Germany and the French Establishment.[17]

Debussy's letters from the first year of WWI clearly show that Debussy experienced the complex array of emotions the experts generally associate with that trauma—fear, anger, guilt, sadness, helplessness, inadequacy, and nervousness. Appearing as well are the related behavioral responses—grief, constant hyperarousal, an inability to concentrate, and a preoccupation with previous traumas.[18] Debussy clearly had good reason to be afraid for his family, his friends, and his country: his stepson Raoul Bardac, stepson-in-law Gaston de Tinan, brother Alfred, and friend André Caplet all served in one capacity or another.[19] But he was also angry, as he revealed to Nicholas Cornio in September 1914: "I won't get on to the subject of German barbarity. It's exceeded all expectations. . . . French art needs to take revenge quite as seriously as the French army does!"[20] In another letter to Durand (August 5, 1915), he decried "those Kultur merchants" for wantonly mowing down the youth of France, thereby precluding them from contributing to French heritage.[21] And in a letter to Godet dated February 4, 1916, he even directed his ire at the French government: "The war continues—as you know—but it's impossible to see why. . . . I realize it's not easy to find a solution but there's something irritating in the way they go about the war so nonchalantly! Death exacts none the less its blind tribute. . . . When will hate be exhausted? Or is it hate that's the issue in all this?"[22] He added, "When will the practice cease of entrusting the destiny of nations to people who see humanity as a way of furthering their careers?"

Nevertheless, Debussy felt guilty that, like his father, Erik Satie had volunteered to defend Paris and that his mother had supported the family during the earlier conflict.[23] Those feelings would have been particularly intense when she died in March 1915, the same week as his mother-in-law.[24] To assuage his guilt and express his empathy, Debussy not only joined Albert Dalimier's committee "to look after the wives and children of the orchestral musicians" but also contributed to the performances listed in table 13.1.[25] Figure 13.1 shows the program for one of these events: a Festival Debussy arranged by *Lyre et palette* on April 8, 1916, to raise money for L'Appui aux artistes, an organization responsible for awarding grants to artists in need.[26] And yet, Debussy never overcame his feelings of helplessness and inadequacy: "As for music . . . I no longer knew what it was; the familiar sound of the piano had become something hateful. Pythagoras (?) [Archimedes] working on his mathematical problems right up until a soldier killed him, Goethe writing *The Elective Affinities* during the French occupation of Weimar, these are admirable intellectual achievements. I can only deduce that I'm inferior, and do some mathematics, possibly?"[27] No wonder his mind temporarily shut down: "The brain is a delicate machine which seizes up at the slightest shock: 'ambience' is more than a cliché."[28]

Although this breakdown left Debussy incapacitated for the final months of 1914 and the first half of 1915, the effects of the trauma wore off in the summer of 1915, thanks to his sojourn in Pourville. It was here that Debussy rekindled his passion for composing music. He explained the therapeutic effects of the visit in a letter to Bernardo Molinari from October 6, 1915: "Your kind letter has reached me in a little spot by the sea where I come to try and forget the war. For the last three months I've been able to work again. When I tell you that I spent nearly a year unable to write music . . . after that I've almost had to *relearn* it. It was like a rediscovery and it's seemed to me more beautiful than ever. Is it because I was deprived of it for so long?"[29] He added, "What beauties there are in music 'by itself,' with no axe to grind or new invention to amaze the so-called 'dilettanti.' . . . The emotional satisfaction one gets from it can't be equaled, can it, in any of the other arts?" Debussy expressed much the same sentiments a week later in a letter to Godet (October 14, 1915): "I've been staying by the sea in a place which regrets its lack of cosmopolitan brilliance: it's called Pourville-sur-mer. There I rediscovered my ability to think in music, which I had lost for a year. . . . Not that my writing music is indispensable but it's the only thing I know how to do, more or less well, and I confess its disappearance made me miserable. . . . Anyway, I've been writing like a madman, or like a man condemned to die the next morning."[30] But Debussy remained angry at the war itself: "Certainly I haven't forgotten the war during these last three months. . . . Indeed, I've come to see the horrible necessity of it. I realized that there was no point adding myself to the number of wounded and, all in all, it was cowardly just to think about the atrocities that had been committed without doing anything in return; by re-fashioning, as far

"Lyre et Palette"

6, Rue Huyghens, XIV·
(Carrefour Raspail et Montparnasse)
Concert privé du Samedi 8 Avril 1916, à 8 h. 3/4 très précises

FESTIVAL DEBUSSY

PROGRAMME

I. Préludes :
 a) Danseuses de Delphes.
 b) Les Collines d'Anacrapi.
 c) Ce qu'a vu le vent d'Ouest.
  M. RICARDO VINES

II. *a)* Air de Lia (L'Enfant prodigue).
 b) Les Cloches.
 c) Fantoches.
  Mᵐᵉ VALLIN-PARDO

III. *a)* Arabesque.
 b) La Fille aux cheveux de lin.
 c) Prélude de la Suite Bergamasque.
  Pour Harpe seule
  Mˡˡᵉ L. WURMSER-DELCOURT

IV. Images :
 a) Reflets dans l'eau.
 b) Hommage à Rameau.
 c) Mouvement.
  M. RICARDO VINES

V. Deux Danses :
 a) Danse sacrée.
 b) Danse profane.
  Mˡˡᵉ L. WURMSER-DELCOURT
  Au Piano : M. DANIEL JEISLER

VI. *a)* Le Promenoir des deux Amants.
 b) Mandoline.
  Mᵐᵉ VALLIN-PARDO

VII. *a)* Poissons d'or.
 b) La Soirée dans Grenade.
 c) L'Isle joyeuse.
  M. RICARDO VINES

Harpe chromatique sans pédales, système Lyon
Piano Erard

*Ce programme est vendu au profit
de " L'APPUI AUX ARTISTES "*

Figure 13.1 Program for "Festival Debussy" (April 8, 1916)

as my strength allowed me, a little of the beauty these 'men' are destroying, with a meticulous brutality that is unmistakably 'Made in Germany.'"[31]

One reason why Debussy overcame the effects of the trauma in the second half of 1915 is that he used musical composition as a form of therapy; music provided a medium within which he could work through the complex array of emotions unleashed by the war. Take, for example, *Noël des enfants*, Debussy's Christmas carol from the fall of 1915. As shown in table 13.2a, Debussy's text describes how many French children have lost their homes and their parents and implores Santa not to visit the homes of enemy children. There's not much Christmas spirit here! The tone of *Ode à la France* isn't much rosier (see tab. 13.2b): "[It] is not one of triumph, let alone of French triumphalism, but rather of desolation and bitterness."[32] The same can be said of the second movement of *En blanc et noir*; dedicated to Lieutenant Jacques Charlot, who died in action on March 3, 1915, the score includes an epigram taken from the end of François Villon's "Ballade contre les ennemis de la France." Indeed, as shown in table 13.2c, the last five lines rebuke those who wish evil on France. Remarkably, the texts of the three works are interrelated: the phrase "Mais donnes la victoire aux enfants de France" from the end of *Noël des enfants* (underlined in tab. 13.2a), recalls the refrain "La grand' pitié du royaume de France" from the first stanza of *Ode à la France* (underlined in tab. 13.2b) and the refrain "Qui mal voudroit au royaume de France" from Villon's ballad (underlined in tab. 13.2c).[33] For the record, Algernon Swinburne, working during the Third Republic, translated Villon's phrase "the kingdom of France" as "the state of France,"

Table 13.2. Debussy's *Noël des enfants qui n'ont plus de maison*

a. Debussy, *Noël des enfants qui n'ont plus de maison*

>Nous n'avons plus de maisons!
>Les ennemis ont tout pris,
>Jusqu'à notre petit lit!
>Ils ont brûlé l'école et notre maître aussi.
>Ils ont brûlé l'église et monsieur Jésus-Christ!
>Et le vieux pauvre qui n'a pas pu s'en aller!
>
>Nous n'avons plus de maisons!
>Les ennemis ont tout pris,
>Jusqu'à notre petit lit!
>Bien sûr! papa est à la guerre,
>Pauvre maman est morte
>Avant d'avoir vu tout ça.
>Qu'est-ce que l'on va faire?
>Noël! petit Noël! N'allez pas chez eux,
>N'allez plus jamais chez eux,
>Punissez-les!
>
>Vengez les enfants de France!
>Les petits Belges, les petits Serbes,
>Et les petits Polonais aussi!
>Si nous en oublions, pardonnez-nous.
>Noël! Noël! surtout, pas de joujoux,
>Tâchez de nous redonner le pain quotidien.
>
>Nous n'avons plus de maisons!
>Les ennemis ont tout pris,
>Jusqu'à notre petit lit!
>Ils ont brûlé l'école et notre maître aussi.
>Ils ont brûlé l'église et monsieur Jésus-Christ!
>Et le vieux pauvre qui n'a pas pu s'en aller!
>Noël! écoutez-nous, nous n'avons plus de petits sabots:
>Mais donnez la victoire aux enfants de France!

b. Louis Laloy, *Ballade de la pit*é *du royaume de France*

Jeanne
>Les troupeaux vont par les champs désertés
>Où les sillons ont gardé les charrues.
>Cette fumée est le feu des cites
>Don't l'ennemi a pris remparts et rues.
>Il prétendait vaincie sans coup féri;
>De mâle rage il se venge en souffrance.
>Dieu! Pourrez-vous voir sans la secourir
>La grand' pitié du royaume de France?
>
>Qui défandait sa maison fut pendu
>Comme voleur au carrefour des routes.
>Cris maternals ils n'ont pas entendu,
>Et profane de sang les saintes voûtes.
>Rester ou fuir, c'est la morte encourir;

Femme ou enfant n'a droit a espérance:
N'y a-t-il baume ou charme pour guérir
<u>La grand' pitié du royaume de France?</u>

Prince éloigné, ne vous fais remontrance.
Vivre sans regne ou sans effet mourir,
Rien ne vous peut alléger de souffrir
<u>La grand' pitié du royaume de France.</u>

Le jour se finit sans entendre
Cloches sonner. [Choeur: Ah!] Quel est ce cri?
[Choeur: Ah!] Qui pleure? J'aperçois s'étendre
Le corps de la France meurtrie.

Sainte vierge, aidez-moi,
Voyez mes mains trop faibles et tremblantes
Pour laver la face sanglante
Et relever ces os broyés.
De votre feu brulez mon âme,
Faites de moi vivante flamme,
Que guerriers s'assemblent autour
Pour porter à France secours.
Le bois craque et fume,
Le bûcher qui me consume s'allume.

Choeur
Clarté vivante victime ardente
Nous arrivons de not' pays pour y combat' les ennemis
Forêt de mort forts bucherons
Taillez, cognez nous les aurons
Nous jetterons hors du pays
Ceux qui à tort l'ont assailli
Il n'est quartier pour ces larrons
Frappez! Marchez! Nous les aurons!
Nous traquerons hors du pays
Ceux qui sans foi l'ont envahi.
Adroits chasseurs, gibier fêlon,
Courez! Tirez! Nous les aurons!
Voix au ciel
Aidez-nous!
Gardez-nous!
Sauvez-nous!
Pardonnez-nous!

Jeanne
Sur vos morts sans tombe,
Voyez! Mes cendres tombent
En linceuil

La moisson future
Verdit aux sépultures
De vos deuils.

Table 13.2. *continued*

Voix sur la terre
Feu du ciel, angoisse
Dont est transi l'espace.
Feu sur terre, alarme,
Mortel effroi sans larmes.
Feu sauveur du monde
Iniquité féconde.

Ah!

c. François Villon, "Ballade contre les ennemis de la France"

Rencontré soit de bêtes feu jetant
Que Jason vit, quérant la Toison d'or;
Ou transmué d'homme en bête sept ans
Ainsi que fut Nabugodonosor;
Ou perte il ait et guerre aussi vilaine
Que les Troyens pour la prise d'Hélène;
Ou avalé soit avec Tantalus
Et Proserpine aux infernaux palus;
Ou plus que Job soit en grieve souffrance,
Tenant prison en la tour Dedalus,
<u>Qui mal voudroit au royaume de France!</u>
Quatre mois soit en un vivier chantant,
La tête au fond, ainsi que le butor;
Ou au grand Turc vendu deniers comptants,
Pour être mis au harnais comme un tor;
Ou trente ans soit, comme la Magdelaine,
Sans drap vêtir de linge ne de laine;
Ou soit noyé comme fut Narcissus,
Ou aux cheveux, comme Absalon, pendus,
Ou, comme fut Judas, par Despérance;
Ou puist périr comme Simon Magus,
<u>Qui mal voudroit au royaume de France!</u>
D'Octovien puist revenir le temps:
C'est qu'on lui coule au ventre son trésor;
Ou qu'il soit mis entre meules flottant
En un moulin, comme fut saint Victor;
Ou transglouti en la mer, sans haleine,
Pis que Jonas ou corps de la baleine;
Ou soit banni de la clarté Phébus,
Des biens Juno et du soulas Vénus,
Et du dieu Mars soit pugni à outrance,
Ainsi que fut roi Sardanapalus,
<u>Qui mal voudroit au royaume de France!</u>

Envoie,
Prince, porté soit des serfs Eolus
En la forêt où domine Glaucus,
Ou privé soit de paix et d'espérance:
Car digne n'est de posséder vertus,
<u>Qui mal voudroit au royaume de France!</u>

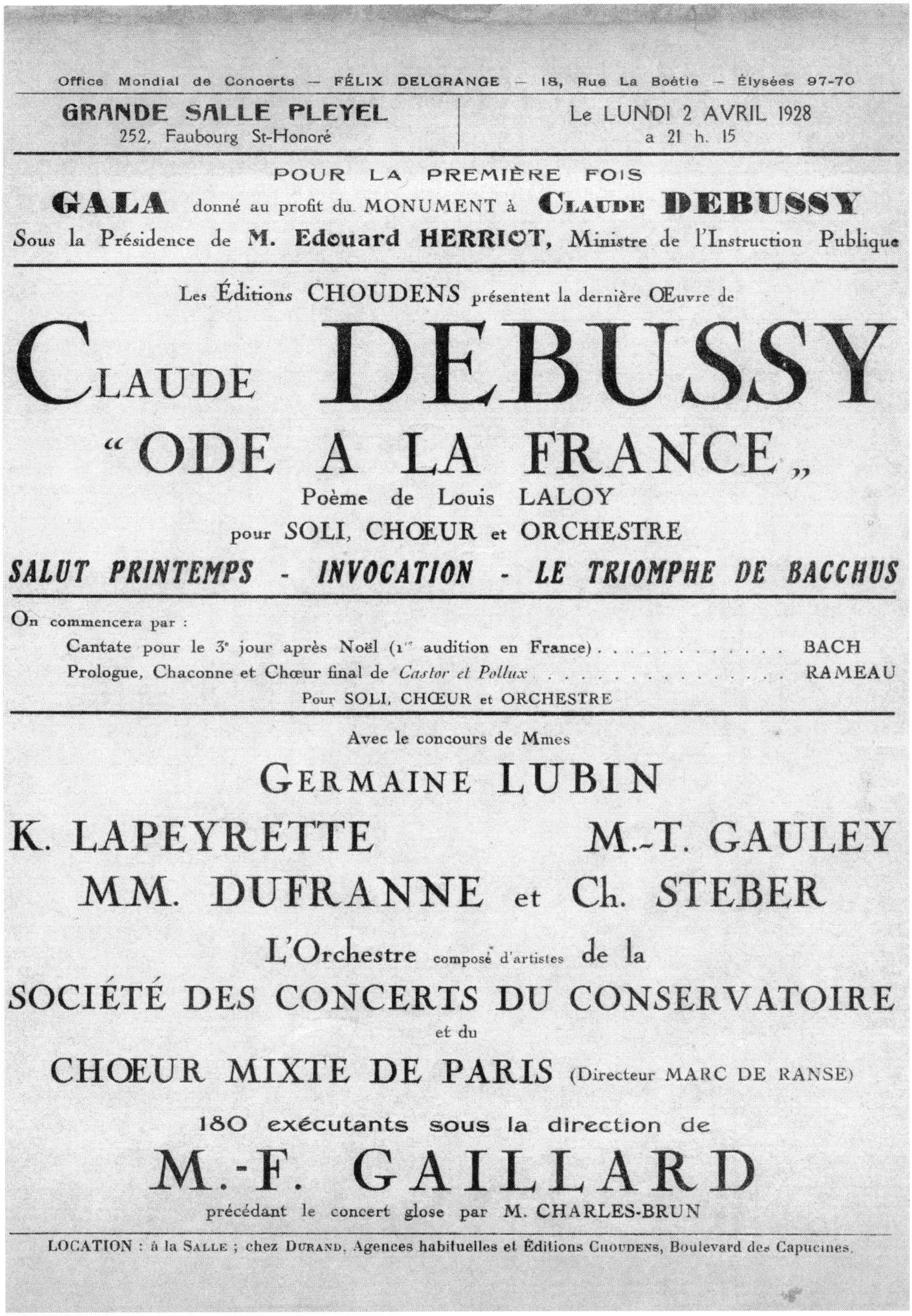

Office Mondial de Concerts — FÉLIX DELGRANGE — 18, Rue La Boétie — Élysées 97-70

GRANDE SALLE PLEYEL
252, Faubourg St-Honoré

Le LUNDI 2 AVRIL 1928
a 21 h. 15

POUR LA PREMIÈRE FOIS

GALA donné au profit du MONUMENT à **Claude DEBUSSY**

Sous la Présidence de **M. Edouard HERRIOT**, Ministre de l'Instruction Publique

Les Éditions CHOUDENS présentent la dernière Œuvre de

Claude DEBUSSY
"ODE A LA FRANCE„

Poème de Louis LALOY

pour SOLI, CHŒUR et ORCHESTRE

SALUT PRINTEMPS - INVOCATION - LE TRIOMPHE DE BACCHUS

On commencera par :

Cantate pour le 3ᵉ jour après Noël (1ʳᵉ audition en France) . . . . BACH
Prologue, Chaconne et Chœur final de *Castor et Pollux* . . . . RAMEAU

Pour SOLI, CHŒUR et ORCHESTRE

Avec le concours de Mmes

Germaine LUBIN

K. LAPEYRETTE   M.-T. GAULEY
MM. DUFRANNE et Ch. STEBER

L'Orchestre composé d'artistes de la

SOCIÉTÉ DES CONCERTS DU CONSERVATOIRE

et du

CHOEUR MIXTE DE PARIS (Directeur MARC DE RANSE)

180 exécutants sous la direction de

M.-F. GAILLARD

précédant le concert glose par M. CHARLES-BRUN

LOCATION : à la SALLE ; chez DURAND, Agences habituelles et Éditions CHOUDENS, Boulevard des Capucines.

Figure 13.2 Poster for an early performance of *Ode à la France* conducted by Marius-François Gaillard

and Debussy transformed it into "the children of France" in his carol.[34] As an aside, figure 13.2 shows that when Marius-François Gaillard gave a rare early performance of *Ode à la France* on April 2, 1928, he placed Debussy's piece alongside the choral works of another esteemed French composer, Rameau, not just those of Bach.[35]

Just as Debussy's anxiety fed his anger, so his anger gave way to sadness, pain, and despair. These feelings led him to create music that often sounds disjunct and recalls the mosaic or collage structures of *La Boîte à joujoux* and *Jeux* or the cellular/cyclic arabesques of *Pelléas et Mélisande*. Take, for example, *Berceuse héroïque*, a short piano piece Debussy wrote in November 1914 for *King Albert's Book*, a compendium put together by Sir Thomas Hall Caine to support the people of Belgium.[36] Set in the remote key of E♭ minor, this melancholy arabesque uses a modal theme and relentless string of quarter notes to convey the image of soldiers trudging to and from the front (see ex. 13.1a); the desolate mood of this music is punctuated by occasional statements of Belgium's national anthem, "The Brabançonne" (see ex. 13.1b). Debussy's *Sonate pour violoncelle*

Example 13.1   Melodic arabesques in Debussy's wartime music

Example 13.1a Debussy, *Berceuse héroïque*, mm. 1–9

Example 13.1b "The Brabançonne," mm. 37–44

Example 13.1c Debussy, *Sonate pour violoncelle et piano*, mvt. 1, mm. 1–4

Example 13.1d Debussy, *Sonate pour violoncelle et piano*, mvt. 1, mm. 27–33

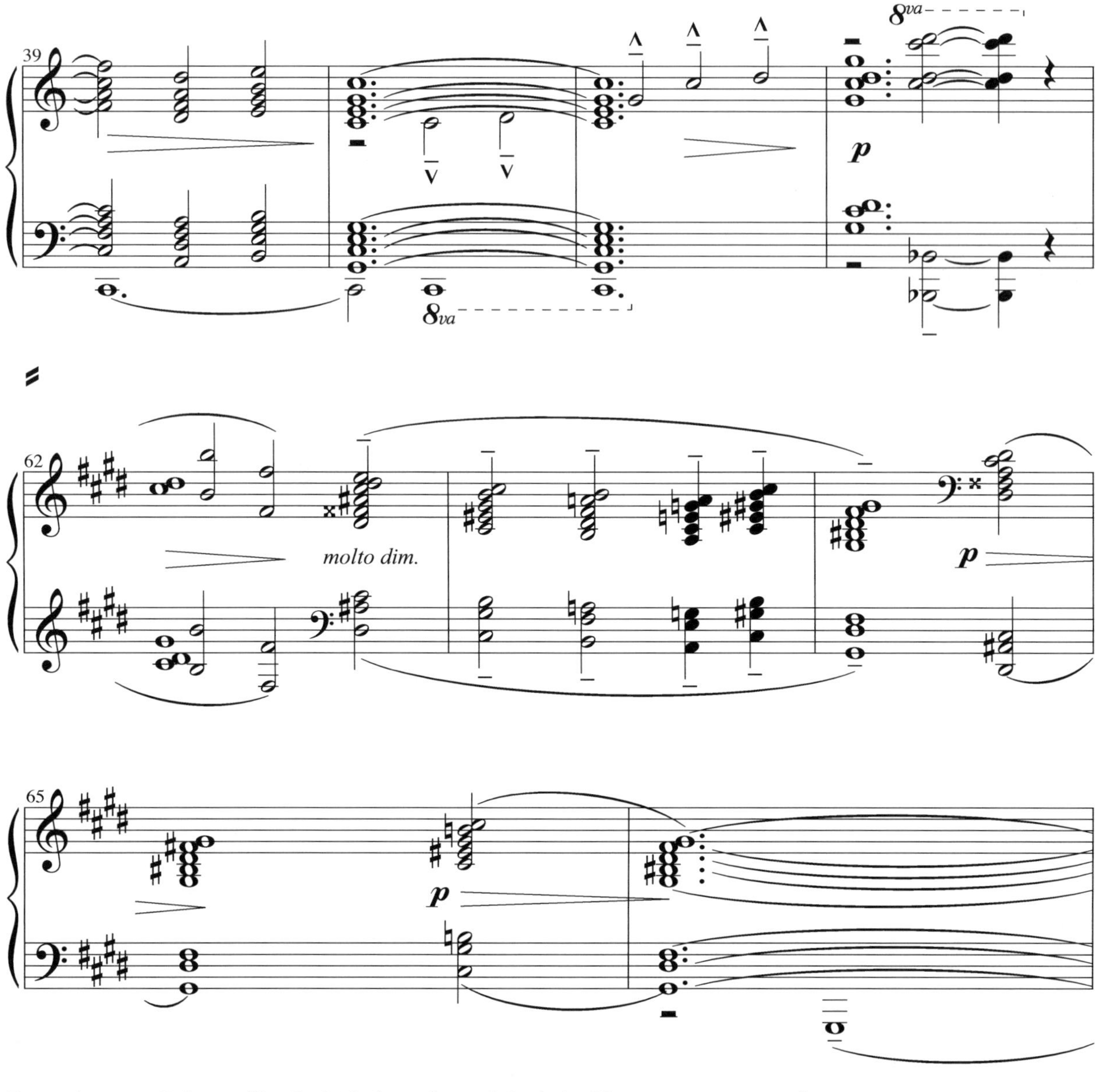

Example 13.1e Debussy, "La Cathédrale engloutie," *Préludes*, Bk. 1, mm. 39–42 and mm. 62–66

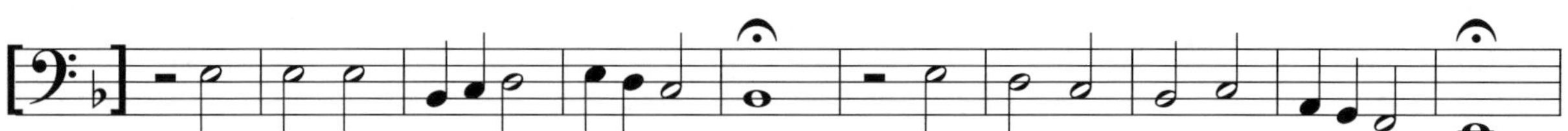

Example 13.1f Debussy's quotation of "Ein feste Bourg" in his sketches for the *Sonate pour violoncelle et piano*

Example 13.1g Debussy, *Élégy*, mm. 1–6

Example 13.1h Debussy, *Sonate pour violoncelle et piano*, mvt. 1, mm. 8–11

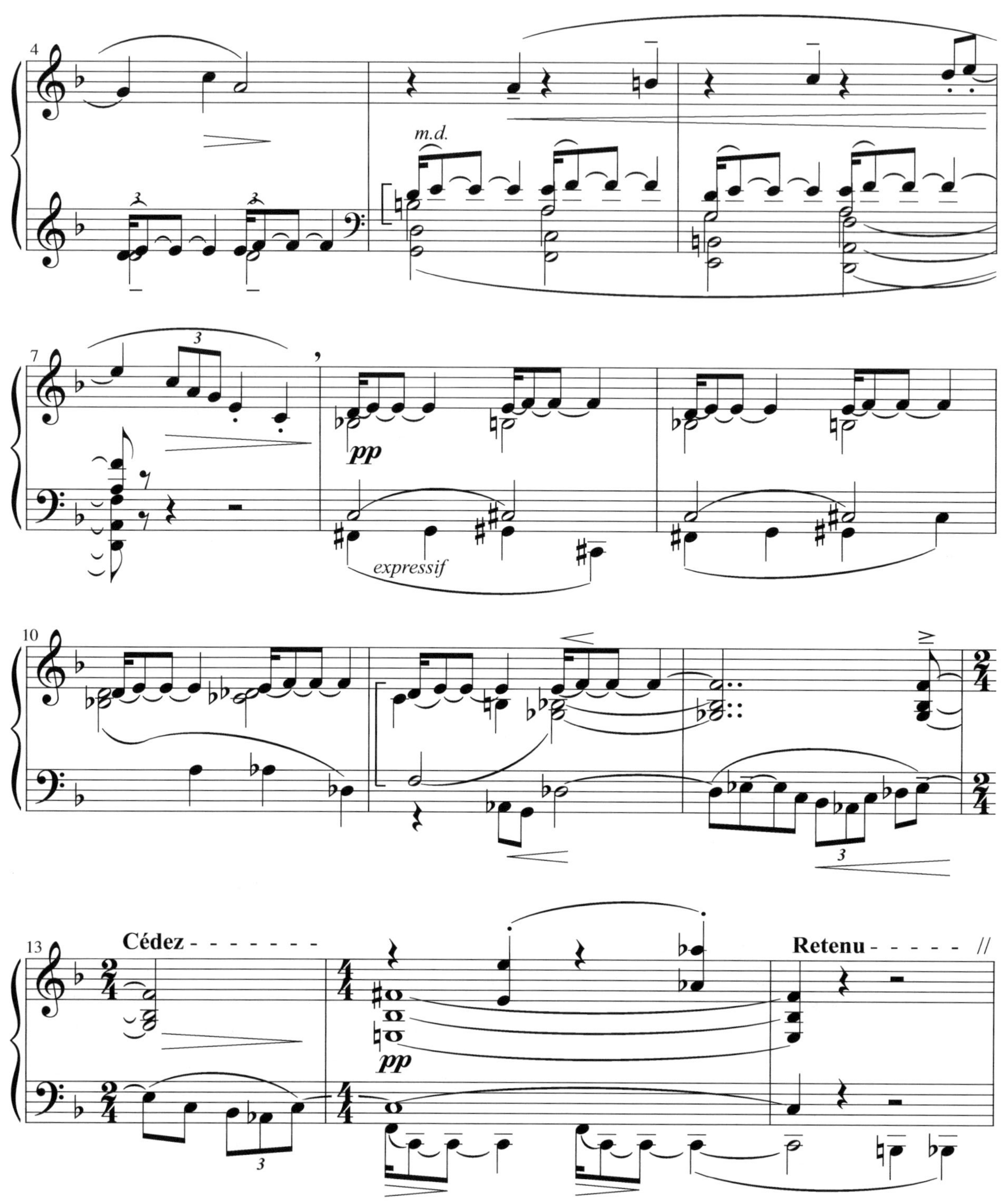

Example **13.1i** Debussy, "Des pas sur la neige," *Préludes*, Bk. 1, mm. 4–15

et piano begins in a similar vein: mm. 1–4, which are shown in example 13.1c, hint at the start of Rameau's opera *Les Fêtes de Polymnie* (1745), a work that Debussy had edited for Durand in 1908. When the music cadences in C major in mm. 27–33, Debussy added a rising pentatonic motive D–F–G–A–C and booming pedal that recall the central section of "La Cathédrale engloutie" (*Préludes*, Bk. 1; see ex. 13.1d–13.1e). Some have even heard allusions to "Ein feste bourg" (see ex. 13.1f).[37] Completed soon after the *Sonate pour violoncelle et piano*, in December 1915, *Élégy* is another dirge in D minor. Debussy wrote this 21-bar score for "Pages inédites sur la Femme et la Guerre," a compendium sponsored by King Edward VII's wife, Alexandra, to raise money for French orphans. Like *Berceuse héroïque*, the work is dominated by a melancholy arabesque in the low register (see ex. 13.1g): examples 13.1h–13.1i show that this gesture resembles similar arabesques from the first movement of the *Sonate pour violoncelle et piano* and "Des pas sur la neige" (*Préludes*, Bk. 1).

The trip to Pourville-sur-mer was clearly a successful one for Debussy; the location provided him with an environment in which he could finally exorcise those childhood demons that had haunted him for so long. Debussy's sense of optimism was so strong that he even resumed work on the libretto of *La chute de la maison Usher* in October 1915. But Debussy's optimism was short lived. On returning to Paris, his health deteriorated rapidly, prompting him to have another round of cancer surgery on December 7, 1915. Debussy had high expectations for the treatment, but these hopes were soon dashed when it became clear that the operation had not been successful. Debussy understandably became depressed. He had been suffering from colorectal cancer at least since early 1909: "For two days I've constantly suffered miserably. Only with the help of a variety of tranquilizers—morphine, cocaine, and other such lovely drugs—was I able to cope, but at the price of total stupor."[38] This was around the same time that he started to work on *La chute de la maison Usher*: "I've been working on [the opera] *Usher* recently and have almost finished a long monologue for Roderick. It's sad enough to make the stones weep for what neurasthenics have to go through. It smells charmingly of mildew, obtained by mixing the sounds of a low oboe and violin harmonics."[39] A year later, the situation was no better: "I live surrounded by memories and regrets. Two gloomy companions, but faithful ones—more so than pleasure and happiness! I'm working as much as I can. There are still moments when I come closest to satisfying my taste for the inexpressible! If, as I hope, I succeed with this exploration of anguish, which is what *La chute de la maison Usher* will be, then I feel I'll have made a successful contribution to music."[40] Debussy's personal struggles made him despondent and bad tempered for much of the next year, impairing his ability to work on his opera.[41]

But the failure of the operation on December 7, 1915, confirmed that Debussy was doomed: there would be no cure; there would be no permanent reprieve from the pain. To quote Stephen Walsh, "Having survived his operation but without much comfort, [Debussy underwent] radium treatment, a new disagreeable process with a high risk of genetic and other undesirable side-effects. The treatment involved sitting on a rubber ring and being given a tincture of opium to cause constipation and avert bowel motion, which could result in the loss of the expensive, not to say dangerous, radium."[42] Debussy described the situation with particular frankness in a letter to Godet (January 4, 1916).

> Recovery will be slow and by natural means. Nature alone has all the time in the world; mine is beginning to run out. So it's not very jolly and I'm complaining—not that there's any point, because Mother Nature is usually deaf to her children's suffering. Ironically, this incident caught me working at full tilt;

as someone said, 'That doesn't happen every day.' One has to take advantage of the good times to make up for the bad. I was on the point—more or less—of finishing *La chute de la maison Usher*, but illness has quashed my hopes.[43]

He added, "Obviously it's not a matter of importance on Aldabaran or Sirius whether I write music or not, but I don't like being crossed and I find it hard to lie down under this blow of fate! And I'm suffering like a condemned man."[44]

As the year wore on, the implications of the failed surgery became increasingly apparent. Sometimes Debussy complained that it prevented him from working properly: "I'm terrified of planning any sort of work whatsoever—that in itself is enough to condemn it to the waste-paper basket, the cemetery of bad dreams. What an existence! I'm exhausted by chasing phantoms but not tired enough to sleep. So I wait for the morrow, for better or for worse; and it starts all over again" (December 11, 1916).[45] Sometimes he reveled in his misery, as on July 21, 1916: "I [must] apologize to Maeterlinck, but very useless 'events' do happen . . . There are always threats! In truth, I wonder how I will [ever] get out of it? Nothing has spared me: illness; Chouchou is ill . . . Mrs. Texier, another patient! One would consider committing suicide if I did not feel anxious as much as duty-bound to finish the two little dramas based on E. Poe."[46] And sometimes he voiced his despair: "I expect you know about the obscure punishment visited on me for nearly two and a half years now? Fear not, I shan't darken your fine horizon with stories that are a meticulous blend of the grotesque and the horrible. The war may not have touched me physically but spiritually it's destroyed me: I'm lost and I don't have the money to offer a realistic reward for my recovery" (May 20, 1917).[47]

But *La chute de la maison Usher* was never far away; Debussy used his score to express the fear, anger, guilt, sadness, helplessness, inadequacy, and nervousness that he clearly felt in his own life. The opening prelude, for example, captures the uneasy atmosphere that pervades the entire opera as well as Debussy's own home. As is clear from example 13.2a, this effect is created by presenting a string of eerie whole-tone chords over a pedal tone B. Examples 13.2b–13.2c then show how Debussy conveyed a similar sense of uneasiness in the opening prelude to his ballet *Jeux*: once again, he presented a string of whole-tone chords over a pedal tone B. And just like the whole-tone harmonies in examples 13.2b–13.2c, those in example 13.2a are brought to life by two surface motives. In *La chute de la maison Usher*, the first of these motives appears in m. 2 and again in mm. 7 and 15–16. The statement in m. 7 spawns a long arabesque that ascends chromatically from B in m. 7, through C♮, D, E, F♮, and F♯ in mm. 8–9, to G♮ and G♯ in m. 10, and is accompanied by a stepwise ascent in a lower voice. When it returns in mm. 15–16, the motive is harmonized by a similar chromatic line that rises from B in mm. 14/16, through C♮, D, D♯, E♯, F♮, F♯, and F× in mm. 16–18. Example 13.2a also suggests that the opening prelude includes another three-note motive: this gesture enters in mm. 3–4 as B–C♮–D♯ and is transposed and augmented in mm. 11–13 as C♮, C♯, E. Finally, examples 13.2d–13.2e show that the first motive recalls the motto theme from the second movement of his *Quatuor à cordes*.

The mood becomes more tender when Lady Madeline sings "The Haunted Palace," though material from the opening prelude also adds a tinge of sadness. Example 13.3a shows that the passage, which features a pedal C♯ and centers on F♯, begins with an arabesque figure starting on D♯ in mm. 20–21. This pattern is followed by a new triadic motive in the voice and a repetition of the motive from mm. 4–5, now G×–A♯–C♯. The triadic motive is particularly striking not only because Roderick sings it transposed down a half step near the climax of the opera (see ex. 13.3b)

Example 13.2 Debussy, "Prelude," *La chute de la maison Usher*

Example 13.2a Debussy, "Prelude," *La chute de la maison Usher*, mm. 1–13

Example 13.2b Debussy, "Prélude," *Jeux*, mm. 1–9

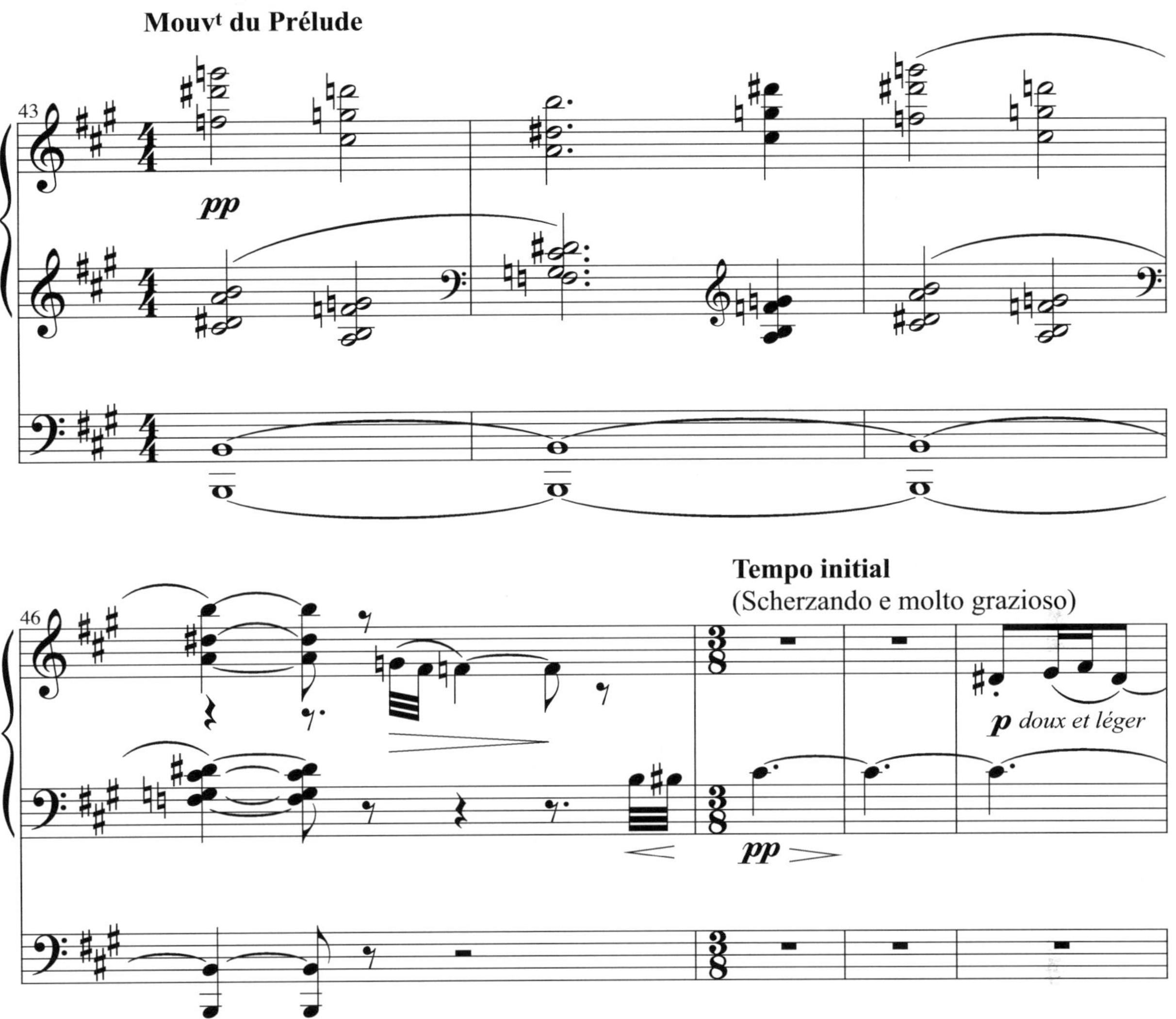

Example 13.2c Debussy, "Prélude," *Jeux*, mm. 43–49

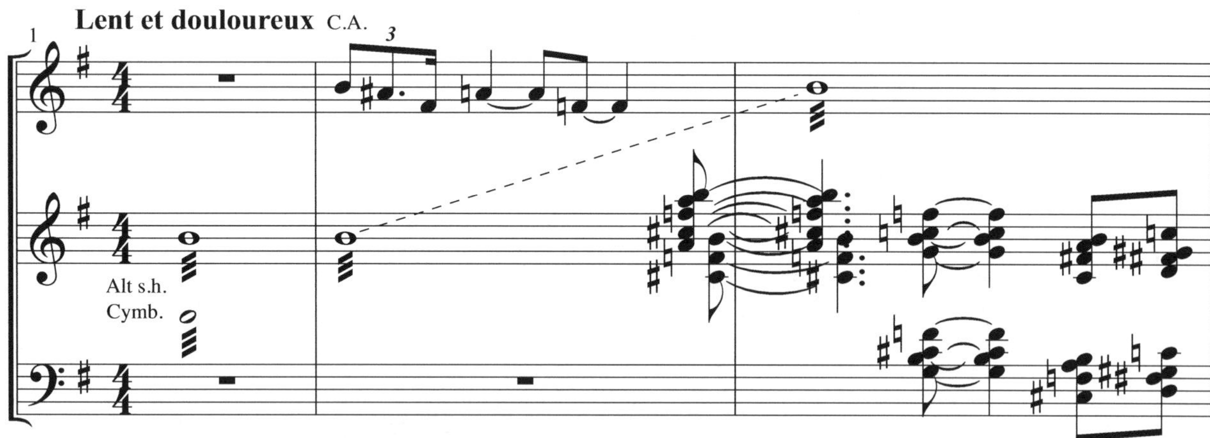

Example 13.2d Debussy, "Prelude," *La chute de la maison Usher*, mm. 1–3

Example 13.2e Debussy, *Quatuor à cordes*, mvt. II, mm. 1–4

but also because it resembles a gesture from m. 2 of Debussy's early song *Le Matelot qui tombe à l'eau* (see ex. 13.3c). Having brought back a variant of the motive from mm. 4–5, example 13.3d shows how Lady Madeline sings another arabesque B–C♮–B–A♯–B–A♯–A♮ in mm. 34–35. Perhaps to convey the abnormal relationship between Lady Madeline and Roderick, this arabesque recalls material from the infamous triple kiss at the climax of *Jeux* (see ex. 13.3e). Examples 13.3f–13.3g then show how the passage ends in m. 37 with a recollection of the opening arabesque from mm. 20–21 and the motto theme from the *Quatuor à cordes* in m. 46. In between, Debussy inserted a somber passage built over an ostinato C♯–G♮ in the bass: examples 13.3h and 13.3i suggest that this material recalls similar passages to Debussy's "La terrasse des audiences du clair de lune" and "Ondine" (*Préludes*, Bk. 2).

The sense of sadness becomes more pronounced when the physician and the friend converse and the music shifts seamlessly to B♭ minor. Example 13.4a shows how this new section is marked by a new wedge motive B♭–B♮–C♮ over B♭–A♭–G♮–G♭ in m. 50. This material returns recomposed starting in m. 76 (see ex. 13.4b) and culminates in a perfect authentic cadence in B♭ minor with a picardy third in mm. 84–85 (see ex. 13.4c). However, Debussy saves some of his most poignant music for the section when the physician describes how he assisted Roderick's mother in the last moments of her life: as shown in examples 13.4d–13.4e, the simple quarter-note gesture is

Example 13.3 Arabesque figures in Debussy, "The Haunted Palace,"
La chute de la maison Usher

Example 13.3a Debussy, "The Haunted Palace," *La chute de la maison Usher*, mm. 20–24

Above, **Example 13.3b** Debussy, *La chute de la maison Usher,* mm. 349–53

Facing, **Example 13.3c** Debussy, *Le Matelot qui tombe à l'eau,* mm. 1–4

454

Andante
On en - tend un chant sur
l'eau Dans la brune:
Ce doit être un ma - te - lot Qui veut

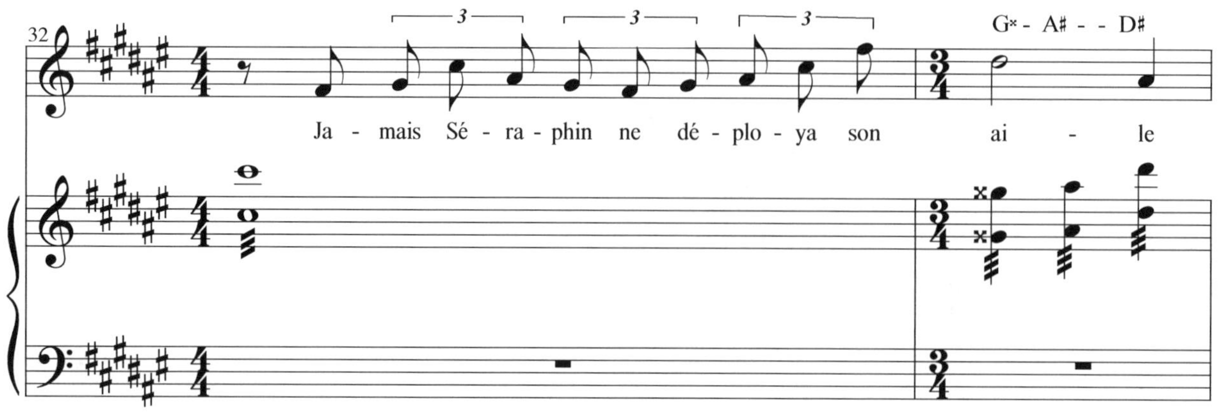

Example 13.3d Debussy, "The Haunted Palace," *La chute de la maison Usher*, mm. 32–36

Example 13.3e Debussy, *Jeux*, mm. 681–87

Example 13.3f Debussy, "The Haunted Palace," *La chute de la maison Usher*, mm. 37–42

Example 13.3g Debussy, "The Haunted Palace," *La chute de la maison Usher*, mm. 45–46

Example 13.3h Debussy, "La terrasse des audiences du clair de lune," *Préludes*, Bk. 2, mm. 15–18

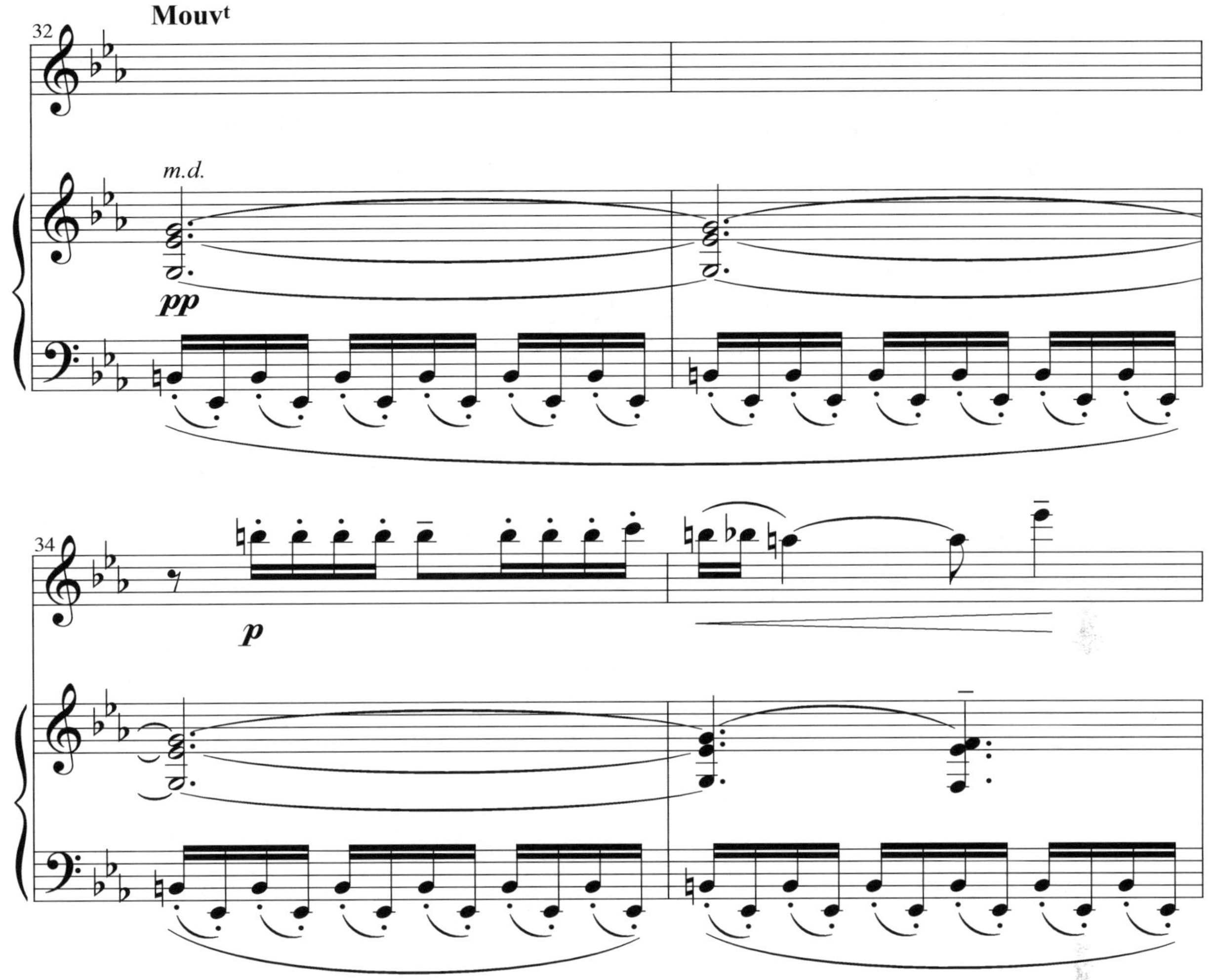

Example 13.3i Debussy, "Ondine," *Préludes*, Bk. 2, mm. 32–35

reminiscent of somber passages in *Pelléas et Mélisande*, such as the one in the interlude between act 4, scenes 2 and 3 that foreshadows Pelléas's death at the end of act 4, scene 4. The mood soon intensifies when the physician expresses his anger at the ways Roderick forced Lady Madeline to sing (ex. 13.4f). The physician's rage is conveyed by distorted variants of the short motive from mm. 4–5 (now A♮–B♭–E♭) and the decorated figure form in mm. 34–35, now E♯–F♯–E♯–E♮–F♮–E♮–E♭. Example 13.4g then shows how anger turns to despair as the scene ends with further variants of the decorated figure reminiscent of the triple kiss from the end of *Jeux*.

The same emotions persist throughout the rest of the opera. As Robert Orledge has noted, Roderick's monologue conveys the same sense of anxiety as act 3, scene 2 of *Pelléas et Mélisande*, when Golaud leads Pelléas down to the castle vaults and warns him not to meet Mélisande again. As mentioned in chapter 8, Maeterlinck specifically alluded to Poe's story in his original play: "Have you noticed the crevices in the walls and in the pillars of the vaults? There is some hidden, unsuspected work; and the whole castle will be engulfed one night if no care be taken."[48] Examples 13.5a–13.5b indicate that both passages use the same pedal tone C and sinister chromaticisms. The first portion of the monologue also features the so-called Usher Chord (C–E–G–F♯) and even culminates in a return of the motto theme from the *Quatuor à cordes* (see ex. 13.5c).[49] Prior to Roderick's hallucination, the score includes new variants of the three-note motive from mm. 4–5 (see ex. 13.5d). The music becomes even more threatening when Roderick laughs at the memory of his mother's death. According to Orledge, the savage string *tremolandos* recall the moment when Golaud murders Pelléas at the end of act 4, scene 4 of *Pelléas et Mélisande* and when Roderick laughs at his mother's death.[50] These passages are given in examples 13.5e–13.5f.

Example 13.4 Debussy, *La chute de la maison Usher*

Example 13.4a Debussy, *La chute de la maison Usher*, mm. 49–52

Example 13.4b Debussy, *La chute de la maison Usher*, mm. 75–78

Example 13.4c Debussy, *La chute de la maison Usher*, mm. 83–86

Example 13.4d Debussy, *La chute de la maison Usher*, mm. 63–68

Example 13.4e Debussy, *Pelléas et Mélisande*, interlude between act 4, scenes 2 and 3, mm. 63–66

Example 13.4f Debussy, *La chute de la maison Usher*, mm. 145–48

Example 13.4g Debussy, *La chute de la maison Usher*, mm. 152–59

Notice, too, how the tremolos in Roderick's monologue accompany transformations of the wedge motive first heard in m. 50 just before the physician laments the passing of Roderick's mother. Not surprisingly, perhaps, Debussy saves some of his angriest music for the end of the opera and the reading of Channing's *Mad Trist*. The passage begins with the wedge motive (see ex. 13.5g) and continues with a veiled recollection of the arabesque figure from Lady Madeline's rendition of "The Haunted Palace" (see ex. 13.5h). The music reaches a fever pitch at the climax of the story, at which point the score fuses the *Quatuor à cordes'* motto and the three-note motive from mm. 4–5 (see ex. 13.5i).

The preceding remarks pinpoint some of the ways in which the score of *La chute de la maison Usher* embodies Debussy's conception of arabesque, moresque, and grotesque. Among other things, they describe the highly decorated character of surface gestures, such as those associated with "The Haunted Palace" (see ex. 13.3) and the extremely disjunct arrangement of the material, much of which alludes to other works by Debussy, such as the "motto" theme from the second movement of Debussy's *Quatuor à cordes* (see ex. 13.2) and passages from *Le Matelot qui tombe à l'eau, Jeux,* "La terrasse des audiences du clair de lune," "Ondine," and *Pelléas et Mélisande* (see ex. 13.3, 13.4, and 13.5). The fragmentary nature and cellular arrangement of these gestures specifically recalls the discussion of grotesques in *La Boîte à joujoux* in chapter 9. The latter qualities

Example 13.5 Debussy, *La chute de la maison Usher* and *Pelléas et Mélisande*

Scène 2

Entre Roderick Usher les vêtements en désordre. Il regarde fixement devant lui, et pourtant ses yeux semblent ne pas voir. Ses gestes song brusques et saccadés, sa voix rauque.

Example 13.5a Debussy, *La chute de la maison Usher*, mm. 159–62

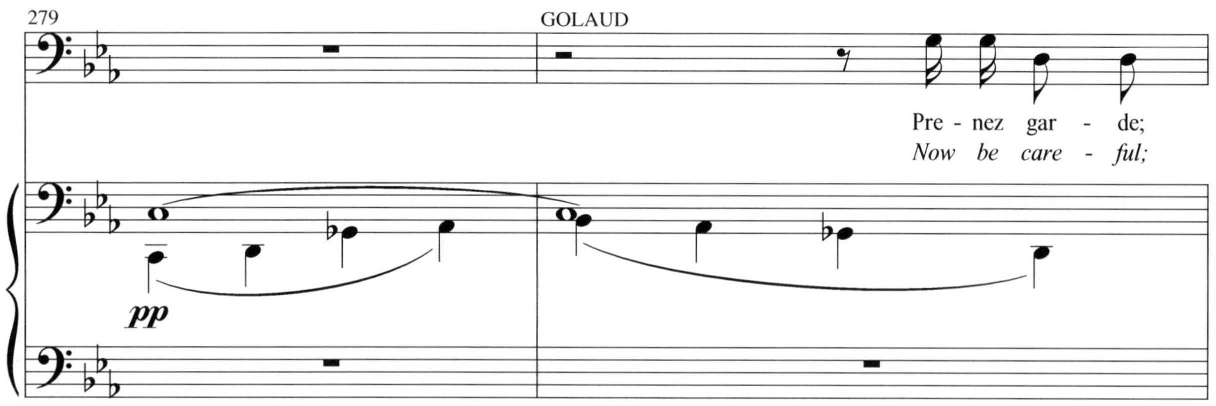

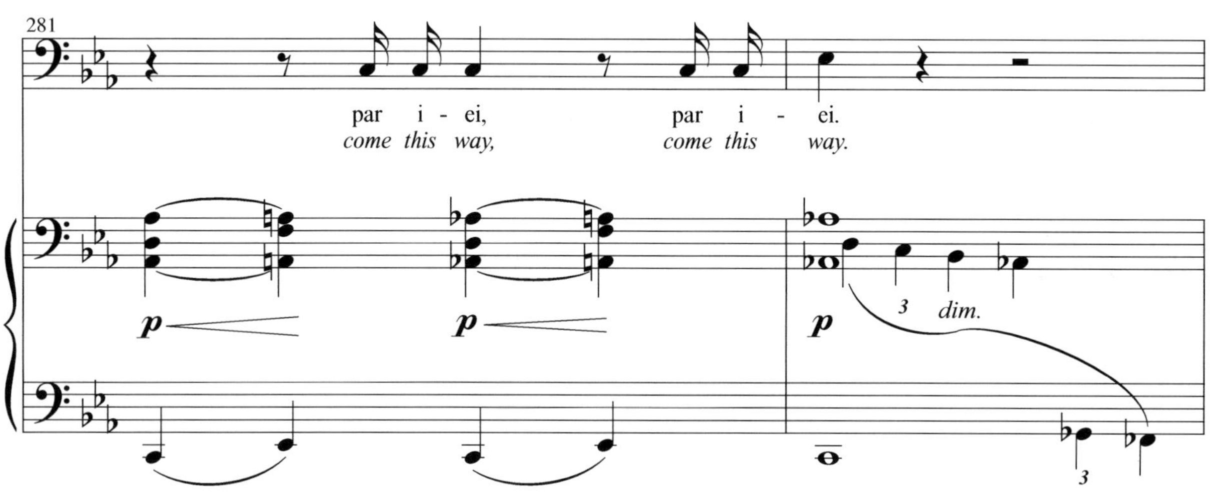

Example 13.5b Debussy, *Pelléas et Mélisande*, act 3, scene 2, mm. 279–82

Example 13.5c Debussy, *La chute de la maison Usher*, mm. 191–97

Example 13.5d Debussy, *La chute de la maison Usher*, mm. 268–72

Example 13.5e Debussy, *La chute de la maison Usher*, mm. 244–47

Example 13.5f Debussy, *Pelléas et Mélisande*, act 4, scene 4, mm. 826–30

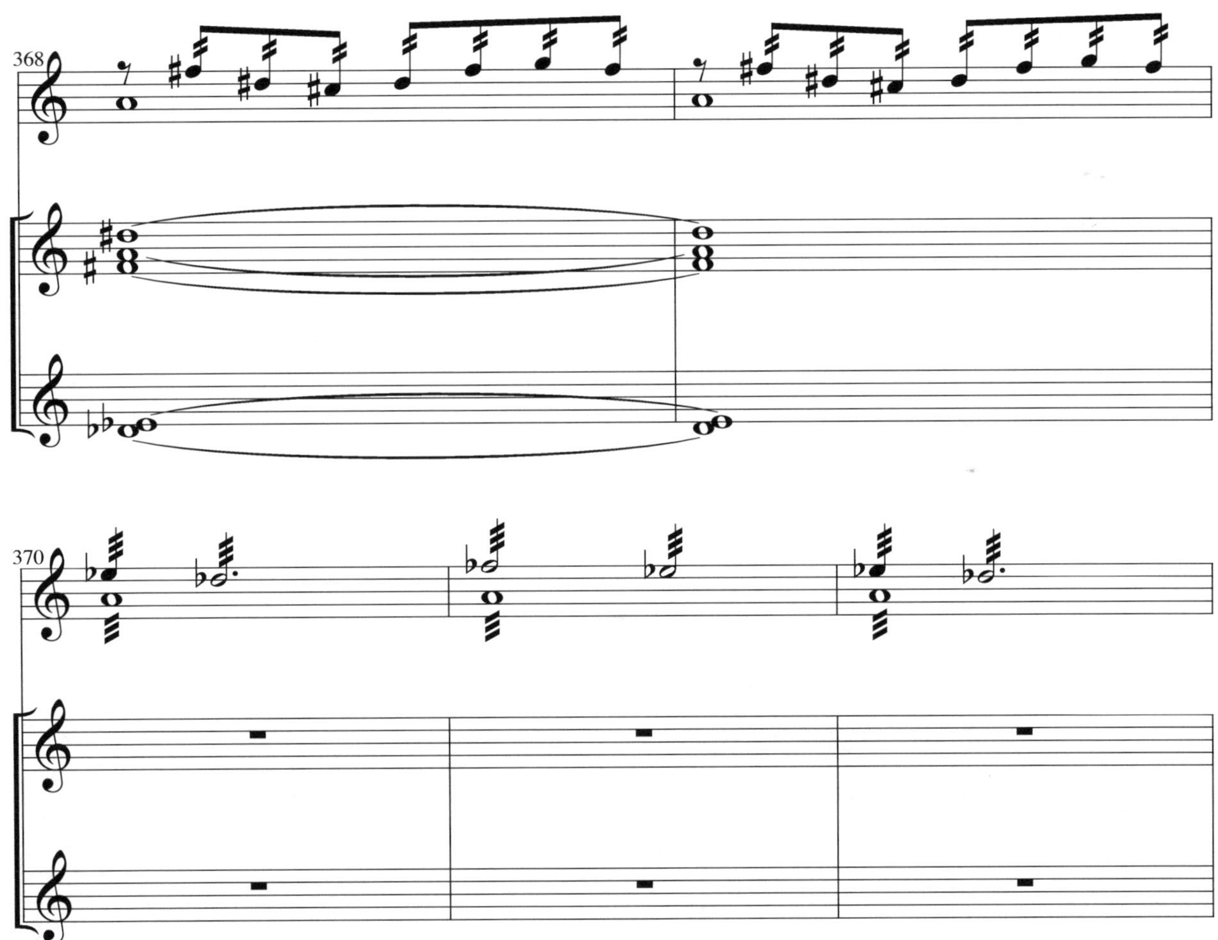

Example 13.5g Debussy, *La chute de la maison Usher*, mm. 244–47, cf. mm. 362–63

Example 13.5h Debussy, *La chute de la maison Usher*, mm. 368–72

Example 13.5i Debussy, *La chute de la maison Usher*, mm. 422–28

also reflect the scattered state of Debussy's mind while he was composing *La chute de la maison Usher*. This mental instability stemmed from the two traumatic experiences that Debussy suffered during WWI: the outbreak of WWI in August 1914 unleashed a stream of suppressed childhood memories about his father's imprisonment after the Paris Commune; the unsuccessful cancer surgery in December 1915 reminded him of the pain he had endured since 1909 and would endure for the rest of his life.

But there is another interesting intersection between Debussy's setting of Poe's story and Schlegel's claim about arabesques and confessions. This point involves Debussy's libretto and the ways in which it modified the original text. As Andrew Porter has noted, Debussy made some drastic changes in transplanting Poe's tale from the page to the stage.[51] For one thing, he confronted the uncomfortable fact that the house serves both as a setting and as a character; this dual role is much easier to pull off in the cinema than in the theater. For another, Debussy needed to find an effective way to portray Lady Madeline; though central to the plot, she is mentioned only briefly in the original story and never utters a single word. Most perplexing of all, Poe's original narrative is cast as a dramatic monologue for the friend and does not subdivide easily into discrete musical units. This problem is most acute in the opening sections where Poe described the friend's arrival, the building's desolate location and dilapidated condition, Roderick's appearance and mental instability, and Madeline's untreatable disease. The second part, which culminates with Madeline's apparent death and premature burial, is more successful and primarily describes Roderick's controversial belief that plants and stones are actually sentient. The only obvious set piece is Roderick's ballad "The Haunted Palace." And, although the final part of the story contains one potential set piece—the friend's recitation from Canning's *Mad Trist* and Madeline's escape from the vault—it takes place in several different locations, making it hard to re-create onstage. This leaves Roderick's final speech in which he realizes that they had "*put her living in the tomb!*"

Debussy's solution was to rewrite Baudelaire's translation of Poe's story. He began by confining the action to Roderick's studio. Like Poe's original, this room has long, narrow windows, an oak floor, somber tapestries, and an array of antique books and musical instruments. Unlike Poe, however, it also has a fireplace and french windows that overlook the tarn outside. This window serves as a conduit through which characters can enter the scene from the outside. Debussy likewise condensed the story's time frame: whereas the original takes place over a period of about two weeks, the libretto shrinks that duration down to less than an hour, about the same time it takes to read the original story out loud.[52] Debussy's changes to the characters were even more drastic and fundamentally altered their interactions.

Since it is extremely hard to portray the house as a character, Debussy decided to develop another character. Poe offered him just two options: the valet and the family physician. Of these, the physician is the more likely suspect. Though he appears in passing in the original story, Poe's brief description casts doubts about the physician's motives: "his countenance wore a mingled expression of low cunning and perplexity." These suspicions were enough for Debussy to transform the physician into "an evil monster" and a "rival to Roderick's unnatural love for his sister."[53] Indeed, not only is the physician responsible for burying Lady Madeline alive, but he is likely to benefit from "the extinction of the interbred Usher line." Roderick is therefore reduced to "a neurasthenic victim."[54] To accomplish this goal, Debussy rewrote the opening to include a lengthy conversation between the physician and the friend. During this conversation, which occurs after Lady Madeline sings portions of "The Haunted Palace" and crosses the back of Roderick's studio, the physician explains both that she is gravely ill and that Roderick is mad and guilty of incest.[55] To quote Andrew Porter, "[Debussy] invested Roderick with a guilty Byronic passion for his sister, which plays no part in Poe's story. . . . By implication, he applied the Béranger couplet set over the Poe story—*Son cœur est un luth suspendu; Sitôt qu'on le touche il résonne*—to [Lady] Madeline, not Roderick, by making the [physician] exclaim angrily that Usher plays upon his sister as if she were a lute."[56]

In light of Schlegel's claim about arabesques and confessions, it is tempting to offer another explanation of Debussy's decision to recast the physician as the villain of *La chute de la maison Usher*. This explanation is biographical in nature. Indeed, just as Poe's original story drew on contemporary fears about premature burial, a fear that was entirely justified given the difficulties nineteenth-century doctors had confirming the death of patients in comas, so Debussy had good reasons for demonizing doctors and for seeing himself as a victim of the medical profession.[57] Naturally suspicious and riddled with self-doubt (Orledge has noted that Debussy often compared himself to Hamlet), he was clearly skeptical of physicians and their diagnoses and prognoses.[58] That skepticism would have been especially strong after the final round of surgery and the subsequent radium treatment. The decision to blame doctors for the demise of the Usher family and the decline in his own health was reinforced by his tendency to identify himself with Roderick Usher: "[My] house has some curious points of resemblance with the House of Usher. . . . Even if I haven't got Roderick Usher's cerebral disorders or his passion for Weber's last Waltz, we share a certain hypersensitivity. . . . I could give you details which would make your beard fall out. . . . It's extremely unpleasant."[59] And, in a moment of extreme irony worthy of Schlegel, he confessed to Paul Dukas (August 10, 1916), "Is it possible that 'The Fall of the House of Usher' is also 'The Fall of Claude Debussy'?"[60]

Notes

1. Mohammed Hamdan, "The Gift of Drugs: Oriental Geographies and Decolonizing Space in Thomas De Quincey's Confessions of an English Opium-Eater," *Janus Unbound: Journal of Critical Studies* II, no. I (Winter 2022): 63–68; Friedrich Schlegel, "Letter about the Novel," *Dialogue on Poetry and Literary Aphorisms*, trans., introduced, and annotated by Ernest Behler and Roman Struc (University Park: Pennsylvania State University Press, 1968), 103.

2. Schlegel, *Dialogue on Poetry*, 103, 104.

3. Schlegel, *Dialogue on Poetry*, 104.

4. Charles Baudelaire, "Le Joujoue du Pauvre," *Le Spleen de Paris* XIX, in *Charles Baudelaire: Œuvres Complètes*, vol. I, ed. Claude Pichois, Bibliothèque de la Pléiade (Paris: Gallimard, 1975): 304–5; Baudelaire, "The Poor Boy's Toy," in *Vol. II: The Poems in Prose and La Fanfarol*, ed. and trans. Francis Scarfe (London: Anvil Press Poetry, 1989), 82–85.

5. Baudelaire, "Morale du joujou," in *Œuvres Complètes*, I:584–85; Baudelaire, "A Philosophy of Toys," in *The Painter of Modern Life*, ed. and trans. Jonathan Mayne (London: Phaidon, 2001), 200.

6. Marie Bonaparte, *The Life and Works of Edgar Allan Poe: A Psycho-Analytic Interpretation*, trans. John Rodker (London: Imago, 1949), 237, 243.

7. Claude Debussy, *Correspondance (1872–1918)*, ed. François Lesure and Denis Herlin, annotated by François Lesure, Denis Herlin, and Georges Liébert (Paris: Gallimard, 2005), 1100; Claude Debussy, *Debussy Letters*, ed. François Lesure and Roger Nichols, trans. Roger Nichols (Cambridge, MA: Harvard University Press, 1987), 194.

8. Robert Orledge, "Liner Notes," in *Claude Debussy: Der Untergang des Hauses Usher* (DVD: Capriccio, 2007), 10.

9. Orledge, "Liner Notes," 10.

10. Those large-scale works included *Le Martyre de Saint Sébastien*, *Khamma*, *Gigues* (*Images*, sér. 3), and *Jeux*.

11. Debussy, *Correspondance*, 1915; Debussy, *Letters*, 298.

12. Debussy, *Correspondance*, 1843; Debussy, *Letters*, 291.

13. Debussy, *Correspondance*, 1862; Debussy, *Letters*, 295.

14. See Federico Lazarro, "Paris and the Nation's Politics," in *Debussy in Context*, ed. Simon Trezise (Cambridge: Cambridge University Press, 2024), 16–24.

15. François Lesure, *Claude Debussy* (Paris: Klincksieck, 1994), 16–17; François Lesure, *Claude Debussy: A Critical Biography*, Eastman Studies in Music 159, ed. and trans. Marie Rolf (Rochester, NY: University of Rochester Press, 2019), 7–8.

16. Lesure, *Claude Debussy*, 16–17; Lesure, *Claude Debussy: A Critical Biography*, 7–8.

17. Marcel Dietschy, *A Portrait of Claude Debussy*, trans. William Ashbrook and Margaret G. Cobb (Oxford: Oxford University Press, 1990), 14–16.

18. US Department of Health and Human Services, *Treatment Improvement Protocol: Trauma-Informed Care in Behavioral Health Services*, HHS Publications No. (SMA) 14–4816 (Rockville, MD: USDHH, 2014), 62–63.

19. Debussy, *Correspondance*, 1852, 2091; Debussy, *Letters*, 293.

20. Debussy, *Correspondance*, 1849; Debussy, *Letters*, 292.

21. Debussy, *Correspondance*, 1915; Debussy, *Letters*, 298.

22. Debussy, *Correspondance*, 1972; Debussy, *Letters*, 314.

23. Debussy, *Correspondance*, 1843; Debussy, *Letters*, 291.

24. Lesure, *Claude Debussy*, 389; Lesure, *Claude Debussy: A Critical Biography*, 321.

25. Debussy, *Correspondance*, 1843, 1844; Debussy, *Letters*, 291, 292.

26. For a general discussion of *Lyre et Palette*'s activities, see Lesure, *Claude Debussy*, 403; Lesure, *Claude Debussy: A Critical Biography*, 332.

27. Debussy letter to Robert Godet dated January 1, 1915, Debussy, *Correspondance*, 1862–63; Debussy, *Letters*, 295.

28. Debussy, *Correspondance*, 1945; Debussy, *Letters*, 305.

29. Debussy, *Correspondance*, 1942–43; Debussy, *Letters*, 303.

30. Debussy, *Correspondance*, 1947; Debussy, *Letters*, 305.

31. Debussy, *Correspondance*, 1947; Debussy, *Letters*, 305.

32. Pieter Mannaerts, "Introduction to Claude Debussy, Ode à la France," in *Repertoire Explorer* 948 (Munich: MPH, 2009).

33. Marianne Wheeldon, "Debussy's Legacy: The Controversy over the *Ode à la France*," *Journal of Musicology* 27, no. 3 (2010): 304–41. Villon's authorship has, however, long been questioned; see Jonathan Dunsby, "The Poetry of Debussy's *En blanc et noir*," in *Analytical Strategies and Musical Interpretation: Essays on Nineteenth- and Twentieth-Century Music*, ed. Craig Ayrey and Mark Everist (Cambridge: Cambridge University Press, 1996), 161–66.

34. Algernon Charles Swinburne, "Ballad against the Enemies of France," in *Poems and Ballads*, 2nd series (New York: R. Worthington, 1878), 212–14. Published in 1878, Swinburne's translation was probably a response to the Franco-Prussian War. See Nick Freeman, "The Gallows Nightingale: Swinburne's Translations of Villon," in *Beyond Arthurian Romances*, ed. Loretta M. Holloway and Jennifer A. Palmgren (Berlin: Springer, 2005), 143.

35. Caroline Rae, "Debussyist, Modernist, Exoticist: Marius-François Gaillard Rediscovered," *Musical Times* 152, no. 1916 (2011): 59–80.

36. [Sir Thomas] Hall Caine, *King Albert's Book: A Tribute to the Belgian King and People from Representative Men and Women throughout the World* (London: Daily Telegraph, 1914).

37. Moray Welsh, "Un Embarras de Richésse," *Strad* 103, no. 1226 (1992): 516–20; Alan Gibbs, "Debussy's Lutheran Side?," *Strad* 103, no. 1228 (1992): 684.

38. Debussy letter to Durand (February 5, 1909). Debussy, *Correspondance*, 1149.

39. See Debussy's letter to Durand (June 26, 1909). Debussy, *Correspondance*, 1193; Debussy, *Letters*, 203.

40. Debussy, *Correspondance*, 1299; Debussy, *Letters*, 220–21.

41. Debussy, *Correspondance*, 1472–73; Debussy, *Letters*, 252.

42. Stephen Walsh, *Debussy: A Painter in Sound* (London: Faber and Faber, 2014), 268–69. See also Eric Frederick Jensen, *Debussy* (Oxford: Oxford University Press, 2014), 115–16.

43. Debussy, *Correspondance*, 1964; Debussy, *Letters*, 310.

44. Debussy, *Correspondance*, 1964; Debussy, *Letters*, 310.

45. Debussy, *Correspondance*, 2058; Debussy, *Letters*, 321–22.

46. Debussy, *Correspondance*, 2008.

47. Debussy, *Correspondance*, 2114; Debussy, *Letters*, 326.

48. Maurice Maeterlinck, "Pelléas et Mélisande (1902)," in *Théâtre*, Vol. II (Brussels: P. Lacomblez; Paris: Per Lamm, 1902), 56.

49. Orledge, "Liner Notes," 10, 11.

50. Robert Orledge, *Debussy and the Theatre* (Cambridge: Cambridge University Press, 1982), 120.

51. To quote Porter, "In refashioning Poe's tale for the stage, the composer destroyed its essential character, and on some level he may have realized this." Porter, "Fragments of the *House of Usher*," *New Yorker*, March 14, 1977, 133.

52. Christopher Lee's reading takes about forty minutes. See Christopher Lee, *Christopher Lee reads Edgar Allan Poe, Tales of Horror*, Listen for Pleasure, Audio Tape (LFP7039, 1979), https://www.youtube.com/watch ?v=Ju1OfKkxMHM, accessed December 28, 2022.

53. Debussy, *Le Roi Lear, Le Diable dans le beffroi, La chute de la Maison Usher*, ed. Robert Orledge, Œuvres Complètes de Claude Debussy, Série VI Œuvres Lyriques, vol. 3 (Paris: Durand, 2006), XXIII.

54. Orledge, "Liner Notes," 11.

55. Debussy's second libretto implies that Roderick might have committed necrophilia. See Robert Orledge, "Debussy's 'House of Usher' Revisited," *Musical Quarterly* 62, no. 4 (1976): 538.

56. Porter, "Fragments of the *House of Usher*," 134.

57. In fact, Poe wrote several stories that involve premature burial—for example, "Berenice" (1835), "The Fall of the House of Usher" (1839), "The Black Cat" (1843), "The Premature Burial" (1844), and "The Cask of Amontillado" (1846). See Gerald J. Kennedy, *Poe, Death, and the Life of Writing* (New Haven, CT: Yale University Press, 1987), 58–59; and Jan Bondeson, *Buried Alive: The Terrifying History of Our Most Primal Fear* (New York: Norton, 2002). For the symbolic significance of the doctor, especially its connections with the occult, see Orledge, *Debussy and the Theatre*, 126–27.

58. Orledge, *Debussy and the Theatre*, 2.

59. Debussy, *Correspondance*, 2022; Debussy, *Letters*, 317.

60. Debussy, *Correspondance*, 2016.

Conclusion

Coming Full Circle

Given this book's focus on arabesques, it seems fitting that the discussion should end by returning to the beginning, just "like a snake biting its own tail." The introduction opened by noting that arabesques played a central role in Symbolist art in general and in Debussy's music in particular. Like other Symbolists, Debussy used them as a source of inspiration as well as a means for challenging common assumptions about the origins, categories, limits, structure, value, emotional impact, and expressive power of art. As the book unfolded, it expanded earlier accounts of the topic in three ways. First, instead of conceiving of arabesques in purely visual terms, it has prioritized literary models, thereby aligning Debussy's aesthetic outlook with that of Poe, Baudelaire, Villiers de l'Isle-Adam, Mallarmé, Verlaine, Huysmans, Maeterlinck, de Régnier, and other nineteenth-century writers. This point is significant because it helps to explain how Debussy exploited the arabesque's propensity for enchainment for narrative purposes. Second, instead of regarding arabesques simply as forms of melodic ornamentation, the book has suggested that Debussy conceived of them in broader terms. As he explained in his review of Ysaÿe's rendition of Bach's Violin Concerto in G minor BWV 1056R on Good Friday 1901, Debussy made five distinct claims about the nature of arabesques and, by extension, moresques and grotesques:

1. Arabesques are forms of ornamentation but are not bound to conventional norms.
2. Arabesques are inherently contrapuntal and create harmony when one contrapuntal thread interacts with another.
3. Arabesques blur the distinction between the ornamental and the structural because they require that local details have global implications.

4. Arabesques introduce an element of fantasy into art, thereby allowing artists to disguise and even replace traditional formal schemes.
5. Arabesques allow artworks to stir emotions and induce images in the mind of the listener.

Third, prior research recognizes the arabesque's aesthetic implications but does not provide an adequate picture of what they might actually be. Indeed, this book has suggested that, for Debussy and other Symbolists, the concept allowed them to erode traditional distinctions between fine art and decorative art, Western and non-Western art, and even art and entertainment. In this way, it helped to dismantle the ways in which art had been institutionalized in France since the mid-seventeenth century and explain why nineteenth-century Symbolism was widely regarded as a precursor of twentieth-century modernism.

With respect to this last point, the influence of Baudelaire, especially his "Le Peintre de la Vie Moderne," cannot be overstated. This seminal essay, originally published in 1863, not only described the changing ways in which nineteenth-century artists engaged with the modern world but also challenged traditional conceptions of art. One way in which it did so was by championing aspects of art that were either downplayed or overlooked by institutions such as the Académie des Beaux-Arts. Take, for example, Baudelaire's discussion of beauty. Although he accepted that traditional aesthetics rightly invoked this concept, Baudelaire rejected "the academic theory of [a] unique and absolute beauty," advocating instead a rational and historical theory.[1] Rather, he proposed "beauty is made up of an eternal, invariable element, whose quantity it is excessively difficult to determine, and of a relative, circumstantial element, which will be, if you like, whether severally or all once, the age, its fashions, its morals, its emotions."[2] This shift away from a notion of aesthetic universals to a relativistic one has become ubiquitous in modern times, though there has certainly been pushback from some on cognitive grounds.[3]

"Le Peintre de la Vie Moderne" also promotes modernism by denying any absolute distinction between fine and decorative art. This move is immediately apparent in Baudelaire's remarks about the commercial art of Constantin Guys. As mentioned earlier, Baudelaire found a "fire" in Guys's manner of execution—"an intoxication of the pencil or the brush, amounting almost to a frenzy"—that captured the transient, fleeting, contingent aspects of modern life.[4] This manner of execution clearly anticipated that of Baudelaire's close friend Édouard Manet and generations of Impressionist, Neo-Impressionist, and Symbolist artists. The same can be said of Baudelaire's response to Poe's short stories, which were meant to be read at a single sitting and often appeared individually in ephemeral media, such as newspapers and literary journals. It was only later that they were reprinted in more durable book form, such as in his *Tales of the Grotesque and Arabesque* and *Tales of Mystery and Imagination & Humour; and Poems*.

Baudelaire's enthusiasm for Guys's *Procession of the Sultan at the Festival of the Bairam, Constantinople* (fig. 3.2) reinforced another essential aspect of modernism: skepticism about how Western art is normally distinguished from non-Western art. Since Baudelaire denied that beauty can be defined in an absolute manner and must be understood contextually, he insisted that beauty often lies in the unfamiliar and the fashionable: "The beautiful is always strange" . . . "every age and every people has enjoyed the expression of its own beauty and ethos."[5] To bolster his point, Baudelaire devoted an entire section of "Le Peintre de la Vie Moderne" to the aesthetic value of cosmetics and to refuting the idea that beauty should be equated with nature and virtue: "I ask you to review and scrutinize whatever is natural—all the actions and desires of the purely natural man: you will find nothing but frightfulness. Everything beautiful and noble is the result of reason and calculation."[6] He added, "Evil happens without effort, *naturally*, fatally; Good is always the product of some art."[7] According to Baudelaire, a woman is "quite within her rights, indeed she is even accomplishing a kind of duty, when she devotes herself to appearing magical and supernatural; she has to astonish and charm us; as an idol she is obliged to adorn herself in order to be adored. Thus, she has to lay all the arts under contribution for the means of lifting herself above Nature, the better to conquer hearts and rivet attention."[8]

By endorsing most, if not all, of Baudelaire's views, Debussy stands out as the modernist composer par excellence. He, too, eroded—though not necessarily eliminated—the boundaries between fine and decorative art, Western and non-Western Art, and art and vernacular entertainment. Debussy began to do so from the outset of his career when he composed esoteric art songs, such as "La Morte des amants" and "L'Ombre des arbres," alongside decorative salon music, such as the *Deux Arabesques*, *Rêverie*, and *Suite bergamasque*, and when he completed traditionally Western compositions, such as *Petite Suite* and *Valse Romantique*, alongside works with exotic and even non-Western allusions, such as *Séguidille* and *Rondel chinois*. As his career progressed, Debussy continued to cultivate such diversity, often including works traditionally labeled as fine art, decorative art, non-Western Art, and vernacular entertainment, within a single collection. His two sets of piano preludes are perfect cases in point: each one contains avant-garde works, such as "Des pas sur la neige" (*Préludes*, Bk. 1) and "Feuilles mortes" (*Préludes*, Bk. 2); salon works, such as "La Fille aux cheveux de lin" (*Préludes*, Bk. 1) and "Bruyères" (*Préludes*, Bk. 2); exotic works, such as "La Sérénade interrompue" (*Préludes*, Bk. 1) and "La Puerta del Vino" (*Préludes*, Bk. 2); and vernacular compositions, such as "Minstrels" (*Préludes*, Bk. 1) and "General Lavine" (*Préludes*, Bk. 2).

Debussy was also the consummate flâneur and something of a night owl.[9] Like Baudelaire before him, he encountered all forms of art on the bustling streets of Paris: non-Western music at the Expositions Universelles of 1889 and 1900, the Galerie Durand-Ruel, the Pavillon Marsan, and numerous other venues just as easily as he could listen to minstrel music, circus music, military marches, children's songs, and other forms of vernacular music. Marguerite Vasnier, for example, recalled a particularly amusing incident that occurred when Debussy visited her mother one summer in Ville d'Avray.[10] When a group of street singers performed outside their villa, Debussy apparently accompanied them on the piano before inviting them to continue inside the house. That being said, his knowledge of non-Western and vernacular music was not based on any systematic study of those repertories; he often lauded such music because it featured elements such as pedals, ostinati, pentatonic scales, and whole-tone collections that he had already absorbed into his own musical language.[11]

One immediate advantage of Debussy's eclecticism was that it made his music attractive to audiences. His stage works and piano music were especially popular. The former were particularly lucrative: *Pelléas et Mélisande* (1902) made a lot of money for him and Durand, as did the score of *La Boîte à joujoux* (1913), something that was ameliorated by Hellé's delightful illustrations.[12] Debussy's piano music was likewise popular with audiences, something he had experienced since the beginning of his career. Indeed, as far back as February 5, 1894, he complained to Ernst Chausson that he sold the score of *Quatuor* "to the Barbarians of the place de la Madeleine" for the same sum of money as his *Deux Arabesques* (1891) and his four-hand transcription of Saint-Saëns Symphony No. 2 (1889).[13] That sum was 250 francs! Orledge has meanwhile noted that sales of Debussy's *Préludes* Bk. 1 easily outstripped those of his orchestral works and their various reductions.[14] Nevertheless, Debussy did come to realize that piano works with evocative titles had the best chance of commercial success.[15] In the case of *Estampes* (1903) and *Images, sér.* 1

(1905), for example, "Jardins sous la pluie," "La Soirée dans Grenade," and "Reflets dans l'eau" sold much better than "Pagodes," "Hommage à Rameau," and "Mouvement."[16] The sales figures for these works stood in sharp contrast to those of Debussy's songs, which never did well in the marketplace. Take, for example, the case of his *Trois Poèmes de Stéphane Mallarmé*: first published in 1913, the same year as *La Boîte à joujoux*, it did not sell a thousand copies until after Debussy's death in 1918.[17]

At the same time, however, Debussy's eclecticism posed countless problems for those interested in analyzing or theorizing about his music. As Douglass Green noted in 1992, no one has ever come up with a "comprehensive theoretical framework" for explaining Debussy's musical language.[18] The problems here are profound. For one thing, although that language has close connections with common practice tonality, individual pieces often violate traditional rules of voice leading and harmony in significant ways.[19] For example, whereas tonal music of the common practice period usually prohibits parallel chords and treats dissonances in narrowly constrained ways, Debussy's works often contain strings of parallel triads, sevenths, and ninths and frequently treat dissonances without preparation or resolution.[20] Similarly, whereas common practice music often focuses on functional progressions and major/minor scales, Debussy's music is often infused with nonfunctional successions, unusual chromaticisms, and modal/exotic inflections. To complicate matters further, they often disrupt the principles of tonal closure and continuity through their use of incomplete structures and interpolations. As a result, particular passages may behave functionally at a local level but nonfunctionally at a global level.[21] These tendencies have prompted the use of terms like *mosaic, collage,* and *braided* to describe Debussy's forms. Furthermore, individual pieces violate common practice norms in different ways and to different degrees. For example, esoteric art songs such as "La Morte des amants" and "L'Ombre des arbres" deviate from tonal norms far more than decorative salon music, such as the *Deux Arabesques, Rêverie,* and *Suite bergamasque.*

The situation is further complicated by the fact that Debussy's style clearly evolved with his early works conforming more closely to common practice norms than his later scores. This evolution did not follow a single trajectory, however, and certainly did not occur at a predictable rate: even late works such as "La Fille aux Cheveux de lin" (*Préludes*, Bk. 1) and "Bruyères" (*Préludes*, Bk. 2) have strong tonal tendencies despite being completed just before the outbreak of WWI.[22] Art critic Jed Perl has recently described a similar evolution in the works of the Swiss artist Alberto Giacometti:

> Most artists who work for many years see their style evolve, sometimes dramatically. In the 1930s and 1940s Giacometti, who had first been admired for Surrealist sculptures in which representational elements are set in essentially abstract structures, found himself increasingly focused on the direct observation of the human figure. What by the 1940s could look like a wholesale transformation of his artistic language was the result of a gradual accretion of individual decisions, all of which, during Giacometti's career of nearly five decades, interlocked. They reinforced one another. They added up.[23]

Such shifts in Debussy's style are entirely consistent with Venturino and Dunsby's claim that Debussy's use of the arabesque passed through different phases—what they refer to as "early," "intermediate," "conventional," and "late."[24]

As if this wasn't enough, there is no reason to suppose that existing analytical tools are rich or flexible enough to cope with the entire range of Debussy's musical styles and idioms. The problem here is that, in comparing Debussy's musical language to the norms of common practice tonality, there is a tendency to describe it in terms of what it doesn't do rather than what it does do. Indeed, as Green put it, "To deal in particular with pitch in music that is not really tonal—however much it may use the vocabulary of tonal music—poses a problem that is not solved by talk of pentatonic, whole-tone, octatonic, or chromatic scales. To speak of non-functional harmony is merely a negative, telling us nothing about how it does function."[25] Schenkerian theory does, of course, helps because it is designed to show how melody, counterpoint, harmony, motive, and form interact in tonal contexts. The theory also has built-in mechanisms for explaining musical surfaces that are almost continuously dissonant and chromatic, that contain parallel chords, and that even include modal and exotic inflections of one sort or another.[26] But it is an open question as to whether the model is able to explain Debussy's most complex and experimental scores. The problems are particularly acute for operas and ballets, genres that pose special issues for Schenkerians.[27] The best that can be done is to evaluate each piece on a case-by-case basis and keep investigating what the limits of the theory may or may not be.

But Debussy's goal wasn't simply to revolutionize the technical aspects of musical composition; he was also interested in redirecting the ways in which music was institutionalized in fin de siècle France.[28] Though well trained at the Paris Conservatoire and a recipient of the Prix de Rome and *Légion d'honneur*, Debussy never regarded himself as part of the musical establishment and always remained one of its staunchest critics. He was perhaps most outspoken on such matters in his critical essays. In his first conversation with Monsieur Croche (*La Revue blanche*, July 1, 1901), for example, Debussy denounced the ways in which composers were traditionally instructed in music conservatories. Following the example of the Symbolist poets and Impressionist painters, he implored musicians "to shake away the dust of tradition" and "search for a discipline within freedom!"[29] Writing as a true modernist, he urged them to stop being governed "by formulae drawn from decadent philosophies" because "they are for the feeble minded." Instead, they should "listen to no one's advice except that of the wind in the trees. This can recount the whole history of mankind."[30] Such ideas also reflected his desire to transform the location of listening experiences: instead of confining music to the salon, the church, the concert hall, or the opera theater, he liked the idea of engaging music in other environments, especially in the "open air."[31]

In Debussy's second conversation with M. Croche (*La Revue blanche*, November 15, 1901), he went on to lambaste the Prix de Rome, which was awarded by members of the Académie des Beaux-Arts: "Among the institutions on which France prides herself, do you know of any more ridiculous? . . . The cool way in which the academic gentlemen of the Institute decide which of these young people will be an artist strikes me as quite naïve. What do they know about it? Are they sure they are artists themselves? From where do they think they inherit the right to decide someone's destiny? It really seems that in this case they'd do better if they tried the simple method of drawing lots with lengths of straw." Instead of remaining in Rome, Debussy implored prize winners to "travel across Europe and choose a teacher themselves."[32] For his part, the most memorable aspect of Debussy's time in Rome was that it allowed him to hear Renaissance vocal polyphony, apparently at the suggestion of Liszt.[33]

One reason why Debussy's complaints were so vociferous is that his conservatory training taught him more about how composers worked in the past than about how they might work in the present. And, of course, Debussy's own career path was anything but traditional.[34] It began after twelve years of professional training at the Paris Conservatoire. On returning to Paris from his Prix de Rome, Debussy set about earning his living as a freelance composer: instead of finding a permanent position as a choral director, conductor, or pedagogue, he relied on financial support from his publishers, first by Georges Hartmann, who supported him between 1895 and 1900, then by Jacques Durand, who gave him an exclusive contract in July 1905.[35] Debussy supplemented his income with commissions, appearances as a conductor, and occasional private students. In the meantime, he earned a name for himself as a critic, writing for *La Revue blanche* in 1901, *Gil blas* and other papers in 1903, *Musica* and other sources in 1908–12, and *SIM* and other journals in 1912–17. Under the guise of M. Croche, Debussy used his essays to denounce the musical establishment, promote French music, and endorse modernism.[36]

The tensions Debussy clearly felt between past and present, old and new, potentiality and actuality, are ones Baudelaire specifically explored in "Le Peintre de la vie moderne": "By modernity, I mean the ephemeral, the fugitive, the contingent, the half of art whose other half is eternal and the immutable."[37] As Baudelaire revealed in "Le Thyrse," the same duality exists in the thyrsus, with the staff metaphorically representing the artists' sense of unity and vision and the floral arabesques their sense of fantasy and imagination. More to the point, the poem is ultimately an homage to Wagner, whose essay "Music of the Future" epitomized Baudelaire's image of modernity in art. His observations about modernity, the ephemeral, and the familiar likewise call to mind his account of Poe's writing: "Now there are certain fugitive and striking impressions—all the more striking in their recurrence as they are the more fugitive—which sometimes take their cue from an external signal, a kind of warning like the sound of a bell, a musical note, or a forgotten scent, and which are themselves followed by a similar event already familiar which occupied the same place in a previously revealed chain."[38]

That artists may be subject to the whims of their audiences was obviously a source of concern to Debussy:

> You must blame the artists. They have to succeed in the fruitless task of both serving the public and at the same time keeping them in a deliberate state of apathy. To this crime, we can add that of knowing how to fight for a place in the market when the time is ripe. But once they're assured of selling their wares they suddenly seem to recoil, asking the public to forgive them for all the trouble they caused when it came to being accepted. Resolutely turning their backs on their younger days, they wallow in their success. Thus they lose all chance of attaining true glory in life—something that is happily reserved for those devoted to the discovery of new worlds of feeling and new forms of expression.[39]

By the end of his career, however, Debussy realized that this advice was easier to bequeath than to achieve. Indeed, he became increasingly concerned that his creative powers might be in decline, that his accomplishments might be eclipsed by those of younger composers and might even be forgotten. Much as he tried, Debussy found it harder and harder to keep producing new works with the level of quality that he demanded. On December 11, 1916, he wrote despairingly to Godet, "I'm terrified of planning any sort of work whatsoever—that in itself is enough to condemn it to the waste-paper basket, the cemetery of bad dreams. What an existence! I'm exhausted by chasing phantoms but not tired enough to sleep. So I wait for the morrow, for better or for worse; and it starts all over again."[40]

Living in the topsy-turvy environment of the modern city, Debussy became acutely aware that his reputation was shaped by the press and the reaction of audiences. Much as he enjoyed the upsurge in his status nationally and internationally following the successful premiere of *Pelléas et Mélisande,* Debussy had to cope with pushback from gossip columnists and hostile critics. The worst scandal erupted in the autumn of 1904, after his affair with his future second wife, Emma Bardac, and the unsuccessful suicide attempt of his first wife, Lily Texier. The popular press had a field day, and the sordid details of what transpired were even parodied in Henry Bataille's play *La Femme nue* (1908). Many of Debussy's old friends deserted him, such as Gustave Doret, Henri Lerolle, Eugène Ysaÿe, and Pierre Louÿs. His mistrust of the press was apparently mutual and became more intense as time passed: Debussy's death was barely covered in the newspapers, and his funeral was attended by only about fifty men and very few women.[41] Except for a couple of political dignitaries and professional colleagues, the list of attendees included family members, close friends, fellow musicians, and some literary types: Jacques Durand, Paul Vidal, Paul Dukas, Maurice Ravel, Henri de Regnier, Louis Laloy, André Caplet, Gabriel Pierné, Pasteur Vallery-Radot, Gustave Samazeuilh, Camille Chevillard, Gustave Charpentier, Rhené Baton, Sylvio Lazzarri, Roger-Ducasse, Florent Schmitt, Ricardo Viñes, Alfred Cortot, Lazare Lévy, and Saint Georges de Bouhélier.[42]

But Debussy's fears about irrelevancy proved completely unfounded. His unique sense of the modern has been a consistent source of inspiration for later generations of composers, performers, and audiences. That modernism, which challenged the ways in which Western art has traditionally been institutionalized and separated from decorative art, non-Western art, and even entertainment, was a consequence of Debussy's fascination with arabesques and their manifestations in the writings of Schlegel, Poe, Wagner, and, above all, Baudelaire. It also fueled his preoccupation with music from other cultures, with new media and technology, such as the phonograph and the cinema, and with vernacular music of the day. Even though his own musical language may not have been as radical as that of younger composers, such as Schoenberg or Stravinsky, Debussy's innovations put him at the forefront of the avant-garde and even foreshadow musicmaking at the start of the twenty-first century. It is hard to think of another twentieth-century composer whose works resonate to the same degree. To quote Paul Léon, "The future will discern which were the classics. Already, [Manet's] *Olympia* is at the Louvre, *Les Fleurs du Mal* in everyone's hand, *Pelléas [et Mélisande]* in everyone's heart."[43] There is no reason to suppose that Debussy's reputation will diminish in the foreseeable future; quite the reverse, it seems likely to flourish for decades to come.

Notes

1. Charles Baudelaire, "Le Peintre de la Vie Moderne: I Le beau, la mode et le bonheur," in *Charles Baudelaire: Œuvres Complètes*, vol. II, ed. Claude Pichois, Bibliothèque de la Pléiade (Paris: Gallimard, 1976), 685; Baudelaire, "The Painter of Modern Life: I Beauty, Fashion, and Happiness," in *The Painter of Modern Life*, ed. and trans. Jonathan Mayne (London: Phaidon, 2001), 3.

2. Baudelaire, "Le Peintre de la Vie Moderne: I Le beau, la mode et le bonheur," 685; Baudelaire, "The Painter of Modern Life: I Beauty, Fashion, and Happiness," 3.

3. For counterarguments, see Matthew Brown, *Debussy Redux: The Impact of His Music on Popular Culture* (Bloomington: Indiana University Press, 2012), 151–53.

4. Baudelaire, "Le Peintre de la vie moderne: V L'Art mnémonique," in *Œuvres Complètes*, II:699; Baudelaire, "The Painter of Modern Life: V Mnemonic Art," in *Painter of Modern Life*, 17.

5. Baudelaire, "Salon de 1846: II. A Qui bon la critique?," in *Œuvres Complètes*, II:419; Baudelaire, "The Salon of 1846: I What Is the Good of Criticism?," in *Art in Paris 1845–1862: Salons and Other Exhibitions Reviewed by Charles Baudelaire*, 2nd ed., ed. and trans. Jonathan Mayne (London: Phaidon, 1995), 45.

6. Baudelaire, "Le Peintre de la Vie Moderne: XI Eloge du maquillage," in *Œuvres Complètes*, II:715; Baudelaire, "The Painter of Modern Life: XI in Praise of Cosmetics," in *Painter of Modern Life*, 32.

7. Baudelaire, "Le Peintre de la Vie Moderne: XI Eloge du maquillage," 715; Baudelaire, "The Painter of Modern Life: XI in Praise of Cosmetics," in *Painter of Modern Life*, 32.

8. Baudelaire, "Le Peintre de la Vie Moderne: XI Eloge du maquillage," 716–17; Baudelaire, "The Painter of Modern Life: XI in Praise of Cosmetics," 33.

9. See Sarah Gutsche-Miller, "Debussy's Noctambule and Parisian Popular Culture," in *Debussy in Context*, ed. Simon Trezise (Cambridge: Cambridge University Press, 2024), 193–200; and Martin Guerpin, "Paris, the City," in *Debussy in Context*, 3–15.

10. See Roger Nichols, *Debussy Remembered* (London: Faber, 1992), 18–19.

11. See Matthew Brown, *Debussy's 'Ibéria': Studies in Genesis and Structure* (Oxford: Oxford University Press, 2003), 61–64.

12. Robert Orledge, "Debussy, Durand et Cie: A French Composer and His Publisher," in *The Business of Music*, ed. Michael Talbot (Liverpool: Liverpool University Press, 2002), 146, 147, 149–50.

13. Claude Debussy, *Correspondance (1872–1918)*, ed. François Lesure and Denis Herlin, annotated by François Lesure, Denis Herlin, and Georges Liébert (Paris: Gallimard, 2005), 168. For Debussy's contract with Durand, see Debussy, *Correspondance*, 166. See also Orledge, "Debussy, Durand et Cie," 127.

14. Orledge, "Debussy, Durand et Cie," 149.

15. Orledge, "Debussy, Durand et Cie," 146, 147.

16. Orledge, "Debussy, Durand et Cie," 147–49.

17. Orledge, "Debussy, Durand et Cie," 150.

18. Douglass M. Green, "Review of Richard S. Parks, *The Music of Claude Debussy* (New Haven, CT: Yale University Press, 1989)," *Music Theory Spectrum* 14, no. 2 (1992): 214.

19. For an extensive discussion of these problems, see Boyd Pomeroy, "Debussy's tonality: a formal Perspective," in *The Cambridge Companion to Debussy,* ed. Simon Trezise (Cambridge: Cambridge University Press, 2003), 155–78, and Matthew Brown, *Explaining Tonality: Schenkerian Theory and Beyond* (Rochester, NY: University of Rochester Press, 2005), 171–208.

20. Debussy's contemporaries were, of course, well aware of these deviations. See, for example, René Lenormand's *Étude sur l'harmonie moderne* (Paris: Propriété du "Monde Musical," 1912).

21. Brown, *Explaining Tonality*, 172.

22. John Koslovsky and Matthew Brown, "History and Tonal Coherence in Debussy's 'La Fille aux Cheveux de lin' and 'Bruyères,'" *Rivista di Analisi e Teoria Musicale* 18, no. 2 (2012): 35–54.

23. Jed Perl, "Between Abstraction and Representation," *New York Review of Books*, November 24, 2022, 6.

24. Stephanie Venturino and Jonathan Dunsby, "The Evolution of Claude Debussy's Arabesque," in *Debussy Studies 2*, ed. Barbara Kelly and David Code (Cambridge University Press, 2025), 58–86.

25. Green, "Review of Richard S. Parks," 214.

26. See Matthew Brown, "The Diatonic and the Chromatic in Schenker's Theory of Harmonic Relations," *Journal of Music Theory* 30, no. 1 (1986): 1–33; and Matthew Brown, Dave Headlam, and Douglas J. Dempster, "The #IV($\flat$V) Hypothesis: Testing the Limits of Schenker's Theory of Tonality," *Music Theory Spectrum* 19/2 (1997): 155–83.

27. It is interesting to note, for example, that Schenker thought that potpourris should follow the same principles of harmony as a sonata or a symphony (see Heinrich Schenker, *Harmonielehre*, Neue musikalische Theorien und Phantasien Vol. 1. [Stuttgart and Berlin: Cotta, 1906], §132, 331–32). As regards opera, he offered penetrating analyses of sections of Mozart's *Don Giovanni* (see Heinrich Schenker, "The Decline of the Art of Composition: A Technical-Critical Study," trans. William Drabkin, *Music Analysis* 24, no. 1–2 (2005): 3–129, esp. 79–85 and 85–92).

28. For Debussy's relationships with the operatic scene in Paris and the Société nationale and other musical institutions, see Hervé Lacombe, "Parisian Opera Institutions: A Framework for Creation," in *Debussy in Context*; and Michel Strasser, "Société nationale and Other Institutions," in *Debussy in Context*, 177–84 and 185–92.

29. Claude Debussy, "Conversation with M. Croche," in *Monsieur Croche et autres écrits*, ed. François Lesure (Paris: Gallimard, 1987), 52–53; Debussy, "Conversation with M. Croche," in *Debussy on Music*, ed. François Lesure, trans. Richard Langham Smith (New York: Knopf, 1977), 48.

30. Debussy, "Conversation with M. Croche," in *Monsieur Croche*, 52–53; Debussy, "Conversation with M. Croche," in *Debussy on Music*, 48.

31. See Debussy's letter to Georges Hartmann (September 16, 1898) in Debussy, *Correspondance*, 419; and Claude Debussy, *Debussy Letters*, ed. François Lesure and Roger Nichols, trans. Roger Nichols (Cambridge, MA:

Harvard University Press, 1987), 100; Debussy, "Concerts Nikisch—La musique en plein air," *La Revue blanche* (July 1, 1901), in *Monsieur Croche*, 46–47; Debussy, "Considérations sur la musique en pleine air.—Les concerts.— Le prince L.-F. de Bavière," *Gils Blas* (January 19, 1903), in *Monsieur Croche*, 74–80; Debussy, "Music in the Open Air," in *Debussy on Music*, 40–41 and 43; Debussy, "Thoughts on Music in the Open Air," in *Debussy on Music*, 92–94.

32. Debussy, "De quelques superstitions et d'un opéra," in *Monsieur Croche*, 56; Debussy, "About a Few Superstitions of Ours, and an Opera," in *Debussy on Music*, 52.

33. Debussy, *Debussy on Music*, 31.

34. See Denis Herlin, "Publishers" and "The Jobbing Composer-Musician," in *Debussy in Context*, ed. Trezise, 143–49 and 169–76.

35. See Christophe Carle, "Debussy in Fin-de-Siècle Paris," in *Debussy and His World*, ed. Jane Fulcher (Princeton, NJ: Princeton University Press, 2001), 271–95; Orledge, "Debussy, Durand et Cie," 121–51; and Denis Herlin, "An Artist High and Low, Or Debussy and Money," trans. Vincent Giroud. in *Rethinking Debussy*, ed. Elliot Antokoletz and Marianne Wheeldon (New York: Oxford University Press, 2011), 149–202.

36. Denis Herlin, "Les mésaventure de *Monsieur Croche Antidilettante*," in *Claude Debussy—Portraits et Études* (Hildesheim: Georg Olms, 2023), 366–91.

37. Baudelaire, "Le Peintre de la vie moderne: La Modernité," in *Œuvres Complètes*, II:695; Baudelaire, "The Painter in Modern Life: IV. Modernity," in *Painter in Modern Life*, 13.

38. Baudelaire, "Edgar Allan Poe, sa vie et ses ouvrages," in *Œuvres Complètes*, II:315; Baudelaire, "Edgar Allan Poe: His Life and Works," in *Painter in Modern Life*, 89.

39. Debussy, "De quelques superstitions et d'un opéra," in *Monsieur Croche*, 57; Debussy, "About a Few Superstitions of Ours, and an Opera," in *Debussy on Music*, 53–54.

40. See Debussy's letter to Robert Godet (December 11, 1916) in Debussy, *Correspondance*, 2058; Debussy, *Letters*, 321–22.

41. Leonard Raines, "Parisians Refuse to Take to Cellar When Shell Explodes Close to Opera Comique," *Musical America* 28 (May 4, 1918): 42.

42. The political dignitaries included Paul Henri d'Estournelle de Constant (diplomat and winner of the Nobel Peace Prize) and Louis Lafferre (minister of public instruction and fine arts), and the professional colleagues included Jacques Rouché, Pierre Gheusi, and Vincent and Émile Isola (directors of the Opéra-Comique).

43. Paul Léon, "Claude Debussy," *Programme Festival de Claude Debussy*, Théâtre des Champs-Élysées, Juin 17, 1932, 3.

Bibliography

Abbate, Carolyn. "Opera as Symphony, a Wagnerian Myth." In *Analyzing Opera: Verdi and Wagner*, edited by Carolyn Abbate and Roger Parker, 96–100. Berkeley: University of California Press, 1989.

Abbate, Carolyn. "*Tristan* in the Composition of *Pelléas*." *19th-Century Music* 5, no. 2 (1981): 117–41.

Abbott, Helen. *Baudelaire in Song: 1880–1930*. Oxford: Oxford University Press, 2017.

Abbott, Helen. *Parisian Intersections: Baudelaire's Legacy to Composers*. Bern: Peter Lang, 2012.

Abel, Richard. *The Ciné Goes to Town: French Cinema 1896–1914*. Expanded edition. Berkeley: University of California Press, 1998.

Abraham, Gerald. *Grieg: A Symposium*. Norman: University of Oklahoma Press, 1950.

Acocella, Joan. "The Faun." *New Yorker*, June 29, 2009. https://www.newyorker.com /magazine/2009/06/29/the-faun.

Acquisito, Joseph. "Uprooting the Lyric: Baudelaire in Wagner's Forests." *Nineteenth-Century French Studies* 32, no. 3–4 (2004): 223–37.

Adlard, Emma. "Debussy, 'Fêtes galantes,' and the Salon of Marguerite de Saint-Marceaux." *Musical Quarterly* 96, no. 2 (2013): 178–218.

Altman, Rick. *Silent Film Sound*. New York: Columbia University Press, 2004.

Arbide, Lola San Martín. "Beyond Paris." In *Debussy in Context*, edited by Simon Trezise, 25–33. Cambridge: Cambridge University Press, 2024.

Ayral-Clause, Odile. *Camille Claudel: A Life*. New York: Abrams, 2002.

Baer, Ulrich. *Remnants of Song: Trauma and the Experience of Modernity in Charles Baudelaire and Paul Celan*. Redwood City, CA: Stanford University Press, 2000.

Bailly, Edmond. *Le Chant des Voyelles comme Invocation des Dieux Planétaires*. Paris: Librarie de l'Art Indépendant, 1912.

Bailly, Edmond. *Le pittoresque musical* à *l'exposition*. Paris: Éditions de l'Humanité Nouvelle, 1900.

Bailly, Edmond. *Le Son dans la Nature*. Paris: Librarie de l'Art Indépendant, 1900.

Bannelier, Charles. *Du beau dans la musique: essai et réforme de l'esthétique musicale par Edouard Hanslick*. Paris: Brandus, 1877.

Barraqué, Jean. *Debussy*. Paris: Seuil, 1962.

Barth, John. *The Friday Book: Essays and Other Nonfiction.* Baltimore: Johns Hopkins University Press, 1984.

Batteux, Charles. *Les Beaux Arts réduits à un même principe.* Paris: Durand, 1746.

Baudelaire, Charles. *Artificial Paradises.* Translated by Stacy Diamond. New York: Carol, 1996.

Baudelaire, Charles. "Crowds." In *Vol. II: The Poems in Prose and La Fanfarol,* edited and translated by Francis Scarfe, 58–59. London: Anvil, 1989.

Baudelaire, Charles. "Les Dons de fées," Le Spleen de Paris XX. In *Charles Baudelaire: Œuvres Complètes,* Vol. I, edited by Claude Pichois, 305–307. Bibliothèque de la Pléiade. Paris: Gallimard, 1975. Translated by Francis Scarfe as "Fairy Gift." In Baudelaire, *Vol. II. The Poems in Prose and La Fanfarol,* edited and translated by Francis Scarfe, 86–89. London: Anvil Press Poetry, 1989.

Baudelaire, Charles. "Edgar Allan Poe: His Life and Works." In *The Painter in Modern Life and Other Essays,* edited and translated by Jonathan Mayne, 70–92. London: Phaidon, 2001.

Baudelaire, Charles. "Edgar Allan Poe: Sa Vie et Ses Ouvrages." In *Charles Baudelaire: Œuvres Complètes,* vol. II, edited by Claude Pichois, 249–318. Bibliothèque de la Pléiade. Paris: Gallimard, 1976.

Baudelaire, Charles. "The Exposition Universelle." In *Art in Paris 1845–1862: Salons and Other Exhibitions Reviewed by Charles Baudelaire,* 2nd ed., edited and translated by Jonathan Mayne, 41–120. London: Phaidon, 1995.

Baudelaire, Charles. "Flares." In *Late Fragments: Flares, My Heart Laid Bare, Prose Poems, Belgium Disrobed,* edited and translated by Richard Sieburth, 80–102. New Haven, CT: Yale University Press, 2022.

Baudelaire, Charles. "Further Notes on Edgar Poe." In *The Painter in Modern Life and Other Essays,* edited and translated by Jonathan Mayne, 93–110. London: Phaidon, 2001.

Baudelaire, Charles. "Fusées." In *Charles Baudelaire: Œuvres Complètes,* vol. I, edited by Claude Pichois, 649–67. Bibliothèque de la Pléiade. Paris: Gallimard, 1975.

Baudelaire, Charles. "La Fanfarlo. Bulletin de la Société des gens de lettres, 1847." In *Charles Baudelaire: Œuvres Complètes,* vol. I, edited by Claude Pichois, 553–80. Bibliothèque de la Pléiade. Paris: Gallimard, 1975.

Baudelaire, Charles. "*La Fanfarlo.*" In *Vol. II: The Poems in Prose and La Fanfarol,* translated by Francis Scharf, 213–63. London: Anvil Press Poetry, 1989.

Baudelaire, Charles. "'Le Joujoue du Pauvre', *Le Spleen de Paris* XIX." In *Charles Baudelaire: Œuvres Complètes,* vol. I, edited by Claude Pichois, 304–305. Bibliothèque de la Pléiade. Paris: Gallimard, 1975.

Baudelaire, Charles, "Le Peintre de la vie moderne." In *Charles Baudelaire: Œuvres Complètes,* vol. II, edited by Claude Pichois, 683–724. Bibliothèque de la Pléiade. Paris: Gallimard, 1976.

Baudelaire, Charles. "*Le Poème du hachisch.*" In *Charles Baudelaire: Œuvres Complètes,* vol. I, edited by Claude Pichois, 401–41. Bibliothèque de la Pléiade. Paris: Gallimard, 1975.

Baudelaire, Charles. "'Le Thyrse', *Le Spleen de Paris* XXXII." In *Charles Baudelaire: Œuvres Complètes,* vol. I, edited by Claude Pichois, 335–36. Bibliothèque de la Pléiade. Paris: Gallimard, 1975.

Baudelaire, Charles. "*Les Fleurs du Mal.*" In *Charles Baudelaire: Œuvres Complètes,* vol. I, edited by Claude Pichois, 1–196. Bibliothèque de la Pléiade. Paris: Gallimard, 1975.

Baudelaire, Charles. "'Les Foules', *Le Spleen de Paris*, XII." In *Charles Baudelaire: Œuvres Complètes*, vol. I, edited by Claude Pichois, 291–92. Bibliothèque de la Pléiade. Paris: Gallimard, 1975.

Baudelaire, Charles. "L'Exposition universelle de 1855 vue par Baudelaire." In *Charles Baudelaire: Œuvres Complètes*, vol. II, edited by Claude Pichois, 575–97. Bibliothèque de la Pléiade. Paris: Gallimard, 1976.

Baudelaire, Charles. "The Life and Works of Eugène Delacroix." In *The Painter in Modern Life*, edited and translated by Jonathan Mayne, 41–68. London: Phaidon, 2001.

Baudelaire, Charles. "L'Œuvre et la vie de Delacroix." In *Charles Baudelaire: Œuvres Complètes*, vol. II, edited by Claude Pichois, 742–70. Bibliothèque de la Pléiade. Paris: Gallimard, 1976.

Baudelaire, Charles. "Mon cœur mis à nu." In *Charles Baudelaire: Œuvres Complètes*, vol. I, edited by Claude Pichois, 676–708. Bibliothèque de la Pléiade. Paris: Gallimard, 1975.

Baudelaire, Charles. "Morale du joujou." In *Charles Baudelaire: Œuvres Complètes*, vol. II, edited by Claude Pichois, 581–87. Bibliothèque de la Pléiade. Paris: Gallimard, 1976.

Baudelaire, Charles. "My Heart Laid Bare." In *Late Fragments: Flares, My Heart Laid Bare, Prose Poems, Belgium Disrobed*, edited and translated by Richard Sieburth, 111–48. New Haven, CT: Yale University Press, 2022.

Baudelaire, Charles. "Notes Nouvelles sur Edgar Poe." In *Charles Baudelaire: Œuvres Complètes*, vol. II, edited by Claude Pichois, 319–37. Bibliothèque de la Pléiade. Paris: Gallimard, 1976.

Baudelaire, Charles, "The Painter of Modern Life: XIII Carriages." In *The Painter of Modern Life*, edited and translated by Jonathan Mayne, 1–40. London: Phaidon, 2001.

Baudelaire, Charles. "A Philosophy of Toys." In *The Painter of Modern Life*, edited and translated by Jonathan Mayne, 197–204. London: Phaidon, 2001.

Baudelaire, Charles. "The Poor Boy's Toy." In *Vol. II: The Poems in Prose and La Fanfarol*, edited and translated by Francis Scarfe, 82–85. London: Anvil Press Poetry, 1989.

Baudelaire, Charles. "Richard Wagner and *Tannhäuser* in Paris." In *The Painter in Modern Life*, edited and translated by Jonathan Mayne, 111–46. London: Phaidon, 2001.

Baudelaire, Charles. "Richard Wagner et *Tannhäuser* à Paris." In *Charles Baudelaire: Œuvres Complètes*, vol. II, edited by Claude Pichois, 779–815. Bibliothèque de la Pléiade. Paris: Gallimard, 1976.

Baudelaire, Charles. "Salon de 1846." In *Charles Baudelaire: Œuvres Complètes*, vol. II, edited by Claude Pichois, 415–524. Bibliothèque de la Pléiade. Paris: Gallimard, 1976.

Baudelaire, Charles. "The Salon of 1846." In *Art in Paris 1845–1862: Salons and Other Exhibitions Reviewed by Charles Baudelaire*, 2nd ed., edited and translated by Jonathan Mayne, 41–120. London: Phaidon, 1995.

Baudelaire, Charles. "The Wand." In *Vol. II: The Poems in Prose and La Fanfarol*, edited and translated by Francis Scarfe, 144–47. London: Anvil Press Poetry, 1989.

Baym, Max I. "Baudelaire and Shakespeare." *Shakespeare Association Bulletin* 15, no. 3 (July 1940): 131–48.

Bellow, Juliet. "Drawing a line with body." In *Arabesque Without End: Across Music and the Arts, from Faust to Shahrazad*, edited by Anne Leonard, 173–202. New York: Routledge, 2022.

Bellow, Juliet, Sophie Biass-Fabiani, François Blanchetière, and Alexandra Gerstein. *Rodin and Dance: The Essence of Movement*. London: Paul Holberton, 2020.

Benjamin, Walter. "Das Kunstwerk im Zeithalter seiner technischen Reproduzierbarkeit." In *Illuminationen. Ausgewählte Schriften 1*, 136–69. Frankfurt am Main: Suhrkamp, 1955.

Benjamin, Walter. "The *Flâneur*." In *Charles Baudelaire: A Lyric Poet in the Era of High Capitalism*, translated by Harry Zohn, 33–66. London: New Left/Verso, 1973/1997.

Benjamin, Walter. "On Some Motifs in Baudelaire." In *Illuminations: Essays and Reflections*, edited by Hannah Arendt, translated by Harry Zohn, 155–200. New York: Harcourt, Brace, and World, 1968.

Benjamin, Walter. "Über einige Motive bei Baudelaire." In *Illuminationen. Ausgewählte Schriften 1*, 185–229. Frankfurt am Main: Suhrkamp, 1955.

Benjamin, Walter. "The Work of Art in the Age of Mechanical Reproduction." In *Illuminations: Essays and Reflections*, edited by Hannah Arendt, translated by Harry Zohn, 217–51. New York: Harcourt, Brace, and World, 1968.

Bent, Ian. "'That Bright New Light': Schenker, Universal Edition, and the Origins of the Erläuterung Series, 1901–1910." *Journal of the American Musicological Society* 58, no. 1 (2005): 69–138.

Bergeron, Katherine. "The Echo, the Cry, the Death of Lovers." *19th-Century Music* 18, no. 2 (1994): 136–51.

Berman, Laurence. "The Evolution of Tonal Thinking in Works of Claude Debussy." PhD diss., Harvard University, 1965.

Berman, Laurence. "'Prelude to the Afternoon of a Faun' and 'Jeux': Debussy's Summer Rites." *19th-Century Music* 3, no. 3 (1980): 225–38.

Bernal, Martin. *Black Athena: The Afroasiatic Roots of Classical Civilization*. New Brunswick, NJ: Rutgers University Press, 1987.

Bernier, Georges, ed. *La Revue blanche. Paris in the Days of Post-Impressionism and Symbolism*. New York: Wildenstein, 1983.

Berry, David Carson. "The Role of Adele T. Katz in the Early Expansion of the New York 'Schenker School.'" *Current Musicology* 74 (2002): 103–51.

Bertelin, Albert. *Traité de composition musicale*. 4 vols. Paris: Editions de la Schola Cantorum, 1931.

Bhogal, Gurminder Kaur. *Details of Consequence: Ornament, Music, and Art in Paris*. AMS Studies in Music. New York: Oxford University Press, 2013.

Bhogal, Gurminder Kaur. "Ephemeral Arabesque Timbres and the Exotic Feminine." In *Arabesque without End: Across Music and the Arts, from Faust to Shahrazad*, edited by Anne Leonard, 129–48. New York: Routledge, 2022.

Bisaro, Xavier. "L'arabesque musicale: un non-sens? Étude de l'applicabilité d'un concept debussyste à la musique du XVIII e siècle." *Musurgia* 17, no. 2 (2010): 21–39.

Bithell, Jethro. *Life and Writings of Maurice Maeterlinck*. London: Walter Scott, 1913.

Blane, Charles. *Grammaire des arts décoratifs*. 2 vols. Paris: Librairie Renouard, 1882.

Bloom, Harold. "Edgar Allan Poe (1809–1849)." In *The American Canon*, edited by David Mikics, 45–60. New York: Library of America, 2019.

Bloom, Peter, ed. "Foreword." In *Claude Debussy Trio for piano, violin and cello, Nocturne et Scherzo for cello and piano, Quatuor à cordes*, Œuvres Complètes, Série III Musique de Chambre, vol. 1. Paris: Durand, 2015.

Boime, Albert. "The Prix de Rome: Images of Authority and Threshold of Official Success." *Art Journal* 44, no. 3, Art and Science: Part II, Physical Sciences (1984): 281–89.

Bois, Jules. *Le Satanisme et la Magie. Avec une Étude de J.-K. Huysmans.* Paris: Léron Chailley, 1895.

Bois, Jules. *Les Noces de Sathan, drame ésotérique.* Avec un dessin de M. Henry Colas. Paris: Chamuel Éditeur, 1892.

Bois, Jules. *Les Petites Religions de Paris.* Paris: Lèon Chailley, 1894.

Bonaparte, Marie. *The Life and Works of Edgar Allan Poe: A Psycho-Analytic Interpretation.* Translated by John Rodker. London: Imago, 1949.

Bondeson, Jan. *Buried Alive: The Terrifying History of Our Most Primal Fear.* New York: Norton, 2002.

Bonneau, Lara. "Trilles, arabesques, et metaphores: À propos de 'L'ornement.'" *Cahiers philosophiques* 162, no. 3 (2020): 1–7.

Botting, Fred. "Poe's Phantasmagoreality." *Edgar Allan Poe Review* 11, no. 1 (Spring 2010): 9–21.

Boulez, Pierre. "Préface, Entretien Pierre Boulez." In *Pelléas et Mélisande cent and après: études et documents.* Palazzetto Bru Zane, Centre de musique contemporaine Française, edited by Jean-Christophe Branger, Sylvie Douche, and Denis Herlin (Lyon: Symétrie, 2013), 1.

Boulez, Pierre. *Relevés d'apprenti.* Edited by Paul Thévenin. Paris: Seuil, 1966.

Boulez, Pierre. *Stocktakings from an Apprenticeship.* Edited by Paule Tilevenin. Translated by Stephen Walsh. Oxford: Clarendon, 1991.

Bourgoin, Jules. *Les Éléments de l'arte arabe.* Paris: Librairie de Fermin-Didot, 1879.

Bourgoin, Jules. *Théorie de l'ornament.* Paris: Ducher, 1883.

Brady, Emily, and Arto Haapala. "Melancholy as an Aesthetic Emotion." *Contemporary Aesthetics* 1 (2003). Accessed July 11, 2025. https://quod.lib.umich.edu/c/ca/7523862.0001.006 ?view=text;rgn=main.

Branger, Christophe, Sylvie Douche, and Denis Herlin, eds. *Pelléas et Mélisande cent and après: études et documents.* Lyon: Symétrie, 2013.

Braswell, Suzanne F. "An Aesthetics of Movement Baudelaire, Poetic Renewal, and the Invitation of Dance." *French Forum* 31, no. 3 (Fall 2006): 23–43.

Breatnach, Mary. "Baudelaire, Wagner, Mallarmé: Romantic Aesthetics and the Word-Tone Dichotomy." In *Word and Music Studies,* 4:69–83. Amsterdam: Rodopi, 2003.

Bribitzer-Stull, Matthew. *Understanding the Leimotif: From Wagner to Hollywood Film.* Cambridge: Cambridge University Press, 2015.

Briscoe, James R. "Debussy 'd'après' Debussy: The Further Resonance of Two Early 'Mélodies.'" *19th-Century Music* 5, no. 2 (1981): 110–16.

Briscoe, James R. "Debussy's Earliest Songs." *College Music Symposium* 24, no. 2 (Fall 1984): 81–95.

Broome, Peter. *Baudelaire's Poetic Patterns.* Amsterdam: Rodopi, 1999.

Brown, Hilda Meldrum. *The Quest for the Gesamtkunstwerk and Richard Wagner.* Oxford: Oxford University Press, 2016.

Brown, Matthew. "An Adaptation of an Adaptation: TableTopOpera's Live Production of *Ariane and Bluebeard.*" In *Ariane & Bluebeard: From Fairy Tale to Comic Book Opera,* edited by Matthew Brown and Th. Emil Homerin, 263–91. Bloomington: Indiana University Press, 2022.

Brown, Matthew. "*Ariane et Bluebeard* and the Legacy of Richard Wagner." In *Ariane & Bluebeard: From Fairy Tale to Comic Book Opera,* edited by Matthew Brown and Th. Emil Homerin, 169–91. Bloomington: Indiana University Press, 2022.

Brown, Matthew. "Chamber Music." In *Debussy in Context*, edited by Simon Trezise, 240–47. Cambridge: Cambridge University Press, 2024.

Brown, Matthew. "Composing with Prototypes: Charting Debussy's *L'Isle joyeuse.*" *Intégral* 16 (2004/2005): 151–88.

Brown, Matthew. *Debussy Redux: The Impact of His Music on Popular Culture.* Bloomington: Indiana University Press, 2012.

Brown, Matthew. *Debussy's 'Ibéria': Studies in Genesis and Structure.* Oxford: Oxford University Press, 2003.

Brown, Matthew. "Debussy's Violin Sonata and the Legacy of J. S. Bach." In *Debussy Studies 2*, edited by Barbara Kelly and David Code. Cambridge University Press, 2025.

Brown, Matthew. "Debussy Today." In *Debussy in Context*, edited by Simon Trezise, 299–310. Cambridge: Cambridge University Press, 2024.

Brown, Matthew. "The Diatonic and the Chromatic in Schenker's Theory of Harmonic Relations." *Journal of Music Theory* 30, no. 1 (1986): 1–33.

Brown, Matthew. *Explaining Tonality: Schenkerian Theory and Beyond.* Rochester, NY: University of Rochester Press, 2005.

Brown, Matthew. "Follow the Leader: Debussy's Contrapuntal Games." In *Debussy's Resonance*, edited by François de Médicis and Steven Huebner, 383–406. Rochester, NY: University of Rochester Press, 2018.

Brown, Matthew. "*Japonism*, Collecting, and the *Expositions Universelles.*" In *Debussy in Context*, edited by Simon Trezise, 98–105. Cambridge: Cambridge University Press, 2024.

Brown, Matthew. "On the Literary Origins of Maeterlinck's *Pelléas et Mélisande.*" *Cahiers Debussy* 39 (2015): 5–17.

Brown, Matthew. "Pelléas, Mélisande, le grotesque et l'Arabesque." In *Regards sur Debussy*, edited by Myriam Chimènes and Alexandra Laederich, 137–50. Paris: Fayard, 2013.

Brown, Matthew. "Review: John Rothgeb ed. and trans., *Beethoven: The Last Piano Sonatas: Edited, with Analytic Commentary, by Heinrich Schenker.*" *Theory and Practice* 41 (2017): 213–28.

Brown, Matthew. "Review of '*Pelléas et Mélisande cent and après: études et documents*,' ed. Christophe Branger, Sylvie Douche, and Denis Herlin." *19th-Century Music Review* 13 (2016): 289–98.

Brown, Matthew. "Tonality and Form in Debussy's *Prélude à 'L'Après-midi d'un faune.*'" *Music Theory Spectrum* 15 (1993): 127–43.

Brown, Matthew, Dave Headlam, and Douglas J. Dempster. "The #IV(♭V) Hypothesis: Testing the Limits of Schenker's Theory of Tonality." *Music Theory Spectrum* 19, no. 2 (1997): 155–83.

Brown, Matthew, Dariusz Terefenko, Christopher Winders, and Kerry Smyth. *Pelléas Redux: Celebrating Debussy, Maeterlinck, and P. Craig Russell.* Rochester, NY: Memorial Art Gallery, 2012.

Brown, Ruth Halle, ed. *Music through Sources and Documents.* Englewood Cliffs, NJ: Prentice-Hall, 1979.

Bruhn, Siglind. *Debussy's Instrumental Music in Its Cultural Context.* Studies in 20th-Century Music: Dimension and Diversity. Hillsdale, NY: Pendragon, 2019.

Buckle, Richard. *Nijinsky.* New York: Simon and Schuster, 1971.

Burkhart, Charles. "Schenker's 'Motivic Parallelisms.'" *Journal of Music Theory* 22, no. 2 (1978): 145–75.

Burkhart, Charles. "A Note on Debussy's *Beau Soir*," *Journal of Schenkerian Studies* 9 (2016), 131–37.

Burkhart, Charles. "Debussy's *Chansons de Bilitis*," *International Forum for Schenkerian Research* 1 (2023), 74–83.

Caddy, Davinia. "Making Moves in Reception Studies: Music, Listening, and Loie Fuller." In *Musicology and Dance: Historical and Critical Perspectives*, edited by Davinia Caddy and Maribeth Clark, 91–117. Cambridge: Cambridge University Press, 2020.

Cahusac, Hector. "Commentaire." *Le Figaro*, May 14, 1913.

Caine, [Thomas Henry] Hall. *King Albert's Book: A Tribute to the Belgian King and People from Representative Men and Women throughout the World*. London: Daily Telegraph, 1914.

Cambiaire, Célestin Pierre. *The Influence of Edgar Allan Poe in France*. New York: Haskell House, 1970.

Carle, Christophe. "Debussy in Fin-de-Siècle Paris." In *Debussy and His World*, edited by Jane Fulcher, 271–95. Princeton, NJ: Princeton University Press, 2001.

Carlson, Marvin. *Theories of the Theater. A Historical and Critical Survey from the Greeks to the Present*. Exp. ed. Ithaca, NY: Cornell University Press, 1993.

Carter, Elliott. "The Three Late Sonatas of Debussy." In *Elliott Carter: Collected Essays and Lectures, 1937–1995*, edited by Jonathan W. Bernard, 122–33. Rochester, NY: University of Rochester Press, 1997.

Cartwright, Mark Anson. "Elision and the embellished final cadence in J. S. Bach's Preludes." *Music Analysis* 26, no. 3 (2007): 267–88.

Chabouille, Louis-Adolphe, ed. *Lettres inédites [à sa mère] de Charles Baudelaire*. Paris: Calmann-Levy, 1891.

Chambers, Ephraim. *Cyclopaedie*. London: J. Knapton et al., 1728.

Chambers, Ross. *The Writings of Melancholy: Modes of Opposition in Early French Modernism*. Translated by Mary Seidman Trouille. Chicago: University of Chicago Press, 1993.

Chambers, Sir William. *Designs of Chinese Buildings, Furniture, Dresses, Machines, and Utensils (1757)*. Facsimile ed. London: Gregg International, 1969.

Chambers, Sir William. *Plans, Elevations, Sections, and Perspective Views of the Gardens and Buildings at Kew in Surry (1763)*. Facsimile ed. London: Gregg International, 1966.

Charlton, David, ed., and Martyn Clarke, trans. *E. T. A. Hoffmann's Musical Writings: Kreisleriana, the Poet and the Composer*. Cambridge: Cambridge University Press, 1989.

Chevenard, Claude-Aimé. *Album de L'Ornemaniste*. Paris: Lenoir, 1845.

Chisholm, A. R. *Mallarmé's L'Après-Midi d'un Faune: An Exegetical and Critical Study*. Melbourne: Melbourne University Press, 1958.

Churton, Tobias. *Occult Paris: The Lost Magic of the Belle Époque*. Rochester, VT: Inner Traditions, 2016.

Cinephilia & Beyond. "'Obsession': When De Palma Stepped Out of Hitchcock's Shadow." Accessed December 26, 2022. https://cinephiliabeyond.org/obsession-de-palma-stepped -hitchcocks-shadow.

Clayson, Hollis. *Painted Love: Prostitution in French Art of the Impressionist Era*. New Haven, CT: Yale University Press, 1991.

Clevenger, John R. "Debussy's Paris Conservatoire Training." In *Debussy and His World*, edited by Jane F. Fulcher, 299–361. Princeton, NJ: Princeton University Press, 2001.

Clevenger, John R. "The Origins of Debussy's Style." PhD diss., University of Rochester, 2002.

Close, A. J. "Commonplace Theories of Art and Nature in Classical Antiquity and the Renaissance." *Journal of the History of Ideas* 30, no. 4 (1969): 467–86.

Cobb, Margaret G., and Richard Miller. *The Poetic Debussy: A Collection of His Song Texts and Selected Letters*. Rev. ed. Rochester, NY: University of Rochester Press, 1994.

Cobb, Palmer. "The Influence of E. T. A. Hoffmann on the Tales of Edgar Allan Poe." *Studies in Philology* 3 (1908): 1–105.

Code, David J. "Debussy, Discourse, Time." *Musical Quarterly* 100, no. 3–4 (Fall–Winter 2017): 340–98.

Code, David J. "Debussy's Quartet in the Brussels Salon of 'La Libre Esthétique.'" *19th-Century Music* 30, no. 3 (2007): 257–87.

Code, David J. "Hearing Debussy Reading Mallarmé: Music *après Wagner* in the *Prélude à l'après-midi d'un faune*." *Journal of the American Musicological Society* 53, no. 3 (2001): 493–554.

Code, David J. "Nijinsky, Modernism, Repression: The Faun Ballet—Once Again—Under Analysis." In *Musicology and Dance: Historical and Critical Perspectives*, edited by Davinia Caddy and Maribeth Clark, 207–30. Cambridge: Cambridge University Press, 2020.

Code, David J. "The 'Song Triptych': Reflections on a Debussyan Genre." In *Debussy's Resonance*, edited by François de Médicis and Steven Huebner, 127–74. Rochester, NY: University of Rochester Press, 2018.

Cogman, Peter. "Claude Debussy, Pierre Louÿs, and the îles sanguinaires." *French Studies Bulletin* 26, no. 97 (2005): 7–9.

Cohn, Danièle. "Préface." In *Sur l'ornement*, edited and translated by Clara Paquet. Paris: Éditions Rue d'Ulm, 2008.

Coleman, Jeremy. *Richard Wagner in Paris: Translation, Identity, Modernity*. Woodbridge: Boydell, 2019.

Collins, Jeffrey. "Watteau and the *Fête galante by Martin Eidelberg, Barbara Anderman, Guillaume Glorieux, Michael Hochmann and François Moureau*." *Eighteenth-Century Studies* 38, no. 4 (2005): 691–96.

Cone, Edward T. *Musical Form and Musical Performance*. New York: Norton, 1968.

Cone, Edward T. "Stravinsky: The Progress of a Method." *Perspectives of New Music* 1, no. 1 (1962): 18–26.

Cook, Bradford, trans. *Mallarmé: Selected Prose Poems, Essays, & Letters*. Baltimore: Johns Hopkins Press, 1956.

Cooper, Kenneth, arr. *Debussy's Sonata 'No. 4' for oboe, horn, and harpsichord*. New York: International Music, 2011.

Cotgrave, Randle. *A Dictionarie of the French and English Tongues* (1611). Columbia: University of South Carolina Press, 1968.

Cowling, Elizabeth. "Feminine/Masculine: The Collages of Picasso, Braque, and Gris. How Did Cubist Artists Use Collage to Probe the Relationship between the Sexes?" *The Met*, November 8, 2022. Accessed November 19, 2023. https://www.metmuseum.org /perspectives/articles/2022/11/feminine-masculine-cubist-collage#:~:text=Inanimate %20objects%20dominated%20the%20imagery,combination%20of%20things%20and %20text.

Cox, David. *Debussy Orchestral Music*. BBC Music Guide. Seattle: University of Washington Press, 1974.

Crane, Walter, and Theo Marzials. *Pan Pipes*. London: George Routledge, 1883.

Culler, Jonathan. "Baudelaire and Poe." In *Critical Insights: The Poetry of Edgar Allan Poe*, edited by Steven Frye, 188–209. Pasadena, CA: Salem, 2011.

Cummins, Linda. *Debussy and the Fragment*. Amsterdam: Rodopi, 2006.

Czerny, Carl. *A Systematic Introduction to Improvisation on the Pianoforte*. Edited and translated by Alice L. Mitchell. Vienna: Diabelli, 1829.

Czerny, Carl. *Systematische Anleitung zum Fantasieren auf dem Pianoforte*, Op. 200. Vienna: Diabelli, 1836.

Dahlhaus, Carl. *Nineteenth-Century Music*. Translated by J. Bradford Robinson. Berkeley: University of California Press, 1989.

Dal Mollin, Paolo Dal, and Jean-Louis Leleu. "Comment composait Debussy: les leçons d'un carnet de travail (à propos de *Soupir* et d'Éventail)." *Cahiers Debussy* 35 (2011): 9–82.

Dällenbach, Lucian. *Le récit spéculaire. Essai sur la mise en abyme*. Paris: Éditions du Seuil, 1977.

Dandrey, Patrick. "Encyclopédisme mélancolique, ou d'un 'miroir terni.'" In *Anthologie de l'humeur noir. Écrits sur la mélancolie d'Hippocrate à l'Encyclopédie*, edited by Patrick Dandrey, 749–54. Paris: Gallimard, 2005.

Dann, Kevin T. *Bright Colors Falsely Seen: Synaesthesia and the Search for Transcendental Knowledge*. New Haven, CT: Yale University Press, 1998.

David, Hans T., and Arthur Mendel, eds. *The New Bach Reader: A Life of Johann Sebastian Bach in Letters and Documents*. Revised and enlarged by Christoph Wolff. New York: Norton, 1998.

Davidian, Teresa Marie. "Debussy's Sonata Forms." PhD diss., University of Chicago, 1988.

De Médicis, Catrina Flint. "Early Music." In *Debussy in Context*, edited by Simon Trezise, 281–90. Cambridge: Cambridge University Press, 2024.

De Médicis, François. "Debussy's *Faun* and the Russian Arabesque." Paper delivered at Claude Debussy in 2018: A Centenary Celebration. Royal Northern College of Music, March 19, 2018.

De Médicis, François. *La Maturation Artistique de Debussy dans son Contexte Historique*. Speculum Musicae XXXVIII. Turnhout: Brepols, 2020.

De Médicis, François. "Symbolism." In *Debussy in Context*, edited by Simon Trezise, 69–78. Cambridge: Cambridge University Press, 2024.

De Quincey, Thomas. *Confessions of an English Opium Eater*. London: Taylor and Hessey, 1822.

De Régnier, Henri. *Le Bosquet de Psyché*. Brussels: Paul Lacomplez, 1894.

Debussy, Claude. *Correspondance (1872–1918)*. Edited by François Lesure and Denis Herlin. Annotated by François Lesure, Denis Herlin, and Georges Liébert. Paris: Gallimard, 2005.

Debussy, Claude. *Danses bohémienne, Dances (Tarentelle styrienne), Ballade (Ballade slave), Valse Romantique, Suite bergamasque, Rêverie, Mazurka, Deux Arabesques, Nocturne*. Edited by Roy Howat. Oeuvres complètes de Claude Debussy, sér. I, vol. 1. Paris: Durand, 2000.

Debussy, Claude. *Debussy Letters*. Edited by François Lesure and Roger Nichols. Translated by Roger Nichols. Cambridge, MA: Harvard University Press, 1987.

Debussy, Claude. *Debussy on Music*. Edited by François Lesure. Translated by Richard Langham Smith. New York: Knopf, 1977.

Debussy, Claude. *Images (1894—dédiées à Y. Lerolle), Pour le piano, Children's Corner*. Edited by Roy Howat. Œuvres Complètes de Claude Debussy, Série I, vol. 2. Paris: Durand, 1998.

Debussy, Claude. *Jeux, Poème dansé.* Edited by Pierre Boulez and Myriam Chimènes. Œuvres Complètes de Claude Debussy, Série V Œuvres d'orchestre, vol. 8. Paris: Durand-Costallat, 1988.

Debussy, Claude. *La Mer.* Edited by Peter Jost. Wiesbaden: Breitkopf & Härtel, 2006.

Debussy, Claude. *La Mer.* Edited by Max Pommer. Leipzig: Peters, 1971.

Debussy, Claude. *La Mer.* Edited by Marie Rolf. Œuvres Complètes de Claude Debussy, Série V Œuvres d'orchestre, vol. 5. Paris: Durand, ca. 1997.

Debussy, Claude. *La Mer.* Edited by Douglas Woodfull-Harris. Barenreiter: Kassel, 2014.

Debussy, Claude. *Monsieur Croche et autres écrits.* Edited by François Lesure. Paris: Gallimard, 1987.

Debussy, Claude. *Pelléas et Mélisande.* Edited by David Grayson. Œuvres Complètes de Claude Debussy. Série VI Œuvres lyriques, vol. 2. Paris: Durand-Costallat, 2010.

Debussy, Claude. *Le Roi Lear, Le Diable dans le beffroi, La chute de la Maison Usher.* Ed. Robert Orledge. Œuvres Complètes de Claude Debussy. Série VI Œuvres Lyriques Vol. 3. Paris : Durand, 2006.

Debussy, Claude. *Trio for piano, violin and cello, Nocturne et Scherzo for cello and piano, Quatuor à cordes.* Edited by Peter Bloom. Œuvres Complètes de Claude Debussy. Série III Musique de Chambre, vol. 1. Paris: Durand, 2015.

Debussy, Claude. "Vendredi Saint—Le neuvième Symphonie." In *Monsieur Croche et autres écrits*, edited by François Lesure, 33–34. Paris: Gallimard, 1987.

Delécluse, François. "Dans l'atelier de Claude Debussy. Processus créateur et méthodes de composition dans les esquisses des dernières oeuvres, 1915–1917." PhD diss., Université Jean Monnet, Saint-Étienne, 2018.

Denis, Maurice. *Henry Lerolle et Ses Amis.* Paris: Duranton, 1932.

Denis, Maurice. *Théories, 1890–1910: Du Symbolisme et de Gauguin vers un Nouvel Ordre Classique.* 3rd ed. Paris: Bibliothèque de L'Occident, 1913.

DeVoto, Mark. *Debussy and the Veil of Tonality: Essays on his Music.* Dimension and Diversity No. 4. Hillsdale, NY: Pendragon, 2004.

Devriè, Anik. "Les musiques d'extrême orient à l'exposition universelle de 1889." *Cahiers Debussy* 1 (1977): 24–37.

Diderot, Denis. *Pensées détachées sur la peinture, la sculpture, l'architecture et la poésie pour servir de suite aux Salons.* In *Œuvres de Denis Diderot*, edited by Hippolyte Walferdin. Vol. 10. Paris: J. L. J. Brière, 1821.

Diderot, Denis, and Jean Le Rond d'Alembert. *Encyclopédie, ou Dictionnaire Raisonné des Sciences, des Arts, et des Métiers.* Paris: Chez Briasson, 1751–65.

Dietschy, Marcel. *A Portrait of Claude Debussy.* Translated by William Ashbrook and Margaret G. Cobb. Oxford: Oxford University Press, 1990.

Donnellon, Déirdre. "Debussy as Musician and Critic." In *The Cambridge Companion to Debussy*, edited by Simon Trezise, 43–58. Cambridge: Cambridge University Press, 2003.

Drabkin, William. "The New *Erläuterungsausgabe.*" *Perspectives of New Music* 12, nos. 1/2 (1973–74): 319–30.

Duchesneau, Michel. "Debussy and Japanese Prints." In *Debussy's Resonance*, edited by François de Médicis and Steven Huebner, 301–25. Rochester, NY: University of Rochester Press, 2018.

Duchesnau, Michel. "Modernism." In *Debussy in Context*, edited by Simon Trezise, 79–87. Cambridge: Cambridge University Press, 2024.

Dujardin, Édouard, ed. *La Revue Wagnerienne.* 1885–1888. Genève: Slatkine, 1993.

Dukas, Paul. "Debussy's Quartet (May, 1894)." In Claude Debussy, *Prelude to "The Afternoon of a Faun,"* edited by William Austin, 151–54. Norton Critical Score. New York: Norton, 1970.

Dunsby, Jonathan. "The Poetry of Debussy's *En blanc et noir.*" In *Analytical Strategies and Musical Interpretation: Essays on Nineteenth- and Twentieth-Century Music*, edited by Craig Ayrey and Mark Everist, 149–68. Cambridge: Cambridge University Press, 1996.

Durand, Jacques. *Quelques souvenirs d'un éditeur.* Paris: Durand, 1924–25.

Duret, Théodore. "The Impressionist Painters" (1878). In *Impressionism and Post-Impressionism 1874–1904*, edited by Linda Nochlin. Sources & Documents in the History of Art Series, 7–10. Englewood Cliffs, NJ: Prentice-Hall, 1966.

Eigeldinger, Jean-Jacques. "Debussy et l'idée d'arabesque musicale." *Cahiers Debussy* 12/13 (1988–89): 5–14.

Eimert, Herbert, "Debussy's *Jeux.*" Translated by Leo Black. *Die Reihe* 5 (1961): 3–20.

Eliot, T. S. "From Poe to Valéry." *Hudson Review* 2, no. 3 (1949): 327–42.

Ellison, David. "Aesthetic Redemption: The Thyrsus in Nietzsche, Baudelaire, and Wagner." In *Ethics and Aesthetic in European Modernist Literature: From the Sublime to the Uncanny*, 87–112. Cambridge: Cambridge University Press, 2001.

Emery, Elizabeth. "Appropriating Japonisme at the 1900 Exposition: Sada Yacco, Loie Fuller, and the 'Geishas' of Le Panorama du Tour du Monde." *Dix-Neuf. Journal of the Society of Dix-Neuviémistes* 24, nos. 2–3 (2020): 221–44.

Emery, Elizabeth. "Madame Desoye, 'First Woman Importer' of Japanese Art in Nineteenth-Century Paris." *Journal of Japonisme* 5, no. 1 (2019): 1–46.

Emery, Elizabeth. *Reframing Japonisme. Women and the Asian Art Market in Nineteenth-Century France, 1853–1914.* London: Bloomsbury, 2022.

Evans, May Garretson. *Music and Edgar Allan Poe.* Baltimore: Johns Hopkins University Press, 1939.

Fauser, Annegret. "Crosscurrents in Debussy's Creative World." In *Debussy in Context*, edited by Simon Trezise, 106–13. Cambridge: Cambridge University Press, 2024.

Fauser, Annegret. *Musical Encounters at the 1889 Paris World's Fair.* Rochester, NY: University of Rochester Press, 2005.

Figueira, Dorothy M. "The Politics of Exoticism and Friedrich Schlegel's 'Metaphorical Pilgrimage to India.'" *Monatshefte* 81, no. 4 (Winter 1989): 425–33.

Filler, Martin. "The Architect of Subtraction." *New York Review of Books* LXX, no. 6 (April 6, 2023): 20–24.

Fischer, Michel. "Le quatuor à cordes en sol mineur de Claude Debussy: de la contraction formelle à la polyvalence de l'idée génératrice." *Musurgia* 8 (2001): 33–68.

Fleischer, Mary. "Theatre and Dance—A Symbolist Dialogue." In *Embodied Texts: Symbolist Playwright-Dancer*, Collaborations Internationale Forschungen zur Allgemeinen und Vergleichenden Literaturwissenschaft 113, 1–18. New York: Rodopi, 2007.

Forrest, William Mentzel. *Biblical Allusions in Poe.* New York: Macmillan, 1928.

Freeman, Nick. "The Gallows Nightingale: Swinburne's Translations of Villon." In *Beyond Arthurian Romances*, edited by Loretta M. Holloway and Jennifer A. Palmgren, 133–46. Berlin: Springer, 2005.

Freud, Sigmund. *Das Unheimliche.* Edited by Oliver Jahraus. Ditzingen: Reclam, 2020.

Freud, Sigmund. "Trauer und Melancholie." *Internationale Zeitschrift für ärztliche Psychoanalyse* 4, no. 6 (1917): 288–301.

Freud, Sigmund. *The Uncanny.* Translated by David McLintock. Introduction by Hugh Haughton. London: Penguin, 2003.

Freud, Sigmund. *Zur Einführung des Narzißmus.* Leipzig: Internationaler Pyschoanalytischer, 1914.

Furetière, Antoine. *Dictionnaire universel des arts et des sciences.* The Hague: Leers, 1702.

Gale, John E. "De Quincey, Baudelaire, and 'Le Cygne.'" *Nineteenth-Century French Studies* 5, nos. 3–4 (1977): 296–307.

Garafola, Lynn. *La Nijinska. Choreographer of the Modern.* New York: Oxford University Press, 2022.

Gautier, Théophile. *Charles Baudelaire: His Life.* Translated by Guy Thorne. London: Greening, 1915.

Geoghegan, Jeffrey C. "Israelite Sheepshearing and David's Rise to Power." *Biblica* 87, no. 1 (2006): 55–63.

Geroud, Daniel. "An Opening on the Unkown and Unknowable." In *A Maeterlinck Reader,* edited by David Willinger and Daniel Gerould, 1–22. New York: Peter Lang, 2011.

Gervais, Françoise. "La notion d'arabesque chez Debussy." *La Revue musicale* 241 (1958): 3–22.

Ghil, René. *Traité du verbe.* Rev. ed. Paris: Alcan Lévy, 1887.

Gibberd, Matt, and Albert Hill. *Ornament Is Crime: Modernist Architecture.* London: Phaidon, 2017.

Gibbs, Alan. "Debussy's Lutheran Side?" *The Strad* 103, no. 1228 (1992): 684.

Godbout, Kevin. "Saturnine Constellations: Melancholy in Literary History and in the Works of Baudelaire and Benjamin." PhD diss., University of Western Ontario, 2016.

Godet, Robert. "En marge de la marge." *La Revue musicale* 7 (May 1, 1926): 71–72.

Godwin, Joscelyn. *Music and the Occult: French Musical Philosophies, 1750–1950.* Rochester, NY: University of Rochester Press, 1995.

Gogröf-Voorhees, Andrea. *Defining Modernism: Baudelaire and Nietzsche on Romanticism, Modernity, Decadence, and Wagner.* 2nd ed. Frankfurt am Main: Peter Lang, 2004.

Gold, Arthur and Robert Fizdale, *Misia. The Life of Misia Sert.* New York: Morrow Quill, 1981.

Goldman, David Paul. "Esotericism as a Determinant of Debussy's Harmonic Language." *Musical Quarterly* 75, no. 2 (Summer 1991): 130–47.

Gordon, Rae Beth. *Ornament, Fantasy, and Desire in Nineteenth-Century French Literature.* Princeton, NJ: Princeton University Press, 1992.

Goubault, Christian. *Claude Debussy.* Paris: Champion, 1986.

Grasset, Eugène. *Méthode de Composition Ornementale.* Paris: Librairie Centrale des Beaux-Arts, ca. 1900.

Grayson, David. "Editing Debussy: Issues *en blanc et noir.*" *19th-Century Music* 13, no. 3 (1990): 243–57.

Grayson, David. *The Genesis of* Pelléas et Mélisande. Ann Arbor, MI: UMI, 1986.

Grayson, David. "The Libretto of Debussy's *Pelléas et Mélisande.*" *Music and Letters* 66, no. 1 (1985): 34–50.

Grayson, David. "The Opera: Genesis and Sources." In *Pelléas et Mélisande,* Cambridge Opera Handbooks, edited by Roger Nichols and Richard Langham Smith, 30–61. Cambridge: Cambridge University Press, 1989.

Grayson, David. "Waiting for Golaud: The Concept of Time in *Pelléas*." In *Debussy Studies*, edited by Richard Langham Smith, 26–50. Cambridge: Cambridge University Press, 1997.

Green, Douglass M. "Review of Richard S. Parks, *The Music of Claude Debussy* (New Haven, CT: Yale University Press, 1989)." *Music Theory Spectrum* 14, no. 2 (1992): 214–22.

Grewe, Cordula. *The Arabesque from Kant to Comics*. Routledge Advances in Art and Visual Studies. New York: Routledge, 2021.

Grey, Thomas. "The 'Splendid and Shameful Art': Dancing in and around the Wagnerian *Gesamtkunstwerk*." In *Musicology and Dance. Historical and Critical Perspectives*, edited by Davinia Caddy and Maribeth Clark, 121–50. Cambridge: Cambridge University Press, 2020.

Griffith, M. "Loie Fuller—The Inventor of the Serpentine Dance." *Strand Magazine* 7 (January 1894): 540–45.

Griffiths, Paul. *The String Quartet*. New York: Thames and Hudson, 1983.

Grøtta, Marit. *Baudelaire's Media Aesthetics: The Gaze of the Flâneur and Nineteenth-Century Media*. London: Bloomsbury 2015.

Gruener, Gustav. "Notes on the Influence of E. T. A. Hoffmann upon Edgar Allan Poe." *Proceedings of the Modern Language Association* 19 (1904): 1–25.

Guerpin, Martin. "Paris, the City." In *Debussy in Context*, edited by Simon Trezise, 3–15. Cambridge: Cambridge University Press, 2024.

Guest, Ann Hutchinson, ed. *Nijinsky's Faune Restored*. Language of Dance Series No. 3. Philadelphia: Gordon and Breach, 1991.

Guiley, Rosemary Ellen. *The Art of Black-Mirror Scrying*. New Milford, CT: Visionary Living, 2014.

Gutsche-Miller, Sarah. "Debussy's Noctambule and Parisian Popular Culture." In *Debussy in Context*, edited by Simon Trezise, 193–200. Cambridge: Cambridge University Press, 2024.

Guye, Jean-Philippe, Philippe Gouttenoire, and Éric Demange. "Le quatuor de Debussy: recherches analytiques et esthétiques." *Analyse Musicale* 37 (2000): 32–60.

Hahn, H. Hazel. "Consumption and Leisure." In *Debussy in Context*, edited by Simon Trezise, 45–55. Cambridge: Cambridge University Press, 2024.

Halls, W. D. *Maurice Maeterlinck. A Study of his Life and Thought*. Oxford: Clarendon, 1960.

Hamdan, Mohammed. "The Gift of Drugs: Oriental Geographies and Decolonizing Space in Thomas De Quincey's Confessions of an English Opium-Eater." *Janus Unbound: Journal of Critical Studies* II, no. I (Winter 2022): 63–68.

Hanslick, Eduard. *The Beautiful in Music*. Translated by Gustav Cohen. Edited by Morris Weitz. Library of the Arts No. 45. New York: Bobbs-Merrill, 1957.

Hanslick, Eduard. *Vom Musikalisch-Schönen*. Ein Beitrag zur Revision der Ästhetik der Tonkunst. 3rd ed. Leipzig: Rudolph Weigel, 1854.

Hartmann, Elwood. "Japonisme and Nineteenth-Century French Literature." In "East-West Issue," special issue, *Comparative Literature Studies* 18, no. 2 (1981): 141–66.

Hartmann, Sadakichi. *Japanese Art*. Boston: L. C. Page, 1904.

Haswell, Richard H. "Poe and Baudelaire: Translations." *Poe Studies* 5, no. 2 (1972): 62–63.

Hays, Michael. "On Maeterlinck Reading Shakespeare." *Modern Drama* 20, no. I (1986): 49–59.

Heard, Mervyn. *Phantasmagoria: The Secret Life of the Magic Lantern*. Hastings: Projection Box, 2006.

Heck, Adeline Anastasia. "Under the Spell of Wagner: *The Revue Wagnérienne* and Literary Experimentation in the Belle Epoque (1878–1893)." PhD diss., Princeton University, 2020.

Hellé, André. *Films pour les tout-petits.* Paris: Librairie Garnier, 1923.

Hellé, André. *French Toys.* Paris: Éditions De L'Avenir Féminin, 1915.

Hellé, André. *Grosses bêtes & petites bêtes.* Paris: Tolmer & Cie, 1912.

Hennion, Antoine, and Joël-Marie Fauquet. "Authority as Performance: The Love of Bach in Nineteenth-Century France." *Poetics* 29 (2001): 75–88.

Hennion, Antoine, and Joël-Marie Fauquet. *La grandeur de Bach: L'amour de la musique en France au XIXe siècle.* Paris: Fayard, 2000.

Henry, Freeman G. "Les Fleurs du Mal and the Exotic: The Escapist Psychology of a Visionary Poet." *Nineteenth-Century French Studies* 8, nos. 1/2 (1979–80): 62–75.

Hepokoski, James. "Beyond the Sonata Principle." *Journal of the American Musicological Society* 55, no. 1 (2002): 91–154.

Hepokoski, James. "Formulaic Openings in Debussy." *19th-Century Music* 8, no. 1 (Summer 1984): 44–59.

Herlin, Denis. "À la librairie de l'Art indépendent: l'univers symboliste de Debussy," In *Claude Debussy—Portraits et Études*, 17–47. Hildesheim: Georg Olms, 2023.

Herlin, Denis. "André Hellé et La Boîte à joujoux: interview, conférence et texte intégrale de *L'Histoire d'une Boîte àjoujoux.*" *Cahiers Debussy* 30 (2006): 97–123.

Herlin, Denis. "An Artist High and Low, or Debussy and Money." Translated by Vincent Giroud. In *Rethinking Debussy*, edited by Elliot Antokoletz and Marianne Wheeldon, 149–202. New York: Oxford University Press, 2011.

Herlin, Denis. *Claude Debussy—Portraits et Études.* Hildesheim: Georg Olms, 2023.

Herlin, Denis. "From Debussy's Studio: The Little-Known Autograph of *De rêve*, the First of the *Proses lyriques* (1892)." Translated by Peter Bloom. *Notes* 71, no. 1 (September 2014): 9–34.

Herlin, Denis. "The Jobbing Composer-Musician." In *Debussy in Context*, edited by Simon Trezise, 169–76. Cambridge: Cambridge University Press, 2024.

Herlin, Denis, "Les mésaventure de *Monsieur Croche Antidilettante*." In *Claude Debussy—Portraits et Études*, 366–91. Hildesheim: Georg Olms, 2023.

Herlin, Denis. "*Les soirs illuminés par l'ardeur du charbon*: de Baudelaire à Debussy," In *Claude Debussy—Portraits et Études*, 497–504. Hildesheim: Georg Olms, 2023.

Herlin, Denis. "L'esquisses du quatuor à cordes." *Cahiers Debussy* 14 (1990): 23–54.

Herlin, Denis. "Publishers." In *Debussy in Context*, edited by Simon Trezise, 143–49. Cambridge: Cambridge University Press, 2024.

Herrmann, Bernard. "Bernard Herrmann. Composer." In *Sound and Cinema. The Coming of Sound to American Film*, edited by Evan William Cameron, 117–35. Pleasantville, NY: Redgrave, 1980.

Herrmann, Bernard. *The Impressionists. Satie, Debussy, Ravel, Fauré, Honegger.* London Philharmonic Orchestra, Phase 4. Decca: London, SPC 21062, 1970.

Hinterberger, Heinrich. *Enthaltend die Bibliothek des Herrn Dr. Heinrich Schenker.* Wien Katalog XII. Vienna: Antiquariat Hinterberger, ca. 1935.

Hitchcock, Alfred. "The Enjoyment of Fear." In *Hitchcock on Hitchcock: Selected Writings and Interviews*, edited by Sidney Gottlieb, 116–21. Berkeley: University of California Press, 1995.

Hitchcock, Alfred. "Why I Am Afraid of the Dark." In *Hitchcock on Hitchcock: Selected Writings and Interviews*, edited by Sidney Gottlieb, 142–45. Berkeley: University of California Press, 1995.

Hodson, Milicent. *Nijinsky's Bloomsbury Ballet. Reconstruction of the Dance and Design for* Jeux. The Wendy Hilton Dance & Music Series No. 12. Hillsdale, NY: Pendragon, 1996.

Hogarth, William. *The Analysis of Beauty* (London: J. Reeves, 1753). A Scolar Press Facsimile. Ilkley, UK: Scolar, 1969.

Holloway, Robin. *Debussy and Wagner*. London: Eulenberg, 1979.

Holme, Charles. *Modern Pen Drawings: European and American*. London: Offices of Studio, 1901.

"How Delacroix Went from Lycée Dropout to Establishment Favourite," *The Art Newspaper*, April 12, 2018, https://www.theartnewspaper.com/2018/04/12/how-delacroix-went-from-lycee-dropout-to-establishment-favourite.

Howat, Roy. "Debussy and the Orient." In *Recovering the Orient. Artists, Scholars, Appropriations*, edited by Andrew Gerstle and Anthony Milner, 45–81. Reading: Harwood, 1994.

Howat, Roy. *Debussy in Proportion: A Musical Analysis*. Cambridge: Cambridge University Press, 1983.

Howat, Roy. "Dramatic Shape and Form in *Jeux de vagues*, and Its Relationship to *Pelléas*, *Jeux* and Other Scores." *Cahiers Debussy* 7 (1983): 7–23.

Howat, Roy. "En route for 'L'île joyeuse': The Restoration of a Triptych." *Cahiers Debussy* 19 (1995): 37–52.

Howat, Roy. "Foreword." In *Debussy: Images (1894—dédiées à Y. Lerolle), Pour le piano, Children's Corner*, Œuvres Complètes de Claude Debussy, sér. 1, vol. 2. Paris: Durand, 1998.

Howat, Roy. "Foreword." In *Deux Arabesques, Œuvres Complètes*, sér. 1, vol. 1, edited by Roy Howat. Paris: Durand, 2008.

Howat, Roy. "The New Debussy Edition: Approaches and Techniques." *Studies in Music* 19 (1985): 94–113.

Huebner, Steven. *French Opera at the Fin De Siècle: Wagnerism, Nationalism, and Style*. Oxford: Oxford University Press, 1999.

Huebner, Steven. "Wagnérisme." In *Debussy in Context*, edited by Simon Trezise, 88–97. Cambridge: Cambridge University Press, 2024.

Huebner, Steven, Brendan King, and Charlotte Mandell. "The *Revue Wagnerienne*: Symbolism, Aetheteticism, and Germanophilia." In *Wagner and His World*, edited by Thomas S. Grey, 372–90. Princeton, NJ: Princeton University Press, 2009.

Huysmans, Joris-Karl. *Against Nature*. Translated by Robert Baldick. Harmondsworth: Penguin, 1959.

Huysmans, Joris-Karl. *À Rebours*. Paris: Garnier-Flammarion, 1978.

IMDb. "Claude Debussy (1862–1918)." Accessed July 25, 2024. http://www.imdb.com/name/nm0006033.

Inwood, Margaret. *The Influence of Shakespeare on Richard Wagner*. Lewiston, NY: Edwin Mellen, 1999.

Jarociński, Stefan. *Debussy: Impressionism and Symbolism*. London: Eulenburg, 1976.

Järvinen, Hanna. "Critical Silence: The Unseemly Games of Love in Jeux (1913)," *Dance Research: The Journal of the Society for Dance Research*, Vol. 27, No. 2, (2009), 199–226.

Jeanne, Paul. *Les Théâtre d'Ombres à Montmartre de 1887–1923*. Paris: Les Éditions des Presses Modernes au Palais-Royal, 1937.

Jensen, Eric Frederick. *Debussy*. Oxford: Oxford University Press, 2014.

Jentsch, Ernst. "On the Psychology of the Uncanny." In *Uncanny Modernity: Cultural Theories, Modern Anxieties*, edited by Jo Collins and John Jervis, translated by Roy Sellars, 216–28. Basingstoke: Palgrave Macmillan, 2008.

Jentsch, Ernst. "Zur Psychologie des Unheimlichen." *Psychiatrisch-Neurologische Wochenschrift* 8, no. 22 (August 25, 1906): 195–98.

Jentsch, Ernst. "Zur Psychologie des Unheimlichen." *Psychiatrisch-Neurologische Wochenschrift* 8, no. 23 (September 1, 1906): 203–5.

Johansson, Niclas. *The Narcissus Theme from* Fin de Siècle *to Psychoanalysis*. Frankfurt am Main: Peter Lang, 2017.

Johnson, Barbara. "About the Book." In *Divagations*, translated by Barbara Johnson, 215–36. Cambridge, MA: Harvard University Press, 2007.

Johnson, Julian. "Vertige!: Debussy, Mallarmé, and the Edge of Language." In *Debussy's Resonance*, edited by François de Médicis and Steven Huebner, 366–92. Rochester, NY: University of Rochester Press, 2018.

Jones, Owen. *The Grammar of Ornament*. London: Day and Son, 1856.

Jordan, Stephanie. "Debussy, the Dance, and the Faune." In *Debussy in Performance*, edited by James Briscoe, 119–34. New Haven, CT: Yale University Press, 1999.

Jullian, Philippe. *Prince of Aesthetes: Count Robert de Montesquiou 1855–1921*. Translated by John Haylock and Francis King. New York: Viking, 1968.

Justo, Mattias. "Spleen and Ideal: Sound and the Language of the Extrarational in Claude Debussy's *La Chute de la maison Usher*." MA KU Leuven, 2023.

Kahane, Martine, and Nicole Wild. *Wagner et La France: Exposition 26 octobre–26 janvier 1984*. Paris: Bibliothèque nationale, Théâtre National de L'Opéra de Paris, Herscher, 1983.

Kandinsky, Wassily. *Concerning the Spiritual in Art* (1912). Translated by M. T. H. Sadler. New York: Dover, 1977.

Katz, Adele. *Challenge to Musical Traditieon*. New York: Knopf, 1945.

Kecskeméti, István. "Claude Debussy, musicien français: His Last Sonatas." *Revue belge de musicology* 16 (1962): 117–49.

Kelly, Barbara L. "Debussy's Homage to Chopin: As Editor, Performer, and Composer." In *Accenting the Classics: Editing European Music in France, 1915–1925*, edited by Deborah Mawer, Barbara L. Kelly, Rachel Moore, and Graham Sadler, 219–52. Woodbridge: Boydell and Brewer, 2023.

Kelly, Barbara L. "Debussy's Parisian Affiliations." In *The Cambridge Companion to Debussy*, edited by Simon Trezise, 25–42. Cambridge: Cambridge University Press, 2003.

Kennedy, Gerald J. *Poe, Death, and the Life of Writing*. New Haven, CT: Yale University Press, 1987.

Kerman, Joseph. *Opera as Drama*. Rev. ed. Berkeley: University of California Press, 1988.

Kermode, Frank. "Poet and Dancer Before Diaghilev." In *Puzzles and Epiphanies*. London: Routledge & Kegan Paul, 1962.

Knapp, Bettina L. "Baudelaire and Wagner's Archetypal Operas." *Nineteenth-Century French Studies* 17, nos. 1/2 (1988–89): 58–69.

Knapp, Bettina L. *Maurice Maeterlinck*. Boston: Twayne, 1975.

Kobel, Peter, and the Library of Congress. *Silent Movies. The Birth of Film and the Triumph of Movie Culture.* New York: Little Brown, 2007.

Koslovsky, John, and Matthew Brown. "History and Tonal Coherence in Debussy's 'La Fille aux Cheveux de lin' and 'Bruyères.'" *Rivista di Analisi e Teoria Musicale* 18, no. 2 (2012): 35–54.

Kremer, Nathalie. "The Broken Lines of Art: Diderot and Baudelaire on Painting." *Nouvelle revue d'esthétique* 25, no. 1 (2020): 145–53.

Kufferath, Maurice. "Commentaire." *Guide Musical*, March 4, 1894.

Lacombe, Hervé. "Parisian Opera Institutions: A Framework for Creation." In *Debussy in Context*, edited by Simon Trezise, 177–84. Cambridge: Cambridge University Press, 2024.

Laforgue, Jules. "Impressionism" (1883). In *Impressionism and Post- Impressionism 1874–1904*, edited by Linda Nochlin. Sources & Documents in the History of Art Series, 14–20. Englewood Cliffs, NJ: Prentice-Hall, 1966.

Laforgue, Jules. *Œuvres Complètes,* vol. I, edited by Jean-Louis Debauve, Daniel Grojnowski, Pascale Pia, and Pierre Olivier Walzer, in collaboration with David Arkell and Maryke de Courten. Lausanne: L'Age d'Homme, 1986.

Laforgue, Jules. *Œuvres Complètes*, vol. II, edited by Maryke de Courten Jean-Louis Debauve, Daniel Grojnowski, and Pierre Olivier Walzer, in collaboration with David Arkell. Lausanne: L'Age d'Homme, 1995.

Laforgue, Jules. *Œuvres Complètes*, vol. III, edited by Jean-Louis Debauve, Mireille Donin-Orsini, Daniel Grojnowski, and Pierre Olivier Walzer, in collaboration with Maryke de Courten and Michèle Hannoosh. Lausanne: L'Age d'Homme, 2000.

Lalo, Pierre. "Claude Debussy et l'universe." *Programme Festival de Claude Debussy*, Théâtre des Champs-Élysées, June 17, 1932, 5–6.

Laloy, Louis. *La musique chinoise.* Collection "Les musiciens célèbres." Paris: Henri Laurens, 1910.

Laloy, Louis. "La Musique de l'Avenir." *Le Mercure de France* 76 (December 1, 1908): 419–34.

Landis, Yvan. *Baudelaire at 20 Years Old. The Journey to India.* Nogent-sur-Marne: Storia Editions, 2019.

Lang, Edith, and George West. *Musical Accompaniment of Moving Pictures.* Boston: Boston Music, 1920.

Langley, Patrick. "Master of Puppets." *Freize*, September 16, 2017. https://www.frieze.com /article/master-puppets. Accessed July 11, 2025.

Lazarro, Federico. "Paris and the Nation's Politics." In *Debussy in Context*, ed. Simon Trezise, 16–24. Cambridge: Cambridge University Press, 2024.

Leaver, Jon. "'Sorcellerie évocatoire': Magic and Memory in Baudelaire and Eliphas Lévi." *Symposium: A Quarterly Journal in Modern Literatures* 66, no. 3 (2012): 139–49.

Lee, Amanda. "The Romantic Ballet and the Nineteenth-Century Poetic Imagination." *Dance Chronicle* 39, no. 1 Dance and Literature, Part II (2016): 32–55.

Lee, Christopher. *Christopher Lee Reads Edgar Allan Poe, Tales of Horror.* Listen for Pleasure, Audio Tape. LFP7039, 1979.

Lees, Heath. *Mallarmé and Wagner: Music and Poetic Language.* Aldershot: Ashgate, 2007.

Lekić, Mirna. "Secrets of a Toy-Box: A Study of Claude Debussy's *La Boîte à joujoux.*" DMA diss., City University of New York, 2014.

Lenormand, René. *Étude sur l'harmonie moderne.* Paris: Propriété du "Monde Musical," 1912.

Léon, Paul. "Claude Debussy." *Programme Festival de Claude Debussy*, Théâtre des Champs-Élysées, June 17, 1932, 3.

Leonard, Anne. Ed. *Arabesque without End: Across Music and the Arts, from Faust to Shahrazad.* New York: Routledge, 2022.

Leroux, Charles. "La musique classique japonaise." *Bulletin de la Société franco-japonaise* XIX–XX (1911): 37–57.

Lesure, François. *Claude Debussy.* Paris: Klincksieck, 1994.

Lesure, François. *Claude Debussy: A Critical Biography.* Eastman Studies in Music 159. Edited and translated by Marie Rolf. Rochester, NY: University of Rochester Press, 2019.

Lesure, François. "Debussy et le Chat Noir." *Cahiers Debussy* 23 (1999): 35–43.

Leydon, Rebecca. "Debussy's Late Style and the Devices of the Early Silent Cinema." *Music Theory Spectrum* 22, no. 2 (2001): 217–41.

Liu, Julia, and Kenji Fujimura. "Music Education and the Prix de Rome." In *Debussy in Context*, edited by Simon Trezise, 159–66. Cambridge: Cambridge University Press, 2024.

Lloyd, Rosemary. *Baudelaire et Hoffmann. Affinités et Influences.* Cambridge: Cambridge University Press, 1979.

Lloyd, Rosemary. "Debussy, Mallarmé, and 'Les Mardis.'" In *Debussy and His World*, edited by Jane Fulcher, 255–69. Princeton: Princeton University Press, 2001.

Lloyd, Rosemary. *Mallarmé: The Poet and His Circle.* Ithaca, NY: Cornell University Press, 1999.

Lloyd, Rosemary. "Richard Wagner: A French Poet's Reverie." In *Music in European Thought 1851–1912*, edited by Bojan Bujić, 242–46. Cambridge Readings in the Literature of Music. Cambridge: Cambridge University Press, 1988.

Locke, Ralph P. "A Broader View of Musical Exoticism." *Journal of Musicology* 24, no. 4 (2007): 477–521.

Lockspeiser, Edward. *Debussy.* London: Dent, 1963.

Lockspeiser, Edward. *Debussy et Edgar Allan Poe. Documents inédits.* Monaco: Éditions du Rocher, 1962.

Lockspeiser, Edward, *Debussy: His Life and Mind.* Vol. 1, *1862–1902.* 2nd ed. Cambridge: Cambridge University Press, 1978.

Lockspeiser, Edward. "Musorgsky and Debussy." *Musical Quarterly* 23, no. 4 (1937): 421–27.

Longstaffe-Gowan, Todd. *English Garden Eccentricities: Three Hundred Years of Extraordinary Groves, Burrowings, Mountains and Menageries.* London: Paul Mellon Centre for Studies in British Art, 2022.

Louÿs, Pierre. *Les Chansons de Bilitis.* Paris: Librairie De L'art Indépendant, 1895.

Lovecraft, H. P. *The Annotated Supernatural Horror in Literature.* Edited by S. T. Joshi. New York: Hippocampus, 2000.

Lubmann, Niklas. *Art as a Social System.* Translated by Eva M. Knodt. Redwood City, CA: Stanford University Press, 2000.

Lubmann, Niklas. *Die Kunst der Gesellschaft.* Frankfurt a.m.: Suhrkamp, 1995.

Macdonald, Hugh. "Georges Hartmann, the 'Ideal Publisher.'" *Journal of Musicological Research* 28, no. 4 (2009): 295–311.

Macdonald, M. Irwin. "The Fairy Faith and Pictured Music." *The Craftsman* XXIII (October 1912): 20–34.

Maeterlinck, Maurice. *Bulles bleues: Souvenirs heureux.* Monaco: Éditions du Rocher, 1948.

Maeterlinck, Maurice. *Carnets de Travail (1881–1890)*. Edited and annotated by Fabrice van de Kerckhove. Archives du Future. Brussels: AMI Editions, 2002.

Maeterlinck, Maurice. *Hothouses*. Translated by Richard Howard. Princeton: Princeton University Press, 2003.

Maeterlinck, Maurice. "Pelléas et Mélisande (1902)." In *Théâtre*, Vol. II, 4–113. Brussels: P. Lacomblez; Paris: Per Lamm, 1902.

Maeterlinck, Maurice. *Serres chaudes*. Paris: Léon Vanier, 1889.

Mahony, Patrick F. *Maurice Maeterlinck: Mystic and Dramatist*. Washington, DC: Institute for the Study of Man, 1979.

Maillet, Arnaud. *The Claude Glass. Use and Meaning of the Black Mirror in Western Art*. Translated by Jeff Fort. New York: Zone Books, 2009.

Mallarmé, Stéphane. "About the Book." In *Divagations*, translated by Barbara Johnson, 215–36. Cambridge, MA: Harvard University Press, 2007.

Mallarmé, Stéphane. "Autumn Lament." In *Divagations*, translated by Barbara Johnson, 13–14. Cambridge, MA: Harvard University Press, 2007.

Mallarmé, Stéphane. "Crayonné au Théâtre." In *Stéphane Mallarmé: Œuvres Complètes*, vol. II, edited by Bertrand Marchal, 160–69. Bibliothèque de la Pléiade. Paris: Gallimard, 2003.

Mallarmé, Stéphane. "Crayonné au Théâtre: Autres études de danse: Les fonds dans le ballet." In *Stéphane Mallarmé: Œuvres Complètes*, vol. II, edited by Bertrand Marchal, 174–76. Bibliothèque de la Pléiade. Paris: Gallimard, 2003.

Mallarmé, Stéphane. "Crayonné au Théâtre: Ballets." In *Stéphane Mallarmé: Œuvres Complètes*, vol. II, edited by Bertrand Marchal, 170–74. Bibliothèque de la Pléiade. Paris: Gallimard, 2003.

Mallarmé, Stéphane. "Crayonné au Théâtre: 'Le seul il le fallait fluie comme *l'enchanteur*.'" In *Stéphane Mallarmé: Œuvres Complètes*, vol. II, edited by Bertrand Marchal, 177–78. Bibliothèque de la Pléiade. Paris: Gallimard, 2003.

Mallarmé, Stéphane. "Crise en verse." In *Stéphane Mallarmé: Œuvres Complètes*, vol. II, edited by Bertrand Marchal, 204–13. Bibliothèque de la Pléiade. Paris: Gallimard, 2003.

Mallarmé, Stéphane. "Crisis of Verse." In *Divagations*, translated by Barbara Johnson, 201–11. Cambridge, MA: Harvard University Press, 2007.

Mallarmé, Stéphane. "The Evolution of Literature." In *Mallarmé: Selected Prose Poems, Essays, & Letters*, translated by Bradford Cook, 18–24. Baltimore: Johns Hopkins Press, 1956.

Mallarmé, Stéphane. "La Musiques et les Lettres." In *Stéphane Mallarmé: Œuvres Complètes*, vol. II, edited by Bertrand Marchal, 62–77. Bibliothèque de la Pléiade. Paris: Gallimard, 2003.

Mallarmé, Stéphane. "Le Corbeau." In *Stéphane Mallarmé: Œuvres Complètes*, vol. I, edited by Bertrand Marchal, 731–34. Bibliothèque de la Pléiade. Paris: Gallimard, 1998.

Mallarmé, Stéphane. "Le Tombeau de Charles Baudelaire." In *Stéphane Mallarmé: Œuvres Complètes*, vol. I, edited by Bertrand Marchal, 38–39. Bibliothèque de la Pléiade. Paris: Gallimard, 1998.

Mallarmé, Stéphane. "Le Tombeau d'Edgar Poe." In *Stéphane Mallarmé: Œuvres Complètes*, vol. I, edited by Bertrand Marchal, 38. Bibliothèque de la Pléiade. Paris: Gallimard, 1998.

Mallarmé, Stéphane. "Music and Letters." In *Divagations*, translated by Barbara Johnson, 173–98. Cambridge, MA: Harvard University Press, 2007.

Mallarmé, Stéphane. "Plainte d'autumne." In *Stéphane Mallarmé: Œuvres Complètes*, vol. I, edited by Bertrand Marchal, 443–44. Bibliothèque de la Pléiade. Paris: Gallimard, 1998.

Mallarmé, Stéphane. *Poèmes de Edgar Poe*. In *Stéphane Mallarmé: Œuvres Complètes*, vol. II, edited by Bertrand Marchal, 727–820. Bibliothèque de la Pléiade. Paris: Gallimard, 2003.

Mallarmé, Stéphane. *Poésies*. 3rd ed. Paris: Éditions de la nouvelle revue français, 1913.

Mallarmé, Stéphane. "Quant au livre." In *Stéphane Mallarmé: Œuvres Complètes*, vol. II, edited by Bertrand Marchal, 214–28. Bibliothèque de la Pléiade. Paris: Gallimard, 2003.

Mallarmé, Stéphane. "Richard Wagner, rêverie d'un poète français." In *Stéphane Mallarmé: Œuvres Complètes*, vol. II, edited by Bertrand Marchal, 153–59. Bibliothèque de la Pléiade. Paris: Gallimard, 2003.

Mallarmé, Stéphane. "Richard Wagner: The Reverie of a French Poet." In *Divagations*, translated by Barbara Johnson, 107–13. Cambridge, MA: Harvard University Press, 2007.

Mallarmé, Stéphane. "Scribbled at the Theater." In *Divagations*, translated by Barbara Johnson, 117–23. Cambridge, MA: Harvard University Press, 2007.

Mallarmé, Stéphane. "Scribbled at the Theater: Another Study of Dance: The Fundamentals of Ballet." In *Divagations*, translated by Barbara Johnson, 135–37. Cambridge, MA: Harvard University Press, 2007.

Mallarmé, Stéphane. "Scribbled at the Theater: Ballets." In *Divagations*, translated by Barbara Johnson, 129–34. Cambridge, MA: Harvard University Press, 2007.

Mallarmé, Stéphane. "Scribbled at the Theater: 'The Only One Would Have to Be as Fluid as the Sorcerer.'" In *Divagations*, translated by Barbara Johnson, 138–39. Cambridge, MA: Harvard University Press, 2007.

Mallarmé, Stéphane. *Selected Letters of Stéphane Mallarmé*. Edited and translated by Rosemary Lloyd. Chicago: University of Chicago Press, 1988.

Mallarmé, Stéphane. "Sur l'evolution littéraire." In *Stéphane Mallarmé: Œuvres Complètes*, vol. II, edited by Bertrand Marchal, 697–703. Bibliothèque de la Pléiade. Paris: Gallimard, 2003.

Maniates, Maria Rika. "Quodlibet Revisum." *Acta Musicoligica* 38, nos. 2–4 (1966): 169–78.

Mannaerts, Pieter. "Introduction to Claude Debussy, Ode à la France." In *Repertoire Explorer*, 948. Munich: MPH, 2009.

Marks, Emerson. *Taming the Chaos: English Poetic Diction Theory Since the Renaissance*. Detroit: Wayne State University, 1998.

Marks, Martin Miller. *Music and the Silent Film: Contexts and Case Studies 1895–1924*. New York: Oxford University Press, 1997.

Marsnan, Eugène. "Champs-Elysées: Nouvelle saison des Ballets Suédois: ODEON; La Paix." *Paris-Journal*, February 20, 1921.

Marston, Nicholas. "Schenker's Concept of a Beethoven Sonata Edition." In *Essays from the Fourth International Schenker Symposium*, vol. 2, edited by Poundie Burstein, Lynne Rogers, and Karen M. Bottge, 91–101. Heidesheim: G. Olms, 2013.

Martins, José Ednardo. "La Vision de L'univers Enfantin chez Moussorgsky et Debussy." *Cahiers Debussy* 9 (1985): 3–16.

Mauclaire, Camille. *Le Soleil des morts*. Paris: P. Ollendorff, 1898.

Maus, Madeleine Octave. *Trente Années de Lutte pour L'Art: Les XX et La Libre Esthétique, 1884–1914*. Rev. ed. Brussels: Éditions Lebeer Hossmann, 1980.

Mawer, Deborah. "Accenting Bach: An Editorial Trajectory from Fauré to Roger-Ducasse." In *Accenting the Classics: Editing European Music in France, 1915–1925*, edited by Deborah

Mawer, Barbara L. Kelly, Rachel Moore, and Graham Sadler, 153–88. Woodbridge: Boydell and Brewer, 2023.

Maynard, Kelly J. "Strange Bedfellows at the *Revue Wagnérienne*: Wagnerism at the Fin de Siècle." *French Historical Studies* 38, no. 4 (2015): 633–59.

McCabe, Ina Baghdiantz. *Orientalism in Early Modern France*. Oxford: Berg, 2008.

McCombie, Elizabeth. *Mallarmé and Debussy: Unheard Music, Unseen Text*. Oxford: Oxford University Press, 2003.

McFarland, Mark. "Debussy and Stravinsky: Another Look into Their Musical Relationship." *Cahiers Debussy* 24 (2000): 79–112.

McFarland, Mark. "Debussy: The Origins of a Method." *Journal of Music Theory* 48, no. 2 (2004): 295–323.

McFarland, Mark. "The Games of *Jeux*." In *Debussy's Resonance*, edited by François de Médicis and Steven Huebner, 476–510. Rochester, NY: University of Rochester Press, 2018.

McGinness, John. "From Movement to Moment: Issues of Expression, Form, and Reception in Debussy's *Jeux*." *Cahiers Debussy* 22 (1998): 51–74.

McGinness, John. "Vaslav Nijinsky's Notes for 'Jeux.'" *Musical Quarterly* 88, no. 4 (Winter 2005): 556–89.

McGuinness, Patrick. *Maurice Maeterlinck and the Making of Modern Theatre*. Oxford: Oxford University Press, 2000.

McKay, James. "The Bréval Manuscript: New Interpretations." *Cahiers Debussy*, nouvelle série 1 (1977): 5–15.

McKinley, Ann. "Debussy and American Minstrelsy." *Black Perspective in Music* 14, no. 3 (Autumn 1986): 249–58.

Medzini, Meron. *French Policy in Japan during the Closing Years of the Tokugawa Regime*. Cambridge, MA: Harvard University Press, 1971.

Mellers, Wilfred. "The Final Works of Claude Debussy or Pierrot fâché avec la lune." *Music and Letters* 20, no. 2 (1939): 168–76.

Meyers, Jeffrey. *Edgar Allan Poe: His Life and Legacy*. New York: Cooper Square, 1992.

Meyers, Mary J. *French Architectural and Ornament Drawings of the Eighteenth Century*. New York: Metropolitan Museum of Art, 1991.

Middleton, Charles. *A New and Complete System of Geography*. 2 vols. London: Henry Rhodes, 1777, 1778.

Millan, Gordon. *A Throw of the Dice. The Life of Stéphane Mallarmé*. London: Secker & Warburg, 1994.

Millan, Gordon. *The Life of Stéphane Mallarmé*. London: Secker & Warburg, 1994.

Miner, Earl. *The Japanese Tradition in British and American Literature*. Princeton, NJ: Princeton University Press, 1958.

Miner, Margaret. *Resonant Gaps: Between Baudelaire and Wagner*. Athens: University of Georgia Press, 1995.

Monroe, Jonathan. *A Poverty of Objects: The Prose Poem and the Politics of Genre*. Ithaca, NY: Cornell University Press, 1987.

Moortele, Steven Vande. *The Romantic Overture and Musical Form from Rossini to Wagner*. Cambridge: Cambridge University Press, 2007.

Moréas, Jean. "The Manifesto of Symbolism (1886)." Accessed July 25, 2025. https://www.poetryintranslation.com/PITBR/French/MoreasManifesto.php.

Moritz, Karl Philipp. *Sur l'ornement*. Edited and translated by Clara Paquet. Paris: Éditions Rue d'Ulm, 2008.

Moritz, Karl Philipp. *Vorbegriffe zur einer Theorie der Ornamente*. Berlin: Karl Matzdorff, 1793.

Morris, D. Hampton. *A Descriptive Study of the* La Revue Wagnérienne *Concerning Richard Wagner*. Lewiston, NY: Edwin Mellen, 2002.

Morrison, Simon. "Debussy's Toy Stories." *Journal of Musicology* 30, no. 3 (Summer 2013): 424–59.

Morrison, Toni. *Playing in the Dark: Whiteness and the Literary Imagination*. New York: Vintage, 1993.

Moss, Howard. *Instant Lives & More*. Hopewell, NJ: Ecco, 1972.

Mourey, Gabriel, trans. *Edgar Poe. Poésies complètes*. Paris: C. Dalou, 1889.

Mourey, Gabriel. "Memories of Claude Debussy." *Musical News and Herald*, June 11, 1921, 747–48.

Mueller, Richard E. *Beauty and Innovation in La Machine Chinoise: Falla, Debussy, Ravel, Roussel*. Hillsdale, NY: Pendragon, 2018.

Mueller, Richard E. "Javanese Influence on Debussy's *Fantaisie* and Beyond." *19th-Century Music* 10, no. 2 (1986): 157–86.

Murkherjee, Madhuri. "When The Saints Go Marching In: Popular Performances of *La Tentation de Sainte Antoine* and *St Geneviève de Paris* at the Chat Noir Shadow Theater." In *Medieval Saints in Late Nineteenth-Century French Culture*, edited by Elizabeth Emery and Laurie Postelwate, 25–44. Jefferson, NC: McFarland, 2004.

Muzelle, Alain. "Arabesque et Roman dans l'oeuvre de Friedrich Schlegel." *Societes & Representations* Éditions de la Sorbonne 3, no. 10 (2000): 23–54.

Nagai, Y., and K. Kobataki. *Japanese Popular Music*. Osaka: Miki, 1893.

Nectoux, Jean-Michel. *Harmonie en bleu et or: Debussy, la musique et les arts*. Paris: Fayard, 2005.

Nectoux, Jean-Michel. "Portrait of the Artist as a Faun." In *Afternoon of a Faun: Mallarmé, Debussy, Nijinsky*, edited by Jean-Michel Nectoux, 7–12. New York: Vendome, 1987.

Needham, Gerald. "Japanese Influence on French Painting 1854–1910." In *Japonisme: Japanese Influence on French Art 1854–1910*, edited by Gabriel P. Weisberg, 115–39. Kent, OH: Kent State University Press, 1975.

Nichols, Roger. *Debussy*. Oxford Studies of Composers 10. Oxford: Oxford University Press, 1973.

Nichols, Roger. *Debussy Remembered*. London: Faber, 1992.

Nichols, Roger. "Synopsis." In *Pelléas et Mélisande*, Cambridge Opera Handbooks, edited by Roger Nichols and Richard Langham Smith, 62–77. Cambridge: Cambridge University Press, 1989.

Nigro, August J. *The Diagonal Line: Separation and Reparation in American Literature*. Cranbury, NJ: Associated University Presses, 1984.

Nijinska, Bronislava. *Early Memoirs*. Translated and edited by Irina Nijinska and Jean Rawlinson. Durham, NC: Duke University Press, 1992.

Nijinsky, Vaslav. *The Diary of Vaslav Nijinsky*. Edited by Romola Nijinsky. Berkeley: University of California Press, 1968.

Nobel Committee. "The Nobel Prize in Literature 1911." Accessed January 6, 2023. https://www.nobelprize.org/prizes/literature/1911/summary/.

Nochlin, Linda. *Impressionism and Post-Impressionism 1874–1904*. Sources & Documents in the History of Art Series. Englewood Cliffs, NJ: Prentice-Hall, 1966.

Olsen, Donald J. *The City as a Work of Art. London. Paris. Vienna*. New Haven, CT: Yale University Press, 1986.

Orledge, Robert. "Another Look Inside Debussy's 'Toybox.'" *Musical Times* 117, no. 1606 (1976): 987–89.

Orledge, Robert. "Debussy, Durand et Cie: A French Composer and His Publisher." In *The Business of Music*, edited by Michael Talbot, 121–51. Liverpool: Liverpool University Press, 2002.

Orledge, Robert. *Debussy and the Theatre*. Cambridge: Cambridge University Press, 1982.

Orledge, Robert. "Debussy's 'House of Usher' Revisited." *Musical Quarterly* 62, no. 4 (1976): 536–53.

Orledge, Robert. "Debussy's Musical Gifts to Emma Bardac." *Musical Quarterly* 60, no. 4 (1974): 544–56.

Orledge, Robert. "Liner notes." *Claude Debussy: Der Untergang des Hauses Usher*. DVD: Capriccio, 2007.

Ovid. *Metamorphosis*. Oxford World Classics. Translated by A. D. Melville. Introduction and notes by E. J. Kenney. Oxford: Oxford University Press, 1986.

Pace, Ian. "From Jean-Luc Godard to Dennis Potter: Finnissy's Cinematic and Televisual Inspirations." In *Critical Perspectives on Michael Finnissy. Bright Futures, Dark Pasts*, edited by Ian Pace and Nigel McBride, 344–72. London: Routledge, 2019.

Painter, William. *The Palace of Pleasure*. Edited by Joseph Jacobs. London: David Nutt, 1890. Reprint, New York: Dover, 1966.

Palmer, Christopher. *The Composer in Hollywood*. London: Marion Boyars, 1990.

Park, Raymond Roy. "The Late Style of Claude Debussy." PhD diss., University of Michigan, 1967.

Parker, Roger. "Debussy, String Quartet in G minor, Op. 10." Gresham College Lecture, January 29, 2008. https://www.gresham.ac.uk/lectures-and-events/debussy-quartet-in-g-minor -op-10.

Parks, Richard S. *The Music of Claude Debussy*. New Haven, CT: Yale University Press, 1989.

Pasler, Jann. "Debussy, 'Jeux': Playing with Time and Form." *19th-Century Music* 6, no. 1 (1982): 60–75.

Pasler, Jann. "Discontinuity and Continuity in Debussy's Jeux." *Musicae Scientiae* 8, no. 1 (2004): 125–40.

Pasler, Jann. "Pelléas and Power: Forces behind the Reception of Debussy's Opera." *19th-Century Music* 10, no. 3 (1987): 243–64.

Pasler, Jann. "Revisiting Debussy's Relationships with Otherness: Difference, Vibrations, and the Occult." *Music & Letters* 101, no. 2 (2020): 321–42.

Pasler, Jann. "Timbre, Voice Leading, Arabesque." In *Debussy in Performance*, edited by James R. Briscoe, 225–55. New Haven, CT: Yale University Press, 2000.

Pastille, William. "The Development of the Ursatz in Schenker's Published Works." In *Trends in Schenkerian Research*, edited by Allen Cadwallader, 71–85. New York: Schirmer, 1990.

Paulin, Scott D. "Cinematic Music: Analogies, Fallacies, and the Case of Debussy." *Music and the Moving Image* 3, no. 1 (Spring 2010): 1–21.

Pearson, Roger. *Beauty of Baudelaire: The Poet as Alternative Lawgiver.* Oxford: Oxford University Press, 2021.

Pearson, Roger. *Unfolding Mallarmé: The Development of Poetic Art.* Oxford: Clarendon, 1996.

Perl, Jed. "The Art of Pleasure." *New York Review of Books* 64, no. 20 (2017). https://www.nybooks.com/articles/2017/12/21/renoir-art-of-pleasure.

Perl, Jed. "Between Abstraction and Representation," *New York Review of Books,* November 24, 2022.

Perrault, Charles. *Le cabinet des beaux Arts.* Paris: G. Edelinck, 1690.

Perrault, Charles. *Memoirs of My Life.* Edited and translated by Jeanne Morgan Zarucchi. Columbia: University of Missouri Press, 1989.

Peters, Rosemary A. *Stealing Things: Theft and the Author in Nineteenth-Century France.* Lanham, MD: Lexington, 2013.

Picart, Bernard. *Cérémonies et coutumes religieuses de tous les peuples du monde.* Amsterdam: J. F. Bernard, 1723–28.

Piccardi, Carlo. "Pierrot at the Cinema: The Musical Common Denominator from Pantomime to Film: Part I." *Music and the Moving Image* 1, no. 2 (Summer 2008): 37–52.

Piccardi, Carlo. "Pierrot at the Cinema: The Musical Common Denominator from Pantomime to Film: Part II." *Music and the Moving Image* 2, no. 2 (Summer 2009): 7–23.

Piccardi, Carlo. "Pierrot at the Cinema: The Musical Common Denominator from Pantomime to Film: Part III." *Music and the Moving Image* 6, no. 1 (Spring 2013): 4–54.

Pierrot, Jean. *The Decadent Imagination 1880–1900.* Translated by Derek Coltman. Chicago: University of Chicago Press, 1981.

Pillaut, Léon. "Le Gamelan javanais." *Le Ménestrel,* July 3, 1887, 244–45.

Poe, Edgar Allan. *The Complete Tales and Poems of Adgar Allan Poe.* New York: Vintage, 1975.

Poe, Edgar Allan. *Derniers Contes.* Translated by F. Rabbe. Paris, Savine, 1887.

Poe, Edgar Allan. *Edgar Allan Poe: Œuvres en prose.* Translated by Charles Baudelaire. Bibliothèque de la Pléiade. Edited by Y.-G. Le Dantec. Paris: Gallimard, 1951.

Poe, Edgar Allan. *Les Poèmes d'Edgar Poe. Traduction de Stéphane Mallarmé.* Edited by Jean-Louis Curtis. Paris: Gallimard, 1982.

Poe, Edgar Allan. "Philosophy of Composition." *Graham's American Monthly Magazine of Literature and Art* 28, no. 4 (1846): 163–67.

Poe, Edgar Allan. *Poésies complètes de E.-A. Poe.* Translated by Gabriel Mourey. Paris, Dalou, 1889.

Poe, Edgar Allan. *Tales of Mystery and Imagination & Humour; and Poems.* London: Henry Vizetelly, 1852.

Poe, Edgar Allan. *Tales of the Grotesque and Arabesque.* 2 vols. Philadelphia: Lea and Blanchard, 1839.

Pollack, Rachel. *Seventy-Eight Degrees of Wisdom: A Tarot Journey to Self-Awareness.* 40th Anniversary Ed. Newburyport, MA: Red Wheel/Weiser, 2020.

Pollin, Burton R. "More Music and Edgar Allan Poe: A Third Annotated Check List." *Poe Studies/Dark Romanticism* 25, nos. 1–2 (1993): 41–58.

Pollin, Burton R. "Music and Edgar Allan Poe: A Fourth Annotated Checklist." *Poe Studies* 36, nos. 1–2 (2003): 77–100.

Pollin, Burton R. "Music and Edgar Allan Poe: A Second Annotated Check List." *Poe Studies (1971–1985)* 15, no. 1 (1982): 7–13.

Pollin, Burton R. "Poe and the Dance." *Studies in the American Renaissance* 4 (1980): 169–82.

Pollin, Burton R. "Shakespeare in the Works of Edgar Allan Poe." *Studies in the American Renaissance* 9 (1985): 157–86.

Pomeroy, Boyd. "Debussy's Tonality: A Formal Perspective." In *The Cambridge Companion to Debussy,* edited by Simon Trezise, 155–178. Cambridge: Cambridge University Press, 2003.

Pomeroy, Boyd. "A Force of Nature: Debussy and the Chromatically Displaced Dominant." In *Explorations in Schenkerian Analysis*, edited by David Beach and Su Yin Mak, 303–27. Eastman Studies in Music. Rochester, NY: University of Rochester Press, 2016.

Porter, Andrew. "Fragments of the *House of Usher.*" *New Yorker*, March 14, 1977, 130–36.

Potter, Caroline. "Debussy and Nature." In *The Cambridge Companion to Debussy*, edited by Simon Trezise, 137–51. Cambridge: Cambridge University Press, 2003.

Potter, Caroline. "Relationships with Poets and other Literary Figures." In *Debussy in Context*, edited by Simon Trezise, 135–42. Cambridge: Cambridge University Press, 2024.

Poulenc, Francis. *Emmanuel Chabrier.* Geneva: La Palatine, 1961.

Poulenc, Francis. *Emmanuel Chabrier.* Translated by Cynthia Jolly. London: Denis Dobson, 1981.

Poulet, Georges. *Les Métamorphoses du cercle.* Paris: Plon, 1961.

Prendergast, Christopher. *Writing the City: Paris and the Nineteenth Century.* Oxford: Blackwell, 1992.

Priest, Deborah. *Louis Laloy (1874–1944) on Debussy, Ravel, and Stravinsky.* Aldershot: Ashgate, 1999.

Prince, Stephen. "Through the Looking Glass: Philosophical Toys and Digital Visual Effects." *Projections* 4, no. 2 (2010): 19–40.

Pritchard, E. H. "The Struggle for Control of the China Trade during the Eighteenth Century." *Pacific Historical Review* 3, no. 3 (1934): 280–95.

Quinn, Patrick F. *The French Face of Edgar Poe.* Carbondale: Southern Illinois University Press, 1971.

Quinn, Patrick F. *Poe and France: The Last Twenty Years.* Baltimore: Edgar Allan Poe Society and Enoch Pratt Free Library, 1970. https://www.eapoe.org/papers/psblctrs/pl19691.htm.

Quinn, Patrick F., and G. R. Thompson, ed. *Edgar Allan Poe: Poetry, Tales, and Selected Essays.* New York: Library of America, 1996.

Radden, Jennifer, ed. *The Nature of Melancholy from Aristotle to Kristeva.* Oxford: Oxford University Press, 2000.

Rae, Caroline. "Debussyist, Modernist, Exoticist: Marius-François Gaillard Rediscovered." *Musical Times* 152, no. 1916 (2011): 59–80.

Raines, Leonard. "Parisians Refuse to Take to Cellar When Shell Explodes Close to Opéra Comique." *Musical America* 28 (May 4, 1918): 42.

Ramade, Patrick, Martin Eidelberg, Virginie Frelin, and Ingrid Lemainque. *Watteau et la Fête galante.* Paris Réunion des Musées Nationaux, 2004.

Rapée, Erno. *Motion Picture Moods for Pianists and Organists.* New York: Schirmer, 1924.

Rasula, Jed. "Endless Melody." *Texas Studies in Literature and Language* 55, no. 1, Special Section: Literary Modernism and Melody (Spring 2013): 36–52.

Rauss, Denis François. "*Ce terrible finale.* Les sources manuscrits de la sonate pour violon et piano de Claude Debussy et la genèse du troisième mouvement." *Cahiers Debussy* 2 (1978): 30–62.

Rearick, Charles. *Pleasures of the Belle Epoque: Entertainment and Festivity in Turn of the Century France*. New Haven, CT: Yale University Press, 1985.

Retté, Adolphe. *Misty Thule*. Translated by Brian Stableford. Snuggly Books, 2018.

Richards, Eliza. "'The Poetess' and Poe's Performance of the Feminine." *Critical Insights. The Poetry of Edgar Allan Poe*, edited by Steven Frye, 258–89. Pasadena, CA: Salem, 2011.

Robb, Graham. *Unlocking Mallarmé*. New Haven, CT: Yale University Press, 1996.

Roberts, David. *The Total Work of Art in European Modernism*. Ithaca, NY: Cornell University Press, 2011.

Rolf, Marie. "Mauclair and Debussy: The Decade from 'Mer Belle aux île Sanguinaires' to *La Mer*." *Cahiers Debussy* 11 (1987): 9–23.

Rolf, Marie. "Oriental and Iberian Resonances in Early Debussy Songs." In *Debussy's Resonance*, edited by François de Médicis and Steven Huebner, 272–308. Rochester, NY: University of Rochester Press, 2018.

Rolf, Marie. "Semantic and Structural Issues in Debussy's Mallarmé Songs." In *Debussy Studies*, edited Richard Langham Smith, 179–200. Cambridge: Cambridge University Press, 1997.

Rolf, Marie. "Symbolism as Compositional Agent in Act IV, Scene 4 of Debussy's *Pelleas et Melisande*." In *Berlioz and Debussy: Sources, Contexts, and Legacies*. Edited by Barbara L. Kelly and Kerry Murphy, 117–48. Aldershot: Ashgate, 2007.

Royle, Nicholas. *The Uncanny*. Manchester: Manchester University Press, 2003.

Safford, Lisa Bixenstine. "Mallarmé's Influence on Degas's Aesthetic of Dance in his Late Period." *Nineteenth-Century French Studies* 21, nos. 3–4 (Spring–Summer 1993): 419–33.

Said, Edward. *Orientalism*. New York: Random House, 1978.

Sala, Emilio. "Hearing the Shadows at the Chat Noir's Pre-cinematic Theatre." In *The Oxford Handbook of Cinematic Listening*, edited by Carlo Cenciarelli, 42–67. Oxford: Oxford University Press, 2021.

Salem Media. "How Many People Died in WW1?" History on the Net. January 24, 2020. https://www.historyonthenet.com/how-many-people-died-in-ww1.

Salzer, Felix. *Structural Hearing*. New York: Charles Boni, 1952.

Saravese, Nicola. *Eurasian Theatre: Drama and Performance between East and West from Classical Antiquity to the Present*. Edited and revised by Vicki Ann Cremona and translated by Richard Fowler. Holstebro: ICARUS, 2010.

Sayer, Robert. *The Ladies Amusement: Or, The Whole Art of Japanning Made Easy*. London: Golden Buck, 1762. Facsimile ed. Newport, Monmouthshire: Ceramic Book, 1966.

Scharfe, Francis, trans. *Baudelaire: The Poems in Prose and La Fanfarlo*. London: Anvil Press Poetry, 1989.

Schelling, F. W. J. *Historical-Critical Introduction to the Philosophy of Mythology*. Translated by Mason Richey and Markus Zisselsberger. Foreword by Jason M. Wirth. Albany: State University of New York Press, 2007.

Schenker, Heinrich. "The Art of Improvisation." In *The Masterwork in Music 1*, edited by William Drabkin, translated by Richard Kramer, 2–19. Cambridge: Cambridge University Press, 1994.

Schenker, Heinrich. "A Contribution to the Study of Ornamentation." Edited and translated by Hedi Siegel. *Music Forum* 4 (1976): 1–139.

Schenker, Heinrich. *Counterpoint I–II*. Rev. ed. Edited by John Rothgeb. Translated by John Rothgeb and Jürgen Thym. Ann Arbor, MI: Musicalia, 2001.

Schenker, Heinrich. "The Decline of the Art of Composition: A Technical-Critical Study." Translated by William Drabkin. *Music Analysis* 24, no. 1–2 (2005): 3–129.

Schenker, Heinrich. *Der freie Satz*. Neue musikalische Theorien und Phantasien. Vol. 3. Vienna: Universal, 1935.

Schenker, Heinrich. "Der Geist der musikalischen Technik" (1895). In *Heinrich Schenker als Essayist und Kritiker: Gesammelte Aufsätze, Rescensionen und kleinere Berichte aus den Jahren 1891–190*, edited by Hellmut Federhofer, 135–54. Hildesheim: Olms, 1990.

Schenker, Heinrich. "Der Kunst der Improvisation." In *Das Meisterwerk in der Musik I*, 11–40. Munich: Drei Masken, 1925.

Schenker, Heinrich. *Ein Beitrag zur Ornamentik*. Vienna: UE, 1904/1908.

Schenker, Heinrich. *Erläuterungsausgabe der Sonate Op. 101, Ludwig van Beethoven*. Vienna: Universal, 1921.

Schenker, Heinrich. *Free Composition*. Edited and translated by Ernst Oster. New York: Longman, 1979.

Schenker, Heinrich. *Harmonielehre*. Neue musikalische Theorien und Phantasien. Vol. 1. Stuttgart: Cotta, 1906. Edited by Oswald Jonas and translated by Elisabeth Mann Borgese. Chicago: University of Chicago Press, 1954.

Schenker, Heinrich. *Kontrapunkt I–II*. Neue musikalische Theorien und Phantasien 2. Stuttgart: Cotta, 1910; Vienna: Universal, 1922.

Schenker, Heinrich. "Miscellanea." In *The Masterwork in Music 2*, edited by William Drabkin, translated by Ian Bent, 130. Cambridge: Cambridge University Press, 1996.

Schenker, Heinrich. *Piano Sonata in A Major, Op. 101. Beethoven's Last Piano Sonatas. An Edition with Elucidations*, vol. 4. Translated, edited, and annotated by John Rothgeb. New York: Oxford University Press, 2015.

Schenker, Heinrich. *Sonate Op. 27, Nr. 2*. Edited by L. Van Beethoven. Facsimile with commentary by Heinrich Schenker. Vienna: Universal, 1921.

Schenker, Heinrich. "The Spirit of Musical Technique." In *The Schenker Project*, edited by Nicholas Cook, translated by William Pastille, 319–32. Oxford: Oxford University Press, 2007.

Schenker, Heinrich. "Vermischtes." In *Das Meisterwerk in der Musik II*. Munich: Drei Masken Verlag, 1926.

Schenker, Heinrich. "Von der Diminution." *Der Dreiklang* 4/5 (1937): 93–98.

Schlegel, Friedrich. *Dialogue on Poetry and Literary Aphorisms*. Translated, introduced, and annotated by Ernest Behler and Roman Struc. University Park: Pennsylvania State University Press, 1968.

Schmidt, Lothar. "Arabeske. Zu einigen Voraussetzungen und Konsequenzen von Eduard Hanslicks musikalischem Formbegriff." *Archiv für Musikwissenschaft* 40, no. 6/2 (1989): 91–120.

Schoenberg, Arnold. *Style and Idea*. Edited by Leonard Stein. Translated by Leo Black. 60th Anniversary ed. Berkeley: University of California Press, 2010.

Schroder, Maurie Z. *ICARUS: The Image of the Artist in French Romanticism*. Cambridge, MA: Harvard University Press, 1961.

Schultz, Gretchen, and Lewis Seifert. *Fairy Tales for the Disillusioned*. Princeton, NJ: Princeton University Press, 2016.

Scullion, Val. "Kinaesthetic, Spastic and Spatial Motifs as Expressions of Romantic Irony in E. T. A. Hoffmann's *The Sandman* and Other Writings." *Journal of Literature and Science* 2, no. 1 (2009): 1–22.

Second-Genovesi, Charlotte. "1914–1918: l'activité musicale a l'épreuve de la guerre." *Revue Musicologie* 93, no. 2 (2007): 399–434.

Sedgwick, Eve Kosofsky. *The Coherence of Gothic Conventions*. London: Methuen, 1986.

Servières, Georges. *Richard Wagner jugé en France*. Paris: La Librairie illustrée, 1898.

Shaw, Mary Lewis. "Apprehending the Idea through Poetry and Dance." *Dance Research Journal* 20, no. 1 (Summer 1988): 3–9.

Shinabargar, Scott. "La Diction du Mal: Baudelaire." In *The Revolting Body of Poetry*, Chiasma 36. Leiden: Brill Rodopi, 2016.

Shinabargar, Scott. *The Revolting Body of Poetry*. Chiasma 36. Leiden: Brill Rodopi, 2016.

Shiner, Larry. *The Invention of Art*. Chicago: University of Chicago Press, 2001.

Sholl, Robert. "James Sibley Watson's The Fall of The House of Usher: Surrealism—Improvisation—Complementary Serendipities." *Perspectives of New Music*, 58, no. 1 (Winter 2020): 23–69.

Simmel, Georg. "Die Großstädte und das Geistesleben." *Jahrbuch der Gehe-Stiftung* 9 (1903): 185–206.

Simmel, Georg. "The Metropolis and Mental Life." In *The Sociology of Georg Simmel*, edited and translated by K. Wolff, 409–24. New York: Free Press, 1964.

Simpson, Juliet. "Symbolist Aesthetics and the Decorative Image/Text." *French Forum* 25, no. 2 (May 2000): 177–204.

Sloboda, John. *The Musical Mind: The Cognitive Psychology of Music*. Oxford: Oxford Press, 1985.

Smith, Richard Langham. "Debussy and the Art of the Cinema." *Music and Letters* 54, no. 1 (1973): 61–70.

Smith, Richard Langham. "Debussy's Impressionism Interrogated." In *Debussy in Context*, edited by Simon Trezise, 59–68. Cambridge: Cambridge University Press, 2024.

Smith, Richard Langham. "The Play and Its Playwright." In *Pelléas et Mélisande*, Cambridge Opera Handbooks, edited by Roger Nichols and Richard Langham Smith, 1–29. Cambridge: Cambridge University Press, 1989.

Smith, Richard Langham. "Tonalities of Darkness and Light." In *Pelléas et Mélisande*, Cambridge Opera Handbooks, edited by Roger Nichols and Richard Langham Smith, 107–39. Cambridge: Cambridge University Press, 1989.

Smith, Steven C. *A Heart at Fire's Center: The Life and Music of Bernard Herrmann*. Berkeley: University of California Press, 2002.

Smith, Thomas Robert, ed. *Baudelaire: His Prose and Poetry*. The Modern Library. New York: Boni and Liveright, 1919.

Śniedziewski, Piotr. *The Melancholic Gazfe*. Translated by Dwight Williams. Berlin: Peter Lang, 2018.

Somer, Avo. "Chromatic Third-Relations and Tonal Structure in the Songs of Debussy." *Music Theory Spectrum* 17, no. 2 (1995): 215–41.

Spitzer, Michael. *Metaphor and Musical Thought*. Chicago: University of Chicago Press, 2004.

Stanley, Patricia. "Hoffmann's 'Phantasiestücke in Callots Manier' in Light of Friedrich Schlegel's Theory of the Arabesque." *German Studies Review* 8, no. 3 (October 1985): 399–419.

Starkie, Enid. *Baudelaire*. New York: New Directions, 1958.

Starobinski, Jean. "Melancholy in the Mirror: Three Readings of Baudelaire." Translated by Charlotte Mandell. *Hyperion* 5 (2010): 118–23.

Sternfeld, Frederick W. "Some Russian Folk Songs in Stravinsky." *Notes* 2, no. 2 (1945): 95–107.

Stockhausen, Karlheinz. "Von Webern zu Debussy, Bemerkungen zur statistischen Form." *Texte zur electronischen und instrumentalen Musik*. Cologne: DuMont, 1963 [75–85].

Stockhem, Michel. *Eugène Ysaÿe et la Musique de Chambre*. Liège: Pierre Mardaga, 1990.

Stoljar, Margaret. "Mirror and Self in Symbolist and Post-Symbolist Poetry." *Modern Language Review* 85, no. 2 (1990): 362–72.

Strasser, Michel. "Grieg, the Société nationale, and the Origins of Debussy's String Quartet." In *Berlioz and Debussy: Sources, Contexts, and Legacies*, edited by Barbara L. Kelly and Kerry Murphy, 103–15. Aldershot: Ashgate, 2007.

Strasser, Michel. "Société nationale and Other Institutions." In *Debussy in Context*, edited by Simon Trezise, 185–92. Cambridge: Cambridge University Press, 2024.

Sucur, Slobodan. "Tales of the Grotesque and Arabesque." *Literary Encyclopedia*. June 27, 2019. https://www.litencyc.com/php/sworks.php?rec=true&UID=1723.

Sullivan, Louis H. *A System of Architectural Ornamentation*. New York: Rizzoli, in cooperation with the Art Institute of Chicago, 1990.

Sullivan, Michael. *The Meeting of Eastern and Western Art*. Berkeley: University of California, 1989.

Swinburne, Algernon Charles. *Poems and Ballads Second* Series. New York: R. Worthington, 1878.

Symonds, Arthur. *The Symbolist Movement in Literature*. London: Dutton, 1899/1919.

Tansman, Pierre Tugal. *Les Ballets Suédois dans l'art contemporain*. Paris: Éditions du Trianon, 1931.

Tardif, Cécile. "Fauré and the Salons." In *Regarding Fauré*, edited by Tom Gordon, 1–14. Amsterdam: Gordon and Breach, 1999.

Taruskin, Richard. "The First Modernist." In *The Danger of Music and Other Anti-Utopian Essays*, 195–201. Berkeley: University of California Press, 2009.

Taruskin, Richard. *Stravinsky and the Russian Traditions*. Berkeley: University of California Press, 1996.

Terrasse, Claude, and Pierre Bonnard. *Petit Solfège illustré*. Paris: Ancienne Maison Quantin, Librairies-imprimeries réunies, 1893.

Theisen, Bianca. "Early Romantic Poetics of Complex Form." *Studies in Romanticism* 42, no. 3 (Fall 2003): 303–21.

Thibaudet, Albert. *La Poésie de Stéphane Mallarmé*. Paris: Éditions de la nouvelle revue français, 1911.

Tiersot, Julien. *Musiques pittoresques: Promenades musicales à l'Exposition de 1889*. Paris: Fischbacher, 1889.

Tiersot, Julien. *Notes D'Ethnographie Musicale*. Série 1. Paris: Fischbacher, 1905.

Tinchant, Albert, and Georges Fragerolle. *La Tentation de Sainte-Antoine*. Illustrated by Henri Rivière. Paris: E. Plon, Nourrit et Cie, s.d. 1888.

Todorov, Tzvetan. *The Fantastic: A Structural Approach to a Literary Genre.* Translated by Richard Howard. Foreword by Robert Scholes. Ithaca, NY: Cornell University Press, 1975.

Todorov, Tzvetan. *Introduction à la littérature fantastique.* Paris: Seuil, 1970.

Toulet, Emmanuelle. *Birth of the Motion Picture.* Translated by Susan Emanuel. New York: Abrams, 1995.

Trezise, Simon. *La Mer.* Cambridge Music Handbook. Cambridge: Cambridge University Press, 1994.

Trezise, Simon. "Review: *La Mer* by Claude Debussy and Marie Rolf." *Notes,* Second series, 56, no. 3 (2000): 782–86.

Tyacke, George W. *Playing to Motion Pictures.* London: Kinematograph Weekly, 1914.

Tyson, Allan. "Sketches and Autographs." In *The Beethoven Companion*, edited by Denis Arnold and Nigel Fortune, 443–58. London: Faber, 1971.

Union Internationale de la Marionette. "Maurice Maeterlinck." *World Encyclopedia of Puppetry.* Accessed October 20, 2022. https://wepa.unima.org/en/maurice-maeterlinck.

Urchueguía, Cristina. "Wie kam die 'Urlinie' in den 'Urtext'? Aporien musikalischer Schrift im Denken Heinrich Schenkers." *Schweizer Jahrbuch Für Musikwissenschaft* Neue Folge 32 (2012): 237–52.

US Department of Health and Human Services. *Treatment Improvement Protocol: Trauma-Informed Care in Behavioral Health Services.* HHS Publications No. (SMA) 14–4816. Rockville, MD: USDHH, 2014.

Valéry, Paul. *Écrits divers sur Stephane Mallarmé.* Paris: Gallimard, 1950.

Vallas, Léon. *Claude Debussy et son temps.* 2nd ed. Paris: Albin Michel, 1958.

Vallas, Léon. *Claude Debussy: His Life and Works.* Translated by Maire and Grace O'Brien. Oxford: Oxford University Press, 1933.

Vallas, Léon. *The Theories of Claude Debussy, Musicien français.* Translated by Maire O'Brien. Oxford: Oxford University Press, 1929.

Vartija, Devin J. *The Color of Equality: Race and Common Humanity in Enlightenment.* Philadelphia: University of Pennsylvania Press, 2021.

Vaughan, Gerard. "Maurice Denis and the Sense of Music." *Oxford Art Journal* 7, no. 1 Correspondences (1984): 38–48.

Venturino, Stephanie. "Arabesque in French Music after Debussy." In *Arabesque without End: Across Music and the Arts, from Faust to Shahrazad,* edited by Anne Leonard, 149–72. New York: Routledge, 2022.

Venturino, Stephanie, and Jonathan Dunsby. "The Evolution of Claude Debussy's Arabesque." In *Debussy Studies 2*, edited by Barbara Kelly and David Code, 58–86. Cambridge: Cambridge University Press, 2025.

Verlaine, Paul. *Oeuvres poétiques complètes.* Edited by Y.-G. Le Dantec and Jacques Borel. Bibliothèque de la Pléiade. Paris: Gallimard, 1962.

Vidal, Paul. "Souvenirs d'Achille Debussy." *Revue Musicale* 7 (1926): 10–16.

Villiers de l'Isle-Adam, Jean Marie Matthias Philippe Auguste, Comte de. Œuvres complètes. Bibliothèque de la Pléiade. Edited by Alan William Raitt, Pierre-Georges Castex, and Jean-Marie Bellefroid. 2 vols. Paris: Gallimard, 1986.

Villiers de l'Isle-Adam, Jean Marie Matthias Philippe Auguste, Comte de. *The Scaffold and Other Cruel Tales.* Edited by Brian Stableford. London: Black Coat, 2004.

Vivier, Robert. *L'Originalité de Baudelaire.* 3rd ed. Brussels: Palais des Académies, 1965.

Vuillermoz, Emile. "La Saison Russe au Theatre des Champs Elysees." *Revue musicale S.I.M.* 9, no. 6 (June 15, 1913): 49–56.

Wagner, Richard. "Lettre sur la musique." In *Quatre poèmes d'opéras traduits en prose française, précédés d'une lettre sur la musique* [à Frédéric Villot, Paris, 15 septembre 1860] *par Richard Wagner. Le Vaisseau fantôme, Tannhäuser, Lohengrin, Tristan et Iseult.* Paris: Librairie Nouvelle, 1861. Reprint, Paris: Durand, 1893.

Wagner, Richard. "Music of the Future." In *Three Wagner Essays*, translated by Robert L. Jacobs, 13–44. London: Eulenberg, 1979.

Waidelich, Till Gerrit. "Das Opern-Potpourri: Musikalisches Kaleidoskop, ars combinatoria oder musikimmanente Pornographie?" In *Jenseits der Bühne: Bearbeitungs- und Rezeptionsformen der Oper im 19. und 20. Jahrhundert. Symposium der IMS Konferenz Zürich 2007*, edited by Hans-Joachim Hinrichsen and K. Pietschmann, 128–38. Schweizer Beiträge zur Musikforschung, vol. 15. Bärenreiter: Kassel, 2010.

Waller, Bret, and Grace Seiberling, ed. *Artists of La Revue blanche: Bonnard, Toulouse-Lautrec. Vallatton, Vuillard.* Rochester, NY: Memorial Art Gallery of the University of Rochester, 1984.

Walsh, Stephen. *Debussy: A Painter in Sound.* London: Faber and Faber, 2014.

Warner, Marina. *Phantasmagoria: Spirit Visions, Metaphors, and Media into the Twenty-First Century.* Oxford: Oxford University Press, 2006.

Wason, Robert W., and Matthew Brown. *Heinrich Schenker's Conception of Harmony.* Rochester, NY: University of Rochester Press, 2020.

Watelet, Claude-Henri, and Pierre-Charles Lévesque. *Dictionnaire des arts de peinture, sculpture et gravure.* Vol. 1. Paris: L. F. Prault, 1792; Geneva: Minkoff Reprints, 1972.

Waters, Robert F. "Emulation and Influence: Japonisme and Western Music in fin de siècle Paris." *Music Review* 55, no. 3 (1994): 214–26.

Watkins, Glenn. *Soundings.* New York: Schirmer, 1988.

Welsh, Moray. "Un Embarras de Richésse." *Strad* 103, no. 1226 (1992): 516–20.

Wheeldon, Marianne. "Debussy and La Sonata Cyclique." *Journal of Musicology* 22 (2005): 644–79.

Wheeldon, Marianne. *Debussy's Late Style.* Bloomington: Indiana University Press, 2009.

Wheeldon. Marianne. "Debussy's Legacy: The Controversy over the *Ode à la France*." *Journal of Musicology* 27, no. 3 (2010): 304–41.

Wheeldon, Marianne. "Debussy's 'Soupir': An Experiment in Permutational Analysis." *Perspectives of New Music* 38, no. 2 (2000): 134–60.

Wheeldon, Marianne. "Debussy's String Quartet." In *Intimate Voices: The Twentieth-Century String Quartet*, vol. 1: Debussy to Villa-Lobos, edited by Evan Jones, 3–26. Eastman Studies in Music, vol. 70. Rochester, NY: University of Rochester Press, 2009.

Wheeldon, Marianne. "Interpreting Discontinuity in the Late Works of Debussy." *Current Musicology* 77 (2004): 97–115.

White, John Albert. *Transition to Global Rivalry. Alliance Diplomacy and the Quadruple Entente, 1895–1907.* Cambridge: Cambridge University Press, 1995.

Whitford, Frank. *Japanese Prints and Western Painters.* New York: Macmillan, 1977.

Whiting, Steven Moore. "Music on Montmartre." In *The Spirit of Montmartre: Cabarets, Humor, and the Avant-Garde, 1875–1905*, edited by Phillip Dennis Cate and Mary Shaw, 159–97. New Brunswick, NJ: Rutgers University Press, 1996.

Whittall, Arnold. "Tonality and the Whole-Tone Scale in the Music of Debussy." *Music Review* 36, no. 4 (1975): 261–71.

Widor, Charles Marie, and M. Bourtet de Monvel. *Vielles chansons et rondes pour les petits enfants*. Paris: E Plon-Nourrit, 1883.

Willson, Flora. "Future History: Wagner, Offenbach, and 'la musique de l'avenir' in Paris, 1860." *Opera Quarterly* 30, no. 4 (2015): 287–314.

Wilson, Eugene N. "Form and Texture in the Chamber Music of Debussy and Ravel." PhD diss., University of Washington, 1968.

Wise, Brian. "A Look Back 100 Years Later on Debussy's Violin Sonata—the Last Piece He Wrote Before His Death." *String Magazine*, March 14, 2018. https://stringsmagazine.com/a-look-back-100-years-later-on-debussys-violin-sonata-the-last-piece-he-wrote-before-his-death.

Woodfield, Richard. "Introductory Note." In *The Analysis of Beauty*, edited by William Hogarth. London: J. Reeves, 1753. A Scolar Press Facsimile. Ilkley: Scolar Press, 1969.

Wrighte, William. *Grotesque Architecture or Rural Amusement*. London: Henry Webley, 1767.

Wrobel, William. "Half-Diminished Seventh: The Bernard Herrmann Chord." 2002, rev. 2017, 3, 8, 16–17. https://archive.org/details/herrmann-chord-filmscorerundowns.

Wrobel, William. "*Obsession*: Music by Bernard Herrmann." 2015, 1–149. https://archive.org/details/obsession-filmscorerundowns.

Wyzéwa, Théodore de. "Descriptive Music." In *Music in European Thought 1851–1912*, edited by Bojan Bujić, translated by Jennifer Day, 247–50. Cambridge Readings in the Literature of Music. Cambridge: Cambridge University Press, 1988.

Wyzéwa, Théodore de. "La Musique descriptive." *La Revue Wagnérienne* 1, no. 3 (April 8, 1885): 74–77.

Yang, Ya-Ju. "The House as Mirrors in Edgar Allan Poe's 'The Fall of the House of Usher.'" Official Proceedings of the Asian Conference on Arts and Humanities, Osaka, Japan. 2013. https://papers.iafor.org/wp-content/uploads/papers/acah2013/ACAH2013_0239.pdf.

Yee, Jennifer. "Baudelaire and the Chinese Object." *L'Esprit Créateur* 58, no. 1 (2018): 101–13.

Yeoland, Rosemary Hamilton. *A Translation from French into English of Camille Mauclair's Le Soleil Des Mort/Sun of the Dead*. Lewiston, NY: Edwin Mellen, 2015.

Yih, Annie K. "Analysing Debussy: Tonality, Motivic Sets, and the Referential Pitch-Specific Collection." *Music Analysis* 19, no. 2 (2000): 203–29.

Yothers, Brian D. "Poe's Poetry of the Exotic." In *Critical Insights: The Poetry of Edgar Allan Poe*, edited by Steven Frye, 19–33. Pasadena, CA: Salem, 2010.

Youens, Susan. "Le Soleil des Morts: A 'Fin-de-siècle' Portrait Gallery." *19th-Century Music* 11, no. 1, Special Issue: Resolutions II (Summer 1987): 43–58.

Zbikowski, Lawrence. *Conceptualizing Music: Cognitive Structure, Theory, and Analysis*. New York: Oxford University Press, 2002.

Zenck, Claudia Maurer. "Form- und Farbenspiele: Debussys 'Jeux.'" *Archiv für Musikwissenschaft* 33 (1976): 28–47.

Zenck, Claudia Maurer. *Versuch über die wahre Art, Debussy zu analysieren*. Berliner musikwissenschaftliche Arbeiten. München: E. Katzbichler, 1974.

Zielonka, Anthony. "'L'Après-midi d'un faune': Towards the Total Work of Art." *L'Esprit Créateur* 40, no. 3, Re-casting Mallarmé/Rejouer Mallarmé (Fall 2000): 14–24.

Index

Matthew Brown is Professor of Music Theory at the Eastman School of Music. He is author of *Debussy Redux: The Impact of His Music on Popular Culture* (IUP, 2011), *Ariane & Bluebeard: From Fairy Tale to Comic Book Opera* (with Th. Emil Homerin [IUP, 2022]), and (with Robert W. Wason) *Heinrich Schenker's Conception of Harmony*.

FOR INDIANA UNIVERSITY PRESS

Sabrina Black *Editorial Assistant*
Tony Brewer *Artist and Book Designer*
Allison Chaplin *Acquisitions Editor*
Anna Garnai *Production Coordinator*
Sophia Hebert *Assistant Acquisitions Editor*
Samantha Heffner *Marketing Production Manager*
Katie Huggins *Production Manager*
Gigi Lamm *Director of Sales and Marketing*
Nancy Lightfoot *Project Manager/Editor*
Alyssa Nicole Lucas *Marketing and Publicity Manager*
Annie L. Martin *Editorial Director*
Dan Pyle *Online Publishing Manager*
Michael Regoli *Director of Publishing Operations*
Jennifer Wilder *Senior Artist and Book Designer*